EVERYMAN'S LIBRARY

244

ESSAYS
&
BELLES-LETTRES

Everyman, I will go with thee, and be thy guide,
In thy most need to go by thy side

HORATIO NELSON, born at Burnham Thorpe, Norfolk, 1758. Entered the Royal Navy, 1771; received his first command, 1778. Married Frances Nisbet, 1787. Sent in command of the *Agamemnon* to Naples, where met Lady Hamilton, 1793. Promoted rear-admiral, 1797. Defeated the French fleet in Aboukir Bay and created Baron Nelson of the Nile, 1798. Victor of Copenhagen and created viscount, 1801. Mortally wounded at Trafalgar, 21st October 1805.

NELSON'S LETTERS

SELECTED AND EDITED BY

GEOFFREY RAWSON

LONDON J. M. DENT & SONS LTD

NEW YORK E. P. DUTTON & CO INC

Printed in Great Britain
by
Lowe & Brydone (Printers) Ltd
London, N.W.10
for
J. M. DENT & SONS LTD
Aldine House · Bedford Street · London
First published in this edition 1960

PREFACE

More than a century has passed since a large collection of the Letters and Dispatches of Lord Nelson was published by Sir Harris Nicolas in 1844–6.

More than half a century has passed since the Morrison Collection of letters between Nelson and Lady Hamilton was privately printed.

Since then a number of Nelson letters has come to light. From all these, totalling about five thousand items, the following selection has been made for this volume. They cover the period from 1777, when Nelson was an unknown lieutenant, to his final victory and death in 1805, and include his own *Sketch of my Life* written subsequent to the Battle of the Nile.

Perhaps the life of any man is best drawn by himself, as his own biographer. Many of these letters were written only for the eyes of those to whom they were addressed, and others deal with public affairs, political, diplomatic and naval business.

The letters exhibit the simplicity of his character, his integrity and humanitarianism. In an age of cruelty and barbarity, he stands forth as a highly civilized commander beloved by his officers and men, even though had they deserved it he would have hanged them on a Sunday.

The letters cover the whole series of his battles and show him in moments of crisis. There is the dramatic and complete failure of his great commando raid on Santa Cruz, and the exquisite courtesies between the rival commanders.

At the Battle of St Vincent, at the moment of crisis, he showed his tactical acumen and moral courage by leaving the line of battle prescribed by his admiral and sailing alone into the enemy's fire.

This was the turning point in his career. Nelson's 'Patent Bridge,' his skill and daring were extolled in story and song. He became Sir Horatio and a Rear Admiral and famous overnight in the Navy and throughout England.

Eighteen months later the Battle of the Nile raised his renown to its highest peak. Here was the classic, the complete victory, the annihilation of the battle fleet of a great sea power. The Hero of the Nile became Lord Nelson of the Nile.

At Copenhagen, at the height of the battle, the moment of crisis arose. The fire from the Danish batteries was fierce; it was doubtful if the British ships could remain in the imminent deadly breach; his admiral had hoisted the signal of recall. With the turn of the battle in the balance, Nelson calmly sent a note to the Danish commander, proposing a truce. It was addressed *To the Brothers of Englishmen, the Danes,* and began: 'Lord Nelson has directions to spare Denmark.' The bold move succeeded and firing ceased.

As for the domestic crisis in his life, the reader will find here the last brief notes to his wife, and his impassioned letters to Lady Hamilton. Nelson enjoined her to destroy his letters, but for reasons of her own she preserved them.

G. R.

1960.

CONTENTS

AUTHORITIES

The authorities for this volume of Letters from Admiral Lord Nelson are:

1. *Despatches and Letters of Vice-Admiral Lord Viscount Nelson with Notes*, by Sir Nicholas Harris Nicolas, G.C.M.G. Seven volumes. London, 1844-46.

2. Clarke and McArthur. *Life of Nelson.* Two volumes. 1809.

3. *Life of Horatio Lord Viscount Nelson*, by Mr. Harrison. Two volumes. 1806.

4. *Letters of Lord Nelson to Lady Hamilton.* Two volumes. 1814.

5. Morrison, Alfred. *The Hamilton-Nelson Papers.* Two volumes. Privately printed. London, 1893-94.

6. Naish, George P. B. *Nelson's Letters to his Wife.* 1958. Published in conjunction with the Navy Records Society by Routledge and Kegan Paul, to whom I am indebted for permission to give here the complete versions of those letters appearing in this volume.

G. R

NELSON'S OWN STORY

[In October, 1799, when he was famous as the victor of the Nile, Nelson wrote the following *Sketch of My Life* for John McArthur, the then editor of the *Naval Chronicle*.]

Port Mahon, *15 October, 1799*

My dear Sir,

I send you a sketch of my life, which I am sensible wants your pruning knife before it is fit to meet the public eye, therefore I trust you and your friend will do that, and turn it into much better language. I have been and am very unwell, therefore you must excuse my short letter. I did not even know that such a book as yours was printed, therefore I beg you will send me the two volumes and consider me as a sincere friend to the undertaking.

Horatio Nelson, son of the Reverend Edmund Nelson, Rector of Burnham Thorpe, in the County of Norfolk, and of Catherine his wife, daughter of Doctor Suckling, Prebendary of Westminster, whose grandmother was sister to Sir Robert Walpole, Earl of Orford.

I was born September 29th, 1758, in the Parsonage-house, was sent to the high-school at Norwich, and afterwards removed to North Walsham; from whence, on the disturbance with Spain relative to the Falkland Islands, I went to Sea* with my uncle, Captain Maurice Suckling, in the *Raisonable* of 64 guns. But the business with Spain being accommodated, I was sent in a West India Ship belonging to the house of Hibbert, Purrier, and Horton, with Mr. John Rathbone, who had formerly been in the Navy, in the *Dreadnought* with Captain Suckling. From this voyage I returned to the *Triumph* at Chatham in July, 1772; and, if I did not improve in my education, I returned a practical Seaman, with a horror of the Royal Navy, and with a saying, then constant with the Seamen, '*Aft the most honour, forward the better man!*'—It was many weeks before I got in the least reconciled to a Man-of-War, so deep was the prejudice rooted; and what pains were taken to instil this erroneous principle in a young mind! However, as my ambition was to be a Seaman, it was always held out as a reward, that if I attended well to my navigation, I should go in the cutter and decked long-boat, which was attached to the Commanding officer's ship at Chatham. Thus by degrees I became a good pilot, for vessels of that description, from Chatham to the Tower of London, down the Swin, and the North Foreland; and confident of myself amongst rocks

* 1770, being twelve years old.

and sands, which has many times since been of great comfort to me. In this way I was trained, till the expedition towards the North Pole was fitted out; when although no boys were allowed to go in the Ships, (as of no use,) yet nothing could prevent my using every interest to go with Captain Lutwidge in the *Carcass*; and, as I fancied I was to fill a man's place, I begged I might be his cockswain: which, finding my ardent desire for going with him, Captain Lutwidge complied with, and has continued the strictest friendship to this moment. Lord Mulgrave, whom I then first knew, maintained his kindest friendship and regard to the last moment of his life. When the boats were fitted out to quit the two Ships blocked up in the ice, I exerted myself to have the command of a four-oared cutter raised upon, which was given me, with twelve men; and I prided myself in fancying I could navigate her better than any other boat in the Ship.

On our arrival in England, being paid off, October 15, I found that a Squadron was fitting out for the East Indies; and nothing less than such a distant voyage could in the least satisfy my desire of maritime knowledge. I was placed in the *Seahorse* of 20 guns, with Captain Farmer, and watched in the foretop; from whence in time I was placed on the quarter-deck: having, in the time I was in this Ship, visited almost every part of the East Indies, from Bengal to Bussorah. Ill health induced Sir Edward Hughes, who had always shown me the greatest kindness, to send me to England in the *Dolphin* of 20 guns, with Captain James Pigot, whose kindness at that time saved my life. This ship was paid off at Woolwich on the 24th September, 1776. On the 26th I received an order from Sir James Douglas, who commanded at Portsmouth, to act as Lieutenant of the *Worcester*, 64, Captain Mark Robinson, who was ordered to Gibraltar with a convoy. In this ship I was at sea with convoys till April 2nd, 1777, and in very bad weather. But although my age might have been a sufficient cause for not entrusting me with the charge of a Watch, yet Captain Robinson used to say, 'he felt as easy when I was upon deck, as any Officer in the Ship.'

On the 8th of April, 1777, I passed my examination as a Lieutenant; and received my Commission the next day, as second Lieutenant of the *Lowestoffe* Frigate of 32 guns, Captain (afterwards Lieutenant-governor of Greenwich hospital) William Locker. In this Ship I went to Jamaica: but even a Frigate was not sufficiently active for my mind, and I got into a schooner, tender to the *Lowestoffe*. In this vessel I made myself a complete pilot for all the passages through the (Keys) Islands situated on the north side Hispaniola. Whilst in this Frigate, an event happened which presaged my character; and, as it conveys no dishonour to the Officer alluded to, I shall insert it.

Blowing a gale of wind, and very heavy sea, the Frigate captured an

American letter of margue. The first Lieutenant was ordered to board her, which he did not do, owing to the very heavy sea. On his return, the Captain said, 'Have I no Officer in the Ship who can board the Prize?' On which the Master ran to the gangway, to get into the boat: when I stopped him, saying, 'It is my turn now; and if I come back, it is yours.' This little incident has often occurred to my mind; and I know it is my disposition, that difficulties and dangers do but increase my desire of attempting them.

Sir Peter Parker, soon after his arrival at Jamaica, 1778, took me into his own Flag-Ship, the *Bristol*, as third Lieutenant; from which I rose by succession to be first. Nothing particular happened whilst I was in this Ship, which was actively employed off Cape François, it being the commencement of the French war.

On the 8th December 1778, I was appointed as Commander of the *Badger* Brig; and was first sent to protect the Mosquito shore, and the bay of Honduras, from the depredations of the American privateers. Whilst on this service, I gained so much the affections of the Settlers, that they unanimously voted me their thanks, and expressed their regret on my leaving them; entrusting me to describe to Sir Peter Parker and Sir John Dalling their situation, should a war with Spain break out. Whilst I commanded this Brig, H.M.S. *Glasgow*, Captain Thomas Lloyd, came into Montego Bay, Jamaica, where the *Badger* was lying: in two hours afterwards she took fire by a cask of rum; and Captain Lloyd will tell you, that it was owing to my exertions, joined to his, that her whole crew were rescued from the flames.

On the 11th of June 1779, I was made Post into the *Hinchinbrook*. When, being at sea, the Count d'Estaing arriving at Hispaniola with a very large Fleet and Army from Martinico, an attack on Jamaica was expected. In this critical state, I was by both Admiral and General intrusted with the command of the batteries at Port Royal: and I need not say, as this place was the key to the whole Naval force, the town of Kingston, and Spanish Town, the defence of it was the most important post in the whole Island.

In January 1780, an Expedition being resolved on against St. Juan's, I was chosen to direct the Sea part of it. Major Polson, who commanded, will tell you of my exertions: how I quitted my Ship, carried troops in boats an hundred miles up a river, which none but Spaniards since the time of the buccaneers had ever ascended. It will then be told how I boarded, if I may be allowed the expression, an out-post of the Enemy, situated on an Island in the river; that I made batteries, and afterwards fought them, and was a principal cause of our success. From this scene I was appointed to the *Janus*, 44, at Jamaica, and went to Port Royal in the *Victor* sloop.

My state of health was now so bad, that I was obliged to go to England in the *Lion*, the Honourable William Cornwallis, Captain; whose care and attention again saved my life. In August 1781, I was commissioned for the *Albemarle*; and, it would almost be supposed, to try my constitution, was kept the whole winter in the North Sea. In April 1782, I sailed with a convoy for Newfoundland and Quebec, under the orders of Captain Thomas Pringle. From Quebec, during a cruise off Boston, I was chased by three French Ships of the Line, and the *Iris* frigate: as they all beat me in sailing very much, I had no chance left, but running them amongst the shoals of St. George's Bank. This alarmed the Line-of-Battle Ships, and they quitted the pursuit; but the Frigate continued, and at sun-set was little more than gun-shot distant: when, the Line-of-Battle Ships being out of sight, I ordered the main-top-sail to be laid to the mast; on this the Frigate tacked, and stood to rejoin her consorts.

In October I sailed from Quebec with a convoy to New York, where I joined the Fleet under the command of Lord Hood; and in November I sailed with him to the West Indies, where I remained till the Peace; when I came to England, being directed in my way to attend H.R.H. the Duke of Clarence on his visit to the Havannah; and was paid off at Portsmouth on July 3rd, 1783. In the autumn I went to France, and remained there till the spring of the year 1784; when I was appointed to the *Boreas* frigate, of 28 guns, and ordered to the Leeward Island station.

This Station opened a new scene to the Officers of the British navy. The Americans, when colonists, possessed almost all the trade from America to our West India Islands: and on the return of Peace, they forgot, on this occasion, that they became Foreigners, and of course had no right to trade in the British Colonies. Our Governors and Custom-house officers pretended, that by the Navigation Act they had a right to trade; and all the West Indians wished what was so much for their interest.

Having given Governors, Custom-house Officers, and Americans, notice of what I would do, I seized many of their vessels, which brought all parties upon me; and I was persecuted from one Island to another, so that I could not leave my Ship. But conscious rectitude bore me through it; and I was supported, when the business came to be understood, from home: and I proved, (and an Act of Parliament has since established it,) that a Captain of a Man of War is bound to support all the Maritime Laws, by his Admiralty commission alone, without becoming a Custom-house officer.

In July, 1786, I was left with the command till June, 1787, when I sailed for England. During the winter H.R.H. the Duke of Clarence visited the Leeward Islands in the *Pegasus* frigate, of which he was Captain. And in March, this year, I married Frances Herbert Nisbet, widow of Dr. Nisbet, of the Island of Nevis; by whom I have no children.

The *Boreas* being paid off at Sheerness, on November the 30th, I lived at Burnham Thorpe, county of Norfolk, in the Parsonage-house. In 1790, when the Affair with Spain, relative to Nootka Sound, had nearly involved us in a war, I made use of every interest to get a Ship, ay, even a boat, to serve my Country, but in vain: there was a prejudice at the Admiralty evidently against me, which I can neither guess at, nor in the least account for. . . .

On the 30th January 1793, I was commissioned in the handsomest way for the *Agamemnon*, 64 guns; and was put under the command of that great man and excellent officer Lord Hood, appointed to the command in the Mediterranean. The unbounded confidence on all occasions placed in me by his Lordship, will show his opinions of my abilities; having served in the command of the seamen landed for the sieges of Bastia and Calvi. His Lordship, in October 1794, left the Mediterranean to Admiral Hotham, who also honoured me with the same confidence. I was in the Actions of the 13th and 14th of March 1795, and 13th of July in the same year. For the share I had in them, I refer to the Admiralty letters. I was then appointed by Admiral Hotham to co-operate with the Austrian General, De Vins, which I did all the time Admiral Hotham retained the command, till November; when he was superseded by Sir John Jervis, now Earl Vincent.

In April 1796, the Commander-in-Chief so much approved my conduct, that he directed me to wear a Distinguishing Pendant. In June I was removed from the *Agamemnon* to the *Captain*; and on the 11th of August had a Captain appointed under me. Between April and October 1796, I was employed in the blockade of Leghorn, taking Porto Ferrajo, the Island of Caprea, and finally in the evacuation of Bastia: when having seen the troops in safety to Porto Ferrajo, I joined the Admiral in St. Fiorenzo Bay, and proceeded with him to Gibraltar; whence in December I was sent in *La Minerve* frigate, Captain George Cockburn, to Porto Ferrajo, to bring down our Naval stores, &c. On the passage we captured a Spanish Frigate, *La Sabina*, of 40 guns, 28 eighteen pounders on her main deck, as will appear by my Letter.

For an account of what passed from our sailing from Porto Ferrajo on the 29th of January 1797, to the finish of the Action, on the 14th of February, I refer to the account published by Colonel Drinkwater. The King for my conduct gave me a gold Medal, and the city of London a gold Box.

In April 1797, I hoisted my Flag as Rear-Admiral of the Blue, and was sent to bring down the garrison of Porto Ferrajo: which service performed, I shifted my Flag from the *Captain* to the *Theseus* on May the 27th, and was employed in the command of the inner Squadron at the blockade of Cadiz. It was during this period that perhaps my personal courage was more conspicuous than at any other part of my life. In an attack of the Spanish gun-boats, I was boarded in my barge with its common crew of ten men, Cockswain, Captain Fremantle, and myself, by the Commander of the gun-boats; the Spanish barge rowed twenty-six oars, besides Officers, thirty men in the whole. This was a service hand to hand with swords, in which my Cockswain, John Sykes, now no more, twice saved my life. Eighteen of the Spaniards being killed and several wounded, we succeeded in taking their Commander.

On the 15th of July 1797, I sailed for Teneriffe: for the event, I refer to my Letter on that Expedition. Having then lost my right arm, for this loss and my former services his Majesty was pleased to settle on me a pension of £1,000 a year. By some unlucky mismanagement of my arm, I was obliged to go to England; and it was the 13th of December 1797, before the surgeons pronounced me fit for service.

On the 19th of December, the *Vanguard* was commissioned for my Flag-ship. On the first of April 1798, I sailed with a convoy from Spithead: at the back of (the Isle of) Wight, the wind coming to the westward, I was forced to return to St. Helen's, and finally sailed on the 9th of April, carrying a convoy to Oporto and Lisbon. I joined Earl St. Vincent off Cadiz, on April 29th; on the 30th I was ordered into the Mediterranean. I refer to the printed Narrative of my proceedings to the close of the Battle of the Nile.

On the 22nd of September 1798, I arrived at Naples, and was received as a deliverer by the King, Queen, and the whole Kingdom. October 12th the blockade of Malta took place, which has continued without intermission to this day. On the 21st of December 1798, his Sicilian Majesty and family embarked in the *Vanguard*, and were carried to Palermo in Sicily. In March 1799, I arranged a plan for taking the Islands in the Bay of Naples, and for supporting the Royalists who were making head in the Kingdom. This plan succeeded in every part. In May I shifted my Flag, being promoted to be Rear-Admiral of the Red, to the *Foudroyant*, and was obliged to be on my guard against the French Fleet. In June and July 1799, I went to Naples, and, as his Sicilian Majesty is pleased to say, reconquered his Kingdom, and placed him on his Throne. On the 9th of August I brought his Sicilian Majesty back to Palermo, having been upwards of four weeks on board the *Foudroyant*.

On the 13th his Sicilian Majesty presented me with a Sword magnificently enriched with diamonds, the Title of Duke of Bronte, and annexed to it the feud of Bronte, supposed to be worth £3,000 per annum. On the arrival of the Russian Squadron at Naples, I directed Commodore Troubridge to go with the Squadron, and blockade closely Civita Vecchia, and to offer the French most favourable conditions, if they would evacuate Rome and Civita Vecchia; which terms the French General Grenier complied with, and they were signed on board the *Culloden*; when a prophecy, made to me on my arrival at Naples, was fulfilled, viz. *that I should take Rome with my Ships*.

Thus may be exemplified by my Life, that perseverance in any profession will most probably meet its reward. Without having any inheritance, or having been fortunate in prize-money, I have received all the Honours of my Profession, been created a Peer of Great Britain, &c. &c. as set forth in the annexed paper: and I may say to the Reader, 'GO THOU, AND DO LIKEWISE.'

NELSON

October 15th, 1799, Port Mahon

THE ANNEXED PAPER

Presents received for my services in the Mediterranean between 1 October 1798, and 1 October 1799:

From my own most gracious Sovereign, a Peerage of Great Britain and a Gold Medal.

From the Parliament of Great Britain, for my life and two next heirs, 2,000£ per annum.

From the Parliament of Ireland, not known, but supposed the same as given to St. Vincent and Duncan, 1,000£ per annum.

From the Honourable East India Company, 10,000£.

From the Turkey Company, a piece of plate.

From Alexander Davidson, Esq., a gold medal.

City of London, a sword.

The captains who served under my orders in the battle of the Nile, a sword.

The Grand Signor, a diamond aigrette or plume of triumph, valued at 2,000£. Ditto, a rich pelisse, valued at 1,000£.

The Grand Signor's mother, a box set with diamonds valued at 1,000£.

Emperer of Russia, a box set with diamonds, and a most elegant letter—2,500£.

King of the Sicilies, a sword richly ornamented with diamonds and a most elegant and kind letter, 5,000£, and the Dukedom of Bronte, with an estate supposed worth 3,000£ per annum.

King of Sardinia, a box set with diamonds, and a most elegant letter, 1,200£.

The island of Zante, a gold-headed sword and cane, as an acknowledgment that had it not been for the battle of the Nile they could not have been liberated from French cruelty.

City of Palermo, a gold box and chain, brought on a silver waiter.

CHAPTER ONE

THE YOUNG CAPTAIN

[The First Section of Nelson's letters covers a period of sixteen years between 1777 when he was nineteen and 1793 when he was appointed to the command of the *Agamemnon*.

During the first nine years of this period Nelson was almost continuously at sea and was promoted from Lieutenant to Commander and from Commander to Captain. He spent several years on the West Indies and Leeward Island stations, during which he was engaged in a bitter struggle with the American traders. It was at this time also that his courtship and marriage took place.

During his seven years service before he passed his examination as Lieutenant, in 1777, Nelson as a youth had already gained considerable practical experience afloat.

At the age of twelve he went to sea with his uncle, Captain Maurice Suckling, in the *Raisonable*. Then he was sent in a merchant ship to the West Indies and on his return spent a considerable time in boat work in the Thames Estuary, learning pilotage and navigation. His next expedition was to the Arctic regions as a boy of fourteen and on his return from this Polar voyage he spent two years on the East Indies station from which he was invalided home. During the hard winter of 1776-77, he was at sea with the Gibraltar convoys and on 9th April, 1777, he passed his examination as lieutenant and was appointed to the *Lowestoft* frigate, captain William Locker.

Thereafter he spent several years on the West Indian and Leeward Islands station and finally returned to England in the *Boreas* in 1787, accompanied by his wife.]

THE LETTERS

1777

To his brother William Nelson, Christ College, Cambridge.

[The first known extant letter from Nelson]

Navy Office, *April 14th, 1777*

Dear Brother,

My father arrived in town on Friday evening in tolerable good health; my sister and brother are both well, and desire their love to you. I suppose you have not heard of my arrival in England yet, but we arrived on Thursday week, but I have been so full of business in preparing to set out again, that I have not had time to write. I passed my Degree as Master of Arts on the 9th instant, (that is, passed the Lieutenant's examination*), and received my Commission on the following day, for a fine Frigate of 32 guns. So I am now left in the world to shift for myself, which I hope I shall do, so as to bring credit to myself and friends. Am sorry there is no possiblity this time of seeing

* From the following copy of his 'Passing Certificate' it appears that Nelson's examination took place on the *ninth*, and not as he states on the *eighth* of April, 1777.

'Lieutenants' Certificates. *June 1762-May 1777.*

'In pursuance, &c., of the 5th April 1777, we have examined Mr. Horatio Nelson, who by certificate appears to be more than twenty years of age, and find he has gone to sea more than six years in the Ships and Qualities undermentioned: (viz.)

(Nelson, in point of fact, was not more than twenty years of age at this time, having been born on 29th September, 1758.)

		Y.	M.	W.	D.
Raisonable	Mid.	0	5	0	1
Tryumph	Captain's Servant	1	2	0	2
	Mid.	0	10	1	5
Carcass	Mid.	0	5	3	0
Tryumph	Captain's Servant	0	0	1	5
Seahorse	Mid.	0	5	2	6
	Able	1	7	1	6
	Mid.	0	4	3	2
Dolphin	Mid.	0	6	3	6
		6	3	1	6

'He produceth Journals kept by himself in the *Carcass*, *Seahorse*, *Dolphin*, and *Worcester*, and Certificates from Captains Suckling, Lutwidge, Farmer, Pigott, and Robinson, of his diligence, &c.: he can splice, knot, reef a sail, &c., and is qualified to do the duty of an Able seaman and Midshipman. Dated the 9th April, 1777. M.S., Captain John Campbell, Captain Abraham North.'

The letters 'M.S.' were the initials of Captain Maurice Suckling, Nelson's uncle, then Comptroller of the Navy, who is said to have been present at the examination by virtue of his office; and of whom the following anecdote is related: 'Captain Suckling purposely concealed his relationship from the examining captains. When his nephew had recovered from his confusion, his answers were prompt and satisfactory, and indicated the talents he so eminently possessed. The examination ended in a manner very honourable to him: upon which his uncle immediately threw off his reserve, and rising from his seat, introduced his nephew. The examining captains expressed their surprise at his not having informed them of this before. "No," replied the independent Comptroller, "I did not wish the younker to be favoured: I felt convinced that he would pass a good examination; and you see, gentlemen, I have not been disappointed." '

each other, but I hope that will come in a few years, when we will spend some merry hours together.
N.B. If it is not too troublesome turn over.

Where we shall go at present, I know not, but wherever it is, I will always write to you. If you ever choose to write, inclose either to Mr. Suckling,* or my brother†, as in all probability they will know where we are gone. I leave London on Wednesday evening, so shall always be glad to hear from you. Believing me to be, dear Brother, your affectionate brother,

HORATIO NELSON

P.S. Pray give my best respects to my old school-fellow, H. Hammond.‡

To Captain William Locker
[Captain Locker then commanded the *Lowestoffe*, of which ship Nelson was second lieutenant. They sailed for the West Indies in May, and anchored at Barbadoes on 4th July, 1777. On the 19th of that month the *Lowestoffe* arrived at Port Royal, in Jamaica. The address of this letter is wanting, but it would appear to have been written during Captain Locker's temporary absence from his ship in consequence of ill health].

Lowestoffe, at Sea, *August 12th, 1777*

My most worthy Friend,

I am exceedingly obliged to you for the good opinion you entertain of me, and will do my utmost that you may have no occasion to change it. I hope God Almighty will be pleased to spare your life, for your own sake, and that of your family: but should any thing happen to you, (which I sincerely pray God, may not,) you may be assured that nothing shall be wanting on my part for the taking care of your effects, and delivering safe to Mrs. Locker such of them as may be thought proper not to be disposed of. You mentioned the word 'consolation,' in your letter—I shall have a very great one, when I think I have served faithfully the best of friends, and the most amiable of women.

All the services I can render to your family, you may be assured shall be done, and shall never end but with my life; and may God Almighty

* His maternal uncle, Captain Maurice Suckling, then Comptroller of the Navy, and M.P. for Portsmouth.

† His eldest brother, Maurice Nelson, then Clerk for Foreign Accounts in the Navy Office. He died in April, 1801.

‡ Apparently, his distant relation, Horace Hamond, son of Dr. Horace Hamond.

of his great goodness keep, bless, and preserve you, and your family, is the most fervent prayer

Of your faithful servant,

HORATIO NELSON

P.S. Though this letter is not couched in the best manner be assured it comes from one entirely devoted to your service.

H. N.

1778

To Captain Locker, *Lowestoffe*

Bristol, Monday afternoon [apparently *31st August, 1778*]

Dear Sir,

Your goodness to me has been more than ever I expected, or had any right to think on in every respect. The man you mentioned I should be very happy to have with me, as the one is very assiduous, the other you know (is) one of my favourites. I will write to Mr. Hodgeson the first opportunity. One of these days we shall meet, but I know you would not have me ask where there is a probability of being refused. Dundas*,— I thought I had mentioned him before: he messes with us, and keeps the fourth watch: he agrees tolerable well, as he has been told the man he has to deal with, but I am sure he has wished himself often on board the *Lowestoffe*. Cunningham has sent me a jar of sweetmeats, which I am much obliged to him for. I heard of you by M'Namara yesterday. I hope it is not true the accounts we have here of the taking the *Minerva*†. May health and happiness attend (you) is the constant sincere wish of your humble Servant,

HORATIO NELSON

[Nelson was appointed Commander of the *Badger* brig on the 8th December, 1778.]

1779

To Captain Locker, *Lowestoffe*

Badger, off the N.E. End, *April 30th, 1779*

Dear Sir,

I hope with all my heart you are much better than when I left you, and that you will not be obliged to go home on account of your health.

* Thomas Dundas, who had been a midshipman of the *Lowestoffe*: he was made a lieutenant in 1798, commanded the *Naiad* frigate in the Battle of Trafalgar, and died a vice-admiral and K.C.B. in March, 1841.

† On the 22nd August, 1778, the *Minerva*, 32, Captain John Stott, was taken by *La Concorde*, 40; and on the 2nd September, in the same year, the *Active*, 28, Captain William Williams, was captured by the French ships mentioned by Nelson. Neither of the captains survived their misfortune many weeks.

I wish sincerely it was in my power in some measure to show some small return for the many favours I have received, but I am sure you do not think me ungrateful. If you come on the North Side, and I hear of it, I will come in. I know you will be pleased with this little earnest of success, but we have had a good deal of plague with her*. Two days before we could find the French papers, at last found them in an old shoe. There is a polacre coming this way; I hope we shall fall in her way. I wish I could give a good character of Mr. Capper: he is a drunkard; I need say no more. We shall part whenever he can get Mate of a Merchant ship. George Cruger behaves very well. If you have heard from Mrs. Locker, I sincerely hope she and all the family are in good health; and that you and they may continue so, and enjoy every blessing of this life, is the real sincere wish of

Your much obliged and faithful Servant,

HORATIO NELSON

[On 11th June, 1779, some months before his twenty-first birthday, Nelson was promoted to and appointed to the command of H.M.S. *Hinchinbrook*.]

1780

To Captain Locker — Port Royal, *January 23rd, 1780*

My dear Sir,

I arrived here from a cruize in the middle of December, and received your letter from London with great pleasure, as I much feared you were in France; and on the 10th of this month, I received your letter from Kent, dated October 3rd, and am sorry you are not quite recovered. I sailed in the *Hinchinbrook* from Port Royal in the middle of September, to join the *Niger* and *Penelope*. We took four Sail, for which I shall share about 800*l*. sterling. We left the *Penelope* at sea, who soon afterwards took a Spanish privateer: the crew rose upon the *Penelope*, and have carried her off: they certainly have killed poor Captain Jones and his Officers.†

I know you will be sincerely sorry for the loss of poor Hill, who died of fever at Rattan. He had entirely recovered of his wounds. I suppose you have heard he lost his right hand in the action. William Forrest,

* On the 28th April, 1779, the *Badger* captured *La Prudente* of eighty tons and nine men.

† This report was not true; but the *Penelope*, Captain James Jones, foundered with all her crew in that year.

your old Coxswain, is amongst the slain. The *Lowestoffe* was the first that stormed, under the command of Dundas.

I am now going to tell you what you and many others will be very sorry to hear—the death of that worthy, good man, Captain Joseph Deane. He died on the 12th of January, and was buried next day, at Green Bay, amidst the tears of his Officers and Ship's company, and his many friends. Captain Cowling is appointed to the *Ruby*. Of that noble Ship's crew, three hundred took boats and are gone off. Every method has been used to bring them back, which I hope will prove successful. The *Salisbury* has brought in a Spanish Storeship, mounting fifty-six guns, four hundred men, from Cadiz to Port Omoa, after a smart action of two hours and a half. The *Salisbury* lost nine men; the *Don* fifty men.

Our mess is broke up. Captain Cornwallis and myself live together. I hope I have made a friend of him, which I am sure from his character you will be glad to hear. Lambert has changed into the *Leviathan*, to go home. I have sent a cask or two of shaddocks by him, and Mr. Taylor sends to him this day, that if convenient to take two casks of old rum for you. I shall take your rum out of the *Lowestoffe* and keep it with me until you send for it. The Spanish Ship is to be made a Ship of 36 guns. The Admiral offered her to me, which I declined. He says he will give me the first Frigate. He has appointed me to go with an Expedition which is now on foot against the city of Grenada, upon the Lake of Niguragua.* How it will turn out, God knows. I do not expect to return before the beginning of June, but I shall always take every opportunity of writing to you. Collingwood† desires to be very particularly remembered to you and Mrs. Locker, to whom I beg you (to) give my best respects.

The Admiral sails with the Fleet on Tuesday next, the 25th January, to meet if he can the Count de Grasse, who has been cruizing these some weeks past between Cape Nicola and Maize with five Sail of the Line.

You must not be surprised to see me in England after this trip; for if my health is not much better than it is at present, I shall certainly come home, as all the Doctors are against my staying so long in this country. You know my old complaint in my breast; it is turned out to be the gout got there. Kitty Crawford sends you two jars of tamarinds. Cuba, and all your old acquaintances in this part of the world, desire to be kindly remembered to you; and none more so than Captain Cornwallis, who has, I assure you, a very high esteem for your character. Caulfield is to stay behind this cruize to take his trial. Captain Pakenham

* *Vide Sketch of my Life.*

† Captain Cuthbert Collingwood, afterwards Vice-Admiral Lord Collingwood.

(Lord Longford's brother) goes in his Ship. Glover is very ill; I hardly think he will get over this cruize. I have been twice given over since you left this country with that cursed disorder, the gout. I must make this a double letter, though against your desire. We have just heard the *Penelope* was carried into St. Jago, in Cuba. She has been cruizing off the West end of Jamaica. I must now bid you Adieu, wishing you every thing you can wish in this life, and believe me to be with real sincerity,

Your much obliged and sincere friend,

HORATIO NELSON

Captain Inglis desires his compliments.

To Sir Peter Parker, Knight,
Vice-Admiral of the Blue, and Commander-in-Chief at Jamaica

Port Royal, Jamaica, *the 30th of August, 1780*

Sir,

Having been in a very bad state of health for these several months past, so bad as to be unable to attend my duty on board the *Janus*, and the faculty having informed me that I cannot recover in this climate; I am therefore to request that you will be pleased to permit me to go to England for the re-establishment of my health.

I am, Sir, &c.

HORATIO NELSON

1781

To William Locker, Esq., Gray's Inn Bath, *February 15th, 1781*

Dear Sir,

It is really so long since I have wrote to you, that I am almost ashamed to write at all; but I know your goodness will forgive me, although I hardly deserve it. My health, thank God, is very near perfectly restored; and I have the perfect use of all my limbs, except my left arm, which I can hardly tell what is the matter with it. From the shoulder to my fingers' ends are as if half dead; but the Surgeon and Doctors give me hopes it will all go off. I most sincerely wish to be employed, and hope it will not be long. I have thought several times you were appointed to a Ship, else you would have wrote, if only to scold me for neglect: if I am not employed, I intend coming to town the beginning of March. I hope when I come to town to see a fine trio in your room. If Mr. Rigaud has done the picture*, send word in the next letter you write to me, and I will inclose you an order upon Mr. Paynter. Tell Mr. Rigaud I wish him joy of his picture being got to the Sardinian Ambassador's Chapel, and to hear it so well spoke of in the public Papers. Captain Kirke's man has just been here to tell me his master, mistress, and family are come down. I am glad of it. I think the bathing will do infinite service to Mrs. Kirke. I must wish you a good night, and drink your health in a draught of my Physician's cordial and a bolus. Adieu, and believe me to be,

Your sincere friend and devoted humble Servant,

HORATIO NELSON

Pray give my best compliments to Captain Pole, and tell him I hope we shall renew our acquaintance. When you get the pictures, I must be in the middle, for God knows, without good *Supporters*, I shall fall to the ground.

To the Rev. Mr. Nelson,
Burnham, Norfolk

Kentish Town,† *May 7th, 1781*

My dear Brother,

I have no doubt but you have scolded me pretty heartily for not having answered your letter before this time, and therefore I will begin to plead my excuse. In the first place, I was thirty miles on the other side London, and did not return here till the 30th of April, at night. On Thursday, I received your second, with the power of attorney, since which time I have been so much engaged that I really have not had a spare moment. I was with Lord Sandwich yesterday, and he could fix no time when I should be employed, although he promised he would employ me the first opportunity, so all these matters are settled, and now you will say, Why does not he come into Norfolk? I will tell you: I have entirely lost the use of my left arm, and very near of my left leg and thigh, and am at present under the care of a Mr. Adair, an eminent Surgeon in London; but he gives me hopes a few weeks will remove my disorder, when I will certainly come into Norfolk, and spend my time there till I am employed. When you write to my father do not mention my complaints, for I know it will make him very uneasy, and can do no good; and if you tell it to my sisters, desire them not to

* A portrait of Nelson, by John Francis Rigaud, R.A., which was placed by Captain Locker, to whom it was presented, between the portraits of Captains, afterwards Admirals, Sir George Montague and Sir Charles Morice Pole.

† The residence of his uncle, Mr. William Suckling, of the Navy Office.

mention it. I saw Maurice* the other day: he is very well, and says he wishes much to pay a visit to Burnham. I beg you will remember me kindly to all those gentlemen who have been so good as to inquire after me, and believe me to be

Your affectionate Brother,

HORATIO NELSON

Pray give my kind love to all my brothers and sisters.

To the Rev. Mr. Nelson, Junr., Burnham

[He was appointed to command the *Albemarle*, a small frigate of twenty-eight guns, early in August, 1781.]

Kentish Town, *August 24th, 1781*

Dear Brother,

According to my promise I sit down to write you an account of the *Albemarle*. Yesterday I went down to Woolwich with Maurice, and hoisted my Pendant; and I am perfectly satisfied with her, as a twenty-eight gun Frigate. She is in dock, alongside the *Enterprise*, and in some respects, I think, excels her. She has a bold entrance, and clean run. The *Enterprise*, a *lean bow*, which does not answer so well with copper, as they always allow for sheathing, which is upwards of an inch more in thickness, therefore, she wants that much. The *Albemarle* is not so wide, upon the gun-deck, by four inches, but the same beam; the gun-deck six feet high; between decks very low indeed, about five feet. She is now coppering, and will not be out of dock this fortnight, at least.

The Admiralty have been very civil, having given me the choice of all my Officers, which I am much pleased with. Now if you will ask Forster to enter for the Ship, he shall be rated Master's-mate, and receive five pounds bounty money; and if he can bring any Seamen with him, shall have two pounds for each man, and they will have the same bounty. They can come by any of the Wells' Ships, who shall be paid for bringing them. I have talked with Mr. Suckling about your going Chaplain in the Navy, and he thinks, as I do, that fifty pounds where you are, is much more than equal to what you can get at Sea; but in that I know you will please yourself, therefore shall not attempt to state any argument to *dissuade* you from it. Your own judgment must rule you. I beg my kind love to my father, and my brothers and sisters. Adieu, and assure yourself that I am in every respect your affectionate Brother,

HORATIO NELSON

* His brother, Maurice Nelson.

To the Reverend Mr. Nelson, Junr.,
Burnham Sheerness, *October 18th, 1781*

Dear Brother,

According to my promise, I sit down to write: I came down to the Nore on Sunday last, and am now full manned, and ready for any service. I have an exceeding good Ship's company. Not a man or Officer in her I would wish to change. She appears to sail also very well. Where I am going, I know not, but suppose I shall be gone from here in the next week, when I will write again. I hope Mrs. Bolton's* troubles are over. Give my kind love to her, and to my father, sister, and Mun;† tell him I would not take either Mr. Wiseman or Walker. I hardly think I have so bad a man in my Ship. I have got John Oliver, belonging to Wells, and have made him a Quarter-master; he is a very good man.

I am, dear Brother, yours affectionately,

HORATIO NELSON

Compliments to the Wells' Club, and all friends in Norfolk.

1782

To William Locker, Esq.,
Gray's Inn *Albemarle*, Downs, *January 2nd, 1782*

My dear Sir,

The instant I received your letter, the latter part struck me so very much, that perhaps I write to you sooner than otherwise I should have done. I need not say it to you, but what in the *name* of *God* could it be to me, whether a Midshipman in my Ship had not a farthing or fifty pounds a-year? therefore now I must tell you, as far as I know, his wish to leave the Ship. When he came on board, I sent him into Mr. Bromwich's mess, where he was two or three days. In that time they spoke to me, that they hoped I would not take it amiss, but they could not think of keeping that young man (I forget his name) in their mess, as he could not pay his part of their small expenses. I am sure that you will not think I should attempt to force any person upon people who were behaving exceedingly well in the Ship, (which would have been

* Nelson's eldest sister, Susannah, who was born 12th June, 1755, and married 5th August, 1780, Thomas Bolton of Cranwich, in Norfolk. She gave birth to twin daughters on 20th November, 1781. Her son Thomas succeeded as second Earl Nelson. Mrs. Bolton died in July, 1813.

† His brother, Edmund, then a lad nineteen years of age. He died unmarried in December, 1789.

tyrannical in the highest degree) against their inclination. Whether the lad sent to speak to me, or I sent for him, I do not recollect; but I told him of what the mess had said. He then seemed very uneasy at what I told him, and said he could not afford to live in a mess that cost anything; and then said he wished to leave the Ship. The next day he pressed me much to discharge him, as he could not live in any of the midmesses. Much against my inclination I did *discharge* him. What he took the idea of 30*l.* a year from, I know not; for I declare I never opened my lips to him upon the subject. A youngster in the Ship, whose friends are Norfolk people, who had not made an allowance for their son, I took upon me to allow 20*l.* a year.

I assure you, I hold myself under very great obligations to you, that you asserted it was an *infamous lie*: had I in the least suspected the story he has told, he should staid on board, and might have lived as he pleased. It was my endeavouring to put him in a comfortable situation, that has made any person speak ill of me. If he had come into the Ship as many hundred youngsters of the kind do, and the Captain had (*a word illegible*) to him, or of him to anybody for. . . months, I should have had no trouble about him. I can't help being a little surprised that Captain Kirke should have such an opinion of me; and I am sure (I) shall always be happy to obey his commands in the fullest meaning of *the words*. I hope both he and Mrs. Kirke are well: if you should write or see them, I beg my best respects. I have never received your letter about discharging Mr. Mitchel; but you know he is, long before this. He is, as I wrote to you by him. I am sorry poor Bradley is taken, and that the other brother is so ill. Fortitude is not here, or I would send after Jack Moore. Adieu, my dear Sir, and believe that I am

Your much obliged obedient Servant,

HORATIO NELSON

I am much afraid we are fixed for the North Seas, as another has orders to take our Convoy.

To William Locker, Esq.,
Gray's Inn

Portsmouth, *February 5th, 1782*

My dear Sir,

Since I received yours, the *Albemarle* is much altered for the worse. An East India Store-Ship came on board us in a gale of wind, and carried away our foremast, bowsprit, head, and quarter gallery, and done considerable damage to her hull. We arrived here two days ago, and are now coming into the harbour to be docked. I was ordered for Foreign service. Charles Pole is here: he is going to Gibraltar with a large Cutter, laden with Gun-boats; I wish he was safe back. I think he runs great risk of going to Cadiz.* Sir Richard Bickerton is here;—*a great man*, he seems to carry it pretty high with his Captains. Jack Moore is with him, and I heard him tell Captain Robinson, who was Admiral Parker's Captain in the *Fortitude*, he would certainly provide for him. I shall certainly see you in Town before the *Albemarle* gets out of the harbour. Mr. White, the builder, has inquired after you. Farewell, my dear Sir, and believe me to be,

Faithfully yours,

HORATIO NELSON

Compliments to the Bradleys, and all that ask after me.

To the Reverend Mr. Nelson,
Burnham

Portsmouth, *February 8th, 1782*

Dear Brother,

Your letter of January 30th I received two nights ago; and am much obliged to you for it; I should have wrote before I did from the Downs, only I expected my orders every day, when I could have told you where I was to have been stationed. You have heard of the accidents that have happened to the poor *Albemarle*, both by my letter and the Papers long before this. I was under orders for Foreign service, and I fancy was going with dispatches to North America. I am now waiting at Spithead for a wind to bring me into the harbour to be docked and repaired; what will become of me afterwards I know not. If I should touch at any wine Countries, you may assure Lord Walpole I will purchase some of the best wines for him. I beg you will make my best respects to him and Lady Walpole, with many thanks for their kind inquiries after me. I regret very much I had not the pleasure of receiving Mr. Walpole on board the *Albemarle*, or if he had been in Yarmouth, I should certainly have paid my respects to him. Apropos of wine:—in my opinion, the expense of sending a cask of wine from this place to Burnham is almost the original cost; but there it is, if you please to have it; only send word. Charles Boyles sailed from here the day before my arrival.

Whatever may be the opinion of the Wells people respecting Captain Gardner's behaviour in the matter of his Lieutenants quitting his Ship, I will answer he was right. There is not a better Officer, or more of a gentleman, this day in the Service. I am much afraid poor Charles will wait a long while with Mr. R—— before he gets promotion, for he is a great *liar*. Sir Richard Bickerton, with the East India Fleet, sailed yesterday afternoon, with six Sail of the Line for India, and three Sail

* That is, of being captured by the Spaniards.

of the Line and two Fifties, to go part of the way with them. The West India Fleet is not yet ready: they will sail Saturday or Sunday, if the wind is fair.

I wish I could congratulate you upon a Rectory instead of a Vicarage: it is rather *awkward* wishing the poor man *dead*, but we all rise by *deaths*. I got my rank by a shot killing a Post-Captain, and I most sincerely hope I shall, when I go, go out of (the) world the same way; then we go all in the line of our Profession—a *Parson* praying, a Captain fighting. I suppose you are returned from Hilborough before this, and taken *Miss Ellen* and the *Living*. As Miss Bec takes so much notice of my respect to her, tell her I think myself honoured by being in her favour. Love to Mrs. Bolton and Mun, not forgetting little Kate.* You have wrote so long a letter, that I must get another half sheet to work.† . . .

To Captain Locker   Cork, *April 20th, 1782*

My dear Sir,

After a very long passage of ten days, owing to very bad weather, we are at last got here; the *Dædalus*, our consort, arrived the same day. To-morrow we sail, if the wind continues fair. Captain Pringle goes upon the Newfoundland station, after having seen us to the entrance of the River St. Lawrence. Our Convoy is between thirty and forty Sail. I know your goodness will say, 'I wonder how Nelson does?' I say, I am quite well, better than for a long time past. I hope by the time I get back, all your complaints will be removed. Remember me kindly to all the Bradleys, and don't forget me to Commissioner Kirke, nor to Charles Pole, when you see him: never a young man bore his own merits with so much modesty. Farewell, my dear Sir, and believe me to to be

Ever faithfully yours,

HORATIO NELSON

The *Preston*, I understand, is to bring out the English Quebec Fleet. I should be happy to hear from you. Will you send to Mr. Paynter, and tell him I am at Cork?

To William Locker, Esq.,   St. John's Harbour,
Gray's Inn   Newfoundland, *June 1st, 1782*

My dear Sir,

We arrived at this disagreeable place last Monday, at daylight (the

* His youngest sister Katherine, who was born 19th March, 1767: she married on the 26th February, 1787, George Matcham of Ashford Lodge, and died 28th March, 1842, leaving a large family.

† The conclusion is not preserved.

27th) with four Sail of the Convoy; we parted from the *Dædalus* on the 7th of May, three hundred leagues to the Westward of Cape Clear, in a hard gale of wind. As the wind has blown strong from the Eastward, ever since our arrival here, I imagine that Captain Pringle could not fetch this Port, and is therefore gone on to the Westward; if he is, this wind will carry him to Quebec, while I am so unfortunate as to be kept here with a fair wind; for the entrance of this harbour is so narrow, that you cannot sail unless the wind blows right out: as soon as the wind changes I shall sail.

Leocadia arrived here three days before us with the Salt Ships from Lisbon. Captain Hope desires his compliments; he took a Ship privateer, the day he made the land, of fourteen guns. We have heard the news from the West Indies, but not particulars: it is reported that the *Duke* blew up in the Action. I hope to God it is not true. I had rather the French were at the devil, than have lost Captain Gardner: he is a real loss to the Service.* You know the particulars long before this. My second Lieutenant was appointed to the *Preston*, and left the Ship at Cork; the other Lieutenant not having joined the Ship, I gave Bromwich an order to act as a Lieutenant: it will in all probability get him some prize-money, and I hope get him confirmed a Lieutenant; he does his duty exceedingly well as an Officer: indeed I am very well off. They are all good.

As to myself, the voyage agrees better with me than I expected. I hope you are much better in your head than when I sailed, and that Mr. James Bradley is got from under the Doctor's hands. Remember me to them all, and all my old friends that you may see. I think the chance is much against your getting this letter, as it goes by way of Lisbon.

Farewell, my dear Sir, and believe me to be

Your much obliged faithful Servant,

HORATIO NELSON

Bromwich desires his best respects. You must not forget mine to Commissioner Kirke when you see him. *June 3.* The remainder of the Quebec Fleet are arrived at a harbour a few leagues to leeward of this, and I am now getting under sail to join them with the other part of the Fleet from this place. The Irish Newfoundland Fleet arrived here on

* Sir George Rodney's engagement with the French Fleet under Count de Grasse, on the 12th April, 1782. The report of the explosion of the *Duke* was unfounded. Captain Alan Gardner, who greatly distinguished himself in that battle, and on numerous other occasions, became an admiral, was raised to the Peerage, both in England and Ireland, and died in December, 1808.

the 1st of June, and the *Arethusa* with the English Fleet at a place where the Quebec Fleet are, on the 2nd Instant, with their whole Fleets: not a Ship taken in any of the Fleets.

Certificate of Release of an American Prize.

On the 14th of July 1782, the *Albemarle* captured an American fishing Schooner, belonging to Cape Cod, and not having any Officer on board who was acquainted with Boston Bay and the adjacent shoals, Captain Nelson ordered Nathaniel Carver, the Master of the Schooner, to come on board the *Albemarle*, and act as her Pilot.

Having obeyed Captain Nelson's orders to his satisfaction, he said to him, 'You have rendered us, Sir, a very essential service, and it is not the custom of English seamen to be ungrateful. In the name, therefore, and with the approbation of the Officers of this Ship, I return your Schooner, and with it this Certificate of your good conduct. Farewell! and may God bless you.'

These are to Certify, that I took the Schooner *Harmony*, Nathaniel Carver, Master, belonging to Plymouth; but, on account of his good Services, have given him up his Vessel again. Dated on board His Majesty's Ship *Albemarle*, 17th of August, 1782.

Boston Bay HORATIO NELSON

To William Locker, Esq.,
Gray's Inn *Albemarle*, Isle of Bic, River St. Lawrence,
October 19th, 1782

My dear Sir,

My letter from Newfoundland, by the way of Lisbon, if you ever will receive, you have got long before this time; but this I most sincerely hope will not find you at Gray's Inn; but that Old England, at this time of need, will have the services of so good an Officer.

We arrived here with the Convoy on the 1st of July, and I sailed upon a cruise the 4th, and returned to Quebec on the 17th of September, knocked up with the scurvy; having (for) eight weeks, myself and all the Officers (lived) upon salt beef; nor had the Ship's company had a fresh meal since the 7th of April. In the end, our cruise has been an unsuccessful one; we have taken, seen, and destroyed more Enemies than is seldom done in the same space of time, but not one arrived in Port. But, however, I do not repine at our loss; we have in other things been very fortunate, for on the 14th of August, we fell in with, in Boston Bay, four Sail of the Line, and the *Iris*, French Man-of-War, part of M. Vaudreuil's Squadron, who gave us a pretty dance for between nine or ten hours; but we beat all except the Frigate, and though we brought to for her, after we were out of sight of the Line of Battle Ships, she tacked and stood from us.* Our escape I think wonderful: they were upon the clearing up of a fog within shot of us, and chased us the whole time about one point from the wind: the Frigate, I fancy, had not forgot the dressing Captain Salter had given the *Amazon*,† for daring to leave the Line of Battle Ships.

About a fortnight ago, when I was at Quebec, with no other expectation or desires than to return to England, arrives the *Drake* Sloop, and *Cockatrice* Cutter, with orders for the Transports to be fitted for the reception of Troops, and to be sent to New York: in consequence thereof, old Worth, has given me orders to carry the Fleet to New York —a very *pretty job* at this late season of the year, for our sails are at this moment frozen to the yards. The wind has at this instant flew round from the Eastward to the N.W., and I have just made the Signal to unmoor: you shall hear from me again when I reach New York. Farewell, my dear Sir, and assure (yourself)

I am your much obliged, and
Obedient humble Servant,
HORATIO NELSON

Give my compliments to the Bradleys, Commissioner Kirke, or any others that ask after me.

To the Reverend Mr. Nelson, Bath

[The Reverend Edmund Nelson was then at Bath for the benefit of his health. He was at that time in his sixtieth year; and died on the 20th of April, 1802.]

Albemarle, Isle of Bic,
River St. Lawrence, *October 19th, 1782*

My dear Father,

I wrote to Mr. Suckling when I was at Newfoundland, but I have not had an opportunity of writing to you till this time. I expected to have sailed for England on the 1st of November, but our destination is now altered, for we sail with a Fleet for New York to-morrow; and

* *Vide, Sketch of my Life.*

† Captain Elliot Salter, in the *Santa Margeretta*, of 32 guns and 220 men, captured on the 29th July, 1782, after a gallant action, the French frigate *l'Amazone* of 36 guns and 301 men, off Cape Henry.

from there I think it very likely we shall go to the *grand theatre* of Actions, the West Indies; but in our line of life we are sure of no one thing. When I reach New York you shall hear what becomes of me; but whilst I have health it is indifferent to me (were it not for the pleasure of seeing you and my brothers and sisters) where I go.

Health, that greatest of blessings, is what I never truly enjoyed till I saw *Fair* Canada. The change it has wrought, I am convinced is truly wonderful. I most sincerely wish, my dear Father, I could compliment you the same way; but I hope Bath has done you a great deal of good this summer. I have not had much success in the Prize way, but it is all in good time, and I do not know I ought to complain; for though I took several, but had not the good fortune to get one safe into Port, yet, on the other side, I escaped from five French Men-of-War in a wonderful manner. This is all the news I can tell you concerning myself. I can hardly say where you may write to me; but I should suppose you may soon learn where we are. If Nanny or Kate* are with you, give my kind love to them, and to all as you write to them. Farewell, my dearest Father, and assure yourself I always am, and ever shall be,

Your dutiful Son,

HORATIO NELSON

If Dr. Woodward is at Bath, give my compliments to him.

To William Locker, Esq.

Albemarle, New York, *November 17th, 1782*

My dear Sir,

My letter, by the Assistance, you must (have) received long ago. It was directed to you at Gray's Inn, but I suppose they will send it to you. I arrived here with all my Fleet safe on the 13th, which is a very fortunate thing at this season of the year. Peacock I saw and dined with the day I landed; I could not do less. He showed me a letter from you in August, where I was sorry to see you had not got perfectly well. Peacock has got the *L'Aigle*, a very fine Frigate, of twenty-eight, eighteen pounders, and three hundred and fifteen men. She had twenty-four, but she is far preferable with eighteen pounders. I wish he may have health, or I am sorry to say, life to enjoy her. The day he went with me to show me his Ship, he was, to all appearance, perfectly well. He was seized with a fit of *apoplexy*, which, if there had not been a Doctor by, who bled him plentifully, might have carried him off: however, he is now pretty well, but not able to get out of

* His sisters, Anne and Katherine.

doors. It is the second attack, but do not give him the least hint that you know of it, as I fancy the Doctors have pretty well persuaded him it was only a *casual* fainting. He is very much beloved by everybody here; and I think from my little personal acquaintance, he is a very genteel man.

I found Lord Hood here upon my arrival, and I have requested him to take me with him to the West Indies: he has wrote to Admiral Digby for me, and I was to have sailed with (the) Fleet as this day, but for some private reasons, when my Ship was under sail from New York to join Lord Hood, at Sandy Hook, I was sent for on shore, and told I was to be kept forty-eight hours after the sailing of the Fleet: it is much to my private advantage, but I had much rather have sailed with the Fleet: if there is wind enough they sail this day. I have told you all that concerns myself: if you write to me, direct it under cover to Mr. Hunt, Lord Hood's Secretary; he is a son of Hunt's, at the Navy Board. Charles Pilfold is here, one of the first to be made a Lieutenant: he is a charming character, beloved by his Captain, and all his acquaintance. I have had him with me almost ever since my arrival: he is taller and stouter than me. Peacock has not got a third Lieutenant as yet; I wish he could get him. I shall speak to him this day about him. He has the same gentle disposition and modesty as when a youngster: you must remember the little fellow well. He desires to be particularly remembered to you. Pray wish Mrs. Dyne* joy for me, and my best compliments to the old lady and all the family.

I am a candidate with Lord Hood for a Line of Battle Ship: he has honoured me highly by a letter, for wishing to go off this Station, to a Station of Service, and has promised me his friendship. Prince William† is with him; I think it is a prelude to the Digby's going off this station; money is the great object here, nothing else is attended to. Peacock will write to-day, he tells me: he will, perhaps, tell you all the news of this place.

* Miss Frances Bradley married on 9th July, 1782, Andrew Hawes Dyne, and died on 5th August, 1842.

† H.R.H. Prince William Henry, third son of King George III, afterwards Duke of Clarence, Admiral of the Fleet, and King William IV. The Prince gave Nelson his warmest friendship, and many letters were addressed to him. The following description of Nelson by the Prince is recorded:

'I was then a Midshipman on board the *Barfleur*, lying in the Narrows off Staten Island, and had the watch on deck, when Captain Nelson, of the *Albemarle*, came in his barge alongside, who appeared to be the merest boy of a Captain I ever beheld: and his dress was worthy of attention. He had on a full-laced uniform: his lank, unpowdered hair was tied in a stiff Hessian tail, of an extraordinary length; the old-fashioned flaps of his waistcoat added to the general quaintness of his figure, and produced an appearance which particularly attracted my notice; for I had never seen anything like it before, nor could I imagine who he was, nor what he came

The French are still in Boston. The Packet sails to-morrow, and I have been so much employed in fitting my Ship, that I could not get time to write before to-day; and you must excuse me for not saying more, though I could fill another sheet very well. When I arrive in the West Indies you will hear from me.

Farewell, my dear Friend, and be assured

I am your obliged humble Servant,

HORATIO NELSON

I have got but a corner, tell all my friends '*how do ye*.'

1783

To William Locker, Esq.

Albemarle, Off Cape Tiberoon, *February 25th, 1783*

My dear Sir,

As I see the Packet is in sight astern, I ought not to miss this opportunity of writing, more especially as I did not write when in Port-Royal harbour, for I was so much hurried in getting my Ship in order for Sea, that I had not time to look round me.

The Fleet arrived the 4th instant, and I suppose will be ready for Sea the last day of this month, although stores are as scarce at Jamaica as ever: sixteen topmasts were wanted for the Line of Battle Ships, and there was not one in the Island of Jamaica; and the Fleet must have been sent to Sea short of masts, had not providentially a French-Mast ship, belonging to Monsieur Vaudreuil's Fleet come alongside the *Albemarle*, and was captured by her. She has nearly a hundred topmasts

about. My doubts were, however, removed, when Lord Hood introduced me to him. There was something irresistibly pleasing in his address and conversation; and an enthusiasm, when speaking on professional subjects, that showed he was no common being. Nelson after this went with us to the West Indies, and served under Lord Hood's flag during his indefatigable cruize off Cape François. Throughout the whole of the American war, the height of Nelson's ambition was to command a Line-of-Battle Ship; as for prize-money, it never entered his thoughts: he had always in view the character of his maternal uncle. I found him warmly attached to my Father, and singularly humane: he had the honour of the King's service, and the independence of the British Navy, particularly at heart; and his mind glowed with this idea as much when he was simply Captain of the *Albemarle*, and had obtained none of the honours of his Country, as when he was afterwards decorated with so much well-earned distinction.'—*From Minutes of a Conversation with the Duke of Clarence at Bushey Park*, Clarke and M'Arthur, Vol. I, p. 53.

for large Ships, with a number of lower masts and yards. She will clear upwards of 20,000*l*. What a good prize if the Fleet had not been in sight. They do not deserve to share for her: we had chased to leeward, and she had passed every Ship in the Fleet without being noticed. The other Mast-ship that the French brought from America was run ashore, and entirely lost by the Fleet. They had parted from Vaudreuil in a gale of wind, and could not fetch St. John's, Porto Rico, which was their *rendezvous*, and therefore very fortunately came in our way. The French Fleet, finding we were off Monti Christi, went through the Mona Passage, and have been in sight of the Island of *Curaçoa*, but where they are God knows. I am sent out by Lord Hood to find them if I can.

We are all in the dark in this part of the world, whether it is *Peace* or War. If I should capture anything this cruize, I have made Hanbury and Shaw my Agents. Many inquiries were made after you at Jamaica, by people of all ranks and *colour*. Captain Reynolds, I think, told me he had heard from you lately, and that you were in good health, which, be assured, gave me great pleasure. The Fleet fell in with Charles Pole, but I was in chase, and could not see him. I had a letter from him ten days ago by a Ship who parted from his Squadron, for he is quite a Commodore here. He has been pretty successful since he came upon this Station, and will be very much so, if a *Neutral*, which he sent in, is given to him. She is condemned in Jamaica, but they have appealed, and in England we are afraid of the cursed Neutral flag.

My situation in Lord Hood's Fleet must be in the highest degree flattering to any young man. He treats me as if I was his son, and will, I am convinced, give me anything I can ask of him: nor is my situation with Prince William less flattering. Lord Hood was so kind as to tell him (indeed I cannot make use of expressions strong enough to describe what I felt), that if he wished to ask questions relative to Naval Tactics, I could give him as much information as any Officer in the Fleet. He will be, I am certain, an ornament to our Service. He is a *seaman*, which you could hardly suppose. Every other qualification you may expect from him. But he will be a *disciplinarian*, and a strong one: he says he is determined every person shall serve his time before they shall be provided for, as he is obliged to serve his. A vast deal of notice has been taken of him at Jamaica: he has been Addressed by the Council, and the House of Assembly were to address him the day after I sailed. He has his *Levées* at Spanish Town: they are all highly delighted with him. With the best temper, and great good sense, he cannot fail to being pleasing to every one.

But I must say God bless you, for the *Endymion's* boat is just coming on board, who is Convoy to the Packet: they sailed seven days before us from Port-Royal. You will remember me kindly to all my acquaintance and friends that you meet with. Farewell my good Sir, and assure yourself I am, and always shall be,

Your most affectionate Friend and Servant,

HORATIO NELSON

If I get safe back to Port-Royal (which is a matter of great doubt to me), I shall get a cask of the best rum on board for you, when you write, which I hope will have been long before you receive this. You may direct them to the care of Mr. Joseph Hunt, Lord Hood's Secretary, which will be a sure way of my getting them. Bromwich is second Lieutenant of the *Albemarle*, and is a very good Officer. Not an Officer has been changed, except the Second Lieutenant, since the *Albemarle* was commissioned, therefore it is needless to say, I am happy in my Ship's company. Once more farewell.

H. N.

To William Locker, Esq.,
West Malling, Kent Portsmouth, *June 26th, 1783*

My dear Friend,

After all my tossing about into various climates, here at last am I arrived safe, and sound. I found orders for the *Albemarle* to be paid off at this place. On Monday next I hope to be rid of her. My people I fancy will be pretty quiet, if they are not set on by some of the Ships here.*

I have on board for you, drawn off, twelve dozen of rum: I intend to put it for the present under Mr. White's care, as I dare say he will take care of it, (provided the Custom House do not seize it), for I do not think rum is worth the expense of the duty. I hope this will find you in perfect health. Captain Gardner tells me you still live at Malling. Farewell, my dear Sir, and assure yourself,

I am your affectionate Friend,

HORATIO NELSON

* On the reduction of the Navy, in consequence of the Peace, the crews of several ships were very insubordinate, insisting on being paid off at Portsmouth, instead of at Spithead; and it was not until strong measures had been adopted that the mutinous spirit was subdued.

To Captain Locker No. 3, Salisbury-street, Strand, *July 12th, 1783*

My dear Friend,

When I look at the date of your letter I received at Portsmouth, I ought to be ashamed at not having wrote to you; but you always knew I was a careless fellow, although, be assured, my great esteem and respect for you can never be lessened. My time, ever since I arrived in Town, has been taken up in attempting to get the wages due to my *good fellows*, for various Ships they have served in the war. The disgust of the Seamen to the Navy is all owing to the infernal plan of turning them over from Ship to Ship, so that Men cannot be attached to their Officers, or the Officers care two-pence about them.

My Ship was paid off last week; and in such a manner that must flatter any Officer, in particular in these turbulent times. The whole Ship's company offered, if I could get a Ship, to enter for her immediately; but I have no thought of going to Sea, for I cannot afford to live on board Ship, in such a manner as is going on at present.

Yesterday, Lord Hood carried me to Saint James's where the King was exceedingly attentive: on Monday or Tuesday I am to be at Windsor, to take leave of Prince William, previous to his embarkation for the continent.

A Captain Merrick, a young man of Lord Hood's bringing up, is to be with him. He is to go over in the *Augusta* yacht, Captain Vandeput. *Maude*, who you remember, is to be Lieutenant of the Yacht, (he came home third Lieutenant of the *Barfleur*), and to be made a Captain upon his return. Bromwich came home second Lieutenant with me; he is an attentive good Officer, indeed nobody could be happier in their Officers than I was. Trail, who came down passenger in the *Lowestoffe* to Jamaica, has been Master ever since the Ship was commissioned. If I had interest with the Comptroller, I would wish to get him to be Superintendent of some of the Ships in Ordinary. He is the best Master I ever saw since I went to Sea.

Frank* tells me he has sent down by the Maidstone waggon, forty gallons of rum, directed for you: he has sent it not in the way I intended, but I must beg your excuse for it. London is exceedingly hot: I shall fly to the Country as soon as I can settle my little matters.

Farewell, my dear Sir, and assure yourself,

I am your sincere Friend,

HORATIO NELSON

Make my compliments to Mrs. Bradley and all that family, if they are in your neighbourhood.

* Frank Lepée, an old and faithful servant, who was with Nelson in the Expedition to San Juan: he is frequently mentioned.

To Hercules Ross, Esq.

[Mr. Ross was a Merchant at Kingston, in Jamaica.]

Salisbury-street, *9th August, 1783*

My dear Friend,

I am sure you are well convinced that nothing but my not knowing where to direct to you, could have hindered you from being troubled with my nonsense. Twice I called at your house, and they could only tell me you were in Scotland: the third time, a man told me he believed if I directed to Edinburgh, you would get the letter, therefore I determined to write, at all events. The innumerable favours I have received from you, be assured I shall never forget; and any opportunity that may offer of making some small return, you may always command: but I have done. You have always looked on me with a favourable eye, and I believe that I don't want gratitude.

I have closed the war without a fortune: but I trust, and, from the attention that has been paid to me, believe that there is not a speck in my character. True honour, I hope, predominates in my mind far above riches. I came home in the *Albemarle*, with Lord Hood, last from Jamaica, where I left Hanbury, as indefatigable in business as ever, (you know best), he is I hope, and think, in a fair way for making a fortune. Shaw was up at Porto Prince; he has, I fancy, done pretty well in the Neutral trade: all our other Jamaica friends are vanished. Wallcoff, who was Agent of Transports, I supped with him last night; he begged I would present his best compliments, and say everything that could be said of his sensibility of your civility to him; your health, I am told, is perfectly good: I hope it will always continue so.

Do you know Captain Pringle, of the *Dædalus*? He lives at Caroline Park, four miles from Edinburgh: he is my particular friend, and a man of great honour. I have had a very pressing invitation to come down to him: but, as I have not seen my relations, I cannot take this opportunity, which I sincerely regret, as it deprives me of the pleasure of seeing you so soon as I wished. In the winter, we shall meet in London, I have no doubt. I had a letter yesterday from Locker; he is perfectly well. I have not seen any of the Parkers* since my arrival: they are in Essex, at an estate they have lately purchased, pulling the old house down and building a new one (thanks to Jamaica for the money). An Irish Peerage is all that is wanted to complete them. Farewell, my dear friend, and assure yourself, I am, most sincerely,

Your devoted, humble Servant,

HORATIO NELSON

* Admiral Sir Peter and Lady Parker.

To Philip Stephens, Esq., Admiralty.

[Having determined to remain unemployed during the peace, Nelson resolved to go to France, accompanied by his friend, Captain James Macnamara, to acquire the French language.]

No. 3 Salisbury-street, Strand,
October 8th, 1783

Sir,

I am to request that you will be pleased to move their Lordships to grant me six months' leave of absence, to go to Lisle, in France, on my private occasions.

I am, Sir, your most humble Servant,

HORATIO NELSON

To William Locker, Esq. St. Omer, *November 2nd, 1783*

My dear Sir,

Our travels, since we left you, have been extended to a much greater length than I apprehended; but I must do Captain Mac the justice to say it was all my doings, and in a great measure against his advice; but experience bought is the best; and all mine I have paid pretty dearly for.

We dined at Canterbury the day we parted from you, and called at Captain Sandys' house, but he was just gone out to dinner, in the country, therefore we did not see him: we slept at Dover, and next morning at seven a clock, put to Sea with a fine North-west wind, and at half-past ten we were safe at breakfast in Monsieur Grandsire's house at Calais. His mother kept it when Hogarth wrote his *Gate of Calais*. Sterne's Sentimental Journey is the best description I can give of our tour. Mac advised me to go first to St. Omer, as he had experienced the difficulty of attempting to fix in any place where there are no English; after dinner we set off, intended for Montreuil, sixty miles from Calais: they told us we travelled *en poste*, but I am sure we did not get on more than four miles an hour. I was highly diverted looking what a curious figure the postillions in their jack boots, and their rats of horses made together. Their chaises have no springs, and the roads generally paved like London streets; therefore you will naturally suppose we were pretty well shook together by the time we had travelled two posts and a-half, which is fifteen miles, to Marquise. Here we (were) shown into an inn—they called it—I should have called it a pigstye: we were shown into a room with two straw beds, and, with great difficulty, they mustered up clean sheets; and gave us two pigeons for supper, upon a dirty cloth, and wooden-handled knives—*O what a transition from happy England.*

But we laughed at the repast, and went to bed with the determination that nothing should ruffle our tempers. Having slept very well, we set off at daylight for Boulogne, where we breakfasted: this place was full of English, I suppose because wine is so very cheap. We went on after breakfast for Montreuil, and passed through the finest corn country that my eyes ever beheld, diversified with fine woods, sometimes for two miles together, through noble forests. The roads mostly were planted with trees, which made as fine an avenue as to any gentleman's country seat. Montreuil is thirty miles from Boulogne, situated upon a small hill, in the middle of a fine plain, which reached as far as the eye could carry you, except towards the sea, which is about twelve miles from it. We put up at the same house, and with the same jolly landlord that recommended Le Fleur to Sterne. Here we wished much to have fixed, but neither good lodgings, or masters could be had here; for there are no middling class of people: sixty noblemen's families lived in the town, who owned the vast plain round it, and the rest very poor indeed. This is the finest country for game that ever was; partridges two-pence halfpenny a couple, pheasants and woodcocks in proportion, and in short, every species of poultry. We dined, supped, lay, and breakfasted next day, Saturday: then we proceeded on our tour, leaving Montreuil you will suppose with great regret.

We reached Abbeville at eight o'clock: but unluckily for us, two Englishmen, one of whom called himself *Lord Kingsland*, I can hardly suppose it to be him, and a Mr. Bullock, decamped at three o'clock that afternoon in debt to every shopkeeper in the place. These gentlemen kept elegant houses, horses, &c.: we found the Town in an uproar; and as no masters could be had at this place that could speak a word of English, and that all masters that could speak English grammatically, attend at the places that are frequented by the English, which is, St. Omer, Lisle, Dunkirk, and Boulogne, to the Northward of Paris, and as I had no intention of travelling to the South of France till the spring at any rate, I determined, with Mac's advice, to steer for St. Omer, where we arrived last Tuesday: and I own I was surprised to find, that instead of a dirty, nasty Town, which I had always heard it represented, to find a large City, well paved, good streets, and well lighted.

We lodge in a pleasant French family, and have our dinners sent from a *traiteur's*. There are two very agreeable young ladies, daughters, who *honour* us with their company pretty often: one always makes our breakfast, and the other our tea, and play a game at cards in an evening. There, I must learn French if 'tis only for the pleasure of talking to them, for they do not speak a word of English. Here are a great number of English in this place, but we visit only two families; for if I did I should never speak French. Two noble Captains are here—Ball and Shepard,* you do not know, I believe, either of them; they wear fine epaulettes, for which I think them great coxcombs:† they have not visited me, and I shall not, be assured, court their acquaintance. If Charles Pole is arrived, and you write to him, give my kind respects to him; I esteem him as a brother, even beyond what I ever felt for them: tell me where I can write to him. You must be heartily tired of this long epistle, if you can read it; but I have the worst pen in the world, and I can't mend it. God bless you, and be assured

I am your sincere Friend,

And affectionate humble Servant,

HORATIO NELSON

Captain Macnamara desires his compliments to you; his and mine to Mrs. Bradley, Mrs. Dyne, &c.—Direct to me, 'A Monsieur Nelson, chez Madame La Mourie, St. Omer, en Artois, France.'

To William Locker, Esq.,
Town Malling, Kent — St. Omer, *November 26th, 1783*

My dear Friend,

Your kind letter I received last night. I concluded you were in London, as I had not the pleasure of hearing from you sooner. Since I wrote last I have been very near coming to England, occasioned by the melancholy account I have received of my dear Sister's death.‡ My Father, whose grief upon the occasion was intolerable, is, I hope, better; therefore I shall not come over. She died at Bath after a nine days' illness, in the twenty-first year of her age; it was occasioned by coming out of the ball-room immediately after dancing. Your time with Captain Reynolds must have been very agreeable: the good opinion he is pleased to entertain of me is highly flattering: it is more than my short acquaintance with him had a right to expect.

* The two captains were Alexander John Ball, afterwards a very distinguished officer, a rear-admiral and a baronet, and Nelson's intimate friend; and Captain James Keith Shepard, who died a Vice-Admiral of the Red, in 1843.

† Epaulettes were first ordered to be worn, as part of the naval uniform, on the 1st June, 1795.

‡ His eldest sister, Anne Nelson, died at Bath, unmarried, on the 15th November, 1784. As she was baptized on the 20th September, 1760, she was probably in her twenty-fifth, and not, as Nelson says, in her twenty-first year.

The French goes on but slowly; but patience, of which you know I have not much, and perseverance, will, I hope, make me master of it. Here are two Navy Captains, Ball and Shepard, at this place, but we do not visit; they are very fine gentlemen with epaulettes: you may suppose I hold them a little *cheap* for putting on any part of a Frenchman's uniform. Macnamara is very much obliged to you for the trouble you have taken about his picture: he will write a postscript at the end of the letter. Captain Young visited me to-day, and to-morrow we meet at dinner; I shall certainly deliver your compliments: he is come over to place his brother, who is a Lieutenant, in a French family. He returns immediately to England. Mac was last evening at a very elegant ball, but my mind is too much taken up with the recent account of my dear sister's death to partake of any amusements.

I am much obliged to Charles Pole for his remembrance; I should have wrote to him if I had known where to have directed a letter. When you write to Captain Reynolds give my best compliments, and to Captain and Mrs. Gardner, when you write. If I am not in England before the winter is over, I shall go to *Paris* in the spring; where I have received a most polite invitation from the Officer who I detained off Porto Caballo.* I did not know his rank at that time, or after, till I came here: he went by the name of Count de Deux Ponts. He is a Prince of the Empire, a General of the French Army, Knight of the Grand Order of St. Louis, and was Second in Command at the capture of York Town. His brother is heir apparent of the Electorate of Bavaria, and of the Palatinate. The present Elector is eighty years of age, and this gentleman's brother is upon his deathbed; so most probably I shall have had the honour of having taken prisoner a man, who will be a Sovereign Prince of Europe,† and brings into the field near a hundred thousand men: his letter is truly expressive of the attention that was paid him when on board my Ship. There are a vast number of English at this place; I visit but few of them. In two of them I am very happy in their acquaintance; one is the brother of Massingberd, who was in the *Lowestoffe*; who is very polite, and his lady a very complete gentlewoman; here we are quite at home:—the other is an English clergyman, who has a very large family, but two very agreeable daughters grown up, about twenty years of age, who play and sing to us whenever we go. I

* In March, 1783, while cruising in the *Albemarle* off Porto Caballo in the Havannah, he captured a Spanish launch with several French officers of distinction on board, who were making a scientific tour round Caracca de Leon, and whom he immediately released. Among them was Maximilian Joseph, son of Frederic, Prince de Deux Ponts, a general in the French Army, who commanded the Regiment de Deux Ponts in the French service in America.

† Nelson's anticipations were greatly surpassed; for the Prince de Deux Ponts not only succeeded to the Electorate of Bavaria 1799, but in 1806 became King of Bavaria.

must take care of my heart I assure you.* God bless you, my dear friend, and be assured,

I am yours most sincerely,

HORATIO NELSON

[Added, in Captain Macnamara's hand.]

Captain Macnamara is exceedingly obliged to Captain Locker for the trouble he has taken respecting the picture; and begs that the picture may be done *justice to*, as a few guineas extraordinary will not be regarded.

To the Rev. Mr. W. Nelson,
Burnham St. Omer, *December 4th, 1783*

My dear Brother,

Yours I received a few days ago, and am exceedingly happy to hear of your preferment, as it will make you an independent man, and also give ease to our good Father. Fortune, you see, now favours us when we least expect it; but I hope this will not hinder the Walpoles giving you something if it should be in their power. I have not heard from our Father since our melancholy loss. My fears from that account are great. Mr. Suckling wrote me the account of that shocking event the 20th of last month. My surprise and grief upon the occasion are, you will suppose, more to be felt than described. What is to become of poor Kate? Although I am very fond of Mrs. Bolton, yet I own I should not like to see Kate fixed in a Well's society. For God's sake write what you have heard of our Father. I am in astonishment at not having heard from him, or of him by Mr. Suckling. If such an event was to take place, for with his delicate constitution, I do not think it unlikely, I shall immediately come to England, and most probably fix in some place that might be most for poor Kitty's advantage. My small income shall always be at her service, and she shall never want a protector and a sincere friend while I exist. But I will quit the subject.

The occasion of my fears will, I hope in God, soon be removed, by a letter from Mr. Suckling or my Father. St. Omer increases much upon me, and I am as happy as I can be, separated from my native Country. My heart is quite secured against the French beauties: I almost wish I could say as much for an English young lady, the daughter of a clergyman, with whom I am just going to dine, and spend the day. She has such accomplishments, that had I a million of money, I am sure I

* Those ladies were the daughters of an English clergyman of the name of Andrews, and the sisters of Captain George Andrews of the Navy, a follower of Nelson's.

should at this moment make her an offer of them: my income at present is by far too small to think of marriage, and she has no fortune. Are our tickets drawn? I wrote you Mr. Paynter had them, and I told you the numbers, I believe, for I have quite forgot them. When you write tell me some Norfolk news. What is to become of Mr. Bolton? Where does he mean to fix? Is Little Brandon a pleasant village? Have you a good Parsonage house? not that I suppose you will go there while our father stays at Bath; and tell me, if he recovers, whether he means to return to Burnham in the summer. I hope most sincerely he does not, for the journey along is enough to destroy him, and a Burnham winter must kill him. French goes on but slowly; time can only make me master of it, and that a long one, some years probably. God bless you.

Your affectionate Brother

HORATIO NELSON

Make my kind love to Mrs. Bolton, Mr. Bolton, &c., and compliments to all my acquaintance at Wells, Burnham, and not forgetting Dr. Poyntz, who, I see by the papers, has at last got the Canonry of Windsor; and if you reach Wolterton, make my best compliments. I have fixed a party for Paris in March or April if I *remain* in this Country; and probably (shall) then proceed to the Southward. You have heard my account of taking the French Officers off Porto Caballo. I have had a letter from the chief of them, giving me an invitation to come to Paris. He is a much greater man than I suspected him to be: he is General in the French Army, Knight of the Grand Order of St. Louis, (similar to our Knights of the Garter,) was second in Command of the French army in America, brother to the Prince De Deux Ponts, who is heir apparent to the Electorates of *Bavaria* and *Palatinate*, the present Elector upwards of eighty years of age, and the Prince, his brother, in a deep consumption; so that most probably I shall have had the honour of having taken prisoner a man who will be a Sovereign Prince of Europe, and an absolute *Monarch*, ruling a country as large again as England, and brings into the field near a hundred thousand infantry. My paper is full, therefore I must have done. A pretty good postscript!

1784

To the Reverend Mr. Nelson,
Burnham

St. Omer, *December 28th, 1783,*
January 3rd, 1783, (1784)

Dear Brother,

Your Letter of the 15th, I received last post with infinite pleasure, as there was many pleasing accounts in it: if you get Sutton and Ulp secured for you, you are a lucky man indeed. And at a time when all your hopes were vanished—Who would be a Parson? was your tone a few months ago, now, I suppose, at least for the present—Who would not be a Parson? You will be surprised, but most probably my next letter may be from London, where I intend going on the first week in January. My health is not very stout this cold winter; and I must come over to get a little good advice from some of the London Physicians. At this place I am as happy in a friendly society as is possible. As you will suppose my time to have been pretty well taken up, as I have been so long in writing this epistle. The frost, thank God, is broke, which has made a vast alteration in me for the better; cold weather is death to me. I hope your plan of getting Ulp, &c., has been accomplished before this change in the Administration;* if not, I suppose the Walpoles have lost the only opportunity that may present itself for a long time. The latter end of next week probably I may be in London, when you may depend I shall write to you; and, if you like it, I shall buy six or seven halves of tickets for the Irish Lottery. Something may turn up by having a number of chances. My stay in England will be but very short, without the First Lord in (the) Admiralty† thinks proper to employ me. I shall offer my services, and probably I shall stretch as far as Bath for a few days. Although I know I am very little further from London than you are at Burnham, yet what a distance I think is the journey. God bless you. I must conclude, as I am engaged to tea and spend the evening with the most accomplished woman my eyes ever beheld;‡ and when a Lady's in the case, all other things they must give place.

Make my compliments to all the Wells' party, and at Burnham, Dr. Poyntz; if Mr. Bolton has not left Wells give my kind compliments and love.

Yours affectionately,

HORATIO NELSON

Do not forget me to Dr. Poyntz if he is in Norfolk

[Nelson had several youthful affairs, among them being his passionate attachment to Mary Simpson, the reigning beauty at Quebec in 1782 when Nelson was there in command of the frigate *Albemarle*. She was the daughter of one of General Wolfe's officers and eventually married a Colonel Matthews. Nelson was twenty-four at the time and contem-

* Mr. Pitt became Prime Minister on the 27th December, 1783.

† Admiral Richard Viscount Howe, who succeeded Admiral Viscount Keppel, as First Lord of the Admiralty, on the 30th December, 1783.

‡ Apparently Miss Andrews.

porary reports state that he was head over heels in love with her and even wished to resign his commission.]

To William Suckling, Esq. *January 14th, 1784*

My dear Uncle,

There arrives in general a time in a man's life (who has friends), that either they place him in life in a situation that makes his application for anything farther totally unnecessary, or give him help in a pecuniary way, if they can afford, and he deserves it.

The critical moment of my life is now arrived, that either I am to be happy or miserable:—it depends solely on you.

You may possibly think I am going to ask too much. I have led myself up with hopes you will not—till this trying moment. There is a lady I have seen, of a good family and connexions, but with a small fortune, £1,000 I understand.* The whole of my income does not exceed £130 per annum. Now I must come to the point:—will you, if I should marry, allow me yearly £100.† until my income is increased to that sum, either by employment, or any other way? A very few years I hope will turn something up, if my friends will but exert themselves. If you will not give me the above sum, will you exert yourself with either Lord North or Mr. Jenkinson, to get me a Guard-ship, or some employment in a Public Office where the attendance of the principal is not necessary, and of which they must have such numbers to dispose of. In the India Service I understand (if it remains under the Directors) their Marine force is to be under the command of a Captain in the Royal Navy: that is a station I should like.

You must excuse the freedom with which this letter is dictated; not to have been plain and explicit in my distress had been cruel to myself. If nothing can be done for me, I know what I have to trust to. Life is not worth preserving without happiness; and I care not where I may linger out a miserable existence. I am prepared to hear your refusal, and have fixed my resolution if that should happen; but in every situation, I shall be a well-wisher to you and your family, and pray they or you may never know the pangs which at this instant tear my heart. God bless you, and assure yourself, I am,

Your most affectionate and dutiful nephew,

HORATIO NELSON

* Apparently Miss Andrews.

† Mr. Suckling immediately complied with the request. Nelson was probably refused by the fair object of his affections.

To the Reverend Mr. W. Nelson, 3, Salisbury-street, Strand,
Burnham *January 20th, 1783, (1784)*

Dear Brother,

I arrived in Town on Saturday week, but my time has been so much taken up by running at the ring of pleasure, that I have almost neglected all my friends;—for London has so many charms that a man's time is wholly taken up. However, amongst other things which I have done, is that I have received £16 16 for our lottery tickets. It ought to have been £17 odd, but they reduce it fifty ways. I have lodged the identical money with Mr. Paynter, tied up in a paper; I have wrote upon it that we request him to purchase as many halfs in the Irish lottery as it will produce—about six, I fancy, or if there is no Irish one, to purchase in the English; if you do not like that way, you can alter it if you please. I received a letter from our Father last night, who says he is perfectly well; I shall make him a visit before I leave England, which will be in about a fortnight or three weeks. I can't write any more, for I am so unwell I know not how to hold my head up. I caught a violent cold upon my first arrival in England, which probably I should have got clear of, had I not been fool enough to have danced attendance at St. James's yesterday, where I increased my cold, till it has brought on a fever, so much that I was obliged to send for Dr. Warren this morning. I hope a day or two will carry it off. Let me hear from you soon. God bless you, and be assured I am,

Your affectionate Brother,

HORATIO NELSON

Give my compliments to all the good folks at Burnham, Wells, &c. The present Ministry will stay in, there is no doubt, in spite of Mr. Fox and all that party. If the Ministry has not a majority to-day, it is confidently asserted the Parliament will be dissolved. I hope it will, that the people may have an opportunity of sending men that will support their interests, and get rid of a turbulent faction who are striving to ruin their Country.

To the Reverend William Nelson,
Rector of Brandon Parva, Norfolk Bath, *January 31st, 1784*

Dear Brother,

Yours I received the morning I left Town, for which I am much obliged to you. You are an exact correspondent, therefore deserve to be wrote to. I wish sincerely your business had been got through before the late Administration were turned out. If you are not to get it before they come into power again, I am afraid you will stay a long while. As to your having enlisted under the banners of the Walpoles, you might as well have enlisted under those of my grandmother. They are altogether the merest set of *cyphers* that ever existed—in Public affairs I mean. Mr. Pitt, depend upon it, will stand against all opposition: an honest man must always in time get the better of a *villain*; but I have done with politics; let who will get in, I shall be left out.

I am happy I can say that our Father never was so well since I can remember; he is grown quite lusty. His cheeks are so much plumped out, that I thought they had been violently swelled when I first saw him, but it is all solid flesh. He gets up to breakfast, eats supper, and never retires till after ten. Keep his mind at rest, and I do not fear but he will live these many years. We have fixed our plan for next winter: you know I mean to come to you; we shall be quite a party. Poor little Kate is learning to ride, that she may be no trouble to us. She is a charming young woman, and possesses a great share of sense. In about a week or fortnight I think of returning to the Continent, till autumn, when I shall bring a horse, and stay the winter at Burnham. I return to many charming women, *but no charming woman* will return with me. I want to be a proficient in the language, which is my only reason for returning. I hate their country and their manners. As to the lottery tickets, I can't trouble Mr. Paynter to do all that you wish. If an Irish lottery is fixed before I leave England, I will do it with pleasure. If you go to Wolterton, I beg my compliments, as also at Creek, Burnham, Wells, &c. Let me hear from you soon. Is the bank down at Wells? Tell me all your Norfolk news. God bless you, and rest assured.

I am your sincere and affectionate Brother,

HORATIO NELSON

Kitty desires her love.
Rev. Wm. Nelson, Rector*

* Nelson jocularly addressed his letter to his brother as 'Rector', and underscored the word in this place, in consequence of William Nelson having then obtained that rank in the Church, by becoming Rector of Little Brandon, in Norfolk.

IN THE WEST INDIES
COURTSHIP AND MARRIAGE

[In 1784, Nelson was appointed to the command of the frigate *Boreas* and sailed for the Leeward Islands station.]

To William Locker, Esq., West Malling

Boreas, English Harbour, *September 24th, 1784*

My dear Friend,

I was in hopes that the first letter I should write you from this country would have given you some information of your Dominica estate, but that is not in my power. I was one day in Prince Rupert's Bay to wood and water; but there, you know, I could get no information. If Sandys should go to Dominica, I shall give Bradley's letter to him, and write to Orde upon the subject. I have a right to trouble him in any business of that sort, as I took on board for him, at Madeira, four casks of wine, on purpose that I might have his hearty assistance in the business.

Collingwood* is at Granada, which is a great loss to me; for there is nobody that I can make a confidant of. The little man, S——, is a good-natured creature, but no more of an Officer as a Captain than he was as a Lieutenant. Was it not for Mrs. Moutray,† who is *very very* good to me, I should almost hang myself at this infernal hole. Our Admiral‡ is tolerable, but I do not like him, he bows and scrapes too much for me; his wife has an eternal clack, so that I go near them as little as possible: in short, I detest this Country, but as I am embarked upon this Station I shall remain in my Ship. Our ears here are full of Wars in the East; is there any likelihood of a War? I am in a fine (condition) for the beginning of one; well Officered and manned. I have not heard from a single creature in England since I arrived. I have (written) to everybody, and to you from Madeira, but not a line.

Give my best remembrance to Kingsmill, and my friends in his neighbourhood, not forgetting me to the Bradleys; and I beg also that you will rest assured, I am, your devoted faithful Friend and Servant,

HORATIO NELSON

* Captain Cuthbert Collingwood, who then commanded the *Mediator*.
† Wife of Captain John Moutray, Commissioner of the Navy at Antigua.
‡ Sir Richard Hughes.

1785

[During the three years Nelson served on the West Indies station, 1784-87, three important events occurred.

The strong stand he took against the American claim to trade in British colonies;

The strong stand he took against the assumption that a civil commissioner took naval precedence of a naval officer;

His engagement and marriage.

As regards the first, Nelson in the following letter protested to the Admiral on the station (Sir Richard Hughes) against 'the admission of foreigners into the ports of the British islands'.]

Boreas, 11th January, 1785

' . . . I beg leave to hope that I may be properly understood when I venture to say that at a time when Great Britain is using every endeavour to suppress illicit Trade at Home, it is not wished that the Ships upon this Station should be singular, by being the only spectators of the illegal Trade, which I know is carried on in these Islands. The Governors may be imposed upon by false declarations; we, who are on the spot, cannot. General Shirley told me and Captain Collingwood how much he approved of the methods that were carrying on for suppressing the illegal Trade with America; that it had ever been his wish, and that he had used every means in his power, by proclamation and otherwise, to hinder it; but they came to him with protests and swore through everything (even as the Sea phrase is, 'through a nine-inch plank.), therefore got admittance, as he could not examine the vessels himself; and further, by the *Thynne* Packet, he had received a letter from Lord Sydney, one of His Majesty's Principal Secretaries of State saying that Administration were determined that American ships and Vessels should not have any intercourse with our West India Islands . . .

Whilst I have the honour to command an English Man-of-War, I shall never allow myself to be subservient to any Governor, nor co-operate with him in doing *illegal acts.* Presidents of Council I feel myself superior to. They shall make proper application to me for whatever they may want to come by water. If I rightly understand your orders of the 29th of December it is founded upon an Opinion of the King's Attorney General, viz.: 'That it is legal for Governors or their Representatives to admit Foreigners into the Ports of their Government if they think fit.' How the King's Attorney General conceives he has a right to give an illegal Opinion, which I assert the above is, he must answer for. I know the Navigation Laws.

I am, Sir, &c.

HORATIO NELSON

[In another private letter to his old friend, Captain William Locker, Nelson had written:]

The longer I am upon this Station the worse I like it. Our Commander has not that opinion of his own sense that he ought to have. He is led by the advice of the Islanders to admit the Yankees to a Trade; at least to wink at it. He does not give himself that weight that I think an English Admiral ought to do. I, for one, am determined not to suffer the Yankees to come where my Ship is; for I am sure if once the Americans are admitted to any kind of intercourse with these Islands, the views of the Loyalists in settling Nova Scotia are entirely done away. They will first become the Carriers, and next have possession of our Island, are we ever again embroiled in a French war. The residents of these Islands are American by connexion and by interest, and are inimical to Great Britain. They are as great rebels as ever were in America, had they the power to show it. After what I have said, you will believe I am not very popular with the people. They have never visited me and I have not had a foot in any house since I have been on the Station, and all for doing my duty by being *true to the interests of Great Britain.* A petition from the President and Council has gone to the Governor-General and Admiral, to request the admission of Americans. I have given my answer to the Admiral upon the subject; how he will like it I know not; but I am determined to suppress the admission of Foreigners all in my power. I have told the Customs that I will complain if they admit any Foreigner to an Entry:—an American arrives; sprung a leak, a mast, and what not, makes a protest, gets admittance, sells his cargo for ready money; goes to Martinico, buys molasses, and so round and round. But I hate them all. The Loyalists cannot do it, consequently must sell a little dearer. God bless you, my dear Sir, and rest assured,

I am ever, your affectionate Friend,

HORATIO NELSON

Remember me to the boys kindly.

[Nelson had a great deal of trouble over this matter and was pursued even to England by litigation and it was not for some years that he was finally rid of the matter.

The second dispute in which he was involved is explained in the following letter to Mr. Phillip Stephens, Secretary to the Admiralty.]

Boreas, Carlisle Bay, Barbadoes,
17 February, 1785

Sir,

Having lately held a correspondence with Sir Richard Hughes, and Mr. Moutray, a Commissioner of His Majesty's Navy resident at the Island of Antigua . . . it is only necessary for me, Sir, to elucidate and explain the motives that have actuated my conduct through the whole of this business.

The matter is grounded upon my idea (for I never saw any Commission whatever) that Mr. Moutray is not commissioned in such a manner as will authorize him to take upon him the liberty of hoisting a Broad Pennant, or the directing the Captains of His Majesty's Ships; but, Sir, let me first beg their Lordships will be assured that I never have received official information that Commissioner Moutray is appointed a Commodore upon this Station or put in any Commission, but that of Commissioner of the Navy. I must beg their Lordships' indulgence to hear reasons for my conduct, that it may never go abroad into the World, I ever had the idea to dispute the orders of my Superior Officer; neither Admiral, Commodore, or Captain.

I arrived in English Harbour the 28th July, 1784, to lay up for the hurricane season. Till the 1st November, 1784, numerous were the orders I received, and eventually with this direction, to 'Horatio Nelson, Esq., Captain of His Majesty's Ship *Boreas*, and Second Officer in the Command of his Majesty's Ships in English Harbour, Antigua.'

At this time, Sir, I need not to say that Mr. Moutray was not a Commodore; the whole of the Squadron did, I am sure, look upon him as a half-pay Captain, Commissioner of the Navy.

Thus, Sir, the matter stood for three times I went into English Harbour. At St. Christopher's I heard that Commissioner Moutray was authorized to hoist a Distinguishing or Broad Pendant. I did not pretend to think upon the matter; it might probably be so, and my answer to the Admiral was, that if Commissioner Moutray was put into Commission, I should have great pleasure in serving under him. I have not doubt that Sir Richard Hughes believed that Mr. Moutray was commissioned as a Commodore; but at the same time I trust that he thought that the Officers under his command knew their duty too well to obey any half-pay Captain; and that he might safely trust the honour of the Navy to those under him (that they would not act improperly upon this business) and that they would be well informed that the man they received orders from was empowered to give them.

On the 5th of February, 1785, upon my arrival in English Harbour I found the *Latona* with a Broad Pendant flying. As her Captain was junior to me, I sent to know the reason for her wearing it. Her Captain came on board, who I asked the following questions:—

'Have you any order from Sir Richard Hughes to wear a Broad Pendant?'

Answer—'No.'

'For what reason do you then wear it in the presence of a Senior Officer?'

Answer—'I hoisted it by order of Commissioner Moutray.'

Question—'Have you seen by what authority Commissioner Moutray was empowered to give you orders?'

'No.'

Question—'Sir, you have acted wrong, to obey any man who you do not know is authorized to command you.'

Answer—'I feel I have acted wrong; but being a young Captain, did not think proper to interfere in this matter, as there were you and other older Officers upon this Station.'

I did not choose to order the Commissioner's Pendant to be struck, as Mr. Moutray is an old Officer of high military character; and it might hurt his feelings to be supposed wrong by so young an Officer.

When Commissioner Moutray sent me orders, I answered him that I could not obey him till he was in Commission. As I never heard further upon the subject from him, I took for granted he saw I was perfectly right, or he would have produced his Commission which would instantly have cleared up the business. . . .

This is the whole and every circumstance that has arisen upon this business, and have from time to time confirmed me in the opinion that I am Second Officer in Command of his Majesty's Ships upon this Station.

I am, Sir,

Your very humble Servant,

HORATIO NELSON

[Subsequently, the Admiralty expressed the view that however improper he might conceive Mr. Moutray's appointment to have been, he should have submitted his doubts to the Admiral instead of taking upon himself to control the exercise of the functions of his appointment. In any case since the appointment of a Commissioner to Antigua had been discontinued, no instructions for preventing anything of the like kind happening in future were necessary.

Throughout this dispute Nelson showed no ill-feeling whatever to Moutray to whom he was greatly attached. As for Mrs. Moutray he adored her. To his brother, William, he wrote:]

Boreas, Carlisle Bay, *February 20th, 1785*

My dear Brother,

. . . You may be certain I never passed English Harbour without a call but alas! I am not to have much comfort. My dear, sweet friend is going home. I am really an April day; happy on her account but truly grieved were I only to consider myself. Her equal I never saw in any country or situation. . . . What an acquisition to any female to be acquainted with; what an example to take pattern from. Moutray has been very ill; it would have been necessary he should have quitted this Country had he not been recalled. All my Children* are well except one, young Andrews. On the 11th of November last he was forced by Mr. Stainsbury to fight a duel, which terminated fatally for the poor lad; the ball is lodged in his back and whether he will ever get the better of it, God knows. He kept his bed ever since. His antagonist and Mr. Oliver, his second, are in irons since the duel. They will stand a good chance of hanging if the youth should unfortunately die.

Come, I must carry you to our love scenes. Captain Sandys has asked Miss Eliot—*refused*. Captain Sterling was attentive to Miss Eliot but never having asked the question, Captain Berkeley is, I hear, to be the happy man. Captain Kelly is attached to a lady at Nevis, so he says; I don't think much of it. He is not steady enough for that passion to hold long.† Rosy has had no offers; I fancy she seems hurt at it. Poor girl! you should have offered. I have not gallantry enough. A niece of Governor Parry's has come out. She goes to Nevis in the *Boreas*. They trust any young lady with me, being an old-fashioned fellow. . . .'

[And yet, within a short time of writing this letter, Nelson himself was to meet his future wife. Writing to his brother again on the 12th of May, he says:]

'I am just come from Nevis where I have been visiting Miss Parry Herbert and a young Widow.'

[The young widow was Fanny Nisbet who had shortly before received from a friend the following account of her future husband.]

* His midshipmen.

† Nelson was wrong here. They were married.

'We have at last seen the Captain of the *Boreas* of whom so much has been said. He came up just before dinner, much heated, and was very silent; yet seemed, according to the old adage, to think the more. He declined drinking any wine, but after dinner when the President as usual gave the following toasts, "the King", "the Queen and Royal family", and "Lord Hood", this strange man regularly filled his glass and observed that those were always bumper toasts with him; which having drank, he uniformly passed the bottle and relapsed into his former taciturnity. It was impossible during this visit for any of us to make out his real character; there was such a reserve and sternness in his behaviour with occasional sallies, though very transient, of a superior mind.

'Being placed by him, I endeavoured to rouse his attention by showing him all the civilities in my power, but I drew out little more than "Yes" or "No". If you, Fanny, had been there, we think you would have made something of him for you have been in the habit of attending to these odd sort of people.'

[And in a letter to his brother, William, dated 28th June, Nelson added a postscript:]

'*Entre-nous*—Do not be surprised to hear I am a *Benedict*, for if at all, it will be before a month. Do not tell.'

[That was written in June and by September Nelson was already engaged. His first extant letter to Fanny Nisbet is dated:]

Boreas, English Harbour,
11th September, 1785

Indeed, my dear Fanny, I had buoyed myself up with hopes that the Admiral's schooner would have given me a line from you. But the tidings she brought of the release of poor Mrs. Herbert from the world* sufficiently apologise for your not thinking of an absentee. Yet this believe from my heart, that I partake in all the sorrows you experience and I comfort myself that however great your grief at this moment, at losing a person who was so deservedly dear to you, as your good Aunt, yet when reason takes place, you must rather have pleasure in knowing she is released from those torments she had undergone for months past. Time ever has a tendency to soften grief into a pleasing remembrance and her unspotted character must afford you real comfort. Call Religion to your aid; and it will convince you that her conduct in this world was such as insures everlasting happiness in that which is to come.

* Fanny's aunt.

I have received a letter from Mr. Herbert in answer to that which I left for him at Nevis. My greatest wish is to be united to you; and the foundation of all conjugal happiness, real love and esteem is, I trust, what you believe I possess in the strongest degree towards you. I think Mr. Herbert loves you too well not to let you marry the man of your choice, although he may not be so rich as some others, provided his character and situation in life render such an union eligible. I declare solemnly that did I not conceive I had the full possession of your heart, no consideration should make me accept your hand. We know that riches do not always insure happiness; and the world is convinced that I am superior to pecuniary considerations in my public and private life; as in both instances I might have been rich.

But I will have done, leaving all my present feelings to operate in your breast:—only of this truth be convinced, that I am,

Your affectionate,

HORATIO NELSON

P.S. Do I ask too much when I venture to hope for a line? or otherwise I may suppose my letters may be looked upon as troublesome.

[A little later he was writing to his uncle, Mr. William Suckling:]

Boreas, Nevis, *November 14th, 1785*

My dear Sir,

. . . When I open my business, you will perhaps smile, in the first instance, and say, 'This Horatio is for ever in love.'

My present attachment is of pretty long standing; but I was determined to be fixed before I broke this matter to any person. The lady is a Mrs. Nisbet, widow of a Dr. Nisbet who died eighteen months after her marriage and has left her with a son (Josiah). From her infancy, for her father and mother died when she was only two years of age, she has been brought up by her mother's brother, Mr. Herbert, President of Nevis, a gentleman whose fortune and character must be well known to all the West Indian merchants, therefore I shall say nothing upon that head. Her age is twenty two; and her personal accomplishments you will suppose *I think* equal to any person's I ever saw; but, without vanity, her mental accomplishments are superior to most people's of either sex; and we shall come together as two persons most sincerely attached to each other from friendship. Her son is under her guardianship, but totally independent of her.

But I must describe Herbert to you, so that you may know exactly how I stand; for when we apply for advice, we must tell all circumstances. Herbert is very rich and very proud—he has an only daughter, and this niece who he looks upon in the same light if not higher. I have lived at his house when at Nevis since June last and am a great favourite of his. I have told him I am as poor as Job; but he tells me he likes me, and I am descended from a good family which his pride likes; but he also says: 'Nelson, I am proud and I must live like myself, therefore I can't do much in my lifetime; when I die she shall have twenty thousand pounds, and if my daughter dies before me, she shall possess the major part of my property. I intend going to England in 1787 and remaining there my life; therefore, if you two can live happily together till that event takes place, you have my consent.'

This is exactly my situation with him; and I know the way to get him to give me most is not to appear to want it; thus circumstanced, who can I apply to but you? The regard you have ever expressed for me leads me to hope you will do something. My future happiness, I give you my honour, is now in your power; if you cannot afford to give me anything for ever, you will, I am sure, trust to me that, if I ever can afford it, I will return it to some part of your family. I think Herbert will be brought to give her two or three hundred a year during his life; and if you will either *give me*, I will call it—I think you will do it—either one hundred a year, for a few years, or a thousand pounds, how happy you will make a couple who will pray for you for ever. Don't disappoint me, or my heart will break; trust to my honour to do a good turn for some other person if it is in my power. I can say no more, but trust implicitly to your goodness, and pray let me know of your generous action by the first Packet. . . .

1786

To Mrs. Nisbet Off the Island of Deseada, *3rd March, 1786*

Separated from you, what pleasure can I feel? All my happiness is centred with thee; and where thou art not, there I am not happy. Every day, hour and act convince me of it. With my heart filled with the purest and most tender affection do I write this: for were it not so, you know me well enough to be certain that even at this moment I would tell you of it. I daily thank God who ordained that I should be attached to you. He has, I firmly believe, intended it as a blessing to me; and I am well convinced you will not disappoint his beneficent intentions.

Fortune, that is money, is the only thing I regret the want of, and that only for the sake of my affectionate Fanny. But the Almighty who brings us together will, I doubt not, take ample care of us and prosper all our undertakings. No dangers shall deter me from pursuing every honourable means of providing handsomely for you and yours; and again let me repeat that my dear Josiah shall ever be considered by me as one of my own. That Omnipotent Being who sees and knows what passes in all hearts knows what I have written to be my undisguised sentiments towards the little fellow. I am uneasy but not unwell. Nothing but the Admiral's orders to be at Barbadoes at a given time hindered me from coming down after my letters. Sir Richard Hughes, I am certain, would have overlooked my disobedience of orders and have thought I had served the friend, who had neglected to bring my letters, very properly. But I cannot bear the idea of disobeying orders; I should not like to have mine disobeyed. However, it was a toss-up, I assure you.

(*Apparently in continuation*)

March 9th

. . . I have received several letters from my sister and brother; the former from Bath where my old friend Scrivener desired to be kindly remembered to me. I don't think my dear sister knows of my intentions of altering my situation, or she would have mentioned it. My friend Moutray is still there; but I have not a line (from him). It is wonderful and I cannot account for it. I know myself to be so steady in my friendships that I cannot bear the least coolness or inattention in others. My brother takes it for granted I am a married man and in consequence desires his love.

From my Uncle Suckling I have a very kind letter saying he will do everything in his power to add to my happiness; and if I should want it, that he will give me pecuniary assistance.* . . .

You must write often, and long letters. I am, &c.

HORATIO NELSON

To William Suckling, Esq.

Boreas, Carlisle Bay,
March 9th, 1786

My dear Uncle,

Your kind letter of January 3rd I received yesterday on my arrival here from Nevis. When I made application to you in November, it was, I assure you, not so much considering you in the light of a near relation, as of a sincere friend who would do everything which was proper for the happiness of one who sincerely regarded and esteemed

* This was liberally done for some years by his uncle.

him, and whose friendship was pure, without any interested views in it; and had it not been for one sentence in your letter, viz., 'Your application has in a great degree deprived me of my free agency', I should have been supremely happy; but my feelings are too quick and I feel sharply what perhaps others would not, so they gained their ends. That sentence would make me suppose that you thought I conceived I had a right to ask pecuniary assistance; if you did think so, be assured you did me great injustice; for I was convinced that whatever you might be kind enough to do for me, must spring from your own generous heart and not from any shadow of right I could be fool enough to suppose I derived from our relationship.

Relations are not always the people we are to look up to for doing friendly offices. O my dear uncle! you can't tell what I feel—indeed I can hardly write, or know what I am writing; you would pity me did you know what I suffer by that sentence—for although it does not make your act less generous, yet it embitters my happiness. You must know me and consequently that I am guided by the strictest rules of honour and integrity; and that had I not been more ambitious of fame than money, I should not most probably have been under the necessity of making the present application to you. No dangers or difficulties shall ever deter me from doing my utmost to provide handsomely for my dearest Fanny, for with the purest and most tender affection do I love her. Her virtues and accomplishments are not more conspicious than her goodness of heart and gentleness of disposition; and you will esteem her for herself when you know her.

Your readiness in giving, my dear Friend, will not make me more anxious to receive; for can I live without your putting yourself to the inconvenience of advancing me money, I certainly shall do it, for my disposition is not that of endeavouring to grasp all it can. The greatest felicity I can enjoy is to make her happy; for myself I can care but little when she is considered; and I could lay down my life with pleasure at this moment for her future happiness. After what I have written, you will believe my love is founded upon that strong basis which must have the appearance of enjoying happiness with her. I will endeavour as much as my indisposed mind will let me to answer all your questions about her son and herself.

When Mrs. Nisbet married, Mr. Herbert promised two thousand pounds with her; but as her husband settled in the Island (Nevis) where he died a few months after, it never has been paid. Mr. H. told me he had given, and should pay to the child one thousand pounds when he grew up; and that he should bring him up at his expense, and put him in a way of providing for himself. Mr. Nisbet (the gentleman whose wife went astray) was a brother. His estate, I understand from Mr.

Herbert, owes for money lent and attending it as Doctor, about £3,000 currency; but Dr. Nisbet dying insane, without a will, or any Papers which were regular, has made this business rather troublesome, as Mr. Nisbet wishes to pay as little as he can help. Mr. Stanley, the Attorney General whose property is next to Mr. Herbert's and who is his particular friend, has undertaken to settle it for her.

She will not get much; but it must, I conceive, make her little fellow independent. Her Uncle, although he is a man who must have his own way in everything, yet I believe has a good and generous heart, and loves her and her son very sincerely; and I have every reason to suppose is as much attached to me as to any person who could pay their addresses to his dear Fanny, as he always calls her. Although his income is immense, yet his expenses must be great, as his house is open to all strangers and he entertains them most hospitably. I can't give you an idea of his wealth, for I don't believe he knows it himself. Many estates in that Island are mortgaged to him. The stock of Negroes upon his estate and cattle are valued at £60,000 sterling; and he sends to England (average for seven years) 500 casks of sugar. His daughter's fortune must be very large; and as he says and told me at first that he looked upon his niece as his child, I can have no reason to suppose that he will not provide handsomely for her. I had rather wish, that whatever he may do at her marriage, may flow spontaneously from himself. . . .

Your obliged Nephew,

HORATIO NELSON

To Mrs. Nisbet *Boreas*, English Harbour, *August 19th, 1786*

My dearest Fanny,

Having seen in this day's newspaper that a vessel cleared out from St. John's to Nevis a few days ago, I feel vexed not to have had a letter in the Office for you; however if I can help it I will not be behindhand again. To write letters to you is the next greatest pleasure I feel to receiving them from you. What I experience when I read such as I am sure are the pure sentiments of your heart, my poor pen cannot express, nor indeed would I give much for any pen or head that could describe feelings of that kind; they are worth but little when that can happen. My heart yearns to you—it is with you; my mind dwells upon nought else but you. Absent from you, I feel no pleasure; it is you, my dearest Fanny, who are everything to me. Without you, I care not for this world, for I have found lately nothing in it but vexation and trouble.

These, you are well convinced, are my present sentiments; God

Almighty grant they may never change. Nor do I think they will; indeed there is, as far as human knowledge can judge, a moral certainty they cannot; for it must be real affection that brings us together, not interest or compulsion which makes so many unhappy . . .

Monday, (*21st August*)
Seven in the Evening

As you begin to know something about Sailors, have you not often heard that salt water and absence always wash away love? Now I am such a heretic as not to believe that Faith; for behold, every morning since my arrival, I have had six pails of salt water at daylight poured upon my head, and instead of finding what the Seamen say to be true, I perceive the contrary effect; and if it goes on so contrary to the prescription, you must see me before my fixed time. At first, I bore absence tolerably, but now it is almost insupportable; and by and by I expect it will be quite so. But patience is a virtue; and I must exercise it upon this occasion whatever it costs my feelings. I am alone in the Commanding Officer's house, while my ship is fitting, and from sunset until bedtime I have not a human creature to speak to; you will feel a little for me I think. I did not use to be over-fond of sitting alone. The moment old *Boreas* is habitable in my cabin, I shall fiy to it, to avoid mosquitoes and melancholies. Hundreds of the former are now devouring me through all my clothes. You will however find I am better; though when you see me, I shall be like an Egyptian mummy for the heat is intolerable. But I walk a mile out at night without fatigue and all day I am housed. A quart of goat's milk is also taken every day, and I enjoy English sleep, always barring mosquitoes which all Frank's care with my net cannot keep out at present. . . .

Your most affectionate

HORATIO NELSON

To Mrs. Nisbet

Off Antigua, *December 12th, 1786*

Our young Prince is a gallant man; he is indeed volatile but always with great good nature. There were two balls during his stay and some of the old ladies were mortified that H.R.H. would not dance with them;

but he says he is determined to enjoy the privilege of all other men, that of asking any lady he pleases.*

Wednesday. We arrived here this morning at daylight. His Royal Highness dined with me, and of course the Governor. I can tell you a piece of news, which is that the Prince is fully determined, and has made me promise him that he shall be at our wedding; and he says he will give you to me. His Royal Highness has not yet been in a private house to visit and is determined never to do it except in this instance. You know I will ever strive to bear such a character as may render it no discredit to any man to take notice of me. There is no action in my whole life but what is honourable and I am the more happy at this time on this account; for I would, if possible or in my power, have no man near the Prince who can have the smallest impeachment as to character; for as an individual I love him, as a Prince I honour and revere him. My telling you this history is as to myself; my thoughts on all subjects are open to you. We shall certainly go to Barbadoes from this Island and when I shall see you is not possible for me to guess; so much for marrying a Sailor. We are often separated but I trust our affections are not by any means on that account diminished. Our Country has the first demand for our services and private convenience or happiness must ever give way to the Public good. Give my love to Josiah. Heaven bless and return you safe to

Yours most affectionate,

HORATIO NELSON

1787

[Early in 1787 the first lieutenant of the *Pegasus*, Lieutenant Isaac (afterwards Captain) Schomberg, author of the *Naval Chronology* in five volumes (1802) incurred his captain's displeasure, and Nelson as senior officer was involved in the affair.]

'*Pegasus*, English Harbour, Antigua,
23rd January, *1787*

From Mr. Schomberg's neglecting to inform me yesterday of his sending a boat on shore, and Mr. Smollett doing the same, I think

* The Duke of Clarence, third son of George III, afterwards King William IV. At this time he was a young man of twenty-one, an officer in the Navy and commander of H.M.S. *Pegasus*. Being junior in rank to Nelson in the *Boreas*, the Prince was under his orders. Nelson always expressed a high opinion of the Prince who remained on very friendly terms with him for many years, and Nelson, on occasion, sought his influential aid.

proper to recommend the reading over of these orders, with attention, to the Officers and Gentlemen; as for the future, I shall make them accountable for their conduct in disobeying any commands or orders I may from time to time give out.

William.'

[Lieutenant Schomberg did not think he had deserved such a rebuke and at once applied to Captain Nelson for a court martial. Nelson ordered him under arrest pending the holding of a court martial but no opportunity for the court martial occurred.

In the following May, the Prince wrote to Nelson:]

'It is highly requisite for his Majesty's service that Lieutenant Schomberg should be brought to trial particularly after having been kept under suspension rather than confinement for one hundred and seven days. Justice calls loudly for a man so long in his situation to be as soon delivered from his captivity as possible. The only means to effect that must be a court martial. You, Sir, are thoroughly acquainted with all the proceedings and know the uneasiness of mind I have suffered and the vast desire I must have to see the affair of this unhappy and deluded man settled. . . . I entirely coincide in opinion with you, Sir, that it is not only for the advantage of his Majesty's service but that justice requires that his Majesty's ship *Pegasus* should proceed, in her way to North America, to Jamaica. . . .'

'*May 13th.*

My going to Jamaica is really necessary, not only for my own ease and peace of mind but for the King's service, to deliver this miserable object from his long confinement. Commodore Gardner being an Officer of experience and judgment will be able to give me good advice how to pursue the best mode through this difficult and disagreeable affair. I wish to God it had never happened, or that Schomberg had seen his error sooner.

William.'

[Nelson appears to have been annoyed by Schomberg's action.]

By Horatio Nelson, Esq.
Captain of His Majesty's Ship *Boreas*

For the better maintaining discipline and good government in the King's Squadron under my command,

I think it necessary to inform the Officers that if any one of them shall presume to write to the Commander of the Squadron (unless there shall be Ships enough present to bring them to immediate trial) for a Court Martial to investigate their conduct on a frivolous pretence, thereby depriving his Majesty of their services by obliging the Commander of the Squadron to confine them, that I shall and do consider such conduct as a direct breach of the 14th, and part of the 19th Articles of War and shall order them to be Tried for the same.

Given under my hand, on board His Majesty's Ship *Boreas*, at Antigua, the 28th of January, 1787.

HORATIO NELSON

[The *Pegasus* sailed for Jamaica accompanied by the sloop *Rattler* with an official statement of the charge against Schomberg and with a private letter from Nelson to the Commodore.]

Private *Boreas*, Nevis, *May 13th, 1787*

My dear Sir,

In a public letter a Commander would be wrong to set forth all the reasons which influence his conduct; but as I hope to have your approbation, I take the liberty of mentioning a few circumstances.

His Royal Highness will give you an account of Lieutenant Schomberg's conduct and of his having put him into Arrest for disobedience of orders &c. and that on Mr. Schomberg's making proper apologies, he forgave him. Indeed, his Royal Highness's narrative is so explicit that I cannot inform you so fully as that will. His Royal Highness, I can have no doubt, gave the orders alluded to, although Mr. Schomberg might have misunderstood them. I am sure, Sir, you will consider his Royal Highness stands in a very different situation to any other Captain; his conduct will be canvassed by the world when ours would never be heard of.

Mr. Schomberg was our friend Cornwallis's First Lieutenant in the *Canada*. I can only suppose that he thought the Prince was determined to take the first opportunity of bringing him to a Court Martial, that he wrote for this for such a trivial matter. Indeed, what leads me to consider *that* as his motive was, when his Royal Highness told him how wrong he was to write for a Court Martial on himself, the Lieutenant told him that every Officer who served under him (the Prince) must be broke, and the sooner he was from under his command the better; and that if a Court Martial acquitted him, he would write to quit the Ship. This matter has made the Prince very uneasy, for he says no person can tell he gave Mr. Schomberg those orders but himself, and Schomberg denies them. The day the matter happened, the Prince dined in the country and I attended him. On the road he told me how unpleasant it was that Schomberg would act in that matter when he had only forgiven him a few days before; but he said, in future if any person committed faults he would insert it in the Public Order Book of the Ship, which he did on this occasion, the next day. On the evening, when I returned from dining I found Mr. Schomberg's letter. I immediately sent for his Royal Highness and I told him that in his elevated situation in life the world looked more to him than any other person, that Mr. Schomberg had neither more nor less than accused him of putting his name to an untruth; therefore I thought it my duty, although the matter was so trivial, to take Lieutenant Schomberg from under his directions, by suspending him from duty, or it might be said I left him in that disagreeable situation merely because he served under the Prince; and that it very much concerned his Royal Highness to show the world he had put his name to nothing but the truth.

In order to show my disapprobation of Officers writing for Courts Martial, to vindicate their conduct for trivial matters, I gave out the enclosed order that others might not fall into the same error. It might soon have risen to such a height, that if a topsail was not thought properly or briskly reefed by a Captain, or some other trivial matter, and he reprimanded the Officer, the Officer would say, 'Sir, I think it properly done, and I shall write for a Court Martial to vindicate my conduct from your unjust accusation.'

If this was to be allowed, farewell Discipline; the Service is ruined; his Majesty may be deprived of the services of his Officers; and the best-laid schemes may be frustrated by the malignity of individuals, or pique against their Commanders.

As the *Rattler* is to sail for England on the 1st of June, I have sent her down with his Royal Highness, not only as there may not be ships enough collected to hold a Court, but to carry home his Royal Highness's despatches, which he must be very anxious should reach the King before any reports get to him. Extraordinary to tell, in the last month, Mr. Schomberg wrote me a letter requesting to know what charges I intended to exhibit against him, as he supposed I was to be his prosecutor, having ordered him into Arrest. My answer of course was, that I thought that I had complied with his wishes in taking him from under the immediate command of his Royal Highness, and that from the tenor of his letter, I took for granted he meant to prove he never had, in the instance alluded to, disobeyed his Captain's commands and it was therefore he supposed himself unjustly accused. I am, &c.

HORATIO NELSON

[During his service on this station, Nelson was several times corrected, reprimanded or rebuked by the Admiralty.

On one occasion he was told that 'their Lordships are much disappointed and dissatisfied at the little attention to the rules and practice of the service' in respect of a matter concerning a Muster book; on another occasion he was told that he had exceeded his authority in pardoning a seaman who was condemned to death, on the intercession of the Prince; and when their Lordships learned that he had sent the *Pegasus* and *Rattler* to Jamaica he was informed: 'My Lords are not satisfied with the reasons you have given for altering the destination of the *Pegasus* and for sending the *Rattler* sloop to Jamaica; and that for having taken upon you to send the latter away from the station to which their Lordships had appointed her, you will be answerable for the consequence if the Crown should be put to any needless expense upon that account.'

It seems, in short, that during this period of service, Nelson could not do right, so far as the Admiralty was concerned.

For the present, however, his immediate difficulties and disappointments were forgotten. He was on his way to his bride.]

Boreas, Sandy Point,
March 6th, 1787

My dear Fanny,

Your kind letter of Friday night I received yesterday having sent Frank to Basseterre to wait the arrival of the packet.

How uncertain are the movements of us sailors! His Royal Highness is rather unwell therefore I have given up the idea of visiting Tortola for the present. Today we dine with Georges at his country house. The Prince admires Mrs. G. very much. I have had a severe scolding from her but as you was the cause I felt perfectly easy. A neglected female does not easily forgive.

I am glad Mr. Forbes has explained everything to Mr. Herbert's satisfaction. The message he delivered must not be too much trusted to as to the complimentary part. Men make those things as they please and we are all fond of flattery. Adye will deliver this letter. I wish Mr. Herbert would let him settle the business with Nisbet for poor Josiah's sake, although he may have stated the business home pretty accurately yet he will not tell the opinion of the lawyers he has employed if it should be against himself.

I am now feeling most awkward. His Royal Highness has been with me all this morning and has told me that as things have changed if I am not married this time we go to Nevis it is hardly probable he should see me there again, that I had promised him not to be married unless he was present and that he did it to show his esteem for me and should be much mortified if any impediments were thrown in the way to hinder his being present. He intends it as a mark of honour to me as such I wish to receive it. Indeed his behaviour to me has ever been that of a friend instead of a person so elevated above me. He told me this morning that since he has been under my command he has been happy, and have given me to understand that there is no doubt whenever he may be placed in a high situation that I will find him sincere in his friendship. By keeping in his esteem there is no doubt but I shall have my right in the service if nothing more.

I hope Mr. Herbert can have no objection, especially if he considers how much it is my interest to be well with the Prince. I beg you will show him this letter and assure him that in this as well as in other matters I have it to him persuaded that he will do everything which is right and proper on the occasion. You may think this an awkward way of speaking to Mr. Herbert thro' you. But I am convinced you are perfectly assured of my affection and that I have no thought which is concealed from you. In this I believe as in our affection we are reciprocal. No sinister views can be in the way.

Heavens bless you and I need scarcely say how much I am your affectionate,

HORATIO NELSON

[This was his last letter to her before their marriage at Nevis on 12th March, 1787, when Prince William gave away the bride. Nelson was twenty-nine and his wife twenty-five.

A few weeks later the *Boreas* was ordered home and on 4th July anchored at Spithead. The ship was kept in commission for some weeks longer owing to the disturbed state of the Continent but was finally paid off on 1st December, 1787, and Nelson's command of the *Boreas* came to an end.]

NELSON THE FARMER

To the Reverend Mr. Nelson,
Hilborough — Cavendish Square, *October 29th, 1787*

My dear Brother,

Many thanks for your kind inquiries about the School: it is quite the thing I wished for, and you will be pleased to tell the Master the child* shall come after the Christmas holidays. We are happy to hear Mrs. Nelson is about again, and desire to be most kindly remembered to her, with many thanks for her obliging offer, when the child may come to school: but we hope *Boreas* will soon be paid off, then we shall come into Norfolk directly. As to news, the Papers are all Peace; but, in my opinion, nothing can prevent a War. In the Naval line every exertion is made use of to man the Fleet. Compliments to all about you, and believe me, ever

Your most affectionate Brother,

HORATIO NELSON

Maurice is well. He has been staying a few days on board with me.

1788

To the Reverend William Nelson,
Hilborough

6, Princes-street,
Cavendish-square,
January 3rd, 1788

My dear Brother,

Our little boy† shall be at Hilborough on Tuesday or Wednesday next, escorted by Frank, who I have desired to stay two or three days till the child becomes reconciled. I am assured of your and Mrs. Nelson's goodness to him—that is, you will not allow him to do as he pleases: it's mistaken kindness where it happens. I wish him at school to have the same weekly allowance as the other boys, and whatever else may be proper for him. We have been very unwell, and shall go to Bath as soon as I can get out. Your rum will come down when I know the best conveyance: send me word. Your pay for the *Boreas* would not amount to the fees of Office. In the Lottery, whatever part of a ticket, or in what proportion you wish to have one, shall be complied with. Maurice is well: he has just left us, and desires to be remembered. Our

* His step-son, Josiah Nisbet.
† Josiah Nisbet.

best compliments to Mrs. Nelson and the old ladies. The wine shall come as soon as I can get it from the Custom-house, and know the best conveyance. Adieu, and believe me ever, your most affectionate Brother,

HORATIO NELSON

To William Locker, Esq.,
Kensington

Bath, *January 27th, 1788*

My dear Sir,

Your kind letter I received yesterday, and am much obliged by your kind inquiries about a house. I fear we must at present give (up) all thoughts of living so near London, for Mrs. Nelson's lungs are so much affected by the smoke of London, that I cannot think of placing her in that situation, however desirable. For the next summer I shall be down in Norfolk, from whence I must look forward. I was rather hurried in getting down here, by Prince William having invited me to Plymouth. I was therefore glad to place Mrs. Nelson here at once, which not only saved me the expense, but the toil, of a journey three hundred miles. I returned from Plymouth three days ago, and found Prince William everything I could wish—respected by all. Those who knew him formerly say he is a most altered young man; and those who were prejudiced against him acknowledge their error. The *Pegasus* is allowed by every one to be one of the best disciplined Ships that ever came into Plymouth. But the great folks above now see he will not be a cypher, therefore many of the rising people must submit to act subordinate to him, which is not so palatable; and I think a Lord of the Admiralty* is hurt to see him so able, after what he has said about him. He has not certainly taken a leaf out of his book, for he is steady in his Command and not violent. He has wrote Lord Hood what I cannot approve, yet am sorry about his taking Lieutenant Schomberg.

When the Lists come out will you be good enough to send me one? Kingsmill will frank it if it can come by the post. I hope he is better; pray give my best wishes to him. Mrs. Nelson desires the same, and unites with me in best wishes to your family. I pray compliments to Bradley, Anderson, &c. You are in debt to Mr. Suckling for the duty on the rum: the wine I desire you will not pay. Charles Pole is not well, I fear he is getting too fat. God bless you, my dear Sir, and be assured

I am your most faithful and affectionate

HORATIO NELSON

I beg my compliments to Lord Ducie when you see him.

* The two naval Lords of the Admiralty were Admiral Viscount Howe, and Rear-Admiral the Hon. John Leveson Gower.

[When he went on shore, in December, 1787, on the paying-off of the *Boreas*, Nelson was twenty-nine. With the exception of a short period of a few months in 1781, during which he had been on half pay, he had spent practically all his life from the age of twelve at sea. He had served in fourteen ships and had commanded four; his service had taken him to the West Indies, to the Artic regions, to Newfoundland and Canadian waters. While in command of the *Boreas* in the Leeward Islands, he had experienced an arduous and unpleasant time in dealing with frauds and in defending the commercial interests of his country during which he had taken risks and incurred heavy legal responsibilities.

He had received several rebukes and reprimands from the Admiralty; he had quarrelled with his Admiral; he had had several bouts of ill-health and finally, on her return to England, the *Boreas* had been made a receiving ship for impressed men at the Nore.

He left the ship angry, annoyed and irritated.

'I rejoice at the *Boreas* being paid off which will release me for ever from an ungrateful service, as it is my firm and unalterable determination never again to set my foot on board a King's ship. Immediately on my arrival in Town, I shall wait on the First Lord of the Admiralty and resign my commission.'

But this intention was happily prevented by his receiving a very civil letter from Lord Howe who presented him to the King at the next Levee when he was graciously received.

After he left the *Boreas*, Nelson remained unemployed on shore for five solid years. For a great part of that time he seems to have been kicking his heels and only six letters are included here which were written during this period. In a letter to his old friend, Captain William Locker, he wrote:]

1789

To William Locker, Esq.,
Kensington — Burnham, *September 10th, 1789*

My dear Sir,

I was exceedingly happy to hear by your letter from Harrogate, that you was so much recovered, and by this time, I take for granted, you are settled again at home, and I most sincerely hope you will never be obliged again to travel in quest of health. When we may meet, time must determine; at present, I have no appearance of being called up to London. Not being a man of fortune is a crime which I cannot get over, and therefore none of the Great care about me. I am now commencing Farmer, not a very large one, you will conceive, but enough for amusement. Shoot I cannot, therefore I have not taken out a license; but notwithstanding the neglect I have met with, I am happy, and now I see the propriety of not having built my hopes on such sandy foundations as the friendships of the Great. The newspapers tell me of fine frolics which both King and Prince of Wales have been making. Pray is Mr. Laforey to be promoted, or is there to be a promotion of Flags? Is there any idea of our being drawn into a quarrel by these commotions on the Continent? whenever that may be likely to happen, I will take care to make my application in time. I wish our friend Kingsmill would retract many of his generous expenses: it is his gifts which has drawn him into difficulties, that I have little doubt of, and not knowing the value of money. Pray, when you write or see him, remember me kindly to him. Mrs. Nelson desires me to present her best respects to you and family, and believe me,

Yours much obliged, and affectionate,

HORATIO NELSON

1790

[To his friend the Duke of Clarence, he wrote:]

Burnham, Norfolk, *June 24th, 1790*

Sir,

. . . My not being appointed to a ship is so very mortifying that I cannot find words to express what I feel on the occasion: and when I reflect on your Royal Highness's condescension in mentioning me to Lord Chatham* I am the more hurt and suprised.

[To Lord Chatham himself he wrote:]

Burnham, Norfolk, *September 26th, 1790*

My Lord,

My wish to be employed is so great that I trespass on your Lordship's time with a letter. I am sensible I have no great interest to recommend me, nor have I had conspicuous opportunities of distinguishing myself; but thus far, without arrogating, I can say that no opportunity has been passed by; and that I have ever been a zealous officer. I am sure Lord Hood† will bear testimony of what I have taken the liberty of saying. If the *Raisonable* is not given away, I should esteem myself highly honoured by the command of her.

I have the honour to remain, &c.,

HORATIO NELSON

* Then First Lord of the Admiralty.

† Then one of the Lords of the Admiralty.

[Throughout this long period of five years during which he led a quiet and sequestered life, Nelson never ceased on the slightest opportunity to apply for a ship, but as the months and even the years passed he seems to have become resigned to his long-continued inactivity. Alone at Burnham with his father and his wife he occupied himself with gardening and farming, read the current periodicals, studied charts, drew plans and speculated upon the Left Wing political activities which he found manifesting themselves all around him.

He had no family of young children to pre-occupy him. Mrs. Nelson's son, young Josiah, was at a boarding school and Nelson took great interest in his education upon which he seems to have had decided views. Some time previously, the Earl of Cork had written to Nelson asking his advice about his son, Courtenay Boyle, then a Midshipman in the *Boreas*. Nelson replied:]

'In the first place, it is necessary that he should be made complete in his Navigation; and if the Peace continues, French is absolutely necessary. Dancing is an accomplishment that probably a Sea Officer may require. You will see almost the necessity of it, when employed in Foreign Countries; indeed, the honour of the Nation is so often entrusted to Sea Officers that there is no accomplishment which will not shine with peculiar lustre in them. He must nearly have served his Time, therefore he cannot be so well employed as in gaining knowledge. If I can at any time be of service to him, he may always call upon me. His charming disposition will ever make him friends.'

[Meanwhile he was interesting himself in the social and economic conditions around him, and he summed up the result of his observations on these matters in a long letter addressed to the Duke of Clarence.]

1792

Burnham, *10th December, 1792*

Sir,

I was honoured by your Royal Highness's letter last night and it shall ever be my pride to deserve your kindness. Respecting my present situation with Lord Hood, I can readily and truly answer. We have not for a long time had any communication with each other. Our familiar correspondence ceased on a difference of opinion. In the Spanish armament, when almost the whole service were called forth, I asked Lord Hood to interest himself with Lord Chatham that I might be appointed to a Ship. His Lordship having declined doing it, has prevented my troubling him again for his interest or influence. However in consideration of our former intimacy, whenever I have gone to

London, I have hitherto thought it right to leave my name at his Lordship's door. I certainly cannot look on Lord Hood as my friend; but I have the satisfaction of knowing that I never gave his Lordship just cause to be my enemy.

Our Lord Lieutenant has summoned a meeting of the Norfolk Justices on Tuesday next the 11th, and I have no doubt they will resolve to do collectively what none of them chose to do individually—to take away the licences from those public houses who allow of improper Societies meeting at them, and to take up those incendiaries who go from ale-house to ale-house, advising the poor people to pay no taxes, &c. In this neighbourhood a person of the name of Priestley*, a clergyman, has held this language to a circle of ten miles round him; and a few days past I asked a Justice of the Peace, 'Why, as such a man's conduct was known, that he was not taken up?' His answer was that 'no Justice would render himself unpopular at this time by being singular; for that his life and property were gone if the mob arose; but that when the Justices all agreed to act in an uniform manner, this man should certainly be taken hold of, if he went on with such conduct.

That the poor labourer should have been seduced by promises and hopes of better times, your Royal Highness will not wonder at, when I assure you they are really in want of everything to make life comfortable. Part of their wants, perhaps, were unavoidable from the dearness of every article of life; but much has arose from the neglect of the Country Gentlemen in not making their farmers raise their wages in some small proportion as the prices of necessaries increased. The enclosed paper will give your Royal Highness an idea of their situation. It is most favourable; but I have been careful that no Country Gentleman should have it in his power to say, I had pointed out the wants of the poor greater than they really are. Their wages have been raised within these three weeks, pretty generally, one shilling a week; had it been done some time past they would not have been discontented, for a want of loyalty is not amongst their faults; and many of their superiors in many instances might have imitated their conduct with advantage. The wise precautions of Government have certainly given a vigour to the loyal of the Nation who are most undoubtedly by far the majority; and the disaffected join them at present for fear of being suspected; therefore I have no doubt that our tranquillity will be restored.

I am, &c.

HORATIO NELSON

* This was the celebrated Dr. Joseph Priestley.

[In the enclosed paper alluded to, Nelson set out an account of]

THE EARNINGS AND EXPENSES OF A LABOURER IN NORFOLK WITH A WIFE AND THREE CHILDREN, SUPPOSING THAT HE IS NOT TO BE ONE DAY KEPT FROM LABOUR IN THE WHOLE YEAR

	£	s	d
One pair of Man's shoes, 7s., one pair of Women's, 4s. 6d., one pair for each of three Children, 10s. 6d., and £1 1s. for mending.			
Shoes and Mending	2	3	0
Shirts, two	0	10	0
Breeches or Jacket	0	3	0
Woman's and Children's clothes	1	6	0
Soap, 12 lbs.	0	8	10
Candles, 6 lbs.	0	4	0
Coals, one chaldron and a half	1	19	0
House rent	2	0	0
	8	13	10

Earnings

	£	s	d
From October 10th to March 31st, at 9s. per week	11	14	0
From March 31st to June 30th, at 8s. per week	5	4	0
From June 30th to August 24th, turnip-hoeing and hay-harvest	3	0	0
Harvest	2	2	0
Woman's gleaning	1	1	0
Total Earnings	23	1	0

	£	s	d
Earnings	23	1	0
Clothes, &c.	8	13	10
For food, five people	14	7	2

Not quite twopence a day for each person; and to drink nothing but water, for beer our poor labourers never taste, unless they are tempted which is too often the case, to go to the Alehouse.

[Such were his conclusions regarding the agricultural labourers' conditions after five years close association with them and while engaged in farming on a small scale himself. Nelson was a true-blue Tory, a Conservative to the core. His devotion to King and country were unbounded. He viewed the Doctor Priestleys and other advanced reformers of the day with suspicion and distrust. But he was also the firm friend of the poor and oppressed, and his quick eye and warm heart led him to take a deep personal interest in the deplorable condition of the East Anglian labourers whose lot, now as then, was the worst in the whole kingdom.

Perhaps he too felt himself poor and neglected. He had no undue affection for 'the great'; he himself was the scion of an ancient and noble family, the Walpoles, but his father was a poor country parson; he had a wife and a step-son to support; he had been unemployed for five years; he felt neglected and saw nepotism in high places; he was in the prime of life being then thirty-five years of age, and he was conscious that his services in the past had been ignored and that his prospects for the future were doubtful.

As each year passed they declined, and those ships which were being commissioned were being offered to other captains.

But now suddenly and almost without warning a great and violent change was at hand—not only in his own fortunes but in those of his country.

War with France was imminent. Every available ship, every man was wanted. Nelson went off to London and from there wrote to his wife:]

London, *January 7th, 1793*

My dear Fanny,

Post Nubila Phoebus—your son will explain the motto—after clouds come sunshine. The Admiralty so smile upon me that really I am as much surprised as when they frowned. Lord Chatham* yesterday made many apologies for not having given me a ship before this time, but that if I chose to take a 64-gun ship to begin with I should be appointed to one as soon as she was ready, and that I should as soon as in his power be removed into a 74. Lord Hood has sent for me to nominate the 1st Lieutenant† and that probably my ship would either be the *St. Albans* or *Intrepid*—one at Portsmouth, other at Plymouth. I want one at Chatham, as it would be convenient on every account and I have just been with the Comptroller‡ to try and get one order at Chatham which I hope to be able to accomplish.

As the Duke of Clarence§ wished to know what passed about me at

* Lord Chatham was First Lord of the Admiralty from 1788 to 1794.
† Nelson chose Martin Hinton, who had served with him in the *Albemarle*.
‡ Sir Henry Martin, Comptroller of the Navy 1790–4.
§ Prince William Henry was created Duke of Clarence in 1789.

the Admiralty I cannot leave town before Thursday or Friday. Perhaps this ship will not be ready before the end of the month. Everything looks war. One of our ships looking into Brest has been fired into. The shot is now at the Admiralty.

Tell my father I had not forgot his hat, it is ordered. You will write him my news, which I am sure will please him. Adair is not come to town if he comes I will certainly see him.*

Love to Josiah and believe me your most affectionate

HORATIO NELSON

* Nelson and his wife had been living at Burnham Thorpe with his father, while he was unemployed.

[War with France was declared one month later, on 11th February, and in the meantime Nelson had received his appointment to the *Agamemnon*, 64, then lying at Chatham.]

CHAPTER TWO

THE *AGAMEMNON*

[The *Agamemnon* was the last ship which was Nelson's own and his sole command. He was appointed to her on 26th January, 1793, and did not leave her until 1st June, 1796, when he was removed from the *Agamemnon* to the *Captain*, and became a squadron commander. His stepson, Josiah Nisbet, now thirteen years old, accompanied him as a midshipman in her.

He was delighted with his ship. He was satisfied with every officer; 'with a good ship and ship's company we can come to no harm'; 'we appear to sail very fast'; 'we are all well; indeed nobody can be ill with my ship's company, they are so fine a set'; '*Agamemnon* sails admirably; we think better than any ship in the fleet'.

Now began that twelve years' struggle with revolutionary France in which the influence of sea power was to play so great a part and of which, in Admiral Mahan's phrase, Nelson was the embodiment.

During this period, from 1793 until 1805, Nelson was almost continuously on active service; it includes the great trinity of his victories at the Nile, Copenhagen and Trafalgar; it includes also a number of minor actions in which he was often in the imminent deadly breach; he rose from a comparatively unknown naval captain to the heights of naval glory and of national renown; from now on, his letters and despatches increase in range, variety, number and importance as the scope of his duties and the brilliant successes which attended him increase in magnitude.

The next section of his letters describes his service in the *Agamemnon* under the successive commands of Lord Hood, Admiral Hotham and Sir John Jervis.

One of the first actions of Lord Hood was to try and take advantage of the situation prevailing in Marseilles and Toulon, which were blockaded by the fleet, were short of food and were prepared to treat for peace. It was hoped that Provence would separate from revolutionary France, where the reign of terror had begun, and proclaim its independence under the protection of Britain. On 27th August, Toulon hoisted the Bourbon flag and Lord Hood's fleet sailed into the harbour; troops took possession of the forts and the fine dockyard, and no fewer than thirty French ships of the line were delivered to Lord Hood.

This extraordinary success deceived even Nelson.]

'I hardly think the war can last' [he wrote to his wife.]

[Later he was despatched by Lord Hood in the *Agamemnon* to Naples to secure 10,000 troops to hold Toulon.]

Begun off the Island of Sardinia, *September 7th*,
finished at anchor off Naples, *September 11th, 1793*

My dear Fanny,

I wrote you a line by Lord Conway* who is gone home with Lord Hood's dispatches. As soon as the treaty was concluded, *Agamemnon* as being a fast sailer was sent off with dispatches to the courts of Turin and Naples for ten thousand troops to secure our possession. I should have liked to have stayed one day longer with the fleet when they entered the harbour but service could not be neglected for any private gratification. I have only to hope I shall succeed with the King of Naples. The last visit he had was from a French Grenadier belonging to Mons. Truguet's† fleet, how different he must feel.

What an event this has been for Lord Hood. Such a one as History cannot produce its equal. That the strongest place in Europe and twenty-two sail of the line etc. should be given up without firing a shot, it is not to be credited. On Sunday August 25th a party deposed Admiral Trogoff‡ and placed St. Julien§ at the head of the fleet, manned sixteen sail of the line and were determined to come out and fight us who were only 12 sail, Lord Hood having sent away the other part of his fleet to give them the option. The fleet regret they did not. The issue we should, I doubt not, have liked better than laying them up dismantled. The perseverance of our fleet has been great and to that only can be attributed our unexampled success. Not even a boat could get into Marseilles or Toulon or on the coast with provisions; and the old saying that hunger will tame a lion was never stronger exemplified. The Spanish fleet arrived as ours was sailing into the harbour and joined in the general joy which this event must give to all Europe. St. Julien with about 4,000 men left the fleet as ours entered, and joined General Corteau who I think it probable by this time has attacked Toulon with the Parisian army. They have made sad work with the Marseillois who were in treaty with us. I hope to God our success may be so used as to give peace to that unhappy distracted country. Nice, Ville Franche, Monaco and Menton which were taken from the King of Sardinia must fall again to him, so soon as our fleet

* Lord Hugh Seymour Conway, captain of the *Leviathan*, died a vice-admiral in 1801.

† Admiral Truguet commanded the Republican fleet; he died in 1839.

‡ Rear-Admiral Trogoff, with his flag in *Commerce de Marseilles*, had been in command Toulon, but retired owing to ill health.

§ Trogoff's successor; he was unable to control his men when Toulon surrendered to the English.

can be liberated from Toulon. No conquests of importance I believe the world is convinced of, can be made without us, and yet as soon as we have accomplished the service we are ordered on, we are neglected. If Parliament do not grant something to this fleet our jacks will grumble, for here there is no prize money to soften our hardships. All we get is honour and salt beef. My poor fellows have not had a morsel of fresh meat or vegetables for near nineteen weeks and in that time I have only had my foot twice on shore at Cadiz. We are absolutely getting sick from fatigue. No fleet I am satisfied ever served their country with greater zeal than this has done from the Admiral to the lowest sailor.

Admiral Goodall* is governor of Toulon, Elphinstone Commander of the grand batteries at the harbour's mouth. I may have lost an appointment by being sent off. Not that I wish to be employed out of my ship. I have sent in a ship from Smyrna bound to Marseilles and I think it probable she will be condemned worth about £10,000. I hope she may it will add something to our comforts. Josiah is well and a good boy. He has got a Turkish sabre of which he is not a little proud. I have inclosed this letter to Mr. Suckling but have not mentioned to him my having sent in any vessel. If she is condemned your knowing it is quite sufficient except my good father for many reasons which you know as well as myself, and if she is not the least that is said about her the better.

We are now in sight of Mount Vesuvius which shows a fine light to us in Naples Bay where we are laying too for the night and hope to anchor early tomorrow. Shall take this letter on shore with me in case the post goes out directly.

You will write to my father to say where we are and my kindest remembrances to him and remember me to all those who wish to hear of me. We were in the Bay all night becalmed and nothing could be finer than the views of Mount Vesuvius. Believe me your most affectionate husband,

HORATIO NELSON

To Mrs. Nelson — Naples, *September 14, 1793*

My dear Fanny,

My other letter will arrive with this. Our news was received here with the greatest satisfaction. The King has twice sent for me, and I dine with him tomorrow after he has made me a visit which he is to do on board the *Agamemnon*. We are called by him the Saviours of Italy, and of his

* Samuel Cranston Goodall was third in command in the Mediterranean.

Dominions in particular. I have acted for Lord Hood with a zeal which no one could exceed and am to carry from the King the handsomest letter, in his own handwriting, which could possibly be. This I got through Sir William Hamilton and the Prime Minister* who is an Englishman. Lady Hamilton† has been wonderfully kind and good to Josiah. She is a young woman of amiable manners, and who does honour to the station to which she is raised. I am to carry Lord Hood six thousand troops from hence. Remember me to my dear Father, also to Lord and Lady Walpole. Believe me, your most affectionate Husband,

HORATIO NELSON

[Meanwhile, a crisis was approaching at Toulon. There were not sufficient troops to defend the extensive lines in the rear of the port; the defending troops were mixed and of questionable efficiency; the French leaders had rapidly assembled superior forces to retake the city and port; evacuation became imperative and 14,000 of the inhabitants took refuge in the British ships. The arsenals were fired and an immense amount of destruction carried out. It was on this occasion that a young and then unknown military genius, a major of artillery, accurately indicated the key to the landward defences of Toulon and with his 'whiff of grapeshot' made the British hold untenable. Nelson describes the event to his clergyman brother, William.]

Agamemnon, Leghorn,
December 27th, 1793

My dear Brother,

You may probably have heard of our evacuation of Toulon by last post, when I wrote Maurice a line, as the report then went. For England the getting rid of such a place is a most happy event. Our money would have gone very fast. The particulars are as follows; that on the 13th a most numerous Army covered the neighbouring hills, that Lord Hood had given notice to the inhabitants of the probable evacuation of the place, that on the 17th at eight o'clock at night a general attack was made on all our outposts which lasted all night; the Foreign troops quitted them sooner than they ought to have, and the others were

* The celebrated Sir John Acton, grandfather of the historian Lord Acton.

† Nelson's first meeting with Lady Hamilton, who was then twenty-six and at the height of her beauty. She had been married to Sir William Hamilton for two years. Nelson was seven years older and had been married for six years.

obliged to be abandoned the next morning, destroying the works, and spiking the guns, as well as a short time would allow. Lord Hood attempted to rally the flying troops but it was impossible; our Army retired into the Town and Fort La Malgue. On the 18th the Neapolitan troops were ordered to embark, together with the Royalists in as many ships as could be found. Then began a scene of horror which may be conceived, not described. The mob rose; death called forth all its myrmidons which destroyed the miserable inhabitants in the shape of swords, pistols, fire and water. Thousands are said to be lost. In this dreadful scene and to complete misery, already at the highest, Lord Hood was obliged to order the French Fleet, twenty Sail of the Line, twenty other Men-of-War, together with the Arsenal, Powder Magazines, &c. to be set on fire. One half of the Town is said to have been consumed with them. Only three of the French Fleet saved; all the Forts are blown up and it is now strongly reported that Lord Hood has sailed for Hieres Bay. Fathers are here without families, and families without fathers, the pictures of horror and despair. *Agamemnon* is here getting provisions, but stationed with a squadron off Corsica. Josiah is well and desires to be remembered. Don't omit my remembrance in the kindest manner to Mrs. Nelson and my Aunt. I expect to see them soon for this war cannot last much longer. Compliments at Swaffham and believe me,

Your affectionate Brother,

HORATIO NELSON

1794

[Early in January, 1794, Lord Hood concluded a convention with General Paoli by which it was agreed that the British forces should assist the Corsicans in expelling the French and that Corsica should be ceded to Britain. Nelson in the *Agamemnon* was then cruising off Calvi with a small squadron to prevent the French from receiving supplies and he was in frequent communication with Paoli.]

To his wife At Sea, *February 13th, 1794*

I am just going into Leghorn to get water. Corsica, I hope, will fall in due time. Commodore Linzee has the command of the Sea-business, Lord Hood is in the offing. I have had the pleasure to fulfil the service

I had been employed upon, neither allowing provisions nor troops to get into Corsica, nor the Frigates to come out. I am next going to cruise off Bastia to prevent succours from getting in there. Corsica is a wonderfully fine Island. We are anxious to hear how Parliament likes the war. I am still of opinion it cannot last much longer; not by the French having an absolute Monarchy again, but by our leaving them alone; perhaps the wisest method we can follow. You will remember me in the kindest manner to my Father. God bless you.

HORATIO NELSON

The Rev. Dixon Hoste,
Godwich Hall, near Rougham

Agamemnon, Leghorn,
February 14, 1794

Dear Sir,

You cannot receive much more pleasure in reading this letter than I have in writing it, to say that your Son is everything which his dearest friends can wish him to be; and is a strong proof that the greatest gallantry may lie under the most gentle behaviour. Two days ago it was necessary to take a small Vessel from a number of people who had got on shore to prevent us. She was carried in high style and your good Son was by my side; we had six men badly wounded.

I am, dear Sir, Your most obedient Servant,

HORATIO NELSON

[The loss of Toulon deprived Lord Hood of a base for the British Fleet and he accordingly looked to Corsica where the port and town of Bastia offered what he wanted. Having reconnoitered the place from seaward, Nelson concluded that the ships could silence the fire of the sea-front, batter down the walls and then five hundred troops could carry the place by assault.

General Dundas commanding the troops took however a different view, declining to move against Bastia and condemning the attempt as rash unless he was first reinforced with 2,000 men from Gibraltar. Lord Hood urgently pressed him; Dundas remained firm and bitter letters passed between them while the French, unmolested except by the insurgent Corsicans, continued to strengthen the defences. In point of fact, Bastia was far more strongly defended than either Nelson or the Admiral knew and proved a tough nut to crack.

On 4th April, 1794, the besieging force, 1,200 Marines and 250 seamen, landed to the north of the town, Nelson with them.]

To the Rev. Dixon Hoste Camp, *May 3rd, 1794*

My dear Sir,

. . . You will have heard that we are before Bastia with 1,000 Regulars and Marines, and 300 Seamen. We landed on the 4th April. The Enemy have force but what we cannot exactly say. General D'Aubant* with 1,100 as fine Troops as ever marched will not join us, declaring that our united force is unequal to the attempt. The Army here is commanded by Lieut-Col. Villettes, a most excellent Officer, and I have the pleasure of giving my assistance. We shall in time accomplish the taking of Bastia. I have no doubt in the way we proposed to attempt it, by bombardment and cannonading, joined to a close blockade of the harbour. We now hear that General D'Aubant will take the field when the reinforcements arrive from England. I am almost afraid to say which I think such conduct merits. The King cannot approve of it. Bastia is a large Town, walled in with a Battery to the north and south of it, a Citadel in the middle, defended by thirty pieces of cannon and eight mortars, four stone redoubts on the nearest hills and three other posts above them. The Town contains about 12,000 inhabitants—it is said 14,000. The Troops we differ about as to numbers. Success, I trust, indeed have little doubt will crown our zealous and well-meant endeavours; if not, our Country will, I believe, sooner forgive an Officer for attacking his Enemy than for letting it alone. This Island, the finest almost in the world, I hope will belong to England. The inhabitants are strongly attached to us, and it will give us the command of the Mediterranean. The Italian States and the Spaniards, I believe, are jealous of our taking it, well knowing its consequence.

The *Agamemnon* is moored off our Camp; your dear boy wished much to come ashore with me, and if I had not thought the danger was too great, I should have brought him. He has been several times to see me. The zeal of our soldiers and seamen is, I believe, almost unexampled; there is not one who does not consider himself as personally interested in the event, and deserted by the General. It has made them equal to double their numbers. . . .

I am, dear Sir,

Your very humble Servant,

HORATIO NELSON

* General D'Aubant had succeeded General Dundas.

FROM NELSON'S JOURNAL

. . . The Seamen always slept on the battery with their pikes and cutlasses. Lord Hood on the 8th sent in another Flag of Truce at eight o'clock which was refused; the Mayor telling the Officer 'that they would return bomb for bomb and shot for shot'. Opened the twenty-four pounder and howitzer with the greatest good effect; nor could all the efforts of the Enemy knock down our works. A continued and increasing fire was kept up on the Town and outworks.

In the night of the 12th a large Boat came out of Bastia; she was closely pursued by our Guard-boats and taken; in her were three deserters, the Captain of *La Fortunée* frigate, twelve Seamen, eight Corsicans and thirty wounded soldiers going to Capraja. Her despatches were thrown overboard but in the morning of the 13th at daylight, Lieutenant Suckling of the *St. Croix* schooner saw the packet floating on the water which he took up and brought to me. Probably in the hurry of throwing them overboard, the weight that had been tied to them had slipped out of the string.

They were all letters from Gentili, the Commander-in-Chief at Bastia saying how much they had been annoyed by our fire, which had been opened on them forty days, and that if succours did not arrive by the 29th of the month, they must look upon the Town as lost to the Republic. These letters were addressed to Salicetti, La Combe St. Michel, and Santelli. Lord Hood sent in the Boat with her crew and wounded men, with a week's provisions; and we got this day a nine-pounder on the ridge.

On the 14th May, the Enemy displayed a picture on Camponella the whole day; they did not treat it with insult and I think it was intended for Lord Hood. (By way of compliment for having returned the Boat with the wounded men.) Our batteries kept up an incessant fire. During the night of the 15th, our Guard boats took a boat from Capraja, bound to Bastia, Galeazzini the Mayor's brother was in her: no despatches could be found. The Enemy were employed preparing Gardiola for a mortar.

On the 16th they got up a thirteen-inch mortar which kept up a constant fire throughout the night. It blowing strong from the northward, three Boats attempted to get into the Town with powder and provisions; two were taken but one got in. From this day until the 19th, the Enemy fired more than usual both night and day. We had also often five shells in the air all at once, going to Bastia.

On the 19th of May, some means had been taken to convey a message to Lord Hood, that if he would condescend to send a boat with a Flag, a negotiation would be entered into for the surrender of the Town and its dependencies. In consequence, at four o'clock that evening, May 19th, a Flag of Truce was hoisted on board the *Victory* and a boat went off from her to the Town, and one from the Town to the *Victory*. The Enemy from Camponella met us without arms, and our Officers advancing, they shook hands and were good friends; they said it was all over and that Bastia was ours. . . .

To Mrs. Nelson Camp, *May 20th, 1794*

I have the pleasure to tell you that yesterday afternoon the 19th the Enemy sent off a Flag of Truce to Lord Hood. The truce still continues and I hope there will be a surrender of the Town in consequence. Our Fiorenzo army, hearing what was going on here, have marched to the tops of the heights, which will probably terrify the Enemy. I always was of opinion, have ever acted up to it, and never have had any reason to repent it, that one Englishman was equal to three Frenchmen; had this been an English Town, I am sure it would not have been taken by them. They have allowed us to batter it without once making any effort to drive us away. I may say truly that this has been a Naval Expedition; our Boats prevented anything from getting in by sea and our Sailors hauling up great guns, and then fighting them on shore.

We expect to take 1,000 Regulars, 1,500 National Guards and a large party of Corsican Troops, 4,000 in the whole; these will lay down their arms to 1,000 Soldiers and Marines and 200 Seamen. There is some difficulty about the terms, and hostilities may recommence for a day or two longer, but they must submit. Josiah has been with me at the head of the British grenadiers taking possession of the Forts and Posts. When I reflect what we have achieved, I am all astonishment. Providence has ever been gracious to me and has been my protector from the many perils incident to my situation.

Yours, &c.

HORATIO NELSON

[So ended the siege and surrender of Bastia in which Nelson had taken a leading, not to say decisive, part. When Lord Hood's despatch describing the operation was published, Nelson was disappointed that he had not been given greater credit. Writing to his uncle Suckling, he said:]

Lord Hood and myself were never better friends—*nor although his Letter does*, did he wish to put me where I never was—in the rear.

Captain Hunt who lost his Ship, he wanted to push forward for another—a young man who never was on a battery, or ever rendered any service during the siege; if any person ever says he did, then I submit to the character of a story-teller. The whole operations of the Siege were carried on through Lord Hood's letters to me. I was the mover of it—I was the cause of its success. Sir Gilbert Elliot will be my evidence, if any is required. I am not a little vexed, but shall not quarrel. . . .

[Having captured Bastia, the next objective was Calvi on the north-west point of the Island, a strongly fortified port, admirably situated for defence from its position and the prevailing on-shore breeze in summer being a lee shore for the attacking ships. It was to this operation that Nelson, working amicably with the military commander, General Stuart, and 'believing ourselves safe under your Lordship's wing' now addressed himself.]

To Mrs. Nelson Camp, near Calvi, *June 27th, 1794*

My dear Fanny,

I sent you a few lines just as we landed, since which nothing particular has occurred. Dragging cannon up steep mountains and carrying shot and shells has been our constant employment. Josiah is very well and I have no fears but he will be a good man. He is affectionate, though warm in his disposition which nothing can cool so thoroughly as being at Sea where nobody has entirely their own way. Corsica, in respect to prizes, produces nothing but honour, far above the consideration of wealth; not that I despise riches, quite the contrary, yet I would not sacrifice a good name to obtain them.

The French here do not know what to make of us. They hear we are landed, yet have not seen us, nor have they any idea about our batteries which, when they open, will be heavy on them. That we shall take Calvi in due time I have no manner of doubt. You know probably that George the Third is King of Corsica, chosen by the unanimous consent of the people themselves, the best of all Titles; they are now our fellow subjects. The first resolution of the Parliament of Corsica was to declare they were Englishmen; they might have been mistaken for Irishmen by their 'bull'. You will hear that Lord Hood fell in with the French Fleet on the 10th but they were too near the shore for him to prevent their getting into Port. His Lordship *wished to attack them*; a Council of Flag Officers prevented him.* You may be assured he will either take or destroy them, but I trust not before Calvi is ours, when I shall

* Nelson's dislike of Councils of War was notorious.

immediately join the Fleet. Be so good as to write a line to my Father to say I am well, never better; also to Mrs. Bolton and that I shall write soon. I expect this will find you at Mr. Matcham's, at Ringwood; remember me kindly. God bless you.

HORATIO NELSON

June 28th

Those people who so liberally abuse everybody but themselves are probably the very persons who deserve abuse. I hope those who are to get so much money will make a proper use of it. Had I attended less than I have done to the service of my Country I might have made some too; however I trust my name will stand on record, when the money-makers will be forgot.

[The siege of Calvi began on 27th June; it did not capitulate until 10th August, six weeks later, during which time Nelson was continuously in the forefront. As at Bastia there was a lack of naval and military co-operation; the place was difficult to attack; the work was tedious and exhausting and malaria was rampant. General Stuart's right-hand man was Colonel Moore, afterwards the hero of Corunna; Lord Hood was anxious to complete the business and to get his ships and men back to the Fleet.

Meanwhile on 1st June, Lord Howe had won a glorious victory 'The First of June' which naturally distracted attention from the siege of Calvi.]

TO H.R.H. The Duke of Clarence.

Camp before Calvi, *August 6th and 10th, 1794*

Sir,

The Gazette will tell your Royal Highness the general outlines of this siege which I believe is novel in its form. We landed about four miles to the Westward of Calvi on the 19th of June; on the 19th of July we were in full possession of every outpost of the Enemy with very trifling loss. Our batteries were erected with impunity in situations which the Enemy ought to have prevented. Had they kept even a moderate look-out, our loss of men must have been great, every battery being within reach of grape-shot from its opponent. On the 19th of July, General Stuart sent in to ask, if they had any terms to propose to him; their answer was the Motto of the Town,—*Civitas Calvis semper fidelis.* We were then only 650 yards from the centre of the Citadel, and they allowed us to erect very strong batteries under a mask—they must and ought to have known what we were after—without firing a single shot or shell.

On the 28th in the morning, our batteries, 560 yards from the Citadel wall, were ready to open their force, consisting of twenty one cannon, five mortars and four howitzers. The General sent in to say he should not fire on the black flags (hospitals). This note produced a negotiation, by which the Enemy wanted to obtain a Truce for twenty-five days; when, if no succours arrived, they agreed to surrender the Town, Frigates, &c. Lord Hood and the General agreed to give them six days; but, while this was going on four small Vessels got in, which gave them hope, I suppose, of more effectual relief; for on the 30th of July they rejected our offer; and our fire opened with all the effect we could expect.

On the 1st of August, at eleven o'clock, when much of the parapet was beaten down, and the houses in the Citadel were either in ruins or in flames, the Enemy hung out a White flag, and requested a suspension of hostilities for a few hours, to prepare terms. In twenty four hours everything was settled,—That on the 10th of August we were to be put in full possession, and the Garrison and such of the Inhabitants as chose were to be transported to Toulon, without being Prisoners of War; provided no effectual succours were thrown in by the French.

Thus is likely to end the attack of Corsica, the possession of which will, I hope, benefit our country. While there are such men as Sir Gilbert Elliot* to point out the advantages, it would be impertinent in me to attempt it. The loss to the French will be great; they got from it all the deals that are excellent for their decks, and timbers for their topsides, with pitch and tar which, although of an inferior quality, they employed at Toulon for many uses. We also get the *Melpomene* the most beautiful frigate I ever saw, fourteen ports, thirteen eighteen-pounders. The *Mignonne* with twelve-pounders, but not a very fine ship, at least if compared with the other.

The climate here, from July to October, is most unfavourable for Military operations. It is now what we call the dog-days, here it is termed the Lion-Sun; no person can endure it; we have upwards of one thousand sick out of two thousand; and the others not much better than so many phantoms. We have lost many men from the season, few from the Enemy. I am here the reed among the oaks; all the prevailing disorders have attacked me, but I have not strength for them to fasten upon; I bow before the storm, while the sturdy oak is laid low. One plan I pursue, never to employ a Doctor; Nature does all for me, and Providence protects me. Always happy if my humble but hearty endeavours can serve my King and Country.

* Afterwards Viceroy of Corsica.

The French Fleet are still at Gourjean Road and so securely moored, that it is said we cannot get at them with our ships. They are guarded as much as possible from Fire-ships by a line of Frigates outside the large Ships, and a line of Gun boats outside them, and at night a line of Launches; the whole is protected by very formidable batteries. When they came out of Toulon, by some mistake, they were represented to Admiral Hotham* as nine Sail of the Line whereas time has shown they were only seven; which induced a most gallant Officer to bear up for Calvi, and there he intended to fight them, sooner than they could throw in succours: had he known they were only an equal force, I am sure he would have given a good account of them.

I have written thus much that your Royal Highness may be assured of my compliance with your desire of knowing what we are about; and that I am ready to obey your orders; being with the highest respect, your Royal Highness's most dutiful servant

HORATIO NELSON

Agamemnon, off Leghorn,
August 18th, 1794

My dear Fanny,

I wrote you a line by the officer who carries home Lord Hood's dispatches and a letter a few days before, but which I find probably went by the same conveyance.

I left Calvi on the 15th I hope never to be in it again. I was yesterday in Fiorenza and today shall be safe moored I expect in Leghorn, where I am to remain and recruit a worn out ship's company. Since the ship has been commissioned this is the first resting time we have had. You may hear, therefore as it is all past I may tell you that on the 10th of July last a shot having struck our battery the splinters of stones from it struck me most severely in the face and breast. Although the blow was so severe as to occasion a great flow of blood from my head, yet I most fortunately escaped by only having my right eye nearly deprived of its sight. It was cut down, but is as far recovered as to be able to distinguish light from darkness, but as to all the purpose of use it is gone. However the blemish is nothing, not to be perceived unless told. The pupil is nearly the size of the blue part, I don't know the name. At Bastia I got a sharp cut in the back.

But what degree of credit may be given to my services I cannot say. General Stuart and Lord Hood are as far asunder as the other generals.

* Vice-Admiral Hotham succeeded Lord Hood as Commander-in-Chief in the Mediterranean.

They hate us sailors, we are too active for them. We accomplish our business sooner than they like. We throw them and I hope ever shall both at sea and on shore in the back ground. Lord Hood has been very ill and no doubt has applied for leave to go home. I hope he will take me with him.

You must not think that my hurts confine me. No—nothing but the loss of a limb should have kept me from my duty and I believe it to have conduced to my keeping up in the general mortality. Mrs. Moutray's son who was on shore with me I am fearful will fall a sacrifice to the climate. He is a lieutenant of the *Victory* a very fine young man who I have a great regard for.* Lord Hood is quite distressed about him. Poor little Hoste is also so extremely ill that I have great fears about him. Bolton very ill, Suckling that giant knocked up and 150 of my people in their beds. Never say I have not a good constitution. Of 2,000 men I am the healthiest. I have been disappointed in not getting a letter but perhaps it is my fault in desiring you to direct to Gibraltar, but I hope to get some letters here.

I see by the papers the death of a Captain Kelly, I hope most sincerely it is not our friend. I have I assure you done with campaigning, it was in some measure forced upon me I never solicited it. Josiah is very well and a clever smart young man so I must call him his sense demands it. As I only expect barely to save post, I leave the saying I am well to my father for you to say. Believe me your most affectionate husband,

HORATIO NELSON

Leghorn, *September 1st, 1794*

My dear Fanny,

I yesterday received your letter of August 4th which I sincerely thank

* Son of the lady in the West Indies whom he called his 'dear sweet friend', and whom he so admired.

Young Moutray died the next day and Nelson placed a memorial to him in the Church of St. Fiorenzo.

(From a copy in Nelson's own hand now in the British Museum)

SACRED TO THE MEMORY
OF LIEUTENANT JAMES MOUTRAY, R.N.
WHO, SERVING ON SHORE AT THE SIEGE OF
CALVI
THERE CAUGHT A FEVER
OF WHICH HE DIED
SINCERELY LAMENTED
ON AUGUST 19TH 1794
AGED 21 YEARS

This Stone is erected by an Affectionate Friend, who well knew his Worth as an Officer, and his Accomplished Manners as a Gentleman. H. N.

you for. The uncertainty of a ship's destination you are now aware off therefore pray continue to direct here. If I should be so happy as to go home I shall leave directions for my letters to be sent to Marsh and Creed. I hope you will apply to them for whatever money you may want, it would indeed grieve me if I thought you wanted for anything. I shall not be in their debt therefore do not be afraid to call on them. Indeed my dear Fanny my love, regard and esteem for you cannot I think be exceeded by any man whatever.

Lord Hood is something better but when he goes home or who goes with him is still uncertain. I think if he can with propriety take me I shall be one of the ships. He has been grievously thwarted in this country by envious people which has added to the load he has had on his mind.

You will be sorry to hear young Moutray is dead. I wrote you he was ill with the Calvi fever. He was 2nd Lieutenant of the *Victory* and at this moment would have been a Captain. What a shock it must be to his poor mother who was all expectation of hearing of his promotion when a very different account will be told her. His own amiable disposition will never be forgot by all who knew him. Lord Hood was his godfather and feels much for the loss of him. Suckling has been very ill but is out of danger. Bolton, Hoste and Weatherhead are recovered. My ship's company are not yet much better but time I hope will restore us. As to my health it never was better. My constitution is absolutely the wonder of the fleet. Nothing hurts it. I have been 5 nights without sleep (at work) and never felt an inconvenience. Josiah has as good health as myself. He is a very good boy and will be an excellent officer. Captain Valiant's son is on board the *Victory* and will soon be made a lieutenant. I have not yet seen him.

I have had a letter from our father who seems pretty well. I hope we shall meet him before the year expires at Burnham but that pleasure I cannot much build upon. From your not mentioning Kelly I hope no accident has happened. I suppose for the same reason you never hear from the West Indies.

The French Squadron are still in Gourjean Bay blocked up by us and the Spaniards but another month must liberate them and they will get I dare say to Toulon. The opportunity was lost by Admirals of fighting them, and it is a thousand to one if we ever have so fair an opportunity. Equal numbers and the British fleet declined battle. Had Lord Hood been there, I am sure he would have given a good account of them. We sailed from Bastia with only 5 sail of the line in search of them and should most certainly have brought them to action had fortune favoured us. Best love where you are. Your most affectionate H. N.

Leghorn, *September 12th, 1794*

My dear Fanny,

I had the happiness of receiving your letter of August 18th yesterday and do most truly rejoice that your mind did not take alarm at Captain Serocold's death, which I feared might have found its way to newspapers without a name. I ever feel the protecting hand of Providence covering me and when it shall be His good will that I am to leave this world I trust I shall leave a fair name behind me. I hope to see you in the fall of the year. Lord Hood's inclination I believe leads him to take me with him if the service will admit of it, and although I shall not bring with me either riches or honours, yet I flatter myself I shall bring a sound constitution and an unblemished character. My ship's company are better but still in a very weak state.

The French are getting on at Toulon rather faster than was expected. They have now 11 sail of the line ready for sea and in a few days will have two more, therefore my going must depend on Elphinstone's reinforcement of ships. It always rejoices me to hear you are comfortable and that my friends are attentive to you. I hope we shall find some snug cottage whenever we may be obliged to quite the Parsonage.

It is probable we shall get to sea in about 3 days from hence with Lord Hood in the *Victory* to Genoa, Port Especia and Vado Bay then off Gourjean Bay, Toulon and I hope to Gibraltar and England. When Lord Hood quits I should be truly sorry to remain. He is the greatest sea officer I ever knew and what can be said against him I cannot conceive. It can only be envy. It is better to be envied than pitied, but it comes from the Army who have also poisoned some of our minds. The taking of Bastia contrary to all military judgement is such an attack on the understandings of these gentry that it is never to be forgiven and the mind to recover itself flies to revenge. General Stuart I am sorry to say has most deeply imbibed this diabolical leven.

Remember me kindly to my sister and Mr. Matcham and to other parts of my family when you write and believe me your most affectionate husband,

HORATIO NELSON

Josiah is very well.

To the same Genoa, *20th September, 1794*

This City is, without exception, the most magnificent I ever beheld, superior in many respects to Naples, although it does not appear quite so fine from the sea, yet on shore it is far beyond it. All the houses are palaces on the grandest scale. However, I trust we shall soon quit these magnificent scenes, and retire to England, where all that I admire is placed.

Yours, &c.

HORATIO NELSON

To Admiral Lord Hood

September 23rd, 1794

My Lord,

On Sunday evening I waited on the Doge and as Mr. Drake* was not arrived, I found it absolutely necessary to say something civil, which I did in the following words: 'That I was come to pay my respects to his Serene Highness, and to assure him that both by duty and inclination I should preserve the strictest attention to the neutrality of Genoa; and should be happy in doing everything in my power to cement the harmony which subsisted between the two Nations'.

The Doge was much pleased and very civil; and answered, 'That he thanked me for my expressions of friendship, and begged to assure me that it should be reciprocal on his part; and that from so pleasing a renewal of our friendship, he had no doubt of its being lasting; that he was always glad to see English Men-of-War in Genoa; and whatever I might find a difficulty in procuring, if I would make it known to him, he should be happy in removing it; and that the gates were always at my disposal.'

I was received in some State, the Doge advancing to the middle of the room. I had the honour also of a Senato. On my departure from the Palace, the orders of the Doge had arrived before me at the gates, where the Captain of the Guard told me he had received the mandate for opening them at whatever time I pleased.

I am, &c.

HORATIO NELSON

[His 36th birthday was two days later]

Agamemnon, Genoa,
September 27th, 1794

My dear Fanny,

We are just going to sea with Lord Hood and Admiral Hotham who came in here 4 days ago. We are going off Gourjean to look at the

* The British Minister.

French ships, from thence to Toulon where the enemy have 6 sail ready for sea and most probably will soon make an effort to join their other ships. The French have taken possession of Vado Bay in the Genoa territories and of course will prevent our ships from anchoring and I have little doubt but if the enemy turn their thoughts to the invasion of Italy but that next spring they will do it. The allied powers seem jealous of each other and none but England are hearty in the cause.

Lord Hood goes from the fleet to Corsica from whence he sails for England. I do not now think we have any chance of going with him. The fleet here cannot be lessened. Admiral Hotham thinks we are too few, therefore I stand no chance of seeing you at present but let's hope whatever is is best. Many here are using their interest to go home when Elphinstone arrives therefore I have not nor do I build too much on my prospect of seeing you till the spring, by which time I hope the war will be over and we shall get to the farm again.

Remember me kindly where you are and believe me your most affectionate husband,

HORATIO NELSON

Josiah is very well 5 feet high he says he is 5 feet 1 inch. I have not wrote my father from hence.

To Admiral Lord Hood *Agamemnon*, at Sea,
October 2nd, 1794

My Lord,

Not any notice having been taken in the Public List of Wounded at the Siege of Calvi, of my eye being damaged, I feel it but justice to myself to transmit to your Lordship two Certificates, one from the Surgeon General of his Majesty's Forces, the other from the Physician of the Fleet, and the Surgeon landed for the care of the Seamen; and I have to request that your Lordship will take such measures as you may judge proper that my Sovereign may be informed of my loss of an eye in His Service; nor do I think that his Majesty will consider that I suffered the less pain from my determination to do my duty in twenty-four hours after the accident, that those laborious duties intrusted by your Lordship to my direction might not slacken.

I submit my case entirely to your Lordship, resting assured you will mention me in this matter as I deserve, and will do ample justice to the gallant Officers and Seamen employed under me.

I am, with great respect,

Your Lordship's most obedient servant,

HORATIO NELSON

CERTIFICATES

These are to Certify that Horatio Nelson, Esquire, Commander of His Majesty's Ship *Agamemnon* did, on the 10th day of July, 1794, while commanding the Seamen before Calvi, receive a wound of the iris of the right eye, which has occasioned an unnatural dilatation of the pupil, and a material defect of sight.

JOHN HARNESS
Physician to the Fleet

MICHAEL JEFFERSON
Surgeon attending on Shore

These are to Certify that Captain Horatio Nelson of his Majesty's Ship *Agamemnon*, now serving on shore at the Siege of Calvi was on the 10th day of July last, wounded in the face and right eye, much injured by stones or splinters, struck by shot from the Enemy.

There were several small lacerations about the face; and his eye so materially injured that in my opinion he will never recover the perfect use of it again.

W. CHAMBERS
Surgeon to the Forces in the Mediterranean

[At this time Nelson was unhappy and discontented on several counts. He considered that his services at Bastia and Calvi had not received due credit; he had lost the sight of his eye; Lord Hood, whom he so admired, was returning to England to be replaced by Vice-Admiral Hotham whom he did not know; he had hoped the *Agamemnon* would have been ordered home but she could not be spared.]

To Mrs. Nelson Off Gourjean, *October 3rd, 1794*

Lord Hood is gone to Leghorn to receive his dispatches by a messenger, who is arrived from England, and most probably we shall only see him to take leave. Admiral Hotham will be Commander-in-Chief; and with new men, new measures are generally adopted, therefore I can at present say nothing about myself, except that I am in most perfect health. We have here eleven Sail of the Line, the Enemy have fourteen; seven here, and seven at Toulon. They will probably before the winter is over effect a junction, when our Fleet will be kept together; but whenever they choose to give us a meeting, the event I have no doubt will be such as every Englishman as a right to expect.

October 10th.—Lord Hood is to join us in a few days; I fear I have no chance whatever of going Home. My Ship's company are by no means recovered; and we are destined to keep the sea, until both Ship and Crew are rendered unfit for service. Pray let me hear often from you: it is my greatest comfort.

October 12th.—Lord Hood left us yesterday: therefore our hopes of my going Home at present are at an end; however, we must not repine: at all events I shall cheat the winter, and, as I understand I am to have a cruise, it may possibly be advantageous. Lord Hood is very well inclined towards me; but the service must ever supersede all private consideration. I hope you will spend the winter cheerfully. The Wolterton family, I am sure, will be happy to receive you for as long a time as you please. Do not repine at my absence; before Spring I hope we shall have Peace, when we must look out for some little cottage: I assure you I shall return to the plough with redoubled glee.

October 15th.—Two of my opponents, whom I fell in with last year about this time, are now in England, or near it, the *St. Fiorenzo*, late *La Minerve*, and *La Melpomene*, both 40 guns, 18-pounders, two as fine Frigates as are in the world. I have been fortunate in being present at the taking and destroying of that whole Squadron; and which, but for our disabling them, intending to have returned to France: they are now better disposed of.

Yours, &c.

HORATIO NELSON

To Mrs. Nelson Leghorn, *October 24th, 1794*

What changes, my dearest Fanny, our life is subject to. The other day, when I wrote, I was going up the Levant: now that is gone by, and I am under different orders. We came in here to get a few refreshments for my people, seventy of whom are still very ill, and I go to sea on the 26th to join the Fleet again. We have but little news here. I wish we could make a Peace on any fair terms, for poor England will be drained of her riches to maintain her Allies, who will not fight for themselves.

[Apparently in continuation]

Leghorn, *October 31st*

It is an ill wind that blows nobody any good: being obliged by a gale to put back last night, I in consequence received your letter of September 30th, which gave me infinite pleasure. Why you should be uneasy about me, so as to make yourself ill, I know not. I feel a confident protection in whatever service I may be employed upon; and as to my health, I don't know that I was ever so truly well: I fancy myself grown quite stout. My Ship, and Ship's Company, though not in half the strength as when I left Spithead, several of my guns that were landed at Corsica having been destroyed, yet I am sure feel themselves equal to go alongside any 74 out of France. Lord Hood sends me word he shall come out here again; I own I don't think so, although he retains the Chief Command. It rejoices me to hear Maurice is so well off. Admiral Hotham cannot keep the sea much longer; the Fleet must return into some Port. We have had three gales of wind in thirteen days, all very strong; neither sails, ships, nor men can stand it. In the Channel, the Fleet goes instantly into Torbay, here we always keep the Sea.

Yours, &c.

HORATIO NELSON

To William Suckling, Esq.

Agamemnon, Leghorn, *October 31st*, *1794*

My dear Sir,

Being driven back to this Port last night by a gale of wind, I got Mrs. Nelson's letter, dated from Kentish Town. Your kindness to her will never be forgotten by me; and to Mrs. Suckling and Miss Suckling I feel infinitely obliged. I shall only tell you, what may not be believed in England, that the French have put together a Fleet at Toulon, which could hardly be credited. Although many of them are old, yet they have fitten them well enough for an Action, if it should be necessary. I send you a list of them on the other side. We don't seem to make much of the war. Our Allies are our burden. Had we left the Continent to themselves, we should have done well, and at half the expense. The gale moderates, and I am just going to get under weigh again.

Believe me, with every affectionate wish and regard,

Yours obliged,

HORATIO NELSON

To H.R.H. The Duke of Clarence

Agamemnon, at Sea, *November 7th, 1794*

Since I had the honour of writing to your Royal Highness, my time has been fully occupied in endeavouring to reinstate the health of my Ship's company, which had been miserably torn to pieces by, without vanity, I hope I may be allowed to say, as hard service as a Ship's crew ever performed. I have lost fifty of my best men since I left Calvi; nor can the others be got round to their proper health, so entirely are their constitutions destroyed. I had been sent into Leghorn for some stores at the latter end of October, and did not join Admiral Hotham off Gourjean Bay until the 3rd of November in the morning, when I found the Enemy's Fleet had given us the slip and that it was determined to unite our Fleet at St. Fiorenzo; the French having given out, that they would eat their new-year's dinner in Corsica. I was immediately detached to look into Hieres Bay and Toulon, and to examine into the state of their Fleet, and where they were got to. On the 5th of November, not finding them in Hieres Bay, I stood close into Toulon Harbour, where are twenty-two Sail of Ships in the inner Harbour: we could only look over a point of land, therefore cannot say how many were of the Line. I see plainly they will keep us in hot water the whole winter, and I think it probable may detach small Squadrons to get, for a few days at intervals, in the track of our Trade upward-bound. Your Royal Highness has probably read the list handed about of their Fleet, fifteen Sail of the Line, ten Frigates, and Corvettes. Many we know must be in very bad condition; but still they may bear a few hours at Sea, which is sufficient for their purpose. Believe me ever with the highest respect,

Your Royal Highness's most dutiful Servant,

HORATIO NELSON

To the Right Honourable Sir Gilbert Elliot, Viceroy of Corsica

Agamemnon, St. Fiorenzo, *November 10th, 1794*

My dear Sir,

As I have been sent by the Admiral to examine into the state of the Enemy's Fleet at Toulon, I think it will be acceptable to your Excellency to have a copy of my Report, more especially as it is given out that Corsica is their object of attack, and very many in our service believe it. I own myself of a different opinion. Neither Calvi, St. Fiorenzo, or Bastia can be attacked by them, unless—what I hope no Englishman will credit—that they are able to beat our Fleet. We know from experience that an Army, thrown ashore without the possibility of being supported by a Fleet to land all the requisites for a Siege, (which are many,) however numerous they may be, cannot subsist long in an Enemy's country. The Corsicans, if we keep them out of fortified places, would harass them to death.

I shall take this opportunity of saying a word of Ajaccio. If the Enemy have an intention of getting a hold in Corsica, that is the place they will attempt; and should they succeed, we shall find it a difficult matter to drive them out again. I never was there; but it strikes me, that by numbers landed, and the appearance of their Fleet for a few hours, they may succeed; for I believe the Corsicans understand nothing of the art of defending fortified Towns.

You will, I am sure, receive what I am going to say as it is meant, *well*, and believe that all my wishes and desires are to see our Country successful, and the schemes of our Enemies frustrated. I am well aware it may be said, and with truth, that we have not Troops in the Island to defend any one place properly. I admit it; but in answer I say—and am satisfied in my mind it will turn out so—if the Enemy make an attempt, that a few Troops and Artillery stationed at Ajaccio, to keep the gates shut for a few days, would render abortive any schemes they may have for establishing themselves there. I think three hundred men, and some Artillery to keep the Guns in order, to which if a Guardship was added, the seamen, in time of need, could go on shore to man the works; (for if the Enemy get Ajaccio, they may lay there with their whole Fleet, or leave a single Frigate, neither of which we could attack; for in the Gulph there is no sounding, and a sea setting constantly in, which would make us keep at a distance.) With this defence, I am confident the place, and I believe I may say the Island, would be perfectly safe, till our Fleet could get to the Enemy, when the event, I have no doubt, would be what every Briton might expect; besides, we have the incitement, (if any is wanted,) of our Home Fleet*, and we shall not like to be outdone by any one.

* The victory of the 1st of June.

I have taken the liberty of mentioning my idea of the importance of Ajaccio, only in the belief which I have, that your Excellency will receive it as a *private* communication, (my situation does not entitle me to give any public opinion on such a point); as such I send it, and shall be happy if it gives rise to a serious consideration of its importance, when, I doubt not, much more proper modes of defence and security will be thought of than I have suggested. But, however that may be, I am bold to say, none can exceed me in the earnest desire of serving well my King and Country; and of convincing your Excellency how much I am, on every occasion, your most sincere, humble Servant,

HORATIO NELSON

Agamemnon, St. Fiorenzo,
November 12th, 1794

My dear Fanny,

I have since I wrote you last been sent to look after the French fleet who had again given Admiral Hotham the slip. I found them in Toulon, 16 sail of the line and several frigates. Our fleet had gone to Fiorenzo to refit and be prepared for any movement of the enemy. I came in here two days ago, and found a most unpleasant circumstance a mutiny on board the *Windsor Castle*, Admiral Linzee's ship. The crew wishing to change their captain and 1st Lieutenant, the officers have been tried at their own requests and most honourably acquitted but the Admiral notwithstanding has removed them and forgiven the ship's company who richly deserved a halter. I am of opinion 'tis mistaken lenity and will be the cause of present innocent people being hanged. I wish Lord Hood was either here or I was in England with him. The French say they will have Corsica again and we have croakers who believe them. I am of a totally different opinion and have no doubt that the enemy will in the first instance not make any attempt and in the next that should they come out, we shall beat them if our Admiral will give us leave, which many doubt so much do characters alter. There has been a most diabolical report here of our being captured and carried into Toulon (owing to my running into the harbour's mouth) I hope it has not reached England. Never believe anything you may see in the papers about us and rest assured that *Agamemnon* is not to be taken easily. Not any two-decked ship in the world is able, we flatter ourselves, to do it.

Josiah tells me he will write you on Monday when the post next goes to England. I am now at Leghorn to get new masts and to endeavour to restore my worn out ship and ship's company. God bless you and believe me your most affectionate

HORATIO NELSON

I don't know I ever had such good health as since I have been in

Italy, not one day's illness. Josiah is quite a man. I am now getting a French master to him, Hoste and myself. Best love and remembrances to Mrs. Suckling, Miss Suckling and Mr. Ramsey.

To H.R.H. the Duke of Clarence *November, 1794*

Sir,

Our Transports, which had been detained at Toulon since the time they carried over the Garrison of Calvi, arrived on the 22nd. No reason was ever given for detaining them; but their sails were taken from them, and during their stay not a man was suffered to go on shore. They were, however, treated tolerably, until the arrival of Jean Bon St. André, who, to the Officer's modest and proper requests, gave insolent answers, the true characteristic of little minds; a generous Enemy would have disdained the withholding medical assistance from the unfortunate, whom chance had put in their power. At eight o'clock in the evening of the 20th, their sails were sent alongside, and a message, that if they were not out of the harbour of twelve o'clock next day, they would keep them. The English, poor fellows, wanted no spur to clear them of such wretches; one Transport, who got aground, they left behind, and she is not yet arrived. The Enemy have fifteen Sail of the Line ready for Sea, with which, they say, they mean to fight our Fleet; and as Admiral Hotham sailed from Fiorenzo on the 25th, to go off Toulon with thirteen Sail of the Line, they will have the opportunity. As to the event I have no doubt it will be victory on the side of the English.

My heart, I assure you, is almost broke to find the *Agamemnon* lying here, little better than a wreck: we hope to get fitted in about three weeks. I own my sincere wish, that the Enemy would rest quiet until we are ready for Sea, and a gleam of hope sometimes crosses me, that they will. At Toulon seven Sail of the Line are to be launched by next March; they get well supplied with timber by the Genoese vessels.

I am, &c.

HORATIO NELSON

To William Suckling, Esq.

Agamemnon, Leghorn, *November 28th, 1794*

My dear Sir,

Perhaps you will say, I am but little obliged for this letter, as it encloses one for my dear wife; but I believe you will give me credit for writing as often as my situation will admit. I shall tell you our news, which will soon be interesting. Matters are fast drawing to a crisis in this Country. Our Transports, which have been detained at Toulon, since they carried over the Garrison of Calvi, were liberated on the 20th November; their sails, which had been taken from them, being sent on board, and sixteen hours allowed them to depart. Not a man allowed to go on shore during their stay, and the answers of Jean Bon St. André were insolent in the highest degree to modest and proper requests. He sent a message to Lord Hood, not knowing of his departure, that, if he sent any more Flags to the Port of the Mountain, he would burn the Vessels. They have fifteen Sail of the Line ready for sea, with which they say they will fight our Fleet. Now, as Admiral Hotham is gone off Toulon with thirteen Sail of the Line, they may if they please. I am, as you will believe, uneasy enough, for fear they will fight, and *Agamemnon* not present,—it will almost break my heart; but I hope the best—that they are only boasting at present, and will be quiet till I am ready.

The Admiral will return here, and I hope to be ready to accompany him the next time he goes to sea: it is misery for me to be laid up dismantled. Our friends in Corsica think the French intend them a visit. I am of a different opinion from the whole Fleet, Army and Viceroy. Port Especia is their object, I am convinced; and, if they get it, they will plague us more than ever. They have seven Sail of the Line on the stocks at Toulon, which will all be launched next March, when they will have twenty-two Sail of the Line for the whole of next summer. The Genoese supply them with everything, and England has submitted to be humbled by such a paltry State. The Danes and Swedes are for ever entering Toulon with timber. If they are stopped, they are bound to Genoa and Leghorn, from which place the wood, &c., is sent with little expense. The rascality of Neutral Powers we all know; therefore I have only to say, they are as bad as ever.

I beg you will present my kindest remembrances to Mrs. Suckling, Miss Suckling, and the rest of the family. Is Captain Suckling still abroad? My remembrance to him when you write, and don't forget me to Mr. Rumsey, and my friends at Hampstead, and believe me ever

Yours most affectionate

HORATIO NELSON

To John M'Arthur, Esq. *Agamemnon*, Leghorn, *November 28th, 1794*

My dear Sir,

I dare say you inquired at Gibraltar about the expense of the Corn vessel, and have directed Littledale and Broderip to pay the amount, although the letter is not yet arrived. This letter is on the subject of our Bastia and Calvi Prize-money.

What I have got at present is nothing: what I have lost is, an eye, £300, and my health, with the satisfaction of my Ship's company being completely ruined: so much for debtor and creditor. It is absolutely necessary you should know how the Prize-money is to be distributed. It may be necessary, and I think must be finally determined by the King in Council. Shall those who were present at the commencement, those who only came time enough to see the Enemy's flags struck, share equal to us who bore the burden of the day? It must be considered as very different to sharing Prize-money at sea. There the object, if resistance was made, could be assisted: with us it was quite different. Far be it from me to be illiberal. Those Ships who rode guard the whole time, as *Victory*, *Princess Royal*, and *Fortitude*, and *Agamemnon*, are the only Ships who remained the whole Siege; *Gorgon*, great part; *L'Imperieuse*, certain; and *Fox* Cutter. How the others are to be discriminated, I cannot say.

I think you ought to get the opinion of two good Counsel, and from their opinion you may form some judgment what may be necessary to be done. Colonel Villettes and myself have talked the matter over, and think, as we were joined together in the same service, that we should be considered as different from the others. Then Brereton and the Captains who blockaded the Port, and served on shore—under what head those (Ships) who accidentally assisted for one moment and were gone the next, is not for me to determine. If it is thought right these points ought, and I must desire may be, inquired into. I know no reason why every one that pleases is to share with us. It may be necessary to speak to Lord Hood on the subject, who, I am sure, will recommend what is just, and that I would have you pursue. Believe me,

Yours very obedient humble Servant,

HORATIO NELSON

Agamemnon, St. Fiorenzo,
January 17th, 1795

My dearest Fanny,

I wrote you a few days past, since which we have had nothing but gales of wind and a heavy sea, so much so that one of the ships lost all her masts last night. In *Agamemnon* we mind nothing. She is the finest ship I ever sailed in and was she a 74 nothing should induce me to leave her whilst the war lasted. I understand Admiral Hotham will not part with a ship till Lord Hood's arrival which I own much disembarrasses me, for my hopes were to be in England whilst Lord Hood was at home and being put into a good 74 with my ship's company that I might be ready for service early in the spring for not an hour this war will I, if possible, be out of active service. My hopes were originally to have gone home, with Lord Hood, to have been placed in a 74, to have got two months' leave of absence and to have my ship ready for sea in March or April, but this plan is all over and I must wait patiently till Lord Hood's arrival, when I shall hear what he says and be guided accordingly. Much as I shall regret being so long parted from you, still we must look beyond the present day, and two or three months may make the difference of every comfort or otherwise in our income. I hope we have many happy years to live together and if we can bring £2,000 round I am determined to purchase some neat cottage, when we shall never have occasion to change. As for Josiah I have no doubts but he will be a comfort to both of us. His understanding is excellent and his disposition really good. He is a seaman, every inch of him.

The fleet is on the eve of going to sea again to cover our reinforcements and although we have lost the use of one 74 still I have no doubts of our superiority over the French fleet, should they give an opportunity of meeting at sea. In three days I dare say we shall sail.

I have really nothing to tell you, not having been but once out of my ship but that I am in most perfect health and ever my dearest Fanny, your most affectionate husband,

HORATIO NELSON

Remember me kindly to my father. Did you send something to my Aunt Mary? I find the letters I wrote you some days past are in quarantine and will be so smoked and dried that probably you will hardly be able to read them.

Agamemnon, Fiorenzo,
January 31st, 1795

My dearest Fanny,

It is with inexpressible pleasure I have received within these two days past your letters of December 16–17th up to 24th and 28th, with our Father's of January 1st. I rejoice my conduct gives you pleasure and I trust that I shall never do anything which will bring a blush on your face or on that of any of my friends. It is very true I have ever served faithfully and ever my fate to be neglected but it is no reason I should be negligent of my duty. I have pride in doing my duty well, and a self approbation, which if not so lucrative yet perhaps give more pleasing sensations—but I trust the time will come when I may be rewarded but really I don't flatter it is near. General Stuart's anger to me arises from no cause but hatred to my Lord Hood, hatred founded on the most diabolical principles, because and because only Lord Hood took Bastia against all army opinions and never gave the army or General one opportunity of complaining of his neglect of them at the siege of Calvi. The refusal of one gun would have been the greatest satisfaction to the General, much more than supplying 700 men to do nothing which has been required. I parted from the General on the best terms possible but my journal of the siege, sent home by Lord Hood, showed what the General must from his conduct wished concealed, that all the heavy work and every gun which was fired, was done by seamen and sea officers. This is my crime and I suppose the Scotchman will do all he can to injure me, so far as not saying anything for me, or any other way I defy his malice.

I have got *Agamemnon* into high order again and was I fully manned, think her equal to any service whatever, and I believe my ship's company are attached to me. Had she 10 more guns nothing should tempt me to part with her.

I think Lord Hood told me that my loss of an eye should be represented to the King. Many have for much less losses handsome pensions. That I do not expect, it would be too good luck for me. However they ought to give me an equivalent. Lord Chatham carried my papers (so Lord Hood tells me but this is secret) to the King. Now he is out,* all those hopes will be done away. I ought to have the Colonel of Marines or King's Yacht, neither of which I expect, or £200 a year pension. My eye as you may conceive is now grown worse and is almost total darkness and very painful at times. But never mind. I can see very well with the other.

I have wrote to Mr. Bailey and Mr. Stanley. Hope you have got the letters and that they will have the desired effect. Get hold of the money or any part of it, if you can. It is very cruel to keep us out of it, particularly the interest of ours and Josiah's. Lord Hood has so many particular friends to serve that I depend but little from that quarter, except public declaration in my favour as an officer. I believe I shall write Lord Hood what I never told him yet, that after everything was fixed for the attack of Bastia, that I had information given me of the enormous number of troops we had to oppose us, but my honour, Lord Hood's honour, and the honour of our country must have all been sacrificed had I told what I knew; therefore you will believe what must have been my feelings during the whole siege, when often I had proposals made to me, by men now rewarded, to write to Lord Hood to raise the siege.

* Lord Chatham was succeeded as First Lord of the Admiralty by Earl Spencer, in December, 1794.

I had improved a good deal in French at Leghorn and brought with me an Italian Frenchman but he is no use to me whatever and I shall return him to the shore again as soon as I go to Leghorn.

Captain Inglefield's is a good place, certainly equal to £1,000 a year but I have no desire to be a commissioner.

I thank you for sending the things to Aunt Mary. We must not neglect her.

Feb. 1st.—The fleet goes to sea on the 3rd to parade off Toulon, where the Spanish fleet are at present, and if the French will not come out to fight them it is not very likely they will come out to us. I am afraid I shall not make prize money enough to make any purchases out of it.

Remember [me] kindly to our friends at Bristol. I shall write to my father whilst we are at sea. Josiah is very well and a very good young man. Hoste tells me he writes sometimes to his father but if you write say he is very well and what is true as amiable a young man as ever lived. Weatherhead has just heard of the death of his brother. Believe me ever my dear Fanny, Your most affectionate husband

HORATIO NELSON

I beg my best respects at Wolterton. Feb. 3rd. All well.

To Mrs. Nelson St. Fiorenzo, *7th February, 1795*

This day twelve months, my dear Fanny, our Troops landed here to attempt the conquest of the Island, at least of those parts which the French were in possession of; and, however lightly the acquisition of Corsica may be deemed by many in England, yet I take upon me to say, it was a measure founded on great wisdom; and during the war must be ever of the most essential service to us, and very detrimental to our Enemies. After the evacuation of Toulon, we had no place whatever of our own for the Fleet to anchor in: Tuscany was wavering, and, although since declared for us, yet we are not certain of her alliance from one day to another. The French Consul at Leghorn, though not received officially, has never quitted that place, and we know that attempts have been made to get Tuscany again acknowledged by the French as a Neutral Power; in which case what security have we for our Fleet, and the numerous Victuallers and Storeships attendant on it? Corsica has always supplied Toulon with all the straight timbers, beams, decks, and sides for their Ships; they are now deprived of that supply, which would have enabled them by this time to have built a small Fleet; and besides, the Corsican tar and hemp formed by no means an inconsiderable resource for the dock-yard at Toulon. Moreover, all our trade, with that of our Allies, is obliged to make the Coasts of this Island, the Ports of which would have been so full of Row-galleys, that no commerce could have been carried on; nor could our Men-of-War have prevented the evil, for half the twenty-four hours is calm, when these Vessels would take the Merchant-men, though the whole of the British Navy were in sight. So much for the value of Corsica—I have done; the recollection of one short year brings it to my mind. It was Lord Hood's plan, and it was accomplished chiefly by seamen.

Yours, &c.

HORATIO NELSON

Agamemnon, at Sea,
March 10th, 1795

My dearest Fanny,

I shall commence a letter at this moment to assure you, although I flatter myself that no assurance is necessary, of my constant love and affection. We are just in sight of the French fleet and a signal out for a general chase. We have but little wind and unfortunately the enemy are in-shore of us, however I hope the Admiral will allow us to go on, and if the French do not skulk under their battery, I trust we shall give a good account of them. Whatever may be my fate, I have no doubt in my own mind but that my conduct will be such as will not bring a blush on the face of my friends. The lives of all are in the hands of Him who knows best whether to preserve it or no, and to His will do I resign myself. My character and good name is in my own keeping. Life with disgrace is dreadful. A glorious death is to be envied, and, if anything happens to me, recollect death is a debt we must all pay, and whether now or in a few years hence can be but of little consequence.

March 11th.—Did not get sight of the French fleet this morning. I suppose they stood to the westward all night. The Admiral has just got information that the French fleet sailed from Toulon on the 1st March and on the 8th off Cape Corse took the *Berwick* of 74 guns. They are certainly out looking for our convoy every moment expected from England.

March 12th.—The French are now within 4 miles of *Agamemnon* and *Princess Royal*, our fleet 10 miles from us, we standing towards our fleet, the enemy attempting to cut us off. God bless you and believe ever your most faithful and affectionate husband,

HORATIO NELSON

To H.R.H. the Duke of Clarence *March 15th, 1795*

Our Fleet closed with *Ça Ira* and *Censeur*, who defended themselves in the most gallant manner; the former lost 400, the latter 350 men; the rest of the Enemy's Ships behaved very ill. Martini, the Admiral, and St. Michael, the Commissioner, were on board a Frigate. The orders of the French were, to defeat us, and to retake Corsica; I believe they will in no respect obey their orders. Every Ship fired red-hot shot; but we now know, from experience, they are useless on board a Ship. Frederick behaved exceedingly well, as did Montgomery in the *Courageux*, and Reeve in the *Captain*; and I must not forget Goodall, who is as gallant an Officer as ever lived. These Ships being the van, had more than their share of the Action. Every Officer, I am sure, would have been happy, had the Enemy given them equal opportunities. The French bore away towards Toulon in the afternoon, and are now out of sight. I am, &c.

HORATIO NELSON

To William Suckling *Agamemnon*, Porto Especia,
March 22nd, 1795

My dear Sir,

The event of our brush with the French Fleet you will know long before this reaches you, and I know you will participate in the pleasure I must have felt in being the great cause of our success. Could I have been supported, I would have had *Ça Ira* on the 13th, which might probably have increased our success on the next day. The Enemy, notwithstanding their red-hot shot and shells, must now be satisfied (or we are ready to give them further proofs) that England yet reigns Mistress on the Seas; and I verily believe our seamen have lost none of their courage; and sure I am, that had the breeze continued, so as to have allowed us to close with the Enemy, we should have destroyed their whole Fleet. They came out to fight us, and yet, when they found us, all their endeavours were used to avoid an Action.

But accidents will happen to us as to others: a few days after the action we met with a very heavy gale of wind which has driven the *Illustrious** on shore; but we have some faint hopes she may yet be saved. Our Prizes are almost refitted; and to-morrow we sail for Corsica. I beg

* The *Illustrious*, 74, Captain Frederick, having lost her main and mizen masts in the action, was taken in tow by *Meleager*, and separated from the Fleet in a violent gale, on the night of the 17th March. The tow-rope carried away, and she drove on shore in Valence Bay, between Spezia and Leghorn, on the 18th, and it being impossible to get her off, was set on fire and destroyed. Captain Frederick and his officers were (as is usual) tried by a court-martial for the loss of their ship, but were honourably acquitted.

leave to trouble you with a letter for Mrs. Nelson, and have to beg you will give my kindest remembrances to Mrs. Suckling, Miss Suckling, and all the family, not forgetting Mr. Rumsey and family.

Believe me ever your most affectionate

HORATIO NELSON

To Mrs. Nelson — Fiorenzo, *1st April, 1795*

I am absolutely, my dearest Fanny, at this moment in the horrors, fearing from our idling here, that the active Enemy may send out two or three Sail of the Line, and some Frigates, to intercept our Convoy, which is momentarily expected. In short, I wish to be an Admiral, and in the command of the English Fleet; I should very soon either do much, or be ruined. My disposition cannot bear tame and slow measures. Sure I am, had I commanded our Fleet on the 14th, that either the whole French Fleet would have graced my triumph, or I should have been in a confounded scrape. I went on board Admiral Hotham as soon as our firing grew slack in the Van, and the *Ça Ira* and *Censeur* had struck, to propose to him leaving our two crippled Ships, the two Prizes, and four Frigates, to themselves, and to pursue the Enemy; but he, much cooler*, than myself, said, 'We must be contented, we have done very well.' Now, had we taken ten Sail, and had allowed the eleventh to escape when it had been possible to have got at her, I could never have called it well done. Goodall backed me; I got him to write to the Admiral, but it would not do: we should have had such a day, as I believe the Annals of England never produced. I verily think if the Admiral can get hold of them once more, and he does but get us close enough, that we shall have the whole Fleet. Nothing can stop the courage of English seamen.

I may venture to tell you, but as a secret, that I have a Mistress given to me, no less a Personage than the Goddess Bellona; so say the French verses made on me, and in them I am so covered with laurels, that you would hardly find my sallow face. At one period I am 'the dear Nelson,' 'the amiable Nelson,' 'the fiery Nelson:' however nonsensical these expressions are, they are better than censure, and we are all subject and open to flattery. The French Admiral is to be tried, and some of the Captains are under arrest: it is reported that the Captain of the *Sans Culotte* has run away. The Toulonese will not allow the French Fleet to enter their port, but make them remain in Hieres Bay, telling them, 'To get out and execute their former orders, or never enter the ports of

* 'I can, *entre nous*', said Sir William Hamilton, in a letter to Nelson, 'perceive that my old friend, Hotham, is not quite awake enough for such a command as that of the British Fleet in the Mediterranean, although he is the best creature imaginable.'

the Republic.' They were very much alarmed in Corsica at the appearance of the Enemy's Fleet. So certain were the French of defeating us, that the Mayor and all the Municipality of Bastia were on board the *Sans Culotte*, to resume their Station.

Yours, &c.

HORATIO NELSON

To Mrs. Nelson St. Fiorenzo, *12th April, 1795*

Rest assured, my dear Fanny, you are never absent from my thoughts. —If the folks will give me the Colonelcy of Marines,* I shall be satisfied; but I fear my interest is not equal to get it: although I will never allow that any man whatever has a claim superior to myself.† We have just got the thanks of the Corsican Parliament and Viceroy, for our gallant and good conduct on the 13th and 14th day of March, which they say, and truly, has saved them from an invasion. The Viceroy's private letter to me has a very flattering compliment, that cannot but be pleasing to you: 'I certainly consider the business of the 13th of March as a very capital feature in the late successful contest with the French Fleet; and the part which the *Agamemnon* had in it must be felt by every one to be one of the circumstances that gave lustre to this event, and rendered it not only useful, but peculiarly honourable to the British Arms. I need not assure you of the pleasure with which I constantly see your name foremost in everything that is creditable and serviceable; nor of my sincere regard and affection.'

So far, all hands agree in giving me those praises, which cannot but be comfortable to me to the last moment of my life. The time of my being left out here by Lord Hood, I may call well spent; had I been absent, how mortified should I now be. What has happened may never happen to any one again, that only one Ship of the Line out of fourteen, should get into Action with the French Fleet, and for so long a time as two hours and a half, and with such a Ship as the *Ça Ira*. Had I been supported, I should certainly have brought the *Sans Culotte* to battle, a most glorious prospect. A brave man runs no more risk than a coward, and *Agamemnon* to a miracle has suffered scarcely anything: three or four of our wounded are dead, the others are in a fair way of doing well.

* Colonelcies of Marines were then conferred upon three, or four, senior post captains, and were, in fact, honourable sinecures, which they relinquished on obtaining their flags. These appointments were later discontinued and 'good service pensions' substituted for them.

† Nelson was then within forty-six of the top of the list of post captains, and he here compared his own services with those of the captains who stood above him.

We have got accounts of the French Fleet, the troops are landed, and their Expedition is given up; the Ships have suffered much, many at this time are shifting their masts. Our Fleet was never in better order. My kindest remembrances to my father. Yours, &c.

HORATIO NELSON

To Mrs. Nelson Off Minorca, *20th May, 1795*

As yet we have no accounts of Lord Hood's having actually sailed from St. Helen's: and what they can mean by sending him with only five Sail of the Line, is truly astonishing; but all men are alike, and we in this Country do not find any amendment, or alteration, from the old Board of Admiralty. They should know that half the Ships in this Fleet require to go to England, and that long ago they ought to have reinforced us. At this moment our operations are at a stand, for want of Ships to support the Austrians in getting possession of the Sea-coast of the King of Sardinia; and behold, our Admiral does not feel himself equal to shew himself, much less to give assistance in their operations.

June 7th.—We have been off here very nearly a month, expecting first Lord Hood, then Admiral Dickson. We have lost much by Lord Hood's going to England, and much more, probably, by his not returning.

June 15th.—Yesterday, Admiral Man joined us, with a Squadron from England. Lord Hood enclosed me a copy of a letter from Lord Spencer about me, acknowledging my pretensions to favour and distinction, when proper opportunities offer. This letter was written before the account of our Action had arrived; that may throw an additional weight into the scale for me. However, I hope to save my pay, which, with a little addition, will buy us a very small cottage, where I shall be as happy as in a house as large as Holkham.

Yours, &c.

HORATIO NELSON

To the Rev. Dixon Hoste,
Godwick Hall, Norfolk *Agamemnon*, off Minorca, *June 22nd, 1795*

My dear Sir,

Although your good son writes the day of receiving a letter from you, yet I will not let the opportunity slip of sending a line to thank you for your news. The changes and politics of Ministers and men are so various, that I am brought to believe all are alike; the loaves and fishes are all the look out. The ins and outs are the same, let them change places. The extraordinary circumstance of the Prince of Wale's debts is much more lamentable: his best friends must be hurt, and the others are, as far as I hear, as much in debt as people will trust them. They are of an age to know better, and if they will not practise what they know, they ought to be punished, by letting them feel that want they are making others so severely partake of. However, I trust if this debt is once more paid, that he will be acquainted by the Nation they will pay no more for him. What a figure would the Duke of Clarence have made had he served, out of debt and beloved by the nation; in short, our profession, *in war*, is so popular, that he might have done what he pleased.

We have just got accounts that the French Fleet is at sea, twenty-two Sail of the Line. Sir Sydney Smith did not burn them all*—Lord Hood mistook the man: there is an old song, *Great talkers do the least, we see.* Admiral Hotham is waiting here with twenty English and two Neapolitan Ships of the Line, for our invaluable Convoy of Stores, Provisions, and Troops from Gibraltar. I hope the Enemy will not pass us to the westward, and take hold of them. This Fleet must regret the loss of Lord Hood, the best Officer, take him altogether, that England has to boast of. Lord Howe certainly is a great Officer in the management of a Fleet, but that is all. Lord Hood is equally great in all situations which an Admiral can be placed in. Our present Admiral is a worthy, good man, but not by any means equal to either Lord Hood or Lord Howe. Fame says I am to have my Flag or the Marines; I hope the latter. The former will most likely throw me out of service, which I should very much regret: I long for one more good Action with this Fleet, and then Peace. I beg my respects to Mrs. Hoste, and also to Mr. and Mrs. Coke: I hope a son will come forth.

I am, dear Sir, Your very faithful servant,

HORATIO NELSON

To H.R.H. the Duke of Clarence *15th July, 1795*

Sir,

Not having had any signification to the contrary, I still presume to suppose, that an account from me of the operations of this Fleet is acceptable to your Royal Highness.

The *Agamemnon* was sent from Fiorenzo with a small Squadron of

* At Toulon, in 1793. Sir Sidney Smith's exalted opinion of his own services (however justified by his undoubted gallantry and zeal) seems to have given offence to many eminent officers both of the Navy and Army.

Frigates to co-operate with the Austrian General de Vins, in driving the French out of the Riviera of Genoa, at the beginning of July. On the 6th, I fell in with the French Fleet of seventeen Sail of the Line and six Frigates; they chased me twenty-four hours, and close over to St. Fiorenzo, but our Fleet could not get out to my assistance. However, on the 8th, in the morning, Admiral Hotham sailed with twenty-three Sail of the Line; and on the 13th, at daylight, got sight of the Enemy, about six leagues south of the Hieres Islands. A signal was then made for a general chase. At noon, the *Victory*, Admiral Man, with *Captain*, *Agamemnon*, *Cumberland*, *Defence*, and *Culloden*, got within gun-shot of the Enemy; when the west wind failed us, and threw us into a line abreast. A light air soon afterwards coming from the Eastward, we laid our heads to the northward, as did the Enemy, and the Action commenced.

It was impossible for us to close with them, and the smoke from their Ships and our own made a perfect calm; whilst they, being to windward, drew in shore; our Fleet was becalmed six or seven miles to the westward. The *Blenheim* and *Audacious* got up to us during the firing. The *Alcide* struck about half-past two, and many others were almost in as bad a state; but she soon afterwards took fire, and only two hundred men were saved out of her. At half-past three the *Agamemnon* and *Cumberland* were closing with an eighty-gun ship with a Flag, the *Berwick*, and *Heureux*, when Admiral Hotham thought it right to call us out of Action, the wind being directly into the Gulf of Frejus, where the Enemy anchored after dark.

Thus has ended our second meeting with these gentry. In the forenoon we had every prospect of taking every Ship in the Fleet; and at noon, it was almost certain we should have had the six near Ships. The French Admiral, I am sure, is not a wise man, nor an Officer: he was undetermined whether to fight or to run away: however, I must do him the justice to say, he took the wisest step at least. Indeed, I believe this Mediterranean Fleet is as fine a one as ever graced the Ocean.

John Holloway is Captain of the Fleet, a good man. The Enemy will have still twenty-one Sail at sea in a month, but I do not believe they can ever beat us in their present undisciplined state: the prisoners we have seen are staunch Royalists, and I really believe the war is almost at an end. I am going to Genoa, to see Mr. Drake, our Minister, and to consult about what assistance the Admiral can afford the Austrians in the Riviera of Genoa. We have just got accounts of Vado Bay being taken from the French.

I am, &c.

HORATIO NELSON

To Earl Spencer, First Lord of the Admiralty

Agamemnon, July 19th, 1795

My Lord,

I have seen in the newspapers that I am appointed one of the Colonels of Marines, an appointment certainly most flattering to me, as it marks to the world an approbation of my conduct. To your Lordship I beg leave to express my gratification, more especially as, by a letter from your Lordship to Lord Hood, you declared your intention to represent my services in the most favourable point of view to the King; for which I beg leave to return your Lordship my most sincere thanks. In the same letter the doubts which had arisen respecting the damage my eye had sustained at the Siege of Calvi, made it, your Lordship said, impossible to say whether it was such as amounted to the loss of a limb. I have only to tell your Lordship, that a total deprivation of sight for every common occasion in life, is the consequence of the loss of part of the crystal of my right eye.

As I mean not to press on your Lordship the propriety of considering my loss, I shall conclude by assuring you, that my endeavours shall never be wanting to merit a continuance of your good opinion, and that I shall ever consider myself your Lordship's most obliged, humble servant,

HORATIO NELSON

Being appointed with a small Squadron of Frigates to co-operate with the Austrian General de Vins, I cannot allow my letter to go, without saying it appears to me that General de Vins is an Officer who perfectly knows his business, and is well disposed to act with vigour on every proper occasion. The Enemy are throwing up strong works near Albinga; but before three days are past, I expect the Army will be to the westward of them.

Agamemnon, off Vado Bay,
July 24th, 1795

My dearest Fanny,

What changes in my life of activity, here I am commenced a co-operation with an old Austrian General, almost fancying myself charging at the head of a troop of horse. As nothing will be wanting on my part towards the success of the common cause I have no doubt but you will hear by autumn that we are in possession of 60 miles of sea coast, including the towns of Monarco and Nice. I have 8 sail of frigates under my command. The service I have to perform is important and, as I wrote you a few days ago from Genoa, I am acting not only without the orders of my commander in chief but in some measure contrary to them. However, I have not only the support and countenance of His Majesty's Ministers both at Turin [and] at Genoa but a consciousness that I am doing what is right and proper for our King and Country's service. Hotham has no political courage which is in an officer abroad as highly necessary as battle courage.

We took three days ago, that is the squadron, a vessel from Marseilles bound to Genoa, deserted when near the shore by the master and crew, who certainly carried off with them great riches. What they left we know not. She is said to be valued when she sailed from Marseilles at the enormous sum of £160,000 sterling. However, we must expect nearly all the money is gone. I have got one large chest of silver, some lumps of gold, 7 and 8 lbs. in the lump, with a great number of diamond rings, loose diamonds and other valuables on board *Agamemnon*, besides a rich cargo of silks, spices, etc. However some may value her, if she gives me 1,000 or 1,500 pounds I shall be well satisfied. I have information of three others but the knowledge of my activity is gone forth and I do not expect much more success. The Ministers want the Admiral to give me an order to wear a distinguishing pendant. Lord Hood would in the present situation of affairs at once order it—No expense but honorary. The Austrian army is composed of 32,000 the finest troops I ever saw, and the General when he gets Nice will have the baton of a Marshal. What shall I get? However, this I can say, that what I have got I owe to myself and to no one else. To you I may say my character stands high almost with Europe, even the Austrians knew my name perfectly. When I get through this campaign I think myself I ought to rest. I hope to God the war will be over and that I may return to you in peace and quietness. A little farm and my good name is all my wants or wishes.

Josiah is very well and a good boy. With kindest remembrances to my father, believe me ever your affectionate

HORATIO NELSON

July 27 Leghorn.

Blown in here in a gale of wind. Now fine weather. Hope to get to sea this night. All my letters gone to the fleet and to Genoa. God bless you.

HORATIO NELSON

To Captain Collingwood

Vado Bay, *August 31st, 1795*

My dear Coll.,

I cannot allow a Ship to leave me without a line for my old friend, who I shall rejoice to see; but I am afraid the Admiral will not give me that pleasure at present. You are so old a Mediterranean man, that I can tell you nothing new about the Country. My command here is so far pleasant as it relieves me from the inactivity of our Fleet, which is great indeed, as you will soon see. From the event of Spain making peace, much may be looked for,—perhaps a war with that Country: if so, their Fleet (if no better than when our Allies) will soon be done for. Reports here say, they mean to protect Genoese and other Vessels from search by our Cruisers, in the Gulf of Genoa. If so, the matter will soon be brought to issue; for I have given positive directions to search such Vessels, denying the right of the Spaniard to dictate to us what Ships we shall or shall not search. The Genoese are going, it is said, to carry a Convoy with provisions to their Towns in the Riviera of Genoa, in possession of the French Army. However cruel it may appear to deprive poor innocent people of provisions, yet policy will not allow it to be done, for if the inhabitants have plenty, so will the Enemy, and therefore I have directed them to be brought into Vado. So far have I gone; and trust I have acted, and shall act, so as to merit approbation. Our Admiral, *entre nous*, has no political courage whatever, and is alarmed at the mention of any strong measure; but, in other respects, he is as good a man as can possibly be.

I hope, my dear friend, you left Mrs. Collingwood well. How many children have you? Did you see Mrs. Moutray lately? Her dear, amiable son was lost by serving under me. I have a stone on board, which is to be erected in the church at St. Fiorenzo to his memory. I hardly ever knew so amiable a young man. Believe me, ever, my dear Collingwood,

Yours most affectionate Friend,

HORATIO NELSON

Tell me a great deal.

Agamemnon, at Sea,
September 21st, 1795

My dear Fanny,

I have not received a letter from you later than the end of July which I cannot account for as our posts are regular, but at present I believe the fault must lay with the people at Leghorn not forwarding my letters, although several ships have joined me from thence. I have had a long letter from Suckling telling me all the Burnham news, which is all new to me and very pleasant to hear. For the moment I fancy myself at the old parsonage. I have been in concert with His Majesty's Minister very hard at work in pushing the Austrian general forward and yesterday morning got them to make an attack which has been successful, and they have carried the centre post on the ridge of mountains occupied by the French troops. The action lasted 10 hours, and if the General will carry one other point we shall gain 33 miles of country. Another is in agitation which, if the Admiral will give me transports to carry a certain number of troops, will astonish the French and perhaps the English. The General, if he can be brought to move, is of great abilities, but generally the politics of his Court so ties his hands that he cannot always do what he thinks proper. However, if this army does not move, the Minister who is fixed at headquarters, will endeavour to withhold the remainder of the Emperor's loan—say gift. This is an all powerful motive with a German Court and for which the lives of their subjects are held in no estimation. I shall now become a politician almost fit to enter the diplomatic line, for the tricks of each Court are so mean that if a private man was to act so, he would be scouted. The common cause has no weight with anyone. England wants to rule all the Courts and by her money does much. They dislike it and take every opportunity of thwarting the schemes proposed by our Ministry.

I am now on my way to Leghorn to get some provisions, where I shall finish my letter. Josiah is very well. Hoste quite recovered and not the worse for his accident. He is without exception one of the finest boys I ever met with.

September 24th, Leghorn.—I am just arrived and received your letters of August 16th, 20th and 27th. I build little on prize money. When it is paid it is time enough to reckon on it. What is to turn up, who can say, but I believe *Agamemnon* cannot much longer be kept on here.

I have just received the most handsome testimony transmitted to our Minister which he has sent home of my conduct from the Austrian General. Much has not been in my power but I have done my all to serve the cause.

I have letters from Lord Hood whose loss we feel every day and should a Spanish war take place Hotham must give up the command.

I will write to our father very soon. I have received his letter. Believe me my dear Fanny, your most affectionate husband,

HORATIO NELSON

To the Rev. Mr. Nelson, Bath

Leghorn, *September 29th, 1795*

My dear Father,

I am this moment receiving the pleasure of your letter of September 3rd, and should be glad, did circumstances so turn out, that I could get to England in the *Agamemnon*, for in no other way can I get home with honour or propriety; and I must say, except the being at home, I know of no Country so pleasant to serve in as this, or where my health is so good. My command at Vado is honorary though expensive, for all Foreigners only consider our rank and not our pay. I have the satisfaction to have received the handsomest testimony of conduct, and as I know you will partake with me that satisfaction, I send you a copy of the Minister's Note to the Admiral—viz., 'I cannot in justice to the abilities, judgment, and activity of Captain Nelson, omit mentioning to your Excellency, the very high opinion in which that Officer is held by General de Vins and the other Austrian General-Officers; and I have thought it my duty to transmit to his Majesty's Ministers at Home this handsome testimony which our Allies bear to the zeal and good conduct of that Officer, whom your Excellency was pleased to select to command the Squadron co-operating with them. This unprejudiced testimony is no less flattering to Captain Nelson than to your Excellency's discernment in having made choice of him for this service.'

I have nothing to write about but myself, for none else attempts to do anything. If our plan can be carried into execution, we shall take Nice, but much must be left to chance: the plan well laid is most likely, but never certain, of success. I came in here four days past and am now under sail for Vado. Our Fleet has arrived at Corsica from a cruize off Toulon, where they permitted six Sail of the Line and eight Frigates to escape out of Toulon, and I believe they have left the Mediterranean. Having talked of myself, I have nothing more to add, except that Admiral Hotham is just going to send six Sail of the Line after the French Ships escaped from Toulon, and supposed to be gone to the West Indies. Josiah is well, never ill. Hoste has almost recovered his broken leg. Parted with Frank* for drunkenness, and when so, mad: never will I keep a drunkard another hour. *Agamemnon* almost worn out, must go home shortly. With best love to my wife, believe me

Your most affectionate and dutiful Son,

HORATIO NELSON

I was not much surprised to hear of Mr. Raven's departure, but very much of poor Edmund Rolfe.†

* Frank Lepée was frequently mentioned in Mrs. Nelson's letters to her husband; and it appears from her letter of the 10th December, 1794, that he had fallen into disgrace: 'Poor Frank! I own I was afraid something was the matter—that he was not so good as formerly; I am very sorry that he is in so deplorable a way; I hope he never is with you; you may be able to get him in Greenwich Hospital. You are sure of Captain Locker.'

Locker had been appointed Lieut.-Governor of Greenwich Hospital.

† His first cousin, son of the Rev. Robert Rolfe and Alice Nelson.

To William Suckling, Esq. *Agamemnon*, off Marseilles, *October 27th, 1795*

My dear Sir,

Although I seldom have the pleasure of hearing immediately from yourself, yet Mrs. Nelson never fails of telling me of your health, the goodness of which, she well knows, give me real satisfaction.

The campaign of our Allies, the Austrians and Piedmontese, is, I suppose, almost over, not that I am in the secret when it commenced. My situation with this Army has convinced me, by ocular demonstration, of the futility of Continental Alliances. The conduct of the Court of Vienna, whatever may be said by the House of Commons to the contrary, is nothing but deception: I am certain, if it appears to that Court to be their interest to make peace with France, it will be instantly done. What is Austria better than Prussia, or *vice versâ*?—in one respect, Prussia perhaps may be better than Austria: the moment he got our money he finished the farce. Austria, I fear, may induce us to give her more, for to a certainty she will not carry on another campaign without more money; but it appears to me that the continuance or cessation of the war depends entirely on the French Nation themselves: it will now be seen whether they are willing to receive and join the Count d'Artois and have Royalty; or if they oppose him, that they are determined to be a Republic. If the first, at this moment of writing all must be clearly finished: if they destroy the Emigrants landed at Charente, it is clear the French Nation wish to be a Republic; and the best thing we can do, is to make the best and quickest peace we can: the landing the Emigrants is our last trial; and if that fail, we have done our utmost to place Louise upon the Throne. To me, I own, all Frenchmen are alike: I despise them all. They are (even those who are fed by us) false and treacherous: Even Louis XVIII receives our money, and will not follow our advice, and keep up the dignity of the King of France at Verona.

Fame, with her wings and long tongue, has proclaimed that prizes (and, of course, riches are imagined,) have fallen most abundantly on the *Agamemnon*. I wish I could tell you it is true; if the *Golden Fleece* is condemned, which I very much doubt, from the number who share for her—nine of us,—if I get 5 or 600 pounds, what a valuable prize she must be! My others, although pretty numerous, are scarcely anything; for I assure you, that if, at the conclusion of the war, I save my pay for the *Agamemnon*, I shall feel myself extremely fortunate. Everything is by comparison: except one or two Line of Battle Ships, we are the only one who has got a pound; and they must, from the expenses of a Fleet, have spent a little fortune—so far I feel highly fortunate.

As the Armies are quiet, the Admiral has given me directions to look after the French Fleet at Toulon (whilst he lies quiet in Leghorn Roads);

and as I know of no person so active as myself, here I am with one Frigate off Marseilles—not a Vessel to be seen; but before I close my letter I hope to say we have a prize.

Remember me most kindly to Mrs. Suckling, Miss Suckling, and every part of the family. Is Captain Suckling still on the Continent?

November 2nd

No success, although I have been indefatigable. The seamen have all deserted the Ships in Toulon, therefore as a Fleet, they cannot come to sea again. In France, they had a very fine harvest, and bread is by no means dear or scarce. The Spanish Vessels now fill Marseilles with every comfort and luxury. Peace, I believe, will yet be with us before next January; at least, I hope so, if it can be had on honourable terms. Believe me

Your most obliged and affectionate Nephew,

HORATIO NELSON

[The address of this letter is not known.]

Agamemnon, Vado Bay, *November 6th, 1795*

Dear Sir,

I have just received your letter of September 29th, and will be open and sincere in my declaration, that I will not attempt to come into Parliament* but in support of the real Whig interest—I mean the Portland interest; and I must know that those principles are truly acceptable to that party which you conceive would give me its support.

My pretensions are only a long series of services performed for my Country; and if that part of my Country who may honour me with their confidence in Parliament, think me an eligible person to serve them in the House of Commons, the same zeal shall manifest itself there as it has done so repeatedly in their service in Action against the French. I have only to say, that I have been more than one hundred times actually engaged in Battle, at sea and on shore, against the French, since the commencement of this war, and that I have been twice wounded. If these gentlemen are satisfied, the Duke of Portland must be applied to, through Lord Walpole and Lady Walpole; for although I have so often seen the French shot, yet truly I have seen little of their money. I can have no doubt of Lord Hood's good wishes to serve me,

* Nothing more is known of the proposition to bring Nelson into Parliament; he never sat in the House of Commons.

and I will write to him on the subject; nor will Admiral Cornwallis, I am confident, withhold his assistance. Lord Conway is my friend and acquaintance, and a more honourable man, I am confident, does not grace the Navy of England; therefore, if I am joined with him, the same Admiralty interest will support us both. If it is necessary that I should be in England, the Duke of Portland must make application for the *Agamemnon* to be ordered home: but I should hope that, being now actually in the most active service in the Mediterranean, it will not be necessary, (for I should not much like a land voyage,) therefore, if it is necessary, I should hope *Agamemnon* will be ordered home.

Thus, my dear Sir, I have been plain, and cannot well be misunderstood. Believe me ever,

Your most obliged, humble servant,

HORATIO NELSON

To Lord Granville, Secretary of State for Foreign Affairs.

[Francis Drake, Minister at Genoa, having informed Nelson that a report was circulated among the Allies, to which the King of Sardinia gave credence, that the British cruisers connived with the enemy to allow coasting vessels to land their cargoes for the supply of the French army in the Riviera of Genoa, Nelson immediately wrote to Lord Granville.]

Agamemnon, Genoa Road, *23rd November, 1795*

My Lord,

Having received, from Mr. Drake, a copy of your Lordship's letter to him of October, enclosing a paper highly reflecting on the honour of myself and other of His Majesty's Officers employed on this Coast under my Orders, it well becomes me, as far as in my power lies, to wipe away this ignominious stain on our characters. I do, therefore, in behalf of myself, and much-injured Brethren, demand, that the person, whoever he may be, that wrote, or gave that paper to your Lordship, do fully, and expressly bring home his charge; which, as he states that this agreement is made by numbers of people on both sides, there can be no difficulty in doing. We dare him, my Lord, to the proof. If he cannot, I do most humbly implore, that His Majesty will be most graciously pleased to direct his Attorney-General to prosecute this infamous libeller in His Courts of Law; and I likewise feel, that, without impropriety, I may, on behalf of my brother Officers, demand the support of His Majesty's Ministers: for as, if true, no punishment can be too great for the traitors; so, if false, none can be too heavy for the villain, who has dared to allow his pen to write such a paper. Perhaps I ought to stop my letter here; but I feel too much to rest easy for a moment, when the honour of the Navy, of our Country, is struck at through us; for if nine (ten) Captains, whom chance has thrown together, can instantly join in such a traitorous measure, it is fair to conclude we are all bad.

As this traitorous agreement could not be carried on but by concert of all the Captains, if they were on the Stations allotted them, and as they could only be drawn from those Stations by orders from me, I do most fully acquit all my brother Captains from such a combination, and have to request, that I may be considered as the only responsible person for what is done under my command, if I approve of the conduct of those under my orders, which in this most public manner I beg leave to do: for Officers more alert, and more anxious for the good, the honour, of their King and Country, can scarcely ever fall to the lot of any Commanding Officer; their Names I place at the bottom of this letter.

For myself, from my earliest youth I have been in the Naval service; and in two Wars, have been in more than one hundred and forty Skirmishes and Battles, at Sea and on shore; have lost an eye, and otherwise blood, in fighting the Enemies of my King and Country; and, God knows, instead of riches, my little fortune has been diminished in the Service: but I shall not trouble your Lordship further at present, than just to say—that at the close of this Campaign, where I have had the pleasure to receive the approbation of the Generals of the Allied Powers; of his Excellency Mr. Drake, who has always been on the spot; of Mr. Trevor, who has been at a distance; when I expected and hoped, from the representation of His Majesty's Ministers, that His Majesty would have most graciously condescended to have favourably noticed my earnest desire to serve Him, and when, instead of all my fancied approbation, to receive an accusation of a most traitorous nature—it has almost been too much for me to bear. Conscious innocence, I hope, will support me.

I have the honour to be

My Lord,

Your Lordship's most obedient, humble servant,

HORATIO NELSON

N.B.—Captains Fremantle, Hope, Cockburn, Hon. Charles Elphinstone, Shields, Middleton, Plampin, Brisbane, Thomas Elphinstone, Macnamara.

To the Rev. Dixon Hoste

Agamemnon, Leghorn, *December 12th, 1795*

My dear Sir,

Your letter of November 1st, I received a few days past, and your good son tells me he has answered his letter. William will have served his two years as rated Mid on the 1st of February next. This time as Mid, is absolutely necessary as a part of the long six years. You had better get out his Time from the Navy Office, and when his six years draw towards an end, I would have him strongly recommended to Sir John Jervis; for whenever peace comes it will be very difficult, with the best interest, to get him made a Lieutenant. I hope he has more than one year's Time: if not, two years is very long to look forward for a continuance of the war. You will have heard of the Austrians being defeated on the Coast of Genoa, and a part of the defeat attributed to a want of a sufficient Naval force. However, on inquiry, things may turn out, I have still had the good fortune, individually, to meet with approbation from our Ministers and the Generals. Our Admirals will have, I believe, much to answer for in not giving me that force which I so repeatedly called for, and for at last leaving me with *Agamemnon* alone.

I was put in a cleft stick: if I quitted where I was at anchor, the French would have landed in the rear of the Austrian Army, and the total defeat of that Army must have been the consequence: if I remained at anchor, the Enemy's Gun-boats in the general attack would harass the left wing of the Austrian Army. Much against my inclination, I took the plan of laying quiet, instead of attacking their Gun-boats; and most fortunate it has been for the Army I did so, for eight or ten thousand men made their escape by the road I protected, and amongst others, General de Vins himself. The Austrians will make the most of a want of Naval force for all purposes. Admiral Hotham kept my Squadron too small for its duty; and the moment Sir Hyde took the command of the Fleet he reduced it to nothing—only one Frigate and a Brig, whereas I demanded two Seventy-four Gun-ships and eight or ten Frigates and Sloops to ensure safety to the Army. However, on inquiry, which I trust and sincerely hope will take place, on my own account, it will turn out that the centre and right wing gave way, and that although it must have been very unpleasant to have a number of Gun-boats firing on them, the left was the only part that was not defeated, but retreated in a body; whereas the others fled, General de Vins, from ill-health, as he says, gave up the command in the middle of the Battle, and from that moment, not a soldier stayed in his post, and many thousands ran away who had never seen the Enemy—some of them thirty miles from the advanced posts. So much for my history.

I tremble at your account of want of bread for our poor. Pray God send us peace. We have established the French Republic, which, but for us, I verily believe would never have been settled by such a volatile, changeable people. I hate a Frenchman. They are equally objects of my detestation, whether Royalists or Republicans—in some points, I believe the latter are the best. Sir John Jervis took the command of the Fleet on the 29th of November, at St. Fiorenzo, but I have not yet heard from him or has anybody here. We sincerely hope he has orders to send *Agamemnon* home. We are worn out. I beg you will present my respects to Mr. and Mrs. Coke, also, though unknown, to Mrs. Hoste and your family, and believe me, Dear Sir,

Yours very faithfully,

HORATIO NELSON

1796

To Mrs. Nelson

[On the 19th of January, the *Agamemnon* joined the Fleet in Fiorenzo Bay, when Nelson had his first interview with Admiral Sir John Jervis, the new Commander-in-Chief.]

Agamemnon, St. Fiorenzo, *20th January, 1796*

We were received, not only with the greatest attention, but with much apparent friendship. Sir John Jervis's offer of either the *St. George*, 90, or *Zealous*, 74, was declined; but with that respect, and sense of obligation on my part, which such handsome conduct demanded of me. I found the Admiral anxious to know many things, which I was a good deal surprised to find had not been communicated to him from others in the Fleet; and it would appear, that he was so well satisfied with my opinion of what is likely to happen, and the means of prevention to be taken, that he had no reserve with me respecting his information and ideas of what is likely to be done: he concluded by asking me if I should have any objection to serve under him, with my Flag. My answer was, that if I were ordered to hoist my Flag, I should certainly be happy in serving under him; but if *Agamemnon* were ordered to go home, and my Flag were not arrived, I should on many accounts wish to return to England; yet still, if the war continued, I should be very proud of the honour of hoisting my Flag under his command: and, I rather believe, Sir John Jervis writes home this day, that if the Fleet is kept here, my Flag, on a promotion, may be sent to the Mediterranean. The credit I derive from all these compliments must be satisfactory to you; and, should I remain until peace, which cannot be very long, you will, I sincerely hope, make your mind easy. Yet, sometimes, notwithstanding all I have said, I think my promotion will be announced, and that I shall have a land voyage: be it as it may, I shall take it easy. *Agamemnon* is just going to sea, and I can assure you that my health was never better than at this moment.

Yours, &c.

HORATIO NELSON

To Mrs. Nelson Gulf of Genoa, *27th January, 1796*

I sent you a line just as I was getting under sail from St. Fiorenzo. The Fleet was not a little suprised at my leaving them so soon, and, I fancy, there was some degree of envy attached to the surprise; for one Captain told me, 'You did just as you pleased in Lord Hood's time, the same in Admiral Hotham's, and now again with Sir John Jervis; it makes no difference to you who is Commander-in-Chief.' I returned a pretty strong answer to this speech. My command here is to prevent any small number of men from making a descent in Italy. I hear no more of this promotion, and I sincerely hope they will put it off a little longer; unless, which I cannot well expect, they should send me out my Flag. My health was never better.

Yours, &c.

HORATIO NELSON

Leghorn, *February 12th, 1796*

My dearest Fanny,

I came in here last night with a convoy from Genoa where I found Sir John Jervis and the whole fleet. I sail again tomorrow for my station. A letter from you, I fancy, went off for Genoa a few hours before my arrival. As to news, we have little more than the great preparations the French are making for opening the campaign in Italy, and if the Austrians and Piedmontese do not exert themselves I think Turin will be lost and of course all Piedmont. Sardinia is in rebellion, therefore Kings will be reduced in Europe. God knows I now see no prospect of peace. Before the King's message to the House I had hopes but from that moment I gave it up. The message was forced and so worded that it was easy to see no peace was intended by it except such a one as the French are not humbled enough to grant. The convoy is not yet ordered for England but I trust *Agamemnon* will be one of the ships. Admiral Linzee goes home certainly and if the *Princess Royal* does not go home he will hoist his flag in the *Agamemnon*, but I believe it will be April before any convoy is ready and from our sailing I think we shall be two months to Spithead—miserable time.

Josiah is very well and is daily threatening to write you a letter. Our new Admiral will not land at Leghorn. The late one was so much here that Sir John is determined to act in the contrary way. Reports say the French will have their fleet at sea again. If they do I think they will now lose the whole of them, for we have a man of business at our head.

With best regards to my father, believe me, your most affectionate

HORATIO NELSON

Agamemnon, off Hieres Islands,
February 17th, 1796

I received your letter of Jan. 18th after mine of Feb. 12th was gone to the Post Office. I hoped Mr. Baillie would from his fair words have at least done as much for you as for Mrs. Kelly but her brother is to be courted. He may probably be useful to the house. However, the four years will soon wear away and then we shall get it all together and peace will by that time, I hope, be arrived, when a cottage of our own and an income to live, if not in luxury, in comfort, I doubt not but we shall possess in an ample degree. I cannot bring myself to believe that jealousy could have been the cause of lessening my force at so critical a time. I attribute it to ignorance and inattention. My conduct has no mystery. I freely communicate my knowledge and observations and wish my Admiral may make proper use of it. God forbid I should have any other consideration on service than to serve my country. I appear to stand well as yet with Sir John Jervis and it shall not be my fault if I do not continue so. I am now sent by him to examine into the state of the ships in Toulon. Their numbers we know full well but the accounts of their state are so contradictory that it leaves us uncertain. I will tell you their state when I finish this letter.

You observe that Lady H. tells you that but little is known in the fleet since Sir John's arrival. So much the better. Lord Hood knows that it is unsafe to open one's mouth in a fleet.

1st April reports say the convoy will be ready, but no ships are yet named and till reinforcements arrive I do not see Sir John can part with a single ship for he is now inferior to the French at Toulon. They have built 5 sail of the line since we left Toulon.

I rejoice to hear poor Aunt Mary is better. If you think of anything pray send it her, £5 or £10 cannot be laid out more to my satisfaction.

I am glad to hear you have so pleasant a party. You know F. Parsons was always a favourite of mine. Remember me to her, Mrs. Estridge, Aunt Webbe, the Tobins etc. This Dr. Randolph must be a wonderful man by your account but really I do not believe the world is one bit worse than when our great-grandmothers rode double, except perhaps from a freer communication with the world people are less ashamed.

February 28th.—I am now on my way to Genoa, having been joined by the Admiral on the 23rd off Toulon. The French have 13 sail of the line and 5 frigates ready for sea and 4 or 5 fitting in the arsenal, two of which are in forwardness. Sir John from his manner I plainly see does not wish me to leave this station. He seems at present to consider me as an assistant more than a subordinate for I am acting without orders. This may have its difficulties at a future day but I make none knowing the uprightness of my intentions. He asked me if I had heard any more of my promotion. I told him no. His answer was 'You must have a larger ship for we cannot spare you either as Admiral or Captain.' However, we keep going on and if *Agamemnon* is ordered home I hope to come in her but if it is right for me to stay, stay I must.

Genoa, March 2nd.—Just arrived. Have received here your letter of Jan. 10th. The pride cannot lay in Holloway, it is in his wife, a very great lady. His makings are savings for he had no occasion to spend anything and I have heard him, he did lay out more than £100 and mine has been full £2,000. As to prize money, he has not received so much as myself, therefore it is all a boast.

Josiah is very well but I almost despair of this letter. He waits probably for some great news to tell you. God bless you. With kind affections to my father and believe me ever your most affectionate husband,

HORATIO NELSON

To Francis Drake, Minister at Genoa *March 15th, 1796*

Having received information, on which I am told I may depend, that Salicetti is now here, with other Commissioners, for the express purpose of expediting the operations of the French Army towards the invasion of Italy; and that one of the three columns, into which that Army is to be divided, is either to penetrate through the Genoese territory, or to be conveyed coastways to take possession of Port Especia; which will instantly give them the flat country as far as Leghorn; and no doubt but a small Army appearing before Leghorn, would, without any difficulty, make themselves masters of it: I therefore feel it my duty, as Commanding Officer of his Majesty's Squadron employed on this Coast, and in the absence of the Naval Commander-in-Chief, to state clearly the fatal consequences which will attend this plan of the French Commissioners. The possession of Port Especia will always give an easy access to every part of Italy, even to the Kingdom of Naples, and also security to Transports, Ships of War, and small Vessels; and I moreover beg it may be understood, that if the French Flotilla proceeds along the Coast, our Ships-of-war cannot molest them; not being able to approach the Coast, from the shallowness of the water. I must besides observe, that the Enemy possessing Leghorn, cuts off all our supplies; and of course our Fleet cannot always be looked for on the northern Coast of Italy. I therefore beg leave to state, that to obviate these misfortunes, two plans are necessary to be attended to; the first, and best, is the possession of Vado Bay; this done, as far as human foresight can discern, Italy is safe: the next is the taking of Especia; and, as a Sea-Officer, I beg leave to say, that unless one of these plans is adopted, my Admiral, and Commander-in-Chief of his Majesty's Fleet, cannot answer for the safety of Italy, from any attempts that may be made on it Coastways.

I am, &c.

HORATIO NELSON

Agamemnon, Gulf of Genoa,
April 24th, 1796

My dear Fanny,

I have just received your letter of March 21st. You did most perfectly right in not trusting to the movements of a sailor, and you will know from my late letters that Sir John Jervis has such an opinion of my conduct that he is using every influence both public and private with Lord Spencer for my continuance on this station. I am sure you will feel how superior is the pleasure of knowing that my integrity and plainness of conduct is the cause of my being kept from you, to receive me as a person whom no Commander-in-chief would wish to keep under his command. Sir John was a perfect stranger to me, therefore I feel the more flattered and when I reflect that I have had the unbounded confidence of three Commanders-in-chief I cannot but feel a conscious pride and that I have abilities. Rest assured, my dearest Fanny, of my unabated and steady affection which if possible is increasing by that propriety of conduct which I know you are pursuing. Whilst the war lasts I must serve somewhere and for health and nearness to England I know of none equal to this. I thank you for telling me of the gown you are working to receive me in but for fear you should not have finished it I have one, lawn I fancy, and worked most elegantly I ever saw. If Admiral Linzee goes home, which I believe is likely to happen, I have some thoughts of sending a parcel by him, but most probably he has so many things of his own that mine would be seized, perhaps I shall keep them to bring home myself, but this I shall think on.

Sir Hyde Parker has left the fleet for England. It seems Lady Parker has behaved infamously ill and almost ruined his future peace of mind as well as his pocket, but the newspapers will soon tell all.

Admiral Linzee has long had leave of absence which he did not choose to accept. It almost makes me laugh. So soon as he heard of Sir Hyde's misfortune he told Sir John Jervis he would accept of the Admiralty leave and go home in the first convoy. His desires will I am pretty sure be complied with and the Admiral has told me in that case I am to hoist a broad pendant with a captain under me and to command a Division of the fleet for now Sir Hyde is gone he has nobody with any nerves about him and therefore, ill as he can spare me from my present very important service, he must have me near him. Pray do not let this go farther than my father, not even to the Rector or the Matchams. It is all pleasant to me and I know must be so to you.

As to the French fleet coming to sea, that cannot be sure, but if they do, depend on it we shall thrash them.

What can I say to Huggins? If I write it can only be a civil letter, but I will do it soon as you wish it. Lt. Berry is not arrived, therefore I have not seen the patterns.

April 28th.—You will soon hear of our little brush at Loana. We took four vessels, of very little value to us although of great loss to the enemy. I hope tomorrow to get a letter. I am steering for Genoa with that expectation.

Do not tell this news to anyone. If it ever gets into the *Gazette* it is time enough.

If my brother is with you say I don't write for that reason but shall when I think he returns to Hillborough. Josiah is very well, indeed he is never sick. Extraordinary, I have not had a line from Mr. Hoste since I drew the last bill, although it must be known I advanced the money every day for 14 months before I asked for it, and another is now rising very fast. I am very angry. Poor Mrs. Kelly; if she is angry at every good deed of mine, I hope she will die of the spleen. From my heart I wish Kelly every success and honour.

29th.—No letter. All bad news armistice with the King of Sardinia, in a few days peace. Austrians retreating, all will before long make peace, then I shall certainly come home.

Believe me, my dear Fanny, your most affectionate

HORATIO NELSON

Kind remembrances to my father.

Agamemnon, Leghorn,
May 20th, 1796

My dearest Fanny,

I received the day of my arrival your affectionate letter of April 18th. What can be the reason of Mr. Baillie's conduct? It certainly was the intention of Mr. Herbert that the interest should be regularly paid and I have no doubt but a Court of Law would order it. I recollect in particular the will says the interest of the £500 for Josiah shall go towards his education but the principal not to be paid till he is 21 I believe. Now how can the will of the donor be complied with if the interest is not regularly paid? It requires no lawyer to give an opinion on this part of the will. I wish you would get from Doctor's Commons a copy of the will and codicils, then you can for 2 or 3 guineas ask a lawyers' opinion whether the interest ought not to be paid by the trustees. If they say yes, it should be regularly demanded of the trustees for us and for Josiah. The paper can be sent to me as a letter. Huggins can do nothing.

Admiral Linzee is sailed this morning for England in the *Egmont* 74, Capt. Sutton, one of the best conditioned ships in this country. It is proof that all still goes by interest. *Egmont* of all ships ought to have been kept in this country. As to myself I can say nothing. If I am not to hoist my flag in this country, most probably I shall be in England before the convoy. If I am ordered to hoist it the compliment is great and therefore we must both rest contented for a little time. The war will not last much longer. The French must be tired and I believe all our Allies are the same.

Lieutenant Berry has joined the ship. He seems a gentleman and an officer from appearances. I have no doubt but I shall like him. How vexed I am about Suckling. He will never now I fear become respectable. If he has again taken to drink the more he drinks the better, it will the sooner finish his disgrace and the part we must all bear in it. My poor father, how he must feel when he knows it. This may find you possibly at Mr. Suckling's. If so, I beg you will say every kind thing for me. We are certainly under greater obligations to him than to anyone. He is a good man and respectable character.

The Duke of Parma and the Duke of Modena have both made treaties with the French, paid large sums of money and in the treaty it is specified that certain pictures are to be delivered to be sent to Paris. The palace of the Louvre is to be the finest gallery of pictures in the world. The pope has sent to offer ten millions of crowns to prevent their coming to Rome. It is said they have refused unless the famous statue of the Apollo of Belvedere is sent to Paris. What a race of people, but they have done wonders, and yet I believe they will not get farther than they are at present. Reinforcements are coming to join General Beaulieu and the inhabitants of the Tirole a hardy and warlike people, are rising to join the General. If all the States of Italy make peace we have nothing to look to but Corsica which, in the present state of its inhabitants, is not, in my opinion, an object to keep us in the Mediterranean. We shall, I hope, quit it and employ our fleet more to our advantage.

I can only say Josiah is well, indeed he is never sick. I am sorry I cannot say so much of Hoste. He is a very delicate boy. I have not heard from his father this long time. Believe me ever, my dear Fanny, your most affectionate husband,

HORATIO NELSON

To Admiral Sir John Jervis — Fiorenzo, *June 4th, 1796*

I feel highly flattered by your desire to have me continue to serve under your command, which I own would afford me infinite satisfaction; and I therefore beg leave to propose some measures that may still give me that pleasure.

The first is, although the *Agamemnon* can certainly remain in this Country for the next three months, she must be in England before the winter. Another is, that if a Sixty-four is ordered to go, although *Diadem* is certainly in much better plight than *Agamemnon*, yet in point of sailing she is much inferior. The third is, if you really think that the Admiralty will order my Flag to be hoisted in this country, that you would direct me to hoist my Pendant on board any Ship you judge proper. You will easily perceive, that my wishes to stay are sincere; were they not, after your kindness to me, I should be ungrateful.

June 5th

I am not, dear Sir, less anxious than yesterday, for having slept since my last letter: indeed, I cannot bear the thoughts of leaving your command. You have placed an unbounded confidence in me, and, I own, I feel that no exertion of mine has been wanting for a moment, to merit so great an honour.

I am, &c.

HORATIO NELSON

[On 11th June, 1796, whilst in the midst of these operations, Nelson shifted his Broad Pendant from the *Agamemnon* to the *Captain*, thus terminating his long association in command of that ship, in which he spent three years and three months.]

CHAPTER THREE

BATTLE OF ST. VINCENT

To Mrs. Nelson *Captain*, at Sea, *13th June*, *1796*

You will see, my dear Fanny, by the date of this letter, that I have at last left poor old *Agamemnon*. Whether it is right or wrong, time must determine. I have remained in a state of uncertainty for a week; and had the Corn-ships, which were momentarily expected from Naples, arrived, I should have sailed for England. The Admiral has on every occasion behaved with the greatest attention to me; and if I am to serve, it is better I should serve in this Country, where I am known and respected, than to take my chance of being sent Home, and ordered to another station. All *Agamemnon's* Officers are changed,* except Suckling, and the Master, who has a wife and large family. Suckling wishes, as his elder brother is dead, to return: I do not believe any one person in the world has a better heart than he has, or who would do more real good, if Providence ordains that he should be master of the Wooton estate. I have sent my small present for you by him, and also something for my father. What is become of George Tobin?† He is a fine young man: it is a pity he has not got more forward.

June 19th, *1796*

I have just left Sir John Jervis: the French are fitting, and, if Richery joins from Cadiz, they may come out: but we shall certainly beat them, if it pleases God to give us the opportunity. Indeed, the French say, they are Masters on shore, and the English at sea. The Pope has paid largely to save Rome: Naples, I suppose, must pay also. Both the Emperor, and Spain are trying which shall succeed with Naples—one for war, the other for peace. The Emperor must either directly have 100,000 men in Italy, or make peace; how that will affect England, I know not. If we can make a good peace, I wish for it, but hope we shall not be so pusillanimous as to give up all our conquests.

Yours, &c.

HORATIO NELSON

* The following officers served with Nelson in the *Captain*, from 11th June, 1796: Lieutenants Richard Dalton, Peter Spicer, James Summers, James Noble, Henry Compton, and Edward Berry. Surgeon: Thomas Eshelby. Master: Philip Thomas.

† George Tobin was made a post captain in April, 1802.

EVACUATION OF LEGHORN

To Sir Gilbert Elliot

Captain, San Fiorenzo, *July 1st*, *1796*

Dear Sir,

I know you must be anxious to hear what has been passing at Leghorn, therefore I send you information just as I received it, without form or order. You may depend Buonaparte is gone, and I hope on the account supposed, that General Beaulieu is reinforced. The English are under infinite obligation to Spannochi, (Governor of Leghorn) who is suffering for it. And to Captain Fremantle they are much obliged, for his great exertions in getting all their shipping out of the Mole. I will not say that any exertions of my own were wanting to get to Leghorn sooner, for it was Thursday noon before we heard the rumour at Genoa, and it was the same day they knew it at Leghorn, when an express was sent to me. Calms prevented my arrival till the Monday morning; fortunately, my assistance was not wanting, and it was to these (apparently to me unfortunate) calms that so much property was saved. As soon as I get a little provision and wood, which will be two days, I shall go to Genoa, to inquire for letters and to hear the news, but pray keep this secret, or I shall be tormented with applications for passages, and I have as many on board as is convenient to me. Whatever commands or letters you may have, I shall take great care of them. From Genoa, I shall proceed directly to the Fleet, and I sincerely hope they may be induced to come out before they know of Buonaparte's retreat; for I have no doubt but the destination of the French Army was Corsica, and it is natural to suppose their Fleet was to amuse ours whilst they cross from Leghorn. Ever believe me, dear Sir,

Your Excellency's most obliged and faithful servant,

HORATIO NELSON

His Excellency the Vice-Roy.

P.S. Your Excellency may wish to send the *Vanneau* or *Sardine* to some place with your dispatches. I will order them to Bastia to receive your commands the moment I receive your wishes; they are perfectly ready for sea.

To Joseph Brame, British Consul at Genoa

Captain, at Sea, *July 6th*, *1796*

Sir,

Being ordered to blockade the Port of Leghorn, I have to desire that you will officially inform the Government of Genoa, and all the Foreign

Ministers and Consuls, that the Port of Leghorn is in a state of blockade, and that any Vessels which may clear out from Genoa for Leghorn, or attempt to enter it after this public declaration, which I desire you will give in its fullest force and form, will be made Prizes of, or fired on, and sunk, as circumstances may make proper: and you will also signify, that the entry of the Road, which includes the space inside the Melora, will be considered as the Port of Leghorn. The Genoese Government will of course make this known to all the Towns in the Riviera of Genoa, as you will write to all your Vice-Consuls, from Port Especia to Ventimiglia.

I have also further to desire that you will acquaint the Government of Genoa, and all the Foreign Ministers and Consuls, that no Vessel will be permitted to leave the Port of Leghorn until it is delivered from the hands of its present tyrannical Rulers, and restored to its legal Government; and you will desire the several parties mentioned to write to their Consuls at Leghorn of this my determination. And as I think it honourable to make known this determination, that no person may plead ignorance, so it will be credited, if my character is known, that this blockade will be attended to with a degree of rigour unexampled in the present war.

I am, Sir,

Your obedient servant,

HORATIO NELSON

ELBA SEIZED

To Admiral Sir John Jervis — *Captain*, off Porto Ferrajo, *July 9th, 1796*

Sir,

It was yesterday, at seven in the morning, I received the Vice-Roy's letter, acquainting me of his intention to possess Porto Ferrajo, then close off the Melora. I instantly dispatched the *Meleager* to Genoa, with my letters, the one to Mr. Brame, and to the Foreign Consuls at Leghorn. I inclose copies, and directed Captain Cockburn to remain in that Port forty-eight hours, in order to receive all the information which is to be collected.

The *Blanche*, *Sardine*, *Le Genie*, a Gun-boat, and two Corsican privateers, I left, to continue the blockade of Leghorn, and proceeded, with the *Peterel*, off this place, where I arrived last night. The Convoy hove in sight this morning, and the *Inconstant* is working up to join me. In the night I sent a boat into Porto Ferrajo, where they found his Majesty's Ship *Southampton*.

I have the honour, &c.

HORATIO NELSON

Sir Gilbert Elliot's reasons for taking possession of Porto Ferrajo in the Island of Elba, are fully shown by his letter to the Governor dated Bastia, 6th July, 1796:

'Sir,

The French troops have taken possession of the City of Leghorn, the cannon of the fortresses have been directed against the ships of the King, in the Road, and the property of his Majesty's subjects at Leghorn has been violated, notwithstanding the neutrality of His Royal Highness the Grand Duke of Tuscany, and the reiterated protestations of the French to respect it. There is likewise reason to believe, that the French have the same design upon the fortress of Porto Ferrajo, hoping by such means to facilitate the designs which they meditate against the Kingdom of Corsica. These circumstances have determined us to prevent the plans of the Enemies of the King, which are equally hostile to his Royal Highness, by placing at Porto Ferrajo a garrison capable of defending that place, our only intention being to prevent that fortress, and the whole of the Island of Elba, from being taken possession of by the French. We invite and request you, Sir, to receive the troops of his Majesty which will appear before the place, under the following conditions . . . '

According to these conditions, Porto Ferrajo and its dependencies were to remain under the government of the Grand Duke, and it was promised that the troops should retire and the place be restored, at the peace.

To Admiral Sir John Jervis — Leghorn Roads, *18th July, 1796*

Dear Sir,

I hope his Holiness the Pope may yet wage war against the French. I have never heard that he has been in actual hostility against them. The blockade of Leghorn is complete, not a Vessel can go in or come out without my permission. Yesterday a Dane came out laden with oil and wine for Genoa: I told him to return, or I should send him to Corsica. His answer was, 'I am a Neutral, and you may take me, but I will not return.' I therefore took possession, and intended giving him to a Corsican privateer; when, in about two hours, he begged I would allow him to return. On this, I sent him back with a letter to the Danish Consul, whence the following is an extract:—'Respect for the Danish flag, and humanity to the owners of this Vessel, impel me to return her into their possession, and not proceed to those extremities which the laws of Nations allow in case of a declared blockaded Port.' This, I am satisfied, was a trial of what I intended; for he said, all the Neutrals were determined to come out. If we are firm, the Grand Duke will sorely repent his admission of the French; his repeated proclamations for the people to be quiet, have given time to the French to lay powder under all the works; and, in case of any disturbance, they say, 'up shall go the works.' Cannon are pointed from the wall to every street, and all the cannon and mortars are mounted: the famous long brass gun is on the Mole-head, and also a mortar. The Grand Duke declares he yet hopes the Directory will order Buonaparte to leave Leghorn; but I believe the French now wish to get into fortified Towns, to prolong the campaign.

The *Captain* has her wants, but I intend she shall last until the autumn; for I know, when once we begin, our wants are innumerable. I hope the Admiralty will send out fresh Ships. The French are fitting out here from four to six Tartans, with thirty-six pounders, to drive me out of the Roads; but I am prepared against Fire Vessels, and all other plans, as well as I am able. The Tartans, it is said, will be out to-night: two thousand French are arrived, and more are expected. I have only now to beg, that whenever you think the Enemy will face you on the water, that you will send for me; for my heart would break to be absent at such a glorious time.

I am, &c.

HORATIO NELSON

To H.R.H. the Duke of Clarence

Captain, Leghorn Roads, under sail for Genoa,
20th July, 1796

Sir,

I was this morning honoured with your Royal Highness's letter of May 30th; and it gives me real satisfaction to be assured of the continuance of your good opinion. Indeed, I can say with truth, that no one whom you may have been pleased to honour with your notice, has a more sincere attachment for you than myself. It has pleased God this war, not only to give me frequent opportunities of shewing myself and Officer worthy of trust, but also to prosper all my undertakings in the highest degree. I have had the extreme good fortune, not only to be noticed in my immediate line of duty, but also to obtain the repeated approbation of His Majesty's Ministers at Turin, Genoa, and Naples, as well as of the Vice-Roy of Corsica, for my conduct in the various opinions I have been called upon to give; and my judgment being formed from common sense, I have never yet been mistaken.

You will hear of our taking possession of Porto Ferrajo; if we had not, to a certainty the French would, and then they would have been too near Corsica, where I fear we have an ungrateful set of people; and one party acknowledged friends to the French, which, although greatly outnumbered by our friends, constantly makes disturbances. The armistice of the Pope and King of Naples will, I believe, come to nothing; it was only done to gain time, and they will be guided by the success or defeat of the Austrians. The King of Naples is firm; he has been by far the most faithful Ally of England.* He is at the head of 80,000 men at Velletri, only two posts from Rome, where the people are ripe for a revolt, and already declare that the busts, statues, and manuscripts, shall not go out of Rome. The French possessing themselves of Leghorn, so contrary to the repeated pledges of the Directory, will afford such an opportunity for all the Italian States to break up with them again, that perhaps they may be induced to give it up: the King of Naples, if they refuse, would march to attack it, and we are sure of the lower order at Leghorn. The garrison is reinforced to 5,000 men, and provisions are getting into the Citadel. The French General has told the inhabitants, that if they are not quiet, he would blow all the works up round the Town, which in fact would blow half the Town up: the mines are laid; large Vessels are also fitting with forty-two pounders, and furnaces, to annoy me; but I am prepared, as much as possible, against whatever may happen.

Genoa, July 23rd.—I arrived here yesterday and rejoice to hear that Marshal Wurmser has commenced offensive operations. I have no doubt but the French will retire to Piedmont as fast as they advanced from it; and I fear they may force the King of Sardinia into an alliance against us. To-morrow I return to Leghorn.

I am, &c.

HORATIO NELSON

To Mrs. Nelson *2nd August, 1796*

Had all my actions, my dearest Fanny, been gazetted, not one fortnight would have passed during the whole war without a letter from me: one day or other I will have a long Gazette to myself; I feel that such an opportunity will be given me. I cannot, if I am in the field for glory, be kept out of sight. Probably my services may be forgotten by the great, by the time I get Home; but my mind will not forget, nor cease to feel, a degree of consolation and of applause superior to undeserved rewards. Wherever there is anything to be done, there Providence is sure to direct my steps. Credit must be given me in spite of envy. Even the French respect me: their Minister at Genoa, in answering a Note of

* Peace was, however, made between the King of Naples and the French Republic on the 10th October following.

mine, when returning some wearing apparel that had been taken, said, 'Your Nation, Sir, and mine, are made to show examples of generosity, as well as of valour, to all the people of the earth.' The following is a copy of the Note I had sent him. 'Generous Nations are above rendering any other damage to individuals than such as the known Laws of War prescribe. In a Vessel lately taken by my Squadron was found an *imperiale* full of clothes belonging to a General Officer of Artillery. I therefore send you the clothes as taken and some papers which may be useful to the Officer, and have to request you will have the goodness to forward them.'

I will also relate another anecdote, all vanity to myself, but you will partake of it: A person sent me a letter, and directed as follows, 'Horatio Nelson, Genoa.' On being asked how he could direct in such a manner, his answer, in a large party, was, 'Sir, there is but one Horatio Nelson in the world.' The letter certainly came immediately. At Genoa, where I have stopped all their trade, I am beloved and respected, both by the Senate and lower Order. If any man is fearful of his Vessel being stopped, he comes and asks me; if I give him a Paper, or say, 'All is right,' he is contented. I am known throughout Italy; not a Kingdom, or State, where my name will be forgotten. This is my Gazette.

Lord Spencer has expressed his sincere desire to Sir John Jervis, to give me my Flag. You ask me when I shall come home? I believe, when either an honourable peace is made, or a Spanish war, which may draw our Fleet out of the Mediterranean. God knows I shall come to you not a sixpence richer than when I set out. I had a letter a few days since from H.R.H. the Duke of Clarence, assuring me of his unalterable friendship. With kindest love to my father, believe me your most affectionate husband,

HORATIO NELSON

To the Rev. William Nelson, Hilborough

Captain, between Bastia and Leghorn,
August 18th, 1796

My dear Brother,

I always have very great pleasure in receiving a letter from you, and I have only to beg that you will write more frequently. I laugh at your fancying my being able to buy, at least, Tofts;* and don't you be uneasy when I assure you that if I have saved my Ship-pay, the Marine I throw in, I shall be content; but I verily believe that will not be the case. It is true I have taken numbers of prizes, but I have always shared with my Squadron, none of whom have I ever received sixpence from; or, had

* A property.

so many Vessels in sight, that they run away with the greater part. I believe had I trusted to my own good fortune and enterprising spirit, I might have been able to think of Tofts; but that gives me not a moment's concern. Happy, happy shall I be to return to a little but neat cottage!

I may tell you as a *secret*, that probably the next letter you see from me will be in the Public Gazette. An expedition* is thought of, and of course I shall be there, for most of these services fall to my lot. I have just been arranging shot, shells, &c., &c., for to give our Enemies. As to rewards, I expect none. I shall not, perhaps, return till a peace, when our services are forgot. I am not surprised that the Linen draper should sell his estate. Almost every one lives beyond his income, and attempts to imitate his neighbour who is richer. However, now, I am a real Commodore having a Captain under me,† I shall share for all prizes, whoever is the taker. A Spanish galleon taken now in this Country will be a capital stroke, but I can hardly bring myself to believe they will venture on a war. If they do, we must give up Corsica, and that is all. Our Fleets will cover every sea but the Mediterranean. The Dons will expect it at home and abroad. America will readily join against them, and they will lose Mexico and Peru. America will find soldiers and privateers, and we must find Ships-of-war. I have my eye on a Spaniard [who] is gone, I fancy, to the mouth of the Tiber, to bring away the tribute of the Pope for the French. I hope to catch her on her return, if she has really their busts and money on board.

I rejoice to hear Aunt Mary is so well recovered. Tell her I hope yet to take her by the hand before the year comes round. Tell me all the Norfolk news that is interesting. How are all our friends at Swaffham? Does Mr. Rolfe live at (I have forgot the name) Saham. I shall keep this letter open till I get to Leghorn, which I keep very warm with my blockade, and hope to be able to tell you good news. I thank my nephew‡ for his letter, and if he works as hard in the Church as I have done on the sea, he may become a Bishop.

August 19th

I am sorry to tell you the Austrians have had a check in Lombardy, by fancying themselves too powerful. It disappoints my hopes for the present. Remember me most kindly to Mrs. Nelson and Aunt Mary,

* Against Leghorn.

† He was appointed a full commodore, having Captain Ralph Willett Miller as his captain on the 11th August, three days before the date of this letter. It appears from the 'Order of Battle' of the 19th August, 1796, that Captain Charles Stuart was his captain until Captain Miller joined.

‡ Horatio, only son of the Rev. William Nelson, who was then but seven years old.

Miss Charlotte, Horace, our friends at Swaffham, and everywhere else. Perhaps you may meet Maurice Suckling: he will now marry Miss Framingham. He may be odd, but I believe none will do more real good with the estate when he comes to it, which I hope he will*. Josiah thanks you all for your inquiries: he is not the least altered. Ever, your most affectionate brother,

HORATIO NELSON

To Mrs. Nelson

[In this letter Nelson informed his wife that as soon as affairs were settled with the Grand Duke, he should pay his Holiness the Pope a visit, and he added:]

Leghorn Road,
August 23rd, 1796

I do not think that he will oppose the thunder of the Vatican against my thunder; and you will, I dare say, hear that I am at Rome in my barge. If I succeed, I am determined to row up the Tiber, and into Rome.

Yours, &c.

HORATIO NELSON

EVACUATION OF CORSICA

To Admiral Sir John Jervis

Diadem†, at Sea, *28th September, 1796*

Sir,

Yesterday morning the *Captain* sailed from Leghorn, according to your orders, as did *L'Eclair*, from necessity, the day before—both for Ajaccio. During the course of yesterday, I received repeated information of the movements of the Privateers with the Corsicans on board; the whole number of Corsicans is nine hundred, including all the Officers; six brass twelve-pounders are embarked, thirty-five cases of small arms, and various other articles, in from fifteen to twenty Privateers, and I am certain they mean to sail the first favourable moment. (On the 25th, each Corsican was paid 100 livres). The Corsicans behave so ill at

* Lieut. Maurice Suckling did marry Miss Framingham.

† The *Captain* being sent from Leghorn to Ajaccio, under the command of Lieut. Berry, Nelson hoisted his broad pendant on board the *Diadem*, 64, Captain George Henry Towry.

Leghorn, that the French are determined to send them off, upon the general principle of action of the French—'If you succeed, so much the better for us; if you do not, we get rid of a set of scoundrels.'

Now, Sir, the point for me to consider is, where will the French land in Corsica? the twelve-pounders can only be to possess a Post, (that they meant to have gone by Capraja, at least to possess it, is now certain; the French Commissary was heard to say to Gentili, I told you long ago to possess Capraja; you now see what you have lost.) This, you will say, the Viceroy, from his information and means of knowledge of every part of his kingdom, ought to know better than any one of us. I am on my way to concert with his Excellency how I can best use my small force to his advantage, considering the other services I have to look to.

My idea runs strong that Porto Vecchio, which is reported to me to be neglected by us, and in which is a fort, is the object the Enemy mean to possess, which, if their friends in the Island support them, is sure refuge for their Vessels, and an opening for the introduction of more troops and supplies. If the Viceroy will put some men in the fort, and I find *Sardine*, I will, with the *Venom*, which I have ordered from Leghorn, place them as Guard-ships in the harbour; and I will endeavour to have a Frigate off that part of the coast. If the Enemy land nearer Bastia, the Vice-Queen's Yacht (but this I don't build upon) may be useful. *Vanneau*, *Rose*, and the four small Feluccas, which the Vice-Roy has purchased, must . . . our communication, and be the searchers for the Enemy about the Islands between the Main and Corsica. (These Vessels, with those which may be there, will be sure to destroy them; although it is possible the men may get on shore: but I hope, from the small craft which may be sent about the Islands between Corsica and the main, we may get accounts of their approach.) If their intention be to land on the western coast of Corsica, I take for granted they will never attempt the route by Cape Corse, which would every hour expose them to the sight of some of our Ships, which of course would be their destruction. In either case, I think I shall act upon the idea that they will proceed to the south-ward, passing the passage of Piombino to Castiglione, the last place in their possession: but if I can find them on that coast, I believe (having knowledge of the whole Coast) I can destroy their *flota*. But, supposing they pass the Islands, if we possess Porto Vecchio, although the people may land, yet there is not shelter for the Vessels the whole Coast to Bastia. But perhaps they will push for the Coast of Sardinia, Madalina Islands, &c., and pass the Straits of Bonafaccio. This must be a work of time, and we shall have I hope many chances for their destruction; (no opportunity for which shall be omitted by, Sir, your most obedient servant,

HORATIO NELSON)

What will the Vice-Roy do? Would it not be well to give notice to the Island that 900 refugee Corsicans are forced by the French to embark, and to attempt the (*imperfect*).

(P.S. The French are very angry at our taking Capraja: the Commissioner was heard to say to Gentili, 'I told you we should have sent 300 men, and taken Capraja; you now see the consequence.')

29th September, in sight of Bastia

The Austrians, under the Archduke, took possession of Frankfort on the 8th; and it is expected that Wurmser will once more attack the French: Mantua stopped him again. All hope for another and younger General. The Neapolitan property is detained by the French at Leghorn.

To Mrs. Nelson About *17th October, 1796*

We are all preparing to leave the Mediterranean, a measure which I cannot approve. They at home do not know what this Fleet is capable of performing; anything, and everything. Much as I shall rejoice to see England, I lament our present orders in sackcloth and ashes, so dishonourable to the dignity of England, whose Fleets are equal to meet the World in arms; and of all the Fleets I ever saw, I never beheld one in point of officers and men equal to Sir John Jervis's, who is a Commander-in-Chief able to lead them to glory.

Yours, &c.

HORATIO NELSON

To Admiral Sir John Jervis *Captain*, Port Ferrajo, *October 21st, 1796*

Sir,

I have the honour to acquaint you that I arrived at Bastia on the 14th, and was joined between that time and the 19th by the *Egmont*, *Captain*, *Excellent*, and *Southampton*. The Ships-of-the-line were moored opposite the Town, the embarkation of provisions and stores commenced on the 15th, and was continued without intermission till the 19th at sunset. In that night every soldier and other person were brought off with perfect good order from the north end of the Town.

It is unnecessary for me to mention to you the fatigue of the whole of this duty, but I cannot omit to state the merits of every officer employed on it, and most particularly that of Lieutenant Day, Agent for Transports; and much which has been saved may be fairly attributed (without disparagement to any one) to his indefatigable attention and ability. The Captains of all the Ships-of-war, although not particularly in their line of duty, never omitted, night or day, their personal exertions.

The cordiality with which the whole of this service was carried on between His Excellency the Vice-Roy, Lieutenant-General de Burgh, and myself, I cannot but think it right to inform you of; and that I have the honour to be with the greatest respect,

Yours most obedient servant,

HORATIO NELSON

To H.R.H. the Duke of Clarence

Captain, 25th October, 1796

Sir,

I was honoured with your Royal Highness's letter of 2nd of September*, a few days past, in the midst of a very active scene, the evacuation of Bastia; which being our first post, was entrusted to my direction, and I am happy to say that not only Bastia, but every other place in the Island is completely evacuated. The Corsicans sent to Leghorn for the French, as was natural for them, in order to make their peace; and the Enemy was in one end of Bastia, before we had quitted the other. The exertions of the Navy on this occasion, as on all others which I have seen, have been great, and beyond the expectations of those who never will believe what we are capable of performing. Our troops are ordered to Porto Ferrajo, which can be defended against any number of the Enemy for a length of time; and the Port, although small, will hold with management our whole Fleet and Transports.

As soon as all our Transports are arrived at Elba, we are to go out to look for Man, who is ordered to come up: we shall then be twenty-two Sail of such Ships as England hardly ever produced, and commanded by an Admiral, who will not fail to look the Enemy in the face, be their

* 'Richmond, September 2nd, 1796

'Dear Sir,

I am to acknowledge the receipt of yours of 20th and 23rd July, which came safe to hand. I congratulate you on being at last in the command of a Ship of 74 guns, and I believe you did not make the exchange before it was requisite. I always was persuaded you would make the best use of any opportunity to distinguish yourself; you have had many, and I hope you will have more, in which the same good fortune, I trust, relative to your person, will attend you. As for the execution, I am confident the King's service will benefit always under your direction.

'Since your last letter, the Austrian affairs both in Italy and Germany have suffered seriously. I am not yet so blind to the French Revolution, as not to be convinced there must be treachery amongst the Imperial Officers, which, it is to be lamented, the Emperor will not or cannot detect. I should think our Fleet, situated as Italy force what it may: I suppose it will not be more than thirty-four Sail of the Line. We may reasonably expect reinforcements from England; for whilst we can keep the combined Fleet in the Mediterranean, so much more advantageous to us; and the moment we retire, the whole of Italy is given to the French. Be the successes of the Austrians what they may, their whole supply of stores and provisions comes from Trieste, across the Adriatic to the Po, and when this is cut off, they must retire. If the Dons detach their Fleet out of the Mediterranean, we can do the same—however, that is distant. I calculate on the certainty of Admiral Man's joining us, and that in fourteen days from this day we shall have the honour of fighting these gentlemen: there is not a seaman in the Fleet who does not feel confident of success. If I live, your Royal Highness shall have no reason to regret your friendship for me, and I will support Sir John Jervis to the utmost of my power. . . . I hope soon to hear that your Flag is flying, which I am sure will be most honourable for yourself, and I trust most advantageous for our King and Country. I am, as ever, your most faithful,

HORATIO NELSON

To William Locker, Lieutenant-Governor, Royal Hospital, Greenwich

Captain, at Sea, *November 5th, 1796*

My dear Friend,

It is true that my time has lately been so fully employed, that I have not had that time I wished for, to write to all my friends. However, as I am attached to the Fleet, I have not so many affairs in hand. Sir John desires me to say, when I write you, that he is sorry he cannot, so much as he wishes, write to you himself. We have now done with Corsica; I have seen the first and the last of that Kingdom. Its situation certainly was most desirable for us, but the generality of its inhabitants are so greedy of wealth, and so jealous of each other, that it would require the patience

now is, from these repeated defeats of the Austrians, cannot be of any more use in the Mediterranean; and, indeed, as a Spanish war seems to be inevitable, the West Indies will require a great Naval force, and it will be proper to augment the Fleet which protects our own coasts, and is known under the denomination of the Channel Fleet. I therefore suppose the Mediterranean Fleet will be divided—part to the West Indies, and the rest come home, leaving a few Frigates, under a very active Officer, at Gibraltar.

'We cannot say dear old England is as we could wish it; however, we are better off than any other nations; and, thank God, there is no treachery amongst our Military, or amongst our people! I wish for the best; and, being clear of all kind of party, I care not who is the Minister, provided he is active, and really anxious to make peace the moment he can. Adieu, my dear friend, and ever believe me, yours sincerely, William.'

of Job, and the riches of Croesus to satisfy them. They say themselves they are only to be ruled by the Ruling Power shooting all its Enemies, and bribing all its Friends. They already regret our departure from them, for no more silver harvests will come to their lot. I remember when we quitted Toulon we endeavoured to reconcile ourselves to Corsica; now we are content with Elba—such things are: however, we have a fine Port, and not expenses for the Government of the Island.

We are anxious to hear what the King of Naples has determined on, in consequence of our remaining to support him: if he is marched, I hope soon to be in possession of Leghorn again. The conduct of the Pope is extraordinary; although he is at war with the French, yet he has not opened his Ports to us: he is fearful of a turn in the present happy prospects. In short, Italy has been lost by the fears of its Princes; had they expended half the money to preserve their Territories, which they have paid the French for entering them, their Countries would have been happy, instead of being filled with present misery and diabolical notions of Government. I have received the third volume of Charnock's book*, but how it came to me I know not, but suppose by the Queen. As the book gets forward, it naturally becomes more interesting. I am in your debt for the subscription.

We left St. Fiorenzo on the 2nd, at night, and are now seeing our Smyrna convoy part of the way down the Straits, and hope to meet Admiral Man, who has, more than a month past, known the situation of our gallant Admiral. Orders have been sent, which fame says, were received October 10th; but Admiral Man could not have sailed on the receipt of them, as Swedes have been spoke only eight, nine, and ten days through the Gut.

So soon as our Fleet is united, I have no doubt but we shall look out for the Combined Fleet, who I suppose are about thirty-four Sail of the Line, badly manned, and worse ordered; whilst ours is such a Fleet as I never before saw at sea. There is nothing hardly beyond our reach. I need not give you the character of Sir John Jervis, you know him well; therefore I only say, he is worthy of such a Fleet, for he knows how to use us in the most beneficial manner for our Country. You will not forget me kindly to every part of your family, and also to Mr. Bradley and our Naval friends; also to Simon Taylor. As I read in the paper, St. Domingo is to be evacuated, I hope Jamaica will be safe. All the French Army in Italy is going to the Devil very fast. We are on shore, upon *velvet*. Ever believe me, your most affectionate,

HORATIO NELSON

I write this to go when opportunity offers.

* *Biographia Navalis.*

Captain, at Sea,
November 7th, 1796

My dear Fanny,

I wrote you a line by the *Camelion* a few days before our sailing from San Fiorenzo, as I had done a short time before from Bastia. The first was a short letter for I dare not trust to paper the plan which was to be pursued. However, by this time you will learn the determination for this fleet to remain in the Mediterranean. As for Corsica I have seen the first and last of it. I was the cause of giving many lucrative employments for the army which they were incapable of getting for themselves and I took them off the island when they were equally helpless. It will appear extraordinary but they allowed the Corsicans at Bastia to sequester and seize all the English property, to lay a privateer across the Mole and in short by every way to insult them, and had I not arrived, I am sure they would have taken the Viceroy from them and have submitted to any terms the townspeople demanded and this with a force of 1,800 men in possession of the citadel, but all were panic struck. In one quarter of an hour I settled the whole matter for I sent to the Council of 30 who acted for the Corsicans or French, and told them if the sequester was not taken off in that time, the armed Corsicans retired and that I was molested in taking off what I thought proper, I would blow the town down. The Corsicans down muskets and run. From this moment all was quiet and I saved £200,000 sterling worth of stores and property. In short it is impossible to say what I did not do. The scrap of paper sent from the General to the captain of the fleet will say more for me than I can say for myself, except that I did bring them off and the two field pieces, which the army brought from the citadel to protect their rear, I brought off as a point of honour, and I landed them all safe at Porto Ferraio, a secure place which I had taken for them. Not a sixpence worth of property belonging to the merchants was left behind. The pleasure of my own mind will be my reward, except having the honour to maintain the Viceroy, Secretary of State and about 40 other persons at an enormous expense, but such things are. So soon as we have defeated the Spanish fleet, which I doubt not with God's help but we shall do, I have two or three little matters to settle in Italy and then I care not how soon I return to you. Do not flatter yourself I shall be rewarded. I expect nothing, therefore shall not be disappointed.

November 11th, off Minorca.—We are so far with our convoy. Perhaps we shall [see] Gibraltar. If we do I shall write you from thence but this goes on board the Admiral to take its chance for a passage. Josiah is most perfectly well. With kindest regards to my father, believe me, your most affectionate husband,

HORATIO NELSON

I shall not forget George Jolliffe. He is on board the *Inconstant*.

N.B. We took Bastia with 1,250 men.

I send the General's note to you as I [am] more interested and feel a greater satisfaction in getting your and my father's applause than that of all the world beside.

To the Rev. Dixon Hoste

Captain, at Sea, *November 25th, 1796*

My dear Sir,

Our friends in England sometimes accuse us of not writing so frequently as they wish us: on many occasions we can retort the charge—so says your good son, William. I can say, which will be enough for a letter, that I have never once had cause to wish him anything *but what he is*. His accidents, I can truly say, have so happily turned out that I hope he is in no way the worse for them, but I have recommended for him not to break any more limbs.

Although this is writing at sea, yet most probably it will leave us at Gibraltar, for which place we are steering; and you will, perhaps, expect a little news from near the fountain-head, did you not know that our future movements are too important to be trusted to a letter; and our past ones, every newspaper tells you *more* than I can, for what is not known they happily guess at. Our evacuation of Corsica was effected beyond our most sanguine expectations, and contrary to the belief of our absent friends, the part allotted to me, the evacuation of Bastia, considered the most important, ended, as our world here, say, much to my credit; for the French and their adherents were round the Town, and the Spanish Fleet only thirty-six miles from us*; but I left

* Towards the end of September, Admiral Don Juan de Langara, with the Spanish Fleet, consisting of nineteen sail-of-the-line, ten frigates, and some corvettes, put to sea from Cadiz, and proceeded to Carthagena, where they were joined by seven line-of-battle ships, thus making twenty-six sail-of-the-line. With this imposing force, Langara appeared off Cape Corse in Corsica, on the 15th October, at which time Sir John Jervis's Squadron, amounting to only fourteen sail of the line (the *Captain* being at Bastia) were at anchor in Mortella Bay. Instead, however, of attacking the English Fleet, the Spanish admiral went to Toulon; and on his arrival there, on the 26th October, the combined fleets formed thirty-eight sail-of-the-line and nearly twenty frigates.

not a man behind, and saved two hundred thousand pounds' worth of cannon, stores, and provisions, and landed the whole Army, &c., &c. safe at Porto Ferrajo, a place of shelter I had contributed to take a few months before. Our gallant Admiral, Sir John Jervis, in vain expected Admiral Man from Gibraltar, but we have been disappointed, and you know where he is by this time, instead of coming to our help who so much needed it, but in this world nothing ought to surprise us. We are only fifty leagues from Gibraltar, and hope there to find reinforcements from England, when, if we are twenty-five Sail of the Line, you may rest perfectly assured under our present Commander, we shall beat the Combined. God send our meeting may be soon, for I should be sorry to have a Peace before we make the Dons pay for meddling. When you see Mr. and Mrs. Coke, I beg you will make my compliments, and present mine to Mrs. Hoste. William tells me he is writing a long letter: therefore, perhaps, he will tell you more news than I can.

November 28th.—I this day delivered to William your letter of October 31st: he says you seem to regret his not going home in the *Agamemnon*; had I thought so, I certainly should not have taken him from her. I am, dear Sir,

Your very obedient servant,

HORATIO NELSON

[The Government having determined to withdraw the garrison from Porto Ferrajo, Nelson was ordered by Sir John Jervis, on 10th December, 1796, to hoist his Distinguishing Pendant on board *La Minerve* frigate, to take the *Blanche* under his command, and to proceed from Gibraltar to Porto Ferrajo. Upon his arrival there, or meeting with them, he was also to take under his command the seventeen ships or vessels named, and 'to carry into execution His Majesty's commands relative to the disposition of the troops and stores lately removed to that garrison from the Island of Corsica'. The British Artillery and the 1st Regiment, or Royal Scotch, were to be disembarked at Gibraltar; and all the other troops, British and foreign, were to be landed at Lisbon. Sir John Jervis's order concluded . . . 'Having experienced the most important effects from your enterprise and ability, upon various occasions since I have had the honour to command in the Mediterranean, I leave entirely to your judgment the time and manner of carrying this critical and arduous service into execution.']

To Mrs. Nelson

About *the 10th December, 1796*

I am going on a most important Mission, which, with God's blessing, I have little doubt of accomplishing; it is not a fighting Mission, therefore be not uneasy. I feel honoured in being trusted, as I am, by Sir John Jervis. If I have money enough in Marsh and Creed's hands, I wish you would buy a Cottage in Norfolk. I shall follow the plough with much greater satisfaction than viewing all the magnificent scenes in Italy.

Yours, &c.

HORATIO NELSON

To Lt. General de Burgh

La Minerve, 30th December, 1796

Sir,

I am honoured with your letter of the 28th, and have most seriously attended to every part of the very wise reasoning contained in it: the difficulty of your deciding on the contrary orders of Government, and of guessing what may be their intentions at present, I clearly perceive*. But my instructions from Admiral Sir John Jervis, both written and verbal, are so clear, that it is impossible for me to mistake a tittle of them, or the sentiments of my Commander-in-Chief; and I am therefore ready to meet the responsibility. I am positively ordered to execute the King's instructions for carrying the troops to the places destined for them. I am advised that the British Fleet will never come to Porto Ferrajo, and that all our Naval establishments here are to be immediately withdrawn, which I shall do as expeditiously as possible.

The King of Naples having made a Peace, the Admiral considers his business with the Courts of Italy as terminated; and that the point he is now instructed to attend to is the protection of Portugal; therefore the utility of Porto Ferrajo, as far as relates to a safe place for our Fleet, is at an end; what its further political consequence may be, does not come within the sphere of my supposed knowledge; nor of what may happen both in Portugal and Gibraltar from the want of this Army. I have sent to collect my Squadron, and as soon as they arrive, unless I should receive other orders, I shall offer myself for embarking the troops, stores, &c.; and should you decline quitting this Post, I shall proceed down the Mediterranean with such Ships of war as are not absolutely wanted for keeping open the communication with the Continent, supposing the Enemy to have no more Naval force in this neighbourhood than at present.

I am, &c.

HORATIO NELSON

* General de Burgh did not think himself authorised to abandon Port Ferrajo until he had received specific instructions to that effect; and in the letter to Nelson, to which this is a reply, he said: 'I will at the same time confess that my only motive for urging delay, arises from a wish to have my proceedings in some measure sanctioned by orders we ought to expect, and by no means from an idea that we assist the Service by staying here; for I have always held the opinion, that the signing of a Neapolitan peace with France ought to be our signal for departure.'

1797

To Lt. General de Burgh

La Minerve, Porto Ferrajo, *20th January, 1797*

Sir,

The whole of the Ships of War which Sir John Jervis has appropriated for the service of the evacuation of this place being now either in the Port or near approaching it, I have therefore to request that you will be pleased to inform me, with as little delay as possible, whether it is your intention to embark the troops and stores now here, or any part of them.

Should your answer be in the affirmative, every measure shall be taken by me for the speedy arrival of the troops in Gibraltar and Portugal; and should it be a negative, in that case I shall, according to my instructions, withdraw all our Naval stores and establishment, and as many Ships of War as I think can possibly be spared from the service which may be required of them here, our Fleet being now particularly instructed to attend to the preservation of Portugal.

[Imperfect]

To Sir John Jervis

La Minerve, Porto Ferrajo, *January 25th, 1797*

Sir,

Although I hope to be with you before *Southampton*, yet it is possible that may not be the case, as I mean to look into Toulon, Mahon, and Carthagena, that I may be able to tell you the apparent state of the Combined Fleet.

The General having declined to evacuate Porto Ferrajo*, as you will observe by the copy of the letter transmitted herewith, I have, notwithstanding withdrawn all our Naval establishment from this place, having first completed every Ship to as much stores as her Captain pleased to take. Every Transport is completely victualled and arranged, that every soldier can be embarked in three days.

* Colonel Drinkwater wrote: 'On the 27th December, Nelson reached Porto Ferrajo. Sir Gilbert Elliot was then absent on his visit to the Italian States, but intelligence of the Commodore's arrival was immediately sent to him. On the return of the Vice-Roy to Elba, a consultation was held between Sir Gilbert Elliot, Lieutenant-General de Burgh (who commanded the troops), and Commodore Nelson, respecting the late orders from Government at home, which Nelson had been specially deputed by the Admiral to carry into effect. The subject was one of great difficulty, involving many interests, and had, of course, the most deliberate consideration, the result of which was that, under existing circumstances, it was deemed of paramount importance that the British troops should, notwithstanding those orders, continue in possession of Elba until His Majesty's Ministers could be fully apprised of the many cogent reasons for that course of proceeding.'

The way in which I have sent down the Storeship and *Dolphin*, as also the Convoy, eight or nine Sail, with my intention of looking into the Enemy's ports, I hope you will approve of.

I shall not enter into further particulars till I have the honour of seeing you, but believe me, with the greatest respect, Sir,

Your most obedient servant,

HORATIO NELSON

P.S. I have sent orders for *Pallas* to join you by the *Dido* and *Southampton*, and have left similar orders at this place.

Ships left at Porto Ferrajo:

Inconstant		*Rose*	Gun-boats
Blanche		*Venom*	Gun-boats
Peterel	Sloops	*Mignonne*	
Speedy	Sloops		
L'Utile	Sloops		

La Minerve, Port Ferraio,
January 27th, 1797

My Dearest Fanny,

The *Minerve* is completely refitted and I am only waiting for the weather moderating to proceed to sea with a small convoy to proceed down the Mediterranean therefore the next letter I shall probably write you will be dated from Lisbon where I hope to arrive safe with my charge, but in war much is left to Providence. However, as I have hitherto been most successful confidence tells me I shall not fail, but as nothing will be left undone by me should I not always succeed my mind will not suffer, nor will the world I trust be willing to attach a blame where my heart tells me none will be due.

Sir Gilbert Elliot and his suite go down in *La Minerve* therefore I shall be sure of a pleasant party let what will happen.

There are four mails now at Florence from England. I long to hear from you, but as I have wrote you in future your letters had better come through the Admiralty till I can tell you what route by post to send them. As for news beyond my immediate concerns the public prints must tell you more than I can therefore the whole I can say which I feel you will prize more than any other news is that I am in most perfect good health. Our winter here has been very disagreeable and on the continent vast falls of snow. I am anxious to know how my father bears it. I do not believe it can be very long before I shall have the happiness of seeing my dear Fanny. Believe me ever your most affectionate husband,

HORATIO NELSON

[At Carthagena Nelson found that the Spanish fleet had left that Port, and he became extremely anxious to join Sir John Jervis. *La Minerve* arrived at Gibraltar on 9th February, when Nelson learned that the Spaniards had passed the Rock, to the westward, on the 5th, and had sent *Le Terrible* and two other Sail of the Line and a frigate with supplies for their Lines before Gibraltar. His two lieutenants, Culverhouse and Hardy, taken in *La Sabina*, were then prisoners on board *Le Terrible*, but an exchange had been effected and they rejoined *La Minerve*. Nelson could remain only one day at Gibraltar and *La Minerve* weighed in the forenoon of the 11th February.]

To Edward Hardman, Private Secretary to Sir Gilbert Elliot

La Minerve, February 11th, 1797

Dear Sir,

The Minerve was most certainly ready for sea, and it is as true, that had Sir Gilbert been on board, the *Minerve* would have been at sea before the lee-tide made. Hope's* Barge attended instead of *Minerve's*. Now the tide is made against us; therefore, I most heartily wish you all a good appetite, and only beg you will be on board as early in the evening as possible—say eight o'clock—for I shall sail the first moment after; but I fear a *westerly* wind.

Yours most truly,

HORATIO NELSON

P.S. I took my leave of the Governor, and refused to dine on shore.

THE BATTLE OF ST. VINCENT

[The preceding letter was written three days before the battle of St. Vincent.

As soon as *La Minerve* sailed from Gibraltar, she was pursued by *Le Terrible* and another of the Spanish Line-of-battle ships. The headmost of the Spanish ships gaining on the frigate, she prepared for action; Colonel Drinkwater asked Nelson's opinion as to the probability of an engagement, to which Nelson said he thought it very possible, and looking up at his Broad Pendant, added, 'But before the Dons get hold of that bit of bunting, I will have a struggle with them, and sooner than give up the Frigate I'll run her ashore.' Nelson and his guests sat down to dinner, and while Colonel Drinkwater was congratulating Lieutenant Hardy on his being no longer a prisoner of war, the cry was heard of 'a man overboard!'

There is perhaps no passage in Naval history of more thrilling interest than the following account of what then occurred:

* Captain George Hope, of the *Romulus*.

'The officers of the ship ran on deck; I, (Colonel Drinkwater) with others, ran to the stern-windows to see if anything could be observed of the unfortunate man; we had scarcely reached them before we noticed the lowering of the jolly-boat, in which was my late neighbour, Hardy, with a party of sailors; and before many seconds had elapsed, the current of the Straits, (which runs strongly to the eastward,) had carried the jolly-boat far astern of the Frigate, towards the Spanish ships. Of course, the first object was to recover, if possible, the fallen man, but he was never seen again. Hardy soon made a signal to that effect, and the man was given up as lost. The attention of every person was now turned to the safety of Hardy and his boat's crew; their situation was extremely perilous, and their danger was every instant increasing, from the fast sailing of the headmost ship of the chase, which by this time had approached nearly within gun-shot of the *Minerve*. The jolly-boat's crew pulled 'might and main' to regain the Frigate, but apparently made little progress against the current of the Straits. At this crisis, Nelson, casting an anxious look at the hazardous situation of Hardy and his companions, exclaimed "By God! I'll not lose Hardy: back the mizen topsail." No sooner said than done, the *Minerve's* progress was retarded, having the current to carry her down towards Hardy and his party, who seeing this spirited manœuvre to save them from returning to their old quarters on board the *Terrible*, naturally re-doubled their exertions to rejoin the Frigate. To the landsmen on board the *Minerve* an action now appeared to be inevitable; and so, it would appear, thought the Enemy, who surprised and confounded by this daring manœuvre of the Commodore, (being ignorant of the accident that led to it,) must have construed it into a direct challenge. Not conceiving, however, a Spanish ship of the Line to be an equal match for a British Frigate, with Nelson on board of her, the captain of the *Terrible* suddenly shortened sail, in order to allow his consort to join him, and thus afforded time for the *Minerve* to drop down to the jolly-boat to take out Hardy and the crew; and the moment they were on board the Frigate, orders were given again to make sail. Being now under studding-sails, and the widening of the Straits allowing the wind to be brought more on the *Minerve's* quarter, the Frigate soon regained the lost distance, and in a short time we had the satisfaction to observe that the dastardly Don was left far in our wake; and at sunset, by steering further to the southward, we lost sight of him and his consort altogether'.

During the night of the 11th February, *La Minerve* found herself surrounded by several large ships, which Nelson believed to be the Spanish Fleet, but from which he extricated himself with his usual skill. Nothing was seen of the Spaniards the next day, and on the 13th, *La Minerve* joined Sir John Jervis's Fleet; Sir Gilbert Elliot and Nelson immediately waited on the Admiral, on board the *Victory*, who, on learning that the enemy was so near, made the signal to 'prepare for action.'

Nelson then left *La Minerve* and hoisted his Broad Pendant on board his own ship, the *Captain*, commanded by Captain Miller. Sir Gilbert Elliot requested to remain with the Admiral in the *Victory*, but was refused; and he with his suite were transferred to the *Lively* frigate, Captain Lord Garlies, who had orders to proceed to England. Sir John Jervis, however, yielded to the joint entreaties of Sir Gilbert Elliot and Lord Garlies, that the *Lively* might remain with the Fleet until she could carry home the news of the expected engagement. Thus Sir Gilbert and Colonel Drinkwater became spectators of one of the most important events of their time, and thus, too, the battle fortunately found an able historian.]

A FEW REMARKS RELATIVE TO MYSELF IN THE *CAPTAIN*, IN WHICH MY PENDANT WAS FLYING ON THE MOST GLORIOUS VALENTINE'S DAY, 1797

On the 13th February, at 6 p.m., shifted my Pendant from *La Minerve* Frigate to *Captain*.

Valentine's day, at daylight, signal to prepare for Battle; at 10, saw some strange Ships standing across the van of our Fleet, on the larboard tack, which was sailing in two divisions, eight in the weather, seven in the lee, on the starboard tack. About 11, signal to form the Line, as most convenient. At twenty-five past 11, the Action commenced in the Van, the passing through the Enemy's Line. About 1 a.m., the *Captain* having passed the sternmost of the Enemy's Ships, which formed their Van, consisting of seventeen Sail of the Line, and perceiving the Spanish Fleet to bear up before the wind, evidently with an intention of forming their Line, going large—joining their separated division,—or flying from us; to prevent either of their schemes from taking effect, I ordered the Ship to be wore, and passing between the *Diadem* and *Excellent*, at ten minutes past 1 o'clock, I was in close Action with the Van, and, of course, leewardmost of the Spanish Fleet. The Ships which I know were the *Santa Trinidad*, *San Josef*, *Salvador del Mundo*, *San Nicolas*, *San Isidro*, another First-rate and Seventy-four, names not known. I was immediately joined and most nobly supported by the *Culloden*, Captain Troubridge. The Spanish Fleet, from not wishing, I suppose, to have a decisive Battle, hauled to the wind on the larboard tack, which brought the Ships above mentioned to be the leewardmost Ships in their Fleet. For an hour the *Culloden* and *Captain* supported this apparently, but not in reality, unequal contest, when the *Blenheim*, passing to windward of us and ahead, eased us a little. By this time the *Salvador del Mundo* and *San Isidro* dropped astern, and were fired into in a masterly style by the *Excellent*, Captain Collingwood, who compelled them to hoist English colours, when, disdaining the parade of taking possession of beaten Enemies, he most gallantly pushed up to save his old friend and messmate, who was to appearance in a critical situation: the *Blenheim* having fallen to leeward, and the *Culloden* crippled and astern, the *Captain* at this time being actually fired upon by three First-rates and the *San Nicolas* and a Seventy-four, and about pistol-shot distance of the *San Nicolas*. The *Excellent* ranged up with every sail set, and hauling up his mainsail just astern, passed within ten feet of the *San Nicolas*, giving her a most awful and tremendous fire. The *San Nicolas* luffing up, the *San Josef* fell on board her, and the *Excellent* passing on for the *Santa Trinidad*, the *Captain* resumed her situation abreast of them, close alongside.

At this time, the *Captain* having lost her fore-topmast, not a sail, shroud, or rope standing, the wheel shot away, and incapable of further service in the Line or in chase, I directed Captain Miller to put the helm a-starboard, and calling for the Boarders, ordered them to Board.

The Soldiers of the 69th Regiment, with an alacrity which will ever do them credit, with Lieutenant Pierson, of the same Regiment, were amongst the foremost on this service. The first man who jumped into the Enemy's mizen-chains was Captain Berry, late my First-Lieutenant. He was supported from our spiritsail-yard; and a soldier of the 69th Regiment having broke the upper quarter-gallery window, jumped in, followed by myself and others, as fast as possible. I found the cabin-doors fastened, and the Spanish Officers fired their pistols at us through the Windows, but having broke open the doors, the soldiers fired, and the Spanish Brigadier (Commodore, with a distinguishing Pendant) fell as retreating to the quarter-deck. Having pushed on the quarter-deck, I found Captain Berry in possession of the poop, and the Spanish Ensign hauling down. The *San Josef* at this moment fired muskets and pistols from the Admiral's stern-gallery on us. Our seamen by this time were in full possession of every part: about seven of my men were killed, and some few wounded, and about twenty Spainards.

Having placed sentinels at the different ladders, and ordered Captain Miller to push more men into the *San Nicolas*, I directed my brave fellows to board the First-rate, which was done in a moment. When I got into her main-chains, a Spanish Officer came upon the quarter-deck rail, without arms, and said the Ship had surrendered. From this welcome information, it was not long before I was on the quarter-deck, when the Spanish Captain, with a bended knee, presented me his Sword, and told me the Admiral was dying with his wounds below. I gave him my hand, and desired him to call to his Officers and Ship's Company that the Ship had surrendered, which he did; and on the quarter-deck of a Spanish First-rate, extravagant as the story may seem, did I receive the Swords of the vanquished Spaniards, which as I received I gave to William Fearney, one of my bargemen, who placed them, with the greatest sang-froid, under his arm. I was surrounded by Captain Berry, Lieutenant Pierson, 69th Regiment, John Sykes, John Thompson, Francis Cook, and William Fearney, all old *Agamemnons*, and several other brave men, Seamen and Soldiers. Thus fell these Ships. The *Victory* passing saluted us with three cheers, as did every ship in the Fleet. The *Minerve* sent a boat for me, and I hoisted my Pendant on board her, directing Captain Dockburn to put me on board the first uninjured Ship of the Line, which was done; and I hoisted my Pendant in the *Irresistible* but the day was too far advanced to venture on taking possession of the *Santa Trinidad*, although she had long ceased to resist, as it must have brought on a night Action with a still very superior Fleet. At dusk, I went on board the *Victory*, when the Admiral received me on the quarter-deck, and having embraced me, said he could not sufficiently thank me, and used every kind expression which could not fail to make me happy. On my return on board the *Irresistible*, my bruises were looked at, and found but trifling, and a few days made me as well as ever.

H. N.

N.B. There is a saying in the Fleet too flattering for me to omit telling—viz., 'Nelson's Patent Bridge for boarding First-rates', alluding to my passing over an Enemy's 80-gun Ship; and another of a Sailor's taking me by the hand on board the *San Josef*, saying he might not soon have such another place to do it in, and assuring me he was heartily glad to see me.

To the Mayor of Norwich

[From the Assembly Book of the Corporation of Norwich]

Irresistible, off Lisbon, *26th February, 1797*

Sir,

Having the good fortune, on the most glorious 14th of February, to become possessed of the Sword of the Spanish Rear Admiral Don Xavier Francisco Winthuysen, in the way set forth in the paper transmitted herewith, and being born in the County of Norfolk, I beg leave to present the Sword to the City of Norwich, in order to its being preserved as a Memento of the Event, and of my Affection for my Native County.

I have the honour to be, Sir,

Your most obedient Servant,

HORATIO NELSON

To Mrs. Nelson *Irresistible*, Lisbon, *28th of February, 1797*

We got up here with our Prizes this afternoon: the more I think of our late Action, the more I am astonished; it absolutely appears a dream. The *Santissima Trinidad*, of four decks, lost five hundred killed and wounded; had not my Ship been so cut up, I would have had her; but it is well, thank God for it! As to myself, I assure you I never was better, and rich in the praises of every man from the highest to the lowest in the Fleet. The Spanish War will give us a Cottage and a piece of ground, which is all I want. I shall come one day or other laughing back, when we will retire from the busy scenes of life: I do not, however, mean to be a hermit; the Dons will give us a little money.

If my father should at any time wish for any part that is in my Agent's hands, I beg he would always take it, for that would give me more real pleasure than buying house or land. I go to sea the day after to-morrow in this Ship, with a Squadron to be off Cadiz, consisting of the *Irresistible*, *Orion*, &c. Sir John Jervis has already spread the Frigates; and I shall return by the time his Fleet is ready for sea.

Yours, &c.

HORATIO NELSON

From Mrs. Nelson

11th March, 1797

My dearest Husband,

Yesterday I received your letter of February 16th. Thank God you are well, and Josiah. My anxiety was far beyond my powers of expression. M. Nelson and Captain Locker behaved humanely, and attentive to me. They wrote immediately, Captain Locker assuring me you were perfectly well, Maurice begging me not to believe idle reports, the Gazette saying you were slightly wounded. Altogether, my dearest husband, my sufferings were great. Lady Saumarez (whose husband, Captain Sir James Saumarez, commanded the *Orion* in the Battle,) came running to tell me she had Letters from her husband—all this was on this day week. He speaks generously and manly about you, and concluded by saying, 'Commodore Nelson's conduct is above praise.' You were universally the subject of conversation.

I shall not be myself till I hear from you again. What can I attempt to say to you about Boarding? You have been most wonderfully protected: you have done desperate actions enough. Now may I—indeed I do—beg that you never Board again. *Leave it for Captains*. How rejoiced Jo. must have been to have seen you, although it was but an absence of two months. To-morrow is our wedding-day, when it gave me a dear husband, my child the best of fathers. I hope he will deserve all the blessings Providence has bestowed on him.

Do come home this summer or in the autumn. It is said a change in Administration would certainly have taken place, had not this wonderful and fortunate Victory taken place. Admiral Parker, it seems, had written the *Captain* and *Culloden* bore the brunt of the Action. This instant have I received a letter from Lord Hood, telling Sir Robert Calder was gone to Portsmouth. Thank you, my dearest husband, a thousand times, for your letter of February 22nd. God bless you and protect you, and my Jo.—crown all your endeavours with success, and grant us a happy meeting. I can bear all my extreme good fortune. Your affectionate Wife,

FRANCES H. NELSON

NELSON KNIGHTED

Admiralty, *17th March, 1797*

Sir,

I have His Majesty's commands to acquaint you, that in order to mark his Royal approbation of your successful and gallant exertions on several occasions during the course of the present War in the Mediterranean, and more particularly of your very distinguished conduct in the glorious and brilliant Victory obtained over the Fleet of Spain by His Majesty's Fleet, under the command of Admiral Sir John Jervis, on the 14th of February last, His Majesty has been pleased to signify his intention of conferring on you the Most Honourable Order of the Bath, with which it is His Majesty's pleasure that you should be invested, when the proper measures can be taken for that purpose. I have great satisfaction in communicating to you this very distinguished mark of the Royal approbation.

I am, &c.

SPENCER

To Earl Spencer, First Lord of the Admiralty

Captain, off Cape St. Mary's,
April 2nd, 1797

My Lord,

Yesterday I had the honour of receiving your Lordship's letter of March 17th, signifying to me his Majesty's most gracious intention to confer on me the Most Honourable Order of the Bath, as a mark of his Royal approbation of my conduct on several occasions during the present War. May I presume, through your Lordship, who have so favourably represented my services to the King, to present my most profound and humble acknowledgments to his Majesty for this most distinguished mark of his Royal Favour?

I feel it would be presumptuous in me to say more than to acknowledge the very handsome manner in which your Lordship has been pleased to execute his Majesty's commands, and that I am,

Your Lordship's most obliged Servant,

HORATIO NELSON

Captain, off Cadiz,
April 2nd, 1797

My dearest Fanny,

You will believe whether my letters are long or short which last they generally are, still my heart is entirely with you. Your letter of March 11th, my father's of the 14th with 40 others came to me yesterday afternoon. It is well when we seem to satisfy all the world for the Spaniards are not less lavish of their praises of me than are the people of England. Lord Spencer (this keep to yourself except my father) has by the King's command signified to me His Majesty's intention to confer on me the most honourable order of the Bath, as a mark of His Royal approbation of my conduct on many occasions during the present war. As to fortune we must be content with a little and the cottage. Near Norwich, or any other place you like better, will I assure you content me. I do not say if the Government offered me £300 or £500 per annum I would refuse on the contrary I should be obliged to them, but it is a thing I cannot ask, but then we could afford no more than a cottage. My chains medals and ribbons with a contented mind are all sufficient. When you write to Josiah you may address yourself to Lieutenant Nisbet and I hope he will be a Captain if the war lasts till October next. William Bolton, and Hoste with Weatherhead will also be promoted by Lord Jervis but I fear about their time. I have sent to Maurice to take out so much of a Capt. William Bolton's time, that is all fair. Weatherhead, Mr. Coke has interested himself about and I hope will get over his want of time, but I fear he has not interest for such a thing.

I have handsome letters from the Duke of Clarence and Lord Hood. I have very many letters to write therefore I must finish for the present.

We have just chased two Spanish ships of the line into Cadiz where we are blockading them up. I do not expect to see them this summer out again. With love to my father, believe me, your most affectionate husband,

HORATIO NELSON

April 3rd.—I forgot to answer one part of your former letter about a young lad. You must explain to the lad and his mother and if he comes out I will certainly do my best for him.

To the American and Danish Consuls at Cadiz

His Britannic Majesty's Ship *Captain*, off Cadiz,
11th April, 1797

Sir,

In consequence of the unprovoked declaration of War by the King of Spain, against his Britannic Majesty and the British Nation, it is thought right that Spain should no longer have any Trade:

I have, therefore, the honour to acquaint you, that no Neutral Vessel will be permitted in future to enter or leave the Port of Cadiz, unless by leave obtained from me, or the Commander-in-Chief of the British Fleet; and that, from this moment, Cadiz is to be considered as a blockaded Port. I have the honour to be, Sir,

Your most obedient servant,

HORATIO NELSON

To Admiral Don Josef de Mazaredo, Cadiz

Theseus, May 30th, 1797

Sir,

I have the honour of sending your Excellency a packet from Sir John Jervis; and I embrace the opportunity of assuring you of my high esteem of your character. The 4th of June being the birthday of my Royal Master, Sir John Jervis intends firing a *feu de joie*, at eight o'clock in the evening; and has desired me to mention it to your

Excellency, that the Ladies of Cadiz may not be alarmed at the firing. Believe me your Excellency's most faithful servant,

HORATIO NELSON

To this letter the Spanish Admiral replied:

On Board the *Conception*, off Cadiz,
1st June, 1797

My dear Sir,

I correspond to the urbanity merited by the letter with which you honoured me, the 30th May last. The Ladies of Cadiz, accustomed to the noisy sounds of salutes of vessels of war, will sit, and will hear what Sir John Jervis means to regale them with, for the evening of the 4th current, in honour of his Britannic Majesty's birthday; and the general wish of the Spanish nation cannot but interest itself in so august a motive.

God preserve you many years. I kiss your hands

Your attentive Servant,

JOSEF DE MAZEREDO

Theseus, June 15th, 1797

My dearest Fanny,

I have received your affectionate letters of May 8th, 15th and 29th and from the complexion of the times I most fervently hope we shall have a tolerable peace. The vessel which brought these letters being to return within an hour of my getting them must make me write a short letter to say we are well and Josiah very much improved. I hope he will make a good man.

Although the fleet has taken some prizes, yet I think you must not reckon on more than £5,000 besides the £2,000 from my agents. Where ever you buy the house, depend on it I shall be content. I am tired of the war and long for nothing but to get to you. On the 1st of October, peace or war I hope to sail for England. Nothing but a conviction in my own mind of enemy's fleet coming out of port in a week afterwards should tempt me to stay one day after that time.

The *Theseus* was one of the ships concerned in the business at home for which scare her late Captain Aylmer left her fancying her crew intended to carry her into Cadiz and had always a party of marines under arms. I have found a more orderly set of men. A few nights ago a paper was dropped on the quarter deck. I send you a copy.

Success attend Admiral Nelson
God bless Captain Miller we thank
them for the officers they have placed over us.
We are happy and comfortable and will shed every drop
of blood in our veins to support them, and the
name of the *Theseus* shall be immortalized as high as the
Captain. Ship's Company.

I must not get too far or you will not get your letter. I command the advanced squadron and have to hope the Dons will have the goodness to come out very soon. Then I stay not one hour after it. I have my dear father's letter of May 22nd. God bless him and you and believe me your most affectionate husband,

HORATIO NELSON

Joliffe is acting lieutenant of the *Bellerophon*. I never have had an opportunity of knowing him personally, but have had the opportunity of being in a small degree useful to him. Lt. Thompson I know very well a most excellent officer is 1st lieutenant of the *Irresistible* and if the Spanish fleet comes out will assuredly be a captain in my squadron. Three last verses of a poem, I know not the author.

True British valour has appalled
The proud insulting foe
What late was Nelson's Olio called
Has laid the Dons full low.

This hero brave old England's boast
Grappled two ships along
Forced them to strike on their own coast
And lasting laurels won.

Long will this fact in history shine
Give me the fair sex say
A Nelson for my valentine
On this auspicious day.

An old sailor.

To Sir John Jervis

Theseus, June 21st, 1797

My dear Sir,

The history of women was brought forward, I remember, in the Channel Fleet last War. I know not if your Ship was an exception, but I will venture to say, not an Honourable but had plenty of them; and they always will do as they please. Orders are not for them—at least, I never yet knew one who obeyed.

Your most faithful,

HORATIO NELSON*

To Mrs. Nelson

29th June, 1797

Rest assured of my most perfect love, affection, and esteem for your person and character, which the more I see of the world, the more I must admire. The imperious call of honour to serve my Country, is the only thing which keeps me a moment from you, and a hope, that by staying a little longer, it may enable you to enjoy those little luxuries which you so highly merit. I pray God it may soon be peace, and that we may get into the cottage.

I have to thank many friends for their kind congratulations, and have had a long letter and genealogy from the York Herald, Mr. Nayler, whom I have referred to my brother Maurice. I have sent my brother my Supporters, Crest, and Motto: on one side a Sailor properly habited, holding in his hand the Broad Pendant on a staff, and trampling on a Spanish flag; on the other side the British Lion tearing the Spanish flag, the remnants hanging down, and the flag in tatters. Motto, what my brother William suggested, turned into English—'Faith and Works.'

I hope you will like them. I intend my next winter's gift at Burnham should be fifty good large blankets of the very best quality, and they will last for seven years at least. This will not take from anything the Parish might give. I wish inquiry to be made, and the blankets ordered of some worthy man; they are to be at my father's disposal in November. I have received my dear father's letter. God bless him and you.

Yours, &c.

HORATIO NELSON

* Sir John Jervis's reply to this letter, dated on the 21st, commenced: 'I perfectly agree with you that the overflow of Honourables and the Disciples they have made among the Plebeians has been the ruin of the Service. I never permitted a woman to go to sea in the ship . . .'

To George Naylor, York Herald and Genealogist of the Order of the Bath

Theseus, off Cadiz, *June 29th, 1797*

Sir,

I am honoured with your letter of May 29, relative to my Pedigree; and I have desired my brother to deliver you this letter, and to arrange such matters as are proper with you. As Government have always, I believe, on occasions like the present, paid all the Fees of Office, Installations, &c., I expect they will do it on the present occasion, for I cannot think of being at one sixpence expense*; but my Brother will express my sentiments fully on this head, and I have the honour to be, Sir,

Your most obedient servant,

HORATIO NELSON

To the Rev. Dixon Hoste,
Goodwicke, near Rougham

Theseus, June 30th, 1797

My dear Sir,

As I have desired my dear William to write you, I shall only express my anxiety that his Time should be sent to me. I hear he was borne some short time on the *Grampus*' books, but of this you know more than I can do. My health is so indifferent, that longer than the 30th September I cannot serve without a short respite from fatigue; but I hope the War will be over by that time; for, unless we are united at Home much good cannot be expected—let it be a War of the Nation, and what signify France, Holland, and Spain.

We are looking at the Ladies walking the walls and Mall of Cadiz, and know of the ridicule they make of their Sea Officers. Thirty Sail are now perfectly ready, and, the first east wind, I expect the Ships from the Mediterranean which will make them forty Sail of the Line. We are now twenty; some of our Ships being always obliged to be absent for water, provisions, &c. However equal we may be to do the business, yet I cannot bring myself to believe that it is good policy to leave us so inferior, whatever honour there may be in it. The merchants of Cadiz have repeatedly petitioned Government to force out the Fleet; and say truly, that ten Sail of the Line had better be sacrificed than the loss of their three Ships from Lima, and their Homeward Convoy, which must fall into the hands of the English, if they are not forced from before the harbour. I am of opinion that some morning, when least expected, I shall see them tumbling out of Cadiz. We in the advance are, night and

* Nelson refused to pay any fees for the honour conferred upon him.

day, prepared for battle: our friends in England need not fear the event. At present we are all quiet in our Fleet; and, if Government hang some of the Nore Delegates, we shall remain so*. I am entirely with the Seamen in their first Complaint. We are a neglected set, and, when peace comes, are shamefully treated; but, for the Nore scoundrels, I should be happy to command a Ship against them. We have reports through Spain that Pitt is out: it is Measures must be changed, and not merely Men. I beg my respects to Mr. Coke and Mrs. Coke, and believe me, dear Sir,

Your very obedient servant,

HORATIO NELSON

BOMBARDMENT OF CADIZ

To Admiral Sir John Jervis *3rd July, 1797*

We will begin this night by ten o'clock; and I beg that all the launches of the Fleet may be with me by eight, or half-past at farthest, also all the barges or pinnaces. I wish to make it a warm night at Cadiz. The Town and their Fleet are prepared, and their Gun-boats are advanced; so much the better. If they venture from their walls, I shall give Johnny his full scope for fighting. Mazaredo will be more than human, if he can keep the Merchants of Cadiz in good humour. I am inclined to think he has been out this afternoon. I intend, if alive, and not tired, to see you to-morrow, and ever to the last believe me your faithful,

HORATIO NELSON

To Admiral Sir John Jervis

Theseus, July 4th, 1797

Sir,

In obedience to your orders, the *Thunderer Bomb* was placed, by the good management of Lieutenant Gourly, her present Commander, assisted by Mr. Jackson, Master of the *Ville de Paris*, who volunteered his able services, within 2,500 yards of the walls of Cadiz; and the shells were thrown from her with much precision, under the directions of Lieutenant Baynes, of the Royal Artillery; but, unfortunately, it was soon found that the large Mortar was materially injured, from its former services; I therefore, judged it proper to order her to return under the protection of the *Goliath*, *Terpsichore*, and *Fox*, which were

* The mutiny at the Nore.

kept under sail for that purpose, and for whose active services I feel much obliged.

The Spaniards having sent out a great number of Mortar Gun-boats and armed Launches, I directed a vigorous attack to be made on them, which was done with such gallantry, that they were drove and pursued close to the walls of Cadiz, and must have suffered considerable loss: and I have the pleasure to inform you, that two Mortar-boats and an armed Launch remained in our possession.

I feel myself particularly indebted, for the successful termination of this contest, to the gallantry of Captains Fremantle and Miller, the former of whom accompanied me in my Barge; and to my Coxswain, John Sykes, who in defending my person, is most severely wounded; as was Captain Fremantle, slightly, in the attack. And my praises are generally due to every Officer and man, some of whom I saw behave in the most noble manner; and I regret it is not in my power to particularize them. I must also beg to be permitted to express my admiration of Don Miguel Tyrason, the Commander of the Gun-boats. In his Barge, he laid my Boat alongside, and his resistance was such as did honour to a brave Officer; eighteen of the twenty-six men being killed, and himself and all the rest wounded. Not having a correct list of killed and wounded, I can only state, that I believe about six are killed and twenty wounded.

I have the honour to be, &c.

HORATIO NELSON

To Admiral Sir John Jervis

Theseus, July 9, 1797

My dear Sir,

In the first place, I congratulate you on the finish, as it ought, of the *St. George's* business*, and I (if I may be permitted to say so) very much approve of its being so speedily carried into execution, even although it is *Sunday*. The particular situation of the service requires extraordinary measures. I hope this will end all the disorders in our Fleet: had there been the same determined spirit at home, I do not believe it would

* On Friday the 7th, and Saturday the 8th July, four mutineers of the *St. George* were tried by a court-martial; on the 8th July, Sir John Jervis wrote two notes respecting them to Nelson. In the first he said: 'If these four unfortunate men receive sentence of death, as there is every reason to believe they will, from the strong and direct evidence which came home to the bosoms of all yesterday, and the court-martial ends this day, they will suffer at 6 o'clock in the evening, therefore,' &c. As the trial did not terminate until after sunset, the sentence was not carried into execution on the 8th, and Sir John Jervis consequently wrote to Nelson: 'The sentence must be carried into execution to-morrow morning, although it is Sunday, and you

have been half so bad, not but that I think Lord Howe's sending back the first petition was wrong.

Yours most affectionately and gratefully,

HORATIO NELSON

To Sir Robert Calder, First Captain to Admiral the Earl of St. Vincent

Theseus, July 9th, 1797

My dear Sir,

I am sorry that you should have to differ with (Vice-Admiral Thompson) but had it been Christmas Day instead of Sunday, I would have executed them. We know not what might have been hatched by a Sunday's grog; *now* your discipline is safe. I talked to our people, and, I hope, with good effect: indeed, they seem a very quiet set. Ever your most faithful,

HORATIO NELSON

To Capt. John Nicholson Inglefield,
Commissioner of the Navy at Gibraltar

July 11th, 1797

My dear Sir,

I am sorry to find, from General O'Hara's letter, that he has the smallest alarm for our success in anything my great Commander-in-Chief plans: had my orders been well executed, not a Spanish gun or mortar boat would have been left at Cadiz. Our loss of men is most trifling; but, however that might have been, I had rather see fifty shot by the Enemy than one hanged by us. It is good at these times to keep the Devil out of their heads.

Mazaredo is alarmed; has drawn all his Ships between St. Mary's and Cadiz; and if you make haste with the sea-mortar, I will bomb him out of Cadiz bay. Three fires were seen in the Town, but they were got under without much difficulty. I laid myself with the Bomb on the strong face of Cadiz, seventy guns and eight mortars. They expected

will take care to have the Boats of the detached squadron up in time.' In a letter to Nelson, dated *Ville de Paris*, Sunday evening, 9th July, 1797, Sir John Jervis said: 'Vice-Admiral Thompson has presumed to censure the execution on the Sabbath, in a public letter; and I have insisted on his being removed from this Fleet immediately, or that I shall be called home.' The Admiralty acknowledged the receipt of Lord St. Vincent's† letter announcing the execution of the mutineers on the Sunday, and expressed 'their very high approbation' of his 'conduct on that unpleasant and urgent occasion'.

† Sir John Jervis was created Earl St. Vincent for his victory at sea.

me on the weak side. The next night I took them on the soft side, and eighty shells fell in the Town, and some over it amongst their Shipping. Yesterday, in the *Theseus*, I had the honour of every gun from the southern part of Cadiz, and of every Gun and Mortar-boat. I could not get them out so far as I wished, or some of them should have paid me a visit. I sent ninety-one prisoners into Cadiz, whom I took on the night of the 3rd; and, as to killed, I know nothing about them: eighteen were killed in the Commanding Officer's boat, that had the presumption to lay my Barge aboard, manned with some of the *Agamemnon's* people. My Squadron is now ten Sail of the Line. If they come out, there will be no fighting beyond my Squadron.

I am, &c.

HORATIO NELSON

THE ATTACK ON SANTA CRUZ

Theseus, July 12th, 1797

My dearest Fanny,

I am always sorry when you are disappointed, but if you recollect that I was absent on service it must be very uncertain when I should return to the fleet. From April 12th to May 23rd was my absence for although a cutter left me when I joined the Port Ferraio convoy to announce my junction and although I wrote one on May 1st yet only the former got to the fleet, the latter I found at Gibraltar and brought it myself to the fleet. Never fancy for a moment you are absent from my thoughts or that I neglect writing. Yesterday after Boyle left me I received yours of June 19th and my father's of June 12th. You will receive my letters wrote since my return in due time but when you know I am sent from the fleet you never ought to calculate on a letter till you know from myself of my return. But you believed the convoy would arrive with the cutter but the fact is the cutter was 7 days in doing what took the convoy 32 days to Gibraltar and there I left them and they did not join the fleet till the 7 or 8 of June, but I have done.

I never saw Sheppards Spring nor do I fancy if it was within our purse it would suit us. A cottage is absolutely all that we can look to, and £2,000 is the fullest extent which we can afford for it, and if you do not object I should like Norfolk in preference to any other part of the kingdom but do as you please and I have no doubt but I shall be satisfied. I should be glad if the house was bought.

I am sure the time is past for doing anything for George Tobin, had he been with me which was offered he would have long since have been a captain, and I should have liked it as being most exceedingly pleased with him. You surprise me about Lieutenant Pierson I never heard a syllable about it. However, they know their own concerns best but I should not have approved of him for a son-in-law, although I believe him to be a very good young man, but I don't think he will make a pleasant husband. He is too nice in his dress and fidgetty and has not the knack of being contented with his situation.

Respecting Hoste I have desired his father to send out his time and he may of course apply where he pleases for interest with Sir John Jervis and if you write him pray say so. I still adhere to my determination of going home on October 1st or immediately as we have an account of peace. Sir John has promised me a frigate to take my body and my rags may travel in due time by the *Theseus*.

It was not Captain Wilsford but a Colonel Drinkwater, who wrote the last siege of Gibraltar, who wrote the history of the action. Capt. W. has not abilities for such a thing. His compliments to me are great but I am confident not a word beyond the truth. My late affair here will not I believe lower me in the opinion of the world and I hope it will be my last exertion this year.

Your former direction was right and this not so, but any direction will find H. N. you will recollect the Italian compliment I told you of. 'There is but one H. N. in the world.' I have had flattery enough to make me vain and success enough to make me confident. Josiah is very well he reads all your letters. He does not believe Mr. P. will marry any one who has not a great deal of money and he believes Mr. P. will turn merchant. I have wrote this long letter to be ready for I never know half an hour. The happy termination of the mutiny at the Nore gives us all great pleasure.

Ever believe me your most affectionate husband,

HORATIO NELSON

July 14.—As I may be absent for a short time* do not be anxious about letters for you cannot hear from me.

Questions submitted to the Captains of the Squadron.

Question 1st

Is it your opinion that from the information we have been able to collect, and from Lieutenant Wably's plan, that the landing should be made in the valley marked E., known by the name of Lion's Mouth,

* The Commander-in-Chief had received news that a Spanish ship called *El Principe d'Asturias*, richly laden, from Manilla to Cadiz, was at Santa Cruz, and he determined to carry Nelson's favourite design of attacking that place into effect.

and endeavour to get over the mountain marked F. and attack the fort marked G? Or is it your opinion that, at least, 600 men should be landed under the Line Wall, and to escalade that wall?

2nd

Supposing the escalade of the Line Wall to be successful, is it your opinion that an immediate attack should be made on the Town and Mole, by turning to the left, or should the attack be made by turning to the right, and attacking the battery G?

The following regulations are recommended by Rear-Admiral Nelson.

July 17th, 1797

1st

That each Ship's Boats should be kept together by towing each other, which will keep the people of each Ship collected, and the Boats will be in six divisions, and nearly got on shore at the same moment.

2nd

The Marines of each Ship of the Line to be put in their Launches, which will carry them.

3rd

The moment the Boats are discovered by a firing being made on them, the Bomb-vessel to commence her fire on the Town, and to keep it up till the flag of truce is hoisted from either the Enemy or from us.

4th

That a Captain should be directed to see the Boats put off from the Beach, that more men may be speedily got on shore with the field-pieces.

5th

Frigates to anchor, as soon as possible after the alarm is given, or the forces ashore, near the battery in N.E. part of the Bay.

6th

Immediately as the forces get on shore, they are to get in the rear of the battery marked G., in the N.E. part of the Bay, and to instantly storm it, and also to take post on the top of the hill which is above it.

Every Ship to land the number of men as against their names expressed, with a proper proportion of Officers and Midshipmen, exclusive of Commissioned Officers and servants.

And the Captains are at liberty to send as many more men as they please, leaving sufficient to manage the Ship, and to man the launch and another boat. Every Captain that chooses, is at liberty to land, and command his seamen, under the direction of Captain Troubridge.

It is recommended to put as many Marine coats or jackets on the seamen as can be procured, and that all should have canvas cross-belts.

The Marines to be all under the direction of Captain Oldfield, the senior Marine Officer; and he is directed to put himself under the direction of Captain Troubridge, as is Lieutenant Baynes, of the Royal Artillery, with his Detachment.

To Thomas Troubridge, Captain of H.M. Ship *Culloden*, and Commander of the Forces ordered to be landed for taking Santa Cruz.

Theseus, at Sea, *20th July, 1797*

Sir,

I desire you will take under your command the number of Seamen and marines named in the Margin, who will be under the command of Captains Hood, Fremantle, Bowen, Miller and Waller, and the Marines under the command of Captain Thomas Oldfield, and a detachment of the Royal Artillery under the command of Lieutenant Baynes, all of whom are now embarked on board his Majesty's Frigates, *Seahorse*, *Terpsichore*, and *Emerald*.

With this detachment you will proceed as near to the Town of Santa Cruz as possible, without endangering your being perceived; when you will embark as many men as the Boats will carry, and force your landing in the north-east part of the Bay of Santa Cruz, near a large battery. The moment you are on shore, I recommend you to first attack the battery; which when carried, and your post secured, you will either proceed by storm against the Town and Mole-head battery, or send in my Letter, as you judge most proper, containing a Summons, of which I send you a copy; and the terms are either to be accepted or rejected in the time specified, unless you see good cause for prolonging such other methods as you judge most proper for speedily effecting my orders, which are to possess myself of all cargoes and treasures which may be landed in the Island of Teneriffe.

Having the firmest confidence in the ability, bravery, and zeal of yourself, and all placed under your command, I have only to heartily wish you success, and to assure you that I am your most obedient and faithful servant,

HORATIO NELSON

To the Governor, or Commanding Officer at Santa Cruz. By Sir Horatio Nelson, Knight of the Most Honourable Order of the Bath; Rear-Admiral of the Blue, and Commander-in-Chief of his Britannic Majesty's Forces by Sea and Land, before Santa Cruz.

Theseus, 20th July, 1797

Sir,

I have the honour to acquaint you, that I am come here to demand the immediate surrender of the Ship *El Principe d'Asturias*, from Manilla bound to Cadiz, belonging to the Philippine Company, together with her whole and entire cargo; and also all such other cargoes and property as may have been landed in the Island of Teneriffe, and not intended for the consumption of its Inhabitants. And, as it is my earnest wish that not one individual inhabitant of the Island of Teneriffe should suffer by my demand being instantly complied with, I offer the following most honourable and liberal Terms; which if refused, the horrors of war, which will fall on the Inhabitants of Teneriffe, must be by the World imputed to you, and to you only; for I shall destroy Santa Cruz, and the other Towns in the Island, by a bombardment, and levy a very heavy contribution on the Island.

Article 1st

The Forts shall be delivered to me; and instantly a party of the British troops shall be put in possession of the gates.

Article 2nd

The Garrison shall lay down their arms; but the Officers shall be allowed to keep their swords, and the Garrison, without the condition of being prisoners of War, shall be transported to Spain, or remain in the Island whilst their conduct is orderly and proper, as the Commanding Officer pleases.

Article 3rd

Upon the express condition that the full and entire cargoes of *El Principe d'Asturias*, and all such other cargoes and property as may have been landed on the Island of Teneriffe, and not intended for the consumption of its Inhabitants, (shall be surrendered,) and the first Article complied with, not the smallest contribution shall be levied on the Inhabitants; but they shall enjoy the fullest protection in their persons and properties.

Article 4th

No interference whatever shall be made in the Holy Catholic

Religion; the Ministers of it, and all its Religious Orders, shall be considered as under my especial care and protection.

Article 5th

The Laws and Magistrates shall be continued as at present, unless by the general wish of the Islanders. These Terms subscribed to, the Inhabitants of the Town of Santa Cruz shall lodge their arms in one house, under the joint care of the Bishop and Chief Magistrate; and it will be my pride to consult with those Gentlemen, what may be most advantageous for the Inhabitants.

HORATIO NELSON

I allow half of one hour for acceptance or rejection.

HORATIO NELSON

NELSON LOSES HIS ARM

[The first attack on Santa Cruz was intended for the night of the 21st July, but the ships were discovered before a landing could be made.

The following letter announced Nelson's intention to renew the attack in person on the night of the 24th July. It is supposed to be the last he wrote with his right hand.

Nelson begged his son-in-law, Lieutenant Nisbet, to remain behind. 'Should we both fall, Josiah, what would become of your poor mother? The care of the *Theseus* falls to you; stay, therefore, and take charge of her.' 'Sir,' replied Nisbet, 'the ship must take care of herself. I will go with you tonight, if I never go again.']

To Admiral Sir John Jervis *Theseus*, off Santa Cruz, *July 24th, 8 p.m.*

My dear Sir,

I shall not enter on the subject while we are not in possession of Santa Cruz; your partiality will give credit that all has hitherto been done which was possible, but without effect: this night I, humble as I am, command the whole, destined to land under the batteries of the Town, and to-morrow my head will probably be crowned with either laurel or cypress. I have only to recommend Josiah Nisbet to you and my Country. With every affectionate wish for your health, and every blessing in this world, believe me your most faithful,

HORATIO NELSON

The Duke of Clarence, should I fall in the service of my King and Country, will, I am confident, take a lively interest for my Son-in-Law, on his name being mentioned.

[The attack on Santa Cruz failed and Nelson was obliged to withdraw his force, losing a large number of officers and men killed, drowned and wounded. The Governor of Santa Cruz behaved in the handsomest manner and Nelson thanks him in the next letter.]

To His Excellency Don Antonio Gutierrez, Commandant-General of the Canary Island

His Majesty's Ship, *Theseus*,
opposite Santa Cruz de Teneriffe, *26th July, 1797*

Sir,

I cannot take my departure from this Island, without returning your Excellency my sincerest thanks for your attention towards me, by your humanity in favour of our wounded men in your power, or under your care, and for your generosity towards all our people who were disembarked, which I shall not fail to represent to my Sovereign, hoping also, at a proper time, to assure your Excellency in person how truly I am, Sir, your most obedient, humble Servant,

HORATIO NELSON

P.S. I trust your Excellency will do me the honour to accept of a Cask of English beer and a cheese.

[In the assault on the Mole, Nelson received a severe wound from grape-shot in the right elbow. Nisbet applied a tourniquet and thereby perhaps saved Nelson's life.]

AFTER THE FAILURE AT SANTA CRUZ

To Admiral Sir John Jervis

Theseus, July 27th, 1797

My dear Sir,

I am become a burthen to my friends, and useless to my Country; but by my letter wrote the 24th, you will perceive my anxiety for the promotion of my son-in-law, Josiah Nisbet. When I leave your command, I become dead to the World; I go hence, and am no more seen. If from poor Bowen's loss, you think it proper to oblige me, I rest confident you will do it; the Boy is under obligations to me, but he repaid me by bringing me from the Mole of Santa Cruz.

I hope you will be able to give me a frigate, to convey the remains of my carcase to England. God bless you, my dear Sir, and believe me, your most obliged and faithful,

HORATIO NELSON

You will excuse my scrawl, considering it is my first attempt.

To Admiral Sir John Jervis

(*see Frontispiece*) *Theseus, August 16th, 1797*

My dear Sir,

I rejoice at being once more in sight of your Flag, and with your permission will come on board the *Ville de Paris*, and pay you my respects. If the *Emerald* has joined, you know my wishes. A left-handed Admiral will never again be considered as useful, therefore the sooner I get to a very humble cottage the better, and make room for a better man to serve the State; but whatever be my lot, believe me, with the most sincere affection, ever your most faithful,

HORATIO NELSON

Turn over.

The papers I sent by Waller were, I find, neither *correct* or all which I wished to send. I send you the total by Captain Miller.

Lord St. Vincent's answer:

Ville de Paris, 16th August, 1797

My dear Admiral,

Mortals cannot command success; you and your Companions have certainly deserved it, by the greatest degree of heroism and perseverance that ever was exhibited. I grieve for the loss of your arm, and for the fate of poor Bowen and Gibson, with the other brave men who fell so gallantly. I hope you and Captain Fremantle are doing well; the *Seahorse* shall waft you to England the moment her wants are supplied. Your Son-in-law is Captain of the *Dolphin* Hospital-ship, and all other wishes you may favour me with shall be fulfilled, as far as is consistent with what I owe to some valuable Officers in the *Ville de Paris*. We expect to hear of the Preliminaries of Peace being agreed on every hour. I have betted 100*l* that they were settled on or before the 12th, and that the Definitive Treaty is signed before that day month. Give my love to Mrs. Fremantle. I will salute her and bow to your stump to-morrow morning, if you will give me leave. Yours most truly and affectionately,

ST. VINCENT

To Lady Nelson

Theseus, at Sea, *August 3rd, 1797*

My dearest Fanny,

I am so confident of your affection, that I feel the pleasure you will receive will be equal, whether my letter is wrote by my right hand or left. It was the chance of war, [the failure at Santa Cruz] and I have great reason to be thankful; and I know that it will add much to your pleasure in finding that Josiah, under God's Providence, was principally instrumental in saving my life. As to my health, it never was better; and now I hope soon to return to you; and my Country, I trust, will not allow me any longer to linger in want of that pecuniary assistance which I have been fighting the whole war to preserve to her. But I shall not be surprised to be neglected and forgot, as probably I shall no longer be considered as useful. However, I shall feel rich if I continue to enjoy your affection. The cottage is now more necessary then ever. You will see by the papers, Lieutenant Weatherhead is gone. Poor fellow! he lived four days after he was shot. I shall not close this letter till I join the Fleet, which seems distant; for it's been calm these three days' past. I am fortunate in having a good surgeon on board; in short, I am much more recovered than I could have expected. I beg neither you or my father will think much of this mishap: my mind has long been made up to such an event. God bless you, and believe me

Your most affectionate husband,

HORATIO NELSON

August 16th

Just joined the Fleet perfectly well, and shall be with you, perhaps, as soon as this letter. Good Earl St. Vincent has made Josiah a Master and Commander. I shall come to Bath the moment permission comes from the Admiralty for me to strike my Flag. Sir Peter feels himself authorised to give me leave of absence, when the first you hear of me will be at the door. God bless you and my father, and ever believe me,

Your most affectionate,

HORATIO NELSON

To William Suckling

Seahorse, off Scilly,
August 30th, 1797

My dear Sir,

As I can write but slowly, I am forced to begin my letter a great way from Portsmouth, where, please God, I am bound. I have ever been a trouble to you, and am likely so to continue, as I have now to request you will have the goodness to ask the Collector of the Customs at Portsmouth to take care of my wine, and such things as I may place under his care, till I can find a hut to put my mutilated carcase in.

It is my intention to set off directly for Bath, if the Admiral can give me leave of absence, but to be in London in one week. Pray, remember me kindly to Mrs. Suckling, and all my good friends near you, and believe me,

Your most affectionate Nephew,

HORATIO NELSON

To Evan Nepean, Secretary to the Admiralty

Seahorse, Spithead, *1st September*, *1797*

Sir,

I have the honour to acquaint you of my arrival here, agreeable to orders, of which the enclosed is a copy. And I have to request their Lordships' permission to go on shore for the recovery of my wounds.

I have the honour to be, &c.

HORATIO NELSON

[Having received permission to strike his Flag on 3rd September, Nelson immediately proceeded to Bath, where he joined his wife and father.]

To the Rev. Mr. Nelson, Hilborough

Bath, *September 6th*, *1797*

My dear Brother,

Yesterday brought me your truly affectionate letter. As to my personal health, it never was better, and my arm is in the fairest way of soon healing. Next week, I intend to be in Town, and it is not impossible, but I may visit Norfolk for a few days, especially if a decent house is likely to be met with near Norwich; but Wroxham very far indeed exceeds my purse. Bath will be my home till next spring. I think our good Father is not in the smallest degree altered. Lady Nelson joins me in kind love to Mrs. Nelson, our Aunt, and friends at Swaffham, and believe me, your most affectionate brother,

HORATIO NELSON

I left Captain Nisbet perfectly well. He saved my life by his recollection in stopping the bleeding.

Letter from Lady Nelson to Mr. William Suckling

Bath, *Wednesday*,
September 6th, *1797*

My dear Sir,

I beg you will accept the united thanks of my dear husband and myself for your kind inquiries and truly friendly invitation to your house, which we would have accepted had it not been for the necessity of my husband's arm being dressed every day by a surgeon. We purpose being in London the middle of next week. I have written to Mr. M. Nelson to take us a lodging, and as soon as my husband can do without a surgeon, we shall spend some time with you. Earl Spencer has written a handsome letter, and is to be in town next week. My husband's spirits are very good, although he suffers a good deal of pain—the arm is taken off very high, near the shoulder. Opium procures him rest, and last night he was pretty quiet. The Corporation have handsomely congratulated him on his safe arrival. Such a letter from Lord Hood!—it does him honour, and I have forgot the ill treatment of former years which my good man received from him. Everything which concerns my husband I know you feel interested in, therefore, shall not make any excuses for what I have told you.

To H.R.H. the Duke of Clarence

September 7th, 1797

Sir,

I trust your Royal Highness will attribute my not having sent a letter since my arrival to its true cause—viz., the not being now a ready writer. I feel confident of your sorrow for my accident; but I assure your Royal Highness, that not a scrap of that ardour with which I have hitherto served our King has been shot away.

I am, &c.

HORATIO NELSON

[It being intended to grant Nelson a Pension of £1,000 a year, custom rendered it necessary that he should state his services in a Memorial to the King.]

TO THE KING'S MOST EXCELLENT MAJESTY,
THE MEMORIAL OF SIR HORATIO NELSON, K.B., AND REAR-ADMIRAL
IN YOUR MAJESTY'S FLEET

Humbly Sheweth,

That, during the present War, your Memorialist has been in four Actions with the Fleets of the Enemy—viz,. on the 13th and 14th of March 1795, on the 13th of July 1795, and on the 14th of February 1797; in three Actions with Frigates; in six Engagements against Batteries; in ten Actions in Boats employed in cutting out of Harbours, in destroying Vessels, and in taking three Towns. Your Memorialist has also served on shore with the Army four months, and commanded the Batteries at the Sieges of Bastia and Calvi;

That, during the War he has assisted at the Capture of seven Sail of the Line, six Frigates, four Corvettes, and eleven Privateers of different sizes, and taken and destroyed near fifty Sail of Merchant Vessels; and your Memorialist has actually been engaged against the Enemy upwards of one hundred and twenty times. In which Service your Memorialist has lost his right eye and arm, and been severely wounded and bruised in his body. All of which Services and wounds your Memorialist most humbly submits to your Majesty's most gracious consideration.

HORATIO NELSON

About October, 1797.

To Lieut. Governor Locker, Royal Hospital, Greenwich

October 11th, 1797

My dear Sir,

Many thanks for your kind letter, I sincerely wish my arm

[The remainder is in Lady Nelson's hand-writing.]

Thus far my husband has begun his letter to you, but an appointment with a friend of his prevent his concluding; therefore, in his name and my own, we shall rejoice to see you on Thursday. I thank Lord St. Vincent for his notice. I wish my Captain* had wrote us a line.

Yours very sincerely,

FRANCES H. NELSON

Sir H. Nelson attends the Drawing-room, therefore you are sure of him.

Pray give our Compliments to Mr. L., and ask him to take a family dinner on Thursday or Friday with us. We expect you.

To the Chamberlain of the City of London.†

Sir Horatio Nelson presents his most respectful Compliments to the Chamberlain of the City of London, and begs leave to acquaint him, that he will attend at his Office on Tuesday next, at one o'clock, unless any other hour should be more agreeable.

* Her son, Captain Nisbet.

† On the 28th December, 1797, Nelson received the Freedom of the City of London, in a gold box valued at 100 guineas.

Wednesday, November 22nd, 1797

Thanksgiving in St. George's Church, Hanover-Square, London.

An Officer desires to return Thanks to Almighty God for his perfect recovery from a severe Wound, and also for the many mercies bestowed upon him.

December 8th, 1797

To Captain Berry, Norwich

Secret, except to Dr. Forster and Miss
December 8th, 1797

My dear Sir,

If you mean to marry, I would recommend your doing it speedily, or the to be Mrs. Berry will have very little of your company; for I am well, and you may expect to be called for every hour. We shall probably be at sea before the *Foudroyant* is launched. Our Ship is at Chatham, a Seventy-four, and she will be choicely manned. This may not happen, but it stands so to-day.

Ever yours most faithfully,

HORATIO NELSON

NELSON HOISTS HIS FLAG IN VANGUARD

To Captain Ralph Willett Miller

December 11th, 1797

My dear Sir,

As I have not the hand of a ready writer, my friends must put up (at the best) with short letters, and oftener excuse my writing anything. I could say nothing of you anywhere, or to any person, that was not pleasant to your friends, and strictly true. John Bull does not forget the *Captain* on the 14th February, for both at the London Tavern and Guildhall after 'Lord Duncan' (the last Action being the best) 'and his Fleet', comes 'Earl St. Vincent and the glorious 14th February'; then 'Sir H. N., and the brave Officers and men who fought on board the *Captain* on the 14th February'; and had our Battle been in the Channel, it would have been so much the better for us.

[The following, except the Signature and Postscript, is in Lady Nelson's writing.]

Lady Nelson and myself called to see your little girl at Mr. Taylor's. She is a very fine girl, and a great favourite with Mr. and Mrs. Taylor, who seem very fond and kind to her. They are, I am sure, good people, and spoke in most affectionate terms of Mrs. Miller. It is fixed I am to have the *Vanguard*. She will be out of dock in ten days; and as there are many Ships paying off at Chatham, I shall be well manned and soon; therefore I am in hopes of joining Lord St. Vincent some time in February. Lady Nelson begs you will accept her compliments.

Believe me, your sincere

HORATIO NELSON

Berry is married, but still goes with me. Many thanks for your letters.

[On 13th December, Nelson being pronounced fit for service, the *Foudroyant* was intended to receive his Flag, but the ship not being in a sufficiently forward state, the *Vanguard* was substituted for her.]

To Earl Spencer, First Lord of the Admiralty

Admiralty, Noon, Monday
(apparently *December 18th, 1797*)

My Lord,

I am just from Chatham. The *Vanguard* will be out of dock at half-past one this day, and ready to receive men whenever your Lordship is pleased to direct her being Commissioned.

Ever your most obedient,

HORATIO NELSON

CHAPTER FOUR

THE NILE CAMPAIGN

[The next section of Nelson's letters cover the period from January, 1798, to August, 1799, the most important and the most critical years of his life—public and private, including as they do the battle of the Nile which made him a world figure and his growing intimacy with Lady Hamilton.

Nelson hoisted his flag as Rear Admiral of the Blue in H.M.S. *Vanguard* on 29th March, 1798, and in the following June he was entrusted with the command of a powerful squadron of twelve Sail of the Line and ordered to seek out the French armament and to take, sink, burn or destroy it.

He carried out all four of these injunctions. Later in the period under notice he became involved in complicated measures associated with the defence of the kingdom of Naples against the French, the execution of the Italian naval officer Caraccioli and a growing and passionate attachment to Lady Hamilton.

It was during this period also that he was created Lord Nelson of the Nile and Duke of Bronte; and it was also at this time that he disobeyed the orders of the Commander-in-Chief in the Mediterranean, Lord Keith, who had directed him to send his squadron for the protection of Minorca. For this failure to obey orders he was censured by the Admiralty.]

To Thomas Lloyd, May's Buildings, London

Bath, *January 29, 1798*

My dear Lloyd,

There is nothing you can desire me to do that I shall not have the greatest pleasure in complying with, for I am sure you can never possess a thought that is not most strictly honourable. I was much flattered by the Marquis's kind notice of me, and I beg you will make my respects acceptable to him. Tell him that I possess his place in Mr. Palmer's box; but his Lordship did not tell me all its charms, that generally some of the handsomest ladies in Bath are partakers in the box, and was I a bachelor I would not answer for being tempted; but as I am possessed of everything which is valuable in a wife, I have no occasion to think beyond a pretty face. I am sorry the King is so poor. Had he been worth what those vile dogs of Opposition think, what a vast sum would have been given to the Nation; but I now hope all the

Nation will subscribe liberally*. You will believe that I do not urge others to give, and to withhold myself; but my mode of subscribing will be novel in its manner, and by doing it, I mean to debar myself of many comforts to serve my country, and I expect great consolation every time I cut a slice of salt beef instead of mutton. The *Vanguard* will be at Sheerness, Saturday, and, if this wind holds, she will be at Portsmouth before Thompson† quits the Channel. I only pray that the French may not be ready to leave Brest. I have been in a fever ever since the *Boadicea's* return with the account of their being ready for sea. Lady Nelson and my father thank you for your kind remembrance of them, and believe me, my dear Lloyd,

Your most affectionate

HORATIO NELSON

To the Rev. Edmund Nelson, Bath

London, *14th March, 1798*

My dear Father,

I thank you for your affectionate letter, as indeed yours always are; and I hope in a few months to return with the olive branch, and to find you in as good a state as when we parted. I have this day taken leave of the King; and on Saturday I expect to be ordered to leave Town for Portsmouth, where I hope I shall not remain forty-eight hours, but my movements now depend on Lord Spencer. Lady Nelson intends setting out for Bath the same moment I do for Portsmouth. At all times, and in all places, believe me ever, with the truest filial affection, your dutiful Son,

HORATIO NELSON

[At 8 p.m. on the 29th March, Nelson hoisted his flag, Blue at the Mizen, on board the *Vanguard*, at Spithead. She stayed some days at St. Helen's and left England on 10th April, with the Portugal, Gibraltar and Mediterranean convoy, to join Lord St. Vincent's Fleet at Lisbon.]

On placing Nelson again under Lord St. Vincent's command, Lord Spencer wrote:

'*30th March, 1798*

'I am very happy to send you Sir Horatio Nelson again, not only because I believe I cannot send you a more zealous, active, and approved

* A voluntary subscription for the support of the war.

† Vice-Admiral Sir Charles Thompson, third in command of the Channel Fleet, under Lord Bridport.

officer, but because I have reason to believe that his being under your command will be agreeable to your wishes. If your Lordship is as desirous to have him with you as he is to be with you, I am sure the arrangement must be perfectly satisfactory.'

Lord St. Vincent wrote in reply, on 1st May:

'I do assure your Lordship that the arrival of Admiral Nelson has given me new life: you could not have gratified me more than in sending him; his presence in the Mediterranean is so very essential, that I mean to put the *Orion* and *Alexander* under his command, with the addition of three or four Frigates, and to send him away the moment the *Vanguard* has delivered her water to the in-shore squadron, to endeavour to ascertain the real object of the preparations making by the French.'

To Lady Nelson — Lisbon, *24th April, 1798*

We arrived here yesterday, in fourteen days from St. Helen's. Lord St. Vincent is at sea off Cadiz, having wished to prevent some Spanish Ships from getting out, but without effect; for one Ship of the Line, the *Monarca*, and two Frigates, escaped on the 12th; the *Neptuno* 84, and two more Frigates, are also on the wing, but I hope they will not escape his vigilance. The *Dolphin* is here, and her Captain, Josiah is very well.* If possible, I shall sail to-morrow to join the Fleet. I can hardly describe to you the miserable appearance of this place after seeing England. I pray fervently for Peace. Yours, &c.

HORATIO NELSON

To the Duke of Clarence — *April 24th, 1798*

The new Viceroy of Mexico has got off. By their Detachments, it does not appear probable that the Spanish Fleet will put to sea for the sake of fighting; therefore, I fear we shall have a dull campaign off Cadiz; and the Earl's force will not, I apprehend, admit of his detaching me up the Mediterranean, to endeavour to get hold of the French Squadron, now masters of that sea. I am, &c.

HORATIO NELSON

* His stepson, Josiah Nisbet, then commanded the *Dolphin*, of 24 guns.

To Lady Nelson Lisbon, *1st May, 1798*

I joined the Fleet yesterday, and found Lord St. Vincent everything I wished him; and his friends in England have done me justice for my zeal and affection towards him. I have my fears that he will not be much longer in this Command, for I believe he has written to be superseded, which I am sincerely sorry for. It will considerably take from my pleasure in serving here; but I will hope for the best. The Dons have, I find, long expected my return with Bomb-vessels, Gun-boats, and every proper implement for the destruction of Cadiz and their Fleet. They have prepared three floating batteries to lie outside their walls, to prevent the fancied attack; and, lo, the mountain has brought forth a mouse:—I am arrived with a single Ship, and without the means of annoying them. The Admiral probably is going to detach me with a small Squadron; not on any fighting expedition, therefore do not be surprised if it should be some little time before you hear from me again. I direct this to our Cottage,* where I hope you will fix yourself in comfort and I pray that it may very soon please God to give us Peace. England will not be invaded this summer. Buonaparte is gone back to Italy, where 80,000 men are embarking for some expedition. With every kind wish that a fond heart can frame, believe me, as ever, your most affectionate husband.

HORATIO NELSON

To the Captains of the *Orion*, *Alexander* and *Vanguard*

Gibraltar Bay, *7th May, 1798*

It being of the very greatest importance that the Squadron should not be separated, it is my positive orders that no temptation is to induce a Line-of-Battle Ship to separate from me, except the almost certainty of bringing a Line-of-Battle Ship of the Enemy to Action; but in common chaces, if the weather is such as to risk separation, or the approach of night, it is my directions you leave off the chace, and rejoin me, even without waiting the signal of Recall, unless I make the signal to continue the pursuit, by No. 104, page 30, S.B.

HORATIO NELSON

* Before Nelson left England, he obtained the object he had so long desired by purchasing a 'cottage' and a few acres of land, called 'Round-Wood', near Ipswich. On 28th May, Lady Nelson wrote to him: 'On Sunday, the 20th of May, we arrived at Round-Wood. The satisfaction I felt was very great on being under your own roof. No thanks to any earthly being. Our Father was for staying, although the house had little or no accommodation. He viewed everything attentively, and I never saw him so thoroughly satisfied as he was, and says the more he examines everything the better he is pleased. The house is quite large enough.'

[The Squadron sailed from Gibraltar on 8th May. On the 11th Lord St. Vincent issued another order to Nelson, which stated that the Admiralty having directed that the whole naval force under his (Lord St. Vincent's) command should be collected 'to prepare for a service of very great importance,' he was, after ranging the coast of Provence and the Western Riviera of Genoa, or before if he discovered that the preparations on the coast were forward, to make the best of his way to Gibraltar with his line of battle ships and worst sailing frigates, and on his arrival there to use all dispatch in completing the water and provisions of the Squadron, and to join him off Cadiz. This order was accompanied by a letter in which St. Vincent said, 'The Admiralty has at last discovered that it is necessary to provide a force to look after the French in the Mediterranean,' and that some ships were expected from England. He added, 'You, and you only, can command the important service in contemplation; therefore make the best of your way down to me, or the first division from England will be here before you. I shall bring Murray from Lisbon, for the *Colossus* is now most powerfully manned, and he is too good a fellow to be left there when so much is to be done. You shall also have some choice Fellows of the in-shore Squadron.']

To Lord St. Vincent. *Vanguard*, off Cape Sicie, *May 17th, 1798*

My Lord,

This morning, the *Terpsichore* captured a small French Corvette, of six guns and sixty-five men, which came out of Toulon at 11 o'clock, last night. From the general report of Vessels spoke, you will observe the uniformity of the reports—viz., that an expedition is preparing to sail from Toulon. We have separately examined the crew of this Corvette, and, from the whole, I believe the following may be depended on as near the truth—that Buonaparte arrived at Toulon last Friday and has examined the troops which are daily embarking in the numerous Transports; that Vessels with troops frequently arrive from Marseilles; it is not generally believed that Buonaparte is to embark, but no one knows to what place the Armament is destined. Fifteen Sail of the Line are apparently ready for sea, but nineteen are in the harbour, and yet it is said only six Sail of the Line are to sail with the Transports now ready; that about 12,000 men are embarked; their cavalry arrived at Toulon, but I cannot learn that any are yet embarked. Reports say they are to sail in a few days, and others that they will not sail for a fortnight. This Corvette was bound to the westward, I believe, with dispatches, but the Commander denies it.

The Admiral Brueys has his Flag in *L'Orient*, 120 guns; *Le Formidable* and *Spartanade*, of 80 guns, are also Flag-ships. The Venetian Ships are considered as very bad in every respect, but I do not learn that the

Fleet is deficient in either men or stores. All this information is but little more than you knew when I left you, but, still, knowing that late information of the state of the Enemy's Fleet is desirable, I send an intelligent young man, Mr. Charles Harford, who has just served his Time, with this letter, and I beg leave to recommend him to your notice. You may rely, my Lord, that I shall act as occasions may offer, to the best of my abilities, in following up your ideas for the honour of His Majesty's Arms, and the advantage of our Country, and believe me, your Lordship's obedient Servant,

HORATIO NELSON

I saw three French Frigates this afternoon, but as they did not see the Squadron, I am in hopes of getting near them. The Squadron is as I wish them.

VANGUARD *DISMASTED IN A GALE*

[On the night of 20th May when off Toulon and almost within sight of the great French Armament under Buonaparte, the *Vanguard* was dismasted in a furious gale, suffered very severe damage and was in the gravest danger of driving on to a lee shore. She was saved by the *Alexander* (Captain Ball) taking her in tow.]

Vanguard, Island of St. Peter's, in Sardinia,
May 24th, 1798

My dearest Fanny,

I ought not to call what has happened to the *Vanguard* by the cold name of accident: I believe firmly, that it was the Almighty's goodness, to check my consummate vanity. I hope it has made me a better Officer, as I feel confident it has made me a better Man. I kiss with all humility the rod.

Figure to yourself a vain man, on Sunday evening at sun-set, walking in his cabin with a Squadron about him, who looked up to their Chief to lead them to glory, and in whom this Chief placed the firmest reliance, that the proudest Ships, in equal numbers, belonging to France, would have bowed their Flags; and with a very rich Prize lying by him. Figure to yourself this proud, conceited man, when the sun rose on Monday morning, his Ship dismasted, his Fleet dispersed, and himself in such distress, that the meanest Frigate out of France would have been a very unwelcome guest. But it has pleased Almighty God to bring us into a safe Port, where, although we are refused the rights of humanity, yet the *Vanguard* will in two days get to sea again, as an English Man-of-War.

The exertions of Sir James Saumarez, in the *Orion*, and Captain A. Ball, in the *Alexander*, have been wonderful; if the Ship had been in England, months would have been taken to send her to sea: here, my operations will not be delayed four days, and I shall join the rest of my Fleet on the rendezvous.

If this letter gets to you, be so good as to write a line to Lord Spencer, telling him that the *Vanguard* is fitted tolerably for sea, and that what has happened will not retard my operations. We are all health and good humour: tell Lady Saumarez Sir James never was in better health. With kind love to my Father, believe me ever your affectionate husband,

HORATIO NELSON

I have wrote to Lord S. by another, but I still wish you to write a line to say we are all well, for yours may arrive and his Lordship's miscarry.

P.S. Mr. Thomas Meek, who was recommended by Mr. Hussey and my brother Suckling, was killed, and several seamen were wounded.

To Lord St. Vincent

Vanguard, Island of St. Peter's, in Sardinia, *May 24th, 1798*

My Lord,

I am sorry to be obliged to inform you of the accidents which have happened to the *Vanguard*. On Saturday, May the 19th, it blew strong from the N.W. On Sunday it moderated so much, as to enable us to get our top-gallant masts and yards aloft. After dark it began to blow strong; but as the Ship was prepared for a gale, my mind was easy. At half-past one A.M. on Monday, the main-top-mast went over the side, as did soon afterwards the mizen-mast. As it was impossible for any night-signal to be seen, I had hopes we should be quiet till day-light, when I determined to wear, and scud before the gale; but about half-past three the fore-mast went in three pieces, and the bowsprit was found to be sprung in three places. When the day broke, we were fortunately enabled to wear the Ship with a remnant of the sprit-sail. The *Orion*, *Alexander*, and *Emerald* wore with us; but the *Terpsichore*, *Bonne Citoyenne*, and a French Smyrna-ship, continued to lay to under bare poles. Our situation was 25 leagues south of the Islands of Hieres; and as we were laying with our head to the N.E., had we not wore, which was hardly to be expected, the Ship must have drifted to Corsica. The gale blew very hard all the day, and the Ship laboured most exceedingly. In the evening, being in latitude 40° 50′ N., I determined to steer for Oristan Bay, in the Island of Sardinia: during the night, the *Emerald* parted company, for what reason I am at present unacquainted with. Being unable to get into Oristan, the *Alexander* took us in tow, and by Captain Ball's unremitting attention to our distress, and by Sir James Saumarez's exertions and ability in finding out the Island of St. Peter's, and the proper anchorage, the *Vanguard* was, on May the 23rd, at noon, brought safely to an anchor into the harbour of St. Peter's.

I have the honour to be, &c.

HORATIO NELSON

To the Viceroy of Sardinia

His Britannic Majesty's Ship *Vanguard*,
At Anchor, off the Island of St. Peter's,
26th May, 1798

Sir,

Having, by a gale of wind sustained some trifling damage, I anchored a small part of his Majesty's Fleet, under my orders, off this Island, and was surprised to hear, by an Officer sent by the Governor, that admittance was to be refused to the Flag of his Britannic Majesty into this Port. When I reflect that my most gracious Sovereign is the oldest, (I believe,) and certainly the most faithful, Ally which his Majesty of Sardinia ever had, I could feel the sorrow which it must have been to his Majesty to have given such an order, and also for your Excellency, who has to direct its execution. I cannot but look at Africa's shore, where the followers of Mahomet are performing the part of the good Samaritan, which I look for in vain at St. Peter's, where it is said the Christian Religion is professed. May I request the favour of your Excellency to forward one Letter for his Britannic Majesty's Minister at Turin, and the other for his Britannic Majesty's Consul at Leghorn. May God Almighty bless your Excellency is the sincere wish of your most obedient servant,

HORATIO NELSON

To Lord St. Vincent

31st May, 1798

My dear Lord,

My pride was too great for man; but I trust my friends will think that I bore my chastisement like a man. It has pleased God to assist us with his favour, and here I am again off Toulon. I am, &c.

HORATIO NELSON

ORDER OF BATTLE AND SAILING

Vanguard 2 Points Order of Sailing		No.	Ships	Captains	Guns	Men
All Frigates to repeat		1	*Culloden*	T. Troubridge	74	590
		2	*Theseus*	R. W. Miller	74	590
		3	*Alexander*	A. J. Ball	74	590
Leander	Starboard Squadron	.4	*Vanguard*	Edward Berry	74	595
		5	*Minotaur*	Thomas Louis	74	640
		6	*Swiftsure*	B. Hallowell	74	590
		7	*Audacious*	David Gould	74	590
		8				
All Frigates to repeat	Larboard Squadron	9	*Defence*	John Peyton	74	590
		10	*Zealous*	Samuel Hood	74	590
		11	*Orion*	Sir J. Saumarez	74	590
		12	*Goliath*	Thomas Foley	74	590
		13	*Majestic*	G. B. Westcott	74	590
		14	*Bellerophon*	H. D'E. Darby	74	590

Given on board his Majesty's Ship *Vanguard*, at Sea, 7th June, 1798.

HORATIO NELSON

A copy of this delivered to each of the Captains of the Line-of-Battle Ships:—Captain Thompson, of the *Leander*.

THE NILE CAMPAIGN

[On the 19th May, 1798, Lord St. Vincent received most secret instructions from the Admiralty, dated the 2nd of that month. 'Your Lordship is to lose no time in detaching from your Fleet a Squadron, consisting of twelve Sail of the Line, and a competent number of Frigates, under the command of some discreet Flag-Officer, into the Mediterranean, with instructions to him to proceed in quest of the said Armament; and on falling in with it, or any other force belonging to the Enemy, to take or destroy it. Your Lordship is to direct the Commanding Officer of the above-mentioned Squadron, to remain upon this service so long as the provisions of the said Squadron will last, or as long as he may be enabled to obtain supplies from any of the ports in the Mediterranean, and when, from want of provisions, or any other circumstance, he shall be no longer able to remain within the Straits, to lose no time in rejoining you.'

These instructions were accompanied by a private and confidential letter from Lord Spencer, dated the 29th April, 1798, which dwelt at some considerable length on the late proceedings of the Cabinet, the state of the Continent, and the probable intentions of the French

Armament at Toulon. The appearance of a British Squadron in the Mediterranean was declared to be a condition on which the fate of Europe at that moment depended; every nerve was to be strained, and considerable hazard incurred, in effecting it: yet the Government entirely left it to Lord St. Vincent's determination, either to make a Detachment from his Fleet, or to take his whole force into the Mediterranean; and the defeat of the purpose of the Toulon Armament, whatever it might be, was to have preference to the great advantages which had hitherto been obtained, from the constant check which St. Vincent had kept on the Spanish Fleet in Cadiz. This check, however, was, if possible, to be continued; and it was hoped that it might be found practicable to send a Detachment from the Fleet into the Mediterranean sufficiently strong to attain the end proposed. 'If you determine', added Lord Spencer, 'to send a detachment, I think it almost unnecessary to suggest to you the propriety of putting it under the command of Sir H. Nelson, whose acquaintance with that part of the world, as well as his activity and disposition seem to qualify him in a peculiar manner for that service. We shall take care to send you out Ships which are the best suited for Foreign service of any that we have to dispose of: in order to make your Fleet as effective as possible . . . I have thought it necessary to enter into this reasoning, to impress your Lordship with the great urgency and importance of the measure which has now been determined upon, and to justify our calling upon you to place yourself, at least for a short time, in a situation of more difficulty than any less pressing emergency would warrant us in doing.'

The selection of so young a Rear-Admiral as Nelson, in preference to his seniors in St. Vincent's Fleet—viz. Sir William Parker and Sir John Orde, naturally gave great offence to those officers. Writing to Nelson, on the 22nd June, St. Vincent said: 'Sir William Parker and Sir John Orde have written strong remonstrances against your commanding the detached Squadron, instead of them. I did all I could to prevent it consistently with my situation; but there is a faction fraught with all manner of ill will to you, that, unfortunately for the two Baronets, domin'd over any argument or influence I could use. They will both be ordered home the moment their letters arrive.'

It had been doubted by whom the selection of Nelson for this important service was actually made. The instructions to St. Vincent would seem to have left the matter entirely in his hands; but Spencer's private letter allowed St. Vincent little discretion, as he was all but ordered to appoint Nelson.

The following Orders from St. Vincent to Nelson, dated 21st May, 1798, were brought by Captain Troubridge, in the *Culloden*: 'In pursuance of instructions I have received from the Lords Commissioners of the Admiralty, to employ a Squadron of his Majesty's Ships within the Mediterranean, under the command of a discreet Officer, (copies of which are enclosed and of other papers necessary for your guidance) in conformity thereto, I do hereby authorize and require

You, on being joined by the Ships named in the margin (*Culloden*, *Goliath*, *Minotaur*, *Defence*, *Bellerophon*, *Majestic*, *Audacious*, *Zealous*, *Swiftsure*, *Theseus*) to take them and their Captains under your command, in addition to those already with you, and to proceed with them in quest of the Armament preparing by the Enemy at Toulon and Genoa, the object whereof appears to be, either an attack upon Naples and Sicily, the conveyance of an Army to some part of the Coast of Spain, for the purpose of marching towards Portugal, or to pass through the Straits, with the view of proceeding to Ireland. On falling in with the said Armament, or any part thereof, you are to use your utmost endeavours *to take, sink, burn, or destroy it*. Should it appear to you, from good authority, on your arrival up the Mediterranean, that the Enemy's force capable of being sent to sea, should be inferior to what is reported by the intelligence herewith transmitted, you are in this case to direct such Ships to rejoin me as may not absolutely be required to insure your superiority the moment you shall find yourself in a situation so to do. You are to remain upon this Service so long as the provisions of your Squadron will last, or as long as you may be enabled to obtain supplies from any of the Ports in the Mediterranean, and when, from the want of provisions or any other circumstance, you shall be no longer able to remain within the Straits, *or that the Enemy's armament should escape to the westward of you, which you shall take especial care to prevent*, you are to lose no time in rejoining me, wherever I may be.']

THE CHASE BEGINS

To Lord St. Vincent *June 11th*

The *Mutine*, Captain Hardy, joined me on the 5th, at day-light, with the flattering account of the honour you intended me of commanding such a Fleet.* *Mutine* fell in with *Alcmene*, off Barcelona on the 2nd. Hope† had taken all my Frigates off the rendezvous, on the presumption that the *Vanguard*, from her disabled state, must return to an Arsenal. I joined dear Troubridge with the reinforcement of ten Sail of the Line, and the *Leander* on the 7th in the evening:‡ it has been nearly calm ever

* 'Tuesday, 5th June, H.M. Brig, *La Mutine*, joined the Squadron, when Captain Hardy came on board with orders for me, and to acquaint me that Captain Troubridge, with ten Sail of the Line, was coming to join me, and that Captain Hope had taken my Frigates off the rendezvous.' 'This intelligence was received,' says Captain Berry, 'with universal joy throughout our little Squadron, and the Admiral observed to me, that he would then be a match for any hostile Fleet in the Mediterranean, and his own desire would be to encounter one.'

† Captain George Hope, of the *Alcmene*.

‡ '7th June.—At 10 m. past 1, discovered a strange Fleet, E. by N., which I supposed to be the Squadron under Captain Troubridge. After I made the Private Signal, I observed it was answered by the *Culloden* shewing her distinguishing Pendants,

since, which grieves me sorely. The French have a long start§ but I hope they will rendezvous in Telamon bay, for the 12,000 men from Genoa in 100 Sail of Vessels, escorted by a Frigate, had not put to sea on the 2nd, nor were all the troops embarked. You may be assured I will fight them the moment I can reach their Fleet, be they at anchor, or under sail, I am, &c.

HORATIO NELSON

To Lord St. Vincent *12th of June, 1798*

As I see no immediate prospect of a Letter, I shall continue my private one in form of a Diary, which may not be unpleasant to refer to: therefore to begin. Being so close to the Enemy, I take the liberty of keeping *Orion* for a few days. Owing to want of wind, I did not pass Cape Corse until this morning; at four we were becalmed. The moment we had passed, I sent the *Mutine* to look into Telamon Bay, which, as all the French troops had not left Genoa on the 6th, I thought a probable place for the rendezvous of a large Fleet; and went with the Squadron between Monte Christi, and Giulio, keeping the Continent close on board.

13th of June.—*Mutine* joined; nothing in Telamon Bay. I then ran the Fleet between Plenosa and Elba, and Monte Christi; and on the 14th at noon, am now off Civita Vecchia; spoke a Tunisian cruiser, who reported he had spoke a Greek, on the 10th, who told him, that on the 4th, he had passed through the French Fleet, of about 200 Sail, as he thought, off the N.W. end of Sicily, steering to the eastward. Am in anxious expectation of meeting with Dispatch-boats, Neapolitan cruisers, &c., with letters for me from Naples giving me information.

15th of June.—Off the Ponza Islands; my hopes of information were vain. Not finding a Cruiser, I shall send Troubridge into Naples, in the *Mutine*, to talk with Sir William Hamilton and General Acton. Troubridge possesses my full confidence, and has been my honoured acquaintance of twenty-five years' standing. I only beg that your Lordship will believe, I shall endeavour to prove myself worthy of your selection of me for this highly honourable Command. Not a moment shall be lost in pursuing the Enemy. I am, &c.

HORATIO NELSON

by which I was satisfied the Ships in sight were the Squadron sent to join me. 30 m. past 6, the under-mentioned Ships having joined me, I hove-to the Fleet.' (*Vanguard's* log). The ships were the *Culloden, Bellerophon, Minotaur, Defence, Zealous, Audacious, Goliath, Majestic, Swiftsure, Theseus, Leander.*

§ The French Fleet sailed from Toulon on 20th May; and on the 14th June, Nelson learnt, from a vessel spoken by the *Leander*, that on the 4th of that month, the French Fleet were seen off Trapani in Sicily, steering to the eastward.

To Earl Spencer — *Vanguard*, off the Island of Ponza, *15th June, 1798*

My Lord,

Not having received orders from my Commander-in-Chief to correspond with the Secretary of the Admiralty, I do not feel myself at perfect liberty to do it, unless on extraordinary occasions, when I shall send copies of my Letters to Lord St. Vincent; but as your Lordships must be anxious to hear of us, I take the liberty of acquainting you that Captain Troubridge joined on the 7th, but it was the 12th before we passed Cape Corse. The last account I had of the French Fleet, was from a Tunisian Cruiser, who saw them on the 4th, off Trapani, in Sicily, steering to the eastward. If they pass Sicily, I shall believe they are going on their scheme of possessing Alexandria, and getting troops to India—a plan concerted with Tippoo Saib, by no means so difficult as might at first view be imagined; but be they bound to the Antipodes, your Lordship may rely that I will not lose a moment in bringing them to Action, and endeavour to destroy their Transports. I shall send Captain Troubridge on shore to talk with General Acton, and I hope the King of Naples will send me some Frigates; for mine parted company on the 20th of May, and have not joined me since. The whole Squadron is remarkably healthy, and perfectly equal to meet the French Fleet. As I send this before I receive accounts from Naples, it is not in my power to say anything more of the Enemy, for I shall make sail and pass the Faro of Messina the moment Captain Troubridge returns.

Highly honoured as I feel with this very important command, I beg you will believe that I shall endeavour to approve myself worthy of it, and that I am, with the highest respect,

Your Lordship's most obedient servant,

HORATIO NELSON

I have taken the liberty of enclosing a letter for Lady Nelson, which I beg your Lordship will have the goodness to order to be sent to her.

To Lord St. Vincent — *Vanguard*, off the Islands of Ponza, *June 15th, 1798*

My Lord,

I have the honour to acquaint you of my arrival here with the whole Line-of-Battle Ships, the Fifty, and Brig, all in the most perfect health. I am sending Captain Troubridge in the *Mutine* to see Sir William Hamilton and General Acton, and to get accounts of the French Fleet. I shall lay with the Squadron off Ischia till Captain Troubridge's return, when not a moment shall be lost in pursuing the Enemy, and bringing them to Action. With the highest respect, believe me, your Lordship's most obedient servant,

HORATIO NELSON

[Captain Troubridge had been sent ahead in the *Mutine* to communicate with the British Minister at Naples, Sir William Hamilton and the Prime Minister of Naples, Sir John Acton. Nelson wished to know if the King of Naples would aid him with supplies, frigates, pilots, &c.

Troubridge returned on 17th June to the Squadron which was hove-to ten miles off Naples. Nelson described the reply which he brought as 'no aid for us—no hostility to the French'.

It was to overcome this 'shivering hesitation' that the wife of the British Minister, Lady Hamilton, employed all her powers and influence with, among others, the Queen of Naples, to gain stores and supplies for the Fleet.]

From Lady Hamilton to Lord Nelson.

17th June, 1798

Dear Sir,

I send you a letter I have received this moment from the Queen. *Kiss it* and send it back by (Captain) Bowen, as I am bound not to give any of her letters.

Ever your

EMMA

To Lady Hamilton

6 p.m.; 17th June, 1798

My dear Lady Hamilton,

I *have* kissed the Queen's letter. I may say I hope for the honour of kissing her hand when no fears will intervene; assure her Majesty that no person has her felicity more at heart than myself and that the sufferings of her family will be a Tower of Strength on the day of Battle, fear not the event, God is with us; God bless you and Sir William; pray say that I cannot stay to answer his letter.

Ever Yours faithfully,

HORATIO NELSON

Lady Hamilton endorsed this letter:

'This letter I received after I had sent the Queen's letter for receiving our ships into their ports, for the Queen had decided to act in opposition to the King, who would not then break with France and our Fleet must have gone back to Gibraltar to have watered, and the battle of the Nile would not have been fought, for the French Fleet would have got back to Toulon.'

[Meanwhile Malta had surrendered to the French Fleet on 15th June, two days earlier.]

To Sir William Hamilton *Vanguard*, off the Faro of Messina, *June 20th, 1798*

My dear Sir,

I have thought so much, and heard so much, of the French, since I left Naples, that I should feel culpable, was I for a moment to delay expressing my sentiments on the present situation of the Kingdom of the Two Sicilies. I trust it will be received as I mean it—as proof of the lively interest I take in the fate of their Sicilian Majesties. I shall begin by supposing myself commanding a Fleet attending an Army which is to invade Sicily. If the General asked if Malta would not be a most useful place for the depot of stores, &c., &c., my answer would be, if you can take Malta, it secures the safety of the Fleet, Transports, stores, &c., and insures your safe retreat should that be necessary; for if even a superior Fleet of the Enemy should arrive, before one week passes, they will be blown to leeward, and you may pass with safety. This would be my opinion. There can be no doubt but the French know as well as you and I do, that their Sicilian Majesties called for our help to save them, (even this is crime enough with the French). Here we are, and are ready, and will shed our blood in preventing the French from ill-treating them. On the arrival of the King's Fleet I find plenty of good will towards us, with every hatred towards the French; but no assistance for us—no hostility to the French. On the contrary, the French Minister is allowed to send off Vessels to inform the Fleet of my arrival, force, and destination, that instead of my surprising them, they may be prepared for resistance. But this being past, I shall endeavour briefly to state what in my opinion is now best to be done, and what Naples ought to do, if it is earnestly wished to save Sicily. I shall suppose the French not advanced since the last accounts, but still on Gozo and Comino, the Fleet anchored between them. By the communication from Naples, they will be formed in the strongest position, with Batteries and Gun-boats to flank them. We shall doubtless injure them, but our loss must be great; and I do not expect to force them from the anchorage, without Fire-ships, Bomb-vessels, and Gun-boats when one hour would either destroy or drive them out. If our Fleet is crippled, the blockade ends; if not, it will be continued, by attention, and sending two Ships at a time to Sicily to get refreshments, for the summer, at least; but whenever this Fleet may be drawn away, and the Ministry find what has passed at Naples—*no co-operation*, although we are come to their assistance—who can say that the Fleet will be kept in these seas? I have said and repeat it, *Malta is the direct road to Sicily.* It has been, and may be yet in the King of Naples' power, by giving me help of every kind, directly to destroy this Armament, and force the Army to unconditional submission. Naples must soon find us masts, yards, stores, ammunition, &c., &c. Will not this be a declaration of War against the French?—therefore why delay sending help, if it is only six Gun-boats at a time. But not a moment must be lost—it can never be regained. I recollect General Acton, in his letter to you calling for our help, says, 'Will the King and Ministry wish to see these fine Countries in the hands of the French?' the answer is, No; and we have sent the means of preventing it. It may now be asked—will the Ministry of their Sicilian Majesties permit these fine Countries to fall into the hands of the French? This will assuredly happen if they do not co-operate with us. If I have wrote my mind too freely, I trust it will be excused. The importance of the subject called for my opinion. I have given it like an honest man, and shall wish to stand or fall with it.

I am, dear Sir, with the highest respect, &c.

HORATIO NELSON

(On the 26th, Alexandria bearing at noon S.68 E.233 miles. 'At 9 a.m. Captain Hardy, of the *Mutine*, came on board, per signal. I gave him orders to proceed to Alexandria, and endeavour to procure intelligence of the French Fleet, then to join me, immediately after having delivered my Dispatches to the British Consul, which I committed to his charge.')

To George Baldwin, Consul at Alexandria

Vanguard, at Sea, *26th June, 1798*

Sir,

The French having possessed themselves of Malta, on Friday, the 15th of this month, the next day, the whole Fleet, consisting of sixteen Sail of the Line, Frigates, Bomb-vessels, &c. and near three hundred Transports, left the Island. I only heard this unpleasant news on the 22nd, off Cape Passaro. As Sicily was not their object, and the wind blew fresh from the westward, from the time they sailed, it was clear that their destination was to the eastward; and I think their object is, to possess themselves of some Port in Egypt, and to fix themselves at the head of the Red Sea, in order to get a formidable Army into India; and, in concert with Tippoo Saib, to drive us, if possible, from India. But I have reason to believe, from not seeing a Vessel, that they have heard of my coming up the Mediterranean, and are got safe into Corfu. But still I am most exceedingly anxious to know from you if any reports or preparations have been made in Egypt for them; or any Vessels prepared in the Red Sea, to carry them to India, where, from the prevailing winds at this season, they would soon arrive; or any other information you would be good enough to give me, I shall hold myself much obliged.

I am, Sir, &c.

HORATIO NELSON

To Sir William Hamilton

Vanguard, Syracuse, *July 20th, 1798*

My dear Sir,

It is an old saying, 'the Devil's children have the Devil's luck.' I cannot find, or to this moment learn, beyond vague conjecture where the French Fleet are gone to. All my ill fortune, hitherto, has proceeded from want of Frigates. Off Cape Passaro, on the 22nd of June, at day-light, I saw two Frigates, which were supposed to be French, and it has been said since that a Line of Battle Ship was to leeward of them, with the riches of Malta on board, but it was the destruction of the Enemy, not riches for myself, that I was seeking. These would have fallen to me if I had had Frigates, but except the Ship of the Line, I regard not all the riches in this world. From every information off Malta I believed they were gone to Egypt. Therefore, on the 28th, I was communicating with Alexandria in Egypt, where I found the Turks preparing to resist them, but know nothing beyond report. From thence I stretched over the Coast of Caramania, where not meeting a Vessel that could give me information, I became distressed for the Kingdom of the Two Sicilies, and having gone a round of 600 leagues at this season of the year (with a single Ship) with an expedition incredible, here I am as ignorant of the situation of the Enemy as I was twenty-seven days ago. I sincerely hope, that the Dispatches which I understand are at Cape Passaro, will give me full information. I shall be able for nine or ten weeks longer to keep the Fleet on active service, when we shall want provisions and stores. I send a paper on that subject herewith. Mr. Littledale is, I suppose, sent up by the Admiral to victual us, and I hope he will do it cheaper than any other person; but if I find out that he charges more than the fair price, and has not the provisions of the very best quality, I will not take them; for, as no Fleet has more fag than this, nothing but the best food and greatest attention can keep them healthy. At this moment, we have not one sick man in the Fleet. In about six days I shall sail from hence, and if I hear nothing more from the French, I shall go to the Archipelago where if they are gone towards Constantinople I shall hear of them. I shall go to Cyprus, and if they are gone to Alexandretta, or any other part of Syria or Egypt, I shall get information. You will, I am sure, and so will our Country, easily conceive what has passed in my anxious mind, but I have this comfort, that I have no fault to accuse myself of. This bears me up, and this only. I send you a Paper, in which a letter is fixed for different places, which I may leave at any place, and except those who have the key, none can tell where I am gone to.

July 21st.—The Messenger has returned from Cape Passaro, and says, that your letters for me are returned to Naples. What a situation am I placed in! As yet, I can learn nothing of the Enemy; therefore I have no conjecture but that they are gone to Syria, and at Cyprus I hope to hear of them. If they were gone westward, I reply that every place in Sicily would have information for us, for it is news too important to leave me one moment in doubt about. I have no Frigate, nor a sign of one. The masts, yards, &c., for the *Vanguard* will, I hope, be prepared directly; for should the French be so strongly secured in Port that I cannot get at them, I shall immediately shift my Flag into some other Ship, and send the *Vanguard* to Naples to be refitted; for hardly any other person but myself would have continued on service so long in such a wretched state. I want to send a great number of Papers to Lord St. Vincent, but I dare not trust any person here to carry them even to Naples. Pray send a copy of my letter to Lord Spencer. He must be very anxious to hear of this Fleet. I have taken the liberty to trouble your Excellency with a letter for Lady Nelson. Pray forward it for me, and believe me, with the greatest respect, your most obedient Servant,

HORATIO NELSON

To Lady Nelson — Syracuse, *July 20th, 1798*

I have not been able to find the French Fleet, to my great mortification, or the event I can scarcely doubt. We have been off Malta, to Alexandria in Egypt, Syria, into Asia, and are returned here without success: however, no person will say that it has been for want of activity. I yet live in hopes of meeting these fellows; but it would have been my delight to have tried Buonaparte on a wind, for he commands the Fleet, as well as the Army. Glory is my object, and that alone. God Almighty bless you.

HORATIO NELSON

To the Commanders of any of His Majesty's Ships

Vanguard, Syracuse, *22nd July, 1798*

Sir,

Resting with the greatest confidence that had the French Fleet proceeded to the westward from Malta, that his Majesty's Minister at

Naples would have taken care to have lodged information for me in every Port in Sicily, knowing I was gone to the eastward, I now acquaint you that I shall steer direct for the Island of Cyprus, and hope in Syria to find the French Fleet. I am, &c.

HORATIO NELSON

Having received some vague information of the Enemy, I shall steer to the north of Candia, and probably send a Ship to Milo, and if the Enemy are not in those seas, I shall pass on for Cyprus, Syria, and Egypt.*

THE BATTLE OF THE NILE

[Nelson sailed from Syracuse on 24th July and proceeded to the Morea where intelligence was gained that the French Fleet had been seen steering to the S.E., whereupon Nelson made all sail for Alexandria.

At 4 p.m. on the afternoon of 1st August, 1798, the *Zealous* made the signal for the French Fleet, sixteen Sail of the Line, at anchor in Aboukir Bay.

The Battle began at sunset (6.30) and was fought after nightfall.]

The rival squadrons were as follows:

ENGLISH

Ship	Guns	Men	Killed	Wounded
Vanguard	74	595	30	75
Orion	74	590	13	29
Culloden	74	590	0	0
Bellerophon	74	590	49	148
Defence	74	590	4	11
Minotaur	74	640	23	64
Alexander	74	590	14	8
Audacious	74	590	1	35
Zealous	74	590	1	7
Swiftsure	74	590	7	22
Majestic	74	590	50	143
Goliath	74	590	21	41
Theseus	74	590	5	30
Leander	50	343	0	14
	1,012	8,068	218	677

* At the end of the copy of this letter in the 'Letter Book', which was long in Lady Hamilton's possession, she wrote: 'The Queen's letter, privately got by me, got him and his Fleet victualled and watered in a few days – EMMA HAMILTON.'

FRENCH

Ship	Guns	Men	How disposed of
L'Orient	120	1,010	Burnt
Le Franklin	80	800	Taken
Le Tonnant	80	800	,,
Le Guerrier	74	700	,,
Le Conquérant	74	700	,,
Le Spartiate	74	700	,,
Le Timoléon	74	700	Burnt
Le Souverain Peuple	74	700	Taken
L'Heureux	74	700	,,
Le Mercure	74	700	,,
L'Artemise	36	300	Burnt
L'Aquilon	74	700	Taken
La Sérieuse	36	300	Sunk
L'Hercule (*Bomb*)		50	Burnt
La Fortune	18	70	Taken
Le Guillaume Tell	80	800	Escaped
Le Généreux	74	700	,,
La Justice	40	400	,,
La Diane	40	400	,,
	1,196	11,230	

Complement of Men on board the French Ships burnt, taken and sunk at the Battle of the Nile, as by certificates from the Commissaries and Officers of the different Ships		8,930
Sent on shore by cartel, including the wounded, as by certificates from Captain Barré of *L'Aceste* ..	3,105	
Escaped from the *Timoléon*	350	
Escaped from *L'Hercule* (Bomb)	50	
Officers, Carpenters, and Caulkers, Prisoners on board the Fleet	200	
		3,705
Taken, drowned, burnt and missing		5,225

HORATIO NELSON

[As Nelson was a Rear-Admiral of the Blue, the Blue Ensign was the proper Colours of his Squadron. Pursuant, however, to an order from the Earl of St. Vincent, the White, or Saint George's Ensign was used in the Battle, because it was more distinct from the French Flag (the tri-colour, blue, white, and red, vertically) than either a Blue or Red Ensign; and thus the Red Cross of Saint George, the ancient Banner of England, witnessed that glorious victory.]

To Lord St. Vincent *Vanguard*, off the Mouth of the Nile,
3rd August, 1798

My Lord,

Almighty God has blessed his Majesty's Arms in the late Battle, by a great Victory over the Fleet of the Enemy, who I attacked at sunset on the 1st of August, off the Mouth of the Nile. The Enemy were moored in a strong Line of Battle for defending the entrance of the Bay, (of Shoals,) flanked by numerous Gun-boats, four Frigates, and a Battery of Guns and Mortars on an Island in their Van; but nothing could withstand the Squadron your Lordship did me the honour to place under my command. Their high state of discipline is well known to you, and with the judgment of the Captains, together with their valour, and that of the Officers and Men of every description, it was absolutely irresistible. Could anything from my pen add to the character of the Captains, I would write it with pleasure, but that is impossible.

I have to regret the loss of Captain Westcott of the *Majestic*, who was killed early in the Action; but the Ship was continued to be so well fought by her First Lieutenant, Mr. Cuthbert, that I have given him an order to command her till your Lordship's pleasure is known.

The Ships of the Enemy, all but their two rear Ships, are nearly dismasted: and those two, with two Frigates, I am sorry to say, made their escape; nor was it, I assure you, in my power to prevent them. Captain Hood most handsomely endeavoured to do it, but I had no Ship in a condition to support the *Zealous*, and I was obliged to call her in.

The support and assistance I have received from Captain Berry cannot be sufficiently expressed. I was wounded in the head, and obliged to be carried off the deck; but the service suffered no loss by that event; Captain Berry was fully equal to the important service then going on, and to him I must beg leave to refer you for every information relative to this Victory. He will present you with the Flag of the Second in Command, that of the Commander-in-Chief being burnt in *L'Orient*.

Herewith I transmit you Lists of the Killed and Wounded, and the Lines of Battle of ourselves and the French. I have the honour to be, my Lord, your Lordship's most obedient Servant,

HORATIO NELSON

To the Respective Captains of the Squadron

Vanguard, off the Mouth of the Nile,
2nd August, 1798

Almighty God having blessed His Majesty's Arms with Victory, the Admiral intends returning Public Thanksgiving for the same at two o'clock this day; and he recommends every Ship doing the same as soon as convenient.

HORATIO NELSON

To the Captains of the Ships of the Squadron

Vanguard, off the Mouth of the Nile,
2nd day of August, 1798

The Admiral most heartily congratulates the Captains, Officers, Seamen, and Marines of the Squadron he has the honour to command, on the event of the late Action; and he desires they will accept his most sincere and cordial Thanks for their very gallant behaviour in this glorious Battle. It must strike forcibly every British Seaman, how superior their conduct is, when in discipline and good order, to the riotous behaviour of the lawless Frenchmen.

The Squadron may be assured the Admiral will not fail, with his Dispatches, to represent their truly meritorious conduct in the strongest terms to the Commander-in-Chief.

HORATIO NELSON

[On 3rd August, the Captains of the Squadron met on board the *Orion*, Captain Sir James Saumarez, the senior Captain, and second in command.]

'The Captains of the Squadron under the Orders of Rear-Admiral Sir Horatio Nelson, K.B., desirous of testifying the high sense they entertain of his prompt decision and intrepid conduct in the Attack of the French Fleet, in Bequier Road, off the Nile, the 1st of August, 1798, request his acceptance of a Sword; and, as a further proof of their esteem and regard, hope that he will permit his Portrait to be taken, and hung up in the Room belonging to the Egyptian Club, now established in commemoration of that glorious day.

'Dated on board of His Majesty's Ship, *Orion*, this 3rd of August, 1798.

Jas. Saumarez — D. Gould
T. Troubridge — Th. Foley
H. D. Darby — R. Willett Miller
Tho. Louis — Ben. Hallowell
John Peyton — E. Barry
Alex. John Ball — T. M. Hardy
Sam. Hood.'

To the Captains of His Majesty's Ships off the Nile

Vanguard, August 3rd, 1798

Gentlemen,

I feel most sensibly the very distinguished honour you have conferred upon me by your Address of this day. My prompt decision was the natural consequence of having such Captains under my command, and I thank God I can say, that in the Battle the conduct of every Officer was equal. I accept, as a particular mark of your esteem, the Sword you have done me the honour to offer, and will direct my Picture to be painted the first opportunity, for the purpose you mention.

I have the honour to be, Gentlemen,

With the highest respect, your most obliged,

HORATIO NELSON

The Rt. Hon. Lord Nelson, K.B.

My Lord,

Herewith I send you a Coffin made of part of *L'Orient's* Main mast, that when you are tired of this Life you may be buried in one of your own Trophies—but may that period be far distant, is the sincere wish of your obedient and much obliged servant,

Ben Hallowell

Swiftsure, May 23rd, 1799'

[Astonishment prevailed among the crew of the *Vanguard* when they saw the coffin brought on board. 'We shall have hot work of it indeed,' said one of the Seamen; 'you see the Admiral intends to fight till he is killed, and there he is to be buried.' Nelson highly appreciated the present, and for some time had it placed upright, with the lid on, against the bulk-head of his cabin, behind the chair on which he sat at dinner. While his Officers were one day looking at it, he came out of the cabin: 'You may look at it, Gentlemen, as long as you please: but, depend on it, none of you shall have it.' Nelson was buried in this Coffin.]

THE BAND OF BROTHERS

Captain Sir James Saumarez, of the *Orion*, which he commanded at the Battle of St. Vincent.

Captain Thomas Troubridge, of the *Culloden*, which he commanded at the Battle of St. Vincent.

Captain Henry D'Esterre Darby, of the *Bellerophon*.

Captain Thomas Louis, of the *Minotaur*.

Captain John Peyton, of the *Defence*.

Captain Alexander John Ball, of the *Alexander*.

Captain Samuel Hood, of the *Zealous*.
Captain Davidge Gould, of the *Audacious*.
Captain Thomas Foley, of the *Goliath*. He was Captain of the *Britannia*, bearing the Flag of Sir Charles Thompson, at the Battle of St. Vincent, and commanded the *Elephant*, which bore Nelson's Flag at Copenhagen in 1801.
Captain Ralph Willett Miller, of the *Theseus*.
Captain George Blagdon Westcott, of the *Majestic*, was killed in the Battle, and a monument was erected to his memory in St. Paul's, at the Public expense.
Captain Thomas Boulden Thompson, of the *Leander*, who again distinguished himself by his 'gallant and almost unprecedented defence' of that ship against *Le Généreux* of 74 guns, on the 18th August, 1799, when he was severely wounded and made prisoner.
Captain Benjamin Hallowell, of the *Swiftsure*, in which he was captured by a French Squadron, in June, 1801, after a gallant defence.
Captain Edward Berry, of the *Vanguard*. He was knighted in December, 1798.
Captain Thomas Masterman Hardy, of the *Mutine* Brig. Though, from the insignificant size of his vessel, Captain Hardy can scarcely be included in the list of Captains who commanded ships in the battle, yet, as he was the only other Captain present, he cannot properly be omitted. He was posted into the *Vanguard*, and was Nelson's Captain in the *Victory*, at Trafalgar.

To the Lord Mayor of London *Vanguard*, Mouth of the Nile, *8th August, 1798*

My Lord,

Having the honour of being a Freeman of the City of London, I take the liberty of sending to your Lordship, the Sword of the Commanding French Admiral, Monsieur Blanquet, who survived after the Battle of the first, off the Nile; and request, that the City of London will honour me by the acceptance of it, as a remembrance, that Britannia still rules the Waves, which, that She may for ever do, is the fervent prayer of your Lordship's most obedient Servant,

HORATIO NELSON

To Earl Spencer, First Lord of the Admiralty

Mouth of the Nile, *9th August, 1798*

My Lord,

Was I to die this moment, 'Want of Frigates' would be found stamped on my heart. No words of mine can express what I have, and am suffering for want of them. Having only the *Mutine* Brig, I cannot yet send off Captain Capel, which I am very anxious to do; for as an accident may happen to Captain Berry,* it is of some importance, I think, for your Lordship to be informed of our success as speedily as possible. If the King of Naples had joined us, nothing at this moment could prevent the destruction of the Store Ships, and all the Transports, in the Port of Alexandria; four Bomb-vessels would burn the whole in a few hours; but, as I have not means, I can only regret the circumstance.

I send you a pacquet of intercepted Letters, some of them of great importance; in particular, one from Buonaparte to his brother. He writes such a scrawl, no one not used to it can read; but luckily, we have got a man who has wrote in his Office, to decipher it. Buonaparte has differed with his Generals here; and he did want—and if I understand his meaning, does want, and will strive to be, the Washington of France. 'Ma mère' is evidently meant 'my Country.' But I beg pardon: all this is, I have no doubt, well known to Administration. I believe our victory will, in its consequence, destroy this Army; at least, my endeavours shall not be wanting. I shall remain here for some time. I have thought it right to send an Officer (by Alexandretta, Aleppo, and Bussarah) over-land to India, with an account of what I have gathered from these Dispatches; which I hope will be approved. I have sent a copy of my Letter to the Board of Control, that they may give the necessary directions for paying the Officer's bills. If it should have gone to the East India Company, I hope that Board will forward it. Ever believe me,

Your Lordship's most obliged, and obedient Servant,

HORATIO NELSON

To the Hon. William Wyndham,
Minister at Florence *Vanguard, 21st August, 1798*

My dear Sir,

I received, three days ago, your letter of June 20th, and I beg leave to thank you for it. I send you a paper which will inform you of the extent of our victory. My health, from my wound, is become so indifferent, that I think of going down the Mediterranean, so soon as I arrive at Naples, unless I should find anything very extraordinary to detain me, when my health is of no consequence. The command, in my absence, will devolve on Captain Troubridge, than whom the King has not a better Sea-Officer. Sir James Saumarez is on his way to Gibraltar, with six of our Prizes; the others I burnt, that the Mediterranean might

* The accident thus provided against, did occur, by Captain Berry being taken prisoner in the *Leander*, nine days after the date of this letter.

not be left without Ships, for each Prize takes a Ship of the Line to man her, and attend to her wants. This you will believe, when I tell you that only two masts are standing, out of nine Sail of the Line. *L'Orient* certainly struck her colours, and did not fire a shot for a quarter of an hour before, unfortunately for us, she took fire; but although we suffer, our Country is equally benefited. She had on board near six hundred thousand pounds sterling; so says the Adjutant-General of the Fleet, who was saved out of her, and although he does not say she struck her colours, yet he allows that all resistance on her part was in vain. Admiral Brueys was killed early in the battle, and from the commencement of the fight, declared all was lost. They moored in a strong position in a Line of Battle, with Gun-boats, Bomb-Vessels, Frigates, and a gun and mortar Battery on an Island in their Van, but my band of friends was irresistible. The French Army is in possession of Alexandria, Aboukir, Rosetta, Damietta, and Cairo; and Buonaparte writes that he is sending a detachment to take possession of Suez and Fayoum.

By the intercepted letters from the Army (for we took the Vessel with Buonaparte's courier) they are grievously disappointed, the Country between their Posts completely hostile. I have little doubt but that Army will be destroyed by plague, pestilence, and famine, and battle and murder, which that it may soon be, God grant. The Turks will soon send an Army into Syria, and as for the present, we block them up by sea, they must soon experience great distress. I hope to find, on my arrival at Naples, that the Emperor and many other Powers are at war with the French, for until they are reduced there can be no peace in this world. The Admiral having sent up Mr. Littledale, the victualling of the Fleet does not rest with me.

September 7th

I feel so much recovered, that it is probable I shall not go home at present. The Turks have seized all French Ships in the Levant, in consequence of the taking a Turkish sixty-gun Ship at Alexandria, and seizing all Turkish property. This was done on the 14th of August. I shall always receive pleasure in hearing from you, both as a public and private man; and believe me, dear Sir, &c.

HORATIO NELSON

To Earl Spencer

Vanguard, 7th September, 1798

My Lord,

On the 15th August, I received Earl St. Vincent's most secret Orders and Letters. As not a moment was to be lost, I determined to destroy the three Prizes (*Guerrier*, *Heureux*, and *Mercure*,) which had not sailed with Sir James Saumarez, and they were set on fire on the 18th. I rest assured that they will be paid for, and have held out that assurance to the Squadron; for if an Admiral is, after a victory, only to look after the captured ships, and not distressing the Enemy, very dearly indeed does the Nation pay for the Prizes, and I trust that £60,000 will be deemed a very moderate sum; and I am bold to say, when the services, time, and men, with the expense of fitting those three Ships for a voyage to England is valued, that Government will save nearly as much as they are valued at. I rejoice, in the present instance, that a particular regard for my own interest cannot be supposed to actuate me, for if the moderate sum of £60,000 is paid, my share can only be £625, while if it is not paid, I have defrauded the Commander-in-Chief and the other Classes, of the sums set off against them—

Commander-in-Chief	£3,750	0	0
Junior Admirals, each	625	0	0
Captains, each	1,000	0	0
Lieutenants' Class, each	75	0	0
Warrant Officers, each	50	0	0
Petty Officers, each	11	0	0
Seamen and Marines, each	2	4	1

Your Lordship will do me the justice to say, that pay for Prizes, in many instances, (it is not a new idea of mine,) would be not only an amazing saving to the State, without taking into calculation what the Nation loses by the attention of Admirals to the property of the Captors, an attention absolutely necessary as a recompence for the exertions of the Officers and men. An Admiral may be amply rewarded by his feelings and the approbation of his superiors, but what reward have the inferior Officers and men but the value of the Prizes? If an Admiral takes that from them, on any consideration, he cannot expect to be well supported. However, I trust, as in all other instances, if, to serve the State, any persons or bodies of men suffer losses, it is amply made up to them; and in this I rest confident my brave associates will not be disappointed. I have the honour to be, &c.

HORATIO NELSON

DISPOSITION OF THE FLEET UNDER MY COMMAND

Vanguard, 13th September, 1798

Vanguard—Wants new masts and bowsprit, but shall defer getting them till I know the situation of

Culloden—To be careened at Naples.

Alexander—When her masts are reduced and secured, to be sent down the Mediterranean, unless particularly wanted for a month or six weeks.

Goliath—Ordered to be sent from Alexandria the moment the *Lion* arrives. Main-mast bad.

Zealous, *Swiftsure*, *Emerald*, *Alcmene*, *Seahorse*, *La Fortune*—Ordered to cruize off Alexandria as long as they can with propriety.

Thalia—Joined me this morning.

Terpsichore—Sent by Captain Dixon to Naples, and from thence to join the Commander-in-Chief. (Parted company 20th May).

Transfer—Never joined. Reported to be gone to Cyprus.

Lion—Joined Captain Hood off Alexandria, the 25th August.

Mutine—Going down with Dispatches.

Bonne Citoyenne—Gone to Naples.

Earl St. Vincent—With Captain Retalick, to join the Portuguese Squadron.

Portuguese Squadron—Returning from Alexandria, and requested to block up Malta.

Minotaur, *Audacious*—Ordered, when Sir James Saumarez gets between Sardinia and Minorca, to join me at Naples.

Orion, *Defence*, *Bellerophon*, *Theseus*, *Majestic*—On their passage to Gibraltar with the Prizes.

Flora, Cutter—Gone to Alexandria.

HORATIO NELSON

Began at Sea,
September 16th, 1798

My dearest Fanny,

It is hardly possible for me to know where to begin.* My head is almost

* About this time, Nelson received the letter from Lady Nelson, in which she mentioned his portrait: 'Round Wood, July 23, 1798. My dearest Husband, I am now writing opposite to your portrait. The likeness is great; I am well satisfied with Abbot. I really began to think he had no intention of letting me have my own property, which I am not a little attached to. Indeed, it is more than attachment—it is real affection. It is my company—my sincere friend, in your absence. Our good father was delighted with the likeness. The room is very near eleven feet therefore, it stands very well, opposite the East window.'

turned by letters already and what am I not to expect when I get on shore. Noise enough to distract me. My head is healed and I am better.

The Kingdom of the two Sicilies are mad with joy from the throne to the peasant all are alike. From Lady Hamilton's letter the situation of the Queen was truly pitiable. I only hope I shall not have to be witness to a renewal of it. I give you Lady Hamilton's words. 'How shall I describe the transports of the Queen? Tis not possible. She fainted, cried, kissed her husband, her children, walked frantic about the room, cried, kissed and embraced every person near here exclaiming "Oh, brave Nelson; Oh God bless and protect our brave deliverer! Oh Nelson, Nelson, what do we not owe you! Oh victor, saviour of Italy! Oh that my swollen heart could not tell him personally what we owe to him." ' You may judge of the rest, but my head will not allow to tell you half. So much for that.

My fag without success would have had no effect. But blessed be God for his goodness to me. I have your letters of May 22nd, June 11th and July 16th. The box you were so good as to send me with places, seal etc. if sent by *L'Aigle* is lost but never mind that, I feel equally your kindness. Do not send any more. What is likely to go on here time only can shew. I am sure I cannot guess, but as the French have only one regular ship of the line, tis not likely I shall see any more fighting. As to Round Wood if the place or neighbourhood is not to your satisfaction, I hope the country will put me in a situation of choosing another, but my dear Fanny unless you can game, and talk scandal, that is lies, most probably your company will never be coveted by country town tabbies. Young people have more goodness than old cats. I put Hoste into a sloop of war. I hope Lord St. Vincent will allow him to remain in her. His father is under no obligation to me. If he writes stuff tell him so. All must go to Earl St. Vincent I have not power to make a cook. The Queen of Naples has given Hoste a very elegant ring value at least £500 sterling. So much for being a messenger of good news. Sir James Saumarez is on his passage home, so that Lady Saumarez will have the pleasure of his company this winter. Had his wound been very little deeper it would have done his business but as it is, he is not the worse. Josiah is in the *Bonne Citoyenne*. I see no prospect of his being made post. I wish he was as great a favourite of Lord St. Vincent's as I wish him, but that is not my fault. However, I hope he will do well in time. He is young and will not endeavour to make him agreeable for his interest or comfort.

September 25th.—The poor wretched *Vanguard* arrived here on the 22nd. I must endeavour to convey to you something of what passed, but if it was so affecting to those only who are united in bonds of friendship what must it be to my dearest wife. My friends say everything which is most dear to me in this world. Sir William and Lady Hamilton came out to sea attended by numerous boats with emblems etc. My most respectable friends had really been laid up and seriously ill, first from anxiety and then from joy. It was imprudently told Lady Hamilton in a moment. The effect was a shot. She fell apparently dead and is not yet perfectly recovered from severe bruises. Alongside my honoured friends came, the scene in the boat appeared terribly affecting. Up flew her ladyship and exclaiming: 'Oh God is it possible,' fell into my arms more dead than alive. Tears however soon set matters to rights, when alongside came the King. The scene was in its way affecting. He took me by the hand, calling me his deliverer and preserver, with every other expression of kindness. In short all Naples calls me 'Nostra Liberatore' for the scene with the lower classes was truly affecting. I hope one day to have the pleasure of introducing you to Lady Hamilton. She is one of the very best women in this world. How few could have made the turn she has. She is an honour to her sex and a proof that even reputation may be regained, but I own it requires a great soul. Her kindness with Sir William to me is more than I can express. I am in their house, and I may now tell you it required all the kindness of my friends to set me up. Her ladyship, if Josiah was to stay, would make something of him and with all his bluntness I am sure he likes Lady Hamilton more than any female. She would fashion him in 6 months in spite of himself. I believe Lady Hamilton intends writing you.

May God Almighty bless you, my dearest Fanny, and give us in due time a happy meeting. Should the King give me a peerage I believe I scarcely need state the propriety of your going to court. Don't mind the expense. Money is trash. Again God Almighty bless you.

Ever your most affectionate

HORATIO NELSON

You cannot write to Naples by common post. The Admiralty or Secretary of State is the only way.

To Earl Spencer

Naples, *September 25th, 1798*

My Lord,

Culloden and *Alexander* arrived here the 16th. The former is at Castel-à-Mare, where every assistance is afforded her. *Alexander* is fitting for two months' service, when from her battered state she must go down the Mediterranean. Captain Ball is so anxious to get at the *Guillaume Tell*, that she will soon be ready. He is emulous to give the final blow to the French Navy in the Mediterranean (for I reckon, nor do the Enemy, the Venetian Ships as anything). I wish my friend Ball was fairly alongside of her: our Country need not fear the event. His activity and zeal are eminently conspicuous even amongst the Band of Brothers—each, as I may have occasion to mention them, must call forth my gratitude and admiration. On the 22nd, the wreck of *Vanguard* arrived in the Bay of Naples. His Sicilian Majesty came out three leagues to meet me, and directly came on board. His Majesty took me by the hand and said such things of our Royal Master, our Country, and myself, that no words I could use would in any degree convey what so apparently came from the Royal heart. From his Majesty, his Ministers, and every class, I am honoured by the appellation of 'Nostro Liberatore.'

You will not, my Lord, I trust, think that one spark of vanity induces me to mention the most distinguished reception that ever, I believe, fell to the lot of a human being, but that it is a measure of justice due to his Sicilian Majesty and the Nation. If God knows my heart, it is amongst the most humble of the creation, full of thankfulness and gratitude! I send your Lordship a correct statement of the loss of the Enemy in the Battle of the Nile. The hand of God was visible from the first to the last. The fate of *Généreux* and miserable condition of *Guillaume Tell* are farther proofs of it. All glory be to Him! Amen!

With my sincerest respects to Lady Spencer, the Dowager Lady Spencer, Lady Lucan, and those of your Lordship's family who have honoured me by their notice, and I beg you will allow me to assure you with what respect I am,

Your most faithful Servant,

HORATIO NELSON

I have this moment Letters from Mr. Wyndham at Florence, telling me, that three of the Venetian Ships (64s) with eleven Transports, are ready to sail from Toulon. I hope Naples is on the eve of declaring: also, *I hope*—but it is a distant one—that the Portuguese are off Malta, when all is right.

CHAPTER FIVE

NELSON AT NAPLES

To Lady Nelson *28th September, 1798*

The preparations of Lady Hamilton, for celebrating my birthday to-morrow, are enough to fill me with vanity; every ribbon, every button, has 'Nelson', &c. The whole service is marked 'H.N. Glorious 1st of August!'—Songs and Sonnetti are numerous beyond what I ever could deserve. I send the additional verse* to God save the King, as I know you will sing it with pleasure. I cannot move on foot or in a carriage, for the kindness of the populace; but good Lady H. preserves all the papers as the highest treat for you. The Queen yesterday, being still ill, sent her favourite son to visit, and bring me a letter from Her of gratitude and thanks.—Miserable accounts of *Le Guillaume Tell.* I trust God Almighty will yet put her into the hands of our King. His all-powerful hand has gone with us to the Battle, protected us, and still continues destroying the unbelievers: All glory be to God! The more I think, the more I hear, the greater is my astonishment at the extent and good consequences of our Victory.

Yours, &c.

HORATIO NELSON

To Lord St. Vincent *September 30th, 1798*

I trust, my Lord, in a week we shall be at sea. I am very unwell, and the miserable conduct of this Court is not likely to cool my irritable temper. It is a country of fiddlers and poets, whores and scoundrels.

I am, &c.

HORATIO NELSON

* 'Join we in Great Nelson's name,
First on the rolls of Fame,
Him let us sing.
Spread we his fame around,
Honour of British ground,
Who made Nile's shore's resound,
God Save the King.'

To Lord St. Vincent

4th October, 1798

My dear Lord,

I cannot, am not able to tell you the quantity I have to communicate. This Country by its system of procrastination will ruin itself: the Queen sees it, and thinks as we do. The Ministry, except Acton, are for putting the evil day off, when it will come with destruction. War at this moment can alone save these Kingdoms. I am decidedly in opposition to Gallo. General Mack is hourly expected here from Vienna, to command the Neapolitan Army: Acton says they are ready to march. I have scolded; anger is necessary. You will not believe I have said or done anything, without the approbation of Sir William Hamilton. His Excellency is too good to them, and the strong language of an English Admiral telling them plain truths of their miserable system may do good. Ball sails, if possible, to-morrow with *Terpsichore* and *Citoyenne*. Murray, who gives us everything he has, very handsomely goes off Malta with him for a few days. *Vanguard*, I hope, will be next, with *Audacious*, &c. Our wants are great, our means few. I need not tell you we cannot get much from this small Arsenal, but they give us all they have. *Culloden* is getting forward, Troubridge indefatigable: none but he could have saved poor *Culloden*. We all dine this day with the King on board a Ship, he is very attentive; I have been with the Queen, she is truly a daughter of Maria Theresa. I am writing opposite Lady Hamilton, therefore you will not be surprised at the glorious jumble of this letter. Were your Lordship in my place, I much doubt if you could write so well; our hearts and our hands must be all in a flutter: Naples is a dangerous place, and we must keep clear of it.

I am, &c.

HORATIO NELSON

To Lord St. Vincent *Vanguard*, Marsala, West End of Sicily, *22nd October, 1798*

My Lord,

On Monday the 15th, at 8 o'clock, the King and Prince Leopold came on board, and did me the honour of breakfasting. At 10, the Squadron named in the margin* weighed anchor, and at 11, his Majesty left the Ship, expressing himself in the most flattering manner towards me. His Majesty had all the respect paid him by the Squadron

* *Vanguard*, *Minotaur*, *Audacious*, *Goliath* and *Mutine*.

which our situation would admit of, and which it was not only our duty, but so much our inclination to pay him.

The King having desired my return to Naples in the first week in November, I shall, after having arranged the blockade of Malta, return to Naples, and endeavour to be useful in the movements of their Army. In thus acquiescing in the desire of the King of Naples, I give up my plan, which was to have gone to Egypt and attended to the destruction of the French Shipping in that quarter: but I hope before Captain Hood quits his Station, that both the Turks and Russian Squadrons will be on that Coast, when all will be right, I hope, although, I own myself not willing to trust any of our Allies to do that which we could do ourselves. I have reason for thinking that a strong wish for our Squadron's being on the Coast of Naples is, that in case of any mishap, that their Majesties' think their persons much safer under the protection of the British Flag than under any other. The *Culloden* would be ready for sea about this time. I have directed Captain Troubridge to wait my arrival, and also directed the Transports not to sail for Syracuse, as was my intention. On my passage, I met the *Emerald* from Egypt; left Captain Hood the 19th September—all going on well, and I have sent all Captain Hood's Letters to Sir William Hamilton. He will tell you their contents.

The *Emerald* is ordered to re-fit, and will be ready to sail on any Service wanted, or wait my arrival. The *Earl St. Vincent* Cutter is left for the express purpose of sailing the moment the Army marches out of the Kingdom. The *Terpsichore* I shall direct to be at Naples by the 20th November, and to sail for Gibraltar directly, as she wants, by her Captain's report, much repair. There being no wine to be bought at Naples for the Squadron, I anchored here yesterday evening, and having got 200 pipes of wine, I shall sail in the evening. Except with the black lion, we have not a sick man in the Squadron. I have the honour to be, &c.

HORATIO NELSON

To Captain Louis, H.M. Ship *Minotaur*

7th November, 1798

Sir,

I have this moment received your letter enclosing a Petition from the Ship's company of the *Minotaur*. In the common course of Service, I ought not to pay attention either to the Petition of your Ship's company, or to your kind interference in their behalf. I am glad, however, that the prisoners* have not presumed to say a syllable on their conduct, which merits the yard-arm.

But, Sir, I can never forget your noble and effectual support to my Flag on the most glorious First of August; and, in remembrance of the gallant conduct of the *Minotaur's* Ship's company, in obedience to your orders, I do, from these considerations alone, permit you to withdraw your letter for a Court-Martial on the prisoners. I am, &c.

HORATIO NELSON

To Captain Louis

7th November, 1798

Private.

I have endeavoured to write such a letter as I wish to be placed in public, and read to your Ship's company. Believe me, I shall never forget your support. 'A friend in need is a friend indeed': never was it better applied than to the *Minotaur*. I have written to Troubridge to stop the Court-Martial according to your request. I am, &c.

HORATIO NELSON

Lady Hamilton to Lady Nelson Naples, *December 2nd, 1798*

I hope your Ladyship received my former Letter, with an account of Lord Nelson's arrival, and his reception from their Sicilian Majesties, and also the congratulations and compliments from this amiable and adorable Queen to your Ladyship, which I was charged with, and wrote a month back, but as the posts were very uncertain, you may not have received that letter. Lord Nelson is gone to Leghorn with the Troops of the King of Naples, and we expect him soon back, as the King is gone to Rome with his Army, and he begged of my Lord Nelson to be as much at or about Naples as he could, not only to advise and consult with her Majesty (who is Regent) for the good of the common cause, but, *in case of accident*, to take care of her and her family. Lord Nelson is adored here, and looked on as the deliverer of this Country. He was not well when he first arrived, but by nursing and asses' milk, he went from Naples quite recovered. The King and Queen adore him, and if he had been their brother, they could not have shown him more respect and attentions. I need not tell your Ladyship how happy Sir William and

* Two men who had been guilty of mutinous conduct.

myself are at having an opportunity of seeing our dear, respectable, brave friend return here, with so much honour to himself, and glory for his Country. We only wanted you to be completely happy. Lord Nelson's wound is quite well. Josiah is so much improved in every respect, we are all delighted with him. He is an excellent Officer and very steady, and one of the best hearts in the world. I love him much, and although we quarrel sometimes, he loves me, and does as I would have him. He is in the way of being rich, for he has taken many prizes. He is indefatigable in his line, never sleeps out of his Ship, and I am sure will make a very great Officer. Lady Knight and her amiable daughter desire to be remembered to your Ladyship. I hope you received the Ode I sent. It is very well written; but Miss K. is very clever in everything she undertakes. Sir William desires his compliments to your Ladyship, and to Lord Nelson's dear respected father. The King is having his picture set with diamonds for his Lordship, and the Queen has ordered a fine set of China, with all the battles he has been engaged in, and his picture, painted on china. Josiah desired his duty to your Ladyship, and says he will write as soon as he has time, but he has been very busy for some time past. May God bless you and yours, my dear Madam, and believe me your Ladyship's ever sincere friend and humble servant,

EMMA HAMILTON

Sir William is in a rage with Ministers for not having made Lord N. a Viscount; for sure this great Action, greater than any other, ought to have been recompensed more. Hang them, I say!

[Before this letter was received by Lady Nelson, some suspicious reports seem to have reached her; for Nelson's intimate friend, Alexander Davison, writing to him on 7th December, said:

'I cannot help again repeating my sincere regret at your continuation in the Mediterranean; at the same time, I would be grieved that you should quit a station, if it in the smallest degree affected your own feelings. You certainly are, and must be, the best and only judge. Yet you must allow your best friends to express their sensations. . . . Your valuable better-half writes to you. She is in good health, but very uneasy and anxious, which is not to be wondered at. She sets off with the good old man to-morrow for Bath. . . . Lady Nelson this moment calls, and is with my wife. She bids me say, that unless you return home in a few months, she will join the Standard at Naples. Excuse a woman's tender feelings—they are too acute to be expressed.']

Naples, *December 11th, 1798*

My dearest Fanny,

You will of course get my letter from Leghorn. I arrived here on the 5th and the poor Queen has again made me promise not to quit her and her family till brighter prospects appear than do at present. The King is with the army and she is sole regent. She is in fact a Great King.

My correspondence has now the additional increase of a Turkish and Russian admiral which with what I had before takes all my time, but Lady Hamilton's goodness forces me out at noon for an hour. What can I say of her and Sir William's goodness to me. They are in fact with the exception of you and my dear father the dearest friends I have in this world. I live as Sir William's son in the house and my glory is as dear to them as their own. In short I am under such obligations that I can never repay but with my eternal gratitude.

The improvement made in Josiah by Lady Hamilton is wonderful. She seems the only person he minds, and his faults are not omitted to be told him but in such a way as pleases him, and his, your and my obligation are infinite on that score. Not but dear Josiah's heart is as good and as humane as ever was covered by human breast, but his manners are so rough, but God bless him I love him dearly with all his roughness.

I have not received the scrap of a pen from England since the 11th October. Lord St. Vincent is in no hurry to oblige me now. I am got he fancies too near him in reputation. In short I am the envied man, but better that than the pitied one. Never mind, it is my present intention if matters are in a good train to leave the country in March and to be in England in the latter end of May or beginning of June and to rest the four months.

May God bless you my dear Fanny and my father is the constant prayer of your most affectionate

NELSON

To Sir William Hamilton

Naples, *14th December, 1798*

Sir,

As I have been informed that this Kingdom is invaded by a formidable French Army, I think it my duty to acquaint your Excellency, for the information of the English Merchants and others residing at Naples, that the three English transports and others in this Bay have my directions to receive such effects of the English as they can stow, and that the whole Squadron is ready to receive their persons, should such an event be found necessary as for them to embark. I have the honour to be, &c.

NELSON

N.B. I need not say that I mean valuable effects, and not household furniture. I also beg leave to recommend that anything sent on board Ship should be done with as little bustle, and as much secrecy as possible.

To Captain Ball

Naples, *December 15th, 1798*

Most Secret.
My dear Ball,

I desire you will send me directly the *Goliath*, and order Foley to come through the Faro of Messina, that he may get information. He may very possibly see me there and some others. The situation of this Country is very critical—nearly all in it are traitors or cowards. God bless you. Keep this secret, except to caution Foley not to approach Naples but with great caution. I have nothing from England—am here with *Alcmene* and the Portuguese. All in this house join in best wishes and regards with your faithful friend,

NELSON

The *Flora* Cutter is lost, and I have nothing to send to you. Can you spare the *Incendiary*? Do not send a Neapolitan Ship: there are traitors in the *Marine*. In short, all is corrupt.

To Captain Troubridge

(On the following day, owing to the state of affairs at Naples, the *Vanguard* shifted her berth out of gun-shot of the Forts, and got one of the Neapolitan ships out of the Mole.)

Naples, *15th December, 1798*

Most Secret.

Things are in such a critical state here, that I desire you will join me without one moment's loss of time, leaving the *Terpsichore* in Leghorn Roads to bring off the Great Duke, should such a measure be necessary. Probably, I shall send Commodore Campbell very soon on that service.

The King is returned here, and everything is as bad as possible. For God's sake make haste! Approach the place with caution. Messina, probably, I shall be found at; but you can inquire at the Lipari Islands if we are at Palermo. Caution Gage to act with secrecy, and desire him to write to Wyndham, and give him those instructions which may be necessary at this time for his guarded conduct and secrecy. All here join in love and best regards with your faithful friend,

NELSON

THE EVACUATION OF NAPLES

Most Secret. Naples, *December 20th, 1798*

Three barges, and the small cutter of the *Alcmene*, armed with cutlasses only, to be at the Victoria at *half past seven* o'clock precisely. Only one barge to be at the wharf, the others to lay on their oars at the outside of the rocks—the small barge of the *Vanguard* to be at the wharf. The above boats to be on board the *Alcmene* before seven o'clock, under the direction of Captain Hope.

Grapnells to be in the boats.

All the other boats of the *Vanguard* and *Alcmene* to be armed with cutlasses, and the launches and carronades to assemble on board the *Vanguard*, under the direction of Captain Hardy, and to put off from her at half-past eight o'clock *precisely, to row half way towards the Mola Figlio. These boats to have 4 or 6 soldiers in them.*

In case assistance is wanted by me, false fires will be burnt.

NELSON

The Alcmene to be ready to slip in the night, if necessary.

EXTRACTS FROM THE VANGUARD'S *JOURNAL*

December 18th. Sailmakers making cots for the Royal Family: Painters painting the wardroom, and offices under the poop; getting ready for sea, and getting off the valuable effects of Her Sicilian Majesty in the night time.

Thursday, 19th. Smuggling on board the Queen's diamonds, &c.

Friday, 21st. At 10 a.m., their Sicilian Majesties and the Royal Family embarked on board, as did the British Ambassador and family, the Imperial Ambassador and suite, several of the Neapolitan nobles and their servants, and most of the English gentlemen and merchants that were at Naples.

Saturday, 22nd. Fresh breezes, unmoored.

Sunday, 23rd. More moderate, came under the stern and alongside, several Deputations from the City of Naples to His Sicilian Majesty: came on board also, General Mack, who had an audience and returned again to the shore. Weighed and made sail, at 7 p.m., in company with a Neapolitan Ship of the Line, a number of Merchant ships and the English transports.

After a stormy passage, in which the *Vanguard* split her three topsails, she anchored in Palermo Mole at two in the morning of Wednesday, 26th December.

At 5, His Sicilian Majesty and the Royal Family went on shore *incog.*, and at 9, His Majesty landed; manned ship, and cheered him until on shore; could not salute him by reason of being in the Mole. Found here two Spanish ships of 54 guns each, and a Frigate of 36 guns, and several Merchant-ships.

To Lord St. Vincent

Palermo, *December 28th, 1798*

My Lord,

On the 22nd, I wrote a line to Commodore Ducksworth, telling him, that the Royal Family of the Two Sicilies were safely embarked on board the *Vanguard*, and requested him to take the first opportunity of acquainting your Lordship of this event. For many days previous to the embarkation it was not difficult to foresee that such a thing might happen, I therefore sent for the *Goliath* from off Malta, and for Captain Troubridge in the *Culloden*, and his Squadron from the north and west Coast of Italy, the *Vanguard* being the only Ship in Naples Bay. On the 14th, the Marquis de Niza, with three of the Portuguese Squadron arrived from Leghorn, as did Captain Hope in the *Alcmene* from Egypt: from this time, the danger for the personal safety of their Sicilian Majesties was daily increasing, and new treasons were found out, even to the Minister of War. The whole correspondence relative to this important business was carried on with the greatest address by Lady Hamilton and the Queen, who being constantly in the habits of correspondence, no one could suspect. It would have been highly imprudent in either Sir William Hamilton or myself to have gone to Court, as we knew that all our movements were watched, and even an idea by the Jacobins of arresting our persons as a hostage (as they foolishly imagined) against the attack of Naples, should the French get possession of it.

Lady Hamilton, from this time to the 21st, every night received the jewels of the Royal Family, &c. &c., and such clothes as might be necessary for the very large party to embark, to the amount, I am confident, of full two millions five hundred thousand pounds sterling. On the 18th, General Mack wrote that he had no prospect of stopping the progress of the French, and entreated their Majesties to think of retiring from Naples with their august Family as expeditiously as possible. All the Neapolitan Navy were now taken out of the Mole, consisting of three Sail of the Line and three Frigates; the seamen from the two Sail of the Line in the Bay left their Ships and went on shore: a party of English seamen with Officers were sent from the *Vanguard* to assist in navigating them to a place of safety. From the 18th, various plans were formed for the removal of the Royal Family from the palace to the water-side; on the 19th, I received a note from General Acton, saying, that the King approved of my plan for their embarkation; this day, the 20th and 21st, very large assemblies of people were in commotion, and several people were killed, and one dragged by the legs to the palace. The mob by the 20th were very unruly, and insisted the Royal Family should not leave Naples; however, they were pacified by the King and Queen speaking to them.

On the 21st, at half-past 8 p.m. three Barges with myself and Captain Hope, landed at a corner of the Arsenal. I went into the Palace and brought out the whole Royal Family, put them into the Boats, and at half-past nine they were all safely on board the *Vanguard*, when I gave immediate notice to all British Merchants that their persons would be received on board every and any Ship in the Squadron, their effects of value being before embarked in the three English transports who were partly unloaded, and I had directed that all the condemned provisions should be thrown overboard, in order to make room for their effects. Sir William Hamilton had also directed two Vessels to be hired for the accommodation of the French emigrants, and provisions were supplied from our Victuallers; in short, everything had been done for the comfort of all persons embarked.

I did not forget in these important moments that it was my duty not to leave the chance of any Ships of War falling into the hands of the French, therefore, every preparation was made for burning them before I sailed; but the reasons given me by their Sicilian Majesties, induced me not to burn them till the last moment. I, therefore, directed the Marquis de Niza to remove all the Neapolitan Ships outside the Squadron under his command, and if it was possible, to equip some of them with jury masts and send them to Messina; and whenever the French advanced near Naples, or the people revolted against their legitimate Government, immediately to destroy the Ships of War, and to join me at Palermo, leaving one or two Ships to cruize between Capri and Iscia in order to prevent the entrance of any English Ship into the Bay of Naples. On the 23rd, at 7 p.m. the *Vanguard*, *Sannite*, and *Archimedes*, with about twenty sail of Vessels left the Bay of Naples; the next day it blew harder than I ever experienced since I have been at sea. Your Lordship will believe that my anxiety was not lessened by the great charge that was with me, but not a word of uneasiness escaped the lips of any of the Royal Family. On the 25th, at 9 a.m., Prince Albert, their Majesties' youngest child, having eat a hearty breakfast, was taken ill, and at 7 p.m. died in the arms of Lady Hamilton; and here it is my duty to tell your Lordship the obligations which the whole Royal Family as well as myself are under on this trying occasion to her Ladyship. They necessarily came on board without a bed, nor could the least preparation be made for their reception. Lady Hamilton provided her own beds, linen, &c., and became *their slave*, for except one man, no person belonging to Royalty assisted the Royal Family, nor did her Ladyship enter a bed the whole time they were on board. Good Sir William also made every sacrifice for the comfort of the august Family embarked with him. I must not omit to state the kindness of Captain Hardy and every Officer in the *Vanguard*, all of whom readily gave their beds for the convenience of the numerous persons attending the Royal Family.

At 3 p.m.,, being in sight of Palermo, his Sicilian Majesty's Royal Standard was hoisted at the main-top gallant-mast head of the *Vanguard*, which was kept flying there till his Majesty got into the *Vanguard's* barge, and every proper honour paid to it from the Ship. As soon as his Majesty set his foot on shore, it was struck from the Barge. The *Vanguard* anchored at 2 a.m. on the 26th; at 5, I attended her Majesty and all the Princesses on shore; her Majesty being so much affected by the death of Prince Albert that she could not bear to go on shore in a public manner. At 9 a.m., his Majesty went on shore, and was received with the loudest acclamations and apparent joy. I have the honour to be, &c.

NELSON

To Lord St. Vincent

Palermo, *31st December, 1798*

My dear Lord,

I do feel, for I am a man, that it is impossible for me to serve in these seas, with the Squadron under a junior Officer:—could I have thought it!—and from Earl Spencer! Never, never was I so astonished as your letter made me. As soon as I can get hold of Troubridge, I shall send him to Egypt, to endeavour to destroy the Ships in Alexandria. If it can be done, Troubridge will do it. The Swedish Knight* writes Sir William Hamilton, that he shall go to Egypt, and take Captain Hood and his Squadron under his command. The Knight forgets the respect due to his superior Officer: he has no orders from you to take my Ships away from my command; but it is all of a piece. Is it to be borne? Pray grant me your permission to retire, and I hope the *Vanguard* will be allowed to convey me and my friends, Sir William and Lady Hamilton, to England. God bless you, my dear Lord, and believe me your most affectionate friend,

NELSON

1799

Lord St. Vincent to Lord Nelson *17th January, 1799*

I am not surprised at your feelings being outraged, at the bold attempt Sir Sidney Smith is making to wrest a part of your Squadron from you. I have received much the same letter from him, as the one you describe to have been addressed to Sir William Hamilton; a copy of which, with my answer, you have enclosed, and orders for you to take him immediately under your command. I have informed Lord Spencer of all these proceedings, and sent him copies of the letters.

DISPOSITION OF THE SQUADRON UNDER MY COMMAND, JANUARY 1st, 1799

Zealous
Swiftsure
Lion
Seahorse
} Egypt.

Culloden
Minotaur
Bomb-Vessels
} Not yet arrived from the N.W. Coast of Italy, but going to Egypt, to relieve Captain Hood, to attempt the destruction of the Transports, and to give up the command to Sir Sidney Smith.

Alexander
Audacious
Goliath
Emerald
Incendiary
} Off Malta

* Sir Sidney Smith was a Knight Grand Cross of the Order of the Sword of Sweden.

Alcmene
and } In Naples Bay, ready to burn the Neapolitan Ships of War.
Portuguese

Bonne Citoyenne—Going to carry the Turkish Ambassador to Constantinople.

Mutine—Gone to Smyrna with dispatches.

Terpsichore and *Alliance*—at Leghorn, to watch events.

Vanguard—At Palermo.

NELSON

To Lord Spencer

Palermo, *January 7th, 1799*

My dear Lord,

The duplicate of my public letter to Earl St. Vincent sent this day to Mr. Nepean, will detail the particulars of our leaving Naples, and of our arrival at Palermo. Our news from Naples has been daily from bad to worse. On the 4th, the Enemy were not at Naples. There are parties in the Capital for a Republic; and another for making the Duke of Parma, who is at Madrid, King; but, I believe, the fighting party is very small. The events which have taken place in the Kingdom of Naples have been so rapid and extraordinary, that it appears a dream. The King, God bless him! is a philosopher; but the great Queen feels sensibly all which has happened. She begs me not to quit Palermo; for that Sir William and Lady Hamilton, and myself, are her only comforts. I shall, as is my duty, do everything in the best manner I am able, for the honour of our Country. General Stuart from *Minorca* calls for me; Mr. Wyndham from Florence does the same; and the affairs of Egypt and Malta are endeavouring to be brought to an issue. Captain Ball has done wonders, and I trust will soon succeed. The Bombs from Malta go to Egypt, and are to make a vigorous attack on the Shipping at Alexandria. These two points successful, will set us quite at our ease on the sea. With every sentiment of respect, believe me, your Lordship's most faithful Servant.

NELSON

To Lord Howe

Palermo, *8th January, 1799*

My Lord,

It was only this moment that I had the invaluable approbation of the great, the immortal Earl Howe—an honour the most flattering a

Sea-Officer could receive, as it comes from the first and greatest Sea-officer the world has ever produced. I had the happiness to command a Band of Brothers; therefore, night was to my advantage. Each knew his duty, and I was sure each would feel for a French ship. By attacking the Enemy's van and centre, the wind blowing directly along their Line, I was enabled to throw what force I pleased on a few Ships. This plan my friends readily conceived by the signals, (for which we are principally, if not entirely, indebted to your Lordship,) and we always kept a superior force to the Enemy. At twenty-eight minutes past six, the sun in the horizon, the firing commenced. At five minutes past ten, when *L'Orient* blew up, having burnt seventy minutes, the six Van ships had surrendered. I then pressed further towards the Rear; and had it pleased God that I had not been wounded and stone blind, there cannot be a doubt but that every Ship would have been in our possession. But here let it not be supposed, that any Officer is to blame. No; on my honour, I am satisfied each did his very best. I have never before, my Lord, detailed the Action to any one; but I should have thought it wrong to have kept it from one who is our great Master in Naval tactics and bravery. May I presume to present my very best respects to Lady Howe, and to Lady Mary; and to beg that your Lordship will believe me ever your most obliged,

NELSON

To the Marquis de Niza

Palermo, *January 9th, 1799*

My dear Marquis,

You have some Turkish slaves on board. I beg, as a friend, as an English Admiral—as a favour to me, as a favour to my Country—that you will give me the Slaves. In doing this, you will oblige your faithful friend,

NELSON

To Lord St. Vincent

(*About 15th January, 1799*)

My Lord,

General Acton has just sent me notice, that General Pignatelli had signed an armistice with the French, in which the name of the King is not mentioned, and that his Majesty has entirely disapproved of this proceeding; and also that the Ligurian Republic had declared war against his Sicilian Majesty. What may arise from day to day is perhaps difficult to say, but unless some great change of measures, in my opinion, Sicily will soon be in great danger. Commodore Campbell is just arrived from Naples: he has burned the Neapolitan ships, before the time specified in my orders to the Marquis de Niza, of which the King has complained to me, and I have entirely disapproved of Commodore Campbell in this matter. The French are in full possession of Capua, and come to Naples as a friendly place. If I get a copy of the Articles before Captain Hope sails, I shall send them. In this new case, I have offered to go to the Bay of Naples myself, but both the King and Queen have so seriously pressed me not to move, that I cannot do it; they have fears, and have confidence in me, for their safety. Sicily is in this state—*free from Jacobins, hate the French, love the English, and discontented with their present situation.*

January 16th.—I send you the three last letters of General Acton, as conveying more information than anything I could write. I am very unwell. God bless you. Ever your affectionate,

NELSON

To Captain Ball

Palermo, *January 21st, 1799*

My dear Ball,

I most heartily pray that your hard fag is over, and that victory has crowned your exertions and perseverance. When Malta is finished, you shall go down when you please. We have a report here that a Russian ship has paid you a visit, with proclamations for the Island. I hate the Russians, and if she came from their Admiral at Corfu, he is a blackguard. Respecting the situation of Malta with the King of Naples, it is this—he is the legitimate Sovereign of the Island; therefore, I am of opinion his Flag should fly. At the same time, a Neapolitan garrison would betray it to the first man who would bribe him. I am sure the King would have no difficulty in giving his Sovereignty to England; and I have lately, with Sir William Hamilton, got a Note that Malta should never be given to any Power without the consent of England. Now, my dear friend, if, happily, Malta falls, and you like it, the regulation as Governor for the King of Naples and our King shall be placed in you. I know none, without a compliment, so fit for a place where jarring interests are to be consulted; therefore, turn this in your mind, and what you do I am confident I shall approve. I send you the papers, therefore shall not touch on English news. Naples was perfectly quiet on the 18th. The Provisional Government is placed by the people in the hands of three very gallant, and, fame says, loyal Officers. All are turned out and obliged to fly who made the infamous armistice with the French. But, alas! my dear Ball, here is no energy in the Government to profit of favourable moments. The mob to-day loyal, may to-morrow turn the contrary. The Portuguese have, contrary to my orders, destroyed the Neapolitan Navy. This caused much anger, both with the King, and people of all descriptions. I am here, nor will the King or

Queen allow me to move. I have offered to go to Naples, and have wished to go off Malta in case the Squadron from Brest should get near you, but neither one or the other can weigh with them. I cannot say I think they will venture a Squadron to certain destruction in the end, even if they get into Malta or Alexandria.

We have all been very unwell; but I can say with truth, that Sir William and Lady Hamilton, and myself, have but one opinion about you, and are equally anxious for your happiness, both as a public man and private friend. Remember me kindly to Gould, Foley, Barker, and Waller. Lady Knight, and the good, the charming Miss Knight, is more amiable than ever, by her kind attention to her mother. Apropos, a very odd thing has happened. By one of the late posts, Lady Knight received a letter from an attorney in England, saying, that one Joseph Knight, a chimney-sweeper of Sherborne in Dorsetshire, had left the family of Sir Joseph Knight a legacy of £2,500. This will make Miss K.'s fortune from her father £7,500, besides expectations from her mother, who cannot live long. Now all this, if I am not mistaken, Miss K. *longs* to give to one of your Squadron.

Send the *Dorothea* back, as I am sure she can be of no use to you as a Frigate, and I shall want her. Lord Keith is arrived as Second-in-Command in the *Foudroyant*. Darby is on his passage up with a Convoy. How will he like this? Not much, but the Earl does not consult his wishes. God bless you, my dear Ball, and believe me ever your most affectionate friend,

NELSON

P.S. In case of the Surrender of Malta, I beg you will not do anything which can hurt the feelings of their Majesties. Unite their Flag with England's, if it cannot, from the disposition of the Islanders, fly alone.

To Henry Addington, Speaker of the House of Commons

Vanguard, Palermo, *January 31st, 1799*

Sir,

Believe me, I feel, as I ought, the noble reward which our Country has bestowed on me by its Thanks; and I beg you will, Sir, have the goodness to express to the Honourable House my gratitude. I can answer for that of my brave Brethren who fought with me in the Battle of the Nile. To you, Sir, who have not only so handsomely, but so elegantly conveyed to me the Resolutions of the House, words are inadequate to express what I feel; but, believe me, Sir, with every sentiment of respect and esteem, your most obliged and faithful servant,

NELSON

To Sir William Anderson, late Lord Mayor of London

Vanguard, Palermo, *31st January*, *1799*

Sir,

I have only this day received the honour of your letter (when Lord Mayor) of the 16th of October; and I beg that you will convey to the Court of Common Council, my sincere gratitude for all their goodness to me; and assure them, it shall be the business of my life, to act in the manner most conducive to the prosperity of the City of London, on which depends that of our Country.

I am truly sensible of your politeness, in desiring me to say what particular devices I should wish on the Sword which is to be presented to me by the City of London; but I beg to leave that to the better judgment of my Fellow-Citizens. Believe me when I assure you, that I feel myself your most faithful and obliged servant,

NELSON

To Captain Ball

Bellerophon, Palermo, *31st January*, *1799*

My dear Ball,

I send you the *Minerve* and *Vanguard* if you want them: you may keep the *Vanguard*, so as not to make her absence from me more than a fortnight: the other if you can spare her, I should also be glad you would send back in a short time afterwards. I am very anxious to hear from you and how you proceed in the blockade. Indeed, I am very anxious to be with you myself, but I am tied so fast here by their Sicilian Majesties that I cannot move.

Sir Sidney Smith, from a letter he wrote Earl St. Vincent, off Malta, has given great offence, having said that he presumed all the Ships in the Levant being junior to him, he had a right to take them under his command. His Lordship has in consequence given him a broad hint, and has taken him down very handsomely; and, to prevent any further mistakes of this kind, has ordered Sir Sidney to put himself immediately under my command, which I suppose the great Plenipo will not like. However, he has brought this upon himself.

From Minorca, Commodore Duckworth presses hard for a Ship or two of the Line, to re-inforce his Squadron, as they are threatened with an invasion of that Island from the Coast of Spain by a large Army and numerous Gun-boats, besides some Ships of the Line. We have no news from Naples since the 15th instant. From Leghorn our news is very bad. Captain Louis in the *Minotaur* is laying there for the protection of the Grand Duke and his Family, if they wish to embark, as well as all the British subjects. The French have republicanized Lucca, and have troops in many parts of the Tuscan territories. I have received information of six French Ships of the Line fitting out at Brest to make a push for the Mediterranean, and it is supposed their object is Malta or Egypt. However, should they attempt it, I trust Lord Keith will fall in with them before they get up. For news, I refer you to Captains Cockburn and Hardy. Sir William (who has been much indisposed) and Lady Hamilton join in best wishes and regards with your faithful and obedient Servant,

NELSON

Tyson* wrote the above. I will send him to you for two days when I can spare him—a difficult thing.

To the Duke of Clarence

Palermo, *2nd February, 1799*

Sir,

I was yesterday honoured with your Royal Highness's kind letter†; and it was with real sorrow that I saw, for one moment, you had been displeased with me. But, like yourself, it passed away—and your friendship, on which I have and always shall pride myself, remains for one who is attached to your Royal Highness inferior to none in this world. Indeed, Horatio Nelson is the same as your goodness has ever known him to be—attached, affectionate, and unchangeable; with one hand to a wounded head, and, I may now add, with my heart full, and the business of fifteen Sail of the Line, besides my near connexion with the shore. I have sent Troubridge and some Bombs to Egypt, to endeavour to do that which could have been done, if I had possessed the means, in forty-eight hours after the Action. It is now doubtful; but my gallant friend will do what man can do. I beg your Royal Highness to believe that I am ever your attached

NELSON

To William Locker

Palermo, *February 9th, 1799*

My dear Friend,

I well know your own goodness of heart will make all due allowances for my present situation, and that truly I have not the time or power to answer all the letters I receive at the moment; but you, my old friend, after twenty-seven years acquaintance know that nothing can alter my attachment and gratitude to you: I have been your scholar;

* His secretary.

† The Prince's displeasure arose from his supposing that Nelson had not written to him after the Battle of the Nile.

it is you who taught me to board a Frenchman, by your conduct when in the *Experiment*;* It is you who always told me, 'Lay a Frenchman close, and you will beat him,' and my only merit in my profession is being a good scholar; our friendship will never end but with my life; but you have always been too partial to me. Pray tell Kingsmill that it was impossible I could attend to his recommendation; indeed I had, not being a Commander-in-Chief, no power to name an Agent; remember me kindly to him. The Vesuvian Republic being formed, I have now to look out for Sicily; but Revolutionary principles are so prevalent in the world, that no Monarchical government is safe, or sure of lasting ten years. I beg you will make my kindest remembrances to Miss Locker and all your good sons, and believe me ever your faithful and affectionate friend,

NELSON

To Lt. General the Hon. Charles Stuart

Palermo, *10th February, 1799*

What a state we are in here!—without troops, and the Enemy at the door; for although there are 4,000 Neapolitan regular troops, these are not to be trusted; 13,000 Sicilian troops are raising, and 26,000 Militia; but I fear, before these are got together, the active French will get possession of Messina, the key of Sicily. There is a good Citadel, and might be defended for a long time; but there is such treachery, that probably it will be given without a shot. I know, my dear Sir, your situation at Minorca, and I regret that you cannot, I fear, send here and save us, for 1,000 English troops in the citadel of Messina would, I am convinced save Sicily. I dare not hope such a thing; but having ventured to mention this subject, I leave it to your excellent judgment. With every sentiment of respect, believe me, my dear Sir, yours, &c.

NELSON

I have sent my letter to Lord St. Vincent open, for Duckworth to read, which tells all the news I can learn.

To Lord St. Vincent Palermo, *13th February, 1799*

Our news from Calabria is very bad, as most of the Towns have planted the Tree of Liberty, and the madness approaches the coast towards Sicily. In this Island are many discontented people, who have

* Captain Locker was First Lieutenant of the *Experiment* of 20 guns and 142 men, commanded by Capt. Sir John Strachan, on the 19th June, 1757, when she fell in with *Le Telemaque*, a large French ship of 26 guns and 460 men, which was boarded and carried by the *Experiment's* crew led by Locker.

shown themselves in various places in a manner contrary to law, and nearly approaching rebellion. Thus situated, who can say but the chance is, that the Royal Family will be obliged once more to take refuge under the British flag? I have letters from Mr. Wyndham at Florence, who represents the situation of Tuscany as very critical. The French make no scruple of declaring their intention of revolutionizing the Grand Duchy. Not content with turning the King of Sardinia out of Piedmont, they intended seizing his person after he left Leghorn, by some of their privateers, and carrying him to Corsica; for if they could have prevented it, His Majesty would never have got to Sardinia.*

Captain Louis had been requested to allow the *Terpsichore* to go, as if by accident, in company with the Vessel; for to such a state of degradation is this Monarch reduced, that he dared not publicly accept of the offered protection of the British flag. His Holiness the Pope is not expected to live.† The French ordered him, although living in Tuscany, to quit that country, and repair to Sardinia; and when he represented his ill state of health, Salicetti was present when the old man's blisters were taken off, to see that he did not sham: however, he will soon be at rest from all his cares and troubles. As to myself, I see but gloomy prospects, look which way I will. We have accounts that sixty thousand Russians are arrived at Saltzburg, the German side of the Tyrol; but as the Russians have been marching the whole war, so they will I fear, arrive too late in Italy. At present I see but little prospect of the fall of Malta; several Vessels with provisions are got in. Ball is indefatigable, and has great hopes. In short, my dear Lord, everything makes me sick, to see things go to the Devil, and not to have the means of prevention.

I am, &c.

NELSON

MEMORANDUM

Palermo, *24th February, 1799*

His Sicilian Majesty having been graciously pleased to order one thousand ounces to be given to the Officers, seamen, and marines of his Majesty's Ship, the *Vanguard*, as a mark of his approbation of their conduct during the time he was on board, one hundred ounces to be given to the two Barges' crews who assisted in bringing off the Royal Family, one hundred ounces to be given to the Admiral's servants, and

* The King of Sardinia and his family, after taking refuge at Florence, sailed in a Danish frigate for Cagliari, the capital of Sardinia, on 23rd February, protected by the *Terpsichore*, Captain Gage.

† Pope Pius VI died at Valence, in France, on 29th August, 1799, aged eighty-one.

one hundred ounces to be given to the Barge's crew of the *Alcmene*,—the Rear-Admiral has thought proper to have the one thousand ounces distributed in the following manner:—

	Ounces
Wardroom	100
27 Gentlemen of the Quarter-deck and Warrant-officers, 4 each	108
579 Seamen and Marines, 1 and $\frac{1}{3}$ each	772
26 Boys, at half each	13
	993
Remains to be laid out for soup, &c.	7
	1000

NELSON

To Sir Sidney Smith and J. Spencer Smith *Vanguard*, Palermo, *March, 7th, 1799*

Gentlemen,

I have received a letter from Sir Sidney Smith, dated January 23rd, which I consider for the most part as a letter from his Majesty's Ministers, and as such I beg leave to answer it, as I shall write to Sir Sidney Smith on the subject proper for me, as an Admiral, to him as a Captain, now put under my command. I have, therefore, to request that your Excellency will, upon all occasions, arrange plans of operations with me, and desire the Minister of the Sublime Porte to establish Corvettes for holding a constant communication between me and Constantinople; and I beg you will assure the Porte of my anxious desire to do everything they can wish me, either by coming, or sending, under such Officers as I can place confidence in, such a force as the service may require. I therefore again urge that good Corvettes may be immediately sent me, to keep open a constant communication.

Captain Sir Sidney Smith is the Officer at present destined to command the blockade of Alexandria, if that force, as my orders tell me, does not exceed two Ships of the Line. With Captain Sir Sidney Smith's zeal and gallantry you are well acquainted; therefore, it is only necessary for me to say, that I shall give the strictest orders to Sir Sidney Smith to do everything in his power to assist in the destruction of the French in Egypt; and, at the same time, I must desire that your Excellency will urge the Porte to send Turkish and Russian Ships sufficient, with Sir Sidney Smith's own Ship, to attend to the business of Egypt; for the service in these Ports demands all the force I can collect. And I shall direct Sir Sidney Smith not to keep a ship, after the force is four Sail of the Line, and three or four Frigates of Russians and Turks, including his own Ship.

I have this day (March 7th) received letters from Sir Sidney Smith, in his Ministerial capacity I believe. I wish that all Ministerial letters should be wrote in your joint names; for it may be difficult for me to distinguish the Captain of the Man-of-War from the Joint Minister, and the propriety of language in one might be very proper to what it is in the other. I beg of your Excellency to forward my letter to Sir Sidney Smith, Captain of the *Tigre*. I have the honour to be your Excellency's most obedient Servant,

NELSON

To Captain Sir William Sidney Smith

Vanguard, Palermo,
8th March, 1799

Sir,

I have received your letters of January 23rd, February the 6th, 10th, and 23rd. Your situation as Joint-Minister at the Porte makes it absolutely necessary that I should know who writes to me—therefore, I must direct you, whenever you have Ministerial affairs to communicate, that it is done jointly with your respectable brother, and not mix Naval business with the other, for what may be very proper language for a Representative of Majesty, may be very subversive of that discipline of respect from the different ranks in our service. A Representative may dictate to an Admiral—a Captain of a Man-of-War would be censured for the same thing; therefore you will see the propriety of my steering clear between the two situations. I have sent you my orders, which your abilities as a Sea-officer will lead you to punctually execute. Not a Ship more than the service requires shall be kept on any particular station; and that number must be left to my judgment, as an Admiral commanding the Squadron detached by the Commander-in-Chief to the extent of the Black Sea. I shall of course keep up a proper communication with the Turkish and Russian Admirals, which no Captain of a Man-of-War under my orders must interfere in. I am, Sir, your very humble Servant,

NELSON

To Lord St. Vincent

Private.

Palermo, *March 8th, 1799*

My dear Lord,

The arrival of the *Bonne Citoyenne* enables me to send the Ministers' letters from Constantinople; but, in truth, I am at a loss to guess when

Sir Sidney Smith writes to me as Minister or Captain in the Navy; as the latter, they are highly indecent to write to an Officer of my rank. You will agree with me, that the manner of saying the same thing makes it proper or otherwise; but Sir Sidney's dictatorial way of writing is what I never before met with. I shall, my Lord, keep a sufficient force in the Levant for the service required of us, but not a Ship for Captain Smith's parade and nonsense—Commodore Smith—I beg his pardon, for he wears a Broad Pendant—has he any orders for this presumption over the heads of so many good and gallant Officers with me?* Whenever Sir Sidney Smith went on board the *Tigre* in state, as he calls it, the *Royal Standard* was hoisted at the mast-head, and twenty-one guns fired. The Turks, however, who love solid sense and not frippery, see into the Knight, and wonder that some of Sir Sidney's superiors were not sent to Constantinople: but I have done with the Knight. I have letters from dear Ball, off Malta; I send you a copy. The moment the *Terpsichore* arrives, she shall join you. The Grand Signior has ordered 10,000 Albanese troops to come to Sicily. God bless you, and ever believe me your affectionate,

NELSON

To Constantino Ypsilanti

Palermo, *8th March, 1799*

Sir,

Your very elegant and friendly letter was delivered to me yesterday by Captain Nisbet; and I return him to Constantinople, to assure the Sublime Porte, that whilst I have the honour of commanding the detached Squadron of his Britannic Majesty's Fleet in the Levant Seas and Coast of Italy, whatever the Sublime Porte wish me to do, it is my duty, and indeed it is my inclination; for I shall, if it is necessary, to myself to serve the Grand Signior. I have given Captain Sir Sidney Smith orders to do everything in his power to serve the Common Cause. It will not escape your Excellency's descerning judgment that the joint Minister Sir Sidney Smith is a different person from Captain Sidney Smith of the *Tigre*. I have directed Captain Nisbet, who is acquainted with my sentiments, to express them to your Excellency.

I have only to beg, through the favour of your Excellency and of the Grand Vizir, to be laid at the feet of the Grand Signior, and that you will ever believe me your most obliged and faithful,

NELSON

* Lord St. Vincent wrote in reply that Sir Sidney Smith had no authority to wear a Distinguishing Pendant, unless Nelson had given it; and he expressed his disapprobation of Sir Sidney's letters to Nelson, and of the 'bombast' in those to Earl Spencer.

To Sir Sidney Smith and J. Spencer Smith

Vanguard, Palermo, *12th March, 1799*

Gentlemen,

I have the pleasure to tell you that his Excellency General Sir Charles Stuart, K.B., arrived here on the 10th with a respectable force—about 2,000 men; but, as more are expected at Messina, I believe the whole force will be 3,000. We are very anxiously waiting the arrival of the promised succour from Russia under General Harman; and from the favourable appearance in the Kingdom of Naples, I shall strongly recommend their going direct to Naples, and taking possession of that Capital—an operation of no difficulty, if 12,000 are the number of troops. All the lower order would immediately join; and all those traitors, who could hope for pardon, would not be glad to get rid of French fraternization; for they, as usual, begun by stripping their friends, upon principles that our 'good friends must have pleasure in giving,—from our enemies we will take.' In short, I can say with truth, that the French and Neapolitans are heartily sick of each other. All Calabria has returned to its loyalty, even to within forty miles of Naples. Apulia and Lecce have never admitted the French amongst them. In the Roman State all is insurrection against the French; in Civita Vecchia the Enemy have been beat off. What a moment for the Emperor to march! I hope he will, and it will give me pleasure to communicate our success in Italy, and am most exceedingly anxious to hear of Buonaparte's destruction in the East. I have the honour to be, your Excellencies' most obedient Servant,

NELSON

To Captain Sir Sidney Smith

Vanguard, Palermo, *18th March, 1799*

Sir,

Captain Troubridge arrived here last evening, and, as he has delivered to me all the papers he received from you, amongst which I see a form of a passport; and Captain Troubridge tells me it was your intention to send into Alexandria, that all French ships might pass to France—now, as this is *in direct opposition to my opinion*, which is, *never to suffer any one individual Frenchman to quit Egypt*—I must therefore *strictly charge and command you*, never to give any French ship or man leave to quit Egypt. And I must also desire that you will oppose by every means in your power, any permission which may be attempted to be given by any foreigner, Admiral, General, or other person; and you will acquaint those persons, that I shall not pay the smallest attention to any such passport after your notification; and you are to put my orders in force, not on any pretence to permit a single Frenchman to leave Egypt. Of course, you will give these orders to all the Ships under your command. As I am very anxious for the return of the *Emma* polacre, I have to request that you will not detain her more than two hours. As I shall hope to have a constant communication with you, through the means of the Turkish or Russian Admirals, all letters for your Squadron I shall direct to be left in the *Vanguard*. I am, Sir, your very humble servant,

NELSON

DISPOSITION OF THE SQUADRON

20th March, 1799

Tigre *Lion* *Theseus*	Blockading Alexandria.
Alexander *Audacious* *Goliath* *La Minerve* *La Bonne Citoyenne* *Incendiary* *Strombolo*	Blockading Malta.
Culloden *Zealous* *Swiftsure* *Seahorse* *Vanguard* *El Corso* *Perseus* *Bull-Dog*	At Palermo.

Bellerophon, gone with Convoy to Leghorn.
Minotaur, hourly expected from Leghorn.
Alliance, on her passage from Egypt.
Emerald, gone to Mahon to repair.
Mutine, daily expected from Mahon.
L'Entreprenant, gone with dispatches to Tunis.
San Leon, gone with Convoy to Venice.

PORTUGUESE SQUADRON

Principe Real, going to Leghorn.
Affonço, with Captain Ball, off Malta.
San Sebastian, ordered from Messina to Palermo.
Rainha, gone with the French Princesses from Brindisi to Trieste.
Benjamin, with Captain Ball, off Malta.
Balloon, Brig, at Leghorn.

NELSON

To the Hon. William Wyndham

Culloden, Palermo, *22nd March, 1799*

My dear Sir,

The Ambassador of Buonaparte being intercepted by my friend Troubridge, on his way to Constantinople, and amongst other articles of his instructions, is a very important one—viz., an offer to enter on terms for his quitting Egypt with his Army. This offer is what I have long expected the glorious Battle of the Nile would produce; but it was my determination from that moment never, if I could help it, to permit a single Frenchman to quit Egypt.

Captain Sir William Sidney Smith, who has the present command of the Squadron off Alexandria, I have reason to believe, thinks differently from me, and will grant passports for the return of that part of the French army which God Almighty permits to remain. I have, therefore, thought it highly proper to send Captain Sir Sidney Smith the order of which I transmit a copy; for I consider it nothing short of madness to permit that band of thieves to return to Europe. *No.;* to Egypt they went with their own consent, and there they shall remain whilst Nelson commands the detached Squadron; for never, never, will he consent to the return of one Ship or Frenchman.

I beg your Excellency will take the earliest opportunity of sending this important information, and a copy of my letter to Captain Sir Sidney Smith; to England, and ever believe me, with the greatest respect, your obliged and faithful servant,

NELSON

To Captain Ball

Palermo, *25th March, 1799*

My dear Ball,

Although Commodore Campbell is going to join his Ship, yet he is to be considered as under your command, and he understands that perfectly. You will not hurt his feelings, I am sure. Tyson* writes you

* Nelson's old follower and secretary. He was afterwards Clerk of the Survey in Woolwich Dockyard, and died at Southampton, on the 16th November, 1814.

all the forms for changes of Ships, &c. Now, my dear friend, Captain Nisbet is appointed to the *Thalia*, a very fine frigate, and I wish he may do credit to himself, and in her. Will you do me the favour of keeping her, and sending me the *Minerve*, for I want Cockburn, for service of *head*? As soon as Captain Barker's surveys &c. are over, make one of the small craft bring him here. I have sent *Vanguard* to Tripoli to scold the Bashaw. Tunis behaves well. As Corfu has surrendered, I hope Malta will follow the example very soon. I am pressed for Ships for other services, but you are sure I shall do everything to make you comfortable. As the mortars are, I believe, of no use to you, I wish they could again be put in the *Strombolo*, and she sent to me; for I am preparing for Naples, where our friend Troubridge goes directly. The French have certainly made war upon the Emperor, and have surprised some of his troops. Serve him right! why did he not go to war before? In Tuscany, the French are expected every moment. Here we are quiet, and in Calabria all goes on well. At Naples they tell me the French are hated: however, we shall very soon know all the truth from experience. *Bellerophon* and *Minotaur* are ordered to Minorca. I am not well, but keep rubbing on, from day to day. God bless you! Finish the business as soon as you can; and ever believe me, your affectionate

NELSON

To Captain Troubridge Palermo, *28th March, 1799*

Whereas it is of the utmost importance that the City and Towns in the Bay of Naples should be immediately blockaded to prevent the French forces in those places from getting any supplies of corn or other articles by sea, and it being expedient that an Officer of your distinguished merit and abilities should command the blockade, in order to render it the more effectual, you are hereby required and directed to take under your command the Ships named in the margin,* embarking on board them the Governor of Procida and two hundred troops, as also such Officers as are ordered by his Sicilian Majesty to embark with them, and proceed to the Bay of Naples. And it being necessary that the Squadron employed on this service should have some safe anchorage, the more effectually to carry on the said blockade, and the Island of Procida affording the anchorage desired, you will use your endeavours to seize and get possession of the said Island of Procida, if possible, and reinstate the Governor in the command thereof, and using every means in your power to conciliate the affections of the

* *Minotaur*, *Zealous*, *Swiftsure*, *Seahorse*, *Perseus* Bomb and *El Corso* Sloop.

loyal part of the inhabitants; and also, those of the Islands of Ischia and Capri, and, if possible, bring them to their former allegiance; and also, to communicate with the loyal inhabitants of Naples, as much as is in your power, and by every opportunity; but by no means to fire upon the City without farther orders from me, or circumstances render it necessary to fire on some parts of it, in case of the loyal taking arms against the French. And you will use every effort to prevent all supplies of corn, or other articles, from entering the City and Ports in the Bay of Naples; and also of Gaeta and its vicinity, and along the Roman coast to Civita Vecchia; and as it is said, the Ponza Islands continue in their allegiance to his Sicilian Majesty, you will direct that all protection and assistance may be given to them, should they stand in need. And you will consider that every means is to be used, not only by yourself but by all those under your command, to communicate with the inhabitants on all the Northern coast of the Kingdom of Naples and the Islands before mentioned, and as much as in your power to cultivate a good understanding with them and conciliate their affections, in order to induce them to return to their allegiance to his Sicilian Majesty, and to take arms to liberate their Country from French tyranny and oppressive contributions.

NELSON

To Earl Spencer

Palermo, *6th April, 1799*

My dear Lord,

I have to thank you for your letters of December 24th and 25th, duplicates of which I also received by sea the same day. I am happy that everything which I have done respecting Malta, has been exactly what has been wished at home. To say the truth, the possession of Malta by England, would be an useless and enormous expense; yet any expense should be incurred, rather than let it remain in the hands of the French. Therefore, as I did not trouble myself about the establishing again the Order of St. John at Malta, Sir William Hamilton has the assurance from his Sicilian Majesty that he will never cede the Sovereignty of the Island to any power, without the consent of his Britannic Majesty. The poor Islanders have been so grievously oppressed by the Order, that many times we have been pressed to accept of the Island for Great Britain; and I know if we had, his Sicilian Majesty would have been contented. But, as I said before, I attach no value to it for us;* but it is a place of such consequence to the French, that any expense ought to be incurred to drive them out.

* Perhaps no opinion expressed by Nelson is more extraordinary than that Malta is not of value to this country.

I have this moment letters from Captain Ball, stating the distress of the Island, and his fears that when harvest comes, which will be in three weeks, they may make their peace with the French, in the belief that Sicily will fall into their hands before winter; on the other hand, the garrison is in great distress, and eat up with the scurvy. The Bashaw of Tripoli, having made a treaty with Buonaparte, on February 24th, and received a present of a diamond, I wrote him a letter on the subject, and sent it by the *Vanguard*; Captain Hardy brought me back a letter of promise of future good conduct.

I can now get to more interesting subjects; being sensible that by a close blockade of Naples with the largest force I could collect, must prevent any French troops from being sent against the Italian Armies (as they are called) in the Provinces, I sent my friend Troubridge, with five Sail of the Line, on this service, and directed him to use every means in his power to take Procida, in order to secure the anchorage: he sailed on the 31st ultimo. Yesterday I had the most satisfactory letters from him, of his complete possession of all the Islands in the Bay of Naples, and of his getting possession of all Jacobin municipality, officers, &c. Some well-timed and speedy punishments will have the happiest effects. The French are not more than 2,000 troops in Naples, and about 2,000 civic troops; the last are weathercocks, and will always be on the side of the conqueror. We are anxious for the promised succours of Russian troops; 10,000 would possess Naples in twenty-four hours. I am, &c.

NELSON

To the Rev. William Nelson

Palermo, *April 10th, 1799*

My dear Brother,

I thank you for your letter of February 5th, enclosing one from Charlotte: those you mentioned to have wrote, and Horace's, came to me in due time by sea, but our communication with Gibraltar and England is not very certain or frequent. You must not, nor any of my friends think, that because my letters are scarce and short that in any way they are forgot: the wonder even to me is, that I am able to write what I do. My public correspondence besides the business of sixteen Sail of the Line, and all our commerce, is with Petersburg, Constantinople, the Consul at Smyrna, Egypt, the Turkish and Russian Admirals, Trieste, Vienna, Tuscany, Minorca, Earl St. Vincent and Lord Spencer. This over, what time can I have for private correspondence? Consider this and I shall stand acquitted. Whenever I can in ANY way be useful to you or my nephew and niece, you know me not to be disinclined. I neither wish to be thought richer or poorer than I am, but of this be assured, that except my pension I am much poorer than when I left England a year ago. I feel that you have cause for complaint that not one relation of the *Victor of the Nile* has been noticed. I wrote to both Mr. Pitt and Mr. Wyndham and Lord Spencer: the two first never answered my letter; the latter has told me he does not know how he can be useful to my brother Maurice.

So much for *my* interest! However, time must I think bring matters round, for I can never bring myself to believe that Nelson's family should be unnoticed by the English Government. I had not heard of poor Mr. Suckling's death till I received your letter.* The desires of his children do not surprise me. I love his memory, and am not sorry that he has forgot me, except as his executor, in which I will be faithful. I loved my dear Uncle for his own worth, and not from any views of interest to myself. As to my going to England, that must depend so much on circumstances that I cannot form any guess on the subject. I should wish to carry the King back to Naples, and then I will think of it.

April 11th, 1799.—I cannot write more; my hands are full; therefore can only say, God bless you all, and believe me, your affectionate brother,

NELSON

To the Bashaw of Tripoli

Vanguard, Palermo, *28th April, 1799*

Sir,

When I received your Highness's letter, by Captain Hardy, of the *Vanguard*, I was rejoiced to find that you had renounced the treaty you had so imprudently entered into with some emissaries of General Buonaparte—that man of blood, that despoiler of the weak, that enemy of all good Musselmen; for, like Satan, he only flatters that he may more easily destroy; and it is true, that since the year 1789, all Frenchmen are exactly of the same disposition. I had sent your letter to the great King, my Master; I had done the same to the Grand Signior; for I never believed that your Highness would say a word that was not most strictly true; a lie is impossible for a true Musselman to tell—at least, I had always believed so. What, then, must have been my astonishment to have heard from his Britannic Majesty's Consul, Mr. Lucas, that the moment the *Vanguard* sailed, the French Consul and all the French, were liberated, and also the French Vessels in the Port allowed to fit for sea, and one, to my knowledge, had sailed for Malta? Why will your Highness be thus led astray by evil councillors, who can have no other object in view but your ruin?

* Mr. William Suckling died at Kentish Town on 15th December, 1798, aged 69. He left Nelson a legacy of £100, and appointed him one of his executors.

Your Highness knows that although a powerful Squadron of Portuguese Ships has been, since last August, under my command, that by every means in my power they have been prevented from cruising against the Ships of your Highness, or from approaching your Coast. It is now my duty to speak out, and not to be misunderstood. That Nelson who has hitherto kept your powerful Enemies from destroying you, can, and will, let them loose upon you, unless the following terms are, in two hours, complied with—viz., that the French Consul at Tripoli, Vice-Consul, and every Frenchman, are delivered on board her Most Faithful Majesty's Ship *Affonço*, to Commodore Campbell, in two hours from Mr. Lucas setting his foot on shore; that hostages are also sent on board, to remain till every Frenchman in the State of Tripoli shall be sent off, which shall not exceed four days. N.B. There shall be no reservation or trick about the French Consul, &c., at Tripoli. He shall be on board in two hours after the demand being made. All French Vessels, or Vessels pretended to be taken from the French, shall be destroyed in two hours. These terms complied with, Commodore Campbell will, as he has done upon the passage, refrain from taking your Vessels, until his arrival at Palermo. If these proper terms are not complied with, I can no longer prevent the Ships of her Most Faithful Majesty from acting with vigour against your Highness.

Your Highness will, without difficulty, write me a letter, the substance of which will be dictated by Mr. Lucas. You will also, as a convincing proof of your detestation of the evil counsels which have been given to you by Hamet Reis, your Captain of the Port, either cause him to be delivered to Commodore Campbell, that I may send him to Constantinople, or *dispose* of him in such a manner, that he may for ever be incapable of giving your Highness any advice; for his heart is so black, that I am informed he can give you no good.

Your Highness will, I am confident, approve of the open and unreserved manner of this letter, and consider it as a proof of the honest, upright intentions of the Great Monarch who I have the honour of serving, and that it comes from your Highness' most attached and faithful servant,

NELSON

To Earl Spencer

Palermo, *29th April, 1799*

My dear Lord,

Since I wrote you last, things have been every day improving in the Kingdom of Naples; and from appearances, I think it very probable that in ten days their Sicilian Majesties may be again in Naples. These happy prospects have been brought about, first, by the war of the

Emperor; secondly, by the wonderful loyalty of the lower order of the people; and lastly, I flatter myself I may say, by the conduct of the English. Captain Troubridge has given a portion of that spirit he so eminently possesses, to all who communicate with him. The Great Devil* who commands a portion of the Christian army, has been on board the *Culloden*, and an attempt was to be made to take Gaeta on the 26th, at night. Captain Hood has taken Salerno; his Marines and a party of Royalists garrison it. The distance from Naples twenty-eight miles. Castel-á-Mare is also now with the King's colours flying. I had just sent the *Minotaur* and *Swiftsure* to support them. These events have determined the French to evacuate Naples, and I hope the whole of the Neapolitan Dominions. On the 25th Macdonald left the Town for Capua, with all the troops, except 500 in the Castle of St. Elmo, who were expected to make off on the 27th.

Orders have been given by the *Jacobin* Government, for the batteries *not* to fire on the English ships. In short, the communication with Naples is so open, that a General took a boat from the city, and came on board Troubridge, to consult about surprising St. Elmo. The Civic Guard have individually declared that they assemble to keep peace in the City, and not to fight. Many of the principal Jacobins have fled, and Caracciolo has resigned his situation as Head of the Marine. This man was fool enough to quit his Master when he thought his case desperate; yet, in his heart, I believe he is no Jacobin. The fishermen, a few days ago, told him publicly, 'We believe you are loyal, and sent by the King; but much as we love you, if we find you disloyal, you shall be amongst the first to fall.' I am not in person in these busy scenes, more calculated for me than remaining here giving advice; but their Majesties think the advice of my incompetent judgment valuable at this moment, therefore I submit, and I can only say that I give it as an honest man, one without hopes or fears; therefore they get at the truth, which their Majesties have seldom heard.

Malta still holds out; but the moment all hopes of getting supplies from Naples cease, I am in great hopes the garrison will surrender to the meritorious and indefatigable Ball, whose good conduct is equalled by few, exceeded by none. As to myself, I shall only say what your partiality has always believed, that I shall do my best, and believe me, my dear Lord, &c.

NELSON

P.S. April 30th.—Castel-á-Mare has the King's colours flying. Our two Ships at anchor there. All the Jacobins retiring to St. Elmo.

* The name given to a Calabrese who distinguished himself in the Royal cause.

May 1st.—Much blood has been shed near Naples since the 28th. We have lost a few men near Salerno. A very handsome order of the King is come out stating the few exceptions to pardon; and even those, or any one which Troubridge says *Pardon*, it is done by the instrument. I am this moment sending 1,200 infantry and 400 horse—sail in two days in the *Haerlem* and *Vanguard*.

To the King of Sardinia

Palermo, *4th May, 1799*

Sire,

I have been honoured with your Majesty's letter of April 21, and I beg you will be assured that in offering services to your Majesty, I do no more than fulfil the wishes of my gracious Sovereign; and was I to fail in showing your Majesty all the attention in my power, I should be sure of my Royal Master's censure; therefore, I presume to request you will lay your commands upon me, and consider me only as a faithful servant, devoted to your Majesty, from the unhappy events which you have so lately experienced from a set of infidels, robbers, and murderers; but the measure of their iniquity is, I believe, full, and that God, in his wisdom, is in the act of punishing them by the hand of the Austrians. The successes of the Emperor's arms, both in Italy and on the Rhine, I shall have the honour of briefly relating, and I send you such papers as have come to my hands. The Archduke Charles, after several severe battles, has forced Jourdan to repass the Rhine with immense loss. His Royal Highness has taken Kehl, and is before Strasburg, where General Massena has retreated. All Switzerland has revolted against the French, and the Austrians' headquarters in that Country, are at Little Basle and Schaffhausen. In Italy everything is victorious, and therefore the fairest prospect presents itself, that before May is over, there will not be a Frenchman from Milan to the Adriatic. Lodi was the last quarter-general of the French, and it is since said, and universally believed, that the French have abandoned Lodi, and returned across the Po. The State of Genoa is in a deplorable situation for corn, which makes all the lower orders desirous of a change in their Government: I therefore submit to your Majesty's wisdom, to check as much as possible, corn being sent from Sardinia. It may be effected by orders for long quarantines, and other means. The messenger you sent to Leghorn with dispatches for London, and who was forced to come here by the French being in Tuscany, sails tomorrow for London, in a Ship of War. Upon this, and all other occasions, I shall be happy in obeying your commands, being your Majesty's faithful and obedient,

NELSON

To Captain Troubridge

Vanguard, Palermo, *8th May, 1799*

My dear Troubridge,

I desire you will express to Captain Hood the true sense I have of his conduct, not only at Salerno, but upon all other occasions, and that I never expect any but the most useful services where he commands; and I beg you will say the same for me to Captains Louis, Hallowell, Foote, and Oswald; not forgetting Captain Harward and Commodore Mitchell, as far as they have been concerned. As to yourself, your conduct is so all of a piece, that I can only say what is true, that the last service seems to eclipse the former ones. You have an arduous task in your present command; and no Officer in his Majesty's service could, I am convinced, perform it with more judgment and advantage for His Majesty's service than yourself, and I beg that you will ever believe me your faithful, affectionate, and obliged friend,

NELSON

Count Thurn will tell you he takes from hence all the shells and 800 shot, and one month's provisions. I hope he will get off to-day.

[On the 12th May, the *Espoir* arrived at Palermo with news that the French Fleet from Brest had been seen off Oporto, on their way to the Mediterranean, intending, it was supposed, to join the Spanish Fleet, and to act against Minorca and Sicily. It was therefore necessary to reinforce our fleet, and Nelson immediately recalled most of the ships from Naples Bay and determined to proceed to sea; but in consequence of a gale of wind, his Squadron did not sail until the 20th, when it proceeded off Maritimo. The Squadron returned to Palermo on the 29th, to complete their provisions.]

To Rear-Admiral Duckworth

Palermo, *May 12th, 1799*

My dear Sir,

I am sending you eight, nine, or ten Sail of the Line with all expedition, that they may be ready to either form a junction with our great and excellent Commander-in-Chief, or proceed down the Mediterranean, and join him, as he may direct. I would venture to offer my opinion, that the Ships had better be under sail off Port Mahon, than in the harbour. With my best wishes for success, for I cannot come to you, believe me, your obliged,

NELSON

To Lord St. Vincent

Palermo, *12th May, 1799*

My dear Lord,

Eight, nine, or ten Sail of the Line shall, in a few days, be off Mahon, ready to obey your orders, (not in the Port.) I hope the Russians are off Malta. If so, I have wrote to the Admiral to send some of his Ships to Minorca. In short, you may depend upon my exertion, and I am only sorry that I cannot move to your help; but this Island appears to hang on my stay. Nothing could console the Queen this night, but my promise not to leave them unless the battle was to be fought off Sardinia. May God Almighty bless and prosper you, is the fervent prayer of your obliged and affectionate,

NELSON

To Lord St. Vincent

Palermo, *13th May, 1799*

My dear Lord,

Should you come upwards without a battle, I hope in that case you will afford me an opportunity of joining you; for my heart would break to be near my Commander-in-Chief, and not assisting him in such a time. What a state I am in! If I go, I risk, and more than risk, Sicily, and what is now safe on the Continent; for we know, from experience, that more depends on *opinion* than on acts themselves. As I stay, my heart is breaking; and, to mend the matter, I am seriously unwell. God bless you. Depend on my utmost zeal to do as I think my dear friend would wish me; for believe me with real affection your faithful friend,

NELSON

To Lady Hamilton *Vanguard, May 19th, 1799*

Eight o'Clock. Calm.

My dear Lady Hamilton,

Lieutenant Swiney coming on board, enables me to send some blank passports for Vessels going to Procida with corn, &c., and also one for the Courier boat. To tell you how dreary and uncomfortable the *Vanguard* appears, is only telling you what it is to go from the pleasantest society to a solitary cell; or, from the dearest friends to no friends. I am now perfectly the *great man*—not a creature near me. From my heart, I wish myself the little man again! You, and good Sir William, have spoiled me for any place but with you. I love Mrs. Cadogan.* You cannot conceive what I feel, when I call you all to my remembrance. Even to Mira,† do not forget your faithful and affectionate

NELSON

* Lady Hamilton's mother.

† Her maid.

To Lady Hamilton

May 20th, 1799

My dear Lady Hamilton,

Many thanks to you and Sir William for your kind notes. You will believe I did not sleep much, with all my letters to read, &c. My letters from Lord St. Vincent are May 6th. He says: 'We saw the Brest Squadron pass us yesterday, under an easy sail. I am making every effort to get information to Lord Keith; who I have ordered here, to complete their water and provisions. I conjecture, the French Squadron is bound for Malta and Alexandria, and the Spanish Fleet for the attack of Minorca.' I must leave you to judge whether the Earl will come to us. I think he will; but, *entre nous*, Mr. Duckworth means to leave me to my fate. I send you (*under all circumstances*) his letter. Never mind; if I can get my eleven Sail together, they shall not hurt me.

God bless you, Sir William, and all our joint friends in your house; Noble, Gibbs, &c., and believe me ever, for ever, your affectionate friend,

NELSON

ORDER OF BATTLE AND SAILING

Vanguard 2 points
Order of Sailing.

		No.	*Ships*	*Captains*	*Guns*	*Men*	
	Starboard or Weather Division	1	*Culloden*	T. Troubridge	74	590	
		2	*Zealous*	S. Hood	74	590	Rear-Admiral Lord Nelson
		3					
		4	*Alexander*	A. J. Ball	74	590	
		5	*Vanguard*	T. M. Hardy	74	595	
Haarlem		6	*Swiftsure*	B. Hallowell	74	590	
		7	*Affonço*	Comm. Campbell	70	625	
	Larboard or Lee Division	8	*Principe Real*	Comm. Conde de Puységur	92	788	Rear-Admiral Marquis de Niza
		9	*St. Sebastian*	Comm. Mitchell	64	600	
		10	*Goliath*	T. Foley	74	590	
		11	*Lion*	M. Dixon	64	500	
		12	*Audacious*	D. Gould	74	590	
		13	*Minotaur*	T. Louis	74	640	
		14					
		15					
		16					
All Frigates to repeat.		17					

Given on board the *Vanguard*, at Sea, 20th May, 1799.

NELSON

To Lord St. Vincent

Palermo, *30th May, 1799*

The *Vanguard* anchored here yesterday; but it has been so calm, that, except the *Emerald*, none have yet got in. After two days, I hope they will all be as ready for service as our means allow of. I have our dear Troubridge for my assistant; in everything we are brothers. Hood and Hallowell are as active and good as ever: not that I mean to say any are otherwise; but you know these are men of resources. Hardy was bred in the old school, and I can assure you, that I never have been better satisfied with the real good discipline of a Ship than the *Vanguard's*. I hope from my heart that you will meet the Dons alone: if the two Fleets join, I am ready, and with some of my Ships in as high order as ever went to sea. The Russian Ships are blocking up Ancona; but again the *Généreux* has escaped them. As to politics, they are my abomination; the Ministers of Kings and Princes are as great scoundrels as ever lived. The brother of the Emperor is just going to marry the great something of Russia; and it is more than expected that a Kingdom is to be found for him in Italy, and that the King of Naples will be sacrificed. I am, &c.

NELSON

[Nelson shifted his Flag from the *Vanguard* to the *Foudroyant* on 8th June, and removed into that ship from the *Vanguard*, Captain Hardy, five lieutenants, the Surgeon, Chaplain, and some Mates and Midshipmen.]

To Lord St. Vincent

Palermo, *10th June, 1799*

My dear Lord,

We have a report that you are going home. This distresses us most exceedingly, and myself in particular; so much so, that I have serious thoughts of returning, if that event should take place. But for the sake of our Country, do not quit us at this serious moment. I wish not to detract from the merit of whoever may be your successor; but it must take a length of time, which I hope the war will not give, to be in any manner a St. Vincent. We look up to you, as we have always found you, as to our Father, under whose fostering care we have been led to fame. If, my dear Lord, I have any weight in your friendship, let me entreat you to rouse the sleeping lion. Give not up a particle of your authority to any one; be again our St. Vincent, and we shall be happy. Your affectionate

NELSON

CHAPTER SIX

EXECUTION OF CARACCIOLI

[After consulting with the King and Queen of Naples at Palermo, Nelson decided to go to Naples in the *Foudroyant* accompanied by Sir William and Lady Hamilton.

On the passage there he received letters informing him that Captain Foote, R.N. of H.M.S. *Seahorse*, the senior Naval officer at Naples had signed a treaty for the surrender of the castles of Uovo and Nuovo. The principal Neapolitan rebels had taken refuge in these forts. Nelson at once cancelled the truce on the ground that he could approve only of unconditional surrender by the rebels, and that he was vested with full authority to act from the King of Naples.]

OBSERVATIONS ON THE ARMISTICE CONCLUDED BETWEEN THE CARDINAL AND THE FRENCH AND REBELS, 24th JUNE, 1799.

Opinion delivered before I saw the treaty of Armistice, &c., only from reports met at sea.

The Armistice I take for granted is, that if the French and Rebels are not relieved by their friends in twenty-one days from the signing the Armistice, then that they shall evacuate Naples, in this infamous manner, to His Sicilian Majesty and triumphant to them, as stated in the Article.

All Armistices signify that either party may renew hostilities, giving a certain notice fixed upon by the contracting parties. In the present instance, I suppose the Cardinal thought that in twenty-one days he had not the power of driving the French from the Castle of St. Elmo, or the Rebels from the lower Castles of Uovo and Nuovo. The French and Rebels thought that if they could not be relieved in twenty-one days, they could, when unable to remain any longer, covenant to be removed to a place where they may be in a situation to renew their diabolical schemes against His Sicilian Majesty and the peace and happiness of his faithful subjects, and their removal to be at the expense of His Majesty; and those Enemies and Rebels to be protected by the Fleet of His Sicilian Majesty's faithful Ally, the King of Great Britain. Therefore evidently this agreement implies that both parties are supposed to remain in *statu quo*; but if either party receive relief from their situation, then the compact of course falls to the ground, and is of no effect; for if one party can be liberated from the agreement, it naturally implies the other is in the same state. And I fancy the question need not be asked whether, if the French fleet arrived this day in the Bay of Naples, whether the French and Rebels would adhere one moment to the Armistice? 'No!' the French Admiral would say, 'I am not come here to look on, but to act.' And so says the British Admiral; and declares on his honour that the arrival of either Fleet, British or French, destroys the compact, for neither can lay idle.

Therefore, the British Admiral proposes to the Cardinal to send, in joint names, to the French and Rebels, that the arrival of the British fleet has completely destroyed the compact, as would that of the French if they had had the power (which, thank God, they have not) to come to Naples.

Therefore, that it will be fixed that in two hours the French shall give possession of the Castle of St. Elmo to His Sicilian Majesty's faithful subjects, and the troops of his Allies; on which condition alone, they shall be sent to France without the stipulation of their being prisoners of war.

That as to the Rebels and Traitors, no power on earth has a right to stand between their gracious King and them: they must instantly throw themselves on the clemency of their Sovereign, for no other terms will be allowed them; nor will the French be allowed even to name them in any capitulation. If these terms are not complied with, in the time above mentioned—viz. two hours for the French, and instant submission on the part of the Rebels—such very favourable conditions will never be again offered.

NELSON

Foudroyant, Naples Bay, *24th June, 1799*.

Read and explained, and rejected by the Cardinal.

To Lord Keith*

Bay of Naples, *June 27th, 1799*

My dear Lord,

Having detailed my proceedings to the 16th of June, by the *Telegraph* brig, I have now to go on with my movements.

On the 17th the *Alexander* and *Goliath* joined me from off Malta; leaving to look out in that quarter, three Sloops of War;—the force

* Nelson wrote this letter to Lord St. Vincent, but seems to have changed the address, on hearing of the Earl's having resigned the command to Lord Keith.

with me was now fifteen Sail of two-decked Ships, English, and three Portuguese, with a Fire-ship and Cutter. On the 20th, the *Swallow*, Portuguese corvette, brought me your Lordship's dispatch of the 17th, acquainting me of the near approach of the Squadron under Sir Alan Gardner, and that Lord Keith was going in search of the French Fleet. As I had now no prospect of being in a situation to go in search of the Enemy's fleet, which at least is twenty-five Sail of the Line, and might be reinforced with two Venetian Ships, although I was firmly resolved they should not pass me without a battle, which would so cripple them that they might be unable to proceed on any distant service, I determined to offer myself for the service of Naples, where I knew the French Fleet intended going. With this determination I pushed for Palermo, and on the 21st, I went on shore for two hours, saw their Majesties and General Acton, who repeated to me what the General had wrote, (but which I had not received,) to request that I would instantly go into the Bay of Naples to endeavour to bring His Sicilian Majesty's affairs in that City to a happy conclusion.

I lost not one moment in complying with the request, and arrived in the Bay of Naples on the 24th, where I saw a Flag of Truce flying on board His Majesty's Ship *Seahorse*, Captain Foote, and also on the Castles of Uovo and Nuovo. Having on the passage received letters informing me that an infamous Armistice was entered into with the Rebels in those Castles, to which Captain Foote had put his name, I instantly made the signal to annul the Truce, being determined never to give my approbation to any terms with Rebels, but that of unconditional submission. The Fleet was anchored in a close line of battle, N.W. by N. and S.E. by S., from the Mole head one and a half mile distant, flanked by twenty-two Gun and Mortar boats, which I recalled from Procida. I sent Captains Troubridge and Ball instantly to the Cardinal Vicar-General, to represent to his Eminence my opinion of the infamous terms entered into with the Rebels, and also two papers which I enclose. His Eminence said he would send no papers, that if I pleased I might break the Armistice, for that he was tired of his situation. Captain Troubridge then asked his Eminence this plain question: 'If Lord Nelson breaks the Armistice, will your Eminence assist him in his attack on the Castles?' His answer was clear, 'I will neither assist him with men or guns.' After much communication, his Eminence desired to come on board to speak with me on his situation. I used every argument in my power to convince him that the Treaty and Armistice was at an end by the arrival of the Fleet; but an Admiral is no match in talking with a Cardinal. I therefore gave him my opinion in writing—viz. 'Rear-Admiral Lord Nelson, who arrived in the Bay of Naples on the 24th June with the British Fleet, found a Treaty entered into with the Rebels, which he is of opinion ought not to be carried into execution without the approbation of His Sicilian Majesty, Earl St. Vincent,—Lord Keith.'

Under this opinion the Rebels came out of the Castles, which was instantly occupied by the Marines of the Squadron. On the 27th Captains Troubridge and Ball, with 1,300 men, landed from the Ships, united with 500 Russians and a body of Royalists, half of whose *Officers* are, I have every reason to believe, *Rebels*,—cowards they have already proved themselves. Our batteries are open on St. Elmo, and a few days will, I hope, reduce it. The *Alexander* and another are just going to resume their station off Malta, which I am confident will very soon surrender, now all hopes of relief are cut off. I shall not fail to keep up a constant communication with your Lordship, and have the honour to be, with the greatest respect, your most obedient and faithful Servant,

NELSON

PROCLAMATION ISSUED AT NAPLES

Foudroyant, Naples Bay, *29th June, 1799*

Horatio Lord Nelson, Admiral of the British Fleet, in the Bay of Naples, gives notice to all those who have served as Officers Civil or Military, in the service of the infamous Neapolitan Republic, that, if, in the space of twenty-four hours for those who are in the City of Naples, and forty-eight hours for those who are within five miles of it, they do not give themselves up to the clemency of the King, to the Officer commanding the Castles Uovo and Nuovo, that Lord Nelson will consider them still as in rebellion, and enemies of His Sicilian Majesty.

NELSON

To Count Thurn

By Horatio Lord Nelson, &c. &c. &c.

Whereas Francisco Caracciolo, a Commodore in the service of his Sicilian Majesty, has been taken, and stands accused of rebellion against his lawful Sovereign, and for firing at his colours hoisted on board His Frigate, the *Minerva*, under your command,

You are, therefore, hereby required and directed to assemble five of the senior Officers under your command, yourself presiding, and proceed to inquire whether the crime with which the said Francisco

Caracciolo stands charged, can be proved against him; and if the charge is proved, you are to report to me what punishment he ought to suffer.

Given on board the *Foudroyant*, Naples Bay, the 29th June, 1799.

NELSON

To Count Thurn

By Horatio Lord Nelson, &c. &c. &c.

Whereas a Board of Naval Officers of his Sicilian Majesty hath been assembled to try Francisco Caracciolo for rebellion against his lawful Sovereign, and for firing at His Sicilian Majesty's Frigate *La Minerva*;

And whereas the said Board of Naval Officers have found the charge of rebellion fully proved against him, and have sentenced the said Caracciolo to suffer death;

You are hereby required and directed to cause the said sentence of death to be carried into execution upon the said Francisco Caracciolo accordingly, by hanging him at the fore yard-arm of His Sicilian Majesty's Frigate *La Minerva*, under your command, at five o'clock this evening; and to cause him to hang there until sunset, when you will have his body cut down, and thrown into the sea.

Given on board the *Foudroyant*, Naples Bay, the 29th of June, 1799.

To Captain Troubridge *Foudroyant*, Naples Bay, *6th July, 1799*

Whereas John Jolly, Private Marine, belonging to his Majesty's Ship *Alexander*, hath this day been tried by a Court Martial, on charges exhibited against him by Lieutenant Pearce, Second Lieutenant of Marines, for having struck the said Lieutenant Pearce while in the execution of his duty, and threatening to shoot him as soon as he should be released; and the Court finding him guilty of the said crimes, have adjudged the said John Jolly to suffer death, in the manner, and at such time and place, as I might think fit; and, whereas I think it proper, in pursuance of the said sentence, and to mark the heinousness of the crime he hath committed, that the said John Jolly should suffer death accordingly, you are here hereby required and directed to cause all the Marine forces that can properly be spared to be assembled at the most convenient place near your Camp on shore, and carry the said sentence into execution upon the said John Jolly on Monday morning next, the 8th instant, by causing him to be shot to death at the head of the said Marine forces, and in the usual manner;—a copy of which sentence you will receive herewith.

NELSON

To Captain Troubridge

Foudroyant, July 9th, 1799

Sir,

You will, in obedience to my orders, prepare everything for the execution of the sentence of the Court-Martial held on John Jolly; but when all the forms, except the last, are gone through, you will acquaint the prisoner, that, although there has been no circumstance to mitigate the severity of the law, yet that I have reason to hope that the sparing of his life will have as beneficial an effect for the discipline of the Service, as if he had suffered death. You will, therefore, respite the prisoner from the sentence of death, till his Majesty's pleasure is known. I hope that this extraordinary mark of lenity will have its full effect on the mind of those under your command, and be a beacon to them to avoid the crime of drunkenness, which brings with it even the punishment of death. And here I pledge myself to them that, if any similar circumstance happens in future, that I will most assuredly order the sentence to be immediately carried into execution. I am, Sir, yours, &c.

(*Vide p. 288 infra*)

NELSON

To Lord Keith

Foudroyant, Bay of Naples, *13th July, 1799*

My Lord,

I have the pleasure to inform you of the surrender of Fort St. Elmo, (on the terms of the enclosed Capitulation,) after open batteries of eight days, during which time our heavy batteries were advanced within 180 yards of the ditch. The very great strength of St. Elmo and its more formidable position, will mark with what fortitude, perseverence, and activity the combined Forces must have acted. Captain Troubridge was the Officer selected for the command of all the forces landed from the Squadron; Captain Ball assisted him for seven days till his services were wanted at Malta, when his place was ably supplied by Captain Hallowell, an Officer of the most distinguished merit, and to whom Captain Troubridge expresses the highest obligation. Captain Hood, with a garrison for the Castle Nuovo, and to keep good order in the Capital, an arduous task at that time, was also landed from the Squadron; and I have the pleasure to tell you that no Capital is more quiet than Naples. I transmit you Captain Troubridge's letter to me, with returns of killed and wounded.

I have now to state to your Lordship, that although the ability and resources of my brave friend Troubridge are well known to all the world, yet even he had difficulties to struggle with in every way, which the state of the Capital will easily bring to your idea, that has raised his great character even higher than it was before! and it is my earnest request that your Lordship will mention him in that way to the Board of Admiralty, that His Majesty may be graciously pleased to bestow some mark of his Royal Favour on Captain Troubridge,* which will give real happiness to your Lordship's most obedient and faithful servant.

NELSON

To Earl Spencer

13th July, 1799

My dear Lord,

I have much to say, but am unable to write or speak half so much as my duty would make it right, therefore I must be brief. On my fortunate arrival here I found a most infamous treaty entered into with the Rebels, in direct disobedience of His Sicilian Majesty's orders. I had the happiness of saving His Majesty's honour, rejecting with disdain any terms but unconditional submission, to Rebels. The Rebels came out of the Castles with this knowledge, without any honours, and the principal Rebels were seized and conducted on board the Ships of the Squadron. The others, embarked in fourteen polacres, were anchored under the care of our Ships. His Majesty has entirely approved of my conduct in this matter. I presume to recommend Captain Troubridge for some mark of his Majesty's favour: it would be supposing you, my dear Lord, was ignorant of his merit, was I to say more, than that he is a first-rate General. The King holds his Levées on the quarter-deck of the *Foudroyant*, at the same hours as he did when in his palace. His Majesty's health is perfect, and he is in the highest spirits and good-humour.

May I offer my kindest respects to Lady Spencer, and believe me, I am sensible of her goodness. Lieutenant Parkinson will, I am sure, meet with your kind protection: he is an Officer of great merit. Lord Keith writes me, if certain events take place, it may be necessary to draw down this Squadron for the protection of Minorca. Should such an order come at this moment, it would be a cause for some consideration whether Minorca is to be risked, or the two Kingdoms of Naples and Sicily? I rather think my decision would be to risk the former. I am told the alteration of the Government is begun in the Capital, by the abolition of the Feudal system, and it is meant to be continued through the Country. Sir John Acton is with his Majesty: I need not say more than he has the wisest and most honest head in this Kingdom. Sir William and Lady Hamilton are, to my great

* Captain Troubridge was created a Baronet, on 30th November, 1799.

comfort, with me; for without them it would have been impossible I could have rendered half the service to his Majesty which I have now done: their heads and their hearts are equally great and good. With every sentiment of respect and attachment, believe me, my dear Lord, your obliged and faithful,

NELSON

NELSON DISOBEYS ORDERS AND IS REBUKED

[On 13th July, 1799, an order reached Nelson from the Commander-in-Chief, Lord Keith (who had replaced Lord St. Vincent), 'requiring and directing you to send such ships as you can possibly spare to Minorca to wait my orders.']

To Lord Keith

Foudroyant, Naples Bay, *July 13th, 1799*

My Lord,

His Sicilian Majesty arrived in this Bay on the 10th, and immediately hoisted his standard on board the *Foudroyant*, where his Majesty still remains with all his Ministers. It has been and is my study to treat his Majesty with all the respect due to so great a personage, and I have the pleasure to believe that my humble endeavours have met with the Royal approbation. I have the honour to be, your Lordship's obedient servant,

NELSON

The effusions of loyalty from the lower order of the people to their *Father*—for by no other name do they address the King—is truly moving: with some *few* exceptions the conduct of the Nobles has been infamous; and it delights me to see that His Majesty remarks the difference in the most proper manner.

To Lord Keith

Foudroyant, Naples Bay, *13th July, 1799*

My Lord,

I have to acknowledge the receipt of your Lordship's orders of June 27th, and as soon as the safety of His Sicilian Majesty's Kingdoms is secured, I shall not lose one moment in making the detachment you are pleased to order. At present, under God's Providence, the safety of His Sicilian Majesty, and his speedy restoration to his Kingdom, depends on this Fleet, and the confidence inspired even by the appearance of our Ships before the City is beyond all belief; and I have no scruple in declaring my opinion that should any event draw us from the Kingdom, that if the French remain in any part of it, disturbances will again arise, for all order having been completely overturned, it must take a thorough cleansing, and some little time, to restore tranquillity. I have the honour to be with great respect, your Lordship's obedient servant,

NELSON

To Earl Spencer

Foudroyant, Naples Bay, *13th July, 1799*

My dear Lord,

You will easily conceive my feelings at the order this day received from Lord Keith; but my mind, your Lordship will know by my letter sent by Lieutenant Parkinson and Mr. Silvester, was perfectly prepared for this order; and more than ever is my mind made up, that, at this moment, I will not part with a single Ship, as I cannot do that without drawing a hundred and twenty men from each Ship now at the Siege of Capua, where an Army is gone this day. I am fully aware of the act I have committed; but, sensible of my loyal intentions, I am prepared for any fate which may await my disobedience. Capua and Gaeta will soon fall; and the moment the scoundrels of French are out of this Kingdom, I shall send eight or nine Ships of the Line to Minorca. I have done what I thought right; others may think differently; but it will be my consolation that I have gained a Kingdom, seated a faithful Ally of his Majesty firmly on his throne, and restored happiness to millions. Do not think, my dear Lord, that my opinion is formed from the arrangements of any one. *No.*; be it good, or be it bad, it is all my own. It is natural I should wish the decision of the Admiralty and my Commander-in-Chief as speedily as possible. To obtain the former, I beg your Lordship's interest with the Board; and, in all events, I shall consider myself your Lordship's, &c.

NELSON

To the Duke of Clarence *13th July, 1799*

You will have heard, Sir, and conversation will naturally arise upon it, that I have disobeyed Lord Keith's orders in not sending or going down with the Squadron under my command; but, by not doing it, I have been, with God's blessing, the principal means of placing a good Man and faithful Ally of your Royal Father on his throne, and securing peace to these two Kingdoms. I am well aware of the consequences of disobeying my orders; but, as I have often before risked my life for the good Cause, so I with cheerfulness did my commission: for although a Military tribunal may think me criminal, the world will approve of my conduct. I regard not my own safety, when the honour of my gracious King is at stake. The Almighty has in this war blessed my endeavours beyond my most sanguine expectations, and never more than in the entire expulsion of the French thieves from the Kingdom of Naples. I am, &c.

NELSON

To Lord Keith

July 14th, 1799

My dear Lord,

I am truly so very unwell that I have not the power of writing so much of our situation here as I could wish, but thank God all goes on well, and I hope this country will be happier than ever; I am sure it is their Majesties' desire to make it so. The feudal system is fast breaking up, the entire change is already made in the Capital. To all your wishes, depend on it, I shall pay the very strictest attention. Hope and a large part of this Squadron shall go to you when they can be spared, but at present the safety of this Kingdom depends on us. Captain Foote, says Mr. Moncton, is not intended to remain at sea, therefore does not recommend his promotion at present; he has very bad health, but a modest well-behaved young man. Ever, my dear Lord, believe me, your obliged,

NELSON

To Lady Nelson

Naples, *14th July, 1799*

My dear Fanny,

I have to thank you sincerely for your letters. I rejoice that you gave Mr. Bolton* the money, and I wish it made up to £500. I never regarded money, nor wanted it for my own use; therefore, as the East India Company have made me so magnificent a present, I beg that £2,000 of it may be disposed of in the following manner;—five hundred pounds to my father; five hundred to be made up to Mr. Bolton, and let it be a *God-send*, without any restriction; five hundred to Maurice, and five hundred to William. And if you think my sister Matcham would be gratified by it, do the same for her. If I were rich I would do more; but it will very soon be known how poor I am, except my yearly income. I am not suprised at my brother's death;† three are now dead, younger than myself, having grown to man's age. My situation here is not to be described, but suffice it to say, I am endeavouring to work for good. To my father say everything which is kind. I love, honour, and respect him

* His brother-in-law.

† The Rev. Suckling Nelson: he died in April, 1799.

as a father and as a man, and as the very best man I ever saw. May God Almighty bless you, my dear father, and all my brothers and sisters, is the fervent prayer of your affectionate

NELSON

To Commodore Troubridge

17th July, 1799

My dear Troubridge,

When you send in a Summons to the Commander of the French troops in Capua, His Sicilian Majesty approves that, on condition the Commander immediately gives up *Capua* and *Gaeta*, that after laying down their arms, colours, &c., the French garrison shall be permitted to go to France without any restrictions. If this is not complied with, prisoners of war, and as degrading terms as it is in your power to give them—no covered wagons, no protection to Rebels—in short, the Allies must dictate the terms. You will as often as possible, but at least once a day, make some person send me a Journal of your proceedings. His Majesty places the firmest reliance on you, and is confident of your exertions in the glorious Cause. That rapid success may crown your labours, and that you may receive those honours so justly your due, is the fervent prayer of your affectionate and faithful Friend,

NELSON

There is a person who has been a NOTORIOUS *Rebel* but now PRETENDS TO SERVE his King faithfully; if he should attempt to come even into your presence, I earnestly request you will never voluntarily admit him to your sight, much less speak to him; for the honour and loyalty which you possess, never ought to be contaminated with infamy and rebellion. His name is said to be *Rocca Romana.*

NELSON

To Lord Keith

Foudroyant, Naples, *July 19th, 1799*

My Lord,

I am this moment honoured with your order of the 9th, directing me to detach from the Island of Sicily, the whole, or such part of the force, as might not be necessary in that Island. Your Lordship, at the time of sending me the order, was not informed of the change of affairs in the Kingdom of Naples, and that all our Marines and a body of Seamen are landed, in order to drive the French scoundrels out of the Kingdom, which, with God's blessing will very soon be effected, when a part of this Squadron shall be immediately sent to Minorca; but unless the French are at least drove from Capua, I think it right not to obey your

Lordship's orders for sending down any part of the Squadron under my orders. I am perfectly aware of the consequences of disobeying the orders of my Commander-in-Chief; but, as I believe the safety of the Kingdom of Naples depends at the present moment on my detaining the Squadron, I have no scruple in deciding that it is better to save the Kingdom of Naples and risk Minorca, than to risk the Kingdom of Naples to save Minorca. Your Lordship will, I hope, approve of my decision, and believe me, with the greatest respect,

Your Lordship's faithful and obedient servant,

NELSON

To Evan Nepean, Admiralty

Foudroyant, Naples, *July 19th, 1799*

Sir,

I send you a copy of Lord Keith's order to me and my answer, and a copy of a letter I have received since my determination was made (not at this moment to send a single man from this Squadron). I feel the importance of the decision I have taken, and know I subject myself to a trial for my conduct: but I am so confident of the uprightness of my intentions for his Majesty's service, and for that of his Sicilian Majesty, which I consider as the same, that, with all respect, I submit myself to the judgment of my superiors, I have the honour to be, &c.

NELSON

From Evan Nepean

'I have to acknowledge the receipt of your Lordship's letter of the 19th July, inclosing the copy of an order you had received from Vice-Admiral Lord Keith, directing you to proceed with the whole, or to detach a part of the Squadron under your command to Minorca, and also the copy of your letter to his Lordship in answer thereto, and I have their Lordships' commands to acquaint you, that although the co-operation of a British Naval Force with the Army of his Sicilian Majesty might be, and it appears to have been necessary, yet, as from the information your Lordship had received from Lord Keith, you must have been satisfied that nothing was to be apprehended from the Enemy's Fleet, it does not appear to their Lordships to have been necessary that the whole of the Squadron under your command should have been kept for such co-operation, but that a part of it would have been sufficient, not only to have inspired that confidence, which your Lordship states to have been the result of its appearance, but also to have afforded effectual assistance to his Sicilian Majesty; and that their Lordships do not, therefore, from any information now before them, see sufficient reason to justify your having disobeyed the orders you had received from your Commanding-Officer, or having left Minorca exposed to the risk of being attacked, without having any Naval force to protect it.'

To Captain Louis

Foudroyant, Naples Bay,
30th July, 1799

You are hereby required and directed to receive on board the Ship you command, such Marines as may be sent to you from the different Ships of the Squadron, and proceed with them to Gaeta; and, on your arrival there, to send to the French Governor of that Fortress the terms of Capitulation entered into between me and the Commandant of Capua for the surrender of Gaeta; which Articles are enclosed herewith, and with which you will comply on your part, and you will embark the French garrison therein on board Polacres, which will be immediately sent you to put them on board; but should the Polacres not arrive in time, you will embark them on board such craft as you may be able to procure there, to convey them round to this place, in order for their embarkation for Toulon.

NELSON

To Earl Spencer

Naples, *August 1st, 1799*

My dear Lord,

I certainly, from only having a left hand, cannot enter into details which may explain the motives which actuate my conduct, and which may be necessary for a Commanding officer, who may wish to have every subject of duty detailed by those under his command. My principle, my dear Lord, is, to assist in driving the French to the Devil, and in restoring peace and happiness to mankind. I feel I am fitter to do the action than to describe it; therefore, briefly, all the French being forced to quit this Kingdom, and some order restored, two more Ships of the Line are to sail this evening for Minorca, which I will take care of. 500 Marines, united with 600 excellent Swiss, are going to attack Civitá Vecchia, and to encourage the insurrection in the Roman State. The sea part of this business will be commanded by Captain Louis of the *Minotaur*, and the land part under Captain Hallowell of the *Swiftsure*, assisted by an excellent Officer, Captain Cresswell of the Marines, to whom it has been necessary for me to give the temporary rank of Major, which I wish the Board would confirm. I trust to your Lordship's goodness to promote Lieutenant Compton, who has been long with me.

The *Northumberland*, Captain Martin, with some Frigates, if they can be found—but I am stripped to the skin—goes on the Coast of Genoa, to co-operate with Field Marshal Suwarrow. The importance of an active Squadron on that Coast no one is better acquainted with than myself. I wish to send the Portuguese Squadron to Lord Keith, as his Lordship seems to consider them as of some consequence. I cordially congratulate you on the happy arrival of the combined Fleets at Cadiz; for having escaped the vigilance of Lord Keith, I was fearful they would get to Brest. His Sicilian Majesty having settled a certain degree of order, returns to Palermo on the 7th.

I send you a letter of Sir John Acton to me, which gives reasons for the continuing the Cardinal at the head of affairs in this Country. My opinion of him has never altered, but, as he is now only Lieutenant-General of the Kingdom, with a Council of eight, without whose consent no act is valid—but we know the head of every Board must have great weight—this man must soon be removed; for all about him have been and are so corrupt, that there is nothing which may not be bought. Acton and Belmonte seem to me the only uncorrupted men in the Kingdom. Lord Keith has told me of Russian and Turkish fleets taking care of the Coast of Italy. I hear of them, but not even a Corvette have I yet seen. I have only to say that with your every indulgence give me credit for my inclination to do what is right, and believe me, your faithful and obliged,

NELSON

To Captain Nisbet*

Foudroyant, Naples Bay, *3rd August, 1799*

My dear Sir,

I herewith enclose you a letter received some days ago, and on the receipt of this, you will keep a good look-out for the *Northumberland*, who is coming your way, and join her as soon as you can, Captain Martin having letters for you. I am sorry to find you have been cruizing off Civitá Vecchia. I was in hopes of your being on the North Coast of Italy, but I am persuaded it was done for the best. I here enclose you the copy of a letter sent open to me from Mr. Smith, at Constantinople, respecting some supplies furnished the *Bonne Citoyenne*, at the Dardanelles, and request that you will give the necessary directions to have it settled, or explain it to me that it may be settled. Mr. Tyson has written the Purser, Mr. Isaacson, to desire he will draw out bills for the amount, and fresh vouchers for your signature, and the settlement of his account.

I am, wishing you ever success, yours very affectionately,

NELSON

* His stepson.

To Captain Louis

Naples Bay, *August 3rd, 1799*

Sir,

You carried with you the treaty, and, in two hours after your arrival, and the Capitulation was presented, you was to take possession of the gates, and in twenty-four hours the garrison were to be embarked. I am hurt and surprised that the Capitulation has not been complied with. It shall be, and the Commander has agreed to it. I have not read your paper enclosed. You will execute my orders, or attack it. The fellow ought to be kicked for his impudence. You will instantly take possession of the gates and the fortress. I had reason to expect it had been done long ago. I am very much hurt that it has not. Tell Captain Darby, who (I taking for granted that the business had been long settled) was directed to take the Marines, that the Marines must not be taken away until we have possession of the place, and that he must assist in doing it.

I am, dear Sir, your faithful servant,

NELSON

To Captain Louis

Foudroyant, Naples Bay, *4th August, 1799*

Dear Sir,

I have received your letter of yesterday, and am happy to find that all matters are settled. I was sorry that you had entered into any altercation with the scoundrel. The Capitulation once signed, there could be no room for dispute. The enclosed order will point out to you how you are to proceed, and believe me, dear Sir, your most obedient

NELSON

There is no way of dealing with a Frenchman but to knock him down. To be civil to them is only to be laughed at, when they are enemies.

Naples, *August 4th, 1799*

My dear Fanny,

A few days ago brought me your letter of May 6th from Clifton, but since then I see by the papers you have been in London. I am glad you went to court on the King's birthday. By the next I have no doubt but the world will be at peace and if Lord Keith had fallen in with the French fleet we should have had it by this time. Thank God all goes well in Italy and the kingdom of Naples is liberated from thieves and murderers, but still it has so overthrown the fabric of a regular government that much time and great care is necessary to keep the country quiet. Their Majesties have confidence in my councils which they know to be disinterested and are fixed in the belief that whatever I undertake is sure of success and indeed this is general to the Kingdom. However flattering this may be, it has its alloys for if anything was to go wrong my popularity would be over.

The first of August was celebrated here with as much respect as our situation would admit. The King dined with me and when his Majesty drank my health a royal salute of 21 guns was fired from all H.S.M.'s ships of war and from all the castles. In the evening there was a general illumination. Amongst others a large vessel was fitted out like a Roman galley. On the oars were fixed lamps and in the centre was erected a rostral column with my name, at the stern elevated were two angels supporting my picture. More than 2,000 variegated lamps were fixed round the vessel, an orchestra was fitted up and filled with the very best musicians and singers. The piece of music was in a great measure my praises, describing their distress, but Nelson comes, the invincible Nelson and we are safe and happy again. Thus you must not make you think me vain so far very far from it and I relate it more from gratitude than vanity.

I return to Palermo with the King tomorrow and what may then be my movements it is impossible for me to say. As to the co-operation of Turks and Russian fleets I see none of them.

May God bless you all. Pray say what is true and I really steal time to write this letter, and my hand is ready to drop, and as to my eyes I cannot see half what I write. My dear father must forgive my not writing so often as I ought and so must my brothers and friends but ever believe me your affectionate

NELSON

[On the 5th August the *Foudroyant* sailed from Naples with the King on board for Palermo, where she arrived on the 8th; on that day 'at 1 p.m. her Sicilian Majesty and Royal Family came on board the *Foudroyant*: saluted with twenty-one guns. At 5, his Sicilian Majesty, the Queen, and all the Royal Family, attended by the Admiral, went on shore: saluted them with twenty-one guns, which was answered from all the forts.']

To Evan Nepean, Admiralty

Foudroyant, Naples Bay, *5th August, 1799*

Sir,

As I am proceeding in his Majesty's Ship *Foudroyant*, with his Sicilian Majesty on board for Palermo, and it being necessary, for the good of his Majesty's service, that the command of this Squadron should be left with an Officer above the rank of Captain, especially as the Russian and Turkish Squadrons are very soon expected in this Bay; I have, therefore, thought it right to give Captain Troubridge an order to wear a Broad Pendant, he being an Officer highly deserving their Lordship's attention, and which I hope they will approve.

I have the honour to be, &c.

NELSON

To the Prince de Luzzi

Palermo, *13th August, 1799*

Sir,

I have this moment received the honour of your Excellency's letter, conveying to me his Sicilian Majesty's most gracious approbation of my conduct, and also, that his Majesty has been pleased to confer upon me the title of Duke of Bronte, together with the estate attached to it. I request that your Excellency will lay me with all humility, and full of gratitude at his Majesty's feet; express to him my attachment to his Sacred Person, the Queen, and Royal Family, and that it shall be the study of my life, by following the same conduct which has gained me his Royal favours, to merit the continuance of them.

I sincerely thank your Excellency for the very handsome manner in which you have executed the Royal Commands, and believe me, with the highest respect, your Excellency's most obliged servant,

BRONTE NELSON

To the Rev. Edmund Nelson

Palermo, *August 15th, 1799*

My dear Father,

His Sicilian Majesty having created me a Duke, by the title of Bronte, to which he has attached a Feud of, it is said, about £3,000 a year, to be at my disposal, I shall certainly not omit this opportunity of being useful to my family, always reserving a right to the possessor, of leaving one third of the income for the payment of legacies. It shall first go to you, my dear father, and in succession to my elder brother and children male, William the same, Mrs. Bolton's boys, Mrs. Matcham's, and my nearest relations. For your natural life, the estate shall be taxed with £500 a year, but this is not to be drawn into a precedent, that the next heir may expect it. Now, my honoured father, receive this small tribute as a mark of gratitude to the best of parents from his most dutiful son,

NELSON

To Alexander Davison

About 15th August, 1799

You will observe in a part of the King's letter, an observation is made, that this present could not hurt my delicate feelings; that is, I might have before received money and jewels, but I rejected them, as became me, and never received one farthing for all the expenses of the Royal Family on board the *Vanguard* and *Foudroyant*. This I expect from the Board of Admiralty, and that they will order me a suitable sum. It has been honour, and not money which I have sought, nor sought in vain. I am, &c.

NELSON

To Rear-Admiral Duckworth

Palermo, *16th August*, *1799*

My dear Admiral,

Send us cables and ropes. The *Seahorse* has been drove on shore for want of both, and half the Squadron will be in the same state. The *Audacious* has not a sail to her yards, and both she and *Goliath* must soon go down, to be entirely refitted. *Alexander* and *Lion* are also in a terrible state. The former must go to England the moment Malta is taken. The Russian Squadron of three Sail of the Line, under Rear-Admiral Kartzow, arrived yesterday; but having 520 sick to land, are for the present, unfit for service. The united Squadrons from Corfu are the Lord knows where, therefore I must desire, if it is possible, that you send at least one Frigate. The *Minerva*, or, if possible, one equally as good, with a good Corvette, to join Captain Martin on the Coast of Genoa; for I must have a respectable Squadron on the Coast, to support Field-Marshal Suwarrow. The *Seahorse*, I hope, got off on the 4th, but this news is not certain; but I rely on Captain Foote's exertions. The *Swiftsure* is gone to her assistance. My Flag is in a Transport—the *Foudroyant* being gone to Malta, where I want to make an exertion to possess it. The Gulf of Spezzia is said to be taken by the Austrians. In Naples everything is quiet; but the Cardinal appears to be working mischief against the King, and in support of the Nobles: he must, sooner or later, be removed for his bad conduct.

We are dying with heat, and the feast of Santa Rosalia begins this day: how shall we get through it? The King sent me a diamond-hilted sword with a most affectionate letter, and also, I received a dispatch that he had created me Duke of Bronte, and attached an estate to it. The Title, of course, I cannot assume, without the approbation of our King, which I now hear has been some time desired. Darby and Hood, I hope, have long joined you. Pray be so good as to deliver to them the Medals, with my best regards. Our dear Lady has been very unwell, and if this fête to-night do not kill her, I dare say she will write you to-morrow, for there is none she respects more than yourself. Good Sir William is much better for his trip. I send the *Aurora* to get everything, and if you cannot supply her she must go to Gibraltar. Our distress for stores is, you know, very great, and we must hold out another winter. Make my best regards acceptable to Sir James St. Clair. I really have not the power of writing, and I am nearly blind; but whilst I have life, believe me, my dear Admiral, your obliged and affectionate,

NELSON

To the Rev. William Nelson — Palermo, *August 21st, 1799*

My dear Brother,

I am truly sorry that Administration have neither done that for me or my family which might have been expected. Lords St. Vincent and Duncan have £1,000 a-year from Ireland: I have heard of no such thing for *Nelson*. You may be assured that I have never forgotten or will forget my family: I think that would be a crime, and if you will tell me to whom and what I am to ask for, for the descent of the Title and the pension goes with it, I will do it. My father, Maurice, yourself and children, Mrs. Bolton's, and Mrs. Matcham's, this is the way I have fixed the Bronte estate, as I have wrote our dear father; that letter you will see. You may be assured, that when a year comes round, and I really know my income, no brother will be more ready to assist than myself. How is Aunt Mary? Assure her she shall want for nothing, and if she does, pray write Lady Nelson, and she will send her anything she desires. Give my kind love to Mrs. Nelson, and when you write, to the children. Kind regards to all our friends at Swaffham, and don't expect a 'turnover the leaf', for that I cannot ever accomplish; but believe me ever your most affectionate brother, NELSON

I do not assume the name of 'Bronte', except in Sicily, till the King's approbation.

To Alexander Davison — *About 23rd August, 1799*

The estate of Bronte is said to be about £3,000 a year; I am determined on one thing, that the inhabitants shall be the happiest in all his Sicilian Majesty's dominions. I have to thank you for the interest you have taken in the business of the India House; their present has been magnificent; but my friend, these presents, rich as they are, do not elevate me; my pride is, that at Constantinople, from the Grand Signior to the lowest Turk, the name of Nelson is familiar in their mouths; and in this Country, I am everything which a grateful Monarch and people can call me. Poor dear Miller is dead, and so will be your friend Nelson; but until death, he will wear your Medal that was intended for Miller. I have the full tide of honour, but little real comfort; could I have that, with a morsel of bread and cheese, it would be all I have to ask of kind Heaven. If the war goes on, I shall be knocked off by a ball, or killed with chagrin. My conduct is measured by the Admiralty by the narrow rule of law, when I think it should have been done by that of common sense. I restored a faithful Ally by breach of orders—Lord Keith lost a Fleet by obedience, against his own sense, yet as one is censured, the other must be approved. I am, &c.

NELSON

CHAPTER SEVEN

HOMEWARD BOUND

[For a short period after Lord St. Vincent had returned to England, Nelson, now Rear-Admiral of the Red, was acting Commander-in-chief in the Mediterranean, but in January, 1800, Vice-Admiral Lord Keith arrived in Italian waters as Commander-in-chief and Nelson at once came under his orders. At this period, Valetta was being blockaded by a British squadron and Nelson spent a considerable time in Maltese waters.

During this period also the two remaining ships of the French Fleet at the Battle of the Nile (*Le Genereux* and *Guillaume Tell*) were captured, the whole of the French Fleet present in that battle thus being either captured or destroyed.

In February, 1800, Nelson's health obliged him to return to Palermo from Malta whence he sailed in June in the *Foudroyant* to Leghorn having on board the Queen of Naples, her children and Sir William and Lady Hamilton. At Leghorn he left his ship and with the Hamiltons set out for England via Trieste, Vienna and Hamburg, arriving in England on 6th November, 1800.

Eight weeks later he was promoted to the rank of Vice-Admiral of the Blue. In March, 1801, a large Fleet was assembled under Admiral Sir Hyde Parker and Nelson was appointed Second in Command in the *St. George.* Then followed the Battle of Copenhagen.

During his brief stay in England, Nelson finally parted from his wife on 13th January. On 30th January, Horatia was born.]

To Earl Spencer

Palermo, *September 4th, 1799*

My dear Lord,

The courier by which I wrote my letter fourteen days since, is still at Palermo, and the time of his departure so uncertain that I am determined to tell you briefly our situation. The Turkish and Russian Squadron, now united with Vice-Admiral Kartzow, are eleven Sail of the Line, Frigates, &c. The object of the Russian Admiral is Malta solely; as to the idea of going to Naples to land troops, in order to go into the Roman State, or to prevent anarchy in the Kingdom, those are to him secondary operations. It is my intention to have six or seven Sail of the Line at Gibraltar, and four at Minorca, but at present I cannot send all this force down, as Commodore Troubridge is at Naples, which he cannot leave, until the Russian Admiral sends Ships to supply the place of these Ships. The Russian Admiral makes no secret that his Ships cannot keep the sea during the winter, and the Turks we know cannot, therefore if the Coast of Naples requires a Naval Force during that season, His Sicilian Majesty is likely to be in a worse state than before the arrival of this United Squadron. The Portuguese Squadron must return home and the *Alexander*, *Audacious*, and *Lion* are in a truly wretched state; therefore the *Foudroyant* will be the only Ship of the present force, this side Minorca, fit for service. I have just heard accounts that the Spaniards have not four Sail of the Line at Carthagena—therefore I shall detain the *Minotaur*, and send Troubridge to arrange a proper Naval protection for the security of Minorca, which I have never yet considered in the *smallest* danger, but it has been a misfortune that others have thought differently from me on that point. I send you a letter from General Acton. It will convey to your Lordship an idea of my situation here. It is indeed an uncomfortable one; for plain common sense points out that the King should return to Naples, but nothing can move him. Believe me I shall do my best in all circumstances, but I am almost blind, and truly very unwell; and, which does not mend matters, I see no King in Europe really assisting these good Monarchs, but our gracious Sovereign. I am, &c.,

NELSON

To Captain Troubridge, H.M. Ship *Culloden*

Most secret.

Palermo, *September 7th, 1799*

My dear Troubridge,

Having secured the free access of the Straits by the force detached to Gibraltar, and, from your account and Hood's, being perfectly at my ease about Minorca, you have my full permission to either immediately send Louis to Civita Vecchia, with what Vessels you can give him, *Perseus*—or to keep under sail when you think the Russians and Turks are approaching, and go direct to Civita Vecchia, and try what can be done; and if you can get possession, then to land not only your Marines, but such other force as you can spare, and not to move till further orders from me; for, as I have before said, I am perfectly easy about Minorca. Now you know my sentiments, you will act and arrange accordingly; but this must be kept secret, or we shall give jealousy to the Russians. As for the Turks, we can do anything with them. They are good people, but perfectly useless. I think if you go, you had better keep Captain Dunn, although I believe he has stock on board for Duckworth. Do you manage this; for he sails with Secret orders. Your Boatswain's mate shall have an Acting order, and Harriman will, of course, travel with you. All here join in regard. I am, &c.,

NELSON

DISPOSITION OF THE SQUADRON UNDER THE COMMAND OF REAR-ADMIRAL LORD NELSON—viz.,

September 11th, 1799

Off Alexandria and coast of Egypt, under Sir Sidney Smith:
Le Tigre, 80 guns
Theseus, 74
Cameleon, 18

Off Malta, under Rear-Admiral the Marquis de Niza:

Principe Real, 92	Portuguese	*Alexander*, 74
Rainha, 74	Portuguese	*Audacious*, 74
Affonco, 70	Portuguese	*Lion*, 64
Benjamin, 18	Portuguese	*Success*, 32
El Corso, 16	Portuguese	*Bonne Citoyenne*, 20
		Strombolo, Bomb, 16

At Palermo:
St. Sebastian, 64
Balloon, 16
Fulminante Cutter, 4

On the coast of Naples, and Roman coast, under Commodore Troubridge:

Culloden, 74	*Transfer*, 16
Minotaur, 74	*Perseus*, Bomb, 20
La Mutine, 18	

On the North coast of Italy, and to go down to Gibraltar as soon as relieved by a Russian Squadron:

Northumberland, 74	*Seahorse*, 38
Thalia, 36	*Santa Teresa*, 36
Peterel, 18	*San Leon*, 14

To blockade Cadiz, and protect the Straits of Gibraltar, Minorca, &c.:

Leviathan, 74	*La Minerve*, 40
Majestic, 74	*Emerald*, 36
Vanguard, 74	*L'Alceste*, 36
Powerful, 74	*Mermaid*, 32
Bellerophan, 74	*Santa Dorothea*, 36
Zealous, 74	*Incendiary Fire Ship*, 18
Goliath, 74	*Salamine*, 18
Swiftsure, 74	*St. Vincent Cutter*, 16

Enemy's Force as reported

At Cadiz—7 Sail of the Line
Carthagena—4 ditto
Toulon—2 ditto
Ancona
} Besides Frigates Corvettes, &c.

Alexandria—2 ships, late Venetians

To His Excellency The Marquis de Niza, Rear-Admiral Commanding the Blockade of Malta.

Palermo, *3rd October, 1799*

As the reduction of the Island of Malta is of the greatest consequence to the interests of the Allied Powers at war with France, and the withdrawing the Squadron of His Most Faithful Majesty under your command, at this time, from the blockade of that Island, will be of the most ruinous consequences to their interests, particularly when an Enemy's fleet of thirteen Sail of the Line are daily expected in those seas, and two Sail of the Line and several other Ships with provisions and stores, for the relief of Malta, are now lading at Toulon; you are hereby required and directed, in consideration of the above circumstances, and notwithstanding the orders you may have received from your Court to return to Lisbon, not ón any consideration whatsoever to withdraw one man from that Island, which may have been landed from the Squadron from under your Excellency's command, or detach one Ship down the Mediterranean, until further orders from me for that purpose; and you are also required to keep the Brig which will bring you these dispatches, and employ her for the good of the service; and the *Balloön* shall be sent to you in a few days which you may, if you think proper, send to Lisbon with your dispatches.

NELSON

To Captain Sir William Sidney Smith

Palermo, *October, 1799*

My dear Sir,

The Admiralty hope, with all the civilized world, from the consequences of your great exertions and bravery at St. Jean d'Acre, that all the French are destroyed in Egypt, together with their Shipping, &c. I am therefore particularly instructed to direct you, that if this has happily taken place, that all the English ships are to join me. You will, therefore, should that be the case, join me immediately, with the *Tigre*, and all the English ships; and as the Enemy have a large force on the Coast of Portugal, it is of the utmost importance that the junction should be made as soon as possible. At all events the *Theseus* cannot be wanted. The frigate carrying Earl Elgin to Constantinople has my orders to return immediately here. You will not therefore on any account detain Captain Morris one moment. The Turks having no object to attend to but their own Coast, I should think are equal to that service. Ever, my dear Sir, your faithful humble servant,

NELSON

To H.R.H. the Duke of Clarence

Port Mahon, *17th August, 1799*

Sir,

Although I have really but a moment, yet I am sure I cannot better bestow it than in assuring your Royal Highness of my respectful attachment; and I shall retrace our late occurrences as fast as my pen and head will allow me.

Having on the 1st of October received the terms on which the French were to evacuate the City of Rome and Civita Vecchia, on the 2nd, the *Phaeton* arrived, bringing me an account, that, on the 8th and 9th of September, thirteen large Ships, supposed to be of the Line, had been seen off Cape Ortegal. On this information, in case they should be bound into the Mediterranean, I directed the *Culloden* and *Minotaur*, with some small Vessels that were off Civita Vecchia, to proceed immediately, and join me off Mahon harbour; the *Foudroyant* arriving the same day, I sailed from Palermo on the morning of the 5th. I had hardly got clear of the Gulf, when I met the *Salamine* with information from Mahon, that on the 28th of September, a Vessel from Tunis to Minorca had fallen in with two strange Sail of the Line, Frigates, and other Vessels, to the amount of twenty, steering towards Malta. As I have seven Sail of the Line, one Frigate, and three Sloops on the service there, I had to send the Brig to ascertain the event. This news, which I still hope is false, did not tend to make me easy, as in truth I required, being very unwell: however, the more difficulty, the more exertion is called for.

On the 12th, I got off Mahon, and, having given all necessary directions for the Ships on that Station, I made sail for Gibraltar. In the evening, between this Island and Majorca, I fell in with the *Bull-dog*, having on board Sir Edward Berry, who brought me letters from Rear-Admiral Duckworth, discrediting the account of the Enemy's ships being off the Coast of Portugal; with this knowledge I instantly returned to Mahon, where so much has required doing, that, except to pay my visit to the General, and to the Naval Yard, I have not been out of the Ship. General Fox being hourly expected, it has not been in my power to arrange a plan of operations for the immediate reduction of Malta, should it not be effectually relieved by these Ships; which is an object of very great importance to us and his Majesty's Allies: but as neither the Brig nor any Vessel is arrived, I am in total darkness; nor are the Ships from Civita Vecchia come in. However, I sail to-morrow for Palermo, to see what is going on, and prepare all the force I can for Malta. I beg that your Royal Highness will believe me, with the truest attachment, your faithful servant,

NELSON

To the Right Honourable Lord Minto

Palermo, *October 24th, 1799*

My dear Lord,

On my return here two days past from the westward, last from Mahon, (where I had been on information of an Enemy's Squadron having been seen on the Coast of Portugal, now gone into Ferrol, and allowed our outward-bound Convoy to pass unmolested; ten days after they returned to Port.) I received your kind and friendly letter of August 31st, which gave equal pleasure to Sir William, Lady Hamilton, and myself. We are the real *Tria juncta in uno*.

Yesterday, your whole letter was read to the Queen. I am charged to say everything which is grateful and thankful, on Her Majesty's behalf. But I know I need not say much, as she intends, I believe, to write you herself. We all have the most affectionate regard for your public and private character, and I should do injustice to my friends, was I to attempt to say my regard exceeded theirs. My conduct, as yours, is to go straight and upright. Such is, thank God, the present plan of Great Britain!—at least, as far as I know; for if I thought otherwise, I am afraid I should not be so faithful a servant to my Country as I know I am at present. As I shall send you my letters to Mr. Nepean and Lord Spencer, they will speak for themselves; therefore, I will only say, believe I am the same Nelson as you knew Captain of the *Agamemnon*; and more than ever your attached and faithful friend,

NELSON

To Lieutenant-General Sir James St. Clair Erskine, Minorca

Palermo, *October 26th, 1799*

My dear Sir James,

I am in desperation about Malta—we shall lose it, I am afraid, past redemption. I send you copies of Niza's and Ball's letters, also General Acton's, so that you will see I have not been idle. If Ball can hardly keep the inhabitants in hopes of relief by the 500 men landed from our Ships, what must be expected when 400 of them, and four Sail of the

Line, will be withdrawn? and if the Islanders are forced again to join the French, we may not find even landing a very easy task, much less to get again our present advantageous position. I therefore entreat for the honour of our King, and for the advantage of the common Cause, that, whether General Fox is arrived or not, at least the garrison of Messina may be ordered to hold post in Malta until a sufficient force can be collected to attack it, which I flatter myself will in time be got together; but while that is effecting, I fear our being obliged to quit the Island; therefore, I am forced to make this representation. I know well enough of what Officers in your situation can do; the delicacy of your feelings on the near approach of General Fox I can readily conceive; but the time you know nothing about; this is a great and important moment, and the only thing to be considered, *is His Majesty's Service to stand still for an instant?* I have no scruple in declaring what I should do, knowing the importance of possessing Malta to England and her Allies, that if even two regiments were ordered from Minorca, yet it must be considered, (for which the Officers certainly must be responsible,) was the call for these troops known at home, would they not order them to proceed where the Service near at hand loudly calls for them? *this is the only thing in my opinion for consideration.* If we lose this opportunity it will be impossible to recall it. If possible, I wish to take all the responsibility.

I know, my dear Sir James, your zeal and ability, and that delicacy to General Fox has been your sole motive for not altering the disposition of the troops; but I hope General Fox is with you, and I am sure, from his character, he will approve of my feelings on the subject. If he is not, I must again earnestly entreat that, at least, you will give directions for Colonel Graham to hold Malta till we can get troops to attack La Valetta. May God direct your counsels for the honour of our King and his Allies, and to the destruction of the French, is the fervent prayer of yours, &c.

NELSON

To His Imperial Majesty The Emperor of Russia

Palermo, *October 31st, 1799*

Sire,

As Grand Master of the Order of Malta, I presume to detail to your Majesty what has been done to prevent the French from re-possessing themselves of the Island, blockading them closely in La Valetta, and what means are now pursuing to force them to surrender.

On the 2nd of September, 1798, the inhabitants of Malta rose against the French robbers, who, having taken all the money in the Island, levied contributions; and Vaubois, as a last act of villany, said, as baptism was of no use, he had sent for all the Church plate. On the

9th, I received a letter from the Deputies of the Island, praying assistance to drive the French from La Valetta. I immediately directed the Marquis de Niza, with four Sail of the Line, to support the Islanders. At this time, the crippled ships from Egypt were passing near it, and 2,000 stand of arms, complete, with all the musket-ball cartridges, were landed from them, and 200 barrels of powder. On the 24th October, I relieved the Marquis from the station, and took the Island of Gozo—a measure absolutely necessary, in order to form the complete blockade of La Valetta, the garrison of which, at this time, was composed of 7,000 French, including the seamen, and some few Maltese; the Inhabitants in the Town, about 30,000; the Maltese in arms, volunteers, never exceeded 3,000. I entrusted the blockade to Captain Alexander John Ball, of the *Alexander*, 74, an Officer not only of the greatest merit, but of the most conciliating manners. From that period to this time, it has fell to my lot to arrange for the feeding of 60,000 people, the population of Malta and Gozo, the arming of the peasantry, and, the most difficult task, that of keeping up harmony between the Deputies of the Island. Hunger, fatigue, and corruption appeared several times in the Island, and amongst the Deputies. The situation of Italy, in particular this Kingdom, oftentimes reduced me to the greatest difficulties where to find food. Their Sicilian Majesties, at different times, have given more, I believe, than £40,000 in money and corn. The blockade has, in the expense of keeping the Ships destined alone for this service, cost full £180,000 sterling. It has pleased God hitherto to bless our endeavours to prevent supplies getting to the French except one Frigate and two small Vessels, with a small portion of salt provisions.

Your Majesty will have the goodness to observe, that, until it was known that you were elected Grand Master, and that the Order was to be restored in Malta, I never allowed an idea to go abroad that Great Britain had any wish to keep it. I therefore directed his Sicilian Majesty's flag to be hoisted, as, I am told, had the Order not been restored, that he is the legitimate Sovereign of the Island. Never less than 500 men have been landed from the Squadron, which, although with the volunteers, not sufficient to commence a siege, have yet kept posts and battery not more than 400 yards from the works. The quarrels of the Nobles, and misconduct of the Chiefs, rendered it absolutely necessary that some proper person should be placed at the head of the Island. His Sicilian Majesty, therefore, by the united request of the whole Island, named Captain Ball for their Chief Director, and he will hold it till your Majesty, as Grand Master, appoints a person to the Office. Now the French are nearly expelled from Italy by the valour and skill of your Generals and Army, all my thoughts are turned towards the placing the Grand Master and the Order of Malta in security in La Valetta, for which purpose, I have just been at Minorca, and arranged with the English General a force of 2,500 British troops, cannon, bombs, &c., &c., for the siege. I have wrote to your Majesty's Admiral, and his Sicilian Majesty joins cordially in the good work of endeavouring to drive the French from Malta. The laborious task of keeping the Maltese quiet in Malta, through difficulties which your Majesty will perfectly understand, has been principally brought about . . .

To Sir Isaac Heard, Garter King of Arms

Palermo, *November 1st, 1799*

My dear Sir,

I am not certain that I answered your kind congratulatory letter on my elevation to the Peerage—if not, I beg your pardon, and probably deferred it at the moment, in expectation of receiving the plan of the Arms you sent to Lord Grenville, but which has never reached me. I should be much obliged to you for them, but now I suppose the Ducal Arms of Bronte must have a place. If His Majesty approves of my taking the Title of Bronte, I must have your opinion how I am to sign my name. At present I describe myself 'Lord Nelson, Duke of Bronte in Sicily.' As the Pelises given to me and Sir Sidney Smith are novel, I must beg you will turn in your mind how I am to wear it when I first go to the King; and, as the Aigrette is directed to be worn, where am I to put it? In my hat, having only one arm, is impossible, as I must have my hand at liberty; therefore, I think, on my outward garment. I shall have much pleasure in putting myself into your management, for, believe me, dear Sir, your most obliged servant,

BRONTE NELSON

I have just received the Imperial Order of the Crescent from the Grand Signior, a diamond Star; in the centre, the Crescent and a small Star.

To The Right Hon. Earl Spencer, K.G.

Palermo, *November 6th, 1799*

My dear Lord,

I had entertained sanguine hopes that troops would have been obtained from Minorca to join the Russians in the attack of Malta; but that hope is much diminished by a letter from General Sir James St. Clair, writing me word that the 28th Regiment was ordered for England, and that he expected General Fox every moment, and that till he was here, the General would not, on any consideration, break his orders for any object.

Much as I approve of strict obedience to orders—even to a Court-Martial to inquire whether the object justified the measure—yet to say that an Officer is never, for any object, to alter his orders, is what I cannot comprehend. The circumstances of this war so often vary, that an Officer has almost every moment to consider—What would my superiors direct, did they know what is passing under my nose? The great object of the war is—*Down, down with the French!*. To accomplish this, every nerve, and by both Services, ought to be strained. My heart is, I assure you, almost broke with that and other things. The moment I get General Fox's answer . . . for General St. Clair cannot lend me even the garrison of Messina, to hold the posts occupied by our and the Portuguese Marines, till a force can be collected to attack it properly. If I am obliged to withdraw from the shore of the Island, what a thorn it will remain to our trade and to our Allies! It will require a constant succession of good Ships, which are very scarce with me, to cruize off it; and if the Enemy get supplies in, we may bid adieu to Malta. This would complete my misery; for I am afraid I take all services too much to heart. The accomplishing of them is my study, night and day.

The services of Captain Ball will not, I am confident, be forgot by you, but I feel sensible that my pen is far unequal to do justice to the merit of my friends; for could I have described the wonderful merit of Sir Thomas Troubridge and his gallant party in the Kingdom of Naples —how he placed his battery, as he would his Ship, close alongside the Enemy—how the French Commander said, 'This man fancies he is on board Ship—this is not the mode a General would adopt;' in what a few days this band went to the siege of Capua, where, whatever was done, was done by the English and Portuguese, for the Russians would *fight*, but *not* work. The Neapolitan corps were in air, and 600 Swiss were all who Troubridge could depend upon. If I had, as their Chief, a looker-on, a pen to describe their extraordinary merits, they would not be diminished by the comparison of our success in Holland, or by the gallant exertions of my friend, Sidney Smith—of whose zeal, judgment, and gallantry, no man is more sensible than myself—and been equally entitled to the thanks of their Country, by its representatives in Parliament. A few days ago, a gentleman from the Grand Signior came here with letters for me, and also a magnificent diamond Star, in the centre of which, on a blue enamel, is the Crescent and a Star. It is desired by the Grand Signior, that I will wear it on my breast. I have, therefore, attached it to my coat, over the Star of the Order of the Bath. This is sent simply as a mark of his . . . (*illegible*)

Palermo, *November 7th, 1799*

My dear Fanny,

Since my arrival from Minorca I received your letters of June 7th and 13th which came by way of Vienna, which shews the uncertainty of the movements of letters. I have now all my newspapers to September 29th but not the scrap of a pen from any one.

My task here is still arduous for I cannot get the General at Minorca to give me some troops for the service of Malta and I have not force enough to attack it. This and other things have half broke my heart but I trust that one day or other, I shall rest from all my labours. I still find it good to serve near home. There a man's fag and services are easily seen. Next to that is writing a famous account of your own actions. I could not do justice to those of my friends who rescued the Kingdom of Naples from the French and therefore Parliament does not think of them.

I have just received from the Grand Signor a diamond star with a crescent in the centre which I wear above that of the Bath. But these jewels give not money meat or drink and from the various circumstances of my having much more expenses than any Commander-in-chief without any one profit it has been a heavy money campaign to me. I shall mention the circumstance to Lord Spencer but I doubt if he will do anything for me. I trust that the war will very soon be over.

May God bless you and my dear father and believe me ever your affectionate

BRONTE NELSON

To Major-General Sir James St. Clair Erskine, Bart

Palermo, *November 12th, 1799*

My dear Sir James,

I am uneasy at not having yet had answers to my last letter of October 26th by the *Salamine*; therefore I must in duty again state the very great importance of driving the French out of Malta, and endeavour to impress my opinion by such arguments as offer themselves to my mind. I consider the great order of all (implied by the commencement of the war) is to destroy the power of the French: to accomplish this in the quietest and easiest way, is the object of all lesser orders; and if it can be proved that a breach of the lesser order is a more strict compliance with the former, then there can be no doubt of the duty of the breach of the lesser order.

I will suppose two Regiments ordered to England from Minorca—certainly they not knowing of the important object of possessing Malta to us and our Allies, and probably believing, from reports, that La Valetta would fall to the present force employed against it,—the detaining these two Regiments for two months would probably, with the assistance of the Russians, give us Malta, liberate us from an Enemy close to our door, gratify the Emperor of Russia, protect our Levant trade, relieve a large Squadron of Ships from this service, and enable me the better to afford Naval protection to the Island of Minorca, and assist our Allies on the Northern coast of Italy, and to annoy the Enemy on the Coast of France. It would give us one 80-Gun Ship, two 40-gun Frigates, French, besides a new Maltese 70-gun Ship and two Frigates, all ready for sea. With these in the scale against sending away the two Regiments, can there be a doubt as to the propriety of keeping them a little longer? In England or on the Continent, they would be like a drop of water in the ocean, and here they would be of the importance I have pointed out. I earnestly hope that you and General Fox will see the object in the same way as I do; if unhappily you do not, nor can allow the garrison of Messina to hold post in Malta till a force can be got to attack it, the worst consequences may be apprehended to our trade and that of our Allies. I have not yet received answers from the Russian Admiral and General at Naples. The weather has been so very bad. God forbid we should be obliged to give up the idea of taking La Valetta, only the thought of it almost breaks my heart.

I have so many Ships looking out for the Ships which sailed from Toulon the 16th October, that I do not think they can easily get to Malta. I beg that this letter, if General Fox is with you, may be considered as addressed to him as yourself; and ever believe me, with great truth and regard, your obliged friend,

NELSON

To His Excellency the Marquis de Niza

Palermo, *November 24th, 1799*

My dear Marquis,

Your Officer who brought your letter yesterday noon, did not wait my arrival from Court, and I did not know where to send to him. This moment he gives me hopes that you will wait my answer before you leave Malta, which has relieved my anxious mind from the deepest affliction, which your letter of the 19th plunged me into. The moment I can get Ships, you shall be relieved; but, for all our sakes, do not draw, in this critical moment, one man from the Island. Do not, my dear Marquis, let any man draw your excellent judgment from doing what is for the good of our respective Sovereigns, and their Allies. They are not your true friends, or faithful servants of their Sovereigns; therefore, again, and ten times again, I direct you, I entreat you, not to abandon Malta. Stay till the Russians, or English troops, arrive; it cannot be many days. You have, my friend, gained more honour by obeying my order against that of your Prince, and for which His Royal Highness will thank you, than ever can be done by obedience, if it is to injure the good Cause. You are a seaman, and we never wish to find shelter, when the public service requires our being exposed; and as we risk our lives, so we willingly risk our commissions, to serve the public. Ever your faithful friend,

BRONTE NELSON

To Evan Nepean, Esq., Admiralty

Palermo, *November 26th, 1799*

Sir,

It was with extreme concern that I read your letter of October 11th, being perfectly conscious that want of communicating where and when it is necessary, cannot be laid to my charge. I find on looking at my Letter-book that I did write to Admiral Duckworth to correspond with you on such points as might be necessary, and which it was impossible I could detail. I also find that by a Neapolitan courier which left Palermo, the same day, that I wrote, not only to you, but to Lord Spencer. I own I do not feel that if Cutters and Couriers go off the same day, that it is necessary to write by a Convoy. I know the absolute necessity of the Board's being exactly acquainted with everything which passes, and they, I beg, will give me credit for attention to my duty.

As a Junior Flag Officer, of course without those about me, as Secretaries, Interpreters, &c., I have been thrown into a more extensive correspondence than ever, perhaps, fell to the lot of any Admiral, and into a political situation I own out of my sphere. It is a fact which it would not become me to boast of, but on the present occasion, that I have never but three times put my feet on the ground, since December, 1798, and, except to the Court, that till after eight o'clock at night I never relax from business.

I have had hitherto, the Board knows, no one emolument—no one advantage of a Commander-in-Chief.

I have the honour to be, &c.,

BRONTE NELSON

To The Right Honourable Earl Spencer, K.G.

Palermo, *28th November, 1799*

My dear Lord,

I am writing a letter to you on the subject of our situation with the Barbary States, but I shall not keep the *Perseus*, by detaining her a moment with this fine levanter. I hope Ball will be able to hold fast a little longer. All the Marines from the *Foudroyant* are on shore at Malta, and nothing has been wanting on my part to second his truly meritorious exertions. The Marquis de Niza has the greatest merit in obeying my orders, in direct disobedience to those of his Court, but by his letter of the 19th—I fear by the advice of some of his English Commodores—he may be induced to quit Malta, which would be ruin to us in that Island. He has quoted Sir James St. Clair Erskine and Colonel Graham as a justification of his obedience of orders; for they would not, he says, disobey their orders, to save Malta—therefore, why should he? But as he would, about that time, receive from me, a stronger order and requisition if possible, than ever, holding out the certain displeasure instead of approbation of His Royal Highness the Prince of Brazil, should he obey, in this critical moment, the order to proceed to Lisbon, I trust he will remain. Commodore Sir Thomas Troubridge will relieve him, and all will then be well.

In General Fox's orders to Colonel Graham, he says, 'you will not incur any expense for stores, or any article but provisions'. What can this mean? But I have told Troubridge that the Cause cannot stand still for want of a little money. This would be what we call 'penny-wise and pound foolish'. If nobody will pay it, I shall sell Bronte and the Emperor of Russia's box; for I feel myself above every consideration but that of serving faithfully. Do not, my dear Lord, let the Admiralty write harshly to me—my generous soul cannot bear it, being conscious it is entirely unmerited; and ever believe me your obliged,

BRONTE NELSON

To Charles Lock, Esq., His Majesty's Consul at Naples

Palermo, *4th December, 1799*

Sir,

Your letter to me of yesterday's date is incomprehensible, except the highly improper language in which it is couched. I shall send it to the Board of Admiralty, that they may either support the dignity of the Admiral they have entrusted with the command of the Mediterranean fleet, or remove him. Your never mentioning the extraordinary price paid for fresh beef, for the several days you were soliciting to have the exclusive privilege of supplying the Fleet, and your refusal afterwards to bring forward any proof of fraud, warrants every expression in my letter to the Victualling Board. If you could bring proof of what you asserted, you are in the highest degree, as a public Officer, criminal; and if you could not, your conduct is highly reprehensible. My letters to you are all directed 'On His Majesty's Service', and I desire yours may be so to me. I am, &c.,

BRONTE NELSON

To Evan Nepean, Esq., Admiralty

Palermo, *December 14th, 1799*

Sir,

I have this moment a letter from Commodore Troubridge, telling me that the *Culloden* and *Foudroyant* arrived off Malta with the two

British regiments from Messina on the 10th. I trust this force will, at least, hold our present advantageous post till a proper force can be got together to attack La Valetta. The Russians had not left Naples on the 9th, and it was thought it would be five or six days before they sailed for Messina. On every account, I am anxious for this business being finished. Our Ships are torn to pieces; the *Audacious* has the knee of her head loose, and in a wretched state; the *Lion* as bad, and the *Alexander* at present absolutely unable to keep the sea; the *Culloden*, although my brave friend never complains, is in such a state, that, for the world, I would not send her to sea by herself. I have had yesterday a very strong call for a British Squadron on the Coast of Genoa. I see the necessity of one as strong as any man in Europe, for the Russians do nothing by sea; therefore, if their Lordships expect any active sea operations from them, they will find their mistake. Captain Martin was relieved by an Admiral, two Sail of the Line, Frigates, &c.; they have never yet been on the Coast since last September; but I will try and get a small Squadron for that service. I was anxious to get more Ships off Cadiz since the departure of Admiral Duckworth; but at this moment it is not possible, from the circumstance of General Fox's orders to Colonel Graham. In addition to my other occupations, I am a Commissary for our Troops. I have pledged Bronte for 12,000 ounces, if any difficulties arise in the payment; and I am obliged to beg, as an individual, of this Government, for those necessary stores, without which, our Troops would stand still, and which are not sent from Minorca, or allowed to be purchased. The Emperor of Russia's magnificent Box is ready to go to market, in order to assist in placing the Grand Master of Malta in his seat of Government. As to myself, I can see, and that is all I can say; therefore, having not been placed in a situation of those who are Commanders-in-Chief, I want many of those helps which they possess, and this must plead my excuse with their Lordships, if I appear wanting in attention. I have the honour to be, &c.,

BRONTE NELSON

To the Marquis de Niza

Palermo, *18th December, 1799*

My Lord,

I cannot allow you to pass from under my command without assuring you of my sincere and cordial thanks for your constant and ready obedience to every order and wish I have directed to your Lordship for the Public service; and allow me to say, that it is impossible for any Officer to have executed them with more alertness and judgment than yourself. I have, in particular, to express to your Lordship my approbation of your judgment in continuing to obey my orders for the Public service in remaining at Malta till I could get Ships to relieve you, instead of an immediate obedience to your orders from the Court of Portugal, which, had you obeyed, the French would, most probably, have been in possession of the whole Island, and the Allies might not have been able to even effect a landing. Your orders, which it would be no longer proper to disobey, forces me with regret to part from you. I have, therefore, again to thank you for all your kindness towards me, and to assure you with what respect and esteem I feel myself your most obliged, humble servant,

BRONTE NELSON

To J. Fagan, Esq., Rome

Palermo, *December 19th, 1799*

Dear Sir,

Sir William Hamilton has been so kind as to communicate to me the distinguished honour intended me by the inhabitants, by you, and other Professors and Admirers of the Fine Arts, at Rome, to erect a Monument. I have not words sufficient to express my feelings, on hearing that my actions have contributed to preserve the works which form the School of Fine Arts in Italy, which the modern Goths wanted to carry off and destroy. That they may always remain in the only place worthy of them, Rome, are and will be my fervent wishes, together with the esteem of, dear Sir,

Your most obliged servant,

BRONTE NELSON

To Evan Nepean, Esq., Admiralty

Palermo, *23rd December, 1799*

Sir,

I beg leave to inform you, for the information of their Lordships, that His Majesty's Ship *Culloden*, on going into the Bay of Marsa Sirocco, in the Island of Malta, to land the cannon, ammunition, &c., taken on board that Ship at Messina for the siege, struck on a rock, and Commodore Sir Thomas Troubridge, Bart., her Commander, has informed me that the rudder and greatest part of the false keel are carried away, and the rudder would have been lost but for the timely exertion in getting a hawser *secured* through it, the pintles are all broke, and the Ship was steered to the anchorage with her sails, where she is now in safety, but very leaky. If I can get her, the *Alexander*, and *Lion*, to England a few months hence, it is all that I can expect from them, as they are not fit to keep the sea.

I have not as yet had the least co-operation or assistance from Admiral Ouschakoff or the Russian Fleet; they are, I believe, still in Naples Bay. and not any of their troops yet arrived at Malta, where their presence is so absolutely necessary. I have the honour to be, Sir, &c.,

BRONTE NELSON

From Lady Nelson to Lord Nelson

54, St. James's Street, *December 26th, 1799*

Capt. Hardy has made us all happy by the flattering accounts he gives us of your health. I mentioned your letters were written quite out of spirits; he assures me *that* is owing to the tiresome people you have to deal with. It is impossible to tell you how much pleasure the arrival of Capt. Hardy has given to *all* our acquaintance. When I enquired after poor George Bolton Capt. H. did not seem to know anything of him, Susanna was surprised, the conversation droped, and Maurice informed me the next morning that the little boy died on his passage from Gibraltar to Minorca; I own at first I was afraid he had fell overboard. Mrs. Bolton and Kitty have been absent from home some weeks, which frets our good father; yr sister assured us Mr. Bolton was quite *easy* & happy in his *circumstances.* I repeat all these things as I find one half of my letters never reach you. Everything you desire to be sent you will receive by the first frigate. Capt. Hardy told me you would be gratified if I sent Lady Hamilton anything, therefore I shall send her ladyship a cap and kerchief such as are worne this cold weather. I have ordered a suit of clothes for her Majesty's birthday. I am frightened to tell you the expense of your new chariot, nothing fine about it, only fashionable, £352, harness, &c., for one pair of horses. Good Capt. Locker desires I would give his love to you, in short, I was to say everything that was kind and affectionate for him, and at ye same time I was to tell you he is grown quite old; one of his hands are stiff, which prevents him from writing. Lord Hood is still at Bath; I must write to him. I have seen Capt. Hardy, for he is wonderfully anxious for your home coming. The Parkers are in town, Lady P. was kind and attentive to me. Unfortunately, Sir Peter in going upstairs with a candlestick in his hand fell backwards, very much bruised, and one of his legs cut in several places; no danger is apprehended from the fall, but altho' this accident happened upwards of a fortnight, he is not out of his room. Adml. Pole looks well, desires to be kindly remembered to you. I am clothed in two suits of flannel, and I hope I shall be the better for it; my health is much mended within this month. And Ad. Pringle desires me to tell you he longs to see you; he has been very ill with a complaint in his head; he is better, and they give him hopes of getting quite well; he has bought a house and land on the borders of England, 7 miles from a town, which he finds very inconvenient. I am now going to take this letter to Mr. A. Stanhope, who sends all your letters, for I cannot bear the idea of your not receiving them when truly I write once a week. God bless my dearest husband. Our father's blessing attend you.

To Brigadier-General Graham, Malta

Palermo, *7th January, 1800*

My dear Sir,

I can assure you it is as grievous to me, as it can be to you, to hear of the distress of the Maltese; but I pray and beg, alas! in vain. Corn is here for Malta, but the Vessels will not go to sea. Sir William and myself are trying to get the corn here exchanged for corn at Girgenti. I have wrote Troubridge about it. Nothing is well done in this Country.

I hope to soon pay you a visit, and I only wish that I could always do all you ask me. It is certain that you cannot go on at Malta without money; therefore I declare sooner than you should want, I would sell Bronte. But I trust, from General Fox's letter to me, that you will have his consent for ordering what money may be necessary. I send you all the Egyptian papers for you, Ball, and Troubridge, and, if you like, in confidence, Italinsky. Suwarrow is at the Prague with his whole Army—ready to act with the Austrians if they come to their senses, or perhaps against them. *Moreau* is at Vienna, treating for peace. What a state the *Allies* bring us into! But it is in vain to cry out. John Bull was always ill-treated. May a speedy success attend you, is the sincere wish of, my dear Sir, your obliged and faithful servant,

BRONTE NELSON

I beg my best respects to Italinsky.

To Brigadier-General Graham

Palermo, *January 15th, 1800*

My dear Sir,

Notwithstanding the very unpleasant circumstance of the Russians not coming at this moment to your help, I hope that you will not think of quitting the Island, till you may receive either positive orders from General Fox, or from England. I believe, and we have it strong in report from Tuscany, that the two Imperial Courts have settled matters, and that the Russians are again marching to the Rhine. If so, these Troops will again be with you; but even should this not be the case, I attach so much importance to the Island not being entirely in the hands of the French, that I never would consent to leave it. The troops from this Country are not good, but it is probable they would save the fatigue of ours. General Acton is preparing 2,600 to go from Sicily. They will, of course, be under your command; and I have told the General that all provisions, &c., they must carry with them, for all that you would do was to order them on service. If you would like to begin by getting these men to the Island, you had better write a line to General Acton, and 500 can be sent at a time. To-morrow, I sail to Leghorn, in order to talk all matters over with Lord Keith; and I am sure he will either come to you immediately, or allow me. General Fox has now 7,000 healthy troops, at Minorca, but will not part with a man, without orders from home.

Secret.—The French troops from Egypt are not to be allowed to return to France under any Capitulation. Excuse this short letter, as I am pressed for time; but ever believe me, my dear Sir, your obliged and faithful,

BRONTE NELSON

To Earl Spencer, K.G.

Leghorn, *23rd January, 1800*

My dear Lord,

I came here in order to meet Lord Keith, and we are going together to Palermo and Malta. If Sir James St. Clair or General Fox had felt themselves authorized to have given us two thousand troops, I think Malta by this time would have fallen, and our poor Ships released from the hardest service I have ever seen. The going away of the Russians has almost done me up, but the King of Naples has ordered two thousand six hundred troops from Sicily to assist Graham, and they are to be under our command. It is true they are not good soldiers, but they will ease ours in the fatigues of duty. The feeding the inhabitants of Malta and paying two thousand of the people who bear arms, has been a continued source of uneasiness to my mind. His Sicilian Majesty has done more than it was possible to expect he had the ability of performing; for the revenues of his Kingdom are hardly yet come round, and his demands are excessive from all quarters of his Dominions. Lord Keith will now be able to judge with his own eyes and ears, and your Lordship will see his report.

The loyalty and attachment of their Sicilian Majesties to our King and Country is such, that I would venture to lay down my head to be cut off, if they would not rather lose their Kingdom of Naples than hold it on terms from Austria and the French, by a separation from their alliance with England. There is not a thing which his Majesty can desire, that their Majesties of the Two Sicilies will not have the greatest pleasure in complying with. I have before ventured an opinion on the character of their Sicilian Majesties. The King is a real good man but inclined to be positive in his opinion: the Queen is certainly a great Monarch and a true daughter of Maria Theresa. I am just favoured with your letter of December 12th, which, although so entirely contrary to my expectations, cannot alter my respect for all your kindness. I am in debt, from my situation; but time and care will get me out of it. Since May 1798, I have had all the expense of a Commander-in-Chief, without even the smallest advantage. Lord Keith shall find in me an Officer ever ready to anticipate his wishes, so long as my health will permit. With every sentiment of regard, believe me, my dear Lord, your obliged,

BRONTE NELSON

To Lady Hamilton

February 3rd, 1800

My dear Lady Hamilton,

Having a Commander-in-Chief,* I cannot come on shore till I have made *my manners* to him. Times are changed; but if he does not come on shore directly, I will not wait. In the meantime, I send Allen to inquire how you are. Send me word, for I am anxious to hear of you. It has been no fault of mine, that I have been so long absent. I cannot command, and now only obey. Mr. Tyson and the Consul have not been able to find out the betrothed wife of the Priore, although they were three days in their inquiries, and desired the Neapolitan Consul to send to Pisa. I also desired the Russian Admiral, as he was going to Pisa, to inquire if the Countess Pouschkin had any letters to send to Palermo; but as I received none, I take for granted she had none to send.

May God bless you, my dear Lady; and be assured, I ever am, and shall be, your obliged and affectionate,

BRONTE NELSON

To The Reverend Mr. Nelson

Palermo, *February 7th, 1800*

My dear Father,

I can assure you that one of the greatest rewards in this world is your approbation of my conduct; and in having done my duty in life so fortunately, I have always recollected what pleasure this will give my father. Although few things in this world could give me so much pleasure as seeing you, yet I see but little prospect of my going to England at this moment of the war; but we shall meet when and where it pleases God, and my only prayer is that your life may be prolonged, and that every moment I may be able to increase your felicity: but whether I am higher or lower in the world, or whatever fate awaits me, I shall always be your dutiful son,

BRONTE NELSON

* Nelson was deeply mortified at a Commander-in-Chief being sent to the Mediterranean.

To Capt. Sir Edward Berry, H.M. Ship *Foudroyant*

Palermo, *February 7th, 1800*

My dear Sir Edward,

You shall rally—you shall be well: young men will be young men, and we must make allowances. If you expect to find anything like perfection in this world, you will be mistaken: therefore do not think of little nonsenses too much. Such strictness as you show to your duty falls to the lot of few, and no person in this world is more sensible of your worth and goodness in every way than myself. Let all pass over, and come and dine here. As you are ready to execute my orders, take this of coming to this house as a *positive* and *lawful* one. When I see a Ship better ordered than the *Foudroyant*, I will allow you to confine yourself on board. Ever, my dear Sir Edward, believe me your truly sincere friend,

BRONTE NELSON

Lady Hamilton humbly insists that you come on shore.

To Lady Hamilton *February 13th, 1800*

I do not send you any news or opinions, as this letter goes by post and may be opened, and as I wrote to you and Sir William yesterday, nothing particular has occurred. We are now off Messina with a fresh breeze and fair. Mr. Roche has had the goodness to come on board. To say how I miss your house and company would be saying little; but in truth you and Sir William have so spoiled me that I am not happy anywhere else but with you, nor have I an idea that I ever can be. All my newspapers are purloined at Gibraltar, and I suspect a gentleman there has sent them to Lord Keith, for they are all stars. I see in Lord Grenville's note to Paris he concludes with saying that the best mode he can recommend for France to have a solid peace is to replace its ancient princes on the throne. May the Heavens bless you and make you ever be satisfied that I am, &c.,

You will make my kindest regards to Sir William and to all the house, also duty to the Queen.

To Vice-Admiral Lord Keith

18th February, 1800

My Lord,

This morning at daylight, being in company with the Ships named in the margin, I saw the *Alexander* in chase of a Line of Battle Ship, three Frigates, and a Corvette. At about eight o'clock she fired several shot at one of the Enemy's frigates, which struck her colours, and leaving her to be secured by the Ships astern, continued the chase. I directed Captain Gould of the *Audacious*, and the *El Corso* brig, to take charge of this prize. At half-past one P.M., the Frigates and Corvette tacked to the westward; but the Line of Battle Ship not being able to tack without coming to action with the *Alexander*, bore up. The *Success* being to leeward, Captain Peard, with great judgment and gallantry, lay across his hawse, and raked him with several broadsides. In passing the French Ship's broadside, several shot struck the *Success*, by which one man was killed, and the Master and seven men wounded. At half-past four, the *Foudroyant* and *Northumberland* coming up, the former fired two shot, when the French Ship fired her broadside, and struck her colours. She proved to be the *Genereux*, of seventy-four guns, bearing the Flag of Rear-Admiral Perree, Commander in Chief of the French Naval force in the Mediterranean, having a number of troops on board from Toulon, bound for the relief of Malta.

I attribute our success this day to be principally owing to the extreme good management of Lieutenant William Harrington, who commanded the *Alexander* in the absence of Captain Ball, and I am much pleased with the gallant behaviour of Captain Peard, of the *Success*, as also with the alacrity and good conduct of Captain Martin and Sir Edward Berry. I have sent Lieutenant Andrew Thomson, First Lieutenant of the *Foudroyant*, to take charge of the *Genereux*, whom I beg leave to recommend to your Lordship for promotion, and have sent her under care of the *Northumberland* and *Alexander* to Syracuse, to wait your Lordship's orders. I have the honour to be, &c.,

BRONTE NELSON

To Lady Hamilton *18th February, 1800*

I feel anxious to get up with these ships & shall be unhappy not to take them myself, for first my greatest happiness is to serve my gracious King and Country, & I am envious only of glory; for if it be a sin to covet glory I am the most offending soul alive. But here I am in a heavy sea & thick fog—Oh, God! the wind subsided—but I trust to Providence I shall have them. 18th, in the evening, I have got her—*Le Genereux*—thank God! 12 out of 13, only the *Guillaume Telle* remaining; I am after the others. I have not suffered the French Admiral to contaminate the *Foudroyant* by setting his foot in her.

[On the 24th of February, Lord Keith issued an Order to Nelson, which stated that he was 'called from the Blockade of Malta, to attend to other services of public importance', and directed Nelson to take the command of the Ships therein named, 'and to adopt and prosecute the necessary measures for contributing to the complete reduction of Malta'.]

To Vice-Admiral Lord Keith

Foudroyant, off Malta,
24th February, 1800

My Lord,

My state of health is such, that it is impossible I can much longer remain here. Without some rest, I am gone. I must therefore, whenever I find the service will admit of it, request your permission to go to my friends, at Palermo, for a few weeks, and leave the command here to Commodore Troubridge. Nothing but absolute necessity obliges me to write this letter, being, with the greatest respect, &c.,

BRONTE NELSON

To Vice-Admiral Lord Keith

Off Malta, *February 24th, 1800*

My dear Lord,

I could no more stay fourteen days longer here, than fourteen years. I am absolutely exhausted, therefore I have been obliged to write you a Public letter. As to the state of the *Foudroyant*, nothing but the exigencies of the service has prevented her being refitted months ago. This very day is a sufficient proof to me that she cannot keep the sea, even if the main topmast stands, which I doubt, in a severe gale. But her rigging, both standing and running, must be overhauled; everything gives way. But I send Sir Edward Berry, and submit to your decision as to the Ship; to myself you will not, I am sure, object. The *Northumberland* and *El Corso* would have been an acquisition, instead of the *Audacious*, *Lion*, or *Alexander*, or *Strombolo*, who is useless as a cruiser. But I wish not to complain; but my incapacity as to health I feel; and, as a Seaman, I think the *Foudroyant* must be refitted. Ever, my dear Lord, &c.,

BRONTE NELSON

JOURNAL FROM THE 26TH OF FEBRUARY TO THE 10TH OF MARCH, 1800, DURING BLOCKADE OF MALTA

February 26th, at 2 p.m.—Ordered the *Foudroyant* to be anchored on St. Paul's bank—she having split her maintopsail and foresail, parted the cable, let go another anchor. The Commander-in-Chief weighed and stood to the North East, leaving in sight the *Lion*, *Minorca*, and *Perseus*, and under my command *Culloden*, *Lion*, *Success*, *Bonne Citoyenne*. All night, hard gales. A.M. Hard gales, no communication with the shore—two Sail in sight, under main-topsails and foresails.

27th.—Strong gales till evening, when it moderated. Governor Ball sent me word that he was sure the French Ships would attempt to put to sea the first favourable moment. No Ship near us, blowing very fresh all night. A.M. In the morning, more moderate; attempted to get our anchor; but the wind freshening, was obliged to give up, leaving a stream cable on it.

28th.—The *Entreprenant* Cutter joined from Corfu: read her dispatches, and directed her to the Commander-in-Chief; but having received seventy Maltese for the *Genereux*, I directed her to call off Marsa Sirocco, as Commodore Troubridge had them all ready, and the way the wind blew, it could not make a difference of two hours. At nine, the *Cameleon* joined from Sir Sidney Smith with dispatches. At half-past ten, sent to Lord Keith to Syracuse, or to follow him to Leghorn.

1st March.—Governor Ball came on board to tell me of the state of the Ships in La Valetta, and that, in his opinion, the wind coming round to the S.W., they would endeavour to put out in the night; directed the *Lion* to anchor off Marsa Scala, the *Alexander* off St. Julian's, *Foudroyant* off La Valetta, the *Success* to keep near us, as also the *Vincejo*, the *Minorca*, and . . . . In the night it came on a sudden squall at N.E., by which, I believe, the Ship was drove in shore; for at daylight she was within reach of shot, which the French fired at her till ten o'clock, when she was warped out of gun-shot without any damage except wounding the fore top-mast.

2nd.—At four, weighed with a light breeze, southerly. In the night, variable winds and squally. Strong gales to the N.W. all day.

3rd.—At four, joined the *Northumberland*; received Lord Keith's letters and orders of the 27th February; heavy gales all night; laying to under a reefed mainsail. A.M. More moderate; directed Captain Martin to carry the powder into Marsa Sirocco, and to desire Commodore Troubridge to dispose of the French prisoners in a Transport, as they have a bad fever.

4th.—The wind coming to W.S.W., got the *Foudroyant* to an anchor on St. Paul's bank; *Bonne Citoyenne* showed his pendants; all night fresh breezes to the southward. At daylight, employed shifting the foretopmast; found two of the main-shrouds on the larboard side carried away, the sails all split and none to replace them, all, except one foresail, being unfit for a gale of wind, all the ropes very bad, and continually breaking. The *Alexander* and *Lion* at anchor, as by order of the

1st; *Vincejo* off La Valetta; *Success* near the *Strombolo*, preparing to go to Tripoli; *Minorca* not in sight; *Bonne Citoyenne* never joined. Wind, southerly.

5th.—The Governor came on board to dinner: at sunset, the wind west; the station of the Ships—*Foudroyant* on St. Paul's bank; *Alexander* off St. Julian's; *Lion* off Marsa Scala; *Success*, *Minorca*, and *Vincejo*, off La Valetta; *Bonne Citoyenne* supposed to be west of Goza, as ordered; *Strombolo* standing to the N.N. West, being bound to Girgenti. All night fresh breezes. A.M. At daylight, increasing to a heavy gale of wind, which lasted till noon.

6th.—Heavy gales till sunset, when it moderated a little. A.M. At 10, a boat came from the Governor to say a Corvette had got into La Valetta the night of the 5th, which I cannot believe from the position of the Ships. At noon, the Governor came on board to say he began to think it was a Vessel attempting to get out.

7th.—It is ascertained the *Polacca* was attempting to get out. All these twenty-four hours, strong breezes to the N.W.

8th.—Strong breezes and variable from S. to N.W. The report from the *Northumberland* very unfavourable. The *Penelope* joined, but brought no dispatches from England.

9th.—Strong gales from the N.W. all these twenty-four hours.

10th.—Hard gales the whole twenty-four hours, from W.S.W. to N.N.E. Only *Alexander* and *Penelope* in sight. A.M. At 8 the *Speedy* joining.

From Admiral Goodall

London, No. 34, South Audley-street,
November 15th, 1799

My good Lord,

I hope, as the sailor says, 'this will find you well, as I am at this present'. I have wrote at different times three letters to you in favour of my protege, Captain Broughton of the *Strombolo* Bomb, and flattered myself that I should have heard you had had an opportunity of giving him Post. Keep him in your mind's eye, and let it be so.

They say here you are Rinaldo in the arms of Armida, and that it requires the firmness of an Ubaldo, and his brother Knight, to draw you from the Enchantress. To be sure 'tis a very pleasant attraction, to which I am very sensible myself. But my maxim has always been—*Cupidus voluptatum, cupidior gloriae*. Be it as it will, health and happiness attend you, and believe me always yours, J. GOODALL. Remember me to Lady Hamilton and Sir William, and all my friends.

To Admiral Goodall

March 11th, 1800, at Sea, off Malta

My dear Admiral,

It was only two days past that I received your letter of November 15th, the day Lord Keith sailed from Spithead, to take from me all opportunity of my rewarding merit and obliging my friends. Captain Broughton, from his merit, was to be amongst the first for being made Post, and I told Lord Keith so. I was happy to find that, as an Admiralty man, Captain Broughton stands very high in the long list they have given Lord Keith. I can assure you, my dear Admiral, that a more modest, excellent Officer does not exist; and it has been a hard case to be kept so long in a d . . . . d *Collier* Bomb Vessel. We have been so long in hopes of the speedy fall of Malta, and, consequently, of my Ships, the *William Tell*, and the *Diane* and *Justice* Frigates, that I doubt you will but little more than believe that I think we are nearer obtaining them than a year past, and then Captain Broughton had my promise of the *Justice*. Don't say I am selling the skin before I have killed the bear; but the bear shall be killed.

As to my health, I believe I am almost finished. Many things, some of which you have felt in your time, contribute towards it. I am now on my route to my friends at Palermo. I shall there rest quiet for two weeks, and then judge by my feelings whether I am *able* to serve well, and with comfort to myself. It is said the Combined fleet is coming this road, confiding it can escape as it did last year; but the pitcher never goes often to the well, but it comes home broke at last. They had better be d . . . . d than come here, for Lord Keith owes them a grudge, which I trust, if that happens, I shall assist him in paying. Our dear friends, Sir William and Lady Hamilton, are as hospitable, as kind, and as good as ever, and you will join with me, they are nonpareils. I shall rejoice to see you, and it is possible it may be very soon. Be that as it may, ever believe me your obliged and affectionate friend,

BRONTE NELSON

Acton is married to his niece, not fourteen years of age; so you hear it is never too late to do well. He is only sixty-seven.

To Vice-Admiral Lord Keith

Palermo, *20th March, 1800*

My dear Lord,

You will know, by the *Speedy*, of my coming to this place, where I arrived on the 16th. It is too soon to form any judgment of what effect it may have on my health; but on the 18th, I had near died, with the swelling of some of the vessels of the heart. I know the anxiety of my mind, on coming back to Syracuse in 1798, was the first cause; and more people, perhaps, die of broken hearts, than we are aware of. The *Foudroyant* sails to-morrow, and will return here in about a fortnight, by which time I hope some decisive turn will take place in my complaint. The weekly report from Malta, which I directed to be sent by *Girgenti*, is not yet arrived, but probably it may before this letter can go; for I have no conveyance to you but by post. The *Valiant* transport is arrived with Lieutenant England from Larnica, in Cyprus; but sailing one day later than the *Cameleon*. I shall, of course, send Lieutenant England to you as soon as his quarantine is performed, and send the Transport to Mahon. I have agreed with Mr. Woodhouse, at Marsala, for 500 pipes of wine, to be delivered to our Ships at Malta, at 1s. 5d. per gallon; and as Mr. Woodhouse runs all risks, pays all freights, &c., I don't think it a bad bargain. The wine is so good that any gentleman's table might receive it, and it will be of real use to our seamen.

I hope from the reports by the *Penelope*, that Sir Charles Stuart is coming to Malta, which will relieve our Ships from a very tedious, and has been hard, service. I put into this, Sir Sidney Smith's letter to me. I cannot exactly approve of his interference as an English Officer with the disputes between the Ottoman Government and the Pacha of Acre, and without much farther communication with Lord Elgin, I should never consent to *our attacking* Acre; but I have formed an opinion on this subject, and I dare say it will agree with yours. Our friends, Sir William and Lady Hamilton, are tolerable; and I am ever, my dear Lord, your faithful and obedient,

BRONTE NELSON

MEMORANDUM

By my Patent of Creation, I find that my Family name of Nelson has been lengthened by the words, 'of the Nile.' Therefore, in future my signature will be,

'Bronte Nelson of the Nile.'

Given on board the *Foudroyant*, at Palermo, 21st March, 1800.

BRONTE NELSON OF THE NILE

To the respective Captains, &c.

From Lady Nelson to Lord Nelson

March 29th, 1800

I have this instant received a note from Adm. Young, who tells me if I can send him a letter for you in an hour he will send it, therefore, I have only time to say I have at last had the pleasure of receiving two letters from you, dated Jan. 20th, 25. I rejoice exceedingly I did not follow the advice of the physician and our good father to change the climate, and I hope my health will be established by hot sea bathing and the warmth of the summer.

I can with safety put my hand on my heart and say it has been my study to please and make you happy, and I still flatter myself we shall meet before very long. I feel most sensibly all your kindnesses to my dear son, and I hope he will add much to our comfort. Our good father has been in good spirits ever since we heard from you; indeed, my spirits were quite worn out, the time had been so long. I thank God for the preservation of my dear husband, and your recent success off Malta. The taking of the *Genereux* seems to give great spirits to all. God bless you, my dear husband, and grant us a happy meeting, & believe me, &c.

Our father's love and blessing attend you.
I don't seal my letter with black lest I should alarm you.
My love to my dear Josiah.

From Captain Sir Edward Berry to Lord Nelson

Foudroyant, 30th March, 1800

In great haste.
My dear Lord,

I had but one wish this morning—it was for you. After a most gallant defence, *Le Guillaume Tell* surrendered. She is completely dismasted. The *Foudroyant's* lower masts and main topmast are standing, but every roll I expect them to go over the side, they are so much shattered. I was slightly hurt in the foot, and I fear about 40 men are badly wounded, besides the killed, which you shall know hereafter.

All hands behaved as you could have wished. How we prayed for you, God knows, and your sincere and faithful friend,

E. BERRY

Love to all. Pray send this to my wife, or write Admiralty.
Within hail before I fired.

To Evan Nepean, Esq., Admiralty

Palermo, *April 4th, 1800*

Sir,

I have received no official reports; but I have letters from Commodore Troubridge, Captain Dixon, and Sir Edward Berry, telling me of the capture of the *William Tell* on the morn of the 30th of March, after a gallant defence of three hours. The *Lion* and *Foudroyant* lost each about forty killed and wounded; the French Ship is dismasted; the French Admiral Decres wounded; the *Foudroyant* much shattered. I send Sir Edward Berry's hasty note.

Thus, owing to my brave friends, is the entire capture and destruction of the French Mediterranean Fleet to be attributed, and my orders from the great Earl of St. Vincent fulfilled. Captain Blackwood of the *Penelope*, and Captain Long of the *Vincejo*, have the greatest merit. My task is done, my health is finished, and, probably, my retreat for ever fixed, unless another French Fleet should be placed for me to look after. Ever, Sir, your most obedient humble servant,

BRONTE NELSON OF THE NILE

To The Rt. Hon. Lord Minto

Palermo, *April 6th, 1800*

My dear Lord and Friend,

A ten times better title, and to me invaluable—I find *Lords* who are not my friends. Our dear great Earl of St. Vincent's orders to me were to follow the French Mediterranean fleet, and to annihilate them: it has been done, thanks to the zeal and bravery of my gallant friends! My task is done, my health lost, and I have wrote to Lord Keith for my retreat. May all orders be as punctually obeyed, but never again an Officer at the close, of what I must, without being thought vain, (for such I am represented by my enemies,) call a glorious career, be so treated! I go with our dear friends Sir William and Lady Hamilton; but whether by water or land depends on the will of Lord Keith. May God bless you, in which joins Sir William and Lady Hamilton with your affectionate friend,

BRONTE NELSON OF THE NILE

To Earl Spencer, K.G.

Palermo, *8th April, 1800*

My dear Lord,

I send you Sir Edward Berry's letter, and am sure your Lordship will not be sparing of promotion to the deserving. My friends wished me to be present. I have no such wish; for a something might have been given me, which now cannot. Not for all the world would I rob any man of a sprig of laurel—much less my children of the *Foudroyant*! I love her as a fond father, a darling child, and glory in her deeds. I am vain enough to feel the effects of my school. Lord Keith sending me nothing, I have not, of course, a free communication. I have wrote to him for permission to return to England, when you will see a broken-hearted man. My spirit cannot submit patiently. My complaint, which is principally a swelling of the heart, is at times alarming to my friends, but not to, my dear Lord, your obliged and faithful,

BRONTE NELSON OF THE NILE

If I may again say it, what would I feel if my brother was a Commissioner of the Navy—for ever grateful!*

To Vice-Admiral Lord Keith, K.B.

Palermo, *8th April, 1800*

My Lord,

I have the happiness to send you a copy of Captain Dixon's letter to Commodore Sir Thomas Troubridge, informing him of the capture of the *William Tell*; the circumstances attending this glorious finish to the whole French Mediterranean Fleet, are such as must ever reflect the highest honour to all concerned in it. The attention of the Commodore in placing Officers and Men to attend the movements of the French Ships, and the exactness with which his orders were executed, are a proof that the same vigour of mind remains, although the body, I am truly sorry to say, is almost worn away. Then came the alacrity of the *Vincejo*, Captain Long, and other Sloops of War; the gallantry and excellent management of Captain Blackwood of the *Penelope* frigate, who, by carrying away the Enemy's main and mizen topmasts, enabled the *Lion* to get up, when Captain Dixon showed the greatest courage and Officer-like conduct in placing his Ship on the Enemy's bow, as she had only 300 men on board, and the Enemy 1,220. The conduct of these excellent Officers enabled Sir Edward Berry to place the *Foudroyant* where she ought, and is the fittest Ship in the world to be, close alongside the *William Tell*—one of the largest and finest two decked Ships in the world—where he showed that matchless intrepidity and able conduct, as a Seaman and Officer, which I have often had the happiness to experience in many trying situations. I thank God I was not present, for it would finish me could I have taken a sprig of these brave men's laurels: they are, and I glory in them, my darling children, served in my school, and all of us caught our professional zeal and fire from the great and good Earl of St. Vincent.

I am confident your Lordship will bestow the promotions in the properest manner, therefore I have done nothing in that respect; and on this occasion I only beg leave to mention, that Governor Ball would be much flattered by the command of the *William Tell*, and Captain Ormsby, a volunteer in the *Penelope*, would be happy in fitting her for

* His brother Maurice.

him during his very necessary attendance at Malta; and in complying with their request, your Lordship will highly oblige, your most obedient servant,

BRONTE NELSON OF THE NILE

To Lieutenant Inglis, on board the *Guillaume Tell*, at Syracuse

16th April, 1800

My dear Sir,

How fortunate I did not permit you to quit the *Penelope*, to be a junior Lieutenant in the *Foudroyant*! You will now get your promotion in the pleasantest of all ways, by the gallant exertions of yourself and those brave friends who surrounded you on that glorious night. What a triumph for you—what a pleasure to me—what happiness to have the Nile Fleet all taken under my orders and regulations! Blackwood's coming to me at Malta, and my keeping him there, were something more than chance. Ever, my dear Sir, believe me your truly sincere friend,

BRONTE NELSON OF THE NILE

From Sir W. Hamilton to Charles Greville

Palermo, *April 22nd, 1800*

I have this day presented my recredential letters to their Sicilian Majesties, and Mr. Paget having presented his credential letters, tomorrow we go with Lord Nelson in the *Foudroyant* to look at Malta, & shall return here in a few days, when Lord Nelson expects an answer from Lord Keith, having asked his Lordship's permission to return home on account of his health, which indeed is much impaired by wounds & such constant exertions his Lordship has been engaged in so many years. Lord Keith will probably grant his Lordship's request for a frigate or ship to carry him home, (and in that case we are to return home with his Lordship, &, which is my ambition, will have to travel together). The taking of the *Guillaume Tell* by the *Foudroyant* has completed Lord Nelson's task, and he has a good right to a little repose, particularly as he has been superceded in the command of the Mediterranean squadron.

[On the 24th of April, Nelson proceeded in the *Foudroyant* from Palermo to Syracuse, at which place he arrived on the 30th of that month.]

To Alexander Davison, Esq.

Malta, *9th May, 1800*

My dear Davison,

When I laid claim to my right of Prize-money, as Commanding Admiral of the Mediterranean Fleet, I had not an idea of Lord St. Vincent attempting to lay in any claim, for I have ever considered him as far from attempting, notwithstanding any law opinion, to take away my undoubted property. I am confident it will be given up, the moment you show his Lordship my manner of thinking respecting the Nile prize-money. No lawyer in Europe can, I am confident, make either the Earl or myself do a dishonourable act, which this claim, if persisted in, would be; let my Earl lay his hand on his heart, and say, whether his Nelson, subject to all the responsibility of this command, is not entitled to the pittance of Prize-money—be it £5, or £50,000, it makes no difference. No Admiral ever yet received Prize-money, going for the benefit of his health from a Foreign station, and Lord St. Vincent was certainly not eligible to have given me any order till his return to this station; and so think the Board of Admiralty, by their directions to me of August 20th, and many subsequent ones, which would have passed through Lord St. Vincent, had they considered him eligible to give orders; but whether they did or not I could not have obeyed. I trust I shall hear no more of this business, which I blush to think should have been brought forward. I shall very soon see you in England, and ever believe me, my dear Davison, your obliged,

BRONTE NELSON OF THE NILE

ANSWER TO MR. TUCKER'S STATEMENT, TRANSMITTED TO ALEXANDER DAVISON ESQ., RESPECTING THE EARL OF ST. VINCENT'S SHARING PRIZE-MONEY, AS COMMANDER-IN-CHIEF ON THE MEDITERRANEAN STATION, WHILE HE WAS IN ENGLAND

1st.—Mr. Tucker says, the Earl St. Vincent had neither resigned or returned from the command of the Mediterranean station, but had come to England on leave from the Lords Commissioners of the Admiralty, for the benefit of his health only:

Answer.—Lord Nelson received a letter from Mr. Nepean, dated the 20th August, 1799, stating, that as the Earl of St. Vincent had returned to England, and Lord Keith, with the other Flag-Officers, having quitted the Mediterranean station, in pursuit of the Enemy, Lord Nelson had become the Senior Officer of his Majesty's Ships there, and that he had all the important duties of the station to attend to; and proceeds to direct his Lordship's attention to the different points of the war, and of the operations to be carried on by the Squadron under his command. Lord Nelson considers this order alone to be sufficient to entitle him to share for all captures, as the Commander-in-Chief for the time being, as he had all the responsibility; and in no instance before, have Admirals claimed to share when they left the station where they commanded, on account of ill health, or otherwise; and, as an instance, Lord Hood's going home for his health, as well as Lord Nelson, who were both retained in pay, but were not allowed to share any Prize-money; and in the case of Lord Hood and Admiral Hotham, there was no claim whatever made by Lord Hood, because neither him nor any Sea-Officer thought he could have a shadow of claim for such.

2nd.—Mr. Tucker says, that after the arrival of the Earl of St. Vincent in England, he was borne and considered by the Admiralty, in every point of view, as the Commander-in-Chief, and corresponded with them as such until the 26th November, when he resigned the command.

Answer.—If the Earl of St. Vincent was considered as Commander-in-Chief, as Mr. Tucker states him to be, why were not all the Admiralty orders sent to Lord Nelson addressed to the Earl of St. Vincent, as is usual, and by him transmitted to Lord Nelson? On the contrary, all orders from the Admiralty were addressed to Lord Nelson, as the Commanding-Officer in the Mediterranean; and in no instance whatsoever did Lord Nelson receive any orders from the Earl of St. Vincent from the time he left the Mediterranean; and it is presumed that the Earl of St. Vincent did not interfere in the command, or give any orders or directions for the carrying on any service on the station.

Answer to 3rd.—With respect to the *Alcmene* being cruizing under the orders of the Earl of St. Vincent, and had not received any directions from any other Officer, this proves nothing, as though the orders from Lord Nelson did not reach the *Alcmene* before the capture of those prizes, yet orders were transmitted from Lord Nelson to Rear-Admiral Duckworth, to be forwarded as well to the *Alcmene* as the other ships on the Station, to put themselves under his Lordship's command; and if Lord Nelson had thought it proper, he was fully authorized to give orders to the *Alcmene* to cruize on any part of the station he might point out. Lord Nelson had it in his power to give directions to any of His Majesty's Ships on the station, in contradiction to any orders given by the Earl of St. Vincent: on the contrary, the Earl of St. Vincent had it not in his power to give any orders in contradiction of those given by Lord Nelson, until his return within the limits of the Mediterranean Station.

BRONTE NELSON OF THE NILE

To Evan Nepean, Esq., Admiralty

Foudroyant, Malta, *May 12th, 1800*

Sir,

I have the pleasure to send you, and to request you will present it to their Lordships, the Flag of the last of the French Squadron who fought at the Battle of the Nile, on the entire destruction of which I most cordially congratulate their Lordships. This Flag has been presented to me in the most flattering manner by the gallant Captors of the *William Tell*. I have the honour to be, &c.,

BRONTE NELSON OF THE NILE

[The *Foudroyant* got under weigh on the 20th May, and continued off Malta until the 1st of June, when she returned to Palermo.]

To Captain Ormsby, Acting Captain of His Majesty's Ship *Alexander*

Foudroyant, at Sea, *22nd May, 1800*

Sir,

I herewith enclose you a letter from the Commander-in-Chief, conveying his Majesty's most gracious pardon for John Jolly, Private Marine, late belonging to the Ship you command, and desire that you will make the same known to him accordingly, and give him such admonitions for his future conduct as you shall judge necessary and proper on the occasion, and return the order from the Lords of the Admiralty to me the first opportunity, and enter the said John Jolly on the books of the *Alexander*, agreeable to the date of his discharge from the *Foudroyant*. I am, &c.,

(*Vide pp. 240 and 241 supra*) BRONTE NELSON OF THE NILE

To His Sacred Majesty The King of the Two Sicilies

Palermo, *2nd June, 1800*

Sire,

Your Majesty's most gracious approbation of my conduct, so marked to the world by the most distinguished Honour* you have conferred

* King Ferdinand wished to confer an Order upon Nelson, and his Captains, Troubridge, Hall, Hood, Louis, and Hallowell, but as it was then considered that Protestants could not be admitted into the Order of St. Januarius, the King instituted the Order of St. Ferdinand and Merit, on the 1st April, 1800. It consisted originally of two classes only, Knights Grand Cross, and Knights Commanders; but a third and inferior class was added in 1810. The first three Knights Grand Cross were Lord Nelson, Field-Marshal Suwarrow, and the Emperor Paul.

upon me, fills me with sensations which no words I can find will in any manner express. I must, therefore, confine myself to simply assuring your Majesty, that there is not that man living who is more attached to your sacred person, the Queen, and your Majesty's whole Royal Family, than your faithful and devoted servant,

BRONTE NELSON OF THE NILE

To Vice-Admiral Lord Keith

Palermo, *2nd June, 1800*

My dear Lord,

The day after I left Malta, I met the *Princess Charlotte*; but as all the arrangements were made for my coming to Palermo, in order to carry the Queen to Leghorn, I sent her to Troubridge, with directions for the execution of your orders, and then to carry him to Leghorn. The state of the *Foudroyant* is such, that I have hitherto avoided saying anything of it, wishing you to see the almost impossibility of fitting her in this Country; and I therefore hope she will be the Ship, when a little refitted, to carry all my party to England.* We sail on the 5th, and hope for a quick passage. Ever, my dear Lord, your obliged servant,

BRONTE NELSON OF THE NILE

To Sir John Acton

Leghorn Roads, Sunday, Noon, *June 15th, 1800*

My dear Sir,

After a very good passage as to time, we arrived here last evening in a fresh gale from the west—so much, that the Ship went eleven miles an hour, at times more. We have with difficulty got a boat on shore, and returned, which is the only communication we have been able to hold with the shore: and the weather is still so bad, that I see no

* On the 9th May, the Admiralty sent orders to Lord Keith, that if Nelson's health rendered him incapable of doing his duty, and that he should be desirous of returning to England, he was to be permitted to do so, and to take his passage in the first ship Lord Keith might have occasion to send home, unless he should prefer returning by land, in which case he was to be at liberty to strike his flag in the Mediterranean and come on shore. On the same day, Lord Spencer wrote to Nelson the following private letter:

Private.

'My dear Lord,

'I have only time to write you a line by the Messenger, who is just going, which I am desirous of doing, in order that the eventual permission, which we now send out for you to come home, in case your health should make it necessary, may not be misunderstood. It is by no means my wish or intention to call you away from service, but having observed that you have been under the necessity of quitting your station off Malta, on account of the state of your health, which I am persuaded you could prospect this day of a boat getting from the shore to us. The contradictory news has a little agitated the Queen; but when particulars, on examination of different persons, are placed before her Majesty, she will be able to form a proper judgment as to the measures to be taken. I have therefore only to request that your Excellency will assure his Majesty, in which join Sir William and Lady Hamilton, that nothing shall make us quit the Queen and Royal Family until all is safe, and their future plans perfectly and securely settled. On every occasion, I only wish for opportunities of proving to their Majesties my desire to show my gratitude for the numerous favours, honours, and magnificent presents they have heaped upon me; and I beg, my dear Sir, that you will believe me your Excellency's most obliged,

BRONTE NELSON OF THE NILE

If the Queen wishes to send any of the Neapolitan vessels under Lord Keith's command, to Palermo, I shall take upon me to give them orders for that purpose.

To His Holiness The Pope

Leghorn, *24th June, 1800*

Holy Father,

As an individual, who from his public situation has had an opportunity of using his utmost exertions to assist in bringing about the happy event of your Holiness's return to Rome, I presume to offer my most sincere congratulations on this occasion; and with my most fervent wishes and prayers that your residence may be blessed with health, and every comfort this world can afford.

Your Holiness will, I am sure, forgive my mentioning a circumstance which, although at the time it was spoken appeared impossible, yet the fact did happen. Father McCormick, a Friar, coming to the House of

not have thought of doing without such necessity, it appeared to me much more advisable for you to come home at once, than to be obliged to remain inactive at Palermo, while active service was going on in other parts of the station. I should still much prefer your remaining to complete the reduction of Malta, which I flatter myself cannot be very far distant, and I still look with anxious expectation to the *Guillaume Tell* striking to your Flag. But if, unfortunately, these agreeable events are to be prevented by your having too much exhausted yourself in the service to be equal to follow them up, I am quite clear, and I believe I am joined in opinion by all your friends here, that you will be more likely to recover your health and strength in England than in an inactive situation at a Foreign Court, however pleasing the respect and gratitude from that Court to you can be, I am convinced, and none too great for the very essential services you have rendered it.

'I trust that you will take in good part what I have taken the liberty to write to you as a friend, and believe me, when I assure you that you have none who is more sincerely and faithfully so than your obedient humble servant, SPENCER.'

Sir William Hamilton, in September, 1798, to congratulate me on the Battle of the Nile, said, (as can be testified,) 'What you have done is great, but you will do a greater thing—you will take Rome with your Ships.' And although I do not believe that the Father had the gift of prophecy, yet his guess was so extraordinary, and has turned out so exactly, that I could not in my conscience avoid telling your Holiness of it. I will now only trespass on your time, by assuring your Holiness with what respect I am your most obedient servant,

BRONTE NELSON OF THE NILE

[On the 24th of June, Lord Keith arrived at Leghorn with the Squadron.]

To Lord Keith

Leghorn, *24th June, 1800*

My dear Lord,

The idea of removing the *Foudroyant* has created an alarm at the Palace, and I send you a letter from thence. If Sir William and Lady Hamilton go home by land, it is my intention to go with them; if by water, we shall be happy in taking the best Ship we can get; but we are all pledged not to quit the Royal Family till they are in perfect security. If the Prince Castelcicala had not been wanted to attend the Queen to this place, the *Dorotea* would certainly have, in obedience, as I conceived, to your orders, gone direct to England, as I understood the King of Naples had asked for a Frigate to carry his Minister to England, and had sent one of his Frigates in her room. To say the truth, I never thought General Acton was to be the Minister, but the present person. Near 300 packages are on board the *Dorotea*; but you will now arrange all matters as you please. Both she and the *Alexander* are still at Especia, and probably I shall see you before then. I own I do not believe the Brest fleet will return to sea; and if they do, the Lord have mercy on them, for our Fleet will not, I am sure.

I shall enter no further on the various subjects of your order, only to assure you that as little as possible do I ever interfere with your orders. I do not recollect I ever did; for I should not like it myself, and I never wrote what could be called a Public letter to Mr. Nepean, since I have been under your command; but I authorized Duckworth, when under my orders, to correspond directly with the Admiralty, and we know that the Admiralty sends orders to Junior Admirals on the station to perform particular services, without even mentioning the circumstance to the Commanding Flag-Officer on this station; therefore, the Admiralty themselves set the example of this new mode of communication to and from the Board. Hoping to see you, my dear Lord, before twentyfour hours pass over, believe me your obliged,

BRONTE NELSON OF THE NILE

I hear all is done as you wish at Port Especia.

NELSON STRIKES HIS FLAG

On quitting the *Foudroyant* Nelson received this letter from his Barge's crew:

Foudroyant, 26th June, 1800

My Lord,

It is with extreme grief that we find you are about to leave us. We have been along with you (although not in the same Ship) in every Engagement your Lordship has been in, both by Sea and Land; and most humbly beg to your Lordship to permit us to go to England, as your Boat's crew, in any Ship or Vessel, or in any way that may seem most pleasing to your Lordship. My Lord, pardon the rude style of Seamen, who are but little acquainted with writing, and believe us to be, my Lord, your ever humble and obedient servants,

BARGE'S CREW OF THE *FOUDROYANT*.

NELSON ARRIVES IN ENGLAND

[Nelson and his friends arrived at Yarmouth on 6th November; and it being the first time he had landed in England since the Battle of the Nile, he was received with enthusiastic admiration. When he stepped on shore 'the populace assembled in crowds to greet the gallant hero of the Nile; and, taking the horses from his carriage, drew him to the Wrestler's Inn amidst applause. The Mayor and Corporation waited on him and presented him with the Freedom of the Town, some time since voted to him for his eminent services. The infantry in the Town paraded before the Inn where he lodged, with their regimental band, &c., &c., firing feux-de-joie of musketry and ordnance till midnight. The Corporation in procession, with the Officers of the Navy, went to church with him, accompanied by Sir William and Lady Hamilton, to join in thanksgiving. On leaving the Town, the corps of cavalry unexpectedly drew up, saluted, and followed the carriage, not only to the Town's end, but to the boundary of the County. All the Ships in the harbour had their colours flying.']

To Evan Nepean, Admiralty

Yarmouth, *November 6th, 1800*

Sir,

I beg you will acquaint their Lordships of my arrival here this day, and that my health being perfectly re-established, it is my wish to serve immediately; and I trust that my necessary journey by land from the Mediterranean will not be considered as a wish to be a moment out of active service. I have the honour to be, &c.,

BRONTE NELSON OF THE NILE

To Marsh and Creed, Navy Agents

Yarmouth, *November 7th, 1800*

£50 for His Worship the Mayor, to be distributed by him.
5 Guineas for the Town Clerk.
1 Guinea for the Officer.
To be paid by Mr. Warmington for Lord Nelson of the Nile.

To John Locker

27th December, 1800

My dear John,

From my heart do I condole with you on the great and irreparable loss we have all sustained in the death of your dear, worthy Father* —a man whom to know was to love, and those who only heard of him honoured. The greatest consolation to us, his friends who remain, is, that he has left a character for honour and honesty which none can surpass, and very, very few attain. That the posterity of the righteous will prosper we are taught to believe; and on no occasion can it be more truly verified than from my dear much lamented friend; and that it may be realized in you, and your sister, and brothers, is the fervent prayer of, my dear John, your afflicted friend,

NELSON

[After much uneasiness and recrimination on both sides, Nelson took his final leave of his wife on the 13th of January, and soon after left London for Plymouth. On quitting her, he emphatically said, 'I call God to witness there is nothing in you or your conduct I wish otherwise.' He was accompanied to Southampton by his brother, the Reverend William Nelson, and from that place wrote the following note:]

To Lady Nelson

Southampton, *13th January, 1801*

My dear Fanny,

We are arrived, and heartily tired; and with kindest regards to my father and all the family, believe me your affectionate

NELSON

* His old friend and Commander, Commodore William Locker, Lieutenant-Governor of Greenwich Hospital, who died on the 26th December, 1800, aged seventy.

CHAPTER EIGHT

BIRTH OF HORATIA

[The following letters cover the period dealing with the birth on or about 30th January, 1801, of Horatia whose father is concealed under the name of 'Mr. Thomson'. Mr. Thomson is represented as being very anxious about his wife's confinement. The baby was secretly placed with a nurse, Mrs. Gibson, in Little Titchfield Street, and was not baptised until 13th May, 1803, in Marylebone Church. The child's date of birth was registered as 29th October, 1800. Horatia always celebrated her birthday on that date.

She remained with Lady Hamilton until the latter's death in 1815, and married, in 1822, the Rev. Philip Ward. They had many children and she died in 1881 at the age of 80.]

To Lady Hamilton *January 25th, 1801*

If you'll believe me, nothing can give me so much pleasure as your truly kind and friendly letters, and where friendship is of so strong a cast as ours, it is no easy matter to shake it—mine is as fixed as Mount Etna, and as warm in the inside as that mountain. The *Audacious*, Gould, will will be paid off tomorrow, and he bears the talking of Miss Knight with good humour. He has inquired where she lives. He is not grown much wiser since we left him, or he never would have wished to leave such a ship and ship's company. I am quite vexed not to have orders for completing the *San Josef's* complement of men, or to proceed to sea, therefore I shall certainly not be at Torbay on Wednesday. I shall write to Troubridge this day to send me your letter, which I look for as constantly and with more anxiety than my dinner. (Let her go to Brighton or where she pleases, I care not; she is a great fool, and, thank God! you are not the least bit like her.* I delivered poor Mrs. Thomson's† note; her friend is truly thankful for her kindness and your goodness. Who does not admire your benevolent heart. Poor man! he is very anxious, and begs you will, if she is not able, write a line just to comfort him. He appears to me to feel very much her situation; he is so agitated, and will be so for 2 or 3 days, that he says he cannot write, and that I must send his kind love and affectionate regards.) What dreadful

* Lady Nelson.
† This is the first mention of Lady Hamilton under this name.

weather we have got: a deep snow. I wish I was just setting off for Bronte. I should then be happy. As I cannot now sail before Thursday, you may direct your letter on Tuesday to me at Plymouth, and if ever so ready will not sail till the post is arrived. On Wednesday direct to Brixham as I mentioned before, and believe me as ever, your obliged, attached, & most affectionate friend, &c.

My brother is as vexed as I am, and fears he shall lose his trip to Torbay. I should have lived on board before, but, as the ship will be paid tomorrow, I hope to get on board on Tuesday. I hate Plymouth. I shall write every day.

To Lady Hamilton *January 26th, 1801*

When I consider that this day nine months was your birthday, and that although we had a gale of wind, yet I was happy, and sung Come Cheer up Fair Emma, &c. Even the thoughts compared with this day makes me melancholy, my heart somehow is sunk within me. I long to hear you are well (keep up your spirits, all will end well), the dearest of friends must part, and we only part, I trust, to meet again. (I own I wonder that Sir Wm. should have a wish for the Prince of Wales to come under your roof; no good can come of it, but every harm. You are too beautiful not to have enemies, and even one visit will stamp you as his chere amie, and we know he is dotingly fond of such women as yourself, and is without one (spark?) of honour in those respects, and would leave you to bewail your folly. But, my dear friend, I know you too well not to be convinced you cannot be seduced by any prince in Europe. You are, in my opinion, the pattern of perfection.)

I have no orders, and can have none before Wednesday, therefore sooner than Thursday or Friday the ship cannot move. I have told my brother of your intentions of giving him a paste. (He would have had a hard matter to get one of mine.) He proposes, if no orders arrive very soon, to leave me, when I shall instantly return on board. I feel no loss in not going to these balls and assemblies. My thoughts are very differently engaged. I know nothing of my destination more than I did when in London, but the papers and reports of my being put in a bad ship which, although I can hardly credit, fills me with sorrow, which, joined to my private feelings, makes me this day ready to burst every moment into tears. I will try and write to the Duke tomorrow; this day I could not if millions lay in my way. Mrs. Thomson's friend is this moment come into my room. He desires me to thank you for your goodness to his friend. He appears almost as miserable as myself. He says you have always been kind to his dear Mrs. Thomson, and he hopes you will continue your goodness to her on this trying occasion. I have assured him of your innate worth and affectionate disposition, and believe, as ever and for ever, your, &c.

My best respects to Sir William, Mrs. Denis, &c., &c.

To Evan Nepean, Esq., Admiralty

San Josef, Plymouth, *28th January, 1801*

Sir,

I have to acknowledge the receipt of their Lordship's order of the 26th instant, directing me to put myself under the command of Admiral the Earl of St. Vincent. I am, &c.,

NELSON

To Lady Hamilton *January 28th, 1801*

What a fool I was, my dear Lady Hamilton, to direct that your cheering letters should be directed for Brixham! I feel, this day, truly miserable, in not having them; and, I fear, they will not come till tomorrow's post. What a blockhead, to believe any person is so active as myself! I have this day got my orders, to put myself under Lord St. Vincent's command; but, as no order is arrived to man the Ship, it must be Friday night, or Saturday morning, before she can sail for Torbay. Direct my letters, now, to Brixham. My eye is very bad. I have had the Physician of the Fleet to examine it. He has directed me not to write, (and yet I am forced this day to write Lord Spencer, St. Vincent, Davison, about my law-suit, Troubridge, Mr. Locker, &c., but you are the only female I write to;) not to eat anything but the most simple food; not to touch wine or porter; to sit in a dark room; to have green shades for my eyes—(will you, my dear friend, make me one or two?—nobody else shall;)—and to bathe them in cold water every hour. I fear, it is the writing has brought on this complaint. My eye is like blood; and the film so extended, that I only see from the corner farthest from my nose. What a fuss about my complaints! But, being so far from my sincere friends, I have leisure to brood over them.

I have this moment seen Mrs. Thompson's friend. Poor fellow! he seems very uneasy and melancholy. He begs you to be kind to her! and I have assured him of your readiness to relieve the dear, good woman; and believe me, for ever, my dear Lady, your faithful, attached, and affectionate,

NELSON AND BRONTE

To Lady Hamilton *San Josef*, Torbay,
February 1st, 1801

I believe poor dear Mrs. Thomson's friend will go mad with joy. He cries, prays, and performs all tricks, yet dare not show all or any of his feelings, but he has only me to consult with. He swears he will drink your health this day in a bumper, and damn me if I don't join him in spite of all the doctors in Europe, for none regard you with truer affection than myself. You are a dear, good creature, and your kindness and attention to poor Mrs. T. stamps you higher than ever in my mind. I cannot write, I am so agitated by this young man at my elbow. I believe he is foolish; he does nothing but rave about you and her. I own I participate of his joy and cannot write anything.

The *San Josef* left Plymouth yesterday at 1 o'clock, and anchored here at 8 this morning, where I found an order to hoist my flag in the *St. George*, as Lord Spencer says I must go forth as the Champion of England in the North, and my *San Josef* is to be held by Captain Wolseley, of the *St. George*, till my return, when I hope to have a knock at the Republicans. In this instance they have behaved handsomely—could not be better. I trust I shall soon be at Portsmouth, and every endeavour of mine shall be used to come to town for three days, and perhaps you and Sir William may like to see Portsmouth. Captain Darby is just come in; he desires me to say everything which is kind, and that he wishes he could see you instead of your picture, which I have handsomely framed and glazed. The post is waiting, and I have been two hours pulling from Lord St. Vincent's house. It is blowing fresh. May the heavens bless you and yours, is the fervent prayer of your unalterable and faithful, &c.

Best regards to Sir William. Instead of under cover, direct as follows: Lord Nelson, &c., &c., to the care of Sir Thomas Troubridge, Bart., Brixham, Devon, which will give them to me four hours sooner.

To Lady Hamilton *February 3rd, 1801*

Your good and dear friend, does not think it proper at present to write with his own hand (but he hopes the time may not be far distant when he may be united for ever to the object of his wishes, his *only* love. He swears before heaven that he will marry you as soon as it is possible, which he fervently prays may be soon.) He charges me to say how dear you are to him, and that you must, every opportunity, kiss and bless for him his dear little girl, which he wishes to be called Emma, out of gratitude to our dear, good Lady Hamilton; but in either its from Lord N. he says, or Lady H., he leaves to your judgment and choice. I have given Lord N. a hundred pounds this morning, for which he will give Lady Hamilton an order on his agents; and I beg that you will distribute it amongst those who have been useful to you on the late occasion; and your friend, my dear Mrs. Thomson, may be sure of my care of him and his interest, which I consider as dearly as my own, and do you believe me ever, &c.

Lady Hamilton must desire at the back for it to be paid to the person who carries it.

To Lady Hamilton *San Josef, February 4th, 1801*

It blows so very hard that I doubt if it will be possible to get a boat on shore, either to receive or send letters, but if it moderates in time for the post of course mine shall go, and I hope from my heart to hear you are better, and it has made my head ache stooping so much, as I have been making memorandums for my will, and, having regularly signed it, if was to die this moment I believe it would hold good. If I am not able to send it, as far as relates to you, this day, I will to-morrow. I have been obliged to be more particular than I would, as a wife can have nothing, and it might be taken from you by will or the heirs of your husband. If you disapprove of any part say so and I will alter it, but I think you must approve; I have done my best that you should. I shall now go to work and save a fortune. Say, shall I bequeath the £2,000 owing me from Sir William for the same purpose? You must keep this letter till you receive a copy of my memo. What a pretty piece of history letting out the French squadron. I was laughed at by some wiseacres in power when I said, if I was a French Admiral I would come out in spite of all the English fleet, as they kept close into Brest, and I would be outside of them before morning.

Your dear, kind letters of Monday are just come on board in a shore boat, and I shall try and get mine ashore, but it is barely possible. (Sir William should say to the Prince that, situated as you are, it would be highly improper for you to admit H.R.H. That the Prince should wish it I am not surprized at, and that he will attempt every means to get into your house and into any place where you may dine. Sir Wm. should speak out, and if the Prince is a man of honour he will quit the pursuit of you. I know his aim is to have you for a mistress. The thought so agitates me that I cannot write. Tell Mrs. T. her friend is grateful for her goodness,) and with my kindest regards to Mrs. Jenkins and Horatia*, and ever believe me your sincere, faithful, and affectionate, &c.

* 'Kindest regards' to a baby of a week old strikes one as a little curious.

We drink your health every day. Believe me, your letter cannot be too long or too minute of all particulars. My mind is a little easier having perfect confidence. Make my respects to Sir Wm, the Duke, and Lord Wm Gordon.

To Lady Hamilton *February 5th, 1801*

Your dear and excellent friend has desired me to say that it is not usual to christen children till they are a month or six weeks old; and as Lord Nelson will probably be in town, as well as myself, before we go to the Baltic, he proposes then, if you approve, to christen the child, and that myself and Lady Hamilton should be two of the sponsors. It can be christened at St. George's, Hanover Square; and, I believe, the parents being at the time out of the kingdom, if it is necessary, it can be stated born at Portsmouth or at sea. Its name will be Horatia, daughter of Johem and Morata Etnorb. If you read the surname backwards, and take the letters of the other names, it will make, very extraordinary, the names of your real and affectionate friends, Lady Hamilton and myself; but, my dear friend, consult Lady Hamilton. Your friend consults me, and I would not lead him wrong for the world; he has not been very well: I believe he has fretted, but his spirit is too high to own it. But, my dear Madam, both him, you, and your little one, must always believe me your affectionate, &c.

The child, if you like it, can be named by any clergyman without its going to church.

To Lady Hamilton *San Josef, February 6th, 1801*

It blows a gale of wind, but which only affects me as it may deprive me of my dearest, most honoured friend's letters. Your letters are to me gazettes, for as yet I have not fixed upon any, nor can they be half so interesting to my feelings, although you know I am not a little fond of a newspaper, and we have almost quarrelled for a first reading, and I trust the time will soon arrive when we shall have those amicable squabbles again. I am now of course very much by myself, for none ever come to me except at meals, or I send for either Hardy or Parker, and they are both so modest and well behaved that it is really a pleasure to have them on board. Parker boasts whenever he drinks your health, which is at least once a day, that he had the honour of being your aid de camp, and that he has given many messages by your orders. Ah! those were happy times. Would to God we were at this moment in the Bay of Naples, and all matters for those good monarchs going on as well as it did at that time.

Noon. This moment has brought me your two kind letters. You may rely I shall not open my mouth on poor dear Mrs. Thomson's business to any creature on this earth. You and I should be very unworthy if we did any such thing, as all the secret of those two people rests solely in our bosoms. He desires me to say that he approves very much of the sum of money, and submits it to your discretion if a small pension should not be promised if the secret is well kept, but desires that nothing should be given under handwriting. He also desires you will now and then give the nurse an additional guinea. He thinks it might be better to omit xtening the child for the present, and even privately baptising it. The clergyman would naturally ask its parent's name which would put poor Mrs. T. in trouble or cause suspicion, but in all these matters he submits himself to your prudence and friendship. He will send you more money as Mrs. T. wants it, only let him know everything. He says, poor fellow, he would have given anything to have seen the child, especially in your charming company. To say the truth, this lad seems to love you not a little; but who does not; I am sure I do. Capt. William's nephew conducts himself very well, and I shall take him into the *St. George* with me, for which ship Capt. Hardy has got his commission, but she is still at Portsmouth.

Saturday noon. Mr. Davison came while I was at dinner yesterday and gave me your letters. He says you are grown thinner, but he thinks you look handsomer than ever. I know he is a very great admirer of yours. He says you told him to tell me not to send any more advice about seeing compy, for that you are determined not to allow the world to say a word agt you, therefore I will not say a word; I rest confident in your conduct. (I was sure you would not go to Mrs. Walpole's, it is no better than a bawdy house.) This morning brought me your letter of Thursday. I am sorry for all your trouble, but poor Mrs. Thompson's friend will never forget the obligation. Ever, my dear Lady, your's, &c.

To Lady Hamilton *February 8th, 1801*

Mr. Davison will deliver this letter and its enclosure. He is very good and kind to me. and perhaps I can never repay the great and heavy obligation I owe him; but if it pleases God that I should retire into the country, I should not want a carriage, for I can walk, and my affairs would soon arrange themselves. I do not think I ever was so miserable as this moment. I own I sometimes fear that you will not be so true to me as I am to you, yet I cannot, will not believe you can be false. No, I judge you by myself; I hope to be dead before that should happen, but it will not. Forgive me, Emma, oh, forgive your own dear, disinterested Nelson. Tell Davison how sensible I am of his goodness; he knows my attachment to you, and I suspect he admires you himself. I cannot express my feelings. May God send me happiness. I have a letter from Sir William; he speaks of the Regency as certain, and then probably he thinks you will sell better—horrid thought. Only believe me for ever your, &c.

To Lady Hamilton *No date (1801)*

Your dear friend, my dear and truly beloved Mrs. T., is almost distracted; he wishes there was peace, or that if your uncle would die, he would instantly then come and marry you, for he doats on nothing but you and his child; and, as it is my godchild, I desire you will take great care of it. He has implicit faith in your fidelity, even in conversation with those he dislikes, and that you will be faithful in greater things he has no doubt. My God bless you both and send you a happy meeting is the wish of yours, &c.

[With superscription to 'Mrs. Thomson'.]

To Lady Hamilton

San Josef, February 8th, 1801

My dear Lady,

Mr. Davison demands the privilege of carrying back an answer to your kind letter; and, I am sure, he will be very punctual in the delivery. I am not in very good spirits; and, except that our Country demands all our services and abilities, to bring about an honourable Peace, nothing should prevent my being the bearer of my own letter. But, my dear friend, I know you are so true and loyal an Englishwoman, that you would hate those who would not stand forth in defence of our King, Laws, Religion, and all that is dear to us. It is your sex that make us go forth; and seem to tell us—'None but the brave deserve the fair.' and if we fall, we still live in the hearts of those females, who are dear to us. It is your sex that rewards us; it is your sex who cherish our memories; and you, my dear, honoured friend, are, believe me, the first, the best of your sex. I have been the world around, and in every corner of it, and never yet saw your equal, or even one which could be put in comparison with you. You know how to reward virtue, honour, and courage; and never to ask if it is placed in a Prince, Duke; Lord, or Peasant: and I hope, one day, to see you in peace, before I set out for Bronte, which I am resolved to do.

Darby's is one of the Ships sent out after the French Squadron; I shall, therefore, give the print to Hardy. I think, they might come by the mail-coach, as a parcel, wrapped up round a stick; any print shop will give you one: and direct it as my letters. The coach stops, for parcels, at the White Bear, I believe, Piccadilly. Pray, have you got any picture from Mrs. Head's? I hope Mr. Brydon has executed the frames to your satisfaction; the bill he is directed to send to me. Only tell me, how I can be useful to you and Sir William; and believe, nothing could give me more pleasure, being, with the greatest truth, my dear Lady, your most obliged and affectionate friend,

NELSON AND BRONTE

I am told, the moment *St. George* arrives, that I am to be tumbled out of this Ship, as the *Ville de Paris* is going to Plymouth, to be paid, and the Earl will hoist his Flag here: and if I am as fortunate in getting a fresh painted cabin, (which is probable,) I shall be knocked up. At all events, I shall be made very uncomfortable by this hurry. It has been very good and friendly of Mr. Davison to travel upwards of two hundred miles to make me a visit. I rather think the great Earl will not much like his not having called on him, but his manner of speaking of Mr. Davison, for his friendship to me, in the matter of the law-suit, Lord St. Vincent states to my solicitors as offensive to him. Why should it? only that Mr. Davison wishes that I should have justice done me, and not to be overpowered by weight of interest and money. Once more, God bless you and Sir William.

N. & B.

Sir Isaac Heard has gazetted Troubridge's, Hood, &c.'s honours, but has not gazetted mine; and he has the King's orders for mine as much as the others.

FEARS OF THE PRINCE REGENT

To Lady Hamilton *February 17th, 1801*

I am so agitated that I can write nothing. I knew it would be so, and you can't help it. Why did you not tell Sir William? Your character will be gone. Good God! he will be next you, and telling you soft things. If he does, tell it out at table, and turn him out of the house. Do not sit long. If you sing a song, I know you cannot help it, do not let him set next you, but at dinner he will hob glasses with you. I cannot write to Sir Wm, but he ought to go to the Prince and not suffer your character to be ruined by him. O, God, that I was dead! But I do not, my dearest Emma, blame you, nor do I fear your inconstancy. I tremble, and God knows how I write. Can nothing be thought of? I am gone almost mad, but you cannot help it. It will be in all the newspapers with hints. Recollect what the villain said to Mr. Nisbet, *how you hit his fancy*. I am mad, almost dead, but ever for ever yours to the last moment, your, only your, &c.

I could not write another line if I was to be made King. If I was in town nothing should make me dine with you that damned day, but, my dear Emma, I do not blame you, only remember your poor miserable friend, that you must be singing and appear gay. I shall that day have no one to dinner; it shall be a fast day to me. He will put his foot near you. I pity you from my soul, as I feel confident you wish him in hell. Have plenty of people and do not say a word you can help to him. He wishes, I dare say, to have you alone. Don't let him touch, nor yet sit next you; if he comes, get up. God strike him blind if he looks at you—this is high treason, and you may get me hanged by revealing it. Oh, God! that I were. I have read your letter, your resolution never to go where the fellow is, but you must have him at home. Oh, God! but you cannot, I suppose, help it, and you cannot turn him out of your own house. He will stay and sup and sit up till 4 in the morning, and the fewer that stay the better. Oh, God! why do I live? But I do not blame you; it is my misfortune. I feel nobody uses me ill. I am only fit to be second, or third, or 4, or to black shoes. I want no better part than I have. I see your determination to be on your guard, and am as fixed as fate. If you'll believe me, don't scold me; I am more dead than alive, to the last breath yours. If you cannot get rid of this I hope you will tell Sir William never to bring the fellow again.

I send a note for Mrs. T.

To Lady Hamilton *February 19th, 1801*

Forgive my letter wrote and sent last night, perhaps my head was a little affected. No wonder, it was such an unexpected, such a knock-down blow, such a death. But I will not go on, for I shall get out of my senses again. Will you sing for the fellow, *The Prince, unable to Conceal His Pain*, &c? No, you will not. I will say no more for fear of my head. It was so good of you to send to thank Mr. Nisbet for his not asking you to meet the fellow, as he knew his vile intent, and yet, the same morning to let him come and dine with you en famille!—but I know it was not my Emma; Sir William always asks all partys to dinner. I forgive you. Forgive, I beseech, your old and dear friend! Tell me all, every word, that passes. He will propose if you—no, you will not try; he is Sir Wm's guest.

Thursday.—I have just got your letter and I live again. DO NOT let the lyar come. I never saw him but once, the 4th day after I came to

London, and he never mentioned your name. May God blast him! Be firm! Go and dine with Mrs. Denis on Sunday. Do not, I beseech you, risk being at home. Does Sir William want you to be a whore to the rascal? Forgive all my letter; you will see what I feel, and have felt. I have eat not a morsel, except a little rice, since yesterday morning, and till I know how this matter is gone off. But I feel confident of your resolution, and thank you 1,000,000 of times. I write you a letter, which may be said as coming from me if you like, I will endeavour to word it properly. Did you sit alone with the villain for a moment? No, I will not believe it! O, God! keep my sences. Do not let the rascal in. Tell the Duke that you will never go to his house. Mr. G.* must be a scoundrel; he treated you once ill enough, and cannot love you, or he would sooner die. Ever for ever, aye for ever, your, &c.

I have this moment got my orders to put myself under Sir Hyde Parker's orders, and suppose I shall be ordered to Portsmouth tomorrow or next day, & then I will try & get to London for 3 days. May Heaven bless us! but do not let that fellow dine with you. Don't write here after you receive this, I shall be gone. You can, in Sir Wm's name, write a note to Sir H. Parker, asking if the *St. George* is ordered to Spithead. If so, write to Portsmouth desiring my letters to be left at the Post Office till the ship's arrival.

Forgive every cross word, I now live.

To Lady Hamilton — No date

[With superscription 'Mrs. Thomson, to the care of Lady Hamilton']

Your friend is at my elbow, and enjoins me to assure you that his love for you and your child is, if possible, greater than ever, and that he calls God to witness that he will marry you as soon as possible, and that it will be his delight to call you his own. He desires you will adhere to Lady H's good advice and, like her, keep those impertinent men at a proper distance. He behaves, I can assure you, incomparably well, and loves you as much as man ever loved woman, and do you, my dear, believe me ever your dear friend.

To Lady Hamilton — No date

[With superscription 'Mrs. Thomson, to the care of Lady Hamilton']

I gave your letter to your friend, who is much pleased with your resolution. He says he feels confident of your conduct, and begs you

* Charles Greville, Emma's former lover.

will follow the admirable conduct of our dear Lady Hamilton, who will send the Prince to the devil. He again begs me to be his bondsman, and that he will marry you the moment your uncle dies or it comes a peace, and he desires his blessing to his child, and you will forgive my desiring you to kiss it for me. Your friend has not been very well, but hopes to be better very soon. Ever believe me, your & his sincere friend.

[In consequence of the Northern Coalition, it had for some time been determined to send a powerful fleet into the Baltic, under Admiral Sir Hyde Parker, with Nelson as Second in Command; and on 17th February, 1801, the Admiralty issued their orders to Lord Nelson 'to put himself under the command of Sir Hyde Parker, Commander-in-Chief of a Squadron of his Majesty's Ships and Vessels, to be employed on a particular service'. On the 18th of February, he was directed to proceed in the *St. George* to Spithead, and remain there until further orders.]

To Lady Hamilton *February 23rd, 1801*

[With superscription 'To the Care of Lady Hamilton']

My dear Mrs. T., poor Thompson seems to have forgot all his ill health, and all his mortifications and sorrows, in the thought that he will soon bury them all in your dear, dear bosom; he seems almost beside himself. I hope you have always minded what Lady Hn has said to you, for she is a pattern of attacht to her love. I daresay twins will again be the fruit of your and his meeting. The thought is too much to bear. Have the dear thatched cottage ready to receive him, & I will answer that he would not give it up for a queen and a palace. Kiss dear H. for me, &c.

Lady Hamilton to Mrs. William Nelson,
afterwards Countess Nelson London, *February 24th, 1801*

My dearest Friend,

Your dear Brother arrived this morning by seven o'clock. He stays only 3 days; so by the time you would be here, he will be gone. How unlucky you went so soon. I am in health *so so*, but *spirits* today excellent. Oh, what real pleasure Sir William and I have in seeing this our great good virtuous Nelson. His eye is better. Tom tit* does not come to town. She offered to go down but was refused. She only

* Lady Nelson, so referred to by the Nelson family. Josiah Nisbet was nicknamed 'The Cub'.

wanted to go to do mischief to all the great Jove's* relations. 'Tis now shown, all her ill-treatment and bad *heart*. Jove has found it out. Apropos, Lady Nelson is at Brighton yet. The King, God bless him, is ill and their are many speculations. Some say it is his *old disorder*. I can only say to you, God bless you. I will write longer tomorrow. Ever, ever yours, etc.

To Lady Hamilton

Portsmouth,
February 27th, 1801

Parting from such a friend is literally tearing one's own flesh; but the remembrance will keep up our spirits till we meet. My affection is, if possible, stronger than ever for you, and I trust it will keep increasing as long as we both live. I have seen Mrs. Thomson's friend, who is delighted at my having seen his dear child. I am sure he will be very fond of it. I arrived here before noon, and have had my hands full of business. Tomorrow we embark troops. I will write you a long letter tonight, and send it under cover to Troubridge; therefore you will have it on Sunday. For ever, aye for ever, believe me, &c.

Hardy, Parker, and Fremantle, desire their remembrances.

To Lady Hamilton

March 1st, 1801

After my letter of 8 o'clock this morning went on shore, on board came Oliver†, and when he was announced by Hardy, so much anxiety for your safety rushed into my mind that a pain immediately seized my heart, which kept increasing for half an hour, that, turning cold, hot, cold, &c., I was obliged to send for the surgeon, who gave me something to warm me, for it was a deadly chill. This morning has brought me your three dear letters by the post, and as many from Troubridge. Parker being appointed to a fine ship, I have charged him to deliver into your own hands, if possible, this letter. Oliver I shall keep till tomorrow. Why, my dear friend, do you alarm yourself? Your own Nelson will return safe, and, under the hand of Providence, is as safe as if walking London streets. The troops are only 800, and are intended for the better manning our ships. Recollect the more force we have the less risk. You may rely we shall return in May—perhaps long before; the sooner we are off, the quicker we return, and the enemy much less prepared to receive us. I wish it was in my power to get leave of absence for James Dugdale, but not even an ad. or captain could get an hour's leave, and Sir Thomas Pasley at Plymouth has no

* Nelson.
† Nelson's servant.

power to grant it. Amongst many cards, I think I saw somebody's rout, but as I cared for no rout, or the writers, I did not trouble my head about it. I am sure neither of us should have gone to Lady D's rout; we could amuse ourselves better at home. Mr. Levington served that fellow right, damn him. That Lady Aber. is a damned bitch; she would pimp for her husband that she might get at her lovers, for I dare say not one satisfies her, but no proper lover but two that I know of. Would to God I had dined alone with you. What a desert we would have had. The time will come, and believe me, that I am, for ever, for ever, your own.

Thanks for the account of my godchild. Heavens bless it! Our activity will make a peace, and then I would not call the King my uncle.

Sir Charles Sexton, the Commissioner, who you & Sir William would have known had you come to Portsmouth, is on board seeing the ship; he is charmed with your picture, and says he did not believe such a handsome woman existed. I told him your equal did not, and your goodness, abilities, and virtues exceeded far away your beauty. He is a rough sailor, 70, and a very old friend of mine. He quite regrets you and Sir William did not come to Portsmouth with me.

HIS DEAR WIFE

To Lady Hamilton *March 1st, 1801*

Now, my dear wife, for such you are in my eyes and in the face of heaven, I can give full scope to my feelings, for I daresay Oliver will faithfully deliver this letter. You know, my dearest Emma, that there is nothing in this world that I would not do for us to live together, and to have our dear little child with us. I firmly believe that this campaign will give us peace, and then we will sett off for Bronte. In twelve hours we shall be across the water and freed from all the nonsence of his friends, or rather pretended ones. Nothing but an event happening to him could prevent my going, and I am sure you will think so, for unless all matters accord it would bring 100 of tongues and slanderous reports if I separated from her (which I would do with pleasure the moment we can be united; I want to see her no more*), therefore we must manage till we can quit this country or your uncle dies†. I love, I never did love any one else. I never had a dear pledge of love till you gave me one, and you, thank my God, never gave one to any body else. I think before

* His wife.
† Sir Wm. Hamilton.

March is out you will either see us back, or so victorious that we shall insure a glorious issue to our toils. Think what my Emma will feel at seeing return safe, perhaps with a little more fame, her own dear loving Nelson. Never, if I can help it, will I dine out of my ship, or go on shore, except duty calls me. Let Sir Hyde have any glory he can catch—I envy him not. You, my beloved Emma, and my country, are the two dearest objects of my fond heart—a heart susceptible and true. Only place confidence in me and you never shall be disappointed. I burn all your dear letters, because it is right for your sake, and I wish you would burn all mine—they can do no good, and will do us both harm if any seizure of them, or the dropping even one of them, would fill the mouths of the world sooner than we intend. (My longing for you, both person and conversation, you may readily imagine. What must be my sensations at the idea of sleeping with you! it setts me on fire, even the thoughts, much more would the reality. I am sure my love & desires are all to you, and if any woman naked were to come to me, even as I am this moment from thinking of you, I hope it might rot off if I would touch her even with my hand. No, my heart, person, and mind is in perfect union of love towards my own dear, beloved Emma—the real bosom friend of her, all hers, all Emma's, &c.

Oliver is gone to sleep, he is grown half foolish. I shall give him £10 in the morning, and I have wrote a letter recommending a friend of his to the Chairman of the East India Company, which he said you would be glad I should do for him. I have nothing to send my Emma, it makes me sorry you & Sir Wm could not come to Yarmouth, that would be pleasant, but we shall not be there more than a week at farthest.) I had a letter this day from the Rev. Mr. Holden, who we met on the Continent; he desired his kind compliments to you and Sir William: he sent me letters of my name, and recommended it as my motto—Honor est a Nilo—HORATIO NELSON. May the Heavens bless you. (My love, my darling angel, my heaven-given wife, the dearest only true wife of her own till death, &c. I know you will never let that fellow or any one come near you.)

Monday Morning.—Oliver is just going on shore; the time will ere long arrive when Nelson will land to fly to his Emma, to be for ever with her. Let that hope keep us up under our present difficulties. Kiss and bless *our* dear Horatia—think of that.

To the Earl of St. Vincent, K.B. *1st March, 1801*

The wind was yesterday at S.S.W., which has prevented *Warrior*, *Defence*, and *Agincourt* from sailing. Time, my dear Lord, is our best Ally, and I hope we shall not give her up, as all our Allies have given us up. Our friend here is a little nervous about dark nights and fields of ice, but we must brace up; these are not times for nervous systems. I want Peace, which is only to be had through, I trust, our still invincible Navy. I have not seen Captain Thesiger here, I shall receive him with much pleasure; if he is still in Town pray send word to him to meet me in the Downs or Yarmouth. I have written to Troubridge relative to Miller's monument.

March 2nd, getting under sail. I am always happy when my conduct meets with your approbation, and whilst I remain in the service my utmost exertions shall be called forth: for although, I own, I have met with much more honours and rewards than ever my most sanguine ideas led me to expect, yet I am so circumstanced that probably this Expedition will be the last service ever performed by your obliged and affectionate friend,

NELSON AND BRONTE

LAST LETTER TO LADY NELSON

St. George, March 4th, 1801

Josiah is to have another ship, and to go abroad, if the *Thalia* cannot soon be got ready. I have done *all* for him, and he may again, as he has often done before, wish me to break my neck, and be abetted in it by his friends, who are likewise my enemies; but I have done my duty as an honest, generous man, and I neither want or wish for any body to care what becomes of me, whether I return, or am left in the Baltic. Living, I have done all in my power for you, and if dead, you will find I have done the same; therefore my only wish is, to be left to myself: and wishing you every happiness, believe that I am, your affectionate, &c.

To Lady Hamilton

St George at Sea,
March 6th, 1801

How tiresome and alone I feel at not having the pleasure of receiving your dear, kind, friendly, and intelligent letters. I literally feel as a fish out of water. Calms and foul winds have already prolonged our passage from what is often done in fourteen hours to three days, and yet no appearance of our arrival this day. It now snows and rains, and nearly calm. All day yesterday I was employed about a very necessary thing; and I assure you it gave me pleasure, instead of pain, the reflection that I was providing for a dear friend. I have given you, by will, £3,000, and three diamond boxes, & the King of Naple's picture in trust, to be at your disposal, so that it is absolutely your own. By the codicil I have given you the money owing me by Sir William, likewise in trust. The trustees are, Mr. Ryder, a very eminent law man, and Mr. Davison; they will be my executors. If you like any body else, say so, and it shall be done. The star I have given you to wear for my sake. You must not think, my dearest friend, that this necessary act hastens our departure, but it is a right and proper measure. (Why should my friends be neglected, and those who I care nothing for have my little fortune, which I have worked so hard and I think so honorably for?)

Half past eight.—Just anchored in the sea, thick as mud. I am really miserable; I look at all your pictures, at your dear hair, I am ready to cry, my heart is so full. Then I think you may see that fellow. I should never forgive it. It would go near to kill me; but I never will believe it till I know it for certain.

Noon.—Under sail, steering for Yarmouth, but cannot arrive before 5 o'clock. How I regret not being in time to save post, for I judge as of my own fleet.

Three o'clock.—In sight of Yarmouth. With what different sensations to what I saw it before! Then I was with all I hold dear in the world; now, unless the pleasure I shall have in reading your dear, dear letters, how different to the approach. Although we are too late for the post, yet Hardy will take this letter on shore. I shall put it under cover to Troubridge as I shall those of tomorrow. May the Heavens bless my own dear friend and let me read happy & good news from her. Kiss my dear, dear godchild for me, and be assured I am for ever, ever, ever, your, your, your, more than ever yours yours, your own, only your, &c.

I am wet through and cold.

To Lady Hamilton *March, 1801*

You say, my dearest Friend, why don't I put my Chief forward?* He has put me in the front of the battle, and Nelson will be first. I could say more; but will not make you uneasy, knowing the firm friendship you have for me. The *St. George* will stamp an additional ray of glory to England's fame, if Nelson survives; and that Almighty Providence, who has hitherto protected me in all dangers, and covered my head in the day of battle, will still, if it be his pleasure, support and assist me. Keep me alive, in your and Sir William's remembrance. My last thoughts will be with you both, for you love and esteem me. I judge your hearts by my own. May the Great God of Heaven protect and bless you and him! is the fervent prayer of your and Sir William's unalterable friend, till death,

NELSON AND BRONTE

* Sir Hyde Parker.

To Lady Hamilton *March, 1801*

You may readily believe, my dearly beloved Mrs. T., how dear you are to me—as much as life, and that every thought and affection is devoted to you alone; and although I am much worn out since we parted, yet, I am sure that the sight of my heaven-given wife will make me again a happy father, and you a mother. Be assured that I love nothing but you in this world, and our dear child. Fancy what would happen, and will happen, when we meet. I can say no more; flattering fancy wafts me to your dear, dear arms. When you see our dear mutual friend, Ly Hamn, say every kind thing for your husband to her, and hug our dear child. God bless you.

CHAPTER NINE

BATTLE OF COPENHAGEN

I had the happiness of witnessing under all its circumstances the most hard-fought battle and the most complete victory (as far as my reading goes) that ever was fought and obtained by the Navy of this country.

NELSON

To Alexander Davison

(The Squadron sailed from Yarmouth on 12th March.)

Latitude 57° N., *16th March, 1801*

Our weather is very cold, we have received much snow and sharp frost. I have not yet seen my Commander-in-Chief, and have had no official communication whatever. All I have gathered of our first plans, I disapprove most exceedingly; honour may arise from them, good cannot. I hear we are likely to anchor outside Cronenburg Castle, instead of Copenhagen, which would give weight to our negotiation: a Danish Minister would think twice before he would put his name to war with England, when the next moment he would probably see his Master's Fleet in flames, and his Capital in ruins; but 'out of sight out of mind', is an old saying. The Dane should see our Flag waving every moment he lifted up his head. I am, &c.,

NELSON AND BRONTE

To Sir Hyde Parker

24th March, 1801

My dear Sir Hyde,

The conversation we had yesterday has naturally, from its importance, been the subject of my thoughts; and the more I have reflected, the more I am confirmed in opinion, that not a moment should be lost in attacking the Enemy: they will every day and hour be stronger; we never shall be so good a match for them as at this moment. The only consideration in my mind, is how to get at them with the least risk to our Ships. By Mr. Vansittart's account, the Danes have taken every means in their power to prevent our getting to attack Copenhagen by the Passage of the Sound. Cronenburg has been strengthened, the

Crown Islands fortified, on the outermost of which are twenty guns pointing mostly downwards, and only eight hundred yards from very formidable batteries placed under the Citadel, supported by five Sail of the Line, seven Floating batteries of fifty guns each, besides Small-craft, Gun-boats, &c. &c.; and that the Revel Squadron of twelve or fourteen Sail of the Line are soon expected, as also five Sail of Swedes. It would appear by what you have told me of your instructions, that Government took for granted you would find no difficulty in getting off Copenhagen, and in the event of a failure of negotiation, you might instantly attack; and that there would be scarcely a doubt but the Danish Fleet would be destroyed, and the Capital made so hot that Denmark would listen to reason and its true interest. By Mr. Vansittart's account, their state of preparation exceeds what he conceives our Government thought possible, and that the Danish Government is hostile to us in the greatest possible degree. Therefore here you are, with almost the safety, certainly with the honour of England more intrusted to you, than ever yet fell to the lot of any British Officer. On your decision depends, whether our Country shall be degraded in the eyes of Europe, or whether she shall rear her head higher than ever: again do I repeat, never did our Country depend so much on the success of any Fleet as on this. How best to honour our Country and abate the pride of her Enemies, by defeating their schemes, must be the subject of your deepest consideration as Commander-in-Chief; and if what I have to offer can be the least useful in forming your decision, you are most heartily welcome.

I shall begin with supposing you are determined to enter by the Passage of the Sound, as there are those who think, if you leave that Passage open, that the Danish Fleet may sail from Copenhagen, and join the Dutch or French. I own I have no fears on that subject; for it is not likely that whilst their Capital is menaced with an attack, 9,000 of her best men should be sent out of the Kingdom. I suppose that some damage may arise amongst our masts and yards; yet perhaps there will not be one of them but could be made serviceable again. You are now about Cronenburg; if the wind be fair, and you determine to attack the Ships and Crown Islands, you must expect the natural issue of such a battle—Ships crippled, and perhaps one or two lost; for the wind which carries you in, will most probably not bring out a crippled Ship. This mode I call taking the bull by the horns. It, however, will not prevent the Revel Ships, or Swedes, from joining the Danes; and to prevent this from taking effect, is, in my humble opinion, a measure absolutely necessary—and still to attack Copenhagen. Two modes are in my view; one to pass Cronenburg, taking the risk of damage, and to pass up the deepest and straightest

Channel above the Middle Grounds; and coming down the Carbar or King's Channel, to attack their Floating batteries, &c. &c., as we find it convenient. It must have the effect of preventing a junction between the Russians, Swedes, and Danes, and may give us an opportunity of bombarding Copenhagen. I am also pretty certain that a passage could be found to the northward of Southolm for all our Ships; perhaps it might be necessary to warp a short distance in the very narrow part. Should this mode of attack be ineligible, the passage of the Belt, I have no doubt, would be accomplished in four or five days, and then the attack by Draco could be carried into effect, and the junction of the Russians prevented, with every probability of success against the Danish Floating batteries. What effect a bombardment might have, I am not called upon to give an opinion; but think the way would be cleared for the trial. Supposing us through the Belt with the wind first westerly, would it not be possible to either go with the Fleet, or detach ten Ships of three and two decks, with one Bomb and two Fire-ships, to Revel, to destroy the Russian Squadron at that place? I do not see the great risk of such a detachment, and with the remainder to attempt the business at Copenhagen. The measure may be thought bold, but I am of opinion the boldest measures are the safest; and our Country demands a most vigorous exertion of her force, directed with judgment. In supporting you, my dear Sir Hyde, through the arduous and important task you have undertaken, no exertion of head or heart shall be wanting from your most obedient and faithful servant,

NELSON AND BRONTE

To Lady Hamilton

Elephant, *March 30th*, *1801*,
off Copenhagen.

We this morning passed the fancied tremendous fortress of Cronenburg, mounted with 270 pieces of cannon. More powder and shot, I believe, never were thrown away, for not one shot struck a single ship of the British fleet. Some of our ships fired; but the *Elephant* did not return a single shot. I hope to reserve them for a better occasion. I have just been reconnoitring the Danish line of defence. It looks formidable to those who are children at war, but to my judgment, with ten Sail of the Line I think I can annihilate them; at all events, I hope to be allowed to try. I am not very well and tired, but Foley is very good to me. I have much to do here, exactly what you said in London. May God, whom I worship, protect and send me victorious. Amen, if it be His good pleasure. May the heavens bless you. My best regards to Sir William. I hope his pictures have sold well. Recommend to Lord William not to make songs about us, for fear we should not deserve his good opinion. Once more, adieu, and may God bless you shall be my last word.

BATTLE OF COPENHAGEN

[That portion of the British Fleet consisting of twelve ships under Nelson's command had anchored overnight in readiness for the attack on the following morning.

At 9 a.m. on 2nd April, the ships weighed and moved up to the attack, *Edgar* leading the British line, but *Agamemnon* was unable to clear the shoal and *Bellona* and *Russell* grounded. Thus three out of the twelve ships were unable to reach their allotted stations.

Throughout the morning a furious cannonade continued, in which weight of metal was the deciding factor. At the height of the action Nelson had put nine ships against the Danish eighteen; *Bellona* and *Russell* were flying signals of distress; the *Agamemnon* one of inability. Sir Hyde Parker made his signal of recall, the gallant Riou and his frigates had been compelled to retire to avoid destruction; *Monarch* and *Defiance* were badly mauled and even if he had been tempted to withdraw at this crisis of the battle, Nelson would have had to take his ships north through a strange and narrow channel under the fire of the massive Trekover forts.

There was also the chance that his second in command, Admiral Graves, might have taken advantage of Sir Hyde Parker's order to retire; in which case Nelson might have been annihilated.

The determination to continue the battle and the terrible weight of metal from the British guns enabled the British ships slowly to gain the upper hand. It was at this juncture that Nelson sent his celebrated note on shore to the Crown Prince beginning: 'To the Brothers of Englishmen, the Danes.' It led to the truce, under cover of which he was able to extricate his squadron from its dangerous situation. The southerly breeze still served and Nelson at once signalled his ships to weigh or slip and proceed. It was agreed the British should take possession of their prizes, and Copenhagen was fought—and won, but only at the greatest risk. Total killed and wounded numbered 943. All the prizes except one were destroyed by the orders of Sir Hyde Parker and to add to Nelson's fury no medal was struck for this action.]

NELSON'S REPORT ON THE BATTLE

To Sir Hyde Parker *Elephant*, off Copenhagen, *3rd April, 1801*

Sir,

In obedience to your directions to report the proceedings of the Squadron named in the margin, which you did me the honour to place under my command, I beg leave to inform you, that having, by the assistance of that able Officer, Captain Riou, and the unremitting exertions of Captain Brisbane, and the Masters of the *Amazon* and *Cruizer* in particular, buoyed the Channel of the Outer Deep, and the position of the Middle Ground, the Squadron passed in safety, and anchored off Draco the evening of the 1st; and that yesterday morning I made the signal for the Squadron to weigh, and to engage the Danish Line, consisting of six Sail of the Line, eleven Floating Batteries, mounting from twenty-six twenty-four pounders to eighteen eighteen-pounders, and one Bomb-Ship, besides Schooner Gun-Vessels. These were supported by the Crown Islands, mounting eighty-eight cannon, and four Sail of the Line, moored in the Harbour's Mouth, and some Batteries on the Island of Amak.

The Bomb-Ship and Schooner Gun-Vessels made their escape. The other seventeen Sail are sunk, burnt, or taken, being the whole of the Danish Line to the southward of the Crown Islands, after a battle of four hours.

From the very intricate navigation, the *Bellona* and *Russell* unfortunately grounded, but although not in the situation assigned them, yet so placed as to be of great service. The *Agamemnon* could not weather the shoal of the middle, and was obliged to anchor, but not the smallest blame can be attached to Captain Fancourt; it was an event to which all the Ships were liable. These accidents prevented the extension of our Line by the three Ships before mentioned, who would, I am confident, have silenced the Crown Islands, the two outer Ships in the harbour's mouth, and prevented the heavy loss in the *Defiance* and *Monarch*; and which unhappily threw the gallant and good Captain Riou, (to whom I had given the command of the Frigates and Sloops named in the margin, to assist in the attack of the Ships at the harbour's mouth) under a very heavy fire. The consequence has been the death of Captain Riou, and many brave Officers and men in the Frigates and Sloops.

The Bombs were directed and took their stations abreast of the *Elephant*, and threw some shells into the Arsenal. Captain Rose, who volunteered his services to direct the Gun-brigs, did everything that was possible to get them forward, but the current was too strong for them to be of service during the Action; but not the less merit is due to Captain Rose, and, I believe, all the Officers and crews of the Gun-Brigs, for their exertions.

The Boats of those Ships of the Fleet who were not ordered on the attack, afforded us every assistance; and the Officers and men who were in them merit my warmest approbation.

The *Desiree* took her station in raking the southernmost Danish

Ship of the Line, and performed the greatest service. The Action began at five minutes past ten—the Van led by Captain George Murray of the *Edgar*, who set a noble example of intrepidity, which was as well followed up by every Captain, Officer, and Man in the Squadron.

It is my duty to state to you the high and distinguished merit and gallantry of Rear-Admiral Graves. To Captain Foley, who permitted me the honour of hoisting my Flag in the *Elephant*, I feel under the greatest obligations; his advice was necessary on many and important occasions during the Battle. I beg leave to express how much I feel indebted to every Captain, Officer, and Man, for their zeal and distinguished bravery on this occasion. The Honourable Colonel Stewart did me the favour to be on board the *Elephant*; and himself, with every Officer and Soldier under his orders, shared with pleasure the toils and dangers of the day.

The loss in such a Battle has naturally been very heavy. Amongst many other brave Officers and men who were killed, I have with sorrow to place the name of Captain Moss, of the *Monarch*, who has left a wife and six children to lament his loss; and among the wounded, that of Captain Sir Thomas Boulden Thompson, of the *Bellona*. I have the honour to be, &c.,

NELSON AND BRONTE

NOTE SENT BY NELSON, WITH A FLAG OF TRUCE, TO COPENHAGEN, DURING THE ACTION OF THE 2ND APRIL, 1801

TO THE BROTHERS OF ENGLISHMEN,
THE DANES.

Lord Nelson has directions to spare Denmark, when no longer resisting; but if the firing is continued on the part of Denmark, Lord Nelson will be obliged to set on fire all the Floating-batteries he has taken, without having the power of saving the brave Danes who have defended them. Dated on board his Britannic Majesty's Ship *Elephant*, Copenhagen Roads, April 2nd, 1801.

NELSON AND BRONTE, Vice-Admiral,
under the Command of Admiral Sir Hyde
Parker.

To The Government of Denmark *Elephant, 2nd April, 1801*

Lord Nelson's object in sending on shore a Flag of Truce is humanity: he, therefore, consents that hostilities shall cease till Lord Nelson can take his prisoners out of the Prizes, and he consents to land all the wounded Danes, and to burn or remove his Prizes. Lord Nelson, with humble duty to His Royal Highness, begs leave to say, that he will ever esteem it the greatest victory he ever gained, if this Flag of Truce may be the happy forerunner of a lasting and happy union between my most gracious Sovereign and his Majesty the King of Denmark.

NELSON AND BRONTE

HYDE PARKER BURNS THE PRIZES

To Lord St. Vincent *Apparently about April 5th, 1801*

Whether Sir Hyde Parker may mention the subject to you, I know not, for he is rich, and does not want it. Nor is it, you will believe me, from any desire I possess to get a few hundred pounds, that actuates me to address this letter to you; but, my dear Lord, justice to the brave Officers and men who fought on that day. It is true, our opponents were in Hulks and Floats only adapted for the position they were placed in; but that made our battle so much the harder, and victory so much the more difficult to obtain. Believe me, I have weighed all circumstances, and in my conscience I think that the King should send a gracious Message to the House of Commons for a gift to this Fleet; for what must be the natural feelings of the Officers and men belonging to it, to see their rich Commander-in-Chief burn all the fruits of their victory, which, if fitted up and sent to England, as many of them might have been by dismantling part of our Fleet, would have sold for a good round sum? Having mentioned the subject, I shall leave it to the better judgment of your Lordship and Mr. Addington. I am, &c.,

NELSON AND BRONTE

To an un-named Lieutenant in H.M.S. *Warrior*

St. George, Copenhagen Roads,
8th April, 1801

Sir,

Most assuredly you did perfectly right in reporting to me (if your assistance was of no use) the *Bellona* and *Russell* being aground, in order that I might direct the necessary measures for getting them afloat. But as the transaction had slipped my memory until reminded of it by you, I must now say, that I think, at such a moment, the delivery of anything, like a desponding opinion, unasked, was highly reprehensible, and deserved much more censure than Captain Foley

(I suppose was the person you allude to) gave you. As far as my opinion goes, I repeat, that, although you were right in acquainting me with the situation of the *Bellona* and *Russell*, if you were not wanted there, yet I think you wrong in giving a desponding opinion unasked, but which I should not have recollected, if your letter had not brought it fresh to my mind. I had so much pleasure in seeing every Officer and man do his duty on the 2nd, that I should not have recollected an unintentional error, much less a slip of the tongue. I am, &c.,

NELSON AND BRONTE

To the Earl of St. Vincent *St. George, 9th April, 1801*

Just returned from getting the Armistice ratified. I am tired to death. No man but those who are on the spot can tell what I have gone through, and do suffer. I make no scruple in saying, that I would have been at Revel fourteen days ago; that without this Armistice the Fleet would never have gone but by order from the Admiralty; and with it, I dare say, we shall not go this week. I wanted Sir Hyde to let me at least go and cruise off Carlscrona, to prevent the Revel Ships from getting in. I said, I would not go to Revel to take any of those laurels which I was sure he would reap there. Think for me, my dear Lord, and if I have deserved well, let me retire; if ill, for heaven's sake supersede me, for I cannot exist in this state. I am &c.,

NELSON AND BRONTE

To Lady Hamilton *St. George, April 9th, 1801*

I have received, my dear Mrs. Thompson, all your truly kind and affectionate letters, which I have read over to your ever-dear friend. Really, between your goodness and our dear amiable Lady Hamilton, my mind is kept easy. Your friend was on shore with me to-day to receive the ratification of the treaty of armistice. I received as a warrior all the praises which could gratify the ambition of the vainest man, and the thanks of the nation, from the King downwards, for my humanity in saving the town from destruction. Nelson is a warrior, but will not be a butcher. I am sure, could you have seen the adoration and respect, you would have cried for joy; there are no honours can be conferred equal to this. Having done my duty, not all the world should get me out of the ship. No! I owe it to my promise, and not all the world shall ever make me in the smallest article break it. You are, my dearest Mrs. Thomson, so good, so right in all that you do, that I will take care your dear friend shall do no wrong. He has cried on account of his child; he begs, for heaven's sake, you will take care that the nurse had no bad disorder, for he has been told that Captain Howard, before he was 6 weeks old, had the bad disorder which has ruined his constitution to this day. He desires me to say he has never wrote his aunt since he sailed, and all the parade about a house is nonsense.* He has wrote to his father, but not a word or message to her. He does not, nor cannot care about her; he believes she has a most unfeeling heart. I only recommend the example of dear, good Lady Hamilton; she is a pattern, & do not let your uncle persuade you to receive bad company. When you do, your friend hopes to be killed. I have received all your and Lady H's letters to April 1st. I have such short notice, & so many letters to write, that is to Lord Minto and Lord Carysfort, Mr. Addn and Lord St. Vincent, with a line to Troubridge. Believe me, my dearest excellent Mrs. Thom, that I am for ever, because I know your worth, most affectionate and devoted till death.

To Sir Brooke Boothby — *St George*, Copenhagen Roads, *April 9th, 1801*

My dear Sir Brooke,

I am well; the Battle was, I must allow, hard fought, but our success was complete. Of the eighteen Vessels of all descriptions, seventeen are sunk, burnt, and taken. I ought to be ashamed, after such a neglect of your kind letter, of writing so short a one, but time is not mine: therefore, forgive me! I but wish to finish Paul, and then retire for ever. Believe me, your most obliged,

NELSON AND BRONTE

To the Earl of St. Vincent — *14th April, 1801*

Captain Bligh† has desired my testimony to his good conduct, which, although perfectly unnecessary, I cannot refuse: his behaviour on this occasion can reap no additional credit from my testimony. He was my second, and the moment the Action ceased, I sent for him, on board the *Elephant*, to thank him for his support. I am sure of your goodness to Thompson. I am, &c.,

NELSON AND BRONTE

* Lady Nelson.

† The hero – or villain – of the mutiny in the *Bounty* who commanded the *Glatton.*

To Lady Hamilton *Elephant*, Baltic, *April 17th, 1801*

Once more I am shifted to the *Elephant*, and Captain Foley is so good as to be placed with me. *St. George* cannot yet be got over the shallows; and as the Swedish fleet was at sea the 14th, Sir Hyde desired me to shift my flag. For my part, I do not expect to fire another gun; the Swedes cannot be such fools as to wait for us. My mind is fixed to be in England the latter end of May; I hope much sooner. Nothing shall keep me here. I cannot write politicks, therefore can only assure you that I am ever, &c.

To Lady Hamilton *St. George, April 23rd, 1801*

My dearest amiable friend, this day twelve months we sailed from Palermo on our tour to Malta. Ah! those were happy times; days of ease and nights of pleasure. How different, how forlorn! Alas, no wonder I so severely feel the difference, but as we are returning to the anchorage near Copenhagen, I hope a very short time will place me in London. Yesterday Sir Hyde Parker wrote me word that the Russian minister at Copenhagen had sent him a letter, saying that the Emperor had ordered his fleet to abstain from all hostilities, therefore Sir H. P. was determined to return to the anchorage near Copenahgen. I am truly anxiously looking out for my leave of absence, or that the whole fleet may be ordered home; stay I will not, if the Admy. would make me Lord High Admiral of the Baltic. Don't you think I am perfectly right? If you were to think the contrary it would break my heart, for I have the very highest opinion of your judgment.

I hope you have had no more pleasures, and that you have lived quiet as you like, if not I hope you have had spirit enough to act properly and decidedly. I will tell you a curious thing. I received a few days ago a present of some ale and dried fish from a person who is naval officer at Leith. He spells his name differently from all Thompsons I have seen except one, he spells his Thomson. However, his ale is excellent, and all the Thomsons who spell their name this way that I know are all excellent people. May God bless you, my dearest friend. God knows how this letter goes, or one which is aboard the *London*, under cover to Troubridge, wrote 3 days ago. I daresay they are all read. Who cares? I glory in your regard and affection, and your friendship has been and ever will be, I hope, the greatest comfort of my life.

Read the enclosed, and send it if you approve. Who should I consult but my friends? Remember me in the most affectionate manner where proper, and respects and compts as the person deserves to whom you give them.

To Alexander Davison *St. George*, Baltic, *April 23rd, 1801*

. . . You will, at a proper time, and before my arrival in England, signify to Lady N. that I expect, and for which I have made such a very liberal allowance to her, to be left to myself, and without any enquiries from her; for sooner than live the unhappy life I did when last I came to England, I would stay abroad for ever. My mind is fixed as fate; therefore you will send my determination in any way you may judge proper.

To Samuel Barker, Yarmouth *St. George*, Kioge Bay,
April 27th, 1801

My dear Sir,

I feel truly sensible of your kind congratulations on the success of His Majesty's Arms; the spirit and zeal of the Navy I never saw higher than in this Fleet, and if England is true to herself, she may bid defiance to Europe. The French have always, in ridicule, called us a Nation of shopkeepers—so, I hope, we shall always remain, and, like other shopkeepers, if our goods are better than those of any other Country, and we can afford to sell them cheaper, we must depend on our shop being well resorted to. If I land at Yarmouth, I shall most assuredly pay my personal respects to you, not only as a gentleman who has shown me great civilities, but also as the Chief magistrate of a Borough of which I have the honour to be a Freeman. I beg you will have the goodness to present my best respects and good wishes to every individual of the Corporate body, and believe me, my dear Sir, your truly obliged,

NELSON AND BRONTE

[On 5th May, dispatches arrived, appointing Nelson successor to Sir Hyde Parker, as Commander-in-Chief. The first signal which Nelson made, as Commander-in-Chief, was to hoist in all launches, and prepare to weigh. This at once showed how different a system was about to be pursued; it having been intended that the Fleet should await at anchor fresh instructions from England relative to the state of the Northern affairs, an account of which had but lately been dispatched. Nelson, who foresaw every bad consequence from this inactive mode of proceeding, owed his bad health more to chagrin than to any other cause. On 7th May, 1801, the fleet left Kioge Bay, and, proceeding towards Bornholm, anchored, in blowing weather, off that Island. The greater part was here left to watch the Swedes; and with a chosen Squadron, consisting of his ten best sailing seventy-fours, two frigates, a brig, and a schooner, Nelson sailed for Revel. He wished for further satisfaction respecting the friendly disposition of the Russians, and thought that the best method of putting this to the proof, would be to try how he should be received in one of their ports. He sincerely desired peace, but had no apprehension of hostilities. Exclusive of a wish to show the activity of his fleet, he had two other objects in view, personally to wait on the Emperor, and congratulate him on his accession to the Throne, and also to promote the release of the British merchant ships and seamen, who had been detained by the late Emperor Paul.]

To Evan Nepean, Admiralty *St. George*, Kioge Bay, *5th May, 1801*

Sir,

I beg leave to acknowledge the receipt of their Lordships' Commission, appointing me Commander-in-Chief; and I request you will assure their Lordships, that I will endeavour to execute the high trust reposed in me, as well as my abilities, and a most wretched state of health, will allow. I am, &c.,

NELSON AND BRONTE

To Alexander Davison

May 5th, 1801

My dear Davison,

A Command never was, I believe, more unwelcomely received by any person than myself. It may be at the expense of my life; and therefore, for God's sake, at least, for mine, try if I cannot be relieved. The time was, a few months ago, that I should have felt the honour, and I really believe that I should have seen more of the Baltic, the consequence of which I can guess. But nothing, I believe, but change of climate can cure me, and having my mind tranquil. I grieve for Maurice*, but I hope he will recover and do well. I hope yet within a month to be in England. With my thankful respects to Mrs. Davison and your family, believe me ever, my dear Davison, your truly obliged friend,

NELSON AND BRONTE

I will endeavour to collect my ideas on the subject of money matters; but, as you observe, every one pulls at me. The Subscription Book of the Fleet to be delivered to the Committee at Lloyd's, and a Clerk, I suppose, will be sent to the different persons for the subscription. I dare say you have paid mine. Sir Hyde has just gone; he is very low.

* His eldest brother, Maurice, who died of brain fever, after a few days' illness, on the 24th April.

To Rt. Hon. Henry Addington

St. George, May 5th, 1801

My dear Sir,

I feel very much flattered by your truly kind letter, and also for the kind expressions you were so good as to send me by Colonel Stewart. I am sorry that the Armistice (at Copenhagen) is only approved under *all* considerations. Now I own myself of opinion that every part of the *all* was to the advantage of our King and Country. I stated many of my reasons for thinking it advantageous. We knew not of the death of Paul, or a change of sentiments in the Court of Prussia, if her sentiments are changed. My object was to get at Revel before the frost broke up at Cronstadt, that the twelve Sail of the Line might be destroyed. I shall now go there as a friend, but the two Fleets shall not form a junction, if not already accomplished, unless my orders permit it. My health is gone, and although I should be happy to try and hold out a month or six weeks longer, yet death is no respecter of persons. I own, at present, I should not wish to die a natural death—but to the last, believe me, dear Sir, your most obliged,

NELSON AND BRONTE

To the Earl of Carysfort, Envoy Extraordinary to the King of Prussia

St. George, Baltic, *May 8th, 1801*

My dear Lord,

Sir Hyde Parker being ordered to England, the command of the Fleet has been, for the moment, given to me, the duties of which I shall endeavour to execute, as well as my abilities and bad health will allow me. It is my intention to send into Carlscrona a letter to the Swedish Admiral; for, under present circumstances, it would be unpleasant to have a battle with the Swedes: therefore, if anything happens after the receipt of my letter, the blame will rest with them.

I hope Lord St. Helens will be at Berlin, on his way to Russia; and it is my intention to proceed with a part of the Fleet into the Gulf of Finland; but in such a moment, and with such notice, that I wish the new Emperor to see its coming to Revel as a great compliment, as I shall carry neither Bomb-ship, Fire-Ship, nor any of the Flotilla—only twelve Sail of the Line, with some Frigates, Sloops, &c.—as fine Ships, and in as good order, as any in Europe. Although this is my present plan, yet much must depend on the reception which Sir Hyde Parker's letter and messenger have met with at Petersburgh. Let matters turn out as they may, we have force enough to bid defiance to the whole Baltic Fleet; but I hope that all will end amicably. I beg your Lordship to believe me, &c.

NELSON AND BRONTE

To Lady Hamilton *May 8th, 1801*

As both my friends and enemies seem not to know why I sent on shore a flag of truce, the former, many of them, thought it was a ruse de guerre, and not quite justifiable; the latter, I believe, attributed it to a desire to have no more fighting, and few, very few, to the cause that I felt, and which, I trust in God, I shall retain to the last moment, humanity. I know it must to the world be proved, and therefore I will suppose you all the world to me.

First, no ship was on shore near the Crown batteries, or anywhere else within reach of any shore when my flag of truce went on shore; the Crown batteries, and the batteries on Amack, and in the dockyard, were firing at us, one half their shot necessarily striking the ships who had surrendered, and our fire did the same, and worse, for the surrendered ships had four of them got close together, and it was a massacre, this caused my note. It was a sight which no real man could have enjoyed. I felt when the Danes became my prisoners, I became their protector, and if that had not been a sufficient reason, the moment of a complete victory was surely the proper time to make an opening with the nation we have been fighting with. When the truce was settled and full possession taken of our prizes, the ships were ordered, except two, to proceed and join Sir Hyde Parker, and in performing this service, the *Elephant* and *Defiance* grounded on the middle ground. I give you verbatim an answer to a part of a letter from a person high in rank about the Prince Royal, which will bear testimony to the truth of my assertions, viz., 'As to your Lordship's motives for sending a flag of truce to our Government it never can be misconstrued, and your subsequent conduct has sufficiently shown that humanity is always the companion of true valour. You have done more, you have shown yourself a friend of the re-establishment of peace and good harmony between this country and Great Britain'.

To His Excellency The Commander-in-Chief of His Imperial Majesty's Ships at Revel.

St. George, May 11th, 1801

Sir,

I beg leave to inform you of my intention to anchor a Squadron of His Britannic Majesty's Ships in the Bay of Revel, of which intention I have informed Count Pahlen, and his Excellency the Governor of Revel. I have therefore to request, that you will have the goodness to allow some of your Officers and Pilots to come on board me, in order that the Squadron may be anchored in a good berth. I have the honour to be, &c.,

NELSON AND BRONTE

From Count Pahlen St. Petersbourg, *le 12 Mai, 1801*

My Lord,

La lettre que votre Excellence m'a fait l'honneur de m'ecrire en date du 9 Mai, a ete pour moi l'objet de la plus grande surprise. Elle me confirme l'assurance des dispositions pacifiques de la Grande Bretagne, et en meme temps elle m'annonce votre intention, Mylord, de venir avec toute la flotte sous vos ordres a la rade de Revel, ou a celle due Cronstadt. L'Empereur, mon Maitre, ne juge point une semblable demarche compatible avec le vif desir manifeste par Sa Majeste Britannique, de retablir la bonne intelligence, qui a regne si longtemps entre les deux Monarchie. Sa Majeste Imperiale la trouve au contraire entirement opposee a l'esprit des instructions de la Cour de Londre, telles qu'elles lui sont annoncees par le Lord Hawkesbury. En consequence, Sa Majeste m'ordonne de vous declarer, Mylord, que le seul garant qu'Elle accepte de la loyaute de vos intentions, est le prompt eloigenment de la Flotte que vous commandez, et qu'aucune negociation avec votre Cour ne pourra avoir lieu, tant qu'une force navale sera a la vue de ses ports. . . .

J'ai l'honneur d'etre, avec une consideration tres distinguee, Mylord, de votre Excellence, le tres humble et tres obeissant serviteur,
LE COMTE DE PAHLEN

To Count Pahlen *St. George*, Revel Bay,
May 16th, 1801

Sir,

I am this moment honoured with your Excellency's letter; and I only beg leave to refer you again to my letter of the 9th of May. You will there see, that not one-seventh part of the Fleet in point of numbers were coming into the Gulf of Finland; and that, as my intention was to pay a very particular respect to His Imperial Majesty, I submitted it to His pleasure, which Port he would wish me to come to, Revel or Cronstadt.

Your Excellency will have the goodness to observe to the Emperor, that I did not even enter the outer Bay of Revel, without the consent of their Excellencies the Governor and Admiral. My conduct, I feel, is so entirely different to what your Excellency has expressed in your letter, that I have only to regret, that my desire to pay a marked attention to His Imperial Majesty has been so entirely misunderstood. That being the case, I shall sail immediately into the Baltic.

Requesting again, that your Excellency will express to His Imperial Majesty my ardent desire to have shown him all the respect in the power of your Excellency's most obedient, &c.,

NELSON AND BRONTE

From Count Pahlen

St. Petersbourg,
le 6 Mai, 1801

Mylord,

Je ne saurais donner a votre Excellence un temoignage plus eclatant de la confiance que l'Empereur mon Maitre lui accorde qu'en lui annoncant l'effet qu'a produit sa lettre du 16 de ce mois. Sa Majeste Imperiale a ordonne sur le champ la levee de l'Embargo mis sur les Navires Anglais. Cette mesure aurait ete remplie depuis longtems si des circonstances anterieures a Son regne n'eussent pas donne lieu a une demonstration hostile de votre Gouvernement, dans le Nord, et mon auguste Maitre se livre avec plaisir a l'impulsion de son amour pour la justice des l'instant ou l'Europe ne peut plus etre abusee par les apparences sur les motifs qui le font agir.

Je regrette vivement, Mylord, que votre letter precedente ait produit un mesentendu, mais celui qui connait comme vous les loiz de l'honneur et de la vraie dignite ne peut en etre surpris. Sa Majeste Imperiale me charge de mander a votre Excellence, qu'elle sera charmee de faire le connaissance personnelle du heros du Nil, et de vous voir a sa Cour, si vos instructions vous permettent de quitter la Flotte et d'aborder avec un seul Vaisseau dans un de nos Ports. J'ai l'honneur d'etre, avec la plus haute consideration, Mylord, de votre Excellence, le tres humble et tres obeissant serviteur, LE COMTE DE PAHLEN.

To Count Pahlen

St. George, Rostock Bay,
26th May, 1801

Sir,

I am this moment honoured with your Excellency's flattering letter of May 6th, and I assure you that his Imperial Majesty's justice has filled the idea I had formed of his excellent heart and head; and I am sure the handsome manner in which the embargo has been taken off the British Shipping, will give the greatest pleasure to my good and gracious Sovereign.

I am truly sensible of the great honour done me by the invitation of his Imperial Majesty, and at a future time I hope to have the pleasure of presenting my humble duty. I have now only to pray, that a permanent (which must be honourable) Peace, may be established between our gracious Sovereigns, and that our august Masters' reigns may be blessed with every happiness which this world can afford; and I beg that your Excellency will believe that I am, with the greatest respect, your most obedient and very humble servant,

NELSON AND BRONTE

To Evan Nepean, Admiralty *St. George*, Gulf of Finland, *May 17th, 1801*

Sir,

I beg you will inform their Lordships, that my state of health is such, that I feel at present unable to execute the high trust reposed in me, with either comfort to myself, or benefit to the State. I have, therefore, to request their Lordships' permission to return to England, in order to try and re-establish my health, I am, &c.,

NELSON AND BRONTE

To Alexander Davison

St. George, May 22nd, 1801

My dear Davison,

By a letter from Sir Andrew Hammond, given to Lord St. Helens, I first heard of the death of my dear brother Maurice. As the dead cannot be called back, it is of no use dwelling on those who are gone. I am sure you will do everything which is right for his poor blind wife. I hope he has left her well provided for; if not, I beg you will take the trouble to arrange a proper and ample subsistence, and I will make it up*. It is the only true regard I can pay to his memory. He was always good and kind to me; but enough on this subject: I know your sincere friendship for him. Your letters are on board *Admiral Totty*, with Parker, and I have not yet joined him. I shall see you in a very few days; till then I shall only say God bless you. I am very unwell. Since April 27th, I have only once been out of my cabin. Ever yours affectionately,

NELSON AND BRONTE

[About this time Nelson received Secret Orders, addressed on 6th May to Hyde Parker (though he had been superseded by Nelson), that, 'as it appears possible the Swedish Squadron, taking advantage of the return of the Fleet under your command to Kioge Bay, might entertain an intention of forming a junction with the Russians, either at Revel or Cronstadt, or with the Danish Fleet at Copenhagen, you should be directed, either with the whole, or with such part of the Fleet as may be adequate to the purpose, to take such a position as you may conceive best calculated to prevent such a movement on the part of the Swedish Squadron.']

* Maurice Nelson lived many years with a Miss Sarah Ford, who accidentally lost her sight and became a cripple. He was supposed to have married her from compassion for her helpless condition, and she bore his name. Nelson always treated her as his brother's widow, allowed her an annuity; and after his death, she received assistance from Lady Hamilton. She died in 1810 or 1811.

To the Earl of St. Vincent *May 22nd, 1801*

I send you a plan of the bay of Revel, drawn by our friend Colonel Stewart, who is an excellent and indefatigable young man, and, depend upon it, the rising hope of our Army. As there is no other plan in existence, perhaps you will direct a copy to be lodged in the Hydrographer's Office. The Fleet when out of the Mole, always moor on the east side of the Bay, the outer Ship is supposed to be protected by the Fort, which is marked; there are, it is true, a number of guns, but as the Officer who goes there is not to be supposed to mind guns, if he can get in and out again, in my opinion the Revel Fleet, whether in or out of the Mole, would be destroyed by a vigorous attack; and that it may, if the Russians again give us offence, is the sincere wish of your affectionate sick friend,

NELSON AND BRONTE

P.S.—You have often spoke of that worthy officer Admiral George Montagu: I own, I long from his character to give up this Fleet to him, or some other good man. May 24th.—The death of my dear brother, which I received only yesterday, has naturally affected me a good deal; and if I do not get some repose very soon, another will go. Six sons are gone, out of eight; but I hope to see you, and to cheer up once more.

To Rt. Hon. Henry Addington *St. George*, Rostock, *May 27th, 1801*

My dear Sir,

I do not trouble you often with letters, as your time must be much more essentially employed than in reading any opinions of mine. As I send the facts themselves to the Admiralty, Ministers can draw much better conclusions from them than a mere Sea-officer; but as it was the wish of Lord St. Helens for me to give my opinion, from what I had seen in Russia, and my communication with them, I readily gave it—viz. the Emperor of Russia and his Ministers wish for peace with us, but at the same time it is wished to hold up his character, therefore it is wished that he should have the appearance of arranging the peace of the North, and I am confident more would be given up by paying the Emperor that compliment than if we attempted to lay down the law; and his Lordship was pleased to say that he should let the negotiation take that turn. Respecting Privateers, I own I am decidedly of opinion that with very few exceptions they are a disgrace to our Country; and it would be truly honourable never to permit one after this war. Such horrid robberies have been committed by them in all parts of the world, that it is really a disgrace to the Country which tolerates them; and the conduct of too many of our Vice-Admiralty Courts has no wonder made neutral Nations think of preventing such iniquitous proceedings; but as I shall, if alive, have the honour of seeing you in a very few days, I will only say that, I am, with the greatest respect, your most faithful and obliged,

NELSON AND BRONTE

Lord St. Helens would be at Petersburgh about yesterday. My complaint, I flatter myself, is better within these last two days; but we have lost so many of our finest young men by the disorders, and I know it is so deceitful, and no one will tell me anything of my disorder, that I only rely on Providence; I own I have no inclination to die a natural death at present; I ought to have returned with my good and excellent friend Colonel Stewart.

To Mr. Richard Booth, Purser of the *London*

St. George, Rostock Bay,
28th May, 1801

Sir,

I have received a letter from Captain Murray, enclosing a statement of the prices of the different articles that can be procured at Dantzic, for the use of the Fleet. With respect to the beef supplied in the Bay, and which may be sent to the Fleet alive, and the bread—provided the Captains think it good in quality—I approve of the prices, and authorize you to furnish what may be required by the Ships that may arrive in the Bay, and also to send to the Squadron off Bornholm such bread and live cattle, which the Ships, as they are ordered away, can conveniently carry; and I shall give directions for the hides and tallow to be taken care of, and returned, as you recommend. I also desire you will purchase 4,000 pounds of cheese, at the price you mention, taking care that it answers to the sample you have sent.

As to the wine and spirits, I disapprove of the price altogether; the flour I think not good in quality, and desire none may be bought, unless better can be got by adding a trifle to the price. In that case, I wish about 4,000 lbs. to be put on board each 74 Gun-ship, and smaller Vessels in proportion, for the purpose of being served in lieu of part of the allowance of bread; but no pease are wanted. The continuance of the Fleet in the Baltic being very uncertain, you must regulate your engagements accordingly, and not purchase more at a time than can be brought away in the Squadron of three or four Sail of the Line, and a few Small-craft, which it is my intention to keep in the Bay of Dantzic.

In order to recompense you for the trouble you may have on this occasion, I shall recommend to the Admiralty to direct, that you be allowed two and a half per cent. on the money laid out, and your expenses paid for living on shore, trusting that you will use your best endeavours to procure everything you are authorized to buy, at the cheapest rate, and of the best quality. You are hereby authorized to draw bills on the Commissioners of the Victualling Board for the amount of what you purchase, taking care to get receipts from the different Pursers for what you may supply, and vouchers from the proper Officers, that it was good in the kind, as well as a certificate from some of the most respectable merchants, that all your purchases were made at the cheapest rate, and bills drawn at the proper Exchange. I am, &c.,

NELSON AND BRONTE

To Captain George Murray

June 1st, 1801

My dear Murray,

Although you like to be a Commodore, I find you have no inclination to be a Contractor. Now as I find no honest men but Commodores, you must necessarily, if you will be a Commodore, become a Contractor. Myself and Hardy are Contractors; Lord Henry Paulet is just established a Commodore and a Contractor; only I charge you, being a brother Contractor, not to let the world know how much you make by it! Be that as it may, ever believe me, my dear Murray, your obliged and faithful friend,

NELSON AND BRONTE

Pylades goes for England the moment any news comes from Lord St. Helens.

Graves has the Red Ribbon, I a Viscount.*

To Alexander John Ball, Esq., Commissioner of His Majesty's Navy, Gibraltar

St. George, Kioge Bay, *June 4th, 1801*

My dear invaluable Friend,

Although I may not answer letters regularly, or perform many other little acts which the world deem as of the very utmost importance, and for the omission of which, it is necessary to cut each other's throats, although I own I fail most miserably (towards my real friends in particular) in those things, yet believe me, Ball, my heart entertains the very warmest affection for you, and it has been no fault of mine, and not a little mortification, that you have not the Red ribbon and other rewards that would have kept you afloat, and not to have made you a

* For Copenhagen.

Commissioner; but as, I trust, the war is at a close, you must, like Lord Hood, take your Flag when it comes to you, for who is to command our Fleets in a future war? for whatever peace we may make under the present government of France cannot be lasting. I pity the poor Maltese; they have sustained an irreparable loss in your friendly counsel and an able director in their public concerns: you was truly their father, and, I agree with you, they may not like step-fathers; however, I hope that you will find as much pleasure in your new office as it is possible for it to afford, although I am sure it will not be equal to your merit.

As I know you have always been kind to me, I know you will be sorry to hear that I have been even at Death's door, apparently in a consumption. I am now rallied a little, but the disorder is in itself so flattering that I know not whether I am really better, and no one will tell me, but all in the Fleet are so truly kind to me, that I should be a wretch not to cheer up. Foley has put me under a regimen of milk, at four in the morning; Murray has given me lozenges, and all have proved their desire to keep my mind easy, for I hear of no complaints, or other wishes than to have me with them. Hardy is as good as ever, and with Domett, join their kindest regards. I have also on board Colonel Stewart, who commands our *little* Army; he remembers you at St. Domingo. I am just returned from the Gulf of Finland, Revel; and met Lord St. Helens at the entrance; by this, I am sure Peace must be signed with Russia, and Denmark and Sweden have so completely lost their consequence by joining against us, that they must submit to what we settle with Russia. The Northern Fleets are only formidable in point of numbers; in every other respect they are insignificant; and, if our Fleet is active, in the spring of the year, may be got at separately; late in the summer they have their numerous Flotilla, who can join in spite of all our efforts to prevent them, for there is a complete navigation inside, and amongst 10,000 Islands. I hope this will find you in England, as I know your American affairs claim your attention; it is, I trust, needless my dear Ball, to assure you, that if it ever should be in my power in any way to be useful, that nothing could give me greater happiness; for believe me at all times, and places, for ever your sincere, affectionate, and faithful friend,

NELSON AND BRONTE

To Hercules Ross, Esq., Rossie Castle, N.B.

St. George, Kioge Bay, *June 9th, 1801*

My dear Friend,

Your kind letter of May 22nd, I received last night, and I sincerely hope that your nephew's affairs with my valuable friend Davison, will end in an amicable manner. I can assure you that Davison is a man of as strict honour as any in Europe.

You do me a great deal of honour in wishing me to stand godfather for your next child; I accept the duty with much pleasure, and hope that the future Horati*o*, or *a*,* will be an addition of happiness to you and Mrs. Ross; and if ever I travel into Scotland, I pledge myself not to pass Rossie Castle; but Peace—the blessings of Peace, must first shed its benign rays over us, and under the present Ruler of France I see but little prospect of that happy event. Buonaparte's power exists by war, and as France must in time be tired of it, I think his life will be cut short. I hope that we are on the eve of peace with Russia, and both Sweden and Denmark have so given up their independence to her, that if Russia makes peace, the others must. I hope very soon to be in England, for the keen air of the North has not agreed with a constitution so long used to Southern climates. I beg you will present my best compliments to Mrs. Ross; I shall never forget the open heart of her good mother; and do you believe me, ever your most faithful and affectionate friend,

NELSON AND BRONTE

To Evan Nepean, Esq., Admiralty

St. George, Kioge Bay, *12th June*, *1801*

Sir,

Herewith, I enclose you remarks made on the passage of the Belt, also drawings of the same, which I beg you will be pleased to lodge in the records of the Admiralty, that they may be referred to, in case they are wanted. I am, &c.,

NELSON AND BRONTE

To Evan Nepean, Esq., Admiralty

St. George, Kioge Bay, *12th June*, *1801*

Sir,

I am to acquaint you, for the information of the Lords Commissioners of the Admiralty, that the general conduct of Denmark has been so entirely different from what the Armistice points out, that I do not think myself at liberty to proceed as I should think right, until I get their Lordship's instructions, which I trust will be soon. The Armistice, except their Ships being absolutely hauled out, has been totally disregarded. Ships have been masted, guns taken on board, Floating batteries prepared; in short, everything is doing, as my reporters say, in defiance of the Treaty, except hauling out, and completing their rigging.

* It proved to be Horatio.

The moment I receive information, that peace is made with Russia, I shall go over the Grounds, and anchor in Copenhagen Roads, ready to act as circumstances may require, and their Lordships may direct, leaving eight Sail of the Line to watch the Swedes. I think it proper to send the *Pylades* immediately on receiving the above intelligence; otherwise I should not have sent her until a Vessel had arrived from Petersburgh, which I have now reason to expect every day, as Lord St. Helens has three small Vessels with him, besides the *Latona*. I am, &c.,

NELSON AND BRONTE

To Vice-Admiral Lord Nelson, K.B.

Admiralty Office,
31st May, 1801

My Lord,

I have received and communicated to my Lords Commissioners of the Admiralty your Lordship's letter of the 17th instant . . . and I have it in command from their Lordships to acquaint you, in answer thereto, that an arrangement will be made, with as little delay as possible, for relieving your Lordship in your command.

I have their Lordships' further commands to acquaint your Lordship, that your services in the Baltic have met their entire approbation, and to assure you that they feel the greatest concern that the state of your health should render it necessary you should quit the command, by which your Country must be deprived (though it is hoped only for a short time) of the advantage of your Lordship's talents and experience, which have been so conspicuous on all occasions. I have the honour to be, &c.,—EVAN NEPEAN

[The *St. George* made her last cruise, with Nelson's Flag on board, off Bornholm, between the 9th and 13th of June, on which latter day he received the sanction of the Admiralty for his return to England.]

To Evan Nepean, Esq., Admiralty

St. George, Kioge Bay, *13th June, 1801*

Sir,

I am to acknowledge the receipt of your letter of the 31st May, signifying to me their Lordships' permission for my return to England, for the re-establishment of my health, agreeably to my request, the 17th of last month. I beg you will assure their Lordships, that I feel much flattered by the very handsome manner, in which they have expressed their acquiescence.

I have the honour to be, &c.,

NELSON AND BRONTE

FAREWELL TO THE FLEET

[Nelson quitted the command in the Baltic on 19th June, and sailed in the *Kite* brig, commanded by Captain Digby, for England, being unwilling to take a larger vessel from the Fleet.]

St. George, Kioge Bay,
18th June, 1801

Lord Nelson has been obliged, from the late very bad state of his health, to apply to the Lords Commissioners of the Admiralty for leave to return to England, which their Lordships have been pleased to comply with. But Lord Nelson cannot allow himself to leave the Fleet, without expressing to the Admirals, Captains, Officers, and Men, how sensibly he has felt, and does feel, all their kindness to him, and also how nobly and honourably they have supported him in the hour of Battle, and the readiness which they have shown to maintain the honour of their King and Country on many occasions which have offered; and had more opportunities presented themselves, Lord Nelson is firmly persuaded, they would have added more glory to their Country.

Lord Nelson cannot but observe, with the highest satisfaction which can fill the breast of a British Admiral, that (with the exception of the glaring misconduct of the Officers of the *Tigress* and the *Cracker* Gun-brigs, and the charges alleged against the Lieutenant of the *Terror* Bomb), out of 18,000, of which the Fleet is composed, not a complaint has been made of any Officer or Man in it; and he cannot but remark, that the extraordinary health of this Fleet, under the blessing of Almighty God, is to be attributed to the great regularity, exact discipline, and cheerful obedience of every individual in the Fleet.

The Vice-Admiral assures them, that he will not fail to represent to the Lords Commissioners of the Admiralty their highly praiseworthy conduct; and if it pleases God that the Vice-Admiral recover his health, he will feel proud, on some future day, to go with them in pursuit of further glory, and to assist in making the name of our King and Country beloved and respected by all the world.

CHAPTER TEN

THE ANTI-INVASION FLOTILLA

[Nelson arrived at Yarmouth on 1st July, immediately visited the Hospitals to which the wounded at Copenhagen had been conveyed, and then proceeded to London.]

To R. Nelson, Esq., Plymouth Dock, Devon

London, *July 7th, 1801*

Dear Sir,

I received your kind letter from Plymouth, and congratulate you on the birth of a grandson, who I am much flattered with your intention to call after me. I trust that the name of Nelson will remain with credit to our Country for many ages, and although I do not yet despair but that I may have fruit from my own loins, yet the honour of the Nelson family will not, I am confident, be lost by yours. I beg my compliments to Colonel Nelson, and that you will believe me, your most obliged servant,

NELSON AND BRONTE

I beg my compliments to Mr. Marshall.

NELSON APPOINTED IN COMMAND OF THE ANTI-INVASION FLOTILLAS

[In the summer of 1801, Napoleon collected a Flotilla and large Army at Boulogne, with the avowed design of invading England. Vigorous measures were accordingly taken to resist the attempt, and it was determined to place a large force consisting of frigates, brigs, and smaller vessels between Orfordness and Beachy Head. Within three weeks of his arrival in England from the Baltic campaign, Nelson was appointed to this command. He assumed his command by hoisting his Flag in *L'Unite* frigate, at Sheerness, on 27th July.]

To Earl of St. Vincent, K.B. Sheerness, *28th July, 1801*

Everything, my dear Lord, must have a beginning, and we are literally at the foundation of our fabric of defence. I agree perfectly with you, that we must keep the Enemy as far from our own Coasts as possible, and be able to attack them the moment they come out of their Ports . . . As soon as all the orders are given, it is my intention to go to Deal, and to consult with Admiral Lutwidge. Should the Enemy approach our Coasts near the Thames, our Dock-yards can man Flat-boats if they are kept in readiness; and this Yard has 100 men, who can man two Flats which are ordered to be fitted out. If the *Unite* arrives at the Nore this day, I shall go on board her, in order to show that we must all get to our posts as speedily as possible. I am, &c.

NELSON AND BRONTE

To the Earl of St. Vincent — Deal, *July 30th, 1801*

As I had arranged everything possible for me to do at Sheerness, I thought it best to set off for the Downs by the way of Feversham, as I wished to see Captain Becher on the subject of the Sea-Fencibles. I had previously sent Captain Shepard to desire that a Mr. Salisbury would meet me; as he was a person of respectability, rich, (got it by the fair trade), and of great influence amongst the Seafaring men on that part of the Coast, particularly about Whitstable. I made him sensible of the necessity of our Ships, which were to be stationed off the Sand-heads, being manned. He thought if the Admiralty, through me, gave the men assurances that they should be returned to their homes, when the danger of the Invasion was passed, that the Sea-folk would go; but that they were always afraid of some trick; this service, my dear Lord, above all others, would be terrible for me: to get up and harangue like a Recruiting Serjeant! I do not think I could get through it; but as I am come forth, I feel that I ought to do this disagreeable service as well as any other, if judged necessary. I hoisted my Flag here this morning. The *Medusa* is sent for, and I propose going over to the Coast of Boulogne, if possible, tomorrow or next day morning, and to take Captain Fyers of the Artillery with me; to return here, and then to go off Flushing with a Captain Owen of the *Nemesis*: I have thoughts of fixing a Squadron of Small Vessels under him, if I find him equal to my expectation from his writing, and of stationing Captain Bedford of the *Leyden*, whose good sense and Officer-like conduct I have heard much commended, to support him off Flushing; and also for Captain Owen to have the chief command of the Ships and Vessels anchored off Margate Sand. I am, &c.

NELSON AND BRONTE

To the Earl of St. Vincent — Deal, *July 31st, 1801*

Our force will, by your great exertions, soon get so formidable, that the Enemy will hardly venture out. I shall endeavour in the morning to ascertain the possibility of destroying their Vessels in the Harbour of Boulogne. I send you the Return of men in the Master-Attendant's department in Sheerness yard, (247), who could man on an emergency the six upper Vessels: for the time must come, if the Enemy approaches, that all work, except fighting, would stand still; therefore I propose, if we have not men to man them at present, that at least the Vessels should be prepared and ready for the Dock-yard men to be put on board, commanded by their own Officers; which could be of the greatest consequence, and they could always get either to the Essex Coast, or towards Margate, in any weather the Enemy would attempt coming over. Other Yards may be also able to do much. I am, &c.,

NELSON AND BRONTE

To the Earl of St. Vincent — Off Boulogne, *2nd August, 1801*

I have been looking at Boulogne this morning, and see their Line of Vessels, all armed, which lie outside the Port. Captain Fyers, of the Artillery, thinks that they are stationed to add strength to the place. The French are erecting Batteries both for guns and mortars on each side of the Town, as if fearful of an attack. All accounts agree, that fifty or sixty is the full number of Boats, large and small, at Boulogne, and that these can be moved out of the reach of shells; however, I have sent for the Bombs, and will try what can be done. I am, &c.,

NELSON AND BRONTE

To Rt. Hon. Henry Addington — *Medusa*, off Boulogne, *August 4th, 1801*

My dear Sir,

I think I may venture to assure you that the French Army will not embark at Boulogne for the invasion of England; they are suffering this morning from allowing a collection of Craft to be assembled in their Port. Five Vessels of different descriptions are sunk on the outside the Pier by our shells; they were all fitted with heavy guns, and full of men. What damage has taken place inside the Pier, cannot be ascertained, but, judging from the outside, we may suppose it considerable. Ever, my dear Sir, your most obliged,

NELSON AND BRONTE

To Lady Hamilton — *Medusa, August 4th, 1801*

Buy the house at Turnham Green, I can pay for it. How can you be angry with me? I do not deserve it. Conscious of that, I think no more of your reproaches. Respecting the seal, it is your pleasure that I have it; you said, 'She has no right to it,' none has a right to me but yourself. I took it as you desired, & now to be abused. But I forgive you, though my heart is almost broken. Damn that Christie, how negligent he has been, for ever your, &c.

I have not a moment.

10,000 kisses were due.

To the Squadron *5th August, 1801*

Lord Nelson has reason to be very much satisfied with the Captains of the Bombs, for their placing of the Vessels yesterday. It was impossible that they could have been better situated; and the Artillery Officers have shown great skill in entirely disabling ten of the Armed Vessels out of twenty-four opposed to them, and many others, Lord Nelson believes are much damaged. The Commander-in-Chief cannot avoid noting the great zeal and desire to attack the Enemy in a closer and different combat, which manifested itself in all ranks of persons, and which Lord Nelson would gladly have given full scope to, had the attempt at this moment been proper; but the Officers and others may rely, that an early opportunity shall be given them for showing their judgment, zeal, and bravery. The *Hired* and *Revenue* Cutters kept under sail, and performed the duty entrusted to them with a great deal of skill.

NELSON AND BRONTE

To Captains Shield, Hamilton, Schombergh, and Edge

Medusa, 6th August, 1801

Sir,

As there can be no doubt of the intention of the French to attempt the Invasion of our Country, and as I trust, and am confident, that if our Seafaring men do their duty, that either the Enemy will give over the folly of the measure, or, if they persist in it, that not one Frenchman will be allowed to set his foot on British soil; it is, therefore, necessary that all good men should come forward on this momentous occasion to oppose the Enemy, and, more particularly, the Sea-Fencibles, who have voluntarily enrolled themselves to defend their Country afloat, which is the true place where Britain ought to be defended, that the horrors of war may not reach the peaceful abodes of our families. And as the Lords Commissioners of the Admiralty have been pleased to appoint me to command the Sea defence of Great Britain, within the limits of your district, it is my duty to request that you will have the goodness to acquaint all the Sea-Fencibles under your command, and all other Sea-faring men and fishermen, that their services are absolutely required at this moment on board the Ships and Vessels particularly appointed to defend that part of the Coast where the Enemy mean to attempt a landing, if unopposed.

I am authorized to assure the Fencibles, and other Sea-faring men who may come forward on this occasion, that they shall not be sent off the Coast of the Kingdom, shall be kept as near their own homes as the nature of the service will admit, and that the moment the alarm of the threatened Invasion is over, that every man shall be returned to their own homes; and also, that during their continuance on board Ship, that as much attention as is possible shall be paid to their reasonable wants. And I flatter myself, that at a moment when all the Volunteer corps in the Kingdom are come forward to defend our land, that the Seamen of Great Britain will not be slow to defend our own proper element, and maintain as pure as our glorious ancestors have transmitted it to us, our undoubted right to the Sovereignty of the Narrow Seas, on which no Frenchman has yet *dared* to sail with impunity. Our Country looks to its Sea defence, and let it not be disappointed.

I shall send Cutters to bring the Sea-Fencibles, and other Sea-faring men to me, in order that I may dispose of them in the way most proper for the defence of our King and Country, and, at the same time, in the most commodious way to the men themselves. I beg your answer as expeditiously as possible, and am, Sir, &c.,

NELSON AND BRONTE

Let me know, as near as possible, the exact numbers; and when they embark correct lists must be sent with them.

To the Earl of St. Vincent

Medusa, Harwich, *10th August, 1801*

My dear Lord,

In truth, I have no desire for anything else, than to get at a proper time clear of my present command, in which I am sure of diminishing my little fortune, which at this moment does not reach 10,000*l*; and never had I an idea of gaining money by accepting it. I wrote to Hardy, to prepare to go into the *San Josef*. Do you still think of sending me to the Mediterranean? If not, I am ready to go, for the spur of the occasion, on the Expedition which is in embryo, but to return the moment it is over, for I am afraid of my strength. I am always ready, as far as I am able. I shall be at the Nore by sunset. Mr. Spence, the Maritime surveyor of this Coast, is going to carry the *Medusa* out by a new Channel. It is necessary I should know all that is to be known of the navigation; and I have been a tolerable Pilot for the mouth of the Thames in my younger days. I am, &c.,

NELSON AND BRONTE

To the Earl of St. Vincent, K.B.

Sheerness, *11th August, 1801*

My dear Lord,

I came here last night, and found not one of the River Barges . . . Our active force is perfect, and possesses so much zeal, that I only wish to catch that Buonaparte on the water, either with the *Amazon* or *Medusa*; but himself he will never trust. He would say, Allez vous en, and not Allons, mes amis! I hope these French, if they come this year, mean to do it before the 14th of September, beyond which I fear the season will be too much for me. I know not, my Lord, at this moment where I had best strike a blow, which I wish to be a very hard one: you have well guessed the place, Flushing, but I must be careful, and not cripple our Gun-Brigs. At Ostend we cannot get at them, therefore I am anxious for our Howitzer Boats; but they will not keep pace with my wishes. No person knows of my ideas except Captain Owen, who has been long stationed there under Admiral Lutwidge, and Captains Bedford and Parker. I am, &c.,

NELSON AND BRONTE

THE RAID ON BOULOGNE FLOTILLA

To Evan Nepean, Admiralty

Medusa, off Boulogne,
August 16th, 1801

Sir,

Having judged it proper to attempt bringing off the Enemy's Flotilla moored in the front of Boulogne, I directed the attack to be made by four Divisions of Boats for boarders, under the command of Captains Somerville, Cotgrave, Jones, and Parker, and a division of Howitzer Boats under Captain Conn. The Boats put off from the *Medusa* at half-past eleven o'clock last night, in the best possible order, and before one o'clock this morning, the firing began, and I had, from the judgement of the Officers and the zeal and gallantry of every man, the most perfect confidence of complete success; but the darkness of the night, with the tide and half-tide, separated the Divisions; and from all not arriving at the same happy moment with Captain Parker, is to be attributed the failure of success. But I beg to be perfectly understood that not the smallest blame attaches itself to any person; for although the Divisions did not arrive together, yet each (except the fourth Division, which could not be got up before day,) made a successful attack on that part of the Enemy they fell in with, and actually took possession of many Brigs and Flats, and cut their cables; but many of them being aground, and the moment of the Battle's ceasing on board them, the Vessels were filled with volleys upon volleys of musketry, the Enemy being perfectly regardless of their own men, who must have suffered equally with us. It was therefore impossible to remain on board, even to burn them; but allow me to say, who have seen much service this war, that more determined, persevering courage, I never witnessed, and that nothing but the impossibility of being successful, from the causes I have mentioned, could have prevented me from having to congratulate their Lordships. But although in value, the loss of such gallant and good men is incalculable, yet in point of numbers it has fallen short of my expectations. I must also beg leave to state that greater zeal and ardent desire to distinguish themselves by an attack on the Enemy, was never shown than by all the Captains, Officers, and Crews of all the different descriptions of Vessels under my command. The Commanders of the *Hunter* and *Greyhound*, Revenue-Cutters, went in their Boats, in the most handsome and gallant manner, to the attack. Amongst the many gallant men wounded, I have, with the deepest regret, to place the name of my gallant, good friend and able assistant, Captain Edward T. Parker, also my Flag Lieutenant, Frederick Langford, who has served with me many years; they were wounded in attempting to board the French Commodore.

To Captain Gore, of the *Medusa*, I feel the highest obligations; and when their Lordships look at the loss of the *Medusa* on this occasion, they will agree with me, that the honour of my Flag, and the cause of their King and Country, could never have been placed in more gallant hands. Captain Bedford, of the *Leyden*, with Captain Gore, very handsomely volunteered their services to serve under a Master and Commander; but I did not think it fair to the latter, and I only mention it to mark the zeal of those officers. From the nature of the attack, only a few prisoners were made; a Lieutenant, eight seaman, and eight soldiers, are all they brought off. Herewith I send the report of the several Commanders of Divisions, and a return of killed and wounded. I have the honour to be, &c.,

NELSON AND BRONTE

Captain Somerville was the Senior Master and Commander employed.

To the Squadron *Medusa*, Downs, *August 18th, 1801*

Vice-Admiral Lord Nelson has the greatest satisfaction in sending to the Captains, Officers, and men under his command, that were employed in the late attempt on the Enemy's Flotilla off Boulogne, an Extract of a Letter which he has received from the First Lord of the Admiralty, not only approving of their zeal and persevering courage, but bestowing the highest praises on them.

The Vice-Admiral begs to assure them that the Enemy will not have long reason to boast of their security; for he trusts ere long to assist them in person in a way which will completely annhilate the whole of them. Lord Nelson is convinced, that if it had been possible for man to have brought the Enemy's Flotilla out, the men that were employed to do so would have accomplished it. The moment the Enemy have the audacity to cast off the chains which fix their Vessels to the ground, that moment Lord Nelson is well persuaded they will be conducted by his brave followers to a British Port, or sent to the bottom.

NELSON AND BRONTE

To Alexander Davison, Esq.

August 31st, 1801

My dear Davison,

Thanks for your truly kind letter of 22nd. Dear Parker is as well as can be expected; but whether he is to live or die, or whether he ever will be able to walk again, even the Surgeons cannot tell. He has youth on his side, and that is all that can be said for him. Your conduct respecting the Head-money is like yourself, and therefore unlike any other Agent for Prizes. I am sure the Captors are obliged to you for getting so much Head money for them; and I suppose the value of the Ship and stores, and brass cannon will be paid for. On the subject of brass guns, I suppose near thirty have been saved; and as they are worth £400 or £500 a piece, they must be looked after. In every Ship I hear they have brass guns: it will come to be plunder, if not looked after. Captain Hancock, of the *Cruizer* Sloop, landed two at Yarmouth, and perhaps has others on board. The *Arrow*, Captain Brodie, has, I am told, five on board; Captain Dixon, of the *Ramilies*, had eighteen on board; and other Ships had guns. We ought to have saved £70,000 worth of brass, and at least two Sail of the Line, more than we did; but that is past.

I agree with you, and all my friends, that this is not a service for me, beyond the moment of alarm; but I am used and abused; and so far from making money, I am spending the little I have. I am after buying a little farm at Merton—the price £9,000; I hope to be able to get through it. If I cannot, after all my labour for the Country, get such a place as this, I am resolved to give it all up, and retire for life. I am aware none of the Ministry care for me, beyond what suits themselves; but my belief is that we shall have Peace. Sir William and Lady Hamilton are with me, and Mrs. Nelson.* They join with me in kindest respects to you and Mrs. Davison, and to the children, and ever believe me, my dear Davison, your most obliged and affectionate friend,

NELSON AND BRONTE

To Alexander Davison, Esq.

Amazon, Downs, *September 14th, 1801*

My dear Davison,

I have to give you ten thousand thanks for your very friendly offer of assisting me in purchasing the Farm.† It is true, it will take every farthing I have in the world, and leave me in your debt, and also in Tyson's; but I hope in a little time to be able at least to pay my debts. Should I really want your help, and know that I have enough in the world to pay you, I shall ask no one else. The Baltic expedition cost me full £2,000. Since I left London it has cost me, for Nelson cannot be like others, near £1,000 in six weeks. If I am continued here, ruin to my finances must be the consequence, for everybody knows that Lord Nelson *is amazingly rich!* Sir William and Lady Hamilton leave me on the 16th. You will easily guess my feelings at their going. Parker is easy, comfortable and cheerful, whether the thigh will ever unite none can say. Langford is suffering much pain, several pieces of bone in his leg have come away, but they both have youth on their side. I look forward with hope but will not be too sanguine. I yet hope the negotiation is not broken entirely off, for we can never alter the situation of France or the Continent, and ours will become a War of defence; but I hope they will do for the best. A man, a few days ago, sent me a letter demanding a bank note of £100, or he would abuse me in the Papers: I sent it of course to Nepean; the Porter who went to the Post-office for my answer, has been taken up, but he knew not his employer and probably never will be caught. Ever, my dear Davison, believe me, your most obliged friend,

NELSON AND BRONTE

Sir William, Lady Hamilton, and Mrs. Nelson, desire to join me in best compliments to yourself and Mrs. Davison.

* His sister-in-law.

† At Merton.

To Lady Hamilton *September, 1801*

[With superscription 'Mrs. Thomson, care of Lady Hamilton]

I came on board, but no Emma. No, no, my heart will break. I am in silent distraction. The four pictures of Lady Hn are hung up, but alas! I have lost the original. But we part only to meet very soon again; it must be, it shall be.

My dearest wife, how can I bear our separation? Good God, what a change! I am so low that I cannot hold up my head. When I reflect on the many happy scenes we have passed together, the being separated is terrible, but better times will come, shall come, if it pleases God. And to make one worse the fate of poor Parker. But God's will be done. Love my Horatia, and prepare for me the farm at Merton. If the furniture will not suit, we must get other; there are sales every day. My head is almost turned. Continue to love me as Lady Hamilton does; she knows my thoughts, and although this letter is incoherent, yet she will explain it all. May the heavens bless you. Amen, amen, amen.

To Lady Hamilton *Amazon, September 28th, 1801*

We are going this noon to pay our last sad duties to dear good Parker. I wish it was over for all our sakes, then we must endeavour to cheer up, and although we cannot forget our Parker, yet we shall have the comfortable reflection how we loved him, and how deserving he was of our love. I am afraid his father is but in very indifferent circumstances; but I doubt if the Admiralty will direct all the expenses of the lodgings, funeral, &c. to be paid—if not, it will fall very heavy upon me. Pray write me when I am to direct my letters to Merton; is it a post town, or are the letters sent from the General Post Office? I wish I could see the place, but I fear that is impossible at present, and if I could you would not, perhaps, think it right for me to come now Sir William is away. I entreat I may never hear about the expenses again. If you live in Piccadilly or Merton it makes no difference, and if I was to live at Merton I must keep a table, and nothing can cost me one-sixth part what it does at present, for this I cannot stand, however honourable it may be. May God bless you and believe me, &c.

If the wind is to the westward, I shall go to Dungeness, but you must not, by Gore's account, which I send, be surprized at not hearing from me regularly, but you know I always shall write and send when it is possible. I only send this that your dear friendly mind should be easy.

Half past one.—Thank God the dreadful scene is past. I scarcely know how I got over it. I could not suffer much more and be alive.

God forbid I should ever be called upon to say or see as much again. Your affectionate letters are just come, they are a great comfort. The worst, thank God, is past. I must have plate, &c. at Davison's, and I agree with you that nothing but what is mine should be there, and that Sir William should always be my guest. I told you so long ago. I will find out what spoons, &c. I have, and send you a list tomorrow, but today I am done for, but ever for ever yours, &c.

I will write to my Father tomorrow, and take not the smallest notice of how he disposes of himself.

To Lady Hamilton *Amazon, September 29th, 1801*

I send by the coach a little parcel containing the keys of the plate chest and the case of the tea urn, and there is a case of Colebrook Dale breakfast sett, and some other things. Mr. Dods had better go to the house, for he is Davison's man. Will you have your picture carried to Merton? I should wish it, and mine of the Battle of the Nile. I think you had better not have Sir William's books, or anything but what is my own. I have sent in the parcel by the coach this day, two salt-cellars, and two ladles, which will make four of each, as two are in the chest. You will also find spoons and forks sufficient for the present. If sheets are wanting for the beds, will you order some and let me have the bill. I also think that not a servant of Sir William's, I mean the cook, should be in the house, but I leave this and all other matters to your good management. Would to God I could come and take up my abode there, and if such a thing should happen that I go abroad, I can under my hand lend you the house so that no person can molest you, not that I have at present any idea of going anywhere but to Merton. Do you take black James? Do as you please. I have no desire one way or the other. Our dear Parker's circumstances are a little out of order, but I have undertaken to settle them if the creditors will give me time, for the poor father is worse than nothing. I have given him money to buy mourning and to pay his passage home again. I trust in God that he will never let me want, for I find no man who starts up to assist me. I can with a quiet conscience when all is gone live upon bread and cheese. Never mind, so long as I have your friendship warm from the heart. I have got some of dear Parker's hair, which I value more than if he had left me a purse of diamonds. I have sent it in the little box, keep some of it for poor Nelson.

Noon. Blows strong. I have just received your kind letters, they indeed comfort me, and I hope we shall live to see many, many happy years, and ever yours, &c.

To the Duke say everything which is kind.

To the Earl of St. Vincent *October, 1801*

Most heartily do I congratulate you on being a Member of that Administration, which has been able to comply with the almost unanimous wishes of the Country. All hands must now try to keep French men and French principles out of our happy Country. I am, &c.,

NELSON AND BRONTE

PLANS FOR MERTON

To Lady Hamilton *Amazon, October 7th, 1801*

I have just got your letter of yesterday, and am very angry with Mr. Haslewood for not having got you into possession of Merton, for I was in hopes you would have arranged everything before Sir William came home. I shall write Mr. Haslewood today on the subject. The Peace seems to make no impression of joy on our seamen, rather the contrary, they appear to reflect that they will go from plenty to poverty. We must take care not to be beset by them at Merton, for every beggar will find out your soft heart, and get into your house. Lord George Cavendish has just been on board to make me a visit before he leaves Walmer tomorrow; if the weather is moderate, I shall return his visit and call on Billy Pitt, as they say he is expected today. I intend to land at Walmer Castle. But for this visit I should not have gone ashore till all was finished. Make my best regards to Sir William. I hope he will be able in bad weather to catch fish in the water you so beautifully describe. You must take care what kind of fish you put into the water, for Sir William will tell you one sort destroys the other. Commodore Sutton has been on board all the morning, but dines with Admiral Lutwidge. Bedford says his wife is an ugly likeness of Mrs. Lutwidge, so you see that ugly women do get husbands, and Sutton is certainly a very good looking man; I recollect S's wife is niece to Lord Hotham. You will see amongst my things return the round table and the wardrobe.—extraordinary that they should return again into your possession. You are to be, recollect, Lady Paramount of all the territories and waters of Merton, and we are all to be your guests, and to obey all lawful commands. What have you done about the turnip field, duck field, &c.? Am I to have them? I wish I could get up for four or five days. I would have roused the lawyers about. The *Isis* is just coming in—Sutton's broad pennant is to be in her. Yawkins has just been on board, and I delivered your compliments as directed. He always enquires after you and Sir William, and he desires me to say that he wishes Sir William was now here, for there were never so many fish in the Downs. The beach for two days has been remarkably smooth —not a curl on the shore. I shall send to Mr. Turner; you will win his heart by your goodness. Your going away made a blank in our squadron. Dr. Baird is very much affected at receiving the cup; it made him really ill, so that he could not come to dinner, but he deserved it for his humanity. Lord St. Vincent never, I dare say, gave him a sixpence. Best regards to Sir William, Mrs. Cadogan, and all our friends. Yours, &c.

To Lady Hamilton

Amazon, October 12, 1801

My dearest Friend,

This being a very fine morning, and smooth beach, at eight o'clock, I went with Sutton and Bedford, and landed at Walmer, but found Billy* fast asleep, so left my card; walked the same road that we came, when the carriage could not come with us that night; and all rushed into my mind, and brought tears into my eyes. Ah, how different to walking with such a friend as you, Sir William, and Mrs. Nelson!

Called at the barracks, on Lord George Cavendish; but he is gone to London. From thence to the Admiral's, found him up; and, waiting half an hour to see Mrs. Lutwidge, who entreated me to stay dinner —came directly on board. I did not even call to see poor Langford, who has been worse these few days past, and God knows when he will be well. I am afraid it will be a long time; for several pieces of bone are lately come away, and more to come. But Troubridge has so completely prevented my ever mentioning anybody's service, that I am become a cipher, and he has gained a victory over Nelson's spirit. I am kept here; for what, he may be able to tell—I cannot; but long it cannot—shall not be.

Sutton and Beford are gone a tour till dinner time; but nothing shall make me, but almost force, go out of the Ship again, till I have done, and the Admiralty in charity, will be pleased to release me. I am, in truth, not over well. I have a complaint in my stomach and bowels, but it will go off. I thank you for the King's letters. I shall write a kind line to Castelcicala, and answer the King's, very soon, and write to Acton, for he can make Bronte everything to me, if he pleases. I dare say I did wrong never to write him; but as he treated Sir William unkindly, I never could bring myself to do it.

NELSON AND BRONTE

* Mr. Pitt.

To Lady Hamilton *Amazon, October 13th, 1801*

Sutton and Bedford would fain persuade me that by the post today the Admiralty will give me leave to go on shore. I own I do not believe it, or I should not begin this letter, for I should certainly be at Merton tomorrow at breakfast: but they have no desire to gratify me. Thank God there is no more than 9 days to the cessation of hostilities, after that they can have no pretence. My complaint is a little better, and you cannot think how vexed I am to be unwell at a time when I desire to come on shore, and to enjoy a good share of health; but in this season and in this place it is impossible that I can be free from colds. The wind is set in very raw from the westward. Mr. Turner came and dined with me yesterday, and brought the trumpet with him, and he has charged me to say how much he feels obliged by your kind remembrance of him. This is the first time for five years that he has been on board.

Eleven o'clock. The letters are arrived, and Troubridge tells me not to think of leaving my station, so here I shall stay miserable, shut-up, for I will not stir out of the ship. I told Dr. Baird yesterday that I was determined never to mention to Troubridge's unfeeling heart whether I was sick or well. I wish to my heart I could get to Merton; I had rather be sick there than well here; but, in truth, I am so disgusted that this day I care but little what becomes of me. I have this day received a curious letter from the Order of Joachim, in Germany, desiring to elect me Knight Grand Commander thereof. I shall send it to Mr. Addington, that he may give me his opinion, and obtain, if proper, the King's approbation; this is very curious. Dr. Baird is just come on board. Although I am not confined to my bed, I should be much better out of a frigate's cold cabin; but never mind, my dear friend, I see and feel all kindnesses and unkindnesses towards me. Make my kindest regards to Sir William, Mrs. Cadogan and all friends, and believe me yours, &c.,

To the Admiralty *Amazon*, Downs, *October 14th, 1801*

Their Lordship's appointment for my particular service being now done away by the preliminary articles of peace, viz., to prevent the invasion of this country, which service I have not only, by their Lordships' appointing so large a force to serve under my command, been enabled effectually to perform, but also to be able to acquaint you that not one boat belonging to this country has been captured by the enemy; and as my state of health requires repose on shore, I have, therefore, to request that their Lordships will, when they think the services will admit of it, allow me permission to go on shore.

To Lady Hamilton *Amazon, October 15th, 1801*

I have wrote by the way of London; but as your letter came regular, mine may go most likely. The Admiralty will not let me move till after the 22nd, and I have got a dreadful cold. I send you a letter for my father; when read, send to London, to be put in the post. I could not say less; I hope you will approve. Forgive my short letter, but the toothache torments me to pieces. Ever yours, &c.

Sutton and Bedford desire their best respects, and will certainly come and eat your brown bread and butter.

To Evan Nepean, Esq., Admiralty *Amazon*, Downs, *October 15th, 1801*

Sir,

I am to acknowledge the receipt of their Lordships' order for the cessation of hostilities against the French Republic; likewise a copy of the Preliminary Articles of Peace between his Majesty and the said Republic.

I beg leave to know whether their Lordships approve of my directing the Ships and Vessels under my command to rendezvous in the Downs after the 22nd instant? I have the honour to be, &c.,

NELSON AND BRONTE

P.S. Orders are sent from the Navy Board, for some of the Hired Cutters to be discharged, although the same has not been signified to me by their Lordships, or the Navy Board. I have not detained them.

Sir W. Hamilton to Lord Nelson Merton, *October 16th, 1801*

We have now inhabited your Lordp's premises some days, & I can now speak with some certainty. I have lived with our dear Emma several years. I know her merit, have a great opinion of the head & heart that God Almighty has been pleased to give her; but a seaman alone could have given a fine woman full power to chuse & fit up a residence for him without seeing it himself. You are in luck, for in my conscience I verily believe that a place so suitable to your views could not have been found, & at so cheap a rate, for if you stay away 3 days longer I do not think you can have any wish but you will find it compleated here, & then the bargain was fortunately struck 3 days before an idea of peace got abroad. Now every estate in this neighbourhood has increased in value, and you might get a thousand pounds tomorrow for your bargain. The proximity to the capital, and the perfect retirement of this place, are, for your Lordship, two points beyond estimation; but the house is so comfortable, the furniture clean & good, and I never saw so many conveniences united in so small a compass. You have nothing but to come and enjoy immediately; you have a good mile of pleasant dry walk around your own farm. It would make you laugh to see Emma & her mother fitting up pig-sties and hen-coops, & already the Canal is enlivened with ducks, and the cock is strutting with his hens about the walks. Your Lp's plan as to stocking the Canal with fish is exactly mine. I will answer for it, that in a few months you may command a good dish of fish at a moment's warning. Every fish, if of any size, has been taken away, even after the bargain was made, for there are many Troubridges in this world, but Nelsons are rare. I think it quite impossible that they can keep you at Deal more than 3 or 4 days longer; it would be ridiculous. This neighbourhood is anxiously expecting your Ldp's arrival, and you cannot be off of some particular attention that will be shewn you, of which all the world know that you have merited above all others. I enclose a letter which I have received from Count Dillon O'Kelly, who supped with me at Coblenzell's at Prague. See how your merit is estimated on the Continent, and shame be it that so little justice is done you at home. Be so good as to bring or return the letters, as I must answer it. Adieu, my dear Lord & most sincere friend I have in this world, yours, &c:

To Lieutenant . . . H.M. Sloop . . .

Amazon, Downs,
October 19th, 1801

Sir,

Notwithstanding your very improper conduct to your Captain, the Lords Commissioners of the Admiralty have been pleased to show their lenity to you, by cancelling their order for the Court-Martial, which I trust will prove a sufficient warning to you to behave, in future, with becoming respect to your superiors, and be a lesson to you not to listen to *bad* advice, for in the event of your erring again, you will inevitably meet with punishment. I am, &c.

NELSON AND BRONTE

To Lady Hamilton

Amazon, October 20th, 1801

My dearest Friend,

Only two days more, the Admiralty could, with any conscience, keep me here; not that I think they have had any conscience. I dare say, Master Troubridge is grown fat. I know I am grown lean with my complaint; which, but for their indifference about my health, would never have happened; or, at least, I should have got well long ago in a warm room, with a good fire, and sincere friends.

I believe I leave this little Squadron with sincere regret, and with the good wishes of every creature in it. . . . I did not think, tell Sir William, that impudence had got such deep root in Wales. I send you the letter as a curiosity; and to have the impudence to recommend a Midshipman! It is not long ago, a person in Yorkshire desired me to lend him three hundred pounds, as he was going to set up a school! Are these people mad; or, do they take me for quite a fool? However, I have wisdom enough to laugh at their folly; and to be, myself, your most obliged and faithful friend,

NELSON AND BRONTE

FIRST VISIT TO MERTON

To Evan Nepean, Esq., Admiralty

Amazon, Downs,
22nd October, 1801

Sir,

Be pleased to acquaint the Lords Commissioners of the Admiralty, that it is my intention to set off this evening for Merton, agreeably to the leave of absence their Lordships have been pleased to grant me. I have the honour to be, &c.,

NELSON AND BRONTE

[Nelson afterwards wrote to the Lord Mayor, desiring to withdraw this letter, because he was advised that it was not proper for him to point out to the City of London what it ought to do.]

To The Rt. Hon. The Lord Mayor

Merton, *20th November, 1801*

My Lord,

I have seen in this day's Paper, that the City of London have voted their Thanks to the brave Army and Navy who have so happily brought the Campaign in Egypt to a glorious conclusion, and no Thanks were certainly ever better deserved. From my own experience, I have never seen, that the smallest services rendered by either Navy or Army to the Country, have missed being always noticed by the great City of London, with one exception—I mean, my Lord, the glorious Second of April—a day when the greatest dangers of navigation were overcome, and the Danish Force, which they thought impregnable, totally taken or destroyed by the consummate skill of the Commanders, and by the undaunted bravery of as gallant a Band as ever defended the rights of this Country.

For myself, I can assure you, that if I were only personally concerned, I should bear the stigma, now first attempted to be placed upon my brow, with humility. But, my Lord, I am the natural guardian of the characters of the Officers of the Navy, Army, and Marines, who fought, and so profusely bled, under my command on that day. In no Sea-action this war has so much British blood flowed for their King and Country. Again, my Lord, I beg leave to disclaim for myself more merit than naturally falls to the share of a successful Commander; but when I am called upon to speak of the merits of the Captains of His Majesty's Ships, and of the Officers and Men, whether Seamen, Marines, or Soldiers, I that day had the happiness to command, *then I say*, that never was the glory of this Country upheld with more determined bravery than upon that occasion; and, if I may be allowed to give an opinion as a Briton, *then I say*, that more important service was never rendered to our King and Country.

It is my duty, my Lord, to prove to the brave fellows, my Companions in dangers, that *I* have not failed, at every proper place, to represent, as well as I am able, their bravery and meritorious services. When I am honoured with your Lordship's answer, I shall communicate it to all the Officers and Men who served under my command on the Second of April last. I cannot close my letter without bearing testimony to the extraordinary exertions of Rear-Admiral Sir Thomas Graves, and the Honourable Colonel Stewart. I am, &c.,

NELSON AND BRONTE

To The Earl of St. Vincent, K.B.

Merton, *November 22nd, 1801*

My dear Lord,

I was this morning thunder-struck by the reading your Lordship's Letter, telling me that you have never given encouragement to the expectation of receiving Medals for the Action of April 2nd (Copenhagen). Had I so understood you, I never should, the same day, have told Mr. Addington how happy you had made me, by the assurance that the King would give us Medals; and I have never failed assuring the Captains, that I have seen and communicated with, that they might depend on receiving them. I own I considered the words your Lordship used as conveying that assurance. It was an apology for their not being given before, which, I understood you, they would have been, but for the difficulty of fixing who was to have them; and, I trust you will recollect that my reply was, that 'certainly they could not be given to any but those who fought'; and we entered into the difficulties of fixing whether they should be confined to the Ships of the Line, or extended to the Frigates, engaged. I could not, my dear Lord, have had any interest in misunderstanding you, and representing that as an intended Honour from the King, which you considered as so improper to be recommended to the King: therefore, I must beg that your Lordship will reconsider our conversation—to me of the very highest concern, and think that I could not but believe that we were to have Medals.

The conduct of the City of London is to me incomprehensible; for Lord Keith, who has not been engaged, has been Thanked, &c., and Sir Hyde Parker for not fighting might, for what matters to me, have been Thanked, too; but surely, my dear Lord, those who fought ought not to have been neglected for any conduct of *others*.

I am truly made ill by your letter. If any person had told me what you wrote, I would have staked my head against the assertion. With every kind wish, believe me, my dear Lord, your most affectionate,

NELSON AND BRONTE

To Alexander Davison, Esq.

Merton, *December 18th, 1801*

My dear Davison,

I am sorry to be disappointed at not coming to you this morning, but General Waltersdorff sent me word he should be here to breakfast to take leave; but I hope to be with you tomorrow, but do not wait for me. The valuation of the diamonds is, as far as I have been told, shameful; therefore, although I am naturally anxious not to obtrude more on your goodness than necessity obliges me, yet I wish to talk to you on the subject of being *even* a little longer in your debt, taking care, which I hope I shall be able, to secure the payment to you: but more of this tomorrow; and I am, as ever, your most obliged and affectionate,

NELSON AND BRONTE

I would sooner beg, than *give* those fellows my diamonds.

[Nelson was obliged to sell the diamonds with which he had been presented by foreign sovereigns.]

CHAPTER ELEVEN

HAPPY DAYS AT MERTON

[The next section includes Nelson's letters to 18th May, 1803. During the whole of this time he was on shore, living at Merton with the Hamiltons. On 10th April on the ending of hostilities with France, he struck his flag and remained on half pay until the renewal of hostilities with France when he was selected for the chief command in the Mediterranean and hoisted his flag in the *Victory* at Spithead on 18th May, 1803.]

From Mr. Matcham to Nelson *April 24th, 1802*

Your good old father is very ill, and I have directions from Dr. Parry and Mr. Spry to say to you that he is certainly in great danger. Whatever orders you send me shall be executed. Believe me, &c.

To Sir W. Hamilton Merton, *April 28th, 1802*

I feel very much obliged by your truly kind and flattering letter. I have a consolation in the loss I have sustain'd that my dear father was a good man, and that I feel I never was wanting in kindness to him. With every kind wish, my dear Sir William, ever yours, &c.

Of course, I cannot go to the Royal Academy, and must request that you will make my apologies.

To Mrs. Bolton

Merton, *June 11th, 1802*

My dear Sister,

Here is £100, which I shall pay you on the 11th June, for three years, towards the education of your children; by that time, other things may turn up, and this is a trifle in case you may want any little thing going through London. All I desire is, that you would not say or write me a syllable on the subject, for I am sorry I cannot do more, being truly your most affectionate brother,

NELSON AND BRONTE

To the Lord Mayor of London

Merton, *June 21st, 1802*

My Lord,

A few days past, I saw in the Newspapers that a Motion had been made in a Court of Common Council, to thank me for my conduct in taking the command of a Force destined to prevent any designs our Enemies might have of approaching the City of London, but which Motion stands over for some future Court. I have therefore to entreat that your Lordship will use your influence that no such Motion may be brought forward.

There is not, my Lord, one individual in the world who appreciates the honour of having their conduct approved by the City of London, higher than myself. I was desired to take the Command in question in a very indifferent state of health, as I was flattered with the opinion that it would keep quiet the minds of all in London, and the Coast between Beech-Head and Orfordness. This would have been a sufficient reason for me to have laid down my life, much less to suffer a little from ill-health; and, my Lord, His Majesty's Government gave me such a powerful Force, that the gallant Officers and Men I had the honour to command, almost regretted that the Enemy did not make the attempt of Invasion. Therefore, you see, my Lord, I have no merit—I only did my duty with alacrity, which I shall always be ready to do when directed.

But, my Lord, if any other reason was wanting to prevent the City of London from thanking me for only showing an alacrity in stepping forth in time of danger, it is this—not four months before I was appointed to this Command, I had the happiness of witnessing, under all its circumstances, the most hard-fought Battle, and the most complete Victory (as far as my reading goes) that ever was fought and obtained by the Navy of this Country. This Battle, my Lord, had not the honour of being approved in the way which the City of London has usually marked their approbation: therefore, I entreat that you will use your influence that no Vote of approbation may ever be given to me for any services since the 2nd of April, 1801; for I should feel much mortified when I reflected on the noble support I that day received, at any honour which could separate me from them, for I am bold to say, that they deserve every honour and favour which a grateful Country can bestow.

I entreat your Lordship's indulgence for thus expressing my feelings, and again request that the intended Motion of Thanks may be withdrawn. I trust your Lordship will give me full credit for the high estimation in which I hold the City of London, and with what respect I am your Lordship's most obedient humble servant,

NELSON AND BRONTE

To Alexander Davison, Esq. Boxhill, *July 9th, 1802*
(A very pretty place, and we are all very happy.)

My dear Davison,

If the Victory of the 2nd was real, the Admirals, Officers, and Men, who fought and obtained the Victory, are from custom entitled to the Thanks of the City of London. Custom has never gone back to the first causers of Victories, but simply to the Victors. Lord St. Vincent had no thanks given him for the Victory of the Nile, and Sir Hyde Parker, except being nearer the scene of action, had no more to do with that of Copenhagen than Lord St. Vincent. I cannot object to any thanks or rewards being bestowed on any man; but I have a fair claim, from custom to be alone considered through the whole of the Battle, as the Commander of the Ships fighting. The Thanks of Parliament went only to Sir Hyde's conduct in *planning*, not for the *fighting*; therefore, I look forward with confidence to a Sword from the City of London; and their Thanks, and the Freedom in a Gold Box, to Admiral Graves. The City of London has never yet failed noticing Sea Victories, and I trust, as the first commercial City in the world, never will. I remember, a few years back, on my noticing to a Lord Mayor, that if the City continued its generosity, we should ruin them by their gifts, his Lordship put his hand on my shoulder and said—*aye, the Lord Mayor of London said*—'Do you find Victories, and we will find rewards.' I have since that time found *two complete Victories*. I have kept my word, and shall I have the power of saying that the City of London, which exists by Victories at Sea, has not kept its promise a promise made by a Lord Mayor in his robes, and almost in the Royal presence? I have a fair and honourable claim: my part of the honourable contract has now doubly been fulfilled. We shall dine in Piccadilly, Saturday, five o'clock, and Lady Hamilton and Sir William beg that you will come to us; and ever believe me, my dear Davison, your obliged and affectionate,

NELSON AND BRONTE

Lady Hamilton to Sir W. Hamilton (*August*)

As I see it is a pain to you to remain here, let me beg of you to fix your time for going. Weather I dye in Picadilly or any other spot in England, 'tis the same to me; but I remember the time when you wish'd for tranquility, but now all visiting and bustle is your liking. However, I will do what you please, being ever your affectionate & obedient, &c., E.H.

Sir Wm. Hamilton to Lady Hamilton *(August) 1802*

I neither love bustle nor great company, But I like some employment and diversion. I have but a very short time to live, and every moment is precious to me. I am in no hurry, and am exceedingly glad to give every satisfaction to our best friend, our dear Lord Nelson. The question, then, is what we can best do that all may be perfectly satisfied. Sea bathing is useful to your health; I see it is, and wish you to continue it a little longer; but I must confess that I regret, whilst the season is favourable, that I cannot enjoy my favourite amusement of quiet fishing. I care not a pin for the great world, and am attached to no one so much as to you.

To Sir John Eamer, Lord Mayor of London

Private. Merton, *8th September, 1802*

My dear Sir John,

I can assure you that I should dine with you in your private capacity with the greatest pleasure; but it is impossible, as I am sure you are sensible of, that Lord Nelson can receive any mark of distinction from the Chief Magistrate of the City of London, the conduct of the brave Captains, Officers, and Men, who so bravely fought, died, and conquered in the Battle of Copenhagen not having had the honour of the approbation of the City of London, in their Corporate capacity. Whatever my demerits might have been on that glorious day, I am bold to say, that British valour never shone more conspicuously, or more successfully, than on the 2nd of April, 1801. Whenever, my dear Sir John, you cease to be Chief Magistrate of the City of London, name your day, and I will dine with you with satisfaction; but never till the City of London think justly of the merits of my brave Companions of the 2nd of April, can I, their Commander, receive any attention from the City of London. Believe me, my dear Sir John, your much obliged,

NELSON AND BRONTE

Sir William Hamilton to Lady Hamilton *(1802)*

I have passed the last 40 years of my life in the hurry & bustle that must necessarily be attendant on a publick character. I am arrived at the age when some repose is really necessary, & I promised myself a quiet home, & altho' I was sensible, & said so when I married, that I shou'd be superannuated when my wife wou'd be in her full beauty and vigour of youth. That time is arrived, and we must make the best of it for the comfort of both parties. Unfortunately our tastes as to the manner of living are very different. I by no means wish to live in solitary retreat, but to have seldom less than 12 or 14 at table, & those varying continually, is coming back to what was become so irksome to me in Italy during the latter years of my residence in that country. I have no connections out of my own family. I have no complaint to make, but I feel that the whole attention of my wife is given to Ld N. and his interest at Merton. I well know the purity of Ld N's friendship for Emma and me, and I know how very uncomfortable it wou'd make his Lp, our best friend, if a separation shou'd take place, & am therefore determined to do all in my power to prevent such an extremity, which wou'd be *essentially detrimental* to all parties, but wou'd be more sensibly felt by our dear friend than by us. Provided that our expences in housekeeping do not encrease beyond measure (of which I must own I see some danger), I am willing to go on upon our present footing; but as I cannot expect to live many years,* every moment to me is precious, & I hope I may be allow'd sometimes to be my own master, & pass my time according to my own inclination, either by going my fishing parties on the Thames or by going to London to attend the Museum, R. Society, the Tuesday Club, & Auctions of pictures. I mean to have a light chariot or post chaise by the month, that I may make use of it in London and run backwards and forwards to Merton or to Shepperton, &c. This is my plan, & we might go on very well, but I am fully determined not to have more of the very silly altercations that happen between us but too often and embitter the present moments exceedingly. If realy one cannot live comfortably together, a wise and well concerted separation is preferable; but I think, considering the probability of my not troubling any party long in this world, the best for us all wou'd be to bear those ills we have rather than flie to those we know not of. I have fairly stated what I have on my mind. There is not time for nonsense or trifling. I know and admire your talents & many excellent qualities, but I am not blind to your defects, & confess having many myself; therefore let us bear and forbear for God's sake.

To Rt. Hon. Henry Addington — Merton, *December 4th, 1802*

My dear Sir,

I send you my thoughts respecting Malta, made as they flow, from my pen, but with the less diffidence, as I feel that you do not consider my thoughts (on paper) as impertinent intrusions on your time, but as the well meaning of your sincere and attached,

NELSON AND BRONTE

* At this time Hamilton was 72, Emma 39 and Nelson 44. Hamilton shared the expenses of Merton with Nelson.

ON MALTA

It must never belong to France—England does not want it. If Russia will not guarantee Malta, then a new negotiation must be set on foot, and we must hold fast until it is settled. But if Russia will guarantee Malta, then it will become a serious consideration in the new state of the Order, whether it can be carried into effect. Malta is materially changed since the Treaty of Amiens, by Spain having (in breach of that Treaty) taken away a great part of that revenue which was to support the expenses of the Order, and if one power can do it, another can do the same, and the Order of Malta, unable to maintain itself, falls of course.

N.B. It is easy to see from whose advice Spain has acted; other Countries may follow the same advice.

The Order of Malta cannot, in keeping the fortifications in repair, ships, galleys, &c., be kept up for less than the former revenue, and by the introduction of the new Langue, the pride of Spaniards will not allow them, nor even the Italians, to enter into the Order; and they brought a vast accession of flowing wealth to the Order, which now will fail.

Under these circumstances, it becomes a consideration what can be done with it to accord to the spirit of the Treaty of Amiens, that neither France or England shall possess it.

The King of the Two Sicilies is the acknowledged Lord of the Island, even the Maltese, after the destruction of the Order, in their addresses style themselves his Subjects; therefore, on the face of the act, there could be no objection to giving it to him; but the consideration is, how a weak State can keep it out of the power of so powerful a one as France—only by guarantees that the King of the Two Sicilies shall hold Malta on the same terms as the Order, (if it is possible that it shall always be neutral,) and tied up by the guarantee that on no consideration of exchange of territory shall it be given up. The Emperor of Russia having guaranteed all the King of Naples' Dominions last year, will not probably object to do the same for Malta. It is so much the interest of the King of the Two Sicilies to keep Malta from France, (for he would lose Sicily if he gave it up) that I think him, under guarantees, the most proper person to have it. France could not object by the spirit of the Treaty of Amiens, to its being placed, (the Order not being possible to be restored,) in the King of Naples' hands under the same restrictions, and this Country would save £300,000 a year, and by as far as human faith and foresight can go, keep Malta out of the hands of France.

The King of Naples can wish for neither France or England to possess Malta. By the first, he must lose Sicily: by the latter, he may be involved in a war about Malta, should France and England go to war; and this, in my opinion, could be the only rational inducement for the King of Naples to pay the great expenses of holding Malta.

If neither of these plans can be accomplished, we have no choice but to keep Malta.

To The Earl of St. Vincent, K.B.

23 Piccadilly, *February 28th, 1803**

My dear Lord,

I take the liberty of inclosing some ideas of mine relative to our Seamen. My reasons for committing them to paper are stated in the first lines of my Paper. I have sent a copy of them to Mr. Addington. Probably you have arranged similar, or better plans, for obtaining the same much to be desired object. If so, they will have the fullest support of, my dear Lord, your most faithful and affectionate,

NELSON AND BRONTE

PLAN FOR MANNING THE NAVY

February, 1803

At a time when, I have been repeatedly told, the Seamen, notwithstanding their good pay, and abundance of the very best provisions, manifest a reluctance to enter into the Naval Service, it becomes, in my humble opinion, a duty for people conversant with the manners and disposition of Seamen, to turn their thoughts on the mode of inducing the Seamen to be fond, and even desirous of serving in the Navy, in preference to the Merchant Service. Their pay and provisions cannot possibly be improved from what they are at present; but, I think, a plan could be brought forward to Register the Certificates given to Seamen; and a form of Certificate to be general, and filled according to regulations issued by the Admiralty under the authority of an Act of Parliament. The greatest good would result, from such a regulation to the Seamen, who are by hundreds in distress in London, for want of Certificates authenticating their persons; for want of which so many wrong Seamen have been paid, that neither the Pay-Office, nor any Prize-Agent, will venture to pay the Seaman his just due; and the benefit to the Seamen producing good characters, &c., never been concerned in mutinies, or deserted, &c., would much benefit them in getting good berths in the Merchant Service.

When we calculate by figures on the expense of raising Seamen, I think it is said, £20 per man, that 42,000 Seamen deserted during the

* Hamilton's town house.

late War, the loss in money, in that point alone, amounts to £840,000; without taking into consideration the greater expense of raising more men—and certainly not so good as those who have been used to the King's Naval Service. I shall therefore propose, that every Seaman who has served faithfully five years in War, and by his Certificates never been concerned in mutinies, nor deserted, shall receive every New Year's Day, or on the King's birth-day, the sum of two guineas; and if he serves eight years, shall have four guineas, exclusive of any pension for wounds. It may appear, at first sight, for the State to pay, an enormous sum; but when it is considered that the average life of a Seaman is, from *old* age finished, at forty-five years, he cannot many years enjoy the annuity; to assist the paying which, the interest of the money saved by their not deserting would go very far, and perhaps as the Merchants give large wages in War, a tax might be imposed, when wages are above such a sum. It would answer one of these two purposes, either making the increase of wages, in the Merchant's Service, beneficial to those who serve their King and Country in the Navy; or, by keeping down the Merchants' wages, render desertion the less desirable. Much, very much, can be said, and is necessary to be considered on this subject; but the more I think of it, the easier it appears to me to be put in practice. Prize-money to be as regularly paid in London, Portsmouth, Plymouth, &c. as Seamen's wages: this is so easy and simple, that a very few days would, in my opinion, complete such a plan.

But the great thing necessary to guard against is desertion; for notwithstanding all I have proposed, to induce Seamen to serve faithfully, yet a sum of money, and liquor, held out to a Seaman, are too much for him: he allows himself to be seduced and hid, he first becomes fearful of apprehension, and then wishes and exerts himself to get out of the Country in the Merchant's employ. It will be found, (if necessary to be inquired into at the Navy-Office,) and I know it, that whenever a large Convoy is assembled at Portsmouth, and our Fleet in Port, not less than 1,000 men desert from the Navy; and I am sure that one-third of this number, from loss of clothes, drinking, and other debaucheries, are lost by death to the Kingdom. I shall only relate one fact, of a thousand, which could be brought forward: a Ship, from London, clears at Gravesend for her voyage to India. Amongst other Papers, the names of her crew and number are necessary; the names, qualities, &c., are properly filled up, the Ship, to a common observer, is fully manned; but the fact is this, the Ship is navigated to Portsmouth by Ticket-men, (men who are protected from the impress for some cause or other.) The Owner or Captain sends to Portsmouth, (to crimps,) I have been told in one instance as far as fifty men—twenty-five able

Seamen, fifteen ordinary, and ten landsmen, the bounty being, of course, different according to their qualifications; the Ticket-men leave the Ship, the deserters to take up the names, and away they go.

Knowing the case, an Act of Parliament would, if not entirely, very nearly prevent this infamous conduct; the regulation, I think, would very plain and easy. I am sensible that no plan for these very important purposes can be matured by any one head, much less by mine; but as the ideas flow from a pure source,. and a sincere desire to benefit our King and Country, I submit them, with deference to much wiser and abler men than

NELSON AND BRONTE

To Mr. Henry Addington

London, *March 8th, 1803*

Sir,

I feel very great reluctance in troubling you with any personal concerns of mine, but I am really compelled to it, by circumstances, which, when explained, will, I think, convince you, that I cannot do otherwise; and knowing the value of your time, I will do it as shortly as I can.

His Majesty was graciously pleased, on account of my services in the Battle of the Nile, to bestow on me the high honour of a Peerage of Great Britain, and to recommend it to Parliament to enable him to grant a Pension of £2,000 a year to me, and eventually for two lives after mine. In the former part of the Message for that purpose, his Majesty expresses a desire to bestow on me the Pension, and to the two next succeeding heirs male of my body. But in the recommendatory part of the Message the words are, 'to consider of a proper method of enabling his Majesty to grant the same, and of extending, securing, and settling such annuity to the said Rear-Admiral Lord Nelson, and to the two next persons on whom the title of Baron Nelson, &c., shall descend, in such manner as shall be thought most effectual for the benefit of the said Lord Nelson and his family'.

The grant was made to me and the two next succeeding heirs male of my body, which was probably done without an attentive consideration of the whole of the Message. But it was then of no importance to me, as the grant followed the Title; but as His Majesty has since been graciously pleased to confer upon me the Title of a Viscount, with the remainder to my brother and nephews, (failing issue of my own,) I must entreat that you will lay me at his Majesty's feet, and that you will have the goodness to express to him, in the most dutiful manner, my humble hope that, as I have not had the good fortune to acquire sufficient wealth to put it in my power to enable my nephews to support in any degree the rank of a Peer, to which they may eventually succeed, his Majesty will be graciously pleased to take such measures as he shall think necessary, for continuing the Pension in the manner it appears to have been his Majesty's gracious intention it should have been originally granted.

In making this application to you, Sir, it is but fair that I should apprise you that Lord St. Vincent is in the same situation, I believe, with myself; but I know of no other case at all similar, as Lord Duncan has male issue. And I also beg leave to state that both Lord St. Vincent and Lord Duncan had a grant from the Irish Parliament of £1,000 a year, which, from not having been recommended by Government here, was not bestowed upon me. I presume to make only one remark: Was it, or not, the intention of his Majesty's Government to place my rewards for services lower than Lord St. Vincent or Lord Duncan? I had the happiness to be a sharer of the glory of the 14th of February; and I had the honour to command the Fleet which gained the Victory of the Nile, which, till that of Copenhagen, was, I believe, the most complete one ever obtained. I have the honour to be, &c.,

NELSON AND BRONTE

[No increase of pension was granted to him.]

LORD NELSON'S INCOME AND PROPERTY

My Exchequer Pension for the Nile	£2,000	0	0
Navy Pension for loss of one arm and one eye	923	0	0
Half-pay as Vice-Admiral	465	0	0
Interest of £1,000 3 per Cents...	30	0	0
	£3,418	0	0

OUTGOINGS OF LORD NELSON

To Lady Nelson	£1,800	0	0
Interest of money owing	500	0	0
Pension to my Brother's Widow	200	0	0
To assisting in education my Nephews	150	0	0
Expenditure	2,650	0	0
Income	3,418	0	0
For Lord Nelson ..	768	0	0

Therefore, Lord Nelson is free of House-rent, but has to pay charities necessary for his station in life, taxes, repairs, servants, and to live upon £768 per annum.

PROPERTY OF LORD NELSON

Merton House, land, plate, and furniture	£20,000 0 0
In 3 per Cents, £1,000 stock	

DEBTS

By Mortgage on Merton, to assist in the purchase ..	6,000 0 0
Fitting out for the Baltic, and again for my Command on the Coast, in summer, 1801	4,000 0 0
	£10,000 0 0

Real Property of Lord Nelson £10,000
In Three per Cents, £1,000 Stock.

To Captain Sir Edward Berry

Piccadilly, *March 26th, 1803*

My dear Sir Edward,

I have only a moment to answer your questions—War or Peace? Every person has a different opinion. I fear perhaps the former, as I hope so much the latter. If War, I go to the Mediterranean in Hardy's Frigate: the *Victory* is to be my Ship—Sam Sutton to fit her out. You know how happy I should be to have you in any Fleet I command, particularly on the day of Battle: I should be sure of being well supported. You must judge for yourself about applying for employment; but I should think you will have no fears for a Ship being forced upon you. In Peace, Mids. may be difficult to get on board Ships; but our establishment, even if blessed Peace continues, will be large. You will be truly sorry to hear that good Sir William is, I fear, very near his last breach: he is all but gone. You may readily conceive Lady Hamilton's and my feelings on such an occasion: indeed, all London is interested. Ever, my dear Sir Edward, yours most sincerely,

NELSON AND BRONTE

Reports say, but I know not how truly, that changes are in agitation.

To Alexander Davison, Esq.

6th April, 1803

My dear Davison,

Our dear Sir William died at ten minutes past ten, this morning, in Lady Hamilton's and my arms, without a sigh or a struggle. Poor Lady Hamilton is, as you may expect, desolate. I hope she will be left properly; but I doubt. Ever yours most affectionately,

NELSON AND BRONTE

To the Duke of Clarence *April 17th, 1801*

I agree with your Royal Highness most entirely, that the son of a Rodney ought to be the protege of every person in the Kingdom, and particularly of the Sea-Officers: had I known that there had been this claimant, some of my own Lieutenants must have given way to such a name, and he should have been placed in the *Victory*—she is full, and I have twenty on my list; but whatever numbers I have, the name of Rodney must cut many of them out. I am well aware that in my Prize plan, Lawyers must remove all the difficulties that will occur in the completion. Much, very much, is necessary to be considered on every part of it, but I think many objections would be overcome by a temperate and serious discussion. I was told the difficulties were insurmountable, or nearly so. My answer was, 'As the thing is necessary to be done, the more difficulties, the more necessary to try to remove them.' I am, &c.,

NELSON AND BRONTE

To Mr. Henry Addington *April 23rd, 1803*

The Pensions to the Admirals St. Vincent, Duncan, and Nelson, were, I suppose, either granted for the great Victories they obtained over the Enemy, or for enabling them to support the dignity of the Peerage, to which his Majesty was pleased to raise them for their Victories, for which their private fortunes were not supposed equal. If Earl St. Vincent obtained the Pension of £2,000 a year in Great Britain, and £1,000 a year in Ireland, for the Victory off Cape St. Vincent, and Viscount Duncan for that off Camperdown, Lord Nelson trusts, that in any comparison, the Victory off the Nile was equal to either of the others; and, therefore, in strict justice, his Pension should have been equal to the other two noble Admirals.

If it is said that the Pensions are not given for the Victories, but to enable the noble Admirals to support their ranks in the Peerage, then Lord Nelson trusts that his wants will be found superior to either of the others; for Earl St. Vincent, at the time his Pension was granted, had realized not a less sum than £100,000, and Viscount Duncan, not less than £50,000; whereas Lord Nelson, at the time his Pension of £2,000 a year was granted, had not realized £5,000; therefore, why Lord Nelson should have had £1,000 a year less Pension than either of the two noble Admirals, is unaccountable. This comparison is only made to the Battle off the Nile. Since which time Lord Nelson was, by his Majesty, raised to the dignity of a Viscount, for his services in commanding his Majesty's Fleet, when the great, important, and decisive victory off Copenhagen was obtained, but no Pension was given with this accession of Title.

NELSON AND BRONTE

To the Earl of St. Vincent, K.B.

May 12th, 1803

Private.

My dear Lord,

Your mention of the *Victory* remaining some time in England, so much according with what I am told of Lord Keith's saying that he was to have her for the present—induces me to hope that if the *Victory* is ready, or as soon as she is, that I may have her; for all my things, servants, wines, &c., &c., are ordered to be sent to her, be where she will—even my sheep, poultry, hay, corn, and every comfort are ordered to her. But if Lord Keith, or any other man is have her, for a given time, I must un-order all these things. I trust, my dear Lord, that I can take a French Admiral as well as any of them, and have as much chance of falling in with one. I will call this morning for one moment on this subject. Ever, my dear Lord, yours faithfully,

NELSON AND BRONTE

CHAPTER TWELVE

RENEWAL OF HOSTILITIES WITH FRANCE

['Monday, 16th May, 1803, A.M. Received my appointment from the Lords Commissioners of the Admiralty, as Commander-in-Chief of his Majesty's Ships and Vessels employed and to be employed on the Mediterranean Station. On the 17th, made several necessary public arrangements previous to my leaving Town; and about 4 a.m. on Wednesday morning, the 18th, set out from London for Portsmouth, where I arrived on that day, about ½ past Noon. Thursday, 19th May, P.M. (i.e., the afternoon of the 18th.) About ½ past 3, hoisted my Flag on board his Majesty's Ship *Victory*. Saluted Admiral Lord Gardner's Flag on board the *Endymion*, with thirteen guns, which was returned with an equal number.'—*Victory's* Log.]

To Lady Hamilton *Victory, May 20th, 1803*

You will believe that although I am glad to leave that horrid place, Portsmouth, yet the being afloat makes me now feel that we do not tread the same element. I feel from my soul that God is good, and in His due wisdom will unite us, only when you look upon our dear child call to your remembrance all you think that I would say was I present, and be assured that I am thinking of you every moment. My heart is full to bursting! May God Almighty bless & protect you, is the fervent prayer of, my dear beloved Emma, your most faithful, affectionate, &c.

[Within a few days of going on board the *Victory* as his flagship, Nelson was obliged to leave her and transfer his flag to the *Amphion*. He had been instructed to leave the *Victory* with Admiral Cornwallis to reinforce that officer's squadron off Ushant. He remained in the *Amphion* until 1st August when the *Victory* arrived in the Mediterranean and he transferred to her.

Nelson's orders from the Government were to go first to Malta and there arrange for the defence of that island after which he was to take up his station with the Fleet off Toulon and to blockade it. He was also to watch Spanish movements and not to permit any Spanish ships to enter French ports as it was feared that Spain was about to join France.]

To Lady Hamilton

May 22nd, 1803

My dearest Emma,

We are now in sight of Ushant, and shall see Admiral Cornwallis in an hour. I am not in a little fret, on the idea that he may keep the

Victory, and turn us all into the *Amphion*. It will make it truly uncomfortable; but I cannot help myself. We are very comfortable. Mr. Elliot is happy, has quite recovered his spirits: he was very low at Portsmouth. George Elliot is very well; say so to Lord Minto. Murray, Sutton—in short, every body in the Ship, seems happy; and, if we should fall in with a French Man-of-War, I have no fears but they will do as we used to do. Hardy is gone into Plymouth, to see our Dutchman safe, I think she will turn out a good Prize. Taetano desires his duty to Miledi! He is a good man, and, I dare say, will come back; for I think it cannot be a long War: just enough to make me independent in pecuniary matters. If the wind stands, on Tuesday we shall be on the Coast of Portugal; and, before next Sunday, in the Mediterranean. To Mrs. Cadogan* say every kind thing; to good Mrs. Nelson, the Doctor, &c., &c. If you like, you may tell him about the entailing of the Pension; but perhaps he will be so much taken up with Canterbury, that it will do for some dull evening at Hillborough.

I shall now stop till I have been on board the Admiral . . . I shall direct to Merton, after June 1st. Therefore, as you change, make Davison take a direction to Nepean; but I would not trouble him with too many directions, for fear of embroil.

May 23rd

We were close in with Brest yesterday, and found by a Frigate that Admiral Cornwallis had a Rendezvous at sea. Thither we went; but to this hour cannot find him. It blows strong. What a wind we are losing! If I cannot find the Admiral by six o'clock, we must all go into the *Amphion*, and leave the *Victory*, to my great mortification. So much for the wisdom of my superiors. I keep my letter open to the last, for I still hope; as, I am sure, there is no good reason for my not going out in the *Victory*. I am just embarking in the *Amphion*—cannot find Admiral Cornwallis. May God in Heaven bless you, prays your most sincere

NELSON AND BRONTE

To Rt. Hon. Henry Addington

Amphion, Gibraltar, *June 4th, 1803*

My dear Sir,

We arrived here in the night, and as the news of actual War had not reached this place, I am anxious to get to the Fleet. Mr. Elliot has been so good as to send a Messenger to Madrid to get information respecting Spain, but although our Consul at Cadiz expects that there must be a

* Lady Hamilton's mother.

War with Spain, yet I do not find that any particular activity prevails in their Naval Arsenal at Cadiz. They have just got two rich Ships from Manilla. You may rely on my activity in getting off Toulon, when all will go on smoothly. Buonaparte's brother Jerome passed from Martinique a few days ago in a Ship of the Line. It would have been pleasant to have laid a little salt on his tail, but I hope to do it yet. Believe me ever, my dear Sir, your most attached and faithful friend,

NELSON AND BRONTE

To the King of the Two Sicilies.

June 10th, 1803

Sire,

I am confident that your Majesty will readily believe how desirous I must be to pay my humble duty at Naples; but consideration for the situation of your Majesty; and your Kingdom of Naples at this moment prevents me from following my inclinations, as I have fully set forth in my letter to General Acton; but I beg leave to assure your Majesty, that one great reason for my being appointed Commander-in-Chief of the British Fleet in the Mediterranean, was my known attachment to your Majesty, the Queen, and Royal Family, and my ardent wish for maintaining the true honour of your Majesty, and the safety and welfare of your Kingdoms.

The sentiments of his Britannic Majesty will be much better expressed by his Representative, Mr. Elliot, than I could possibly find words for, but your Majesty's good faith and attachment to the British Nation are known and acknowledged by the whole Nation.

It only remains for me to apologize for addressing a letter to your Majesty; but, from your former goodness to me, I cannot resist assuring your Majesty how devotedly I am your most grateful, attached, and faithful servant,

NELSON AND BRONTE

To Rt. Hon. Henry Addington

Amphion, June 28th, 1803,
between Sardinia and Naples

My dear Sir,

Knowing how very much you are pressed for time, I shall, as briefly as possible, consistent with telling you, as a friend, my sentiments on all the topics which I shall necessarily touch upon, with that sincerity which becomes me to you, by my opinion right or wrong.

I shall only say one word of Gibraltar, on which I had a serious conversation with Sir Thomas Trigee, on the impropriety of placing Dillon's Regiment as part of the Garrison of Gibraltar. When we reflect how that Regiment is composed, and that fifty men, the usual Guard at Land Port Gate, by being corrupted, might lose the place, who shall say Gibraltar is secure with those Troops? If it is said, do not trust them with the Guard, then you show your distrust, and, naturally, they become your enemies. The Regiment of Rolle is a fine Corps, and will serve faithfully; but I would not trust them at Gibraltar.

The next point I come to is Algiers. Mr. Falcon the Consul having sent home his own account of the transaction, it rests with Government to determine what steps are to be taken. All that I entreat, if the matters are left to me to settle, is that our demands for satisfaction be fixed; for if we give way in the smallest thing, the insolence of the Dey will but increase. Whatever the wisdom of the Government directs shall be attended to. The alternative must be instantaneous War on a refusal to our demands, or an entire acquiescence. Mr. F. thinks that the Dey never will receive him. He knows best the reasons why he thinks so.

Malta.—I arrived there the 15th of June, in the evening. The French Minister, General Vial, had left it in a Ragusa Vessel in the morning. The Maltese are in the highest spirits, and sincerely hope that they will now be never separated from England. My opinion of Malta, as a Naval station for watching the French in Toulon, is well known; and my present experience of what will be a three weeks' passage, most fully confirms me in it. The Fleet can never go there if I can find any other corner to put them in: but having said this, I now declare, that I consider Malta as a most important outwork to India, that it will ever give us great influence in the Levant, and indeed all the Southern parts of Italy. In this view, I hope we shall never give it up. I carried out orders from Lord Hobart, that General Villettes was to hold 2,000 men at my requisition, if they could be spared from the defence of Malta, for the service of Sicily. The language of General Villettes was natural: 'The Garrison appointed for Malta is not more than on the most economical number of men was judged sufficient; and, looking to the assistance of the Maltese in case of a siege, that these numbers of British troops were only sufficient for the ordinary duties, and that, when the Neapolitan Troops went away, (and he was ordered to send them away,) the duty would be very severe; that the addition of Maltese Troops when trained and formed, would be little better than a well-formed Militia; and, however much they undoubtedly would assist, yet they could not be counted as British Troops; however, that he should not hesitate in providing 1,200 men, and a Corps of Artillery, to be under the command of General Oakes, a most excellent Officer, for the service of Messina, whenever I might call for them:' and the General wished that I should mention this conversation, when I had any opportunity of communicating with Ministers, (but which opportunity

I never can have, but in this private, confidential way.) Sir Alexander Ball thinks, that if half the Troops were gone on other services, particularly to Sicily, that the Maltese would defend the Island, against any force the French could send, supported by our Fleet. Truth probably lays between; but, my dear Sir, these sort of orders should never be left discretionary. You make an Officer responsible for the safety of the place, yet tell him in the same breath, 'Send away so many men, if you can spare them without evident risk.' The conduct of the Officer must be naturally to secure himself from the very great responsibility thrown upon him by such an order.

Sicily.—The state of Sicily is almost as bad as a civilized Country can be. There are no Troops fit to be called such, with a scarcity of corn never known, and of course bread so dear that the lower class of People are discontented. The Nobles are oppressors, and the middle rank wish for a change; and although they would prefer us to the French, yet I believe they would receive the French, rather than not change from the oppression of the Nobles. The Citadel of Messina is strong and in good order, but with a few miserable Troops badly paid, if paid at all; therefore, what could be expected from them? A French Frigate has been there lately, a French Aide-de-camp to the Grand Master, and, lastly, General Vial; they have good eyes, and many at Messina are seduced by them; and if the Neapolitan Troops at Malta were removed there, I fear we should find more enemies and the French more friends. (On these Troops I shall touch in another place.)

On the 17th, at daylight, I left Malta; on the 20th, I passed the Faro of Messina. The lower class of Boat-people came on board with fruit, &c.—their expressions were strong, and ought to be received with caution, yet with their hearts in their hands, you may gather sentiments to form a pretty accurate opinion. 'Viva il Re! Viva Inglese! When will the English come back to Messina?' On asking them if they had any Jacobins in the City, 'Yes, the gentry who wear their hats so—on one side the head'—vide Bond-street loungers. On the 25th, I was at the entrance of the Bay of Naples, where I had appointed the Frigate which carried Mr. Elliot to Naples to join me. I send you copies of my letters to Sir John Acton, the King and Queen, with their answers, Mr. Elliot's, and likewise those I have sent to Lord St. Vincent, for him to lay them before the Cabinet. Here it is necessary to observe to you, that a Sea-Officer cannot hold any official correspondence but with the Secretary of the Admiralty, without an order for that purpose, which is often given: therefore, I have certainly irregularly sent them to Lord St. Vincent, as a Cabinet Minister—conceiving they are on subjects which the Board of Admiralty can have nothing to do with, much less the Clerks of that Office, through whose hands they must pass. When you, my dear Sir, take into your consideration all the letters sent me, with the liberal conduct towards my judgment, I trust that you will agree with me, that under all circumstances at this moment, I did right to give the opinion which I have done; but I stand open to the correction of the Cabinet. I felt that it was our wish to make Naples feel that we were her true friends, and sincerely wished to preserve as much as possible for her, and not to hasten the loss of any part of the Kingdom of Naples.

Sardinia is declared Neutral, but that no Foreign Troops would be allowed to land. I wish they may keep off the French. We have no Troops to assist them, if they wanted our assistance. This reminds me of a word about more Troops for Naples: should the King of Naples, which is most probable, be obliged to quit his Capital and retire to Palermo, what General Acton suggests would be attended with the very happiest consequences,—the possession of Gaeta, a very strong fortified Frontier Town, with a fine Bay and Port, the country people hostile to inveteracy against the French: 1,500 British would secure this post, and always give us an entry into the country. I am not Military man sufficient to say how long our Troops could hold St. Elmo and the other Castles at Naples; but they would give that energy to the people, which might, and probably would be attended with the happiest effects. I regret the necessity of withdrawing the last part of that fine Egyptian Army, and am aware of the influence it will have on the timid Council of Naples.

Rome.—By a letter from Mr. Jackson, his Majesty's Minister to the King of Sardinia, of June 17th, he says:—'I have seen the Secretary of State of this Government, and his Eminence told me there was no doubt that this State would be suffered to remain Neuter, and, consequently, that the Ships of the belligerent Powers will be received in the Ports of the Pope's States.' This may be the case for the moment; but if we were to receive the least advantage by it, I am sure we should be turned out as heretofore.

Tuscany.—It is difficult to know how to consider this State; they are not our friends, and it would, perhaps, be hard to consider them as enemies. Yet why should France use them against us, and we are to suffer Leghorn to enjoy its commerce for the advantage, ultimately, of the French? for it is they who receive the fruits of the Tuscan labour and commerce. And as the French have declared Leghorn in a state of siege, I can see no impropriety of considering it so likewise, and for our Government to place it in a state of blockade whilst the French remain in it. This is for the wise and grave consideration of our Government.

Genoa or Liguria.—The same as the Italian Republic; it is France as much as Toulon; it has not even a name of independence. Therefore I shall, as far as I see at this present moment, have no hesitation in considering all Genoese Vessels as French. Everything at Genoa is French; therefore I hope that not a moment will be lost in declaring Genoa so considered. The blockade of Genoa ought to be declared instantly; if not, it will be what it always has been, the granary of the South of France, and the North part of Italy, which will be much distressed by such a measure, and I hope it will induce the Piedmontese, Genoses, &c., to rise against the French. Be that as it may, I do not think that we ought to allow the French Armies and friends to be maintained and enriched by our not blockading all the Genoese Ports. I therefore hope that this will instantly be done. The Imperial and Greek flag are filling it and Leghorn with corn.

Morea.—It is perfectly clear that the French are at work in that Country, either to prepare for their own reception, or to induce the Greeks to revolt against the Porte, and either way, it is a chain for their getting again to Egypt. If the French or their friends conquer the Morea, Egypt would be the price of returning it, unless by an alliance with the Mamelukes they can possess both. This brings to my mind the Bey, who is going to England to solicit our justice against Turkish oppression. It appears very clear that the Territory assigned them in Upper Egypt, will not maintain them and their flocks. Government will know how to steer between the Turks and Mamelukes.

July 2nd. To this long letter, I shall only beg to call your attention, for what purpose the French are collecting such an Army in Italy, where at present there can be no prospect of an Army able to face them: 13,000 are in the Kingdom of Naples, 8,000 are at this moment in Leghorn, 6,000 marched in on the 28th June, the other parts of Italy are filling with Troops, even drawing them from Switzerland. The objects must be the conquest of Naples (perhaps Sicily,) and certainly getting over to the Morea; therefore I request the removal of our Egyptian Army, which in any of these enterprises have kept the French in check: for I am sure they are afraid of that Army, and the Italians have the greatest confidence in it, and would make a struggle in their mountains; and time gained to us would be very desirable.

July 9th.—I joined our Fleet yesterday. With the casual absence of one or two Ships, we shall be always seven Sail of the Line; and as the French have at least seven—I believe nine—nearly ready, we are in hopes that Buonaparte may be angry, and order them out, which, I have no doubt, will put our Ships in high feather; for I never knew any wants after a Victory, although we are always full of them before. I will only add, that no endeavours of mine shall be wanted to gain one more, for I am worn up; and be assured that I am ever, my dear Sir, your most faithful and attached friend,

NELSON AND BRONTE

To Sir Evan Nepean, Admiralty *Amphion*, off Toulon, *8th July, 1803*

Sir,

You will please to acquaint the Lords Commissioners of the Admiralty, that I arrived off here yesterday forenoon, and was joined by Rear-Admiral Sir Richard Bickerton, with his Majesty's Ships named in the margin.

Captain Gore, of the *Medusa*, having reconnoitred the harbour of Toulon, yesterday, acquaints me that there are seven Sail of the Line in the Inner and Outer Roads, fully rigged, or nearly so, together with five Frigates, and six or seven Corvettes, in the same state of forwardness, and that there is reason to believe there is one or two Sail of the Line in the Arsenal. There is an Admiral's Flag at the main, a Rear-Admiral, and Commodore in a Line-of-Battle Ship, and a Commodore in one of the Frigates. I shall take a very early opportunity of sending a Frigate off the harbour of Toulon, in order to ascertain their state of forwardness, and watch their motions accordingly. I am, Sir, &c.,

NELSON AND BRONTE

To Sir Evan Nepean, Admiralty

Amphion, off Toulon, *12th July, 1803*

Sir,

As there is no Agent Victualler attached to the Fleet under my command, and as most of the supplies of fresh beef and other necessary refreshments for the Ships' Companies, must be procured from Sardinia, Barbary, or, clandestinely, from Spain, where Victualling or other Bills are not negotiable; and as the great distance from Malta or Gibraltar renders the getting such refreshments from those places, in a regular manner, absolutely impossible; and at all seasons, from the length of passage to Malta, must ever preclude a very frequent intercourse, I, therefore, beg leave to submit to their Lordships, (if they do not judge proper to appoint an Agent Victualler to the Fleet,) the propriety of lodging Public money on board the Fleet, for the purpose of paying for the fresh beef and vegetables which may be appropriated for this service, provided, but on no account otherwise, that their Lordships will give orders that the simple receipt from the Captain of the Ship, to whom any sum or sums of money is given, for the payment of such fresh supplies, may be a sufficient Voucher for the disbursement of such money, and a full discharge from any impress against me. And as this measure will attach a responsibility upon the Captains who may be sent for procuring fresh beef, &c., for the Fleet, I also beg that their Lordships will exonerate them from the charge, and direct the Victualling Board not to impress their Accounts for such purchases, provided the Vouchers for them are regular and correct, and that the usual forms in procuring provisions have been duly attended to, and executed accordingly.

I shall on all occasions, where live cattle, &c., are purchased for the individual Ship, or Fleet, direct the Captains to send their Masters on shore with their respective Pursers, to ascertain the prices and quality thereof, and shall direct that every pound of beef, vegetables, &c., so purchased, may be weighed on its coming on board, and entered in the Log-Book immediately, and that the Signing Officer shall examine the Vouchers with that Book, previous to their putting their signatures to them, in order that every species of fraud (should any be intended) may be detected, and the possibility of doing wrong prevented, as much as possible. I am, Sir, &c.,

NELSON AND BRONTE

To Rt. Hon. Henry Addington *27th July, 1803*

Europe seems so degraded, that I declare I would rather die with my sword in my hand resisting, than hold any Territory by means of a degenerate guarantee. Can a Kingdom be said to be free, which pays contributions at the order of a Foreign Power? No; yet such is the state of Naples, Tuscany, and Genoa. General Murat demanded at Genoa a contribution of five millions of livres on the 7th; the Government said they could only raise three; the rest must be paid in men for the Army: 1,600 men marched into Genoa on the 17th of July. Yesterday and to-day, three Corvettes have been trying to proceed to the Eastward: I am confident they want to get to the Heel of Italy and the Adriatic, and it is very difficult to prevent their passing along shore. At Marseilles they are fitting, as reports say, eighty or ninety Gun-boats, and intend sending them, by the Canal of Languedoc, to Bordeaux; but I am sure this is not true. They are to go along shore to the Heel of Italy, and to embark and protect their Army either to Sicily or the Morea, or to both; and the Navy of Europe can hardly prevent these along-shore voyages. However, I am placing an addition to the Squadron I have already stationed upon that Coast; but from Cape St. Vincent, where it is absolutely necessary I should have a look-out for the Ships of War coming from the Mediterranean, to the Head of the Adriatic, I have only eight Frigates; which, with the Service of watching Toulon, and the necessary Frigates with the Fleet, are absolutely not one half enough. I mean this as no complaint, for I am confident the Admiralty are hard pressed, and will send me more when the Service will admit it. I am, &c.,

NELSON AND BRONTE

To Sir Evan Nepean, Admiralty

Amphion, off Toulon, *27th July, 1803*

Sir,

From the various circumstances of service attached to the Naval part of my duty in these seas, which imposes upon me a correspondence from several quarters that requires a knowledge of the different languages, I have felt it necessary to apply to the Rev. Alexander John Scott, Chaplain of His Majesty's Ship *Victory*, who very handsomely offered his services as Interpreter, and as this imposes upon Mr. Scott a very laborious duty, and Interpreters having been rewarded on former occasions*, I am, therefore, to request you will please to communicate this letter to the Lords Commissioners of the Admiralty, and move them to grant such salary to the Office as they may think proper. I am, Sir, &c.,

NELSON AND BRONTE

THE VICTORY *ARRIVED AND NELSON JOINED HER ON 30th JULY*

['Saturday, 30th July. The *Victory* made her number. At 10.30 bore up and made sail.—*Amphion's* Log. 5 p.m. joined this Ship, Captain T. M. Hardy, and superseded Captain Sutton. Hoisted Lord Viscount Nelson's Flag.'—*Victory's* Log.]

To Lady Hamilton

Victory, off Toulon, *August 1st, 1803*

I do not know that you will get this letter.

My dearest Emma,

Your letter of May 31, which came under cover to Mr. Noble, of Naples, inclosing Davison's correspondence with Plymouth, arrived by the *Phoebe* two days ago: and this is the only scrap of a pen which has been received by any person in the Fleet since we sailed from England. . . .

Sutton joined me yesterday, and we are all got into the *Victory*; and a few days will put us in order. Everybody gives a very excellent character of Mr. Chevalier, the servant recommended by Mr. Davison; and I shall certainly live as frugal as my station will admit. I have known the pinch, and shall endeavour never to know it again. I want to send £2,100

* Mr. Scott was allowed £100 per annum, as in former instances of an Admiral's interpreter.

to pay off Mrs. Greaves on October 1st; but I have not received one farthing: but I hope to receive some soon. But Mr. Haslewood promised to see this matter kept right for me. Hardy is now busy, hanging up your and Horatia's picture; and I trust soon to see the other two safe arrived from the Exhibition. I want no others to ornament my cabin. I can contemplate them, and find new beauties every day, and I do not want anybody else.

You will not expect much news from us. We see nothing. I have great fear, that all Naples will fall into the hands of the French; and, if Acton does not take care, Sicily also. However, I have given my final advice so fully and strongly, that, let what will happen, they cannot blame me. Captain Capel says, Mr. Elliot cannot bear Naples. I have no doubt, but that it is very different to your time. The Queen, I fancy, by the seal, has sent a letter to Castelcicala; her letter to me is only thanks for my attention to the safety of the Kingdom. If Dr. Scott has time, and is able, he shall write a copy for you. The King is very much retired. He would not see the French General St. Cyr, who came to Naples to settle the contribution for the payment of the French Army. The Queen was ordered to give him and the French Minister a dinner, but the King stayed at Belvidere.

I think he will give it up soon, and retire to Sicily, if the French will allow him. Acton has never dared give Mr. Elliot, or one Englishman, a dinner. The Fleet are ready to come forth; but, they will not come for the sake of fighting me. I have this day made George Elliot, Post; Lieutenant Pettet, a Master and Commander; and Mr. Hindmarsh, Gunner's son, of the *Bellerophon*, who behaved so well this day five years, a Lieutenant. I reckon to have lost two French Seventy-fours, by my not coming out in the *Victory;* but I hope they will come soon, with interest. This goes to Gibraltar, by Sutton, in the *Amphion.* I shall write the Doctor* in a day or two. I see, by the French papers, that he has kissed hands. With kindest regards to your good mother, and all at Merton, &c., ever yours, most faithfully and affectionately,

NELSON AND BRONTE

To Rt. Hon. Henry Addington — *Victory*, off Toulon, *August 10th, 1803*

My dear Sir,

I have wrote to you so fully on every occasion, and so late as the 4th, that I will not take up your time by Mr. A'Court, except to say that we are all well, and only want the French Fleet to come out to make us all happy. I am making what use I can of Spain, to get water

* His brother on taking his degree of D.D., and obtaining a Prebendal Stall.

and refreshments, and shall do so as long as they will allow us; but I suppose the French will not suffer it very long. The Spaniards are selling Vessels, taken from us by the French, at public auction. I have given Mr. A'Court the advertisement to show Mr. Frere, and to carry it to England. The *Kent* is just joining from Malta. I wait her arrival before I close my letter. Sir Richard Bickerton is just come on board. All is well at Malta, therefore I will not detain Mr. A'Court one moment; and have only to assure you, that I am ever, my dear Sir, your most faithful and attached,

NELSON AND BRONTE

To Lady Hamilton

Victory, off Toulon,
August 10th, 1803

My dearest Emma,

I take the opportunity of Mr. A'Court's* going through Spain, with Mr. Elliot's dispatches for England, to send this letter; for I would not for the world miss any opportunity of sending you a line. By Gibraltar, I wrote you, as lately as the 4th; but all our ways of communicating with England, are very uncertain; and, I believe, the Admiralty must have forgot us; for not a Vessel of any kind or sort has joined us since I left Spithead. News I absolutely am ignorant of; except that a Schooner belonging to me, put her nose into Toulon, and four Frigates popped out, and have taken her, and a Transport loaded with water for the Fleet. However, I hope to have an opportunity, very soon, of paying them the debt, with interest. Mr. A'Court says, at Naples, they hope that the mediation of Russia will save them; but I doubt if Russia will go to War with the French for any Kingdom; and they, poor souls! relying on a broken reed, will lose Sicily.

As for getting anything for Bronte, I cannot expect it; for the finances of Naples are worse than ever. *Patienza*, however: I will . . .

I see, many Bishops are dead. Is my brother tired of Canterbury? I wish I could make him a Bishop. If you see him, or write, say that I have not ten minutes to send away Mr. A'Court, who cannot be detained. I hope Lord St. Vincent has sent out Sir William Bolton. As soon as I know who is First Lord, I will write him.

To Captain Moubray, H.M. Ship *Active*

August 12th, 1803

Dear Sir,

It is not my intention to close watch Toulon, even with Frigates; for I see the gentlemen want one of our Frigates. When we come in sight

* Secretary of Legation at Naples.

of Sicie, join me, and I will further explain my intentions; but I beg you will not keep too close to Sepet or Sicie in the night. I am, dear Sir, your most obedient servant,

NELSON AND BRONTE

To the French Officers, Prisoners of War, at Malta

Victory, August 13th, 1803

Gentlemen,

I have sent to offer the French Admiral in Toulon an exchange of Prisoners. After keeping the Boat waiting three hours, a message came down that the French Admiral would receive no letter or message, and ordered the Boat to return; therefore, you must blame the cruelty of your own Admiral for keeping you Prisoners. At the same time, I shall be happy to do all in my power to render your captivity as easy as possible—always remembering, Do as you would be done by. I am, Gentlemen, with great respect, your most obedient servant,

NELSON AND BRONTE

To Admiral Lord Radstock

Victory, off Toulon, *August 22nd, 1803*

My dear Lord,

Your kind letter of July 5th, I received a few days ago by George Campbell. I have had the pleasure of making acquaintance with your son. He sent me a drawing of the *Esquerques* as a present. Whenever the *Medusa* joins I will consult with Gore as to his coming directly into the *Victory*; but you may rely that he shall be made as soon after he has served his time as is in my power. The sons of Brother-Officers have an undoubted claim to our protection, and when to that is added the son of a very old friend, nothing can, my dear Lord, weigh stronger with me. Your conduct to me on the 14th of February,* has proved you a noble man; and I am sorry to say that I fear we have some Peers who do not answer that description. We are watching the coming out of the French Squadron: they are ready, and I do not think Buonaparte will allow them to remain longer in Port. Believe me ever, my dear Lord, your faithful and attached friend,

NELSON AND BRONTE

* In the Battle of St. Vincent in which Lord Radstock was third in command.

To Rt. Hon. Henry Addington *Victory*, off Toulon,
August 24th, 1803

My dear Sir,

Your time is too precious to be wasted reading unnecessarily, therefore I begin:—By the inclosed letter from the *Morea*, you will see the good disposition of Ali Vizir towards us. You will be the best judge, as things are at present, how he can be made most useful to us. The French will have him, if we do not. You will recollect this is the person who I ventured to recommend our Government sending a present of a handsome pair of pistols to, and you also thought it proper. I was so referred from the Treasury to other places, and at last to the Admiralty, who I knew could have nothing to do with it, that I gave it up, and had only to regret that it was not accomplished: a few hundred pounds would have made him ours for ever. I must apprise you, that General Villettes, although a most excellent Officer, will do nothing but what he receives, 'You are hereby required and directed'; for to obey, is with him the very acme of discipline.

With respect to Sicily, I have no doubt, from what is passing at Naples and in Sicily, but that the French will have it. My former reasons for inducing General Villettes to keep the Neapolitan Troops in Malta, was to prevent what has happened; but, in a month after my back was turned, Villettes obeyed his orders, and now the Governor of Messina says we can defend it, and want no assistance. His whole conduct, I am bold to say, is either that of a traitor or a fool; and being either one or the other is the same in its effects to the poor King of Naples. Not to use every exertion to put the fortifications in repair, when a Foreign Army is in one part of the Kingdom, is nothing short of treason; and the sixteen Gun-boats rotting at Messina, without a man, when they ought to be exercising in the Straits every day. I see clearly, if we have not a little Army to take it, the French will, I am sorry to say, and concluded that the mass of Sicilians wish for a change of Government. They wish for us; but if we will not go there, they will gladly, I fear, receive the French. The middle and lower class will be relieved from the oppression of the Nobles; they love their King and English—hate the Nobles and the French.

Sardinia.—I had a Ship from thence yesterday. The King fancies that he can point out his Neutrality. Alas, he can do nothing but what the French please! You may rely that 5,000 French, or rather Corsicans, are preparing for the invasion (say conquest) of Sardinia. They are forced to enlist from particular districts—five districts, 1,000 men each. All their camp equipage consists of nothing—a light linen jacket, trowsers, red cap, and a pair of shoes, is the whole expense of Government; a musket, accoutrements such as our gentlemen go shooting with, and a short sword. The plunder of the Sardinian Anglo-Sardes is held out as the reward. Not all our Navy can prevent it. Sardinia will be lost without a struggle, and yet the majority of the Sardinians would fly to receive us; but if we will not, then the French, in preference to remaining as they are—oppressed with taxes, and no protection from the Barbary States. I need not say what a loss it will be to us. The mode and manner of allowing us to possess the Madalena Islands, and the North part of Sardinia must be left to other heads than mine.

Corsica.—I am told, is so much oppressed by requisitions of men from that Island, that I am told they would gladly again shake off the French yoke; and this last order for the 5,000 men for the conquest of Sardinia has made them outrageous. But Buonaparte cares for nothing; he sets all his engines to work. If they succeed, it is well; and if not, he is no worse than he was.

Pardon my remarks. I am looking out for the French Squadron—perhaps you may think impatiently; but I have made up my mind never to go into Port till after the Battle, if they make me wait a year, provided the Admiralty change the Ships who cannot keep the Sea in the winter, except *Victory*, *Canopus*, *Donegal*, and *Belleisle*. The Admiralty knows the state of the others, and will relieve them as soon as they can. The *Triumph*, *Superb*, *Monmouth*, *Agincourt*, *Kent*, *Gibraltar*, and *Renown*, are certainly the very finest Ships in our Service—the best commanded, and the very best manned, yet I wish them safe in England, where they would man, filled up with landsmen, fourteen Sail of the Line, and that I had Ships not half so well manned in their room; for it is not a Store-Ship a week which could keep them in repair. This day, only six men are confined to their beds in the whole Squadron. With every good wish for your brilliant success, and for getting us an honourable and permanent Peace, believe me, my dear Sir, with the truest esteem, your most obliged and faithful,

NELSON AND BRONTE

To Sir Evan Nepean, Admiralty

Victory, off Toulon,
24th August, 1803

Sir,

I am to request you will be pleased to represent to the Lords Commissioners of the Admiralty, the situation of the Fleet under my command off this place, with respect to fuel; at present, there is not more upon an average than a month's fuel on board for each Ship, that should we be cut off from supplies of fire-wood, &c., from Sardinia, it is easy to judge the distress the Ships must naturally experience from want of fuel. I therefore beg you will suggest to their Lordships the propriety of sending out Vessels loaded with coals for the use of His Majesty's Ships under my command, together with such quantities of candles as may be deemed necessary for the supply of those Pursers who may stand in need of them, as was done during the time Earl St. Vincent and Lord Keith commanded the Fleet in these Seas. I am, &c.,

NELSON AND BRONTE

To Mr. Drummond, Constantinople *27th August, 1803*

According to the reports of Vessels spoken from Marseilles and Genoa, the War is very unpopular, and I hope it will end in the destruction of that man of tyranny, Buonaparte; but I detest Europe for being so mean-spirited as to submit to the mandates of this Corsican—I blush for their meanness. In Ireland, the Militia have vied with the Regulars who should act best. If we are but true to ourselves, a fig for the great Buonaparte. I am, &c.,

NELSON AND BRONTE

To Mr. Drummond, Constantinople *27th August, 1803*

I have the honour to address your Excellency on a subject which calls loudly for redress and prevention in future. It is the acknowledged right of all lawful Cruisers to examine the Papers of Vessels hoisting Neutral Colours, in order to ascertain whether the property of Enemies, not contraband articles, be carried on board them; and it is the acknowledged Law of Nations, that resistance to such search is confiscation of Ship and Cargo on the principle that such act of hostility makes the Ship and Crew Enemies. It has, I am sorry to say, been invariably the practice of the Greeks, whenever they fancied themselves superior, for their Vessels or Boats to fire on the English flag; and to endeavour to kill the English, who were only executing their bounden duty in examining all Ships and Vessels. When I had the command of the *Agamemnon*, I had sixteen men killed by these Greeks . . . I have earnestly to request that your Excellency will obtain an order to the Greek Islands that their Vessels do not fire on the English flag; for certainly the smaller the Vessel coming, the less cause for firing. I am, &c.,

NELSON AND BRONTE

To James Tough, Esq.,
H.M. Consul-General in Sicily

Victory, off Toulon,
2nd September, 1803

Sir,

A convoy will sail from Malta on the 25th instant, or as soon after as possible for England, and, therefore, if there are any Vessels intended to avail themselves of such protection, they must be at Malta by that time: you will please to inform the Merchants of Sicily, and desire them to acquaint the senior Naval Officer at Malta, on what day the Ships from the different ports of Sicily will be ready, that he may send a Ship of War for them. The Merchant Ships, I understand, have been in the habit of proceeding without Convoy to England and Malta. The consequence has been that several have fallen into the hands of the Enemy; I must therefore desire you will be so good as acquaint the Merchants of Sicily, that should any of their Trade proceed without Convoy, after this public notice, I shall send an account to Lloyd's Coffee-House of the circumstance. I am, &c.,

NELSON AND BRONTE

To William Haslewood, Craven St., Strand

About 6th September, 1803

Private for yourself—and most secret.

My dear Haslewood,

I send you home a Codicil to my Will, which you will not communicate to any person breathing; as I would wish you to open, read it, and if not drawn up properly, send me a copy, and I will execute it. It is possible that my personal estate, after the disposal of the furniture at Merton, may not amount to £4,000; and sooner than this legacy, or any other, should go unpaid, I would saddle Bronte, or any other estate with the legacies. I only mention this as a thing which might happen; and I want to give several other small legacies, and continue the annuity of £100 a year to poor blind Mrs. Nelson.* I may congratulate you on the favourable termination (I hope) of my law-suit†. You have acted not only as able lawyers, but a most friendly part through the whole business, I beg you will express my thanks to Serjeant Shepherd, who has done so much justice to the cause; and be assured, I am ever, my dear Haslewood, your obliged friend,

NELSON AND BRONTE

* The widow of his brother, Maurice Nelson.
† With the Earl of St. Vincent.

To the respective Captains and Commanders
of His Majesty's Ships and Vessels
on the Mediterranean Station.

Victory, off Toulon,
13th September, 1803

When British Seamen and Marines so far degrade themselves in time of War, as to desert from the Service of their own Country, and enter into that of Spain; when they leave one shilling per day, and plenty of the best provisions, with every comfort that can be thought of for them —for twopence a day, black bread, horse-beans, and stinking oil for their food;—when British Seamen or Marines turn Spanish Soldiers, I blush for them: they forfeit in their own opinion, I am sure, that character of love of their own Country, which Foreigners are taught to admire. A Briton to put himself under the lash of a Frenchman or Spaniard must be more degrading to any man of spirit than any punishment I could inflict on their bodies. I shall leave the punishment to their own feelings, which, if they have any, and are still Englishmen, must be very great. But, as they thought proper to abandon, voluntarily, their wives, fathers, mothers, and every endearing tie, and, also, all prospect of returning to their native Country, I shall make them remain out of that Country, which they do not wish to see, and allow others, who love their Country, and are attached to their families, to return in their stead. And, as they have also thought proper to resign all their pay, I shall take care that it is not returned to them, nor their 'R' taken off, but it shall be noted against their names, 'Deserted to the Spaniards', or 'Entered as a Spanish Soldier,' as the case was.

NELSON AND BRONTE

The above Memorandum respecting the desertion of British Seamen or Marines is to be read to the respective Companies of His Majesty's Ships and Vessels under my command, and copies thereof, to be stuck up in the most public places of the Ships, in order that the magnitude of the crime may be properly impressed on their minds.

NELSON AND BRONTE

To Lady Hamilton

Victory, off Toulon,
September 18th, 1803

My dear Lady Hamilton,

The furniture and linen which was left behind at Palermo and Naples, when you came to England, is, I hope, by this time, safe at Malta. I have desired Mr. Noble to unpack, dry them, and send you a list of the contents, which you must send to the Treasury, in order to obtain an order for their being allowed to come direct to you, without passing through the Custom-House. I believe the cases are eighteen in number. I have requested the favour of Mr. Brown, Commander of the *Prevoyante* Store-Ship, who will carry them either to Portsmouth or the Nore, to whichever place he may be ordered. If you will apply by letter to my friend, Mr. Vansittart, of the Treasury, I am sure he will send an order directly for their delivery. Only tell me, my dear Friend, in what manner I can be useful to you in this Country, and believe me, I shall be truly proud in obeying your commands, being for ever, your most obliged, faithful, and affectionate,

NELSON AND BRONTE

To Sir Evan Nepean, Admiralty

Victory, off Toulon,
24th September, 1803

Sir,

As it is more than probable that the Fleet under my command will be obliged to keep the seas during the whole of the winter season, for the purpose of watching the Enemy's Ships at Toulon, and as there is in the Gulf of Lyons and its vicinity, upon an average, three days' gale of severe blowing weather out of the seven, which frequently comes on suddenly, and thereby exposes the topmasts, topsails and sails to great hazard, under every care and attention; I am therefore to desire you will be pleased to communicate this circumstance to the Lords Commissioners of the Admiralty, and suggest to their Lordships the propriety of sending out a sufficient number of topmasts, topsail-yards, and spare sails for the ships, they may judge necessary for the service before-mentioned, as early as possible, there being none of the two former in store, either at Gibraltar or Malta. I am, &c.,

NELSON AND BRONTE

To Lady Hamilton

September 26th, 1803

My dearest Emma,

We have had, for these fourteen days past, nothing but gales of wind, and a heavy sea. However, as our Ships have suffered no damage, I hope to be able to keep the sea all the winter. Nothing, but dire necessity, shall force me to that out of the way place, Malta. If I had depended upon that Island for supplies for the Fleet, we must all have been knocked up long ago; for, Sir Richard Bickerton sailed from Malta, the same day I left Portsmouth, so that we have been a pretty long cruise; and, if I had only to look to Malta for supplies, our Ships companies would have been done for long ago. However, by management, I have got supplies from Spain, and also from France; but it appears, that we are almost shut out from Spain, for they begin to be very uncivil to our Ships. However, I suppose, by this time, something is settled; but, I never hear from England. My last letters are July 6th, near three months. But, as I get French newspapers occasionally, we guess how matters are going on.

I have wrote Mr. Gibbs, again, a long history about Bronte; and, I hope, if General Acton will do nothing for me, that he will settle something; but, I know, whatever is settled, I shall be the loser. Till next year, the debt will not be paid off; how . . .

To the Earl of St. Vincent *Victory*, off Toulon, *September 27th, 1803*

My dear Lord,

It is now near three months since my last letters were dated from England; and but for a French newspaper, which hitherto we have procured through Spain from Paris, we should not have known how the world went on; and reports have so often changed the First Lord of the Admiralty, that I know not if I am now writing to him; but that does not matter; I trust I am writing to an old friend, who sincerely wishes me as well as I do him.

I have said all my say long ago on the subject of the Ships here; therefore, I shall not bore you on that subject again. The fact is this—all the Ships have expected every day before the War, to go to England; therefore, when the War came, they wanted for everything—more especially to go to England. However, a good deal of that fever is wore off, and we are really got to a state of health which is rarely witnessed. I have exerted myself to get all the good things we could from Spain, and latterly our cattle and onions have been procured from France; but from the apparent incivilities of the Spaniards, I suppose we are on the eve of being shut out. Our length of passage from Malta is terrible. We have not procured one single article of refreshment from thence since the Fleet sailed (May 18th); therefore, if a Fleet here had only Malta to trust to, the Fleet must go to Malta, for the good things of Malta could never come to us; and in that case the French might do as they pleased, between here and Gibraltar for two months together. At this moment, I think the Squadron, as far as relates to me, are fit to go to Madras. Their hulls want docking. I hope to be able to keep the sea all the winter—in short, to stay at sea till the French choose to come to sea; and then I hope to send many of our Ships who want what I cannot give them, to England, towing a Line-of-Battle Ship. I believe we are uncommonly well disposed to give the French a thrashing, and we are keen; for I have not seen a French flag on the sea since I joined the Squadron. A fortnight ago, three or four Sail of the Line were under sail, and some had got a few miles from Sepet, but I believe it was only for an exercise. Reports say they are hard at work, fitting out two new 80-gun Ships. Their lower rigging is over the mast-heads. I wish they would make haste, for our gales of wind, Admiral Campbell says, are harder and more frequent than ever. I believe them much the same—always very violent, and a heavy sea. But it is time to finish; therefore I shall only say that I am ever, my dear Lord, your most faithful friend,

NELSON AND BRONTE

To Admiral Sir Peter Parker *14th October, 1803*

Your grandson* came to me, with your kind letter of August 20th, on October 6th; nothing could be more grateful to my feelings than receiving him. I have kept him as Lieutenant of the *Victory*, and shall not part with him until I can make him a Post Captain; which you may be assured I shall lose no time in doing; It is the only opportunity ever offered me, of showing that my feelings of gratitude to you are as warm and alive as when you first took me by the hand: I owe all my Honours to you, and I am proud to acknowledge it to all the world. Lord St. Vincent has most strongly and kindly desired your grandson's promotion; therefore I can only be the instrument of expediting it. Believe me ever, my dear Sir Peter, your most grateful and sincerely attached friend,

NELSON AND BRONTE

To the Duke of Clarence Off Toulon, *15th October, 1803*

I am absolutely, Sir, beginning this letter in a fever of the mind. It is thick as butter-milk, and blowing a Levanter; and the *Narcissus* has just spoke to me to say, 'She boarded a Vessel, and they understood that the men had seen, a few days before, twelve Sail of Ships of War off Minorca. It was in the dusk, and he did not know which way they were steering.' This is the whole story, and a lame one. On the 8th, the French Fleet, as counted by Captain Boyle, was eight Sail of the Line; four Frigates, and some Corvettes. On the 9th, it blew a tremendous storm at N.W. which lasted till the 12th, since which time, although *Seahorse* and *Renown* are endeavouring to reconnoitre, it is so thick that I do not think they can either see into Toulon, or find me if they do. Your Royal

* Afterwards Captain Sir Peter Parker, Bart., who fell at the storming of an American camp, near Baltimore, on the 30th of August, 1814.

Highness will readily imagine my feelings, although I cannot bring my mind to believe they are actually out; but to miss them—God forbid! They are my superior in numbers, but in everything else, I believe, I have the happiness of commanding the finest Squadron in the world—*Victory*, *Kent*, *Superb*, *Triumph*, *Belleisle*, and *Renown*. Admiral Campbell is gone to Sardinia, and I have been anxiously expecting him these ten days. If I should miss these fellows, my heart will break: I am actually only now recovering the shock of missing them in 1798, when they were going to Egypt. If I miss them, I will give up the cudgels to some more fortunate Commander; God knows I only serve to fight those scoundrels; and if I cannot do that, I should be better on shore.

October 16th.—*The Seahorse* spoke me in the night; and made known that the Enemy were in the same state as when last reconnoitred on the 8th. I believe this was the only time in my life, that I was glad to hear the French were in Port. I think Captain Keats is very much better in his health; he is a most valuable Officer, and does honour to your friendship. Every day increases my esteem for him, both as an Officer and a man, I am, &c.,

NELSON AND BRONTE

To His Excellency John Hookham Frere, Madrid

Apparently about 20th October, 1803

I trust that Spain will be too wise to go to War with us. We ought, by mutual consent, to be the very best friends, and both to be ever hostile to France . . . As probably this letter will be read before it gets to you, I can only tell the reader, that a British Fleet never was in higher order, health, and good humour, than the one I have the happiness to command; and if the French do not rue the day when we get alongside of them, it will not be the fault of the Captains, Officers, or Men, but must be that of your Excellency's most obedient servant,

NELSON AND BRONTE

To Miss Horatia Nelson Thomson
(*age* $2\frac{1}{2}$)

Victory, off Toulon,
October 21st, 1803

My dear Child,

Receive this first letter from your most affectionate Father. If I live, it will be my pride to see you virtuously brought up, but if it pleases God to call me, I trust to Himself: in that case, I have left Lady H. your guardian. I therefore charge you, my Child, on the value of a Father's blessing, to be obedient and attentive to all her kind admonitions and instructions. At this moment I have left you, in a Codicil* dated the 6th of September, the sum of four thousand pounds sterling, the interest of which is to be paid to your guardian for your maintenance and education. I shall only say, my dear Child, may God Almighty bless you and make you an ornament to your sex, which I am sure you will be if you attend to all Lady H's kind instructions; and be assured that I am, my dear Horatia, your most affectionate Father,

NELSON AND BRONTE

To Alexander Davison, Esq.

Victory, off Toulon,
October 21st, 1803

My dear Davison,

Your original letter of the 15th of August I received by the *Childers*, and I have not seen a single Vessel since, that could give me the least news. We are looking out for a Spanish War, and for the sailing of the French Fleet, both very great events to us. Our weather has never been good, but it is now terrible. Such a place for storms of wind I never met with, and I am unfortunately in bad weather, always sea-sick. We ought to be amply repaid some day for all our toil. I trust before next winter that we shall have Peace, and be all quiet at home. By a Vessel just spoke from Marseilles, they report that 40,000 Troops are marching into the South of Italy, but we can believe nothing these Neutrals say; and yet it may be true enough, if they intend to cross to the Morea, or Egypt. I am ever, my dear Davison, most affectionately yours,

NELSON AND BRONTE

Hardy desires his compliments.

* In a codicil to his will, dated 6th September, 1803, Nelson made the bequest to his daughter:

'I give and bequeath to Miss Horatia Nelson Thomson (who was baptized on the 15th day of May last, in the Parish of St. Mary-le-bone, and whom I acknowledge as my adopted daughter) the sum of £4,000 to be paid at the expiration of six months after my decease, or sooner, if possible; and I leave my dearest friend Emma Lady Hamilton, sole guardian of the said Horatia Nelson Thomson, until she shall have arrived at the age of eighteen years; and the interest of the said £4,000 to be paid to Lady Hamilton for her education and maintenance. This request of guardianship I earnestly make to Lady Hamilton, knowing that she will educate my adopted child in the paths of religion and virtue, and give her those accomplishments which so much adorn herself, and I hope make her a fit wife for my dear nephew, Horatio Nelson, who I wish to marry her, if he should prove worthy, in Lady Hamilton's estimation, of such a treasure as I am sure she will be.'

To His Excellency Hugh Elliot *Victory*, Madalena Islands, *November 1st, 1803*

My dear Sir,

The Fleet being very much in want of water, I have taken the opportunity of the moonlight nights to come here, in order to obtain it, and some refreshments for our crews, who have now been upwards of five months at sea. But our health and good humour is perfection, and we only want the French Fleet out. This day week they had eight Sail of the Line ready, and a ninth fitting; so that we shall surely meet them some happy day, and I have no doubt but that we shall be amply repaid for all our cares and watchings. I have left Frigates to watch them. The *Raven* goes to Naples in order to obtain candles, and other things of which we stand in need, and I hope she will be favoured with the winds, and catch us here.

I have not a word of news from any quarter, and I have only to hope that all goes well in the Two Sicilies. I should be happy, was it in my power, to communicate oftener with you, and dire necessity only obliges me to send the *Raven*, and I am left without a small Vessel. Pray, tell me, can I write to England through Naples with safety? How do your dispatches go? I am ever, my dear Sir, your Excellency's most faithful and obliged servant,

NELSON AND BRONTE

Captain Murray, Hardy, and Dr. Scott, desire their compliments. My letters I send as I can, generally to Gibraltar. The other routes are uncertain, and I have no spare Vessels. I feel even parting with the *Cameleon*, and he has strict orders to join me as soon as possible.

To Sir Alexander John Ball, Malta *Victory*, Madalena Islands, *November 7th, 1803*

My dear Ball,

I do not think a Spanish War so near. We are more likely to go to War with Spain for her complaisance to the French; but the French can gain nothing, but be great losers, by forcing Spain to go to War with us; therefore, I never expect that the Spaniards will begin, unless Buonaparte is absolutely mad, as many say he is. What! he begins to find excuses! I thought he would invade England in the face of the Sun! Now he wants a three days' fog, that never yet happened! and if it did, how is his Craft to be kept together? He will soon find more excuses or there will be an end of Buonaparte, and may the Devil take him!

Our two last reconnoiterings: Toulon has eight Sail of the Line, apparently ready for sea, five or six Frigates, and as many Corvettes—they count twenty-two Sail of Ships of War; a Seventy-four is repairing;

whether they intend waiting for her I can't tell, but I expect them every hour to put to sea, and with Troops, but their destination?—is it Ireland or the Levant? That is what I want to know. However, out they will come, and I trust, we shall meet them. The event, with God's blessing on our exertions, we ought not to doubt; I really believe that we are the 'strong pull and pull together'. With this force opposed to me, I cannot with prudence leave myself with less than six Sail of the Line, and from various circumstances, Ships going to water, &c., I am too often with only five Frigates, and Smaller Vessels I am most distressed for. However, I send the *Raven* to be under Captain Schomberg's particular orders, for upon every occasion I had rather leave myself bare than have my friends complain. Lord St. Vincent's words are, 'We can send you neither Ships or Men, and with the resources of your mind, you will do without them very well.' Bravo, my Lord. I have all the inclination in the world to send Sir Richard Bickerton to Malta, but I dare not do it at this moment—not so much for the want of the Ship, but from my sincere esteem for the Admiral, and in charity to them both; for if the Battle took place, and Sir Richard absent, they would have reason to curse me for ever. But you may assure her Ladyship, that I know what attachment is, and that the Admiral shall be the first detached after the Battle; and if I can, on any belief that the Enemy are not coming immediately to sea, he shall go before the Battle. Remember me kindly to Macaulay and all our friends at Malta. I admire your Malta Gazettes; it is the custom and a very bad one, for the English, never to tell their own story, and you have put it well together. This Anchorage is certainly one of the best I have met with for a Fleet—water, brooms, sand, onions, some beef, plenty of sheep, and but little of aqua denta; but I suppose the French will take it now we have used it. I am ever, my dear Ball, most sincerely and faithfully yours,

NELSON AND BRONTE

No wonder Neutral Powers complain, when we do not send out a Judge of the Admiralty; it is cruel both to the Detainer, and the Neutral.

To the respective Captains nd Commanders
of His Majesty's Ships and Vessels
on the Mediterranean Station.

Victory, Madalena Islands,
7th November, 1803

Memorandum.

Lord Nelson is very sorry to find that notwithstanding his forgiveness of the men who deserted in Spain, it has failed to have its proper effect, and that there are still men who so far forget their duty to their King and Country, as to desert the Service, at a time when every man in England is in arms to defend it against the French. Therefore Lord Nelson desires that it may be perfectly understood, that if any man be so infamous as to desert from the Service in future, he will not only be brought to a Court-Martial, but that if the sentence should be Death, it will be most assuredly carried into execution.

NELSON AND BRONTE

To Sir Evan Nepean, Admiralty

Victory, off Toulon,
24th November, 1803

Sir,

The Fleet being very short of wood and water, you will please to acquaint the Lords Commissioners of the Admiralty, that I judged it better to go to the Madalena Islands in order to obtain it, than to separate the Fleet, as by experience it is found almost impossible, in the continued gales of wind at this season, for any Ship to be certain of joining in any given time; I therefore left Frigates off Toulon, and proceeded to the Madalena Islands, where having procured wood and water and some refreshments I returned to my Rendezvous. The Chart of Captain Ryves, which the Board has received, is the most correct thing I ever met with. The Fleet worked up from Asinara, with a strong East wind, to the anchorage, with perfect ease, from the Chart and directions; and Captain Ryves deserves the greatest credit for the accuracy of his Chart and remarks. The remarks I send you, and I would recommend their insertion in the Chart. I am, Sir, &c.,

NELSON AND BRONTE

To the Duke of Clarence

Off Toulon,
December 7th, 1803

The French Fleet keep us waiting for them during a long and severe winter's cruise; and such a place as all the Gulf of Lyons, for gales of wind from the N.W. to N.E. I never saw; but by always going away large, we generally lose much of their force and the heavy sea of the gulf. However, by the great care and attention of every Captain, we have suffered much less than could have been expected. I hope now to be allowed to call Keats my friend. He is very much recovered, and cheerful; he is a treasure to the Service. By the French Papers, which we have to November 19th, we are in momentary expectation of Buonaparte's descent upon England; and although I can have no fears for the event, yet there is, I hope, a natural anxiety to hear what is passing at so critical a moment, when everything we hold dear in this world is at stake. I trust in God, Buonaparte will be destroyed, and that then the French may be brought, if the Powers of Europe have either spirit or honour, to reasonable terms of Peace: that this may be soon, and with honour to our Country, is my fervent prayer, and shall ever be my most ardent endeavour. I am, &c.,

NELSON AND BRONTE

To the respective Captains and Commanders
of H.M. Ships and Vessels
of the Mediterranean Station.

Victory, at Sea,
10th December, 1803

Whereas, Robert Dwyer, a Private Marine belonging to His Majesty's Ship *Belleisle*, was, by the sentence of a Court-Martial held on him the 4th ultimo, to receive 500 lashes for disobedience of orders and insolence to his Superior Officer, crimes of the most serious nature, and for which the delinquent no doubt looked forward to the awful sentence of death being pronounced upon him, instead of the corporal punishment above-mentioned; and, although the said Robert Dwyer has received only part of his punishment, yet it being the first offence of a public nature which has been brought to trial since my taking upon me the command of His Majesty's Fleet in the Mediterranean, and the respective Captains having particularly mentioned to me the very orderly conduct and good behaviour of their Ship's Companies, I am, therefore, induced from these circumstances to remit the remainder of the said Robert Dwyer's punishment; but I must desire it to be perfectly understood and to warn the respective Ships' Companies against the commission of crimes of a similar or any other nature, as well as against the shameful, disgraceful crime of Desertion as the sentence of the Court-Martial for either of these offences, be it death or otherwise, will most certainly be inflicted without mitigation.

NELSON AND BRONTE

To James Cutforth,
Agent Victualler, Gibraltar

Victory, Gulf of Palma,
13th December, 1803

Sir,

As rice and sugar are but poor substitutes for butter and cheese, and, in general, not much liked by the Ships' Companies, I am to desire you will (if the price does not exceed that of rice and sugar) purchase cocoa and sugar, in lieu of butter and cheese, for the Fleet under my command —at least, for occasional supplies, and provided the stores under your charge are not over-stocked with rice, in which case you will submit my letter to the Commissioners of the Victualling for their direction. I am, &c.,

NELSON AND BRONTE

To Charles Connor, H.M. Ship *Niger*

December, 1803

Dear Charles,

As Captain Hillyar has been so good as to say he would rate you Mid., I sincerely hope that your conduct will ever continue to deserve his kind notice and protection, by a strict and very active attention to your duty. If you deserve well, you are sure of my assistance. Mr. Scott will furnish you with money to begin your mess, and I shall allow you thirty pounds a year, if it be necessary, which Captain Hillyar will supply you with. And as you from this day start in the world as a man, I trust that your future conduct in life will prove you both an Officer and a Gentleman. Recollect that you must be a Seaman to be an Officer, and also, that you cannot be a good Officer without being a Gentleman. I am always, with most sincere good wishes, your true friend,

NELSON AND BRONTE

To the Reverend Dr. Nelson

Victory, December 14th, 1803

My dear Brother,

I thank you much for your letter, and am always sure of your unalterable regard and affection. Most certainly, if you send out Charles Brown, I will (if he has served his Time during my stay here) if opportunity offers, promote him; but next Christmas, please God, I shall be at Merton; for, by that time, with all the anxiety attendant on such a Command as this, I shall be done up. The mind and body wear out, and my eye is every month visibly getting worse, and, I much fear, it will end in total blindness. The moment the Battle is over, if I am victorious I shall ask for my retreat,—if, unfortunately, the contrary, I hope never to live to see it. In that case, you will get an early Seat in the House of Lords. If Mr. Addington does not give me the same Pension as Government gave to the rich Lord St. Vincent and Duncan, I shall consider no great favour done me, and the Country never could avoid giving the Pension to you: therefore, unless the other is tacked to it, I would not give thanks or sixpence to have it brought before Parliament to benefit Lord St. Vincent's heirs, and certainly, from circumstances, not mine. The putting the stone over poor Maurice was well done, and I approve very much. I do not know that you owe me anything respecting Hillborough; but if you do, I fully acquit you of the debt, and so let it be considered.

The Ministers ought to have done more for you; but if you are made more comfortable, that is well. I have wrote to Horace at Eton, as I suppose his holidays will be over before this letter gets to Canterbury. I desire my kindest regards to Mrs. Nelson; and believe me ever your most affectionate brother,

NELSON AND BRONTE

1804

To Captain T. F. Fremantle *About the beginning of January, 1804*

I trust, my dear Fremantle, in God and in English valour. We are enough in England, if true to ourselves. He may by chance injure us, but can never conquer a determined people. It would be well if the generality of Englishmen would remember that they who know the whole machine, can better keep it going than we who only see a very small part. Although I am naturally anxious for the issue of the attempt, yet I cannot doubt of the final event—it will be the ruin of that infamous Buonaparte, and give us an honourable Peace. I should most assuredly rejoice to have you here, but we none of us see the inside of a Port: I have twice taken shelter under the Madalena Islands on the North end of Sardinia, which form a very fine anchorage. The Village, I am told, for I have not set my foot out of the *Victory*, contains forty or fifty small houses. As to Malta, it is a perfectly useless place for Great Britain; and as a Naval Port to refit in, I would much sooner undertake to answer for the Toulon Fleet from St. Helens, than from Malta; I never dare venture to carry the Fleet there. I know your friends think differently from me, but they talk of what they know nothing about in that respect, and I know it from dear-bought experience. During the winter, generally speaking, I cannot get even a Frigate from Malta, the Westerly winds are so prevalent; and as they approach the Gulf of Lyons they are blown to the South end of Sardinia. Perseverance has done much for us, but flesh and blood can hardly stand it. I have managed to get some fresh provision from Rosas in Spain, which with onions and lemons have kept us remarkably healthy. We are longing for the French Fleet, which is to finish our hard fate. I am, &c.,

NELSON AND BRONTE

To Sir Evan Nepean, Admiralty

Victory, at Sea,
10th January, 1804

Sir,

You will please to acquaint the Lords Commissioners of the Admiralty, that the Enemy's Squadron at Toulon is still in Port, and that by Captain Donnelly's account, who reconnoitred them on the 6th Instant, they are apparently ready for sea; their force nine Sail of the Line and Frigates, the same as when last reported to you. From the information I have received, there is every reason to believe that the Enemy intend sending a force from Corsica, to take possession of the Madalena Islands, with a view to prevent us from using that place as an anchorage. I have, therefore, left the *Amazon* to bring me an account of their proceedings, and have ordered the *Cameleon* to proceed there and remain for the protection of the Inhabitants, and endeavour, if possible, to frustrate the Enemy's intention of landing. I am, Sir, &c.,

NELSON AND BRONTE

To Mrs. Bolton

Victory, January 11th, 1804

My dear Sister,

Your kind letter of October 9th, is just arrived; and you may rest assured that, although I may not write or make all sorts of professions, which I might never have the power of accomplishing, yet I am not less anxious for your and Mr. Bolton's interest in every respect. Sir William Bolton has not yet been fortunate; and if I knew where to place him in fortune's way, he should go. If a Spanish War comes on, he is sure of one, or he must be truly unlucky. With respect to Tom, although I do not know if it be absolutely in my power to say I will entirely keep him at College, yet you may be sure of my assistance; and when poor blindy goes the way of all flesh, and please God some other vacancies which at present drain my pocket very deeply, I shall be more at my ease in pecuniary matters, and, of course, better able to afford permanent assistance. You know, my dear Sister, how I have teazed and teazed for that paltry Prebendary, and I really believe no Minister would give me a place of £50 a year; but if I know what Mr. Bolton looks to, I shall then know how to act. My sincere friendship for him, independent of his relationship, would induce me to do everything in my power to meet his wishes, and that, I trust, he is sure of; but he knows I have had, in reality, not an atom of interest. The French having no trade in the Mediterranean, but very little has been done in the Prize way; indeed, I am afraid my pursuits lays another way. I never did, or could, turn my thoughts to money-making. With most affectionate regards to Mr.

Bolton and all your family, believe me ever, my dear Sister, your most affectionate brother,

NELSON AND BRONTE

I am glad to hear such a good account of Mr. Suckling of Wootton. He is most perfectly right to keep his carriage and live comfortably. Remember me kindly to him, and assure him that no person rejoices more at his comfortable situation than myself.

To Lady Hamilton *Victory, January 20th, 1804*

I send a very neat watch for our god-child, and you will see it is by a good maker, that is, I suppose it will tick for a year instead of a month or two. You will impress her that it is only to be worn when she behaves well and is obedient. I am very sorry that your comb is not arrived; the brig is at Malta, but I daresay it will arrive sometime, and you shall have it at the first opportunity. I send you Mr. Falconet's letter. You will see how very civil both of them are. Mr. Elliot is a great Minister, but I doubt whether the Queen has much real friendship for him. Acton has him fast, but I believe that Mr. Elliot had rather that Acton and the King and Queen looked to him for my services than applying to myself; but circumstanced as I have been and am with that Court Sir William Hamilton gave it up, and no other person shall deprive me of the immediate communication. No, my dear Emma, what I do for them shall be from myself, and not through him. They are in very great fears at this moment.

I have been towards Algiers, where I sent a ship with Mr. Falcon, our Consul, who the Dey turned away; but the Dey has been made so insolent by Mr. North's conduct in giving him 30,000*l.*, that nothing I suppose but a flogging will put him in order, and with the French Fleet ready to put to sea that I have not time for. I have been, my own Emma, but very indifferent, a violent cold upon my breast. Asses milk would have done me much service, but I am better, and I hope to continue so till the Battle is over, then I hope my business here will be finished; that it may be soon is the sincere wish of, my dearest Emma, your ever most faithful and affectionate, &c.,

I send you the Queen's last letter. Dr. Scott, I fear, will not have time to copy the other. I am hard pressed for time, and am not very stout to-day.

To Admiral . . .

[In reply to a friend of Admiral Sir John Borlase Warren, requesting Nelson's intercession on behalf of a young Officer who had behaved improperly to his Captain, and who was, in consequence, to be brought to a Court-Martial.]

About January, 1804

We would all do everything in our power, to oblige so gallant and good an Officer as our friend Warren; but what would he do, if he were here? exactly what I have done, and am still willing to do. The young man must write such a letter of contrition as would be an acknowledgment of his great fault, and with a sincere promise, if his Captain will intercede to prevent the impending Court-Martial, never to so misbehave again. On his Captain's enclosing me such a letter, with a request to cancel the order for the Trial, I might be induced to do it; but the letters and reprimand will be given in the Public Order-Book of the Fleet, and read to all the Officers. The young man has pushed himself forward to notice, and he must take the consequence. We must recollect, my dear Admiral, it was upon the Quarter-deck, in the face of the Ship's Company, that he treated his Captain with contempt; and I am in duty bound to support the authority and consequence of every Officer under my command. A poor ignorant Seaman is for ever punished for contempt to *his* superior. I am, &c.,

NELSON AND BRONTE

To Captain Ryves, H.M. Ship *Gibraltar*

Victory, Madalena,
February 10th, 1804

My dear Sir,

It is with sincerest sorrow that I am to be the bearer of such news as will distress you very much, but, for the sake of your dear children, you must bear up against the heavy misfortune. To attempt consolation at such a time is, I know, out of the question: therefore, I can only assure you of my sincere condolence, and that I am, your most faithful friend,

NELSON AND BRONTE

To Sir John Acton

Victory, Madalena,
February 10th, 1804

My dear Sir John,

Since my letter of January 30th (which has never left the Ship) I have been off Toulon, but it blew such a violent storm of wind and snow, that I was obliged to bear up, and passing round Cape Corse, was glad to get here again, and shall sail the 13th at furthest.

I am now rather led to believe that the Ferrol Squadron of French Ships will push for the Mediterranean. The French Ship at Cadiz is ready to join them. I shall try to intercept them, but I cannot go so far to the Westward as is necessary; for I will not lose sight of the Toulon Fleet. What a most zealous man can do to meet all points of difficulty, shall be done. My Squadron is the finest for its numbers in the world, and much may be expected from it; and should superior numbers join, we must look it in the face. Nil desperandum! God is good, and our cause is just. The assemblage of Troops at Nice is going on; and, although Sardinia, Naples, and Sicily, may be some of the objects, yet I have no doubt by Egypt is the favourite and ultimate object of the Corsican tyrant. I beg you will assure their Majesties that Nelson is Nelson still, and most zealously attached to their service; and I am, my dear Sir John, your Excellency's most faithful friend,

NELSON AND BRONTE

P.S. I send two letters from Dumourier. Your Excellency will judge from his character whether he could at any period be useful to Naples: I have a very high opinion of his abilities. I had, to December 29th, letters from Lady Hamilton, who desires me to present her best compliments to your Excellency, and to Lady Acton.

To Sir Alexander John Ball, Malta

Victory, February 11th, 1804

Private.

My dear Ball,

Many, many thanks for your kind letters, oranges, &c., &c., as Hallowell has been with you he will tell you all the English news, therefore, I have little to say, except that now all my force, except Gibraltar, is united, and for our numbers none better can be. If the Ferrol Squadron joins the Toulon, they will much outnumber us; but in that case I shall never lose sight of them; and Sir Edward Pellew will soon be after them. The loss of the *Raven* is very great, and the Admiralty seem determined not to increase my force. I, at this moment, want ten Frigates or Sloops, when I believe neither the Ferrol or Toulon Squadron could escape me; the *Diana* is ordered home from Gibraltar—it is shameful: Lord St. Vincent was not treated so. The moment I can possibly part with a Vessel, you shall have another in the room of the *Raven*. We are, my dear friend, on the eve of great events; the sooner they come the better; 12,000 men are ready for embarkation at Toulon, and 16,000 at Nice, and as they have not Transports, they must naturally expect more Ships of War; the Admiralty tells me nothing, they know nothing; but my private letters say, that the Brest Squadron, as well as Ferrol, is bound here—if so, we shall have work enough upon our hands.

But, I am sure of my present force as far as it will go; we shall come to no harm. I send a packet for Mr. Drummond; when opportunity offers, pray send it to Patras, Corfu, or Smyrna, and ever believe me, dear Ball, yours most truly and faithfully,

NELSON AND BRONTE

We are all well.

To Captain Gore, H.M. Ship *Medusa* *17th February, 1804*

The Admiralty seem to think that the Spaniards may be hostile to us, and therefore have put me on my guard. Do not let it escape your lips—I am determined to have the first blow; even if they come with their whole eighteen, they shall not join the French. If they come up the Mediterranean, and you have a mind for a shooting party, come with your Frigates. Every part of your conduct is like yourself, perfect. Your letters will be answered formally. I am, &c.,

NELSON AND BRONTE

To Doctor Moseley, Chelsea Hospital

Victory, 11th March, 1804

My dear Dr. Moseley,

Yesterday I received the favour of the fourth edition of your invaluable work on Tropical diseases, &c., and with it your most kind letter; and though I know myself not equal to your praises, yet I feel that my honest intentions for the good of the Service have ever been the same; and as I rise in rank, so do my exertions. The great thing in all Military Service is health; and you will agree with me, that it is easier for an Officer to keep men healthy, than for a Physician to cure them. Situated as this Fleet has been, without a friendly Port, where we could get all the things so necessary for us, yet I have, by changing the cruizing ground, not allowed the sameness of prospect to satiate the mind—sometimes by looking at Toulon, Ville Franche, Barcelona, and Rosas; then running round Minorca, Majorca, Sardinia, and Corsica; and two or three times anchoring for a few days, and sending a Ship to the last place for *onions*, which I find the best thing that can be given to Seamen; having always good mutton for the sick, cattle when we can get them and plenty of fresh water. In the winter it is the best plan to give half the allowance of grog, instead of all wine. These things are for the Commander-in-Chief to look to; but shut very nearly out from Spain, and only getting refreshments by stealth from other places, my Command has been an arduous one.

Cornwallis has great merit for his persevering cruise off Ushant, but he has everything sent him: we have nothing. We seem forgotten by the great folks at home. Our men's minds, however, are always kept up with the daily hopes of meeting the Enemy. I send you, as a curiosity, an account of our deaths, and sent to the Hospital, out of six thousand men. The Fleet put to sea on the 18th of May, 1803, and is still at sea; not a Ship has been refitted, or recruited, excepting what has been done at sea. You will readily believe that all this must have shaken me. My sight is getting very bad; but I must not be sick until after the French Fleet is taken. Then, I shall soon hope to take you by the hand and have further recourse to your skill for my eye.

I am always glad to hear good accounts of our dear Lady Hamilton. That she is beloved wherever she is known, does not surprise me; the contrary would, very much. I am sure she feels most sincerely all your kindness. Believe me for ever, my dear Doctor, your much obliged friend,

NELSON AND BRONTE

To Lady Hamilton *Victory, March 14th, 1804,* off Toulon

Young Faddy*, my dearest Emma, brought me, two days ago, your dear and most kind letter of November 26th, and you are sure that I shall take a very early opportunity of promoting him; and he appears to be grown a fine young man, but vacancies do not happen very frequently in this station. However, if he behaves well, he may be sure of me.

With respect to Mr. Jefferson, I can neither say nor do anything. The Surgeon of the *Victory* is a very able, excellent man, and the Ship is kept in the most perfect state of health; and, I would not, if I could—but, thank God I cannot—do such an unjust act, as to remove him. He is my own asking for; and, I have every reason to be perfectly content. Mr. Jefferson got on, by my help; and, by his own misconduct, he got out of a good employ, and has seen another person, at Malta Hospital, put over his head. He must now begin again; and act with much more attention and sobriety, than he has done, to ever get forward again: but, time may do much; and, I shall rejoice to hear of his reformation . . . A thousand pounds a year will not go far; and, we need be great economists, to make both ends meet, and to carry on the little improvements. As for making one farthing more Prize-money, I do not expect it, except by taking the French Fleet: and, the event of that day, who can foresee? With respect to Mrs. Graefer—what she has done, God and herself know; but I have made up my mind, that Gibbs will propose an hundred pounds a year for her: if so, I shall grant it, and have done. I

* Son of Captain Faddy, of the *Vanguard*, who was killed at the Battle of the Nile.

send you Mrs. Graefer's last letter. Whilst I am upon the subject of Bronte I have one word more—and your good, dear, kind heart, must not think that I shall die one hour the sooner; on the contrary, my mind has been more content ever since I have done it; I have left you a part of the rental of Bronte, to be first paid every half year, and in advance. It is but common justice; and whether Mr. Addington gives you anything, or not, you will want it.

I would not have you lay out more than is necessary, at Merton. The rooms, and the new entrance, will take a great deal of money. The entrance by the corner I would have certainly done; a common white gate will do for the present; and one of the cottages, which is in the barn, can be put up, as a temporary lodge. The road can be made to a temporary bridge; for that part of the Nile, one day, shall be filled up. Downing's canvas awning will do for a passage. For the winter, the carriage can be put in the barn; and, giving up Mr. Bennett's premises, will save fifty pounds a year: and, another year, we can fit up the coach-house and stables, which are in the barn.

The foot-path should be turned. I did show Mr. Haslewood the way I wished it done; and Mr. . . . . will have no objections, if we make it better than ever it has been: and, I also beg, as my dear Horatia is to be at Merton, that a strong netting, about three feet high, may be placed round the Nile, that the little thing may not tumble in; and, then, you may have ducks again in it. I forget, at what place we saw the netting; and either Mr. Perry, or Mr. Goldsmid, told us where it was to be bought. I shall be very anxious until I know this is done. I have had no very late opportunities of sending to Naples: but, via Malta, I wrote to Gibbs, to desire he would send over and purchase the amorins. They will arrive in time. I hope the watch is arrived safe. The *British Fair* Cutter, I hope, is arrived safe. She has three packets, from me, to England. The expenses of the alterations at Merton you are not to pay from the income. Let it all be put to a separate account, and I will provide a fund for the payment . . . All I long for, just now, is to hear that you are *perfectly* recovered; and, then, I care for nothing: all my hopes are, to see you, and be happy, at dear Merton, again; but, I fear, this miscarriage of Pichegru's in France, will prolong the War. It has kept the French Fleet in Port, which we are all sorry for.

Sir William Bolton was on board yesterday. He looks thin. The fag in a Brig is very great; and I see no prospect of his either making Prize-money, or being made Post, at present: but I shall omit no opportunity. I wrote to Mrs. Bolton a few months ago; and I gave her letter, yesterday, to Bolton. He conducts himself very well, indeed. Although, I cannot well afford it, yet I could not bear that poor blind Mrs. Nelson should be in want in her old days, and sell her plate; therefore, if you will find out what are her debts, if they come within my power, I will certainly pay them. Many, I dare say, if they had commanded here, would have made money; but, I can assure you, for Prizes taken within the Mediterranean, I have not more than paid my expenses. However, I would rather pinch myself, than she, poor soul, should want. Your good, angelic heart, my dearest beloved Emma, will fully agree with me, everything is very expensive; and even we find it, and will be obliged to economise, if we assist our friends: and, I am sure, we shall feel more comfort in it than in loaded tables, and entertaining a set of people who care not for us. An account is this moment brought me, that a small sum is payable to me, for some Neutral taken off Cadiz in May, 1800; so that I shall not be poorer for my gift. It is odd, is it not?

I shall, when I come home, settle four thousand pounds in trustees' hands, for Horatia; for I will not put it in my own power to have her left destitute; for she would want friends, if we left her in this world. She will be independent of any smiles or frowns. I am glad you are going to take her home; and, if you will take the trouble with Eliza and Ann, I am the very last to object. Tom, I shall certainly assist at College; and, I am sure, the Doctor expects that I should do the same for Horace: but I must make my arrangements, so as not to run in debt.

April 9th.—I have wrote to the Duke; but, by your account, I fear he is not alive. I write because you wish me, and because I like the Duke, and hope he will leave you some money. But for myself, I can have no right to expect a farthing; nor would I be a legacy-hunter for the world: I never knew any good come from it.

NELSON AND BRONTE

To Sir Evan Nepean, Admiralty

Victory, at Sea,
15th March, 1804

Sir,

I have this day received your duplicate most secret letter of the 13th January last, acquainting me that in consequence of the hostile preparations which are now making in the different Ports of Spain, it has been deemed expedient to reinforce the Squadron under my command with the *Royal Sovereign*, and that the *Leviathan* is to follow her with the Mediterranean Convoy, appointed to sail on the 10th of last month; and as it is probable Sir Richard Bickerton would be desirous of shifting his flag to the *Royal Sovereign*, their Lordships conceive it a mark of attention due to his rank and services, that he should be allowed to do so.

In answer to which, you will please to acquaint the Lords Commissioners of the Admiralty that Sir Richard Bickerton is to shift his flag to the *Royal Sovereign*, the moment the weather and other circumstances will admit, and that I shall appoint Captain Malcolm to the *Kent*, agreeably to their direction. And in further obedience to their Lordships' instructions communicated in your said letter, the strictest regard shall be paid to the conduct of Spain; and I have the pleasure to acquaint you that the Squadron under my command is all collected, except the *Gibraltar*, complete in their provisions and stores to near five months, and in a perfect state of readiness to act as the exigency of the moment shall render necessary. I am, &c.,

NELSON AND BRONTE

To the Russian Gentlemen on board
His Majesty's Ship *Royal Sovereign*

Victory, at Sea,
16th March, 1804

Gentlemen,

Far removed from your Country and relations, and placed to serve in the Fleet under my command, I desire that you will, on every occasion, both in public and private concerns, consult with me, and let me know your wants and wishes, and always consider me as your sincere friend,

NELSON AND BRONTE

To Admiral the Earl of St. Vincent

March 17th, 1804

My dear Lord,

Whilst I have your support, and the Officers of the Fleet look up to me, I can do anything which the number of Ships can allow the warmest wishes of my friends to anticipate. Take that from me, and I am nothing. I am the child of opinion, and the Admiralty can with their breath destroy it. But I rely with confidence upon you, my dear Lord, and that alone keeps me up. My general health, I think, within this last fortnight is better; but my sight is much fallen off,—I have always thought I should be blind. If I can but meet the French Fleet, and do the thing well, I shall certainly ask for rest; it is necessary for me. I have sent your nephew* this morning, to see if he can lay salt upon the tail of a French Frigate; I every day see new and excellent traits in him. Hardy is his great pattern about his Ship, and a better he could not have. I have only to hope the restless animal, Buonaparte, will be upset by Frenchmen, and then we may have some quiet. I am, &c.,

NELSON AND BRONTE

* Captain Parker, of the *Amazon*.

To Lady Hamilton *March 18th, 1804*

We have been expecting the French Fleet at sea to relieve me from some anxiety, but many think (but I do not) that the Spanish fleet is to join them; but let us meet them in any reasonable numbers, and you shall, my dear Emma, have no reason to be ashamed of your own Nelson. I send you the comb, which looks handsome, and a pair of curious gloves, they are made only in Sardinia of the beards of mussles. I have ordered a muff; they tell me they are very scarce, and for that reason I wish you to have them. I must write a line to Mrs. Denis, but, in truth, say, although I am much obliged by her kind letter and good wishes, that I can do nothing more, and barely that, to acknowledge the receipt. I do not think I can answer my brother by this opportunity, I will write him soon.

Remember me most kindly to the Duke of Queensbury, I love the old man and would give up everything but you to him; and to all our *joint* friends, for I can have none separate from being yours, say everything that is kind. Never mind Mr. Addington, if he does not do what is right the more shame for him. Thank God I have both the power and inclination. I shall not close this till the last. The destination of the enemy has as many opinions as there are countrys. Sir Alex Ball is sure they are bound again to Egypt—time will shew. I send you, my beloved Emma, a note, in order that you may, upon your birthday, make some little presents, and if you do not give it all away it will look in bank notes very pretty in your pocket-book. Kiss dear Horatia for me, and the other. Call him what you please, if a girl, Emma. Kindest regards to your good mother, affection to Charlotte and all our friends. It now blows a gale of wind.

March 19th.—The gale seems abating, and I shall get off the vessel for Gibraltar. I have been very restless, my dearest Emma, for these several days and nights, and shall not be better till I hear you are quite recover'd. I am yours for ever and ever, &c.

P.S. Hardy is well, and desires his best respects.

To William Marsden, Admiralty
(Who succeeded Sir Evan Nepean as Secretary) *Victory*, at Sea,
20th March, 1804

Sir,

I have to request you will be pleased to acquaint the Lords Commissioners of the Admiralty, that in consequence of Lieutenant William Miller (2nd) of the *Triumph* being appointed an Agent of Transports, and ordered to England by the Commissioners of that Board, I have given Mr. William Faddy, Midshipman of the *Victory*, a Commission in his room, (a copy of which is herewith transmitted,) and trust their Lordships will order the appointment to be confirmed. I am satisfied when I call to their Lordships' recollection, that this deserving young man is son to the late Captain of the Marines who was killed on board the *Vanguard*, in the Battle of the Nile, they will feel as much pleasure in confirming the appointment, as I do in making the request on his behalf. I beg leave also to observe that his widowed mother is alive, with the charge of a large family unprovided for, and naturally looks up to him for assistance. I am, Sir, &c.,

NELSON AND BRONTE

To His Excellency Hugh Elliot

Victory, March 23rd, 1804

My dear Sir,

Yesterday I received a letter from Mr. Frere of March 9th, in which, after having put us so much upon our guard that we expected a Spanish War every day, the name of Spain is not mentioned: therefore, I must suppose his alarm is gone off, or we may be lulled, by his neglect to say anything, into a fatal security. To me it matters not: I am prepared for all events.

The King, Mr. Frere says, by advices from London of February 26th, is fast recovering. I wish it may be so, but I fear very much to the contrary. I believe the Prince will be sole Regent; and I see, through the French papers—'London News, February 7th'—that Lord Grenville had been three hours with Mr. Fox, supposed forming a new Administration. Georges, I see, is also arrested, and he and Pichegru are to be tried by Military Tribunals. The Invasion must be over before this time, which I still hope will overturn Buonaparte's despotic Government. My reports say that the French have taken up at Leghorn a number of Greek Vessels as Transports. If they leave Leghorn without Troops, it is natural to suppose they are destined to take the French Troops from the Coast of the Adriatic. If so, they must either be destined for the Morea or Egypt. Information upon these points is so important, to enable me to form a probable guess at the destination of the Toulon Fleet, that no money or trouble ought to be spared to obtain it. At eight o'clock yesterday morning, our Frigates saw the French Fleet quite safe. I am going to Madalena to get some refreshments; for I am sorry to say the scurvy has made its appearance in several Ships.

The *Belleisle* will stay four days at Naples; and if the *Gibraltar* is sent away, I may occasionally, to relieve each other, send Ships; but of this the King shall judge; for I never will deprive him of the protection and services of an English Ship. Yesterday, I received from Major Lowe a copy of his letter to your Excellency. There will be no resistance in

Sardinia worth mentioning, should the French land in any force. Major Lowe is probably with you by this time.

Captain Hargood of the *Belleisle* has just joined her from England, in the room of Captain Whitby, gone home to be Admiral Cornwallis's Captain. Captain Hargood is a very old acquaintance and Ship-mate of mine, and an eleve of the Duke of Clarence, and, what is better than all, a very good man. I am ever, my dear Sir, your most obedient, faithful servant,

NELSON AND BRONTE

I have heard nothing from 888.

To Alexander Davison, Esq.

Victory, March 28th, 1804

My dear Davison,

Last night, to my surprise, Mr. Chevalier* sent to speak to me, and said—'I beg pardon, my Lord, but I find myself so disagreeably situated in the Ship, that I beg of your Lordship to send me to England by the first opportunity.' To which I answered, 'Certainly, Mr. Chevalier.' I can have no conception to what this is owing. I never said a harsh thing to him, nor any one else, I am sure. He is very much respected, and an excellent servant. He is his own master in all his department; but was he, if possible, a better servant, I never would ask a servant to stay. It is some vagary or other; so he must follow his own fancy. So much for that.

Day by day, my dear friend, I am expecting the French Fleet to put to sea—every day, hour, and moment; and you may rely that if it is within the power of man to get at them, it shall be done; and, I am sure, that all my brethren look to that day as the finish of our laborious cruize. The event no man can say exactly, but I must think or render great injustice to those under me, that let the Battle be when it may, it will never have been surpassed. My shattered frame, if I survive that day, will require rest, and that is all I shall ask for. If I fall on such a glorious occasion, it shall be my pride to take care that my friends shall not blush for me. These things are in the hands of a wise and just Providence, and His will be done. I have got some trifle, thank God, to leave those I hold most dear, and I have taken care not to neglect it. Do not think I am so low-spirited on this account, or fancy anything is to happen to me. Quite the contrary: my mind is calm, and I have only to think of destroying our inveterate foe.

April 7th.—A Frigate has just brought me an account that she saw the French Fleet outside Toulon, thirty-four hours ago, and she does

* His steward.

not know that they returned. I have two Frigates gone for more information, and we all hope for a meeting with the Enemy. Nothing can be finer than the Fleet under my command. Whatever be the event, believe me ever, my dear Davison, your most obliged and sincere friend,

NELSON AND BRONTE

To Rear-Admiral Sir Richard Bickerton *7th April, 1804*

As the Enemy's Fleet has been out, and may still be at sea, and as I should be very sorry to baulk their inclinations of a Battle by your superiority of numbers, You will, therefore, whenever I make the signal, haul from us to the Southward, furl your top-gallant sails so as not to be discovered from the shore, and just keep sight of us from the masthead; and make the signal for your Division, (except *Excellent*, who is going towards Toulon) and do you call in *Belleisle*, unless I should call her by signal to me. I am, &c.,

NELSON AND BRONTE

To the Rt. Hon. George Rose

Victory, April 8th, 1804

My dear Sir,

I was favoured with your kind letter of December 15th, a few days ago. I have not as yet heard a word of the entailing the English pension; and if common justice is done me, Parliament ought to give me the £1,000 a year that your Administration gave to Lords St. Vincent and Duncan; but, if our reports are true about the King, very great alterations must take place.

We are on the eve of great events. Last week, at different times, two Sail of the Line put their heads outside Toulon; and on Thursday the 5th, in the afternoon, they all came out. We have had a gale of wind and calm since; therefore, I do not know whether they are returned to Port or have kept the sea. I have only to wish to get alongside of them with the present Fleet under my command; so highly officered and manned, the event ought not to be doubted. That the event shall, if possible, be useful to your recommendation, Captain Strachey, who I shall be glad of an opportunity of promoting. With many thanks for your obliging offers of service, for which I hope to thank you soon in London, believe me ever, my dear Sir, your much obliged friend,

NELSON AND BRONTE

To Miss Horatia Nelson Thomson

Victory, April 13th, 1804

My dear Horatia,

I send you twelve books of Spanish dresses, which you will let your Guardian Angel, Lady Hamilton, keep for you, when you are tired of looking at them. I am very glad to hear, that you are perfectly recovered; and, that you are a very good child. I beg, my dear Horatia, that you will always continue so; which will be a great comfort to your most affectionate,

NELSON AND BRONTE

To Lord Hobart, Secretary of State for the War Department

Victory, April 16th, 1804

My Lord,

I have been honoured with your letter of January 7th, and it has given me most sincere pleasure that my whole conduct in my Command here has been such as to meet his Majesty's approbation, and which it shall always be my study to deserve.

Your Lordship will probably hear something of Sardinia through Mr. Elliot at Naples, and Mr. Jackson at Rome. I send your Lordship a copy of my last letter to Mr. Jackson. My line of conduct, in obedience to the spirit of his Majesty's instructions communicated through your Lordship, has been simply this,—to conciliate all, to protect all from French rapacity—and I have the satisfaction to think that I have completely succeeded.

My eye is constantly fixed upon Toulon; and I have no great reason to believe that the French will escape me, whatever may be their destination: and it is with real pleasure I can state to your Lordship, and request you will state it to the King, that no Fleet ever was in higher discipline, and health, and good humour, than the one I have the honour to command; and whenever we fall in with the Enemy's Fleet, (if I do my duty), the happiest result will, I may venture to say, accrue. I have the honour to be, &c.,

NELSON AND BRONTE

The French Fleet safe in Toulon this day at noon.

To Lady Hamilton

Victory, April 19th, 1804

My dearest Emma,

I had wrote you a line, intended for the *Swift* Cutter; but, instead of her joining me, I had the mortification, not only to hear that she was taken, but that all the dispatches and letters had fallen into the hands of the Enemy; a very pretty piece of work! I am not surprised at the capture, but am very much so that any dispatches should be sent in a Vessel with twenty-three men, not equal to cope with any Row-Boat Privateer. As I do not know what letters of yours are in her, I cannot guess what will be said. I suppose, there will be a publication.* The loss of the *Hindostan*, was great enough; but, for importance, it is lost, in comparison to the probable knowledge the Enemy will obtain of our connexions with Foreign Countries! Foreigners for ever say, and it is true—'We dare not trust England; one way or other, we are sure to be committed!' However, it is now too late to launch out on this subject. Not a thing has been saved out of the *Hindostan*, not a second shirt for any one and it has been by extraordinary exertions, that the people's lives were saved.†

Captain Hallowell is so good as to take home for me, wine as by the enclosed list; and, if I can, some honey. The Spanish honey is so precious, that if any one has a cut, or sore throat, it is used to cure it. I mentioned this, in case you should wish to give the Duke a jar. The smell is wonderful! It is produced nowhere but in the mountains near Rosas. The Cyprus wine—one hogshead, was for Buonaparte,—I would recommend the wine-cooper drawing it off: and you can send a few dozens to the Duke; who, I know, takes a glass every day at two o'clock. I wish I had anything else to send you; but, my dearest Emma, you must take the will for the deed. I am pleased with Charlotte's letter; and, as she loves my dear Horatia, I shall always like her. What hearts those must have, who do not! But, thank God, she shall not be dependent on any of them.

Your letter of February 12th, through Mr. Falconet, I have received. I know they are all read; therefore, never sign your name. I shall continue to write through Spain; but never say a word that can convey any information—except, of eternal attachment and affection for you; and that I care not who knows, for I am, &c.,

NELSON AND BRONTE

Poor Captain Le Gros had your Note to him in his pocket-book, and that was all he saved (from the *Hindostan*).

Mr. Este left him at Gibraltar, and went to Malta in the *Thisbe*. Captain Le Gros is now Trying.‡ I think it will turn out that every person is obliged to his conduct for saving their lives. She took fire thirteen leagues from the land.

* The *Swift* was captured by a French privateer 3 April. The despatches for Nelson were thrown overboard before capture.

† *Hindostan* storeship caught fire and was destroyed 2 April.

‡ Trying — Court Martial. He was honourably acquitted.

To Miss Charlotte Nelson*

Victory, April 19th, 1804

My dear Charlotte,

I thank you very much for your kind letters of January 3rd and 4th; and I feel truly sensible of your kind regard for that dear little orphan, Horatia. Although her parents are lost, yet she is not without a fortune; and I shall cherish her to the last moment of my life, and curse them who curse her, and Heaven bless them who bless her! Dear innocent! she can have injured no one. I am glad to hear that she is attached to you; and, if she takes after her parents, so she will to those who are kind to her. I am ever, dear Charlotte, your affectionate uncle,

NELSON AND BRONTE

To Lord Hobart

Victory, April 10th, 1804

Private.

My dear Lord,

I rely with confidence that, although the Admiralty for ever send their dispatches, of whatever consequence, without the use of cipher, and trust to their being thrown overboard in case of capture, yet, as I know the other Departments of Government always use cipher if of importance, and although Admirals are never entrusted with ciphers, yet I rely that your Lordship would not trust any dispatch of consequence in a Vessel with twenty-three men, much less commit the interests and schemes of other Powers to such a conveyance. This is the only consolation I derive from all the dispatches being this day read by the First Consul; I wish they were in his throat. I think a great deal on this matter, but it may be prudent to hold my tongue, except to say, I am, &c.,

NELSON AND BRONTE

[On 23rd April, St. George's Day, 1804, a promotion of Admirals took place, when Nelson became a Vice-Admiral of the White—the highest rank he ever attained.]

To Lady Hamilton

Victory, April 23rd, 1804

My dearest Emma,

Hallowell has promised me, if the Admiralty will give him leave to go to London, that he will call at Merton. His spirit is certainly more

* His niece, only daughter of the Reverend Doctor Nelson, afterwards Earl Nelson.

independent than almost any man's I ever knew; but, I believe, he is attached to me. I am sure he has no reason to be so to either Troubridge, or any one at the Admiralty. I have sent, last night, a box of Maraschino veritabile of Zara, which I got Jemmy Anderson to buy for me, and twelve bottles of Tokay. I have none for myself—being better pleased that you should have it. I am, &c.,

NELSON AND BRONTE

Hallowell parted last night; but, being in sight, I am sending a Frigate with a letter to the Admiralty.

May God Almighty Bless you, and send us a happy meeting.

To the Respective Captains

Victory, at Sea, *28th April, 1804*

Memorandum.

As it is my determination to attack the French Fleet in any place where there is a reasonable prospect of getting fairly alongside of them, and as I think in Hieres Bay, Gourjean Bay, Port Especia, Leghorn Roads, Ajaccio, and many other places, opportunities may offer of attacking them, I therefore recommend that every Captain will make himself, by inquiries, as fully acquainted with the above-mentioned places as possible—viz., for Hieres Bay, the Petite Passe, Grande Passe, and Passage from the Eastward; Gourjean Bay, (of which I send a Chart from the latest surveys made,) Port Especia, and, in particular, the Northern Passage into Leghorn Roads, from which side it is only, in my opinion, possible to attack an Enemy's Fleet to advantage; and with the Gulf of Ajaccio.

In going in to attack an Enemy's Fleet, it is recommended, if possible, to have the Launch out, and hawsers and stream-anchors in her; and, with any other Boats, to lay out of gun-shot, ready to act as circumstances may require. Ships, in bringing up, will anchor as the Captains may think best, from circumstances of wind and weather, and the position of the Enemy; but I would recommend strongly having the four large anchors clear for letting go; because I know, from experience, the great difficulty, with crippled masts and yards, getting an anchor over the side; and it is probable that it may be necessary to remove the Ship after an Action, and to leave some of her anchors behind. The Ships will anchor in such a manner as to give each other mutual support for the destruction of the Enemy.

NELSON AND BRONTE

A Chart of Gourjean Bay to be delivered to each Line-of-Battle Ship.

To Lady Hamilton *April 28th, 1804*

I did not, my dearest Emma, pass over the 26th without thinking of you in the most affectionate manner, which the truest love and affectionate regard of man to a dear beloved woman, which could enter into my mind.

I have been for some days, and am still, very unwell, without being seriously ill, but I fret absolutely like a fool for the faults of others. It was no fault of mine that the dispatches were taken, but of those who sent them in a vessel not fit to trust my old shoes in; nor is it my fault that the *Kent*, the finest ship in the fleet, is kept so long from England, notwithstanding my representations that she is now obliged to leave the fleet, to lay guard-ship at Naples, and more will very soon be in as bad a plight. My only wish is for the coming out of the French fleet to finish all my uneasinesses. But I yet trust that the reign of Buonaparte will soon be over, and then that we shall have a few years of peace and quietness.

Remember me kindly to all we hold most dear, and be assured, my dear Emma, that I am for ever and ever, and if possible more than ever, yours most faithfully, &c.,

Captain Layman, Captain Hallowell, and I believe another packet of letters for you, are now at Gibraltar.

CHAPTER THIRTEEN

THE BLOCKADE OF TOULON

[The next section of Nelson's letters covers a period of fifteen months, from May, 1804, to July, 1805, during the whole of which time he was Commander-in-Chief in the Mediterranean, watching the French Fleet in Toulon until it emerged, in April, 1805, and sailed for the West Indies whither Nelson pursued it with an inferior force.

It was not for some time, however, that Nelson received definite information that Admiral Villeneuve had passed the Strait of Gibraltar and was westward bound. He followed and arrived at Barbadoes on 4th June, but Villeneuve had gone to Martinique whence he returned to Europe. Nelson arrived back at Gibraltar after his fruitless chase on 19th July.

On 15th August, 1805, he joined the Channel Fleet under Admiral Cornwallis with whom he left all his ships except *Victory* and *Superb* and sailed for England where he arrived, at Spithead, on 18th August. The next day he struck his flag and went to join Lady Hamilton at Merton.]

To the Earl of St. Vincent *25th May, 1804*

There is no real happiness, my dear Lord, in this world: with all content and smiles around me, up start these Artillery boys; I understand they are not beyond that age, and set us all at defiance—speaking in the most disrespectful manner of the Navy and its Commanders, &c. I know you my dear Lord, so well, that with your quickness, the matter would have been settled, and perhaps some of them been broke. I am perhaps more patient, but I do assure you not less resolved, if my plan of conciliation is not attended to. You and I are on the eve of quitting the theatre of our exploits; but we owe it to our successors, never, whilst we have a tongue to speak, or a hand to write, to allow the Navy to be in the smallest degree injured in its discipline by our conduct. If these continued attacks upon the Navy are to be carried on every two or three years, it would be much better for the Navy to have its own Corps of Artillery*: the present case is indeed with lads; but they are set on by men, I can see that very clearly. The new Emperor (bravo, Corsican!) will, I hope begin his reign by ordering his Fleet to

* Later, the Royal Marine Artillery was formed.

come out; for if they do not very soon, they will wear us out, and most particularly myself. My health has suffered very much, but I am as happy in the command as man can be: I am, &c.,

NELSON AND BRONTE

To Captain Sir Thomas Troubridge, Admiralty

About 25th May, 1804

My dear Troubridge,

You will see that I have been obliged to write a letter to the Admiralty, on the subject of Soldiers embarked on board Ships of War; and I have written it strong, as I know it must go further than your Board. It is the old history—trying to do away the Act of Parliament; but I trust they will never succeed—for when they do, farewell to our Naval superiority! We should be prettily commanded! You may say, 'they are not intended to command the Navy, but that the Navy is not to command Soldiers on board a Ship.' Let them once gain the step of being independent of the Navy on board a Ship, and they will soon have the other, and command us. It may be said, 'if the Soldiers behave improperly, they would be tried by a Court-martial on shore;' were that possible, of what Members would that Court be composed? Mostly Subalterns, I fancy, who, although we might think the Officer had behaved very improperly, might, and probably would think that he had behaved very properly to us Sea-brutes. But, thank God, my dear Troubridge, the King himself cannot do away the Act of Parliament. Although my career is nearly run, yet it would embitter my future days and expiring moments, to hear of our Navy being sacrificed to the Army. I can readily conceive the attempts of the Army at this moment, when they think themselves of such great importance. The Admiralty order might lead those wrong who do not know that nothing but an Act of Parliament can do away an Act of Parliament. Ever, my dear Troubridge, yours most faithfully,

NELSON AND BRONTE

To Spiridion Foresti, Esq., Corfu *About May 31st, 1804*

The only place to guard against a coup de main from, was Toulon, where 12,000 Troops are ready for embarkation: this I have taken effectual care to prevent, by a perseverance at sea never surpassed in the annals of the world—not a Ship in this Fleet has been into any Port to refit since the War, and to this moment I never have had my foot out of the Ship. I am, &c.,

NELSON AND BRONTE

To the Grand Vizir *13th June, 1804*

Buonaparte, by whatever name he may choose to call himself—General, Consul, or Emperor—is the same man we have always known, and the common disturber of the human race; it is much more dangerous to be his friend than his enemy. With the appearance of friendship he deceives; to be on the latter terms, the hand should be always on the sword. May God grant his Imperial Majesty health and length of days, and may your Highness for many, many years, guide his councils with your wisdom. I beg of your Highness to assure his Imperial Majesty, that I am penetrated with his condescension in remembering my former exertions in the execution of my duty: whilst my health remains, they shall never cease. Other Admirals will readily be found of probably more abilities, but none with more zeal to cement the harmony and perfect good understanding between our two good Sovereigns. The French Fleet is quite safe in Toulon, and for the summer they cannot readily escape without a Battle. May God give the victory to the just cause. I am &c.,

NELSON AND BRONTE

To the Commissioners for Victualling His Majesty's Navy, London

Victory, at Sea, *19th June, 1804*

Gentlemen,

As the substitution of rice for cheese is not in general liked by the Ships' Companies, who do not take up near their allowance of that species of provision, it may, therefore, shortly be expected that lists of the savings of rice as cheese, will be delivered to me, by the respective Captains of the Fleet under my command, for payment. I must, therefore, desire to acquaint you therewith; and that as it has been the custom of this country to pay the Ships' Companies their savings of oil as butter and cheese, and the measure appearing to me so just and reasonable, that the savings of rice as cheese should be paid for as savings of the latter, that I can have no doubt of its propriety. But as the quantities may be considerable, it is my wish that the payment of such savings should have the approbation and authority of your Board, and, therefore, I request that you will furnish me with your regulations on this subject accordingly. I am, &c.,

NELSON AND BRONTE

To the Rt. Hon. Lord Melville, First Lord of the Admiralty

21st June, 1804

My dear Lord,

In case Earl St. Vincent and Sir Thomas Troubridge should not send you my letters to them, respecting the conduct of Soldiers embarked to serve in his Majesty's Ships, I think it of great consequence to the Naval Service, you should be informed of my sentiments upon that subject. It requires not the gift of prescience to assert, if Soldiers embarked in Ships of War are not, as heretofore, left subject to the Act of Parliament for the Government of his Majesty's Ships, Vessels, and Forces by Sea, whereon, as our forefathers said, 'the safety, wealth, and prosperity of the Kingdom chiefly depend,' that the Navy, which we have all heretofore looked up to, will be ruined. The absolute power must remain; there cannot be two Commanders in one Ship, nor two sets of laws to regulate the conduct of those embarked in the same bottom. I will not, my Lord, take up your time in debating, whether it would be better for the Navy to be subject to the same Articles of War as the Army; but we may take a lesson from the epitaph, 'I was well; I would be better, and here I am:' my opinion is, 'Let well alone.' I am, &c.,

NELSON AND BRONTE

To Rt. Hon. Lord Melville *22nd June, 1804*

It is to redeem the solemn pledge I have made, never to omit, upon any change of Administration stating the just claim which I consider the Battle of Copenhagen has to the reward of Medals, such as have been given for other great Naval victories; I therefore inclose for your Lordship's perusal a statement of facts, and the letters which passed between me and Earl St. Vincent upon that occasion; and when your Lordship has leisure time, I request your perusal of them . . . I am aware, my Lord, that his Majesty has the most undisputed right to bestow Medals, or to withhold them, as he pleases. No man admits it more fully than myself; but, my Lord, I turn back to the 1st of June, 1794; from that moment I have ever considered, that his Majesty, by implication, pronounced these words to his Fleet, holding forth the Medal—'This, my Fleet, is the great reward which I will bestow for great and important Victories like the present.' Considering this as a solemn pledge, his Majesty gave it as the reward for the Battles of St. Vincent, of Camperdown, and the Nile: then comes the most difficult achievement, the hardest-fought battle, the most glorious result that ever graced the Naval Annals of our Country: the Medal is withheld, for what reason Lord St. Vincent best knows. Could it be said that the Danes were not brave? the contrary has always been shown. Was our force so superior that there was no merit in gaining the Victory? If guns made the superiority, the Danes were very superior. If it be said, 'Ay, but your Ships were superior:' to that I can answer, that the force placed by the Danes for the preservation of their Arsenal, their Fleet, and the City of Copenhagen, was such, and of that description of Vessels, which they thought inexpugnable by any force that could be brought against it. I have no more to say, but beg to refer your Lordship to the papers sent herewith; and I hope, in the name of those brave Commanders who were under my orders on the glorious 2nd of April, 1801, for your recommendation to his Majesty, that he may be pleased to bestow that mark of honour on the Battle of Copenhagen, which his goodness has given to the Battles of St. Vincent, the 1st of June, of Camperdown, and the Nile. I am, &c.,

NELSON AND BRONTE

To Rt. Hon. Henry Addington

Victory, 30th June, 1804

My dear Sir,

Friend I may call thee now, without the suspicion of adulation to a Minister; but believe me, that your constant friendship for me as a man, have ever held the same place in my heart. I feel pride in avowing it, now you are a private gentleman. I will not say too much, because when a change takes place, if honourable men are to take the helm, I am sure amongst the foremost will be placed one Henry Addington, whose sincere friend is ever his attached and obliged,

NELSON AND BRONTE

I shall see you before Christmas; for I am almost worn out and blind.

To the Rt. Hon. The Lord Mayor

Victory, August 1st, 1804

My Lord,

This day, I am honoured with your Lordship's letter of April 9th, transmitting me the Resolutions of the Corporation of London, thanking me as commanding the Fleet blockading Toulon. I do assure your Lordship that there is not a man breathing who sets a higher value upon the thanks of his Fellow-Citizens of London than myself; but I should feel as much ashamed to receive them for a particular service marked in the Resolution, if I felt that I did not come within that line of service, as I should feel hurt at having a great Victory passed over without notice.

I beg to inform your Lordship that the Port of Toulon has never been blockaded by me: quite the reverse—every opportunity has been offered the Enemy to put to sea, for it is there that we hope to realize the hopes and expectations of our Country, and I trust that they will not be dissappointed.

Your Lordship will judge of my feelings upon seeing that all the Junior Flag-Officers of other Fleets, and even some of the Captains, have received the thanks of the Corporation of London, whilst the Junior Flag-Officers of the Mediterranean Fleet are entirely omitted. I own it has struck me very forcibly; for, where the information of the Junior Flag-Officers and Captains of other Fleets was obtained, the same information could have been given of the Flag-Officers of this Fleet and the Captains; and, it is my duty to state, that more able and zealous Flag-Officers and Captains do not grace the British Navy, than those I have the honour and happiness to command.

It likewise appears, my Lord, a most extraordinary circumstance, that Sir Richard Bickerton should have been, as Second in Command in the Mediterranean Fleet, twice passed over by the Corporation of London; once after the Egyptian Expedition, when the First and Third in Command were thanked; and now again! Conscious of high desert, instead of neglect, the Rear-Admiral resolved to let the matter rest until he could have an opportunity personally to call upon the Lord Mayor, to account for such an extraordinary omission; but from this second omission, I owe it to that excellent Officer not to pass it by. I do assure your Lordship, that the constant, zealous, and cordial support I have had in my Command, from both Rear-Admiral Sir Richard Bickerton and Rear-Admiral Campbell, has been such as calls forth all my thanks and admiration. We have shared together the constant attention of being fourteen months at sea, and are ready to share the dangers and glory of a day of Battle; therefore, it is impossible that I can ever allow myself to be separated in Thanks from such supporters. I have the honour to remain, with the very highest respect, your Lordship's most faithful and obedient servant,

NELSON AND BRONTE

To the Masters of His Majesty's Ships
Victory, *Amazon*, and *Phoebe*

Victory, Gulf of Palma,
Sardinia, *2nd August*, *1804*

Captain Bayntun, of his Majesty's Ship *Leviathan*, having represented to me by letter of this date, that in receiving bread from the *Amity* Transport, a bag of it, said to contain 112 lbs., by accident fell overboard into the sea, and that in consequence of the great swell and the Boats pitching considerably, the said bag of bread was completely wet, and thereby rendered unfit for issue, and requested a survey thereon; You are hereby required and directed to repair on board his Majesty's Ship *Leviathan*, and strictly and carefully survey the bag of bread complained of as above, taking care to see every particle of it particularly picked and the dust wiped off, in order that as much as possible of it may be saved for further use, reporting to me, from under your hands, a very correct and distinct account of your proceedings herein, stating the quantity that may be fit for issuing, which you will leave in charge of the Purser for that purpose, and also, the unserviceable bread to be dried, and returned into his Majesty's Store; and you are further hereby directed strictly to inquire whether blame is to be attached to any individual for the said loss, in order that it may be charged against his growing wages.

NELSON AND BRONTE

To Count Mocenigo, at Corfu *4th August, 1804*

In Sea affairs, nothing is impossible, and nothing improbable. I am, &c.,

NELSON AND BRONTE

To Admiral Sir Robert Kingsmill

Victory, August 4th, 1804

My dear Kingsmill,

It gave me a twitch of pleasure to see your handwriting again; and believe me, my dear friend, that there is nothing that you can desire me to do, that I should not fly to do with the greatest pleasure. Can I forget all your former kindness to me? No, Horatio Nelson is (all that is left of him) the same as you formerly knew him; nor do I forget all Mary's goodness to me.

Bastard is a very fine young man, and I will remove him out of the Bomb. Independent of your friendship, Mr. Bastard, Member for Devon, is a character that we must all respect for his high worth and principles. I can readily believe the pleasure you must have had, in meeting some of my friends at good Admiral and Mrs. Ludwidge's. I am sorry to tell you that my health, or rather constitution, is so much shook, that I doubt the possibility of my holding out another winter, without asses' milk, and some months' quiet; then I may get on another campaign or two; but, my dear Kingsmill, when I run over the undermentioned wounds—Eye in Corsica, Belly off Cape St. Vincent, Arm at Teneriffe, Head in Egypt—I ought to be thankful that I am what I am. If Monsieur La Touche will give me the meeting before I go home, it will probably finish my Naval career. He is ready, and, by their handling their Ships, apparently well manned; but I command, for Captains and Crews, such a Fleet, as I never have before seen; and it is impossible that any Admiral can be happier situated. Rotten Ships neither rests with me nor them. God bless you, my dear Kingsmill, and believe me ever your most faithful and affectionate friend,

NELSON AND BRONTE

To the Reverend Dr. Nelson

Victory, August 8th, 1804

My dear Brother,

Mr. C. B. Yonge had joined the *Victory* long before your letter was wrote, and he is a very good, deserving young man, and when he has served his time, I shall take the earliest opportunity of putting him into a good vacancy; but that will not be until October, the very finish, I expect, of my remaining here, for my health has suffered much since I left England, and if the Admiralty do not allow me to get at asses' milk and rest, you will be a Lord before I intend you should. I am glad the wind was good and acceptable. I have been expecting Monsieur La Touche to give me the meeting every day for this year past, and only hope he will come out before I go hence. Remember me kindly to Mrs. Nelson and believe me ever, your most affectionate brother,

NELSON AND BRONTE

You must excuse a short letter. You will have seen Monsieur La Touche's letter of how he chased me and I *ran*. I keep it; and, by God, if I take him, he shall *Eat* it!

To H.R.H. The Duke of Clarence *15th August, 1804*

If anything the least new was to occur here, your Royal Highness is sure that I should have written to you; but we have an uniform sameness, day after day, and month after month—gales of wind for ever. In July, we had seventeen days very severe weather; the Mediterranean seems altered. However, with nursing our Ships, we have roughed it out better than could have been expected. I have always made it a rule never to contend with gales; and either run to the Southward to escape its violence, or furl all the sails and make the Ships as easy as possible. Our friend Keats is quite well; in his own person he is equal in my estimation to an additional Seventy-four; his life is a valuable one to the State, and it is impossible that your Royal Highness could ever have a better choice of a Sea friend, or Counsellor, if you go to the Admiralty. Keats will never give that counsel which would not be good for the Service. I am, &c.,

NELSON AND BRONTE

To Captain Ross Donnelly, H.M. Ship *Narcissus*

Victory, off Cape St. Sebastians,
20th August, 1804

Sir,

Whereas it is my intention to try every possible means to induce the French Fleet at Toulon to put to sea, You are hereby required and directed to take his Majesty's Ships named in the margin under your command, and proceed off the West end of Porquerolle, in order to induce the Enemy to get to the Eastward, as it is my intention to get into the Gulf of Lyons, and to push round Cape Sicie the first favourable wind. Your appearance may, therefore, tempt them to come out, and stand to the Eastward, or to anchor in Hieres Bay, which may afford the Squadron under my command an opportunity of bringing them to Action.

NELSON AND BRONTE

To Captain Charles Marsh Schomberg, H.M. Ship *Madras*

Victory, at Sea,
2nd September, 1804

Sir,

Lord Elgin having requested through Sir Alexander Ball that I would allow a Ship to call at Cerigo, to bring from thence to Malta some marble antiquities*, and as I am perfectly disposed to meet his Lordship's wishes on this occasion, I am to desire you will send a small Transport to Cerigo, with the first Convoy going up the Levant, and leave her there, for the purpose of receiving the antiquities beforementioned on board (provided it is a safe place for her to remain at) till the return of the Convoy, when you will direct the Officer in charge thereof to call at Cerigo, and bring the Transport with his Lordship's antiquities on board, safe under his protection to Malta, when Sir Alexander Ball will direct the disposal of them; and if it is intended to send them, to England, you will give the necessary orders accordingly. I am, &c.,

NELSON AND BRONTE

* The Elgin Marbles, now in the British Museum.

To Lady Hamilton *Victory, September 29th, 1804*

This day, my dearest Emma, which gave me birth, I consider as more fortunate than common days, as, by my coming into this world, it has brought me so intimately acquainted with you, who my soul holds most dear. I well know that you will keep it, and have my dear Horatia to drink my health. Forty-six years of toil and trouble! How few more the common lot of mankind leads us to expect; and, therefore, it is almost time to think of spending the few last years in peace and quietness!

By this time, I should think, either my successor is named, or permission is granted me to come home; and if so, you will not long receive this letter before I make my appearance; which will make us, I am sure, both truly happy. We have had nothing for this fortnight, but gales of Easterly winds and heavy rains; not a Vessel of any kind or sort joined the Fleet. I was in hopes Dr. Scott would have returned from Naples, and that I could have told you something comfortable for you, from that quarter; and it is now seven weeks since we heard from Malta, therefore I know nothing of what is passing in the world. I would not have you, my dear Emma, allow the work of brick and mortar to go on in the winter months. It can all be finished next summer; when I hope we shall have Peace, or such an universal War as will upset that vagabond Buonaparte. I have been tolerably well, till this last bad weather, which has given me pains in my breast; but, never mind, all will be well when I get to Merton. Admiral Campbell, who is on board, desires to be remembered to you. He does not like much to stay here, after my departure. Indeed, we all draw so well together in the Fleet, that I flatter myself the sorrow for my departure will be pretty general. Admiral Murray will be glad to get home; Hardy is as good as ever; and Mr. Secretary Scott is an excellent man. God bless you, my dearest Emma! and be assured I am ever your most faithful and affectionate,

N. & B.

Kiss dear Horatia. I hope she is at Merton, *fixed*.

To Lieut. Harding Shaw,
Commanding His Majesty's Brig *Spider* *Victory*, at Sea,
4th October, 1804

Sir,

I have received your letter of the 6th ultimo, acquainting me with the circumstance of your having flogged John Carter, Seaman, belonging to the *Spider*, on the 5th of that month; that soon after, a shot was flung from forward by some of the people, which fell close by you, and Mr. Langdon, the Master; and, in order to discover the offender, you judged it necessary to threaten them with individual punishment, which, as they would not confess, you had inflicted upon each of your company, by calling them over by the watch-bill, and giving them a dozen each. In answer to which, I cannot approve of a measure so foreign to the rules of good discipline and the accustomed practice of his Majesty's Navy, and therefore caution you against a similar line of conduct. Had you fixed upon one or more guilty individuals, and punished them severely, it might have had the desired effect, or put them into confinement, and brought them to a Court-Martial. I trust your watchful conduct will prevent any such confusion, or disposition to riot, from happening again. I am, &c.,

NELSON AND BRONTE

To Lieut. The Hon. Henry Duncan,
H.M. Ship *Royal Sovereign* *Victory, October 4th, 1804*

My dear Sir,

There is no man who more sincerely laments the heavy loss* you have sustained than myself; but the name of Duncan will never be forgot by Britain, and, in particular, by its Navy, in which service, the remembrance of your worthy father will, I am sure, grow up in you. I am sorry not to have a good Sloop to give you; but still an opening offers, which I think will insure your confirmation as a Commander. It is occasioned by the very ill state of health of Captain Corbet of the *Bittern*, who has requested a few weeks leave to reside on shore at the Hospital. You will be confirmed before he resumes his command. You had better get your things on board the *Seahorse* this afternoon, as she will go to Malta in the morning. I am ever, my dear Sir, with every kind wish, most faithfully yours,

NELSON AND BRONTE

To Rt. Hon. Earl Spencer *Victory, 10th October, 1804*

I do assure you, my dear Lord, that not one of all your Naval friends, and you ought to have many, loves, honours, and respects you more than myself, or is more grateful for all your kindness. Circumstances may have separated us; but my sincere respect and attachment can never be shaken by either political or other considerations; and it will always give me pleasure, in showing my regard for the Father by attentions to the Son. The sight of your letter called forth feelings of which I have reason to be proud, but which cannot be readily expressed; therefore I shall only say for myself, that Nelson never has, nor can change. I am, &c.,

NELSON AND BRONTE

* Death of his father, Admiral Viscount Duncan.

To Rt. Hon. Viscount Melville *30th October, 1804*

The weather was very thick when I looked into Toulon, but I believe a Vice-Admiral has hoisted his Flag; his name I have not yet heard. They now amuse themselves with night-signals, and by the quantity of rockets and blue lights they show with every signal, they plainly mark their position. These gentlemen must soon be so perfect in theory, that they will come to sea to put their knowledge into practice. Could I see that day, it would make me happy. I am, &c.,

NELSON AND BRONTE

WAR WITH SPAIN

To William Marsden *Victory*, at Sea, *8th November, 1804*

Sir,

I herewith transmit you a copy of a letter and paper therin referred to, from Captain Gore, of his Majesty's Ship *Medusa*, dated the 6th October, (a copy of which, he acquaints me, has also been transmitted to you) giving an account of the capture of three Spanish Frigates with treasure on board, as therein mentioned, which you will be so good as to lay before the Lords Commissioners of the Admiralty, for their information: and, at the same time acquaint their Lordships that I very highly approve of the meritorious conduct of that excellent Officer, Captain Gore, upon the present, as well as upon all former occasions, since he has been under my command, in the important trust of watching the Enemy outside the Straits, and for the great and perfect security which he has afforded with his little Squadron to our Trade to, and from, this Country; and when the very bad state of the *Medusa* is considered, his constantly keeping at sea previous to this, and after an opportunity offered for his returning to England, with the Spanish Frigate *Fama*, deserves particular approbation. I am, Sir, &c.,

NELSON AND BRONTE

To the respective Captains and Commanders
of His Majesty's Ships and Vessels
on the Mediterranean Station. *Victory*, at Sea, *15th November, 1804*

Whereas Hostilities have commenced between Great Britain and the Court of Spain; You are hereby required and directed, on falling in with any Spanish Ship or Vessel of War, or Merchantman belonging to the Subjects of his Catholic Majesty, or which may have Spanish property on board, and on doing so, you will use your utmost endeavour to capture, seize, burn, sink, or destroy them. In the event of your capturing any of their Merchant Vessels, or which may have Spanish property on board, I must desire that the strictest orders are given to the Officers sent into Port with such Merchant Vessels, to see that their hatches are immediately locked and sealed up, and also that all the Ship's papers are sealed up and taken care of, that no embezzlement of any kind whatever do take place, as they will answer the contrary at their peril. As condemnation cannot take place until his Majesty's pleasure is signified, it is my most positive direction that all Vessels having perishable cargoes on board are, immediately on their arrival in Port, delivered into the hands of the Vice-Admiralty Court, to be disposed of as the Judge shall think proper to direct.

NELSON AND BRONTE

To the Commissioners of the Navy

Victory, at Sea,
20th November, 1804

Gentlemen,

In further answer to your Letter of the 25th June last, relative to my opinion of the Guernsey jackets of a new manufacture, as therein mentioned, (which were issued to the Seamen on the 14th October,) and what further supply of them may be necessary for the Squadron under my command, I must beg leave to observe that the quality of the said Guernsey jackets is most excellent, but that they are considerably too narrow and short to be tucked into the Men's trowsers. It is, therefore, my opinion, that they ought to be at least three inches wider, and six longer. Indeed, if they were ten inches of a foot, it would be so much better, as they shrink very considerably in washing; and when the Seamen are on the yards, reefing or furling sails, the jackets rubs out of their trowsers, and exposes them to great danger of taking cold in their loins; so that, with this alteration, which is particularly necessary, they certainly would be the best and most valuable slops that ever were introduced into the Service, and be the means of saving many a good Seaman's life. With respect to the quantity required, it would not be too many to send out one for every Seaman in the Fleet. Perhaps the Guernsey jackets, in its present state, might answer the largest of the boys. I am, Gentlemen, &c.,

NELSON AND BRONTE

To Lady Hamilton *Victory, November 23rd, 1804*

As all our communication with Spain is at an end, I can now only expect to hear from my own dear Emma by the very slow mode of Admiralty Vessels, and it is now more than two months since the *John Bull* sailed. I much fear, something has been taken; for they never would, I am sure, have kept me so long in the dark. However, by management, and a portion of good luck, I got the account from Madrid, in a much shorter space of time than I could have hoped for; and I have set the whole Mediterranean to work, and think the Fleet cannot fail of being successful; and if I had had the spare Troops at Malta at my disposal, Minorca would at this moment have had English colours flying. . . . Where is my successor? I am not a little surprised at his not arriving. A Spanish War, I thought, would have hastened him. Ministers could not have thought that I wanted to fly the Service; my whole life has proved the contrary: and if they refuse me now, I shall most certainly leave this Country in March or April; for a few months' rest I must have, very soon. If I am in my grave, what are the mines of Peru to me! But, to say the truth, I have no idea of killing myself. I may, with care, live yet to do good service to the State. My cough is very bad; and my side, where I struck on the 14th of February, is very much swelled; at times a lump as large as my fist, brought on occasionally by violent coughing; but I hope and believe my lungs are yet safe. Sir William Bolton is just arrived from Malta. I am preparing to send him a cruise, where he will have the best chance I can give him of making ten thousand pounds. He is a very attentive, good, young man.

I have not heard from Naples this age. I have, in fact, no Small Craft to send for news. If I am soon to go home, I shall be with you before this letter. . . . As our means of communicating are cut off, I have only to beg you will not believe the idle rumours of Battles, &c. . . .

To Sir Alexander John Ball

Victory, December 5th, 1804

My dear Ball,

No Sir John Orde, no orders, no letters from England; very extraordinary. I almost begin to think that he is sent off Cadiz to reap the golden harvest, as Campbell was sent off Cadiz by Cornwallis (by orders from England) to reap my sugar harvest. It's very odd, two Admiralties to treat me so: surely I have dreamt that I have 'done the State some service.' But never mind; I am superior to those who could treat me so. When am I to be relieved? Seventy-six days since my last letter from the Admiralty. Poor Admiral Campbell sailed yesterday for England, very ill with debility, hectic fever, &c., but he cheered up on going away. I shall not trouble you with all my conjectures about Sir John Orde's never communicating with me for the three weeks he has been off Cadiz. I am ever, my dear Ball, yours most faithfully,

NELSON AND BRONTE

A Man of War is in sight, South.

To the Queen of the Two Sicilies

Gulf of Palma, *19th December, 1804*

Although I have addressed a letter to the King, to assure him of my unalterable attachment, yet I cannot resist declaring the same to your Majesty, for my obligations are equal to both, and so is my gratitude. Never, perhaps, was Europe more critically situated than at this moment, and never was the probability of universal Monarchy more nearly being realized, than in the person of the Corsican. I can see but little difference between the name of Emperor, King, or Prefet, if they perfectly obey his despotic orders. Your Majesty's illustrious Mother would not have so submitted. Prussia is trying to be destroyed last—Spain is little better than a Province of France—Russia does nothing on the grand scale. Would to God these great Powers reflected, that the boldest measures are the safest! They allow small States to fall, and to serve the enormous power of France, without appearing to reflect that every Kingdom which is annexed to France makes their existence, as independent States, more precarious. Your Majesty sees all this, and much more than I can; for your Majesty is the true daughter of the great Maria Theresa. Your good heart will forgive my free manner of writing, it may be the last I shall ever address to you; for if I do not very soon get quiet on shore, my thread of feeble life will break: but God's will be done. My last breath will be for the felicity of your Majesty, the King, and Royal Family. I am, &c.,

NELSON AND BRONTE

To William Marsden, Admiralty

Victory, December 30th, 1804

Sir,

I have been honoured with your letter of October 6th, on Christmas day, acquainting me that their Lordships had been pleased to comply with my request for permission to return to England for the re-establishment of my health; and that I am to leave Rear-Admiral Sir Richard Bickerton in the command of the Squadron. I am much obliged by their Lordships' kind compliance with my request, which is absolutely necessary from the present state of my health, and I shall avail myself of their Lordships' permission, the moment another Admiral, in the room of Admiral Campbell, joins the Fleet, unless the Enemy's Fleet should be at sea, when I should not think of quitting my Command until after the Battle. I have the honour to be, &c.,

NELSON AND BRONTE

FRENCH FLEET PUTS TO SEA

To Captain Thomas, H.M. Ship *Aetna*

Victory, January 19th, 1805

Sir,

The French Fleet put to sea yesterday, and were seen last night at twelve o'clock, steering South, or S. b W., then supposed in the latitude of Ajaccio, going ten or eleven miles per hour. They are therefore, from this account, bound round the South end of Sardinia. It is therefore my intention to proceed to the Southward, and endeavour to incercept them. If you do not hear of us in a few days, you must take the Transports to Malta, and then endeavour to join me, wherever you may hear I may be. I am, Sir, &c.,

NELSON AND BRONTE

To William Marsden, Admiralty

Victory, Faro of Messina, *January 29th, 1805*

Sir,

From the middle of December, I had information from various places, and amongst others, from the King of Sardinia, that the French were assembling Troops near Toulon, and had taken some of the best Troops and a corps of Cavalry from the Riviere of Genoa. Captain Capel obtained information that every Seaman was pressed and sent to Toulon. On the 16th, the *Active* spoke a Vessel from Marseilles, who reported that seven thousand Troops embarked on board the French Fleet. The wind had been nearly fourteen days Easterly, from N.E. to S.E.; therefore, if the Enemy had been bound to the Westward, they could not have gone with a fair wind. On the 18th, the Enemy put to sea, steering for the South-end of Sardinia. On the 19th, I was informed of it, and put to sea from the Madalena Island, that evening. On the 21st, a French Frigate was seen off the South-end of Sardinia by the *Seahorse*; but the weather was so thick and gale so strong, that Captain Boyle could not see their Fleet, and he joined me the 22nd with the information; but it was from heavy gales the 26th, before I could communicate with Cagliari, at which place they knew nothing of the Enemy. On the same day, the *Phoebe* joined with information that a French Ship of eighty guns had put into Ajaccio on the 19th, in the evening, with the loss of her topmasts, and otherwise much crippled. The *Seahorse* was detached to Naples the 25th, with information.

On the 28th, I was off Palermo and communicated with Sir John Acton; and the news which the Court of Naples has from Paris of January 5th, makes them fear that Sicily might be the object of the Enemy's armament.

One of two things must have happened, that either the French Fleet must have put back crippled, or that they are gone to the Eastward, probably to Egypt, therefore, I find no difficulty in pursuing the line of conduct I have adopted. If the Enemy have put back crippled, I could never overtake them, and therefore, I can do no harm in going to the Eastward; and if the Enemy are gone to the Eastward, I am right. My future movements must be guided by such information as I may be able to obtain, but their Lordships may rely that every exertion shall be used to find them out and bring them to Battle. I am, Sir, &c.,

NELSON AND BRONTE

To Viscount Melville, First Lord of the Admiralty

14th February, 1805

Feeling, as I do, that I am entirely responsible to my King and Country for the whole of my conduct, I find no difficulty at this moment, when I am so unhappy at not finding the French Fleet, nor having obtained the smallest information where they are, to lay before you the whole of the reasons which induced me to pursue the line of conduct I have done. I have consulted no man, therefore the whole blame of ignorance in forming my judgment must rest with me. I would allow no man to take from me an atom of my glory, had I fallen in with the French Fleet, nor do I desire any man to partake of any of the responsibility—all is mine, right or wrong. Therefore, I shall now state my reasons, after seeing that Sardinia, Naples, and Sicily were safe, for believing that Egypt was the destination of the French Fleet; and at this moment of sorrow, I still feel that I have acted right.

1. The wind had blown from N.E. to S.E. for fourteen days before they sailed; therefore they might without difficulty have gone to the Westward. 2. They came out with gentle breezes at N.W. and N.N.W. Had they been bound to Naples, the most natural thing for them to have done would have been to run along their own shore to the Eastward, where they would have had Ports every twenty leagues of Coast to

take shelter in. 3. They bore away in the evening of the 18th, with a strong gale at N.W. or N.N.W. steering S. or S. b W. It blew so hard that the *Seahorse* went more than thirteen knots an hour, to get out of their way. Desirable as Sardinia is for them, they could get it without risking their Fleet, although certainly not so quickly as by attacking Cagliari . . . however, I left nothing to chance in that respect, and therefore went off Cagliari. . . . Having afterwards gone to Sicily, both to Palermo, and Messina, and thereby given encouragement for a defence, and knowing all was safe at Naples, I had only the Morea and Egypt to look to: for although I knew one of the French Ships was crippled, yet I considered the character of Buonaparte; and that the orders given by him, on the banks of the Seine, would not take into consideration winds or weather; nor indeed could the accident of even three or four Ships alter, in my opinion, a destination of importance: therefore such an accident did not weigh in my mind, and I went first to the Morea, and then to Egypt. The result of my inquiries at Coron and Alexandria confirm me in my former opinion; and therefore, my Lord, if my obstinacy or ignorance is so gross, I should be the first to recommend your superseding me; but, on the contrary, if, as I flatter myself, it should be found that my ideas of the probable destination of the French Fleet were well founded, in the opinion of his Majesty's Ministers, then I shall hope for the consolation of having my conduct approved by his Majesty; who will, I am sure, weigh my whole proceedings in the scale of justice. The Pacha of Coron informed me, that the French Ambassador was to leave Constantinople on the 17th or 18th of January, which tallying with the sailing of the French Fleet, might probably be a plan of Buonaparte not to subject himself to the charge of invading the Country of a friendly Power, as the French Government had been charged with, when he went before to Egypt. I am, &c.,

NELSON AND BRONTE

To William Marsden, Admiralty — *Victory*, at Sea, *22nd February, 1805*

Sir,

Since my letter of the 12th of this month, I have to acquaint you, for the information of the Lords Commissioners of the Admiralty, that I arrived with the Fleet off Malta on the morning of the 19th instant, and received information from Captain Schomberg of the Enemy's Fleet having put back to Toulon in a very crippled state; and yesterday, off Maritimo, I received by the *Bittern* the accompanying letter from Mr. Elliott, his Majesty's Minister at the Court of Naples, which you will please communicate to their Lordships, and acquaint them that all the

Frigates and other Vessels are at present detached to obtain intelligence of the Enemy's Fleet, and that the moment I receive a more particular account of their state, I shall send a Sloop of War with information thereof to their Lordships.

The Fleet under my command is in excellent good health, and the Ships, although we have experienced a great deal of bad weather, have received no damage, and not a yard or mast sprung or crippled, or scarcely a sail split. I am, Sir, &c.,

NELSON AND BRONTE

To Lady Hamilton *Victory, March 9th, 1805*

I do assure you, my dearest Emma, that nothing can be more miserable or unhappy, than your poor Nelson. From the 19th of February, have we been beating from Malta to off Palma; where I am now anchored, the wind and sea being so very contrary and bad. But I cannot help myself, and no one in the Fleet can feel what I do: and, to mend my fate, yesterday Captain Layman arrived—to my great surprise —not in his Brig, but in a Spanish Cartel; he having been wrecked off Cadiz, and lost all the dispatches and letters. You will conceive my disappointment! It is now from November 2nd that I have had a line from England. Captain Layman says, he is sure the letters are sunk, never to rise again; but, as they were not thrown overboard until the Vessel struck the rock, I have much fear that they may have fallen into the hands of the Dons.

My reports from off Toulon, state the French Fleet as still in Port; but I shall ever be uneasy at not having fallen in with them. I know, my dear Emma, that it is in vain to repine; but my feelings are alive to meeting those fellows, after near two years' hard service. What a time! I could not have thought it possible that I should have been so long absent; unwell, and uncomfortable, in many respects. However, when I calculate upon the French Fleet's not coming to sea for this summer, I shall certainly go for dear England, and a thousand times dearer Merton. May heaven bless you, my own Emma. I cannot think where Sir William Bolton is got to; he ought to have joined me before this time. I send you a trifle, for a birthday's gift. I would to God, I could give you more; but I have it not. I get no Prize-money worth naming; but, if I have the good fortune to meet the French Fleet, I hope they will make me amends for all my anxiety; which has been, and is, indescribable.

How is my dear Horatia? I hope you have her under your guardian wing, at Merton. May God bless her! Captain Layman is now upon his trial. I hope he will come clear, with honour. I fear it was too great confidence in his own judgment that got him into the scrape; but it was impossible that any person living could have exerted himself more, when in a most trying and difficult situation.

March 10th

Poor Captain L. has been censured by the Court; but I have my own opinion. I sincerely pity him; and have wrote to Lord Melville and Sir Evan Nepean, to try what can be done. Altogether, I am much unhinged.

Tomorrow, if the wind lasts, I shall be off Toulon. Sir William Bolton is safe; I heard of him this morning. I hear that a Ship is coming out for him; but as this is only rumour, I cannot keep him from this opportunity of being made Post; and, I dare say, he will cause, by his delay, such a tumble, that Louis's son, who I have appointed to the *Childers*, will lose his promotion; and then Sir Billy will be wished at the devil! But I have done with this subject: the whole history has hurt me. Hardy has talked enough to him, to rouse his lethargic disposition. I have been much hurt at the loss of poor Mr. Girdlestone. He was a good man; but there will be an end of us all. What has Charles Connor been about? His is a curious letter. If he does not drink, he will do very well. Captain Hillyar has been very good to him. Colonel Suckling, I find, has sent his son to the Meditarranean, taking him from the *Narcissus*, where I had been at so much pains to place him. I know not where to find a Frigate to place him. He never will be so well and properly situated again. I am more plagued with other people's business, or rather nonsense, than with my own concerns. With some difficulty, I have got Suckling placed in the *Ambuscade*, with Captain Durban, who came on board at the moment I was writing.

March 31st

The history of Suckling will never be done. I have this moment got from him your letter, and one from his father. I shall say nothing to him; I don't blame the child, but those who took him out of the most desirable situation in the Navy. He never will get into such another advantageous Ship; but his father is a fool; and so, my dear Emma, that ends. The box which you sent me in May, 1804, is just arrived in the *Diligent* Store-ship. I have sent the Arms to Palermo, to Gibbs. The clothes are very acceptable. I will give you a kiss for sending them. God bless you. Amen.

April 1st

I am not surprised that we should both think the same about the kitchen; and, if I can afford it, I should like it to be done; but, by the fatal example of poor Mr. Hamilton, and many others, we must take care not to get into debt; for then we can neither help any of our relations, and must be for ever in misery. But of this we will talk more, when we walk upon the poop at Merton. Do you ever see Admiral and Mrs. Lutwidge? You will not forget me when you do. To Mrs. Cadogan, say everything that is kind; and to all our other friends; and be assured I am, &c.,

NELSON AND BRONTE

As I know that all the Mediterranean letters are cut and smoked, and perhaps read, I do not send you a little letter in this; but your utmost stretch of fancy cannot imagine more than I feel for my own dear Emma. God bless you. Amen.

To Viscount Melville

Victory, at Sea, *10th March, 1805*

My dear Lord,

I inclose some remarks made by Captain Layman whilst he was in Spain, after the very unfortunate loss of that fine Sloop, which your Lordship was so good as to give him the command of. Your Lordship will find the remarks flow from a most intelligent and active mind, and may be useful should any expedition take place against Cadiz; and, my dear Lord, give me leave to recommend Captain Layman to your kind protection; for, notwithstanding the Court-Martial has thought him deserving of censure for his running in with the land, yet, my Lord, allow me to say, that Captain Layman's misfortune was, perhaps, conceiving that other people's abilities were equal to his own, which, indeed, very few people's are.

I own myself one of those who do not fear the shore, for hardly any great things are done in a small Ship by a man that is; therefore, I make very great allowances for him. Indeed, his station was intended never to be from the shore in the Straits: and if he did not every day risk his Sloop, he would be useless upon that station. Captain Layman has served with me in three Ships, and I am well acquainted with his bravery, zeal, judgment, and activity; nor do I regret the loss of the *Raven* compared to the value of Captain Layman's services, which are a National loss.

You must, my dear Lord, forgive the warmth which I express for

Captain Layman; but he is in adversity, and, therefore, has the more claim to my attention and regard. If I had been censured every time I have run my Ship, or Fleets under my command, into great danger, I should long ago have been out of the Service, and never in the House of Peers. I am, my dear Lord, most faithfully your obedient servant,

NELSON AND BRONTE

FRENCH PUT TO SEA AGAIN

To Captain Thomas, H.M. Bomb *Aetna*

Victory, *April 4th, 1805*

Sir,

The French Fleet is at sea, steering to the Southward, Proceed off Cagliari, fire guns, and call out the *Seahorse*, and desire Captain Boyle to join me. I am now standing to the Westward, as I do not think the French will make Toro. I can tell him no more, as my movements must be very uncertain; but, I believe, the French, if they do not make Toro, will make Galita. I am, Sir, yours faithfully,

NELSON AND BRONTE

To Captain Durban, H.M. Ship *Ambuscade* *4th April, 1805*

Proceed to Galita, communicate with the fishermen, and try and find out if they have seen the French Fleet. I shall lie-to all night, and drift for Galita, and I shall try to keep within Sardinia and Galita till you join. If I am led away by information, I shall endeavour to send a letter to Palma, St. Pierres, or Cagliari. I am, &c.,

NELSON AND BRONTE

To Viscount Melville

5th April, 1805, Midway between the Coast of Barbary and Sardinia

My dear Lord,

Although I feel so far comfortable that the French Fleet is at sea, yet I must have a natural, and I hope a laudable anxiety of mind, until I have the happiness of seeing them. However, I have covered the Channel from Barbary to Toro, with Frigates and the Fleet. The French could not pass before today, if this be their route. I must leave as little as possible to chance, and I shall make sure they are to the Eastward of me, before I risk either Sardinia, Sicily, or Naples; for they may delay their time of coming even this distance, from an expectation that I shall push for Egypt, and thus leave them at liberty to act against Sardinia, Sicily, or Naples. I have taken everything into my most serious consideration; and although I may err in my judgment, yet your Lordship may rely, that I will do what I think is best for the honour of my King and Country, and for the protection of his Majesty's Allies. I will not say more. I am, &c.,

NELSON AND BRONTE

To Alexander Davison, Esq.

Victory, at Sea, *May 7th, 1805*

My dear Davison,

God only knows, my dear friend, what I have suffered, by not getting at the Enemy's Fleet, and when I naturally consoled myself that, at least, time would be given for Sir John Orde's Frigates, who were naturally sent after them, to return to Gibraltar with information for me, I had the mortification yesterday to find that none had been sent there. Nor was it generally believed that Sir John Orde had sent after them; but this I cannot believe, and I must suppose that they have all been unfortunately captured. I think it more than probable I shall go to the West Indies; for, I believe, from what I have yet heard of their course, &c., that is their destination, and there I hope to get hold of them, and to save our valuable West India possessions, and then I shall immediately return to England. But my health, or even my life must not come into consideration at this important crisis; for, however I may be called unfortunate, it never shall be said that I have been neglectful of my duty, or spared myself.

The business of Merton still will call for your kind and friendly attention. The kitchen I hope will be built before even this letter reaches you, and I must trouble you, my friend, to pay the bills; but I hope soon to repay you with many, many kind thanks. I have just heard that Lord Melville has left the Admiralty,* owing to the Tenth Report of the Navy Inquiries. His Lordship was doing much for the Service, and now we have to look forward to some one else. I shall write a line to our friend Nepean, who must be harassed by these changes. God bless you, my dear Davison, and believe me ever, with the truest friendship, yours most faithfully and affectionately,

NELSON AND BRONTE

* Viscount Melville was succeeded as First Lord of the Admiralty on 30th April, 1805, by Admiral Lord Barham. Sir Evan Nepean and all the other Lords remained.

All my letters by *Niger* and *Avenger* are gone up the Mediterranean, and will never be received by me. But salt beef and French Fleet, is far preferable to roast beef and champagne without them. May God prosper my exertions, I pray most fervently, and I think He will in the end.

To Mrs. Bolton

Victory, May 9th, 1805

My dear Sister,

God only knows where I may be on July first, and, therefore, I send you a bill for one hundred pounds; and when I get home, I hope to be able to keep Tom at College without one farthing's expense to Mr. Bolton; and both you and him may be assured, that I would do more, if in my power. I should have been a very rich, instead of a poor man, if Lord Melville had not given the Galleons to Sir John Orde. God bless you, Mr. Bolton, and family; and believe me ever, your most affectionate brother,

NELSON AND BRONTE

I have sent Sir William a cruize, and I hope he will be more fortunate than he has hitherto been.

CHAPTER FOURTEEN

THE CHASE TO THE WEST

To Sir Alexander John Ball

Victory, May 10th, 1805, off Lagos

My dear Ball,

My lot is cast, and I am going to the West Indies, where, although I am late, yet chance may have given them a bad passage, and me a good one: I must hope for the best. A number or Troops are now at Lisbon; but, except that they are destined for the Mediterranean, I know nothing. I am still very unwell. May God bless you, my dear Ball; and be assured I am, &c.,

NELSON AND BRONTE

To the Commander of any of His Majesty's Ships or Vessels in search of the Mediterranean Squadron.

Victory, in Lagos Bay,
10th May, 1805

Most Secret.

Sir,

I desire to acquaint you that I am proceeding with the Squadron;* under my command, to the West Indies, in search of the Enemy's Fleet, and request that you will, without a moment's loss of time, communicate the same to the Lords Commissioners of the Admiralty, and to the Commander-in-Chief of the Channel Fleet, in the event of your falling in with him. I am, Sir, &c.,

NELSON AND BRONTE

N.B.—Barbadoes will be the first place I shall call at.

To William Haslewood *Victory, May 16th, 1805*

It is my desire that Mrs. Gibson is given an annuity of twenty pounds a year, when that she gives up my adopted daughter, Horatia Nelson Thompson, to the guardianship of my dear friend, Lady Emma

* The squadron with which Nelson pursued the enemy's fleet of eighteen Ships of the Line to the West Indies, consisted only of ten Sail of the Line – viz, *Victory, Canopus, Superb, Spencer, Donegal, Tigre, Leviathan, Belleisle, Conqueror, and Swiftsure;* and three frigates, *Decade, Amphion*, and *Amazon*.

Hamilton, and promises not to have anything more to do with the child, either directly or indirectly; and I leave my estate chargeable with this annuity.

NELSON AND BRONTE

To Lady Hamilton

Victory, at Sea, *May 16th, 1805*

My dearest Lady Hamilton,

As it is my desire to take my adopted daughter, Horatia Nelson Thompson, from under the care of Mrs. Gibson, and to place her under your guardianship, in order that she may be properly educated and brought up, I have, therefore, most earnestly to entreat that you will undertake this charge; and as it is my intention to allow Mrs. Gibson, as a free-will offering from myself, (she having no claim upon me, having been regularly paid for her care of the child,) the sum of twenty pounds a year, for the term of her natural life; and I mean it should commence when the child is delivered to you. But should Mrs. Gibson endeavour, upon any pretence, to keep my adopted daughter any longer in her care, then I do not hold myself bound to give her one farthing; and I shall, most probably, take other measures.

I shall write to Mr. Haslewood, upon your telling him that you have received the child, to settle the annuity upon Mrs Gibson; and if you think Miss Connor disposed to be the governess of Horatia, I will make her any allowance for her trouble which you may think proper. I, again and again, my dearest friend, request your care of my adopted daughter, whom I pray God to bless. I am ever, for ever, my dear Lady Hamilton, your most faithful and affectionate,

NELSON AND BRONTE

To Captain Keats, H.M. Ship *Superb*

Victory, *May 9th, 1805*

My dear Keats,

I am fearful that you think that the *Superb* does not go as fast as I could wish. However that may be, (for if we all went ten knots, I should not think it fast enough,) yet I would have you be assured that I know and feel that the *Superb* does all which is possible for a Ship to accomplish; and I desire that you will not fret upon the occasion. I hope, and indeed feel confident, that very soon you will help me to secure the *Majesteux*, I think we have been from Cape St. Vincent very fortunate, and shall be in the West Indies time enough to secure Jamaica, which I think is their object. Whatever may happen, believe me ever, my dear Keats, your most obliged and sincere friend,

NELSON AND BRONTE

PLAN OF ATTACK

[Drawn up by Nelson during his pursuit of the French Fleet to the West Indies]

The business of an English Commander-in-Chief being first to bring an Enemy's Fleet to Battle, on the most advantageous terms to himself, (I mean that of laying his Ships close on board the Enemy, as expeditiously as possible;) and secondly, to continue them there, without separating, till the business is decided; I am sensible beyond this object it is not necessary that I should say a word, being fully assured that the Admirals and Captains of the Fleet I have the honour to command, will, knowing my precise object, that of a close and decisive Battle, supply any deficiency in my not making signals; which may, if extended beyond these objects, either be misunderstood, or, if waited for, very probably, from various causes, be impossible for the Commander-in-Chief to make: therefore, it will only be requisite for me to state, in as few words as possible, the various modes in which it may be necessary for me to obtain my object, on which depends, not only the honour and glory of our Country, but possibly its safety, and with it that of all Europe, from French tyranny and oppression.

If the two Fleets are both willing to fight, but little manoeuvring is necessary; the less the better;—a day is soon lost in that business: therefore I will only suppose that the Enemy's Fleet being to leeward, standing close upon the wind on the starboard tack, and that I am nearly ahead of them, standing on the larboard tack, of course I should weather them. The weather must be supposed to be moderate; for if it be a gale of wind, the manoeuvring of both Fleets is but of little avail, and probably no decisive Action would take place with the whole Fleet. Two modes present themselves: one to stand on, just out of gun-shot, until the Van-Ship of my Line would be about the centre Ship of the Enemy, then make the signal to wear together, then bear up, engage with all our force the six or five Van-Ships of the Enemy, passing, certainly, if opportunity offered, through their Line. This would prevent their bearing up, and the Action, from the known bravery and conduct of the Admirals and Captains, would certainly be decisive: the second or third Rear-Ships of the Enemy would act as they please, and our Ships would give a good account of them, should they persist in mixing with our Ships. The other mode would be, to stand under an easy but commanding sail, directly for their headmost Ship, so as to prevent the Enemy from knowing whether I should pass to leeward or windward of him. In that situation, I would make the signal to engage the Enemy to leeward, and to cut through their Fleet about the sixth Ship from the

Van, passing very close; they being on a wind, and you going large, could cut their Line when you please. The Van-Ships of the Enemy would, by the time our Rear came abreast of the Van-Ship, be severely cut up, and our Van could not expect to escape damage. I would then have our Rear Ship, and every Ship in succession, wear, continue the Action with either the Van-Ship, or second Ship, as it might appear most eligible from her crippled state; and this mode pursued, I see nothing to prevent the capture of the five or six Ships of the Enemy's Van. The two or three Ships of the Enemy's Rear must either bear up, or wear; and, in either case, although they would be in a better plight probably than our two Van-Ships (now the Rear) yet they would be separated, and at a distance to leeward, so as to give our Ships time to refit; and by that time, I believe, the Battle would, from the judgment of the Admiral and Captains, be over with the rest of them. Signals from these moments are useless, when every man is disposed to do his duty. The great object is for us to support each other, and to keep close to the Enemy, and to leeward of him.

If the Enemy are running away, then the only signals necessary will be, to engage the Enemy as arriving up with them; and the other Ships to pass on for the second, third, &c., giving, if possible, a close fire into the Enemy in passing, taking care to give our Ships engaged, notice of your intention.

PRIVATE DIARY

21st June, 1805

Midnight, nearly calm, saw three planks, which I think came from the French Fleet. Very miserable, which is very foolish.

NELSON AND BRONTE

PRIVATE DIARY

Wednesday, 17th July, 1805

Our whole run from Barbuda, day by day, was 3,459 miles: our run from Cape St. Vincent to Barbadoes was 3,227 miles, so that our run back was only 232 miles more than our run out—allowance being made for the difference of the latitudes and longitudes of Barbadoes and Barbuda; average, per day, thirty-four leagues, wanting nine miles.

18th July, 1805

Cape Spartel in sight, but no French Fleet, nor any information about them: how sorrowful this makes me, but I cannot help myself.

PRIVATE DIARY

20th July, 1805

I went on shore for the first time since the 16th of June, 1803; and from having my foot out of the *Victory*, two years, wanting ten days.

NELSON AND BRONTE

To William Marsden, Admiralty *About 20th July, 1805*

I am, my dear Mr. Marsden, as completely miserable as my greatest enemy could wish me; but I neither blame fortune or my own judgment. Oh, General Brereton! General Brereton! Pray forward the inclosed, I shall see and thank you very soon. Ever your obliged,

NELSON AND BRONTE

To Alexander Davison

Victory, July 24th, 1805

My dear Davison,

As all my letters have been sent to England, I know nothing of what is passing; but I hope very, very soon to take you by the hand. I am as miserable as you can conceive. But for General Brereton's damned information, Nelson would have been, living or dead, the greatest man in his Profession that England ever saw. Now, alas! I am nothing—perhaps shall incur censure for misfortunes which may happen, and have happened. When I follow my own head, I am, in general, much more correct in my judgment, than following the opinion of others. I resisted the opinion of General Brereton's information till it would have been the height of presumption to have carried my disbelief further. I could not, in the face of Admirals and Admirals, go N.W., when it was *apparently* clear that the Enemy had gone South. But I am miserable. I now long to hear that they are arrived in some Port in the Bay; for until they are arrived somewhere, I can do nothing but fret. Then I shall proceed to England. I can say nothing, or think of anything, but the loss my Country has sustained by General Brereton's unfortunate, ill-timed, false information. God bless you; and believe me ever, my dear Davison, your most faithful and affectionate friend,

NELSON AND BRONTE

To Rt. Hon. Admiral Lord Gardner

Victory, off Cape St. Mary's,
July 27th, 1805

My Lord,

I am proceeding to the Northward, as I have no doubt that the Enemy's Fleet from the West Indies are gone into some Port in the Bay. Should I receive any information which may lead me to suppose the destination of the Enemy is Ireland, I shall form a junction with you; and it is most probable that I shall, if I receive no intelligence, make Cape Clear; therefore, I shall be obliged if you will order some of your Cruizers to look out for me, with such information as may enable me to direct my further proceedings. I have with me eleven Sail of the Line. I cannot be many days after the *Pickle* Schooner, who is directed to put this letter on board any Frigate of your Squadron, or any one looking out for information near the Channel, which she may fall in with. I have the honour to be, with the highest respect, &c.,

NELSON AND BRONTE

CHAPTER FIFTEEN

LAST DAYS AT MERTON

['19 August, 1805. At 9 p.m. hauled down Lord Nelson's Flag.'—*Victory's* Log.

Nelson proceeded immediately to Merton and arrived there on the following morning.

He remained at Merton from 20 August, 1805, to 13 September, 1805, when he left to join the *Victory* at Portsmouth. Thereafter followed the Campaign of Trafalgar.]

To William Beckford

Merton, *August 31st, 1805*

My dear Mr. Beckford,

Many thanks for your kind letter. Nothing could give me more pleasure than paying my respects at Fonthill, but I cannot move at present, as all my family are with me, and my stay is very uncertain; and, besides, I have refused for the present all invitations. Every Ship, even the *Victory*, is ordered out, for there is an entire ignorance whether the Ferrol Fleet is coming to the Northward, gone to the Mediterranean, or cruizing for our valuable homeward-bound Fleet. I hope they will be met with and annihilated. Lady Hamilton desires me to present her kind regards.—And believe me ever, my dear Mr. Beckford, your much obliged friend,

NELSON AND BRONTE

To the Rev. Robert Rolfe

September 5th, 1805

My dear Mr. Rolfe,

I hope you have not been angry at my not having answered your truly kind letter, but in truth I have not a moment. All my things are this day going off for Portsmouth. Accept my best regards and good wishes, and say every kind thing to your good mother and sister; and be assured I am ever, my dear Rolfe, your most affectionate cousin.

NELSON AND BRONTE

Lady Hamilton to Lady Bolton, Lord Nelson's Niece

4th September, 1805

My dear Friend,

I am again broken-hearted, as our dear Nelson is immediately going. It seems as though I have had a fortnight's dream, and am awoke to all the misery of this cruel separation. But what can I do? His powerful arm is of so much consequence to his Country. But I do, nor cannot say more. My heart is broken. Your father goes today. Mr. William Bolton came yesterday. God bless you. Ever your affectionate,

E. HAMILTON

To Alexander Davison

Merton, *September 6th, 1805*

My dear Davison,

I much fear that I shall not have the pleasure of seeing you before my departure, and to thank you for all your kind attentions. I wish you could name any one to settle my long Account; for although I may not be able to pay off at this moment the balance due to you, still it would be a satisfaction to me to have it settled; and then I could give you a Bond for the amount, until I may be able to pay it, which I still hope to be able to do in spite of Sir John Orde. I hope my absence will not be long, and that I shall soon meet the Combined Fleets, with a force sufficient to do the job well; for half a Victory would but half content me. But I do not believe the Admiralty can give me a force within fifteen or sixteen Sail of the Line of the Enemy; and therefore, if every Ship took her opponent, we should have to contend with a fresh Fleet of fifteen or sixteen sail of the Line. But I will do my best; and I hope God Almighty will go with me. I have much to lose, but little gain; and I go because it's right, and I will serve the Country faithfully.

I send you a Memorandum, which I am sure you will comply with. Poor blind Mrs. Nelson I must assist. This morning a Mr. Brand, an apothecary, called upon me for £113 2s. 6d. as due from my brother Maurice to him. I shall refer him to you, and if it is a just demand, he must have it. I shall leave the bill in St. James's-square.—Ever, my dear Davison, your most obliged and affectionate Friend,

NELSON AND BRONTE

To Vice-Admiral Collingwood

Admiralty, *September 7th, 1805*

My dear Coll.,

I shall be with you in a very few days, and I hope you will remain

Second in Command. You will change the *Dreadnought* for *Royal Sovereign*, which I hope you will like. Ever, my dear Collingwood, most faithfully yours,

NELSON AND BRONTE

PRIVATE DIARY

Friday Night, 13th September

At half-past ten drove from dear dear Merton, where I left all which I hold dear in this world, to go to serve my King and Country. May the Great God whom I adore enable me to fulfil the expectations of my Country; and if it is His good pleasure that I should return, my thanks will never cease being offered up to the Throne of His Mercy. If it is His good providence to cut short my days upon earth, I bow with the greatest submission, relying that He will protect those so dear to me, that I may leave behind.—His will be done: Amen, Amen, Amen.

Saturday, September 14th, 1805

At six o'clock arrived at Portsmouth, and having arranged all my business, embarked at the Bathing Machines with Mr. Rose and Mr. Canning at two; got on board the *Victory* at St. Helens, who dined with me; preparing for sea.

CAMPAIGN OF TRAFALGAR

['September 14. a.m. at 11.30, hoisted the Flag of the Right Honourable Lord Viscount Nelson, K.B., Sunday, 15th: 8 a.m. weighed and made sail to the S.S.E. *Euryalus* in company.'—*Victory's* Log.]

To William Marsden, Admiralty

Victory, at St. Helens,
14th September, 1805

Sir,

You will please to acquaint the Lords Commissioners of the Admiralty that I arrived at Portsmouth this morning at six o'clock, and hoisted my Flag on board the *Victory* at this anchorage about noon. The *Royal Sovereign*, *Defiance*, and *Agamemnon*, are not yet ready for sea, so that I must leave them to follow, the moment they are complete. The Ships named in the margin only accompany me. I am, Sir, &c.,

NELSON AND BRONTE

To Lady Hamilton

Victory, off Plymouth,
September 17th, 1805

Nine o'clock in the Morning, Blowing fresh at W.S.W., dead foul wind.

I sent, my own dearest Emma, a letter for you, last night, in a Torbay Boat, and gave the man a guinea to put it in the Post Office. We have had a nasty blowing night, and it looks very dirty. I am now signalling the Ships at Plymouth to join me; but I rather doubt their ability to get to sea. However, I have got clear of Portland, and have Cawsand Bay and Torbay under the lee. I intreat, my dear Emma, that you will cheer up; and we will look forward to many, many happy years, and be surrounded by our children's children. God Almighty can, when he pleases, remove the impediment. My heart and soul is with you and Horatia. I got this line ready in case a Boat should get alongside. For ever, ever, I am yours, most devotedly,

NELSON AND BRONTE

Mr. Rose said he would write to Mr. Bolton, if I was sailed; but I have forgot to give him the direction: but I will send it today. I think I shall succeed very soon, if not at this moment.

Wednesday, September 18th

I had no opportunity of sending your letter yesterday, nor do I see any prospect at present. The *Ajax* and *Thunderer* are joining; but it is nearly calm, with a swell from the Westward. Perseverance has got us thus far; and the same will, I dare say, get us on. Thomas seems to do very well, and content. Tell Mr. Lancaster that I have no doubt that his son will do very well. God bless you, my own Emma. I am giving my letters to Blackwood, to put on board the first Vessel he meets going to England or Ireland. Once more, heavens bless you! Ever, for ever, your

NELSON AND BRONTE

To James Gambier, Consul at Lisbon

Victory, September 25th, 1805

Sir,

I entreat that it may not be known that I am off Lisbon, for I hope to see our Enemy at sea; and I have further to request that every man which can be raised at Lisbon may be placed for the Fleet under my command. I shall write to Lord Strangford from Lagos. I am, Sir, with great respect, &c.,

NELSON AND BRONTE

To Captain Sutton, H.M. Ship *Amphion*, Tagus

Victory, September 25th, 1805

(Most secret.)

My dear Sutton,

Get every man, in every way, for the Fleet under my command; and beg Mr. Gambier to secure all he can for the Fleet.—I am ever, my dear Sutton, most faithfully yours,

NELSON AND BRONTE

Pray, do not mention my near approach to Cadiz.

GENERAL ORDER

To all Junior Flag Officers, and the Captains or Commanders of any of His Majesty's Ships or Vessels, in search of me.

Victory, off Cape St. Vincent,
27th September, 1805

Secret Rendezvous.

The Rendezvous of the Fleet under my command will be between Cape St. Mary's and Cadiz. Ships, therefore, in search of me, not falling in with the Fleet off the former place, must approach the latter with the utmost caution; and should I have left Cadiz in pursuit of the Enemy, a Vessel of War will be stationed off Cape Spartel with information where I am gone to.

N.B. Tangier Bay will always give information.

NELSON AND BRONTE

To Alexander Davison, Esq. *Victory, about 30th September, 1805*

Day by day, my dear friend, I am expecting the Enemy's Fleet to put to sea—every day, hour, and moment; and you may rely that, if it is within the power of man to get at them, that it shall be done; and I am sure that all my brethren look to that day as the finish of our laborious cruise. The event no man can say exactly; but I must think, or render great injustice to those under me, that, let the Battle be when it may, it will never have been surpassed. My shattered frame, if I survive that day, will require rest, and that is all I shall ask for. If I fall on such a glorious occasion, it shall be my pride to take care that my friends shall not blush for me. These things are in the hands of a wise and just Providence and His will be done! I have got some trifle, thank God, to leave to those I hold most dear, and I have taken care not to neglect it. Do not think I am low-spirited on this account, or fancy anything is to happen to me; quite the contrary—my mind is calm, and I have only to think of destroying our inveterate foe. I have two Frigates gone for more information, and we all hope for a meeting with the Enemy. Nothing can be finer than the Fleet under my command. Whatever be the event, believe me ever, my dear Davison, your much obliged and sincere friend,

NELSON AND BRONTE

To Lady Hamilton

Victory, October 1st, 1805

My dearest Emma,

It is a relief to me, to take up the pen, and write you a line; for I have had, about four o'clock this morning, one of my dreadful spasms, which has almost enervated me. It is very odd; I was hardly ever better than yesterday. Fremantle stayed with me till eight o'clock, and I slept uncommonly well; but was awoke with this disorder. My opinion of its effect, some one day, has never altered. However, it is entirely gone off, and I am only quite weak. The good people of England will not believe that rest of body and mind is necessary for me. But perhaps this spasm may not come again these six months. I had been writing seven hours yesterday; perhaps that had some hand in bringing it upon me.

I joined the Fleet late on the evening of the 28th of September, but could not communicate with them until the next morning. I believe my arrival was most welcome, not only to the Commander of the Fleet, but also to every individual in it; and, when I came to explain to them the '*Nelson touch*,' it was like an electric shock. Some shed tears, all approved —'It was new—it was singular—it was simple!'; and, from Admirals downwards, it was repeated—'It must succeed, if ever they will allow us to get at them. You are, my Lord, surrounded by friends whom you inspire with confidence.' Some may be Judas's; but the majority are certainly much pleased with my commanding them.

To Captain Duff, H.M. Ship *Mars* *4th October, 1805*

As the Enemy's Fleets may be hourly expected to put to sea from Cadiz, I have to desire that you will keep, with the *Mars*, *Defence* and *Colossus*, from three to four leagues between the Fleet and Cadiz, in order that I may get the information from the Frigates stationed off that Port, as expeditiously as possible. Distant Signals to be used, when Flags, from the state of the weather, may not readily be distinguished in their colours. If the Enemy be out, or coming out, fire guns by day or night, in order to draw my attention. In thick weather, the Ships are to close within signal of the *Victory;* one of the Ships to be placed to windward, or rather to the Eastward of the other two, to extend the distance of seeing; and I have desired Captain Blackwood to throw a Frigate to the Westward of Cadiz, for the purpose of any easy and early communication.

NELSON AND BRONTE

To William Marsden, Admiralty *About 5th October, 1805*

I am sorry ever to trouble their Lordships with anything like a complaint of a want of Frigates and Sloops; but if the different services require them, and I have them not, those services must be neglected to be performed. I am taking all Frigates about me I possibly can; for if I were an Angel, and attending to all the other points of my Command, let the Enemy escape for want of the *eyes of the Fleet*, I should consider myself as most highly reprehensible. Never less than eight Frigates, and three good fast-sailing Brigs, should always be with the Fleet to watch Cadiz; and to carry Transports in and out to refit it, would take at least ten and four Brigs, to do that service well. At present I have only been able to collect two, which makes me very uneasy. I am, &c.,

NELSON AND BRONTE

To the Rt. Hon. George Rose

Victory, 16 leagues West from Cadiz,
October 6th, 1805

My dear Mr. Rose,

Your two letters of September 17th (have arrived), and I feel much obliged by your kind intentions for my dear Mr. Bolton, and I think Mr. Pitt will do what he can to oblige me. I verily believe the Country will soon be put to some expense for my account, either a Monument, or a new Pension and Honours; for I have not the very smallest doubt but that a very few days, almost hours, will put us in Battle; the success no man can ensure, but the fighting them, if they are to be got at, I pledge myself, and if the force arrives which is intended. I am very, very, very anxious for its arrival, for the thing will be done if a few more days elapse; and I want for the sake of our Country that it should be done so effectually as to have nothing to wish for; and what will signify the force the day after the Battle? it is, as Mr. Pitt knows, annihilation that the Country wants, and not merely a splendid Victory of twenty-three to thirty-six,—honourable to the parties concerned, but absolutely useless in the extended scale to bring Buonaparte to his marrow-bones: numbers only can annihilate. I think, not for myself, but the Country, therefore I hope the Admiralty will send the fixt force as soon as possible, and Frigates, and Sloops of War, for I am very destitute. I do not mean this as any complaint, quite the contrary; I believe they are doing all they can, if interest does not interfere; therefore, if Mr. Pitt would hint to Lord Barham, that he shall be anxious until I get the force proposed, and plenty of Frigates and Sloops in order to watch them closely, it may be advantageous to the Country: you are at liberty to mention this to Mr. Pitt, but I would not wish it to go farther. I am ever, my dear Mr. Rose,

Your most obliged and faithful friend,

NELSON AND BRONTE

The Treasury should order me to land the money, 150,000 dollars in Spanish, in the Mediterranean. I mentioned it to Mr. Pitt, but I am ordered to land it in England, and the Ships are here.

To Vice-Admiral Collingwood

Victory, October 9th, 1805

My dear Coll.,

I send you Captain Blackwood's letter; and, as I hope *Weazle* has joined, he will have five Frigates and a Brig: they surely cannot escape us. I wish we could get a fine day, and clear our Transports, at least of the bread, and by that time water will come. *Niger* is with the Transports. *Sovereign*'s cables can go into the *Malabar*. I shall be glad to see you mounted in her. I send you my Plan of Attack, as far as a man dare venture to guess at the very uncertain position the Enemy may be found in. But, my dear friend, it is to place you perfectly at ease respecting my intentions, and to give full scope to your judgment for carrying them into effect. We can, my dear Coll., have no little jealousies. We have only one great object in view, that of annihilating our Enemies, and getting a glorious Peace for our Country. No man has more confidence in another than I have in you: and no man will render your services more justice than your very old friend,

NELSON AND BRONTE

P.S.—Keep Blackwood's letter: the Schooner goes off Cadiz from you, and if you have not disposed of the Paper of the 23rd, send them to Blackwood.

To the respective Captains *Victory*, off Cadiz, *10th October, 1805*

Mem.:

When in presence of an Enemy, all the Ships under my command are to bear white Colours, and a Union Jack is to be suspended from the fore top-gallant stay.

NELSON AND BRONTE

[As Collingwoood was a Vice-Admiral of the *Blue*, his Division bore *blue* Ensigns; but in consequence of this Order all the Fleet wore *white* Ensigns in the Battle.]

To Captain Blackwood, H.M. Ship *Euryalus*

Victory, October 10th, 1805

My dear Blackwood,

Keep your five Frigates, *Weazle*, and *Pickle*, and let me know every movement. I rely on you, that we can't miss getting hold of them, and I will give them such a shaking as they never yet experienced; at least I will lay down my life in the attempt. We are a very powerful Fleet, and not to be held cheap. I have told Parker, and do you direct Ships bringing information of their coming out, to fire guns every three minutes by the watch, and in the night to fire off rockets, if they have them, from the mast-head. I have nothing more to say, than I hope they will sail tonight.

Ever yours most faithfully,

NELSON AND BRONTE

To Lady Hamilton *Victory, October 19th, 1805*

My dearest beloved Emma, the dear friend of my bosom. The signal has been made that the Enemy's Combined Fleet are coming out of Port. We have very little wind, so that I have no hopes of seeing them before tomorrow. May the God of Battles crown my endeavours with success; at all events, I will take care that my name shall ever be most dear to you and Horatia, both of whom I love as much as my own life.

And as my last writing before the Battle will be to you, so I hope in God that I shall live to finish my letter after the Battle. May Heaven bless you prays your

NELSON AND BRONTE

October 20th. In the morning, we were close to the Mouth of the Straits, but the wind had not come far enough to the Westward to allow the Combined Fleets to weather the Shoals off Trafalgar; but they were counted as far as forty Sail of Ships of War, which I suppose to be thirty-four of the Line, and six Frigates. A group of them was seen off the Lighthouse of Cadiz this morning, but it blows so very fresh and thick weather, that I rather believe they will go into the Harbour before night. May God Almighty give us success over these fellows, and enable us to get a Peace.

PRIVATE DIARY

October 19th

Fine weather, wind Easterly. At half-past nine, the *Mars*, being one of the look-out Ships, repeated the Signal, 'that the Enemy was coming out of Port'—made the signal for a 'General Chase S.E.'; wind at South, Cadiz bearing E.N.E. by compass, distant sixteen leagues. At three the *Colossus*, made the Signal, 'that the Enemy's Fleet was at sea.' In the evening directed the Fleet to observe my motions during the night, and for *Britannia*, *Prince*, and *Dreadnought*, they being heavy sailers, to take their stations as convenient; and for *Mars*, *Orion*, *Belleisle*, *Leviathan*, *Bellerophon*, and *Polyphemus*, to go ahead during the night, and to carry a light, standing for the Straits' Mouth.

MEMORANDUM

Victory, off Cadiz,
20th October, 1805

Captain Blackwood to keep with two Frigates in sight of the Enemy in the night. Two other Frigates to be placed between him and the *Defence*, Captain Hope. *Colossus* will take her station between *Defence* and *Mars*. *Mars* to communicate with the *Victory*.

Signals by Night

If the Enemy are standing to the Southward, or towards the Straits, burn two blue lights together, every hour, in order to make the greater blaze. If the Enemy are standing to the Westward three guns, quick, every hour.

NELSON AND BRONTE

PRIVATE DIARY

Sunday, October 20th, 1805

Fresh breezes S.S.W. and rainy. Communicated with *Phoebe*, *Defence*, and *Colossus*, who saw near forty Sail of Ships of War outside of Cadiz yesterday evening; but the wind being Southerly, they could not get to the Mouth of the Straits. We were between Trafalgar and Cape Spartel. The Frigates made the signal that they saw 9 Sail outside the Harbour; gave the Frigates instructions for their guidance, and placed *Defence*, *Colossus*, and *Mars*, between me and the Frigates. At noon fresh gales and heavy rain, Cadiz N.E. 9 leagues. In the afternoon Captain Blackwood telegraphed that the Enemy seemed determined to go to the Westward; and that they shall *not* do if in the power of Nelson and Bronte to prevent them. At 5 telegraphed Captain B., that I relied upon his keeping sight of the Enemy. At 6 o'clock *Naiad* made the signal for 31 Sail of the Enemy N.N.E. The Frigates and look-out Ships kept sight of the Enemy most admirably all night, and told me by signals which tack they were upon. At 8 we wore, and stood to the S.W., and at four A.M. wore, stood to the N.E.

PRIVATE DIARY

Monday, October 21st, 1805

At daylight saw the Enemy's Combined Fleet from East to E.S.E.; bore away; made the signal for Order of Sailing, and to Prepare for Battle; the Enemy with their heads to the Southward; at seven the Enemy wearing in succession. May the Great God, whom I worship, grant to my Country, and for the benefit of Europe in general, a great and glorious Victory; and may no misconduct in any one tarnish it; and may humanity after Victory be the predominant feature in the British Fleet. For myself, individually, I commit my life to Him, who made me, and may his blessing light upon my endeavours for serving my Country faithfully. To him I resign myself and the just cause which is entrusted to me to defend. Amen. Amen. Amen.

CODICIL TO LORD NELSON'S WILL

October the twenty-first, one thousand eight hundred and five, then in sight of the Combined Fleets of France and Spain, distant about ten miles.

Whereas the eminent services of Emma Hamilton, widow of the Right Honourable Sir William Hamilton, have been of the very greatest service to our King and Country, to my knowledge, without her receiving any reward from either our King or Country;—first, that she obtained the King of Spain's letter, in 1796, to his brother, the King of Naples, acquainting him of his intention to declare War against England; from which Letter the Ministry sent out orders to then Sir John Jervis, to strike a stroke, if opportunity offered, against either the Arsenals of Spain, or her Fleets. That neither of these was done is not the fault of Lady Hamilton. The opportunity might have been offered. Secondly, the British Fleet under my command, could never have returned the second time to Egypt, had not Lady Hamilton's influence with the Queen of Naples caused letters to be wrote to the Governor of Syracuse, that he was to encourage the Fleet being supplied with everything, should they put into any Port in Sicily. We put into Syracuse, and received every supply, went to Egypt, and destroyed the French Fleet. Could I have rewarded these services I would not now call upon my Country; but as that has not been in my power, I leave Emma Lady Hamilton, therefore, a Legacy to my King and Country, that they will give her an ample provision to maintain her rank in life. I also leave to the beneficence of my Country my adopted daughter, Horatia Nelson Thompson; and I desire she will use in future the name of Nelson only. These are the only favours I ask of my King and Country at this moment when I am going to fight their Battle. May God bless my King and Country, and all those who I hold dear. My relations it is needless to mention: they will of course be amply provided for.

NELSON AND BRONTE

Witnessed—Henry Blackwood.
T. M. Hardy.

[A few hours later Nelson was mortally wounded.]

FINIS

APPENDIX

1. The Nelson-Shirley Correspondence
2. Case of Wm. Clark, A.B.
3. Nelson's appeal for cheaper postage
4. Respect for the British flag
5. Facsimile of Nelson's first letter written after losing his right arm

APPENDIX

1. THE NELSON-SHIRLEY CORRESPONDENCE

When Captain Nelson arrived on the Leeward Islands station in command of H.M.S. *Boreas* in the spring of 1784, he found himself, though only twenty-five, senior captain on the station. He found also that the Admiral, Sir Richard Hughes, was taking no steps to check the contraband trade in which American vessels were actively engaged. Nelson pressed the Admiral to issue orders enforcing the Navigation Act which excluded American vessels from trading with British colonies, Americans being no longer loyal subjects of King George. The Admiral reluctantly issued such orders, but later he issued a supplementary order. This directed naval officers afloat not to take hostile action against American traders but to report the matter to the Governor, for his instructions.

Nelson suspected that Governor Shirley, among others, was in favour of admitting American vessels to the ports, the trade being of as great importance to the Islanders as to the Yankees.

When, therefore, Nelson received the following letter from Governor Shirley he became very angry, and the subsequent correspondence between them traces the course of the dispute, from which Nelson emerged fully vindicated.

Some may think the Nelson-Shirley correspondence exhibits Nelson in an unfavourable light as a presumptuous young man who addressed impertinent letters to His Excellency the Governor and who was, in consequence, properly rebuked for so doing.

Governor Shirley to Nelson

Antigua, *January 15th, 1785*

Sir,

I take the liberty of informing you that a few days ago I received from Sir R. Hughes a copy of an Order dated 30 December 1784 which he informs me he has lately issued, concerning the carrying into execution some Acts of Parliament relative to the Trade. I shall beg leave from time to time to communicate to you what shall appear to me 'for the good of the Service' in general. On this particular point, it does not appear clearly from Sir Richard's order by whom the situation of any foreign ship or vessel wishing to come into port is to be enquired into.

It will be the surest mode of preventing any Deceptions if you will permit some of your people, whose province it is to be capable of judging how far a vessel is injured by any damage sustained at sea, to make the inquiry and to report to you accordingly. You would then direct the Master of such vessel to convey that Report to me.

If it shall be very manifest that there is not a necessity for such vessels coming into Port to repair, you would send them about their business and be kind enough to communicate the same to me. I have thought it proper, Sir, to say this much, as it appears to me that by our joint endeavours the Acts of Parliament may be most eligibly carried into execution.

THOS. SHIRLEY

To Captain Nelson.

Nelson to Shirley

Boreas, Basseterre Road, St. Christopher's,
January 29th, 1785

Sir,

Your letter dated January 15 I only received yesterday as I was absent upon Service.

In answer to which I beg leave to say that I shall always be ready to receive and to communicate such matters as may be necessary we should mutually be acquainted with, for effectively suppressing Illicit Trade, or on other matters for the honour and good of our Sovereign and Country.

In a paragraph in your letter, you say it does not appear clearly from Sir Richard's order by whom the Situation of Foreigners wishing to come into Port is to be enquired into.

I conceive it the duty of all Governors, officers of the Navy, in short all Officers under the Crown to suppress illicit trade, and to take care that the Laws, which the Wisdom of our Parliament has made, be not evaded, either by Oaths, Protests, or Otherwise.

It cannot be supposed that the Man who is regardless of the duty he owes his country will stop at any means to get his wish accomplished, however injurious to his native country, and was there not Bad Principled Men settled in our Islands, Foreigners could have no inducements to visit our Ports.

The Wisdom of our Legislature has directed the Act of Navigation to Admirals and Captains of the Navy, well knowing that those whose profession is the sea must be the best judges of the accidents which may happen upon that element.

Now, Sir, I must beg leave to answer a part of your letter very fully relative to acquainting the Presidents of the reports which may be made to me by the Officers examining Foreigners, Ships and Vessels wishing to come into Port; As I am sure General Shirley has not the smallest idea of offering an Insult to the Navy, I am answering his letter. Had I the least idea any such thing had been meant, I should not have deigned to notice the receipt of it. Captains of Men-of-War receive orders and make reports to *none* but the Admiralty, Admirals, or Senior Officers in their own Service.

Therefore, it is totally out of my power to send any reports to Mr. Presidents. If the Presidents wish to know the situation of any vessel coming into the Roads, and send an officer of a certain rank to enquire on board the *Boreas*, I shall take care he is answered by an officer of equal rank, and such information it is proper he should know be acquainted with.

When the Men of War are in port, you may be assured no Foreigner shall be admitted, unless in Distress.

When the Men of War are absent, if the Presidents of Council and the Officers of His Majesty's Customs do their duty, they will still be excluded. Thus, by our joint endeavours will Illegal Trade be suppressed, the British trader find a market for his commodities which they have not been able to do till lately, and the Act of Parliament most eligibly carried into execution.

Since I have been appointed to the Station among these Islands, I know that several Americans have received Permits from the Custom House here to sell their cargoes, and these Permits obtained upon very frivolous pretexts. And what is worse, Sir, American-built vessels have been registered by the Custom House and the Collector seems to think that it is not illegal to register vessels that were built in America during the Rebellion, as at that time the King called them his 'rebellious subjects.'

It is a very serious matter, and must ruin our Shipbuilding in England where hundreds of Shipwrights are now wanting Bread.

I have troubled you with this narrative that you may, if you think fit, take methods to hinder that what I conceive to be illegal act. I have, since my being upon this Station, transmitted Home such accounts relative to the Trade and Navigation of these Colonies as I have thought fit, and shall from time to time continue that practice whenever it is necessary,

I am, Sir, with great respect
Your Most obedient, humble Servant
HORATIO NELSON

His Excellency General Shirley.

Shirley to Nelson

Monday, *February 5th, 1785*

Sir,

Your letter of the 29th January I have this moment received, and felt myself so Hurt and Insulted by the Contents of it that I shall immediately transmit it to your Admiral from whom I doubt not I shall receive proper redress for such indignant behaviour.

I am etc.

THOS. SHIRLEY

To Captain Nelson
Boreas.

Nelson to Shirley

Boreas, English Harbour, *February 8th*

Sir,

Your letter of yesterday's date I have this moment received. I cannot help being much surprised with the contents as it never was my intention to hurt the feelings or insult General Shirley.

Your letter, Sir, called forth such an answer, but I have read it again and again, but cannot find out any word that is insulting to you.

What I have said are facts, proofs of which I have in my possession for the inspection of Sir Richard Hughes to whom those under his command render an account of all their transactions.

I must again repeat, Sir, that it was never my intention to hurt or insult the feelings of General Shirley by any words spoken or written by me, being with great respect

Your very humble servant

HORATIO NELSON

His Excellency General Shirley.

Shirley to Nelson

Clarke's Hill, *February 9th, 1785*

Sir,

In consequence of the receipt of your letter of yesterday's date mentioning that it was never your intention to hurt my feelings or insult me, I shall think no more of what has passed between us but to convince you that I had some grounds for being hurt and thinking myself ill-treated, I must refer you to the following passages in your letter of the 29 Jan. last where you say; 'That you conceive it the duty of all Governors etc. to suppress Illicit Trade and to take care that the Laws which the Wisdom of our Parliament has made be not evaded either by Oaths, Protests or otherwise.'

This to me clearly conveys an insinuation that you thought either I connived at the Malpractices of others, or was negligent of my own duty. Then you say; 'As I am sure General Shirley has not the smallest idea of offering an insult to the Navy, I am answering his letter. Had I the least idea any such thing was meant, I should not have answered it,' and yet your whole answer is couched in a stile as if I had been affrontive in the highest degree.

You then go on to say that 'Captains of Men-of-War receive orders and make reports to *none* but the Admiralty, Admirals or Senior Officers in their own Service, wherefore it is totally out of my power to send any reports to Mr. Presidents.'

No Paragraph in my original letter of 15 January could bear the construction you put upon it, for the words of my letter are; 'I shall beg leave from time to time to communicate to you what shall appear for the good of the Service in general, and I think on this particular point as it does not appear very clearly from Sir Richard Hughes' order by whom the situation of any Foreign ship or Vessel wishing to come into port is to be enquired into, that it will be the surest mode of effectually preventing any deception if you will *permit* some of your people, whose province it is to be capable of judging how far a vessel is injured by any Damage sustained at Sea to make the enquiry, and to report to you accordingly, and that you would *direct the Commander* (*Master*) *of such vessel to convey that Report to me.*

'If it is very manifest that there is no necessity for such vessels coming into Port, you would send them about their business and be kind enough to communicate the same to me.' You also mention that you have, since being upon this Station, transmitted Home such accounts relative to the Trade and Navigation of these Colonies as you have thought fit. If I am at all concerned or mentioned in such accounts, I make no doubt but you will have candour enough to inform me of it.

I am, Sir, your most obedient humble servant

THOS. SHIRLEY

To Captain Nelson.

Nelson to Shirley

Boreas, English Harbour, *March 1st, 1785*

Sir,

Your letter of the 9th I have this moment received and will explain with great pleasure the meaning I put upon the passages of my letter that were unpleasant to you.

First, I conceive it the duty of all Governors etc. to suppress Illicit Trade.

My meaning is that it was equally the duty of every person holding an office under the Crown to suppress Illegal Trade and that it was not the duty of any particular station. As to Oaths and Protests, if you recollect, Sir, a conversation we had once on the subject, that the Masters of Americans came to you with their protests and that many, you doubted not, were false; but it was not in your power to remedy the evil. The Second Part, as to insulting the Navy, I never had the smallest idea anything improper was meant, but the Navy are ever jealous of receiving directions from any but their own Service. Thirdly, relative to the Americans. I told Sir R. Hughes that I hoped we should be ordered to admit, or exclude totally all Foreigners except in cases of urgent distress, of which Distress none could be such proper judges as Sea Officers. Therefore, it was not necessary the Masters of such Foreigners should have access to the shore unless in distress, for Sir, I have seen at Barbadoes and Monserrat that if a vessel arrived without papers on an old excuse, the Master is gone on shore with them though most likely he (the Master) is at that moment speaking to you—and the Colours blown away, in those instances if any person went on shore from those vessels, what with Oaths, Protests etc. they have uniformly procured what they wanted, either to be made English for the time being or to sell their Cargo..

Fourth, as to my transmitting home the accounts of the Trade &c of these colonies, I have almost every Packet sent accounts chiefly concerning the American trade, for most sincerely do I wish that the Americans may be effectually kept from our Colonies. And that if Nova Scotia and Canada can fully supply our wants in any particular article, then that article to be prohibited being brought from the American States, in any Bottom.

Mine have been private letters but have, I believe, been produced before the Minister, but let me assure you that if ever your name has been mentioned it has always been with great respect, for I am, with sincere esteem

Your much obliged, sincere humble servant

HORATIO NELSON

His Excellency
General Shirley.

Shirley to Nelson

Clarke's Hill, *March 1st, 1785*

Sir,

In answer to your letter of this day's date, I must beg leave to say that there was no occasion for you to have explained yourself further upon this subject, since my letter to you was in answer to a letter whereby you had done away the offensive part of your former letter by assuring me you meant no improper or insulting behaviour personally to me, in which letter I told you I was satisfied.

I must however observe to you, Sir, that old respectable officers of high rank, long service, and of a certain life are very jealous of being dictated to in their duty by young Gentlemen whose service and experience do not entitle them to it.

With respect to the most exceptionable part of your letter, I shall convince you of the unreasonableness of your fears by informing you that neither your Admiral nor your brother officers were at all alarmed for the Dignity of the Service by anything I had mentioned.

Indeed, Sir Richard Hughes informed me that he should give orders to the officers under him to co-operate with me in the plan I had proposed when I sent him a copy of the letter which you were pleased to animadvert upon so much.

And I will appeal to my own Secretary if I did not consult with him on the mode of wording the letter so as to avoid even the appearance of giving an order.

With respect to your correspondence which you suppose the Minister has got to the knowledge of it, it corresponds very much to what I have directly wrote to him, it being my duty and having it very much in my power to send him Intelligence without it going through a multiplicity of hands.

It will appear, I believe that Captain Nelson has not been the only Alert, Active, Patriotic servant of the Crown upon this occasion.

I have received orders from Lord Sydney, I apprehend from your information and that of others as zealous as you, Sir, to enquire into these matters. But as his Lordship mentions it only in a general way, I beg leave to know if I am at liberty (as your letter to me is Private) to acquaint the officers of the Port here as well as those dependant on the other parts of my government with the particular charges mentioned in your letter to me, that they may have it in their power to make such answer as they shall think necessary.

And I am sure, Sir, after the instruction and explanation you have sent me with respect to some part of the King's Service, you will think I have a right, as Chancellor, to put you in mind that there is a maxim both in Law and Equity; *Audi alteram partem*, or else the subject would be deprived of every right that the Laws of his Country intitle him to.

I have the honour to be with great respect, Sir

Your obedient humble servant

THOS. SHIRLEY

Nelson to Shirley

Undated

Sir,

Your letter of March 1 I received last night. From the letters I have received, I believe it right that I should not hold any further correspondence with your Excellency upon this subject.

General Shirley and Sir Richard Hughes will understand the ideas of each other, I doubt not, and the distinction of Old and Young be obliterated.

I am, Sir &c

HORATIO NELSON

I have made no Charges to you against any Individual but, Sir, you are certainly to make what use you please of my whole letters, as they are Publick Ones.

Nelson to Captain Wm. Locker

Boreas, March 5th, 1786

' . . . In December, to my astonishment, comes down an order from the Admiral telling us he had received good advice and requiring us not to hinder the Americans from coming in, and having free egress and regress, if the Governors chose to allow them.

And a copy of the orders he sent to the Governors and the Presidents of the Islands.

The General Shirley and others began by sending letters not far different from orders, that he should admit them in such and such situations, telling me the Admiral had left it to them, but they thought it right to let me know it.

Mr Shirley I soon trimmed up and silenced.

Sir Richard Hughes' was a more delicate business; I must either disobey my orders or disobey Acts of Parliament which the Admiral was disobeying. I determined upon the former, trusting to the uprightness of my intention, and believed that my Country would not allow me to be ruined, by protecting her Commerce. I first, to Sir Richard, expatiated upon the Navigation Laws to the best of my ability and told him I was certain that some person had been giving him advice which he would be sorry for having taken against the positive directions of an Act of Parliament. . . .

. . . and in short that I should decline obeying his orders till I had an opportunity of seeing and talking to him, at the same time making an apology. . . .

Nelson Petitions the King

Boreas, Nevis, *June 23rd, 1785*

The Right Hnble Lord Sydney

My Lord,

Herewith you will receive a Memorial which I beg your Lordship will be pleased to lay before my most gracious Sovereign. Your Lordship will know of the Irritation of the Inhabitants of these Islands for my having done what was my duty. Your Lordship will now perceive by the Memorial that the anger of some people in these Colonies is not lessened, and therefore they have taken the first opportunity of making me suffer pecuniary Punishment although what they have charged me with is as false as anything can possibly be, for one of the partys I never saw.

My Persecution, I must call it, is I have every reason to believe carried on by certain disaffected People, settled in these Islands since the Peace.

If from the state of my case, you think me worthy of some attention, may I hope for your interest that the King may be graciously pleased to redress my grievance.

My constitution is but weak and from being obliged to lay at anchor, under the lee of this Island, and being confined so closely to my ship, it is so much worse that I fear it may ultimately oblige me to quit my ship; but my health is a loss I must be content to suffer, my only consolation is that I have lost it in the service of my country.

I should do injustice to the Attorney General, Mr Stanley and the other Crown lawyers did I not say they have used every endeavour to stop this Persecution against me, but it is out of their power. The President of Nevis and the Judge of the Admiralty have also done what was in their power to have justice rendered to me. By the advice of the Crown Lawyer, I have not stood trial, for the People are so irritated at present that I should be, they fear, condemned against all the evidence I could produce, that what they have laid to my charge is wholly false.

The Officers and ship's crew serving under my command ever have been and are faithful servants to their Country, and I am sure they feel as much for the unfortunate situation of their Commander as I can possibly do for myself.

Pray, my Lord, let my cruel situation be my apology for troubling you and permit me to assure you that I am with every sentiment of Respect

Your Lordship's most devoted, humble Servant

HORATIO NELSON

Nelson to Lord Sydney

Boreas, English Harbour, *September 29th 1785*

My Lord,

Permit me through your Lordship most humbly to express to His Majesty my everlasting thanks for his great condescension and goodness in supporting the conduct of his faithful servant upon an idea that he had done nothing but what was right, and what the office he bears instructs him to do. To you, my Lord, my most unfeigned thanks are due for your great goodness in supporting me through this business which eventually might have ruined my name and fortune.

Allow me, without placing Vanity in view, to say that however Alert and Active I have been in the execution of my duty, this mark of attention from Great Officers of State will bind me faster than ever to the service of my Country

From your Lordship's known character, I always conceived the most fervent hopes of support. Now I am convinced that while I do my duty to my Country I shall always experience the same flattering marks of attention.

When I fail in that, may I fall unpitied!

I have the pleasure to acquaint you that the latter end of July all the prosecutions against me were dropped, the Lawyers on the side of my Prosecutors declaring they would no longer be concerned against me.

I have &c.

HORATIO NELSON

[The Shirley-Nelson correspondence ends here.]

2. CASE OF WM. CLARK, A.B.

Wm. Clark had been condemned to death for desertion by a Court Martial presided over by Captain Nelson. Subsequently he had been both reprieved by Nelson and discharged from his ship, *Rattler*.

Nelson to the Admiralty

Boreas, August 17th, 1787

Sir,

I am at this moment honoured with your letter wherein you acquaint me of their Lordships' surprise at finding William Clark discharged from the *Rattler* by my order, and desiring to know my reasons for giving the order. In return, I beg leave to acquaint you that it was at the request of the poor man, backed by the desire of Captain Collingwood.

I certainly thought it was proper, as I exactly followed the step of the later Commander-in-chief on the Leeward Islands station in a similar case of William Ray, Seaman, deserter from the *Unicorn*.

I had always understood that when a man was condemned to suffer death, he was from that moment dead in law. If he was pardoned, he became as a new man; and there being no Impress, he had the choice of entering, or not, His Majesty's service. There was no want of a good man to supply his place.

If I have erred in discharging him, I am sorry; but I had at that time no doubts, as I conformed to the manner of the later Commander-in-chief's treatment of a man in a similar situation.

And I beg that you will assure their Lordships that I only wish to know the exact Rules of the Service in this respect to have conformed most strictly to them.

3. NELSON'S APPEAL FOR CHEAPER POSTAGE

Boreas, English Harbour, Antigua,
October 10th, 1785

Sir,

I beg leave to trouble you, for the information of the Postmaster General, but before I advance further on the letter let me apologize if I have not taken the proper mode for conveying my feelings of the Situation of the Seamen who are serving their Country under my command.

The enormous Price of Letters received in this country is so very far above what a petty officer can afford to pay—much more so the poor seamen who have no Prize Money, or ever receive any pay while serving abroad, I enclose you the cover of two letters that you may have ocular proofs of the emence expense attending letters. Since my serving here, I have paid much more largely for letters than my fortune will allow of for the comforts of the Seamen hearing from their Wives and famillies.

And at this moment are laying in the Post Office at St. John's near 100 letters which they never can afford to pay for. Nor have I the means to relieve their distress which, by our own feelings, we know must be great.

And I can't help supposing that ye married men who have a familly are very often induced to desert the Service by not having the means of hearing from their famillies.

The crew serving under my command are mostly from the same Country as myself, and look to me as their Protector and Guardian, and have therefore very modestly and properly requested me to transmit their situation home.

Allow me to say one word against an objection which may be thrown up. It may be said that Post Office revenues may be diminished, that abuses will creep into such an indulgence, that many who are not serving their country will receive letters free, or under cover.

To obviate those objections, let the Captain grant a certificate to the Postmaster, with a list of the letters received that the people who they are directed to are now serving on board the ship under my command.

For myself, I will pledge my honour that I will see all the letters opened and if any are under cover, I will send them back to the Post Office.

Your faithful obliged servant

HORATIO NELSON

P.S. If it cannot be done but by Parliament, I am sure they will allow of the indulgence to the (I hope I may be allowed to say without being Accus'd of Vanity) Guardians of their Country.

4. RESPECT FOR THE BRITISH FLAG

Nelson was very punctilious about salutes being properly made, and returned.

When the *Boreas* was lying in Carlisle Bay, Barbadoes, a French schooner of war sailed and the Fort omitted to salute her by hoisting the national colours. Nelson immediately fired two shotted 9-pounders at the Fort as a sharp reminder of their duty.

Six months later, on 20th June 1785, the *Boreas* anchored at St. Eustatia, the Netherlands island. The following letter to the Dutch Governor shows what followed.

Sir,

The British flag not having received even the same marks of respect which has this day been paid to that of the French King (and which Your Excellency promised to the Lieutenant of my Royal Master's ship to pay immediately to his Flag) obliges me to write to you upon that subject.

I hope and believe the British flag not having that respect paid to it which you know, Sir, is so justly its due, has proceeded in some great neglect from Officers under your command, and not from intention in Your Excellency.

In expectation that the former is the case, I shall remain here till tomorrow morning Sun Rise when, if a Salute of at least as many guns as that paid the French is not given to the King's Flag, I must suppose it as an intended insult, and as such an insult as I am sure will be properly noticed.

The Message with which I have the Honour to be intrusted with by the British Admiral I must return to him again, Your Excellency not having allowed me an opportunity of delivering it.'

[The Governor was quick to make amends.]

Log of *Boreas:* '21 June. Saluted the Fort which was returned. Weighed and proceeded to Nevis.'

Theseus Augt 16th 1797,

My Dear Sir,

I rejoice at being once more in sight of your flag, and with your per=
=mission will come on board the Ville de Paris & pay you my respects. If the Emerald has joined, you know my wishes, a left handed Admiral will never again be considered as useful therefore the sooner I get to a very humble cottage the better and make room for a better man to serve the State but whatever be my lot Believe me with the most sincere affection Ever Your Most faithful

Turn over — Horatio Nelson

Reverse side of letter

The papers I sent by Waller, were I find neither correct or all which I wished to send. I send you the whole by Captn Miller

Facsimile of Nelson's first letter written after losing his right arm.

INDEX TO PERSONS NAMED IN THE LETTERS

I

J

K

L

M

N

O

P

R

S

T

EVERYMAN'S LIBRARY: A Selected List

BIOGRAPHY

Baxter, Richard (1615–91).
THE AUTOBIOGRAPHY OF RICHARD BAXTER. 868
Boswell, James (1740–95). *See* Johnson.
Brontë, Charlotte (1816–55).
LIFE, 1857. By *Mrs Gaskell.* Introduction by *May Sinclair.* (*See also* Fiction.) 318
Burns, Robert (1759–96).
LIFE, 1828. By *J. G. Lockhart* (1794–1854). With Introduction by *Prof. James Kinsley,* M.A., PH.D. (*See also* Poetry and Drama.) 156
Byron, Lord (1788–1824).
LETTERS. Edited by *R. G. Howarth,* B.LITT., and with an Introduction by *André Maurois.* (*See also* Poetry and Drama.) 931
Canton, William (1845–1926).
A CHILD'S BOOK OF SAINTS, 1898. (*See also* Essays.) 61
Cellini, Benvenuto (1500–71).
THE LIFE OF BENVENUTO CELLINI, written by himself. Translated by *Anne Macdonell.* Introduction by *William Gaunt.* 51
Cowper, William (1731–1800).
SELECTED LETTERS. Edited, with Introduction, by *W. Hadley,* M.A. 774
(*See also* Poetry and Drama.)
Dickens, Charles (1812–70).
LIFE, 1874. By *John Forster* (1812–76). Introduction by *G. K. Chesterton.* 2 vols. (*See also* Fiction.) 781–2
Evelyn, John (1620–1706).
DIARY. Edited by *William Bray,* 1819. Intro. by *G. W. E. Russell.* 2 vols. 220–1
Fox, George (1624–91).
JOURNAL, 1694. Revised by *Norman Penney,* with Account of Fox's last years. Introduction by *Rufus M. Jones.* 754
Franklin, Benjamin (1706–90).
AUTOBIOGRAPHY, 1817. With Introduction and Account of Franklin's later life by *W. Macdonald.* Reset new edition (1949), with a newly compiled Index. 316
Goethe, Johann Wolfgang von (1749–1832).
LIFE, 1855. By *G. H. Lewes* (1817–78). Introduction by *Havelock Ellis.* Index. (*See also* Poetry and Drama.) 269
Hudson, William Henry (1841–1922).
FAR AWAY AND LONG AGO, 1918. Intro. by *John Galsworthy.* 956
Johnson, Samuel (1709–84).
LIVES OF THE ENGLISH POETS, 1781. Introduction by *Mrs L. Archer-Hind.* 2 vols. (*See also* Essays, Fiction.) 770–1
BOSWELL'S LIFE OF JOHNSON, 1791. A new edition (1949), with Introduction by *S. C. Roberts,* M.A., LL.D., and a 30-page Index by Alan Dent. 2 vols. 1–2
Keats, John (1795–1821).
LIFE AND LETTERS, 1848. By *Lord Houghton* (1809–85). Introduction by *Robert Lynd.* Note on the letters by Lewis Gibbs. (*See also* Poetry and Drama.) 801
Lamb, Charles (1775–1834).
LETTERS. New edition (1945) arranged from the Complete Annotated Edition of the Letters. 2 vols. (*See also* Essays and Belles-Lettres, Fiction.) 342–3
Napoleon Buonaparte (1769–1821).
HISTORY OF NAPOLEON BUONAPARTE, 1829. By *J. G. Lockhart* (1794–1854). 3
(*See also* Essays and Belles-Lettres.)
Nelson, Horatio, Viscount (1758–1805).
LIFE, 1813. By *Robert Southey* (1774–1843). (*See also* Essays.) 52
Outram, General Sir James (1803–63), 'the Bayard of India.'
LIFE, 1903. Deals with important passages in the history of India in the nineteenth century. By *L. J. Trotter* (1827–1912). 396
Pepys, Samuel (1633–1703).
DIARY. Newly edited (1953), with modernized spelling, by *John Warrington,* from the edition of Mynors Bright (1875–9). 3 vols. 53–5
Plutarch (46?–120).
LIVES OF THE NOBLE GREEKS AND ROMANS. Dryden's edition, 1683–6. Revised, with Introduction, by *A. H. Clough* (1819–61). 3 vols. 407–9
Rousseau, Jean Jacques (1712–78).
CONFESSIONS, 1782. 2 vols. Complete and unabridged English translation. New Introduction by *Prof. R. Niklaus,* B.A., PH.D., of Exeter University. 859–60
(*See also* Essays, Theology and Philosophy.)
Scott, Sir Walter (1771–1832).
LOCKHART'S LIFE OF SCOTT. An abridgement by *J. G. Lockhart* himself from the original 7 volumes. New Introduction by *W. M. Parker,* M.A. 39

Swift, Jonathan (1667–1745).
JOURNAL TO STELLA, 1710–13. Deciphered by *J. K. Moorhead.* Introduction by *Sir Walter Scott.* Sir Walter Scott's essay 'Swift, Stella and Vanessa' is included. 757
(*See also* Essays, Fiction.)

Walpole, Horace (1717–97).
SELECTED LETTERS. Edited, with Introduction, by *W. Hadley,* M.A. 775

Wellington, Arthur Wellesley, Duke of (1769–1852).
LIFE, 1862. By *G. R. Gleig* (1796–1888). 341

CLASSICAL

Aeschylus (525–455 B.C.).
PLAYS. Translated into English Verse by *G. M. Cookson.* New Introduction by *John Warrington,* and notes on each play. 62

Aristophanes (450 ?–385 ? B.C.).
THE COMEDIES. Translated by *J. Hookham Frere,* etc. Edited, with Introduction, by *J. P. Maine* and *J. H. Frere.* 2 vols. (*Vol. 1 temporarily out of print.*) 516

Aristotle (384–322 B.C.).
POLITICS and THE ATHENIAN CONSTITUTION. Edited and translated by *John Warrington.* 605
METAPHYSICS. Edited and translated by *John Warrington.* Introduction by *Sir David Ross,* K.B.E., M.A., D.LITT. 1000

Caesar, Julius (102 ?–44 B.C.).
WAR COMMENTARIES. 'The Gallic Wars' and 'The Civil War.' Newly translated and edited by *John Warrington.* 702

Cicero, Marcus Tullius (106–43 B.C.).
THE OFFICES (translated by *Thomas Cockman,* 1699); LAELIUS, ON FRIENDSHIP; CATO, ON OLD AGE; AND SELECT LETTERS (translated by *W. Melmoth,* 1753). With Note on Cicero's Character by De Quincey. Introduction by *John Warrington.* 345

Demetrius (fl. late first century A.D.). (*See under* Aristotle.)

Demosthenes (384–322 B.C.). (*See under* Oratory, p. 11.)

Epictetus (*b. c.* A.D. 60).
MORAL DISCOURSES. THE ENCHIRIDION AND FRAGMENTS. Translated by *Elizabeth Carter* (1717–1806). Edited by *W. H. D. Rouse,* M.A. 404

Euripides (484 ?–407 B.C.).
PLAYS. New Introduction by *John Warrington.* Translated by *A. S. Way,* D.LITT. 2 vols. 63, 271

Herodotus (484 ?–425 ? B.C.).
HISTORY. The 'History' deals with the period covering the Persian invasion of Greece, 492–480 B.C. Rawlinson's Translation, additional notes and Introduction by *E. H. Blakeney.* 2 vols. (*Vol. II temporarily out of print.*) 405–6

Homer (? ninth century B.C.).
ILIAD. New verse translation by *S. O. Andrew* and *Michael Oakley.* 453
ODYSSEY. The new verse translation (first published 1953) by *S. O. Andrew* Introduction by *John Warrington.* 454

Juvenal (*c.* A.D. 50–*c.* 130).
SATIRES; with THE SATIRES OF PERSIUS. Introduction by *Prof. H. J. Rose,* M.A. F.B.A. William Gifford Translation, 1802. Revised by *John Warrington.* 997

Lucretius (*c.* 99 ?–50 ? B.C.).
ON THE NATURE OF THINGS. Metrical Translation by *W. E. Leonard.* 750

Ovid (43 B.C.–A.D. 18).
SELECTED WORKS. Chosen by *J. C.* and *M. J. Thornton.* Selections from the *Metamorphoses, Heroical Epistles,* the *Festivals,* the *Ibis,* and his epistles written in exile: also his *Art of Love.* 955

Persius (34–62). *See* Juvenal.

Plato (427–347 B.C.).
THE REPUBLIC. Translated, with an Introduction, by *A. D. Lindsay,* C.B.E., LL.D. The greatest achievement of the Greek intellect in philosophy. 64
SOCRATIC DISCOURSES OF PLATO AND XENOPHON. Introduction by *A. D. Lindsay* C.B.E., LL.D. 45
THE LAWS. The last of Plato's dialogues is here printed in the A. E. Taylor (1869–1945) Translation. 27

Sophocles (496 ?–406 B.C.).
DRAMAS. This volume contains the seven surviving dramas. 11

Thucydides (*c.* 460–401 B.C.).
HISTORY OF THE PELOPONNESIAN WAR. Translation by *Richard Crawley.* Introduction by *John Warrington.* Index and five plans. 45

Virgil (70–19 B.C.).
AENEID. Verse translation by *Michael Oakley.* Introduction by *E. M. Forster.* 161
ECLOGUES AND GEORGICS. Verse Translation by *T. F. Royds.* The 'Eclogues' were inspired by Theocritus; the 'Georgics' describe a countryman's life. 22

Xenophon (430 ?–360 ? B.C.). (*See under* Plato.)

ESSAYS AND BELLES-LETTRES

Anthology OF ENGLISH PROSE, FROM BEDE TO STEVENSON. **675**

Bacon, Francis, Lord Verulam (1561–1626).
ESSAYS, 1597–1626. Introduction by *Oliphant Smeaton*. Index of Quotations and Foreign Phrases and Glossary. (*See also* Theology and Philosophy.) **10**

Bagehot, Walter (1826–77).
LITERARY STUDIES, 1879. Introduction by *George Sampson*. 2 vols. **520–1**

Belloc, Hilaire (1870–1953).
STORIES, ESSAYS AND POEMS. Edited with Introduction by *J. B. Morton*, C.B.E., the volume now contains a new selection from the *Sonnets, Verses* and celebrated *Epigrams*. **948**

Burke, Edmund (1729–97).
REFLECTIONS ON THE REVOLUTION IN FRANCE (1790) AND OTHER ESSAYS. Introduction and Notes by *A. J. Grieve*, M.A. (*See also* Oratory.) **460**

Canton, William (1845–1926).
THE INVISIBLE PLAYMATE, 1894; W. V., HER BOOK, 1896; and IN MEMORY OF W. V., 1901. (*See also* Biography.) **566**

Carlyle, Thomas (1795–1881).
ESSAYS. Introduction by *J. R. Lowell*. 2 vols. Essays on men and affairs. **703–4**
PAST AND PRESENT, 1843. New Introduction by *Douglas Jerrold*. **608**
SARTOR RESARTUS, 1838; and HEROES AND HERO-WORSHIP, 1841. (*See also* History.) **278**

Castiglione, Baldassare (1478–1529).
THE BOOK OF THE COURTIER, 1528. *Sir Thomas Hoby's* Translation, 1561. Introduction by *W. H. D. Rouse* and Notes by *Prof. W. B. Drayton Henderson*. **807**

Century. A CENTURY OF ENGLISH ESSAYS, FROM CAXTON TO BELLOC. **653**

Chesterfield, Philip Dormer Stanhope, Earl of (1694–1773).
LETTERS TO HIS SON; AND OTHERS. Introduction by *Prof. R. K. Root*. **823**

Chesterton, Gilbert Keith (1874–1936).
STORIES, ESSAYS AND POEMS. Introduction by *Maisie Ward*. An 'omnibus' volume including four 'Father Brown' stories. **913**

Coleridge, Samuel Taylor (1772–1834).
BIOGRAPHIA LITERARIA, 1817. Edited with a new Introduction by *George Watson*, M.A. Coleridge described the work as 'sketches of my literary life and opinions.' **11**
SHAKESPEAREAN CRITICISM, 1849. Edited with a long Introduction by *Prof. T. M. Raysor* (1960), a distinguished Coleridge scholar of the University of Nebraska. 2 vols. (*See also* Poetry and Drama.) **162, 183**

De la Mare, Walter (1873–1956).
STORIES, ESSAYS AND POEMS. An anthology arranged by *Mildred Bozman*. **940**

De Quincey, Thomas (1785–1859).
CONFESSIONS OF AN ENGLISH OPIUM-EATER, 1822. Edited with Introduction by *Prof. J. E. Jordan* (1960). **223**

Eckermann, Johann Peter (1792–1854).
CONVERSATIONS WITH GOETHE, 1836–8. Translated by *John Oxenford*, 1850. Edited by *J. K. Moorhead*, with Introduction by *Havelock Ellis*. **851**
(*See also* Poetry and Drama, Biography.)

Emerson, Ralph Waldo (1803–82).
ESSAYS, 1841–4. New Introduction by *Prof. Sherman Paul*. **12**

Florio, John (1553?–1625). (*See* Montaigne.)

Gilfillan, George (1813–78).
A GALLERY OF LITERARY PORTRAITS, 1845–54. **348**

Gray, Thomas (1716–71).
ESSAYS. (*See* Poetry.)

Hamilton, Alexander (1757–1804), and Others.
THE FEDERALIST, OR THE NEW CONSTITUTION, 1787–8. Introduction by *Prof. W. J. Ashley*. **519**

Hazlitt, William (1778–1830).
LECTURES ON THE ENGLISH COMIC WRITERS, 1819; and MISCELLANEOUS ESSAYS. Introduction by *W. E. Henley*. **411**
LECTURES ON THE ENGLISH POETS, 1818; and THE SPIRIT OF THE AGE, 1825. Introduction by *Catherine Macdonald Maclean*, M.A., D.LITT., F.R.S.L. **459**
THE ROUND TABLE and CHARACTERS OF SHAKESPEAR'S PLAYS, 1817–18. New Introduction by *Catherine Macdonald Maclean*. **65**
TABLE TALK, 1821–2, 1824. New Introduction by *Catherine Macdonald Maclean*. **321**

Holmes, Oliver Wendell (1809–94).
THE AUTOCRAT OF THE BREAKFAST-TABLE, 1858. Introduction by *Van Wyck Brooks*. **66**

Hunt, Leigh (1784–1859).
SELECTED ESSAYS. 78 essays with Introduction by *J. B. Priestley*. **829**

Huxley, Aldous Leonard (*b.* 1894).
STORIES, ESSAYS AND POEMS. **935**

Johnson, Samuel (1709–84).
THE RAMBLER. Introduction by *S. C. Roberts*. (*See also* Biography, Fiction.) **994**

Lamb, Charles (1775–1834).
ESSAYS OF ELIA AND LAST ESSAYS OF ELIA, 1823–33. Introduction by *Augustin Birrell*. Includes the first and the last Essays of Elia. 14
(*See also* Biography, Fiction.)

Landor, Walter Savage (1775–1864).
IMAGINARY CONVERSATIONS, AND POEMS, 1824–9, 1853. Edited, with Introduction by *Havelock Ellis*. 890

Lawrence, David Herbert (1885–1930).
STORIES, ESSAYS AND POEMS. Selected by *Desmond Hawkins*. Poetry, Essays Travel Sketches and Letters. 958
(*See also* Fiction.)

Locke, John (1632–1704).
AN ESSAY CONCERNING HUMAN UNDERSTANDING, 1690. Abridged and edited by *Raymond Wilburn*, presenting the whole sweep of the work. 984
(*See also* Theology and Philosophy.)

Lynd, Robert (1879–1949).
ESSAYS ON LIFE AND LITERATURE. Introduction by *Desmond MacCarthy*. 990

Macaulay, Thomas Babington, Lord (1800–59).
CRITICAL AND HISTORICAL ESSAYS, 1843. New Introduction by *Douglas Jerrold*. 2 vols. 225–6
MISCELLANEOUS ESSAYS, 1823–59; LAYS OF ANCIENT ROME, 1842; and MISCELLANEOUS POEMS, 1812–47. Introduction by *Prof. G. M. Trevelyan*, O.M. 439
(*See also* History.)

Machiavelli, Niccolò (1469–1527).
THE PRINCE, 1513. New Introduction by *Prof. H. Butterfield*, M.A., HON. D.LITT. Translated by *W. K. Marriott*. 280

Mazzini, Joseph (1805–72).
THE DUTIES OF MAN (translated by *Miss E. Noyes*); and OTHER ESSAYS. New Introduction by *Dr Thomas Jones*, C.H., LL.D. 224

Milton, John (1608–74).
PROSE WRITINGS. Introduction by *K. M. Burton*, M.A. The contents of this volume include 'Areopagitica,' 1644, and other important prose works. 795
(*See also* Poetry, etc.)

Mitford, Mary Russell (1787–1855).
OUR VILLAGE, 1824–32. Edited, with an Introduction, by *Sir John Squire*. 927

Modern Humour. An Anthology in Prose and Verse from over sixty authors. 957

Montaigne, Michel de (1533–92).
ESSAYS, 1580–8. John Florio's version, 1603. Edited (from the third edition, 1632) with Intro. by *A. R. Waller*, 3 vols. (*Vol. I temporarily out of print.*) 440–2

Napoleon Buonaparte (1769–1821).
LETTERS. Some 300 of the most interesting of the Emperor's letters, chosen and translated by *J. M. Thompson*, F.B.A., F.R.HIST.S. (*See also* Biography.) 99

Nelson, Horatio, Viscount (1758–1805).
NELSON'S LETTERS. Compiled by *Geoffrey Rawson*. (*See also* Biography.) 244

Newman, John Henry (1801–90).
ON THE SCOPE AND NATURE OF UNIVERSITY EDUCATION; and CHRISTIANITY AND SCIENTIFIC INVESTIGATION, 1852. Introduction by *Wilfrid Ward*. 723
(*See also* Theology and Philosophy.)

Poe, Edgar Allan (1809–49).
ESSAYS. (*See* Poetry.)

Quiller-Couch, Sir Arthur (1863–1944).
CAMBRIDGE LECTURES, from 'Q.'s' well-known books *The Art of Reading*, 1920 *The Art of Writing*, 1916; *Studies in Literature*, 1918; and *Shakespeare's Workmanship*, 1918. (*See also* Fiction.) 974

Rousseau, Jean Jacques (1712–78).
ÉMILE; OR, EDUCATION. Translated by *Barbara Foxley*, M.A. Intro. (1955) by *Prof André Boutet de Monvel*. (*See also* Biography, Theology and Philosophy.) 518

Ruskin, John (1819–1900).
SESAME, AND LILIES, 1864; THE TWO PATHS, 1859; and THE KING OF THE GOLDEN RIVER; or THE BLACK BROTHERS, 1851. Introduction by *Sir Oliver Lodge*. 219
THE SEVEN LAMPS OF ARCHITECTURE, 1849. With an Introduction (1956) by *Sir Arnold Lunn*. Illustrated with 14 plates of engravings. 207

Sévigné, Marie de Rabutin-Chantal, Marquise de (1626–96).
SELECTED LETTERS. Selected and translated by *H. T. Barnwell*, M.A. 98

Spectator, The, 1711–14. By Joseph Addison (1672–1719), Sir Richard Steele (1672–1729) and Others. Edited by *Prof. Gregory Smith*. New Introduction by *P. Smithers* D.PHIL., M.P., and a Biographical and General Index by *Prof. Gregory Smith*. Reset with minor revisions, 1945. 4 vols. (*See also* Essays *under* Steele.) 164–7

Spencer, Herbert (1820–1903).
ESSAYS ON EDUCATION, 1861. Introduction by *C. W. Eliot*. 50

Steele, Sir Richard (1672–1729).
THE TATLER, 1709–11. 99

Sterne, Laurence (1713–68).
A SENTIMENTAL JOURNEY THROUGH FRANCE AND ITALY, 1768; JOURNAL TO ELIZA written in 1767; and LETTERS TO ELIZA, 1766–7. Introduction by *Daniel George*
(*See also* Fiction.) 79

Stevenson, Robert Louis (1850–94).
VIRGINIBUS PUERISQUE, 1881; and FAMILIAR STUDIES OF MEN AND BOOKS, 1882. (*See also* Fiction, Poetry and Drama, Travel.) 765

Swift, Jonathan (1667–1745).
A TALE OF A TUB, 1704; THE BATTLE OF THE BOOKS, 1704; and OTHER SATIRES. Introduction by *Louis Melville.* (*See also* Biography, Fiction.) 347

Swinnerton, Frank (*b.* 1884).
THE GEORGIAN LITERARY SCENE, 1935. A panorama, revised 1951, of English writers (novelists, essayists, dramatists, poets) from 1919. 943

Thackeray, William Makepeace (1811–63).
THE ENGLISH HUMORISTS, 1851; CHARITY AND HUMOUR, 1853; and THE FOUR GEORGES, 1855. Introduction by *Walter Jerrold.* (*See also* Fiction.) 610

Thoreau, Henry David (1817–62).
WALDEN, OR LIFE IN THE WOODS, 1854. Introduction by *Prof. Basil Willey.* 281

Trench, Richard Chevenix (1807–86).
ON THE STUDY OF WORDS, 1851; and ENGLISH PAST AND PRESENT, 1855. Introduction by *George Sampson.* 788

Tytler, Alexander Fraser (1747–1814).
ESSAY ON THE PRINCIPLES OF TRANSLATION, 1791. 168

Walton, Izaak (1593–1683).
THE COMPLETE ANGLER, 1653. Introduction by *Andrew Lang.* 70

FICTION

Ainsworth, William Harrison (1805–82).
OLD SAINT PAUL'S, 1841. Introduction by *W. E. Axon,* LL.D. Great Fire of London. 522
ROOKWOOD, 1834. Introduction by *Frank Swinnerton.* Dick Turpin. 870
THE TOWER OF LONDON, 1840. Lady Jane Grey. 400
WINDSOR CASTLE, 1843. Intro. by *Ernest Rhys.* Henry VIII and Ann Boleyn. 709

American Short Stories of the Nineteenth Century. Edited, with an Introduction, by *John Cournos.* Twenty stories from representative writers. 840

Andersen, Hans Christian (1805–75).
FAIRY TALES AND STORIES. This represents a completely new selection and in the Reginald Spink Translation. 4

Austen, Jane (1775–1817). Each volume has an Introduction by *R. Brimley Johnson.*
EMMA, 1816. 24
PRIDE AND PREJUDICE, 1823. 22
MANSFIELD PARK, 1814. 23
SENSE AND SENSIBILITY, 1811. 21
NORTHANGER ABBEY, 1818; and PERSUASION, 1818. 25

Balzac, Honoré de (1799–1850).
AT THE SIGN OF THE CAT AND RACKET, 1830; and OTHER STORIES. Translated by *Clara Bell.* Introduction by *George Saintsbury.* 349
EUGÉNIE GRANDET, 1834. Translated by *Ellen Marriage.* New Introduction by *Prof. Marcel Girard.* 169
OLD GORIOT, 1835. Translated by *Ellen Marriage.* New Introduction by *Prof. Marcel Girard.* 170
THE WILD ASS'S SKIN, 1831. A youth makes a bargain with destiny. New Introduction by *Prof. Marcel Girard.* 26

Barbusse, Henri (1874–1935).
UNDER FIRE, THE STORY OF A SQUAD, 1916. Introduction by *Brian Rhys.* 798

Beaconsfield, Benjamin Disraeli, Earl of (1804–81).
CONINGSBY, 1844. Introduction and Notes (with a Key to the Characters) by *B. N. Langdon-Davies.* 535

Bennett, Arnold (1867–1931).
THE OLD WIVES' TALE, 1908. The most durable novel of Bennett's. 919

Blackmore, Richard Doddridge (1825–1900).
LORNA DOONE: A ROMANCE OF EXMOOR, 1869. Introduction by *Ernest Rhys.* 304

Borrow, George (1803–81).
THE ROMANY RYE, 1857. Practically a sequel to *Lavengro.* (*See also* Travel.) 120

Brontë, Anne (1820–49).
THE TENANT OF WILDFELL HALL and AGNES GREY. With a new Introduction by *Margaret Lane.* 685

Brontë, Charlotte (1816–55). For Mrs Gaskell's 'Life' *see* Biography.
JANE EYRE, 1847. Introduction by *Margaret Lane.* 287
THE PROFESSOR, 1857. Introduction by *Margaret Lane.* 417
SHIRLEY, 1849. Introduction by *Margaret Lane.* 288
VILLETTE, 1853. Introduction by *Margaret Lane.* 351

Brontë, Emily (1818–48).
WUTHERING HEIGHTS, 1848; and POEMS. Introduction by *Margaret Lane.* 243

Burney, Fanny (Madame Frances d'Arblay, 1753–1849).
EVELINA, 1778. Introduction by *Lewis Gibbs.* 352

Butler, Samuel (1835–1902).
EREWHON, 1872 (revised 1901); and EREWHON REVISITED, 1901. Introduction by *Desmond MacCarthy.* 881
THE WAY OF ALL FLESH, 1903. Introduction by *A. J. Hoppé.* 895

Collins, Wilkie (1824–89).
THE MOONSTONE, 1868. Introduction by *Dorothy L. Sayers.* 979
THE WOMAN IN WHITE, 1860. New Introduction by *Maurice Richardson.* 464

Conrad, Joseph (1857–1924).
LORD JIM, 1900. Characteristically set in the East Indies. Introduction by *R. B. Cunninghame Graham.* 925
THE NIGGER OF THE 'NARCISSUS,' 1897; TYPHOON, 1903; and THE SHADOW LINE, 1917. Introduction by *A. J. Hoppé.* Three of Conrad's best-known stories. 980
NOSTROMO, 1904. New edition of Conrad's greatest novel with an Introduction by *Richard Curle.* 38

Cooper, James Fenimore (1789–1851).
THE LAST OF THE MOHICANS, 1826, A NARRATIVE OF 1757. With an Introduction by *Ernest Rhys.* 79
THE PRAIRIE, 1827. The last of the 'Leatherstocking Tales.' 172

Craik, Mrs. *See* Mulock.

Daudet, Alphonse (1840–97).
TARTARIN OF TARASCON, 1872; and TARTARIN ON THE ALPS, 1885. Two light episodic novels, some of the funniest episodes ever written in French. 423

Defoe, Daniel (1661?–1731).
THE FORTUNES AND MISFORTUNES OF MOLL FLANDERS, 1722. Introduction by *G. A. Aitken.* One of Defoe's greatest books, famous for its picture of low life. 837
JOURNAL OF THE PLAGUE YEAR, 1722. Introduction by *G. A. Aitken.* 289
LIFE, ADVENTURES AND PIRACIES OF THE FAMOUS CAPTAIN SINGLETON, 1720. Introduction by *Edward Garnett.* A supposed record of a journey across Africa. 74
ROBINSON CRUSOE, 1719. Parts 1 and 2 complete. Introduction by *Guy N. Pocock.* (*See also* Travel.) 59

De Rojas, Fernando (15th century).
CELESTINA: OR THE TRAGI-COMEDY OF CALISTO AND MELIBEA, attributed to Fernando de Rojas. Translated, with an Introduction, by *Phyllis Hartnoll,* M.A., L. ÉS L. This is a new translation (1958). 100

Dickens, Charles (1812–70). Each of the following volumes of Dickens's works has an Introduction by *G. K. Chesterton*:

BARNABY RUDGE, 1841. 76
BLEAK HOUSE, 1852–3. 236
CHRISTMAS BOOKS, 1843–8. 239
CHRISTMAS STORIES, 1850–67. 414
DAVID COPPERFIELD, 1849–50. 242
DOMBEY AND SON, 1846–8. 240
GREAT EXPECTATIONS, 1861. 234
HARD TIMES, 1854. 292
LITTLE DORRIT, 1857. 293
MARTIN CHUZZLEWIT, 1843–4. 241
NICHOLAS NICKLEBY, 1838–9. 238
OLD CURIOSITY SHOP, 1841. 173
OLIVER TWIST, 1838. 233
OUR MUTUAL FRIEND, 1864–5. 294
PICKWICK PAPERS, 1836–7. 235
A TALE OF TWO CITIES, 1859. 102
(*See also* Biography.)

Disraeli, Benjamin. *See* Beaconsfield.

Dostoyevsky, Fyodor (1821–81).
THE BROTHERS KARAMAZOV, 1879–80. Translated by *Constance Garnett.* Introduction by *Edward Garnett.* 2 vols. 802–3
CRIME AND PUNISHMENT, 1866. *Constance Garnett* translation. 501
THE IDIOT, 1873. Translated by *Eva M. Martin.* New Introduction by *Richard Curle.* 682
LETTERS FROM THE UNDERWORLD, 1864; and OTHER TALES (THE GENTLE MAIDEN; THE LANDLADY). Translated, with Introduction, by *C. J. Hogarth.* 654
POOR FOLK, 1845; and THE GAMBLER, 1867. Translated, with Introduction, by *C. J. Hogarth.* 711
THE POSSESSED, 1871. Translated by *Constance Garnett.* Introduction by *Nikolay Andreyev,* PH.D., M.A. 2 vols. 861–2

Dumas, Alexandre (1802–70).
THE BLACK TULIP, 1850. The brothers De Witt in Holland, 1672–5. New Introduction by *Prof. Marcel Girard.* 174
COUNT OF MONTE CRISTO, 1844. 2 vols. Napoleon's later phase. New Introduction by *Prof. Marcel Girard.* 393–4
MARGUERITE DE VALOIS, 1845. The Eve of St Bartholomew. 326
THE THREE MUSKETEERS, 1844. The France of Cardinal Richelieu. 81

Du Maurier, George Louis Palmella Busson (1834–96).
TRILBY, 1894. Illustrated by the author. Preface by *Sir Gerald Du Maurier. Trilby* breathes the air of Paris in the eighties and is drawn largely from the author's own experience. 863

Edgeworth, Maria (1767–1849).
CASTLE RACKRENT, 1800; and THE ABSENTEE, 1812. Introduction by *Prof. Brander Matthews.* 410

Eliot, George (pseudonym of Mary Ann Evans, 1819–80).
ADAM BEDE, 1859. New Introduction by *Robert Speaight.* 27
MIDDLEMARCH, 1872. New Introduction by *Gerald Bullett.* 2 vols. 854–5
THE MILL ON THE FLOSS, 1860. Introduction by *Sir W. Robertson Nicoll.* 325
ROMOLA, 1863. Intro. by *Rudolph Dircks.* The Florence of Savonarola. 231
SILAS MARNER, THE WEAVER OF RAVELOE, 1861. Introduction by *A. Matheson.* 12

English Short Stories. Thirty-six selected stories from Middle Ages to present time. Introduction by *Richard Wilson*, B.A., D.LITT. 743

Fielding, Henry (1707–54). *George Saintsbury* has written an Introduction to the Everyman Fielding.
AMELIA, 1751. 2 vols. Amelia is drawn from Fielding's first wife. 852–3
JONATHAN WILD, 1743; and JOURNAL OF A VOYAGE TO LISBON, 1755. *Jonathan Wild* is a satire on false hero-worship; the *Journal* (published posthumously) narrates the incidents of Fielding's last voyage. 877
JOSEPH ANDREWS, 1742. A skit on Richardson's *Pamela*. 467
TOM JONES, 1749. 2 vols. The first great English novel of humour. 355–6

Flaubert, Gustave (1821–80).
MADAME BOVARY, 1857. Translated by *Eleanor Marx-Aveling*. Introduction by *George Saintsbury*. 808
SALAMMBO, 1862. Translated by *J. C. Chartres*. Introduction by *Prof. F. C. Green*, M.A., PH.D. The war of the Mercenaries against Carthage. 869
SENTIMENTAL EDUCATION, 1869. Modern translation, with Introduction and Notes by *Anthony Goldsmith*. 969

Forster, Edward Morgan (*b.* 1879).
A PASSAGE TO INDIA, 1924. With an Introduction by *Peter Burra*. 972

Galsworthy, John (1867–1933).
THE COUNTRY HOUSE. 917

Gaskell, Mrs Elizabeth (1810–65).
CRANFORD, 1853. Introduction by *Frank Swinnerton*. (*See also* Biography.) 83

Ghost Stories. Introduction by *John Hampden*. Eighteen stories. 952

Gogol, Nikolay (1809–52).
DEAD SOULS, 1842. Introduction by *Nikolay Andreyev*, PH.D., M.A. 726

Goldsmith, Oliver (1728–74).
THE VICAR OF WAKEFIELD, 1766. Introduction by *J. M. Dent*. 295
(*See also* Poetry.)

Goncharov, Ivan (1812–91).
OBLOMOV, 1857. First complete English translation by *Natalie Duddington*. New Introduction by *Nikolay Andreyev*, PH.D., M.A. 878

Gorky, Maxim (pseudonym of Alexei Maximovitch Pieshkov, 1868–1936).
THROUGH RUSSIA. Translated, with an Introduction, by *C. J. Hogarth*. 741

Grossmith, George (1847–1912), and **Weedon** (1853–1919).
THE DIARY OF A NOBODY, 1894. With Weedon Grossmith's illustrations. 963

Hawthorne, Nathaniel (1804–64).
THE HOUSE OF THE SEVEN GABLES, 1851. New Introduction by *Prof. Roy Harvey Pearce*. 176
THE SCARLET LETTER: A ROMANCE, 1850. With new Introduction by *Prof. Roy Harvey Pearce*. 122
TWICE-TOLD TALES, 1837–42. With a new Introduction by *Prof. Roy Harvey Pearce*. 531

Hugo, Victor Marie (1802–85).
LES MISÉRABLES, 1862. Introduction by *Denis Saurat*. 2 vols. 363–4
NOTRE DAME DE PARIS, 1831. Introduction by *Denis Saurat*. 422
TOILERS OF THE SEA, 1866. Introduction by *Ernest Rhys*. 509

Huxley, Aldous.
STORIES, ESSAYS AND POEMS. (*See under* Essays.)

James, Henry (1843–1916).
THE AMBASSADORS, 1903. Introduction by *Frank Swinnerton*. 987
THE TURN OF THE SCREW, 1898; and THE ASPERN PAPERS, 1888. Two famous short novels. Introduction by *Prof. Kenneth B. Murdock*, A.M., PH.D. 912

Jefferies, Richard (1848–87).
AFTER LONDON, 1884; and AMARYLLIS AT THE FAIR, 1886. Introduction by *Richard Garnett*. 951

Jerome, Jerome K. (1859–1927).
THREE MEN IN A BOAT and THREE MEN ON THE BUMMEL. Introduction by *D. C Browning*, M.A., B.LITT. 118

Kingsley, Charles (1819–75).
HEREWARD THE WAKE, 1866. Introduction by *Ernest Rhys*. 296
WESTWARD HO!, 1855. Introduction by *Dr J. A. Williamson*, M.A. 20

Lamb, Charles (1775–1834), and **Mary** (1764–1847).
TALES FROM SHAKESPEARE, 1807. Illustrated by *Arthur Rackham*. 8
(*See also* Biography, Essays.)

Lawrence, David Herbert (1885–1930).
THE WHITE PEACOCK, 1911. (*See also* Essays.) 914

Loti, Pierre (1850–1923).
ICELAND FISHERMAN, 1886. Translated by *W. P. Baines*. 920

Lover, Samuel (1797–1868).
HANDY ANDY, 1842. Lover was a musician, portrait-painter, song-writer and actor who also wrote four novels of which this is generally accounted the best. 178

Lytton, Edward Bulwer, Baron (1803–73).
THE LAST DAYS OF POMPEII, 1834. A romance of the first century A.D. 80

Mann, Thomas (1875–1955).
STORIES AND EPISODES. Introduction by *Prof. Erich Heller*, PH.D. 962

Manzoni, Alessandro (1785–1873).
THE BETROTHED (*I Promessi Sposi*, 1840, rev. ed.). Translated (1951) from the Italian by *Archibald Colquhoun*, who also adds a preface. 999

Marryat, Frederick (1792–1848).
MR MIDSHIPMAN EASY. New Introduction by *Oliver Warner*. 82
THE SETTLERS IN CANADA, 1844. Introduction by *Oliver Warner*. 370

Maugham, W. Somerset (*b.* 1874).
CAKES AND ALE, 1930. The finest novel of the author's inter-war period. 932

Maupassant, Guy de (1850–93).
SHORT STORIES. Translated by *Marjorie Laurie*. Intro. by *Gerald Gould*. 907

Melville, Herman (1819–91).
MOBY DICK, 1851. Intro. by *Prof. Sherman Paul*. 179
TYPEE, 1846; and BILLY BUDD (*published* 1924). South Seas adventures. New Introduction by *Milton R. Stern*. 180

Meredith, George (1828–1909).
THE ORDEAL OF RICHARD FEVEREL, 1859. Introduction by *Robert Sencourt*. 916

Mickiewicz, Adam (1798–1855).
PAN TADEUSZ, 1834. Translated into English prose, with Introduction, by *Prof. G. R. Noyes*. Poland's epic of Napoleonic wars. 842

Modern Short Stories. Selected by *John Hadfield*. Twenty stories. 954

Moore, George (1852–1933).
ESTHER WATERS, 1894. The story of Esther Waters, the servant girl who 'went wrong.' Introduction by *C. D. Medley*. 933

Mulock [Mrs Craik], Maria (1826–87).
JOHN HALIFAX, GENTLEMAN, 1856. Introduction by *J. Shaylor*. 123

Pater, Walter (1839–94).
MARIUS THE EPICUREAN, 1885. Introduction by *Osbert Burdett*. 903

Poe, Edgar Allan (1809–49).
TALES OF MYSTERY AND IMAGINATION. Introduction by *Padraic Colum*. 336
(*See also* Poetry and Drama.)

Priestley, J. B. (*b.* 1894).
ANGEL PAVEMENT, 1931. A finely conceived novel of London. 938

Quiller-Couch, Sir Arthur (1863–1944).
HETTY WESLEY, 1903. Introduction by the author. (*See also* Essays.) 864

Radcliffe, Mrs Ann (1764–1823).
THE MYSTERIES OF UDOLPHO, 1794. Intro. by *R. A. Freeman*. 2 vols. 865–6

Reade, Charles (1814–84).
THE CLOISTER AND THE HEARTH, 1861. Introduction by *Swinburne*. 29

Richardson, Samuel (1689–1761).
PAMELA, 1740. Introduction by *George Saintsbury*. 2 vols. 683–4
CLARISSA, 1747–8. Introduction by *Prof. W. L. Phelps*. 4 vols. 882–5

Russian Short Stories. Translated, with Introduction, by *Rochelle S. Townsend*. Stories by Pushkin, Gogol, Tolstoy, Korolenko, Chehov, Chirikov, Andreyev, Kuprin, Gorky, Sologub. 758

Scott, Sir Walter (1771–1832).
The following Waverley Novels each contain an Introduction, biographical and bibliographical, based upon Lockhart's *Life*:
THE ANTIQUARY, 1816. Introduction by *W. M. Parker*, M.A. 126
THE BRIDE OF LAMMERMOOR, 1819. A romance of life in East Lothian, 1695. New Introduction by *W. M. Parker*, M.A. 129
GUY MANNERING, 1815. A mystery story of the time of George III. New Introduction by *W. M. Parker*, M.A. 133
THE HEART OF MIDLOTHIAN, 1818. Period of the Porteous Riots, 1736. New Introduction by *W. M. Parker*, M.A. 134
IVANHOE, 1820. A romance of the days of Richard I. 16
KENILWORTH, 1821. The tragic story of Amy Robsart, in Elizabeth I's time. New Preface and Glossary by *W. M. Parker*, M.A. 135
OLD MORTALITY, 1817. Battle of Bothwell Bridge, 1679. New Introduction by *W. M. Parker*, M.A. 137
QUENTIN DURWARD, 1823. A tale of adventures in fifteenth-century France. New Introduction by *W. M. Parker*, M.A. 140
REDGAUNTLET, 1824. A tale of adventure in Cumberland, about 1763. New Introduction by *W. M. Parker*, M.A. 141
ROB ROY, 1818. A romance of the Rebellion of 1715. 142
THE TALISMAN, 1825. Richard Cœur-de-Lion and the Third Crusade, 1191. New Preface by *W. M. Parker*, M.A. (*See also* Biography.) 144

Shchedrin (M. E. Saltykov, 1826–92).
THE GOLOVLYOV FAMILY. Translated by *Natalie Duddington*. Introduction by *Edward Garnett*. 908

Shelley, Mary Wollstonecraft (1797–1851).
FRANKENSTEIN, 1818. With Mary Shelley's own Preface. 616

Shorter Novels.
Vol. I: ELIZABETHAN. Introduction by *George Saintsbury* and Notes by *Philip Henderson*. Contains: Deloney's 'Jack of Newberie' and 'Thomas of Reading'; Nashe's 'The Unfortunate Traveller'; Green's 'Carde of Fancie.' 824

VOL. II: SEVENTEENTH CENTURY. Edited, with Introduction, by *Philip Henderson.* Contains: Emanuel Ford's 'Ornatus and Artesia'; Aphra Behn's 'Oroonoko'; Neville's 'The Isle of Pines'; Congreve's 'Incognita.' 841

VOL. III: EIGHTEENTH CENTURY. Edited, with Introduction, by *Philip Henderson.* Contains: Beckford's 'Vathek'; Horace Walpole's 'The Castle of Otranto'; Dr Johnson' 'Rasselas.' 856

Sienkiewicz, Henryk (1846–1916).
QUO VADIS? 1896. Translated by *C. J. Hogarth.* Intro. by *Monica Gardner.* 970
TALES. Edited, with Introduction, by *Monica Gardner.* 871

Smollett, Tobias (1721–71).
THE EXPEDITION OF HUMPHRY CLINKER, 1771. Introduction by *Howard Mumford Jones,* and 36 pages of Notes by *Charles Lee.* 975
PEREGRINE PICKLE, 1751. Introduction by *Walter Allen.* 2 vols. 838–9
RODERICK RANDOM, 1742. Introduction by *H. W. Hodges.* 790

Somerville, E. Œ. (1858–1949), and **Ross, Martin** (pseudonym of Violet Florence Martin, 1862–1915).
EXPERIENCES OF AN IRISH R.M. Contains the authors' two books, *Some Experiences of an Irish R.M.,* 1897, and *Further Experiences of an Irish R.M.,* 1908. 978

Stendhal (pseudonym of Henri Beyle, 1783–1842).
SCARLET AND BLACK, 1831. Translated by *C. K. Scott Moncrieff.* Introduction by *Prof. F. C. Green,* M.A., DR.PHIL. 2 vols. 945–6

Sterne, Laurence (1713–68).
TRISTRAM SHANDY, 1760–7. Intro. by *George Saintsbury.* (*See also* Essays.) 617

Stevenson, Robert Louis (1850–94).
DR JEKYLL AND MR HYDE, 1886; THE MERRY MEN, 1887; WILL O' THE MILL, 1878; MARKHEIM, 1886; THRAWN JANET, 1881; OLALLA, 1885; THE TREASURE OF FRANCHARD. Introduction by *M. R. Ridley.* 767
THE MASTER OF BALLANTRAE, 1869; WEIR OF HERMISTON, 1896. New Introduction by *M. R. Ridley.* 764
ST IVES, 1898. Completed by Sir Arthur Quiller-Couch. Introduction (1958) by *M. R. Ridley.* 904
TREASURE ISLAND, 1883; and KIDNAPPED, 1886. Introduction by *Sir Arthur Quiller-Couch.* (*See also* Essays, Poetry, Travel.) 763

Story Book for Boys and Girls. Edited by *Guy Pocock* (1955). 934

Surtees, Robert Smith (1803–64).
JORROCKS'S JAUNTS AND JOLLITIES, 1838. 817

Swift, Jonathan (1667–1745).
GULLIVER'S TRAVELS, 1726. An unabridged edition; with an Introduction by *Sir Harold Williams,* F.B.A., F.S.A., M.A. (*See also* Biography, Essays.) 60

Tales of Detection. Introduction by *Dorothy L. Sayers.* Nineteen stories, tracing the development of the genuine detective story during the last hundred years. 928

Thackeray, William Makepeace (1811–63).
HENRY ESMOND, 1852. Introduction by *Walter Jerrold.* 73
THE NEWCOMES, 1853–5. 2 vols. Introduction by *Walter Jerrold.* 465–6
PENDENNIS, 1848–50. 2 vols. Introduction by *M. R. Ridley,* M.A. 425–6
VANITY FAIR, 1847–8. Introduction by *Hon. Whitelaw Reid.* 298
THE VIRGINIANS, 1857–9. 2 vols. Introduction by *Walter Jerrold.* 507–8
(*See also* Essays and Belles-Lettres.)

Tolstoy, Count Leo (1828–1910).
ANNA KARENINA, 1873–7. Translated by *Rochelle S. Townsend.* With Introduction by *Nikolay Andreyev,* PH.D., M.A. 2 vols. 612–13
MASTER AND MAN, 1895; and OTHER PARABLES AND TALES. Introduction (1958) by *Nikolay Andreyev,* PH.D., M.A. 469
WAR AND PEACE, 1864–9. Introduction by *Vicomte de Vogüé.* 3 vols. 525–7

Trollope, Anthony (1815–82).
THE WARDEN, 1855. The first of the 'Chronicles of Barset.' Introduction by *Kathleen Tillotson,* M.A., B.LITT. 182
BARCHESTER TOWERS, 1857. The second of the 'Chronicles of Barset.' Introduction (1956) on Anthony Trollope's 'Clergy' by *Michael Sadleir.* 30
DOCTOR THORNE, 1858. The third of the 'Chronicles of Barset.' 360
FRAMLEY PARSONAGE, 1861. The fourth of the 'Chronicles of Barset.' Introduction by *Kathleen Tillotson.* 181
THE SMALL HOUSE AT ALLINGTON, 1864. The fifth of the 'Chronicles of Barset.' 361
THE LAST CHRONICLE OF BARSET, 1867. 2 vols. 391–2

Turgenev, Ivan (1818–83).
FATHERS AND SONS, 1862. Translated by *Dr Avril Pyman.* 742
SMOKE, 1867. A new translation, with Introduction, by *Natalie Duddington.* 988
VIRGIN SOIL, 1877. Translated by *Rochelle S. Townsend.* 528

Twain, Mark (pseudonym of Samuel Langhorne Clemens, 1835–1910).
TOM SAWYER, 1876; and HUCKLEBERRY FINN, 1884. Introduction by *Christopher Morley.* 976

Verne, Jules (1828–1905).
FIVE WEEKS IN A BALLOON, 1862, translated by *Arthur Chambers;* and AROUND THE WORLD IN EIGHTY DAYS, translated by *P. Desages.* 779
TWENTY THOUSAND LEAGUES UNDER THE SEA, 1869. 319

Voltaire, François Marie Arouet de (1694–1778).
CANDIDE, AND OTHER TALES. Smollett's translation, edited by *J. C. Thornton*. 936
(*See also* History.)
Walpole, Hugh Seymour (1884–1941).
MR PERRIN AND MR TRAILL, 1911. 918
Wells, Herbert George (1866–1946).
ANN VERONICA, 1909. Introduction by *A. J. Hoppé*. 997
THE WHEELS OF CHANCE, 1896; and THE TIME MACHINE, 1895 915
Wilde, Oscar.
THE PICTURE OF DORIAN GRAY, 1891. (*See* Poetry and Drama.)
Woolf, Virginia (1882–1941).
TO THE LIGHTHOUSE, 1927. Introduction by *D. M. Hoare*, PH.D. 949
Zola, Émile (1840–1902).
GERMINAL, 1885. Translated, with an Introduction, by *Havelock Ellis*. 897

HISTORY

Anglo-Saxon Chronicle. Translated and Edited by *G. N. Garmonsway*, F.R.HIST.SOC. Foreword by *Prof. Bruce Dickins*. 624
Bede, the Venerable (673–735).
THE ECCLESIASTICAL HISTORY OF THE ENGLISH NATION. Translated by *John Stevens*, revised by *J. A. Giles*, with notes by *L. C. Jane*. Introduction by *Prof. David Knowles*, O.S.B., M.A., LITT.D., F.B.A., F.S.A. 479
Carlyle, Thomas (1795–1881).
THE FRENCH REVOLUTION, 1837. Introduction by *Hilaire Belloc*. 2 vols. 31–2
(*See also* Biography, Essays.)
Chesterton, Cecil (1879–1918). A HISTORY OF THE U.S.A., 1917. Edited by *Prof. D. W. Brogan*, M.A. 965
Creasy, Sir Edward (1812–78).
FIFTEEN DECISIVE BATTLES OF THE WORLD, FROM MARATHON TO WATERLOO, 1852. With Diagrams and Index. New Introduction by *Audrey Butler*, M.A. (OXON.). 300
Gibbon, Edward (1737–94).
THE DECLINE AND FALL OF THE ROMAN EMPIRE, 1776–88. Notes by *Oliphant Smeaton*. Intro. by *Christopher Dawson*. Complete text in 6 vols. 434–6, 474–6
Green, John Richard (1837–83).
A SHORT HISTORY OF THE ENGLISH PEOPLE, 1874. Introduction by *L. C. Jane*. English history from 607 to 1873. Continued by: 'A Political and Social Survey from 1815 to 1915,' by *R. P. Farley*, and revised to 1950. 727–8
Holinshed, Raphael (*d.* 1580 ?).
HOLINSHED'S CHRONICLE AS USED IN SHAKESPEARE'S PLAYS, 1578. Introduction by *Prof. Allardyce Nicoll* and *Josephine Nicoll*. 800
Joinville, Jean de. *See* Villehardouin.
Lützow, Count Franz von (1849–1916).
BOHEMIA: AN HISTORICAL SKETCH, 1896. Introduction by *President T. G. Masaryk*. H. A. Piehler covers events from 1879 to 1938. 432
Macaulay, Thomas Babington, Baron (1800–59).
THE HISTORY OF ENGLAND. The complete text in four volumes, which together contain 2,450 pages. Introduction by *Douglas Jerrold*. 34–7
(*See also* Essays.)
Maine, Sir Henry (1822–88).
ANCIENT LAW, 1861. Introduction by *Prof. J. H. Morgan*. 734
Mommsen, Theodor (1817–1903).
HISTORY OF ROME, 1856. Translated by *W. P. Dickson*, LL.D. Introduction by *Edward A. Freeman*. 4 vols. (Vols. III and IV only.) 544–5
Motley, John (1814–77).
THE RISE OF THE DUTCH REPUBLIC, 1856. Intro. by *V. R. Reynolds*. 3 vols. 86–8
Paston Letters, The, 1418–1506. 2 vols. A selection. 752–3
Prescott, William Hickling (1796–1859).
HISTORY OF THE CONQUEST OF MEXICO, 1843. 2 vols. 397–8
Stanley, Arthur (1815–81).
LECTURES ON THE HISTORY OF THE EASTERN CHURCH, 1861. Introduction by *A. J. Grieve*, M.A. 251
Thierry, Augustin (1795–1856).
THE NORMAN CONQUEST, 1825. Introduction by *J. A. Price*, B.A. 2 vols. (*Vol. I temporarily out of print.*) 198–9
Villehardouin, Geoffrey de (1160 ?–1213 ?), **and Joinville, Jean, Sire de** (1224–1317).
MEMOIRS OF THE CRUSADES. Translated, with an Introduction, by *Sir Frank T. Marzials*. 333
Voltaire, François Marie Arouet de (1694–1778).
THE AGE OF LOUIS XIV, 1751. Translation by *Martyn P. Pollack*.
(*See also* Fiction.) 780

ORATORY

British Orations. The 1960 edition of this selection of British historical speeches contains selections from four of the most famous of Sir Winston Churchill's World War II speeches. 714

Burke, Edmund (1729–97).
SPEECHES AND LETTERS ON AMERICAN AFFAIRS. New Introduction by the *Very Rev. Canon Peter McKevitt*, PH.D. (*See also* Essays and Belles-Lettres.) 340

Demosthenes (384–322 B.C.).
THE CROWN, AND OTHER ORATIONS. Translated with an Appendix on Athenian economics by *C. Rann Kennedy*. Introduction by *John Warrington*. 546

Lincoln, Abraham (1809–65).
SPEECHES AND LETTERS, 1832–65. A new selection edited with an Introduction by *Paul M. Angle*. Chronology of Lincoln's life and index. 206

POETRY AND DRAMA

Anglo-Saxon Poetry. English poetry between A.D. 650 and 1000, from 'Widsith' and 'Beowulf' to the battle-pieces of 'Brunanburh' and 'Maldon.' Selected and translated by *Prof. R. K. Gordon*, M.A. Reset, and revised by the translator, 1954. 794

Arnold, Matthew (1822–88).
COMPLETE POEMS. Introduction by *R. A. Scott-James*. 334

Ballads, A Book of British. Introduction and Notes by *R. Brimley Johnson*. Ballads from the earliest times to those of Yeats and Kipling. 572

Beaumont, Francis (1584–1616), and **Fletcher, John** (1579–1625).
SELECT PLAYS. Introduction by *Prof. G. P. Baker*. 'The Knight of the Burning Pestle,' 'The Maid's Tragedy,' 'A King and No King,' 'The Faithful Shepherdess.' 'The Wild Goose Chase,' 'Bonduca,' with a glossary. 506

Blake, William (1757–1827).
POEMS AND PROPHECIES. Edited, with special Introduction, by *Max Plowman*. 792

Brontë, Emily.
POEMS. (*See* Fiction.)

Browning, Robert (1812–89).
POEMS AND PLAYS, 1833–64. With a new Introduction by *John Bryson*, M.A., dealing with the four-volume Everyman Browning set. 2 vols. Volume III, containing *The Ring and the Book*, Browning's long dramatic poem (No. 502), is temporarily out of print. 41–2
POEMS, 1871–90. Introduction by *M. M. Bozman*. 964

Burns, Robert (1759–96).
POEMS AND SONGS. A very full selection and a very accurate text of Burns's copious lyrical output. Edited and introduced by *Prof. James Kinsley*, M.A., PH.D. 94
(*See also* Biography.)

Byron, George Gordon Noel, Lord (1788–1824).
THE POETICAL AND DRAMATIC WORKS. 3 vols. Edited with a Preface by *Guy Pocock* (*See also* Biography.) 486–8

Century. A CENTURY OF HUMOROUS VERSE, 1850–1950. Edited by *Roger Lancelyn Green*, M.A., B.LITT. 813

Chaucer, Geoffrey (*c.* 1343–1400).
CANTERBURY TALES. New standard text edited by *A. C. Cawley*, M.A., PH.D., based on the Ellesmere Manuscript, with an ingenious system of glosses, page by page. 307
TROILUS AND CRISEYDE. Prepared by *John Warrington* from the Campsall Manuscript. 992

Coleridge, Samuel Taylor (1772–1834).
THE GOLDEN BOOK. (*See also* Essays, etc.) 43

Cowper, William (1731–1800).
POEMS. Intro. by *Hugh I'Anson Fausset*. (*See also* Biography.) 872

Dante Alighieri (1265–1321).
THE DIVINE COMEDY, first printed 1472. H. F. Cary's Translation, 1805–14. Edited, with Notes and Index, by *Edmund Gardner*. Foreword by *Prof. Mario Praz*. 308

De la Mare, Walter (1873–1956). (*See* Essays.)

Donne, John (1573–1631).
COMPLETE POEMS. Edited, with a revised Intro., by *Hugh I'Anson Fausset*. 867

Dryden, John (1631–1700).
POEMS. Edited by *Bonamy Dobrée*, O.B.E., M.A. 910

Eighteenth-century Plays. Edited by *John Hampden*. Includes Gay's 'Beggar's Opera,' Addison's 'Cato,' Rowe's 'Jane Shore,' Fielding's 'Tragedy of Tragedies, or, Tom Thumb the Great,' Lillo's 'George Barnwell,' Colman and Garrick's 'Clandestine Marriage,' and Cumberland's 'West Indian.' 818

English Galaxy of Shorter Poems, The. Chosen and Edited by *Gerald Bullett*. 959

English Religious Verse. Edited by *G. Lacey May*. An anthology from the Middle Ages to the present day, including some 300 poems by 150 authors. 937

Everyman, and Medieval Miracle Plays. New edition edited by *A. C. Cawley*, M.A., PH.D. Forewords to individual plays. 381

Fitzgerald, Edward (1809–83). *See* 'Persian Poems.'

Fletcher, John (1579–1625). *See* Beaumont.
Ford, John (1586–1639). *See* Webster.
Goethe, Johann Wolfgang von (1749–1832).
FAUST. Both parts of the tragedy which are the core of Goethe's life-work, in the re-edited translation of *Sir Theodore Martin*. (*See also* Biography, Essays.) 335
Golden Book of Modern English Poetry, The. Edited by *Thomas Caldwell* and *Philip Henderson*, containing some 300 poems by 130 poets, from T. E. Brown to Stephen Spender and C. Day Lewis. 921
Golden Treasury of English Songs and Lyrics, The, 1861. Compiled by Francis Turner Palgrave (1824–97). Enlarged edition, containing 88-page supplement. 96
Golden Treasury of Longer Poems, The. Revised edition (1954) with new supplementary poems. An anthology ranging from Chaucer to Walter de la Mare. 746
Goldsmith, Oliver (1728–74).
POEMS AND PLAYS. Edited, with Introduction, by *Austin Dobson*. 415
(*See also* Fiction.)
Gray, Thomas (1716–71).
POEMS: WITH A SELECTION OF LETTERS AND ESSAYS. Introduction by *John Drinkwater*, and biographical notes by *Lewis Gibbs*. 628
Heine, Heinrich (*c*. 1797–1856).
PROSE AND POETRY. With Matthew Arnold's essay on Heine. 911
Ibsen, Henrik (1828–1906).
A DOLL'S HOUSE, 1879; THE WILD DUCK, 1884; and THE LADY FROM THE SEA, 1888. Translated by *R. Farquharson Sharp* and *Elanor Marx-Aveling*. 494
GHOSTS, 1881; THE WARRIORS AT HELGELAND, 1857; and AN ENEMY OF THE PEOPLE, 1882. Translated by *R. Farquharson Sharp*. 552
PEER GYNT, 1867. Translated by *R. Farquharson Sharp*. 747
THE PRETENDERS, 1864; PILLARS OF SOCIETY, 1877; and ROSMERSHOLM, 1887. Translated by *R. Farquharson Sharp*. 659
Ingoldsby Legends, or *Mirth and Marvels*, by 'Thomas Ingoldsby, Esq.' Edited by *D. C. Browning*, M.A., B.LITT. 185
International Modern Plays. August Strindberg's 'Lady Julie,' Gerhard Hauptmann's 'Hannele,' Brothers Čapek's 'The Life of the Insects,' Jean Cocteau's 'The Infernal Machine,' and Luigi Chiarelli's 'The Mask and the Face.' Introduction by *Anthony Dent*. 989
Jonson, Ben (1573–1637).
PLAYS. Introduction by *Prof. F. E. Schelling*. 2 vols. Complete collection. 489–90
Keats, John (1795–1821).
POEMS. Revised, reset edition (1944). Edited by *Gerald Bullett*. 101
(*See also* Biography.)
Kingsley, Charles (1819–75).
POEMS. With Introduction by *Ernest Rhys*. (*See also* Fiction.) 793
La Fontaine, Jean de (1621–95).
FABLES, 1668. Presented complete in the renowned Sir Edward Marsh translation. 991
'Langland, William' (1330?–1400?).
PIERS PLOWMAN, 1362. Translation into modern English by *Donald* and *Rachel Attwater*. 571
Lawrence, David Herbert (1885–1930). (*See* Essays.)
Lessing, Gotthold Ephraim (1729–81).
LAOCOÖN, 1766, AND OTHER WRITINGS. Introduction by *W. A. Steel*. Contents: 'Laocoön'; 'Minna von Barnhelm,' 1767, a comedy in five acts; and 'Nathan the Wise,' 1779, his philosophical drama. 843
Longfellow, Henry Wadsworth (1807–82).
POEMS, 1823–66. 382
Marlowe, Christopher (1564–93).
PLAYS AND POEMS. New edition with an Introduction by *M. R. Ridley*, M.A. 383
Milton, John (1608–74).
POEMS. New edition by *Prof. B. A. Wright*, M.A., based on Milton's editions and manuscripts. With a new Introduction by *Prof. Wright*. (*See also* Essays.) 384
Minor Elizabethan Drama. 2 vols. Vol. I. Tragedy. Norton and Sackville's 'Gorboduc,' Kyd's 'Spanish Tragedy,' Peele's 'David and Bethsabe,' and 'Arden of Feversham.' Vol. II. Comedy. Udall's 'Ralph Roister Doister,' Lyly's 'Endimion,' Peele's 'Old Wives' Tale,' Greene's 'Friar Bacon and Friar Bungay,' etc. Introduction by *Prof. A. Thorndike*. Glossary. 491–2
Minor Poets of the Seventeenth Century. The Poems of Thomas Carew, Sir John Suckling, Lord Herbert, Richard Lovelace. Edited and revised by *R. G. Howarth*, B.A., B.LITT., F.R.S.L. 873
Modern Plays. R. C. Sherriff's 'Journey's End,' W. Somerset Maugham's 'For Services Rendered,' Noel Coward's 'Hay Fever,' A. A. Milne's 'The Dover Road,' Arnold Bennett and Edward Knoblock's 'Milestones.' Introduction by *John Hadfield*. 942.
Molière, Jean Baptiste de (1622–73).
COMEDIES. Introduction by *Prof. F. C. Green*. 2 vols. 830–1
New Golden Treasury, The. Introduction by *Ernest Rhys*. A companion to Palgrave (q.v.), giving earlier lyrics than he did, and also later. 695
Omar Khayyám (*d*. 1123?). (*See under* Persian Poems.)

Palgrave, Francis Turner (1824–97). *See* 'Golden Treasury of English Songs and Lyrics, The.' 96

Persian Poems. Selected and edited by *Prof. A. J. Arberry*, M.A., LITT.D., F.B.A. 996

Poe, Edgar Allan (1809–49).
POEMS AND ESSAYS. Introduction by *Andrew Lang*. (*See also* Fiction.) 791

Poems of our Time. An Anthology edited by *Richard Church*, C.B.E., *M. M. Bozman* and *Edith Sitwell*, D.LITT., D.B.E. Nearly 400 poems by about 130 poets. 981

Pope, Alexander (1688–1744).
COLLECTED POEMS. Edited with Intro. (1956) by *Prof. Bonamy Dobrée*, O.B.E., M.A. 760

Restoration Plays. Introduction by *Edmund Gosse.* Includes Dryden's 'All for Love,' Wycherley's 'The Country Wife,' Congreve's 'The Way of the World,' Otway's 'Venice Preserved,' Farquhar's 'Beaux-Stratagem,' Vanbrugh's 'Provoked Wife,' Etherege's 'Man of Mode.' 604

Rossetti, Dante Gabriel (1828–82).
POEMS AND TRANSLATIONS. Introduction by *E. G. Gardner.* 627

Shakespeare, William (1564–1616).
A Complete Edition, based on Clark and Wright's Cambridge text, and edited by *Oliphant Smeaton.* With biographical Introduction, Chronological Tables and full Glossary. 3 vols.
Comedies, 153; Histories, Poems and Sonnets, 154; Tragedies, 155

Shelley, Percy Bysshe (1792–1822).
POETICAL WORKS. Introduction by *A. H. Koszul.* 2 vols. 257–8

Sheridan, Richard Brinsley (1751–1816).
COMPLETE PLAYS. Introduction and notes by *Lewis Gibbs.* 95

Silver Poets of the Sixteenth Century. Edited by *Gerald Bullett.* The works of Sir Thomas Wyatt (1503–42), Henry Howard, Earl of Surrey (1517?–47), Sir Philip Sidney (1554–86), Sir Walter Ralegh (1552–1618) and Sir John Davies (1569–1626.) 985

Spenser, Edmund (1552–99).
THE FAERIE QUEENE. Introduction by *Prof. J. W. Hales*, and Glossary. 2 vols. The reliable Morris text and glossary are used for this edition. 443–4
THE SHEPHERD'S CALENDAR, 1579; and OTHER POEMS. Introduction by *Philip Henderson.* 879

Stevenson, Robert Louis (1850–94).
POEMS. A CHILD'S GARDEN OF VERSES, 1885; UNDERWOODS, 1887; SONGS OF TRAVEL, 1896; and BALLADS, 1890, Introduction by *Ernest Rhys.* 768
(*See also* Essays, Fiction, Travel.)

Swinburne, Algernon Charles (1837–1909).
POEMS AND PROSE. A selection, edited with an Intro. by *Richard Church.* 961

Synge, J. M. (1871–1909).
PLAYS, POEMS AND PROSE. Introduction by *Michaél Mac Liammóir.* 968

Tchekhov, Anton (1860–1904).
PLAYS AND STORIES. 'The Cherry Orchard,' 'The Seagull,' 'The Wood Demon,' 'Tatyana Riepin' and 'On the Harmfulness of Tobacco' are included, as well as 13 of his best stories. The translation is by *S. S. Koteliansky.* Introduction by *David Magarshack.* 941

Tennyson, Alfred, Lord (1809–92).
POEMS. A comprehensive edition (1950), with an Introduction by *Mildred Bozman.* 2 vols. 44, 626

Twenty-four One-Act Plays. Enlarged edition, new Introduction by *John Hampden.* Contains plays by T. S. Eliot, Sean O'Casey, Laurence Housman, W. B. Yeats, James Bridie, Noel Coward, Lord Dunsany, Wolf Mankowitz and others. 947

Webster, John (1580?–1625?), and **Ford, John** (1586–1639).
SELECTED PLAYS. Introduction by *Prof. G. B. Harrison*, M.A., PH.D. In one volume: 'The White Devil,' 'The Duchess of Malfi,' 'The Broken Heart,' ''Tis Pity She's a Whore.' 899

Whitman, Walt (1819–92).
LEAVES OF GRASS, 1855–92. New edition (1947) by *Dr Emory Holloway.* 573

Wilde, Oscar (1854–1900).
PLAYS, PROSE WRITINGS, AND POEMS. Edited, with Introduction, by *Hesketh Pearson.* Including the two plays, 'The Importance of Being Earnest' and 'Lady Windermer's Fan'; his novel, 'The Picture of Dorian Gray'; the poem, 'The Ballad of Reading Gaol'; the essay, 'The Soul of Man,' etc. 858

Wordsworth, William (1770–1850).
POEMS. Edited, with Introductory study, notes, bibliography and full index, by *Philip Wayne*, M.A. 203, 311, 998

REFERENCE

Reader's Guide to Everyman's Library. Compiled by *A. J. Hoppé.* This volume is a new compilation and gives in one alphabetical sequence the names of all the authors, titles and subjects in Everyman's Library and its supplementary series, Everyman's Reference Library and the Children's Illustrated Classics. 889

Many volumes formerly included in Everyman's Library reference section are now included in Everyman's Reference Library and are bound in larger format.

ROMANCE

Aucassin and Nicolette, with other Medieval Romances. Translated, with Introduction, by *Eugene Mason.* 497

Boccaccio, Giovanni (1313–75).
DECAMERON, 1471. Translated by *J. M. Rigg*, 1903. Introduction by *Edward Hutton*, 2 vols. Unabridged. 845–6

Bunyan, John (1628–88).
PILGRIM'S PROGRESS, Parts I and II, 1678–84. Reset edition. Introduction by *Prof. G. B. Harrison*, M.A., PH.D. (*See also* Theology and Philosophy.) 204

Cervantes, Saavedra Miguel de (1547–1616).
DON QUIXOTE DE LA MANCHA. Translated by *P. A. Motteux*. Notes by *J. G. Lockhart*. Introduction and supplementary Notes by *L. B. Walton*, M.A., B.LITT. 2 vols. 385–6

Chrétien de Troyes (fl. 12th cent.).
ARTHURIAN ROMANCES ('Erec et Enide'; 'Cligés'; 'Yvain' and 'Lancelot'). Translated into prose, with Introduction, notes and bibliography, by *William Wistar Comfort.* 698

Kalevala, or The Land of Heroes. Translated from the Finnish by W. F. Kirby. 2 vols. 259–60

Mabinogion, The. Translated with Introduction by *Thomas Jones*, M.A., D.LITT., and *Gwyn Jones*, M.A. 97

Malory, Sir Thomas (fl. 1400?–70).
LE MORTE D'ARTHUR. Introduction by *Sir John Rhys*. 2 vols. 45–6

Marie de France (12th century), LAYS OF, AND OTHER FRENCH LEGENDS. Eight of Marie's 'Lais' and two of the anonymous French love stories of the same period translated with an Introduction by *Eugene Mason*. 557

Njal's Saga. THE STORY OF BURNT NJAL (written about 1280–90). Translated from the Icelandic by *Sir G. W. Dasent* (1861). Introduction (1957) and Index by *Prof. Edward Turville-Petre*, B.LITT., M.A. 558

Rabelais, François (1494?–1553).
THE HEROIC DEEDS OF GARGANTUA AND PANTAGRUEL, 1532–5. Introduction by *D. B. Wyndham Lewis*. 2 vols. A complete unabridged edition of Urquhart and Motteux's translation, 1653–94. 826–7

SCIENCE

Boyle, Robert (1627–91).
THE SCEPTICAL CHYMIST, 1661. Introduction by *M. M. Pattison Muir*. 559

Darwin, Charles (1809–82).
THE ORIGIN OF SPECIES, 1859. The sixth edition embodies Darwin's final additions and revisions. New Introduction (1956) by *W. R. Thompson*, F.R.S. 811
(*See also* Travel and Topography.)

Eddington, Arthur Stanley (1882–1944).
THE NATURE OF THE PHYSICAL WORLD, 1928. Introduction by *Sir Edmund Whittaker*, F.R.S., O.M. 922

Euclid (fl. *c.* 330–*c.* 275 B.C.).
THE ELEMENTS OF EUCLID. Edited by *Isaac Todhunter*, with Introduction by *Sir Thomas L. Heath*, K.C.B., F.R.S. 891

Faraday, Michael (1791–1867).
EXPERIMENTAL RESEARCHES IN ELECTRICITY, 1839–55. With Plates and Diagrams, and an appreciation by *Prof. John Tyndall.* 576

Harvey, William (1578–1657).
THE CIRCULATION OF THE BLOOD. Introduction by *Ernest Parkyn.* 262

Howard, John (1726?–90).
THE STATE OF THE PRISONS, 1777. Intro. and Notes by *Kenneth Ruck.* 835

Marx, Karl (1818–83).
CAPITAL, 1867. Translated by *Eden* and *Cedar Paul*. 2 vols. Introduction by *Prof. G. D. H. Cole.* 848–9

Mill, John Stuart (1806–73). *See* Wollstonecraft.

Owen, Robert (1771–1858).
A NEW VIEW OF SOCIETY, 1813; and OTHER WRITINGS. Introduction by *G. D. H. Cole.* 799

Pearson, Karl (1857–1936).
THE GRAMMAR OF SCIENCE, 1892. 939

Ricardo, David (1772–1823).
THE PRINCIPLES OF POLITICAL ECONOMY AND TAXATION, 1817. Introduction by *Prof. Michael P. Fogarty*, M.A. 590

Smith, Adam (1723–90).
THE WEALTH OF NATIONS, 1766. Intro. by *Prof. Edwin Seligman*. 2 vols. 412–13

White, Gilbert (1720–93).
A NATURAL HISTORY OF SELBORNE, 1789. New edition (1949). Introduction and Notes by *R. M. Lockley.* 48

Wollstonecraft, Mary (1759–97), THE RIGHTS OF WOMAN, 1792; and **Mill, John Stuart** (1806–73), THE SUBJECTION OF WOMEN, 1869. New Introduction by *Pamela Frankau.* 825

THEOLOGY AND PHILOSOPHY

Ancient Hebrew Literature. Being the Old Testament and Apocrypha, arranged by *R. Bruce Taylor*. 4 vols. *Volumes I and IV only in print.* 253, 256

Bacon, Francis (1561–1626).
THE ADVANCEMENT OF LEARNING, 1605. Introduction, Notes, Index and Glossary, by *G. W. Kitchin.* (*See also* Essays.) 719

Berkeley, George (1685–1753).
A NEW THEORY OF VISION, 1709. Introduction by *A. D. Lindsay*, C.B.E., LL.D. 483

Browne, Sir Thomas (1605–82).
RELIGIO MEDICI, 1642. New Introduction by *Halliday Sutherland*, **M.D., F.R.S.L.** 92

Bunyan, John (1628–88).
GRACE ABOUNDING, 1666; and THE LIFE AND DEATH OF MR BADMAN, 1658. Introduction by *Prof. G. B. Harrison*, M.A., PH.D. (*See also* Romance.) 815

Chinese Philosophy in Classical Times. Covering the period 1500 B.C.–A.D. 100. Edited and translated, with Introduction and Notes. 973

Descartes, René (1596–1650).
A DISCOURSE ON METHOD, 1637; MEDITATIONS ON THE FIRST PHILOSOPHY, 1641; and PRINCIPLES OF PHILOSOPHY, 1644. Translated by *Prof. J. Veitch.* Introduction by *A. D. Lindsay*, C.B.E., LL.D. 570

Ellis, Havelock (1859–1939).
SELECTED ESSAYS. Sixteen essays, with an Introduction by *J. S. Collis.* 930

Gore, Charles (1853–1932).
THE PHILOSOPHY OF THE GOOD LIFE, 1930. 924

Hindu Scriptures. Edited by *Nicol Macnicol*, M.A., D.LITT., D.D. Foreword by *Rabindranath Tagore.* 944

Hobbes, Thomas (1588–1679).
LEVIATHAN, 1651. Introduction by *A. D. Lindsay*, C.B.E., LL.D. 691

Hooker, Richard (1554–1600).
OF THE LAWS OF ECCLESIASTICAL POLITY, 1597. Introduction by *G. C. Morris*, M.A. 201–2

Hume, David (1711–76).
A TREATISE OF HUMAN NATURE, 1739. Intro. by *A. D. Lindsay*, C.B.E., LL.D. 2 vols. 548–9

James, William (1842–1910).
PAPERS ON PHILOSOPHY. Introduction by *Prof. C. M. Bakewell.* 739

Kant, Immanuel (1724–1804).
CRITIQUE OF PURE REASON, 1781. With an Introduction by *A. D. Lindsay*, C.B.E., LL.D. Translated by *J. M. D. Meiklejohn.* 909

King Edward VI (1537–53).
THE FIRST (1549) AND SECOND (1552) PRAYER BOOKS. Introduction by *Bishop Gibson.* 448

Koran, The. Rodwell's Translation, 1861. Intro. by *Rev. G. Margoliouth*, M.A. 380

Law, William (1686–1761).
A SERIOUS CALL TO A DEVOUT AND HOLY LIFE, 1728. Introduction by *Prof. Norman Sykes*, F.B.A., M.A., D.PHIL. 91

Leibniz, Gottfried Wilhelm (1646–1716).
PHILOSOPHICAL WRITINGS. Selected and translated by *Mary Morris*, with an Introduction by *C. R. Morris*, M.A. 905

Locke, John (1632–1704).
TWO TREATISES OF CIVIL GOVERNMENT, 1690. Introduction by *Prof. W. S. Carpenter.* (*See also* Essays.) 751

Malthus, Thomas Robert (1766–1834).
AN ESSAY ON THE PRINCIPLE OF POPULATION, 1798. New Introduction by *Prof. Michael P. Fogarty*, M.A. 2 vols. 692–3

Mill, John Stuart (1806–73).
UTILITARIANISM, 1863; LIBERTY, 1859; and REPRESENTATIVE GOVERNMENT, 1861. Introduction by *A. D. Lindsay*, C.B.E., LL.D. (*See also* Science.) 482

More, Sir Thomas (1478–1535).
UTOPIA, 1516; and DIALOGUE OF COMFORT AGAINST TRIBULATION, 1553. Introduction by *John Warrington.* Revised edition (1951). 461

New Testament, The. 93

Newman, John Henry, Cardinal (1801–90).
APOLOGIA PRO VITA SUA, 1864. Introduction by *Sir John Shane Leslie.* 636 (*See also* Essays.)

Nietzsche, Friedrich Wilhelm (1844–1900).
THUS SPAKE ZARATHUSTRA, 1883–91. Translated by *Prof. A. Tille* and revised by *M. M. Bozman.* Introduction (1957) by *Prof. Roy Pascal*, M.A., D.LITT. 892

Paine, Thomas (1737–1809).
RIGHTS OF MAN, 1792. Introduction by *Arthur Seldon.* 718

Pascal, Blaise (1623–62).
PENSÉES, 1670. Translated by *John Warrington.* Introduction by *Louis Lafuma.* This translation is from Lafuma's second edition. 874

Ramayana and Mahabharata. Condensed into English verse by *Romesh Dutt*, C.I.E. 403

oinson, Wade (1838–76).
THE PHILOSOPHY OF ATONEMENT, AND OTHER SERMONS, 1875. Introduction by *F. B. Meyer*. 637

Rousseau, Jean Jacques (1712–78).
THE SOCIAL CONTRACT, 1762; and OTHER ESSAYS. Introduction by *G. D. H. Cole*. (*See also* Biography, Essays.) 660

Saint Augustine (353–430).
CONFESSIONS. Dr Pusey's Translation, 1838, with Introduction by *A. H. Armstrong*, M.A. 200
THE CITY OF GOD. Complete text of John Healey's Elizabethan Translation, 1610. Edited by *R. V. G. Tasker*, M.A., B.D., with an Introduction by *Sir Ernest Barker*. 2 vols. 982–3

Saint Francis (1182–1226).
THE LITTLE FLOWERS; THE MIRROR OF PERFECTION (by Leo of Assisi); and THE LIFE OF ST FRANCIS (by St Bonaventura). Introduction by *Thomas Okey*. 485

Spinoza, Benedictus de (1632–77).
ETHICS, 1677; and ON THE CORRECTION OF THE UNDERSTANDING, 1687. Translated by *Andrew Boyle*. New Introduction by *T. S. Gregory*. 481

Swedenborg, Emanuel (1688–1772).
THE TRUE CHRISTIAN RELIGION, 1771. New and unabridged translation by *F. Bayley*. Introduction by *Dr Helen Keller*. 960 pages. 893

Thomas à Kempis (1380?–1471).
THE IMITATION OF CHRIST, 1471. 484

Thomas Aquinas (1225–74).
SELECTED WRITINGS. Selected and edited by *Father M. C. D'Arcy*. 953

TRAVEL AND TOPOGRAPHY

Borrow, George (1803–81).
THE BIBLE IN SPAIN, 1842. Introduction by *Edward Thomas*. 151
WILD WALES: the People, Language and Scenery, 1862. Introduction by *David Jones*, C.B.E., the painter and Borrovian. (*See also* Fiction.) 49

Boswell, James (1740–95).
JOURNAL OF A TOUR TO THE HEBRIDES WITH SAMUEL JOHNSON, 1786. Edited, with a new Introduction, by *Lawrence F. Powell*, M.A., HON. D.LITT. 387

Calderón de la Barca, Mme (1804–82).
LIFE IN MEXICO, 1843. Introduction by *Manuel Romero De Terreros*. 664

Cobbett, William (1762–1835).
RURAL RIDES, 1830. Introduction by *Asa Briggs*, M.A., B.SC. 2 vols. 638–9

Cook, James (1728–79).
VOYAGES OF DISCOVERY. Edited by *John Barrow*, F.R.S., F.S.A. Introduction by *Guy Pocock*, M.A. 99

Crèvecœur, J. Hector St John de (1735–1813).
LETTERS FROM AN AMERICAN FARMER, 1782. Intro. and Notes by *W. Barton Blake*. 640

Darwin, Charles (1809–82).
THE VOYAGE OF THE 'BEAGLE,' 1839. (*See also* Science.) 104

Defoe, Daniel (1661?–1731).
A TOUR THROUGH ENGLAND AND WALES, 1724–6. Intro. by *G. D. H. Cole*. 2 vols. (*See also* Fiction.) 820–1

Kinglake, Alexander (1809–91).
EOTHEN, 1844. Introduction by *Harold Spender*. 337

Lane, Edward William (1801–76).
MANNERS AND CUSTOMS OF THE MODERN EGYPTIANS, 1836. With a new Introduction by *Moursi Saad el-Din*, of the Egyptian Ministry of Education. 315

Park, Mungo (1771–1806).
TRAVELS. Introduction (1954) by *Prof. Ronald Miller*, M.A., PH.D. 205

Polo, Marco (1254–1324).
TRAVELS. Introduction by *John Masefield*. 306

Portuguese Voyages, 1498–1663. Edited by *Charles David Ley*. 986

Stevenson, Robert Louis (1850–94).
AN INLAND VOYAGE, 1878; TRAVELS WITH A DONKEY, 1879; and THE SILVERADO SQUATTERS, 1883. New Introduction by *M. R. Ridley*, M.A. 766 (*See also* Essays, Poetry, Fiction.)

Stow, John (1525?–1605).
THE SURVEY OF LONDON. The fullest account of Elizabethan London. 589

Wakefield, Edward Gibbon (1796–1862).
A LETTER FROM SYDNEY, AND OTHER WRITINGS ON COLONIZATION. Introduction by *Prof. R. C. Mills*. 828

Waterton, Charles (1782–1865).
WANDERINGS IN SOUTH AMERICA, 1825. Introduction by *Edmund Selous*. 772